LAW FOR THE LAND

This book follows the rise of the public trust doctrine – which obligates government to protect critical natural resources – from its ancient Roman origins to a modern force of environmental law. Focusing on California's enchanting Mono Lake, it tells the story of a group of everyday people who used the law to save it, spawning a legal revolution that reverberates globally. Their case pitted local advocates against thirsty Angelenos hundreds of miles away, in a dispute that stretches back to the dawn of Western water woes. Their story exemplifies the challenges of balancing legitimate needs for public infrastructure with competing environmental values, within systems of law still evolving to manage conflicting public and private rights in natural resources. Today, public trust principles infuse both common and constitutional law to protect water, wildlife, ecosystems, and climate – marrying sovereign obligations with environmental rights and raising open questions of legal theory, strategy, and meaning.

Erin Ryan is an internationally regarded expert in environmental law, constitutional law, negotiation, and collaborative governance. After long service as the Atkinson Professor and Associate Dean for Environmental Programs at the Florida State University College of Law, she joins the faculty at the University of Southern California Gould School of Law in 2026. She presents widely in the United States, Europe, and Asia and has served as a fellow at the Harvard Negotiation Research Project, at the Rachel Carson Center in Munich, and as a Fulbright Scholar in China. After graduating from Harvard Law School, she clerked on the U.S. Court of Appeals for the Ninth Circuit and practiced environmental law in San Francisco. Before law school, she was a United States Forest Service ranger at Mono Lake, just east of Yosemite National Park.

Law for the Land

THE PUBLIC TRUST DOCTRINE, MONO LAKE,
AND A QUIET REVOLUTION IN
ENVIRONMENTAL RIGHTS

ERIN RYAN

Shaftesbury Road, Cambridge CB2 8EA, United Kingdom

One Liberty Plaza, 20th Floor, New York, NY 10006, USA

477 Williamstown Road, Port Melbourne, VIC 3207, Australia

314–321, 3rd Floor, Plot 3, Splendor Forum, Jasola District Centre, New Delhi – 110025, India

103 Penang Road, #05–06/07, Visioncrest Commercial, Singapore 238467

Cambridge University Press is part of Cambridge University Press & Assessment, a department of the University of Cambridge.

We share the University's mission to contribute to society through the pursuit of education, learning and research at the highest international levels of excellence.

www.cambridge.org
Information on this title: www.cambridge.org/9781316622858

DOI: 10.1017/9781316761427

© Erin Ryan 2026

This publication is in copyright. Subject to statutory exception and to the provisions of relevant collective licensing agreements, no reproduction of any part may take place without the written permission of Cambridge University Press & Assessment.

When citing this work, please include a reference to the DOI 10.1017/9781316761427

First published 2026

Cover image: Magic sunset on Mono Lake in California, USA. By anderm / Adobe Stock

A catalogue record for this publication is available from the British Library

Library of Congress Cataloging-in-Publication Data
NAMES: Ryan, Erin author
TITLE: Law for the land : the public trust doctrine, mono lake, and a quiet revolution in environmental rights / Erin Ryan, Florida State University College of Law.
DESCRIPTION: Cambridge, United Kingdom ; New York, NY : Cambridge University Press, 2026. | Includes bibliographical references and index.
IDENTIFIERS: LCCN 2025036388 (print) | LCCN 2025036389 (ebook) |
ISBN 9781107171527 hardback | ISBN 9781316761427 ebook
SUBJECTS: LCSH: Environmental law – California – Mono Lake | Climatic changes – Law and legislation – California – Mono Lake | Environmental protection – California – Mono Lake
CLASSIFICATION: LCC KFC610 .R93 2026 (print) | LCC KFC610 (ebook) |
DDC 344.04/60979448–dc23/eng/20250807
LC record available at https://lccn.loc.gov/2025036388
LC ebook record available at https://lccn.loc.gov/2025036389

ISBN 978-1-107-17152-7 Hardback
ISBN 978-1-316-62285-8 Paperback

Cambridge University Press & Assessment has no responsibility for the persistence or accuracy of URLs for external or third-party internet websites referred to in this publication and does not guarantee that any content on such websites is, or will remain, accurate or appropriate.

For EU product safety concerns, contact us at Calle de José Abascal, 56, 1°, 28003 Madrid, Spain, or email eugpsr@cambridge.org

Dedication

This book is dedicated to my family, who have shared me with it for so long, and to the memory of Joseph Sax, whose work changed my life, as it has so many others.

It is also dedicated to the countless people who have devoted themselves to protecting Mono Lake – and so many other treasured public trust resources around the world.

I write it with the hope that whatever inspiration this story provides will help make that world a little bit better for my son, together with all the other children who will inherit it.

Contents

Preface	page xi
Acknowledgments	xvii
About the Author	xxi
How to Use This Book	xxiii
Table of Cases	xxv
Table of Authorities	xxxvii

    Introduction: The Public Trust Doctrine and the Foundations of Environmental Governance   1
    A. The Missing Constitutional Foundations of Environmental Law   4
    B. The Public Trust as an Emerging Foundation for Environmental Governance   13
    C. The Turning Point: Mono Lake and Beyond   16
    D. Public Trust Principles and Environmental Rights   17
    E. A Brief Synopsis of What Follows   21

1   **The Historical Origins of the Modern Public Trust Doctrine**   25
    A. Roots in Roman, English, and Continental Law   28
    B. Reception in the United States   35
    C. Conflicts with Water Allocation Law   48
    D. Setting the Stage for the Mono Lake Story   58

2   **Building the Los Angeles Aqueduct**   60
    A. Water Scarcity in Los Angeles   61
    B. The Early 1900s: Tapping the Owens River Valley   63
    C. An Alternative Account of the Owens Valley Water Transfer   73
    D. After the Aqueduct   75

3	The Mono Basin Extension	83
	A. The Mono Lake Basin	84
	B. Acquiring the Mono Basin Water Rights	93
	C. The Impacts of Water Exports on the Basin	97
4	Saving Mono Lake: The Political Mobilization	101
	A. For the Love of Place: Science Begets Activism	102
	B. A Coalition of Resistance: The Mono Lake Committee Forms	105
	C. The Rural–Urban Partnership: MLC Reaches Out to Angelenos	108
	D. Joseph Sax and the Power of a Good Idea	110
	E. The Path to Litigation	116
5	*National Audubon Society*: The "Mono Lake Case"	125
	A. The Historic Mono Lake Case: *Audubon Society v. Superior Court*	126
	B. Unpacking the *Mono Lake* Decision: Legal Elements and Innovations	146
6	In the Wake of *Audubon*: The Legal and Political Aftermath	158
	A. Protecting the Mono Basin Land	159
	B. Other Mono Lake Litigation	165
	C. State and Federal Funding for Water Conservation	172
	D. Decision 1631: Implementation by the Water Board	174
	E. A Reprieve for Mono Lake?	181
7	The *Mono Lake* Doctrine	197
	A. Public Trust and Distrust: The Scholarly Discourse Erupts	198
	B. The *Mono Lake* Doctrine Develops	211
	C. Ordinary Common Law or Quasi-Constitutional?	223
8	Beyond Mono Lake: The Development of the Public Trust across the United States	236
	A. The Planes of Public Trust Development across the United States	239
	B. The Public Trust in Federal Law	267
9	Public Trust Principles, Environmental Rights, and Trust-Rights Climate Advocacy	281
	A. Public Trust Principles and Environmental Rights in the Literature	287
	B. Trust-Rights Advocacy in Action: Atmospheric Trust and Climate Rights Litigation	300
	C. Climate Claims on State Constitutional Grounds	333
	D. Constitutional and Pragmatic Concerns with Emerging Climate Advocacy	344

10	Environmental Rights around the World: Public Trust Principles and the Rights of Nature Movement	361
	A. Public Trust Principles around the World	364
	B. The Rights of Nature Movement	380
	C. Comparing the Public Trust and Rights of Nature	405
	D. Which Is Better?	415
	Conclusion: A Quiet Revolution in Environmental Law	422
	A. Foundations for Environmental Governance	423
	B. Open Questions	426
	C. The Mono Lake Story, beyond California	445
	D. Coda: Save Mono Lake?	459

Index   463

Preface

The visitors collect at the parking lot, breathlessly absorbing the magnificent escarpment of the Yosemite–Inyo Sierra before them, admiring the defiant cones of the Mono Crater volcanoes behind them, and settling their gazes over the crystalline edges of the body of water between, a vast inland sea twice the size of San Francisco – the mythical Mono Lake of newspaper headline and bumper-sticker fame. As they gradually descend the volcanic ash trail a few hundred yards out to shore, the ranger explains that the parking lot had been submerged twice their standing height in lakewater only a few decades ago, before the lake's tributaries were first diverted into the Los Angeles Aqueduct for the 350-mile journey south to the City....

And then, just a few yards from the foaming water's edge, the ranger stops them and explains that thanks to important legal decisions between 1983 and 1994, the water level is now rising again – the salinity falling, the birds returning, the shrimp safe from extinction, and the people breathing clean air again – all because of an ancient article of common law, the public trust doctrine, according to which the California Supreme Court finally decided that to allow the death of Mono Lake for the benefit of one city [c]ould violate the State's duty to protect it as an ecological resource belonging to all. Parents' eyes grow as wide as their children's in sudden wonder of the power of ideas, and in awe of the devastation of near loss and the grace of last-minute salvation. And as they stand in the midst of such unparalleled natural splendor, rejoicing in a happy ending so rare in like stories of environmental crisis, the visitors experience ... genuine gratitude for [the law].[1]

So I once described the experience of introducing Mono Lake to visitors as a Forest Service ranger in the mid-1990s, in a law review article about the public trust doctrine that I wrote as a student after leaving the Mono Basin to attend law school. Decades later, the Mono Lake story that first propelled me to law school has continued to reverberate throughout the country and even the world, instilling a quiet

---

[1] Erin Ryan, *Public Trust & Distrust: Theoretical Implications of the Public Trust Doctrine for Natural Resource Management*, 31 ENVTL. L. 477, 493–94 (2001) (describing the standard United States Forest Service ranger-led tour of the South Tufa trail on the southwest shore of Mono Lake).

revolution in the development of natural resources law and environmental rights that continues to this day.

This book is the culmination of a thirty-year personal journey that began for me as that grunt-level US Forest Service ranger in the Mono Lake District of the Inyo National Forest, just east of Yosemite National Park, in northeastern California. There, for several precious years, it was my job to explain the Mono Lake story – or "The Water Issue," as we called it then – to astonished visitors from around the world, either on the balcony overlooking the sprawling alkaline lake, or along the sandy shores of the South Tufa trail, itself exposed by decades of water exports to Los Angeles. I introduced visiting families, elementary school groups, and foreign tourists to the geology and biology of the Mono Lake Basin, explained how the steady southbound diversions had drained the lake to the point of ecologic collapse, and then how a ragtag group of local residents, scientists, birders, fishers, and hunters had improbably convinced the state's highest court to intervene.

I would explain how they accomplished this unlikely feat, basing their lawsuit on an ancient and seemingly obscure legal doctrine – the public trust doctrine – which obligated the state to protect the public's interests in certain natural resource commons, like navigable waterways. Like Mono Lake. Almost uniformly, these visitors reveled in the rare happy ending to a familiar tale of conflict between environmental and economic values, precariously balancing the needs of a great city against the preservation of a spectacular natural system.

Indeed, in the mid-1990s, just as the State Water Board finalized plans to protect Mono Lake after the California Supreme Court's decision in its favor, I had the great fortune of finding myself among a handful of rangers, Mono Lake Committee staff, and other locals working at Mono Lake from the tiny mountain hamlet of Lee Vining, California (elevation: 7,000 feet, population: 315). The Water Board had called for carefully calibrated water sharing, ongoing scientific assessment, and collaborative restoration of damaged ecosystems, partnering with the City of Los Angeles, Mono Basin advocates, and public land managers such as the Forest Service in regional natural resource planning as well as hands-on maintenance and repair work. We spent our days alternating between studying the Mono Basin resources, interpreting them for the public, protecting them from misuse, and restoring them from the brink – usually with sleeves rolled up and hat brims down, feet planted in soggy soils, and hands raw with the burn of Mono Lake brine.

Living in the Mono Basin was every bit as enchanting, and every bit as difficult, as working there. Nestled between the western edge of Mono Lake and the eastern slope of the Yosemite–Inyo Sierra crest, Lee Vining is mostly surrounded by 10,000–14,000-foot mountains on three sides, snowed in beyond automobile passage for more than half the year. Back then, before home satellites were available, there was no television, scant Internet, and only one radio station broadcasting intermittently from Mammoth Lakes, a small ski town thirty miles to the south. To pass the time at night, we played a lot of card games (fetishizing variations on Doppelkopf and President), camped tentless under the Eastern Sierra stars, and sang to the moon. On off-days, local residents cultivated various outdoor skills – mountain climbing, kayaking, or birding – but my friends and I invented a wholly new Mono Basin sport: aqueducting.

Propelled by strong legs and even stronger curiosity, we made it our project to find all the points of historic, geologic, and mechanical interest along the 400-mile-long Los Angeles Aqueduct that initiated the Mono Lake drama, all the way from the northernmost intake in the Mono Basin down to its symbolic end at the Department of Water and Power's reflecting pool in Los Angeles. Some, like the point at which the aqueduct begins tunneling below the Mono Crater volcanoes, were easily accessible. Others, as where the Owens River shifts entirely into its concrete bed at Aberdeen, were under lock and key. Still others were almost purposefully hard to find, like the unheralded canyon site where the St. Francis Dam had catastrophically failed early in the aqueduct's history, drowning entire communities as they slept. In all aspects of our lives, we were thus fully immersed in the Mono Lake story, and we became evangelists for the possibilities it suggested for resolving resource conflicts across wide gulfs of conflicting interests and ideologies.

At some point, inspired by the public trust doctrine at the heart of the Mono Lake litigation, I applied to law school and accepted a place at Harvard – but I found myself so in love with the Mono Basin that I could not bring myself to leave it. For an additional year after that, I didn't, choosing to just stay in the job that I loved. When I asked the lawyers I met there about jettisoning the Forest Service for law school, they cried aloud that this was a terrible idea, as they were all dreaming of leaving the law to become forest rangers! It was easy to imagine living out my days happily as a Mono Lake ranger, and perhaps I would have done so had I not been seriously injured the following year. At that point, my romance with the western wilds was undercut by my needs for medical care and less physically demanding work. After many months on crutches behind a visitor center desk, I reconsidered my plans and later began law school with both enthusiasm and gratitude. When my hometown was requested for the 1L Facebook, despite my family origins in the east, I firmly responded, "Lee Vining, CA."

As wrenching as the decision to leave the Mono Basin was for me, it was also a decision germinated in hope. The Mono Lake case inspired me to believe in the power of the legal system and the political process to offer meaningful solutions to complex problems. My decision to study law was the direct result of my experiences there, bearing witness to the ability of ordinary people to wield the power of ideas to resolve critical social and environmental crises through legal processes. Especially in the aftermath and implementation of the Mono Lake litigation, I was inspired by the efforts of citizens, lawyers, scientists, and governments working together to make progress in the best possible way, even when no perfect way was available.

Moreover, as difficult as it was to leave, doing so opened up an entirely new lens for understanding the majesty and difficulty of the Mono Lake decision. After practicing land use and environmental law in California, I became a professor of property law, water law, natural resources law, and negotiation – all distinct fields of the law that are deeply implicated in the Mono Lake story. Over two decades later, even though I still miss the Mono Basin like a hole in my heart, it can feel as though I never left, because I teach the case in every one of my courses (in varying levels of detail). I show photos taken while I lived and worked at Mono Lake, some of which I have included in the inset here, and these classes are always among the most popular of the year. The Mono Lake saga remains one of my favorite stories in the world, and one that I have enjoyed sharing in all corners of the world since leaving the Mono Basin for academia. Much more importantly, that story has inspired environmental advocates globally, leading to the development and evolution of public trust principles around the nation and the world, as reported in Chapters 8, 9, and 10.

For that reason, this is a book that has been brewing within me for the better part of the last twenty-five years – though it has grown far beyond its origins, just as the public trust doctrine has grown over the same time period. The narrative exposes these complex personal roots for me at times, alternating between the academic analysis of a law professor and the personal narrative of a local storyteller. But throughout, my objective is to share this classic story of American environmental law that continues to inspire advocates worldwide, the long legal tradition from which it came, and the new legal pathways it has helped open up for environmental advocacy more generally. This book began as an article for a symposium on the public trust, itself based on a lecture about Mono Lake that I have given countless times – drawing on my expertise as both the Mono Lake ranger I once was and the property, water, and environmental law professor I later became. Then it grew.

In addition to the Mono Lake story, the book grew to explore the public trust doctrine and environmental rights more generally. It considers the doctrine's relationship with other areas of law, as well as its potential expanse and limits in application to other public natural resource commons that are also subject to private appropriation – such as the atmosphere, or biodiversity, or a healthy environment more generally. It explores different ways of conceptualizing environmental rights – from the anthropocentric public trust doctrine, which puts human needs at the center of legal consideration, to the rights of nature doctrine, which recenters environmental rights around the natural world itself. The book grew to encompass the many different facets of the public trust that had developed long before the Mono Lake case, were reshaped at Mono Lake, then metamorphosized in different jurisdictions in application to different resources, and have continued to evolve along multiple dimensions across the states of the union and nations of the world ever since.

In that wider legal world today, the doctrine is no longer just about traditional rights of access and navigation, if it ever was. It is no longer just about navigable waterways, if it ever was. The subject of a robust legal and political discourse, questions about the nature of the doctrine, its ethical orientation, and its relationships with other areas of law remain under vigorous exploration and debate. Even where the doctrine is unwritten as a formal matter, public trust principles have entered the legal lexicon and populate the language of lawsuits, statutes, and increasingly, constitutions. Environmental advocates, in particular, have learned to partner public trust principles with independent constitutional promises in seeking to protect public commons from undue private expropriation – even the atmospheric commons from private appropriation as a sink for carbon pollution. Once a doctrine that empowered sovereign authority over trust resources, the public trust has gradually evolved into a doctrine that obligates sovereign authority to protect those resources – and empowers citizens to demand it. It has been an enormously significant shift.

Even when the most ambitious public trust claims fail, the doctrine serves its underlying legal values by facilitating the open deliberation of complex environmental policy between citizens and the various branches of government that represent them. As explored here, the public trust doctrine emerges as a powerful platform to advance separation-of-powers values, and not for the reasons that concern skeptics, who question the wisdom of a doctrine that enables the judiciary to second-guess legislative decisions through an arguably quasi-constitutional constraint on sovereign authority. Yet the alternative view is that the doctrine empowers citizens to engage their representatives in government with legitimate questions and concerns in transparent and accountable public forums, through multiple ports of entry. If the executive ignores the undue expropriation of rightfully public resources, then the people can ask the legislature to remind them. And if legislators fall deaf to the same concern, perhaps co-captured by benefiting private industry, the public trust doctrine enables the people to remind them in court. And if all representatives of government should fall deaf to public concern, then the people can elevate public trust principles to the relevant constitution – as many communities have now done, both at the state level domestically and at the national level abroad.

This unique provenance certainly makes the public trust doctrine worthy of close study, hopefully in as fulsome a treatment as this is. But no matter how long the public trust saga grows – even with thousands of years in the making – the Mono Lake story, a critical inflection point within it, will remain a worthy chapter in that epic tale. It is one of the all-time great stories of American law, and the rarest of birds in environmental law, with an essentially "win-win" outcome (when – spoiler alert! – the ecosystem was spared but the metropolis salvaged all water losses through conservation). It showcases all the grit, glory, and controversy that always characterizes human efforts to solve critical societal problems through the rule of law. Whatever one's perspective on the outcome, may we all learn from its model, and carry that spirit of problem-solving with us to future environmental conflicts.

Acknowledgments

This book is based on exhaustive primary and secondary research, and it draws from several previously published works, which I wish to acknowledge up front. The genesis of the book was the storytelling and analysis in *The Public Trust Doctrine, Private Water Allocation, and Mono Lake: The Historic Saga of* National Audubon Society v. Superior Court, 45 ENVTL. L. 561 (2015), an article reviewing the significance of the Los Angeles–Mono Lake water conflict and its implications for future public trust conflicts, written for a 2015 symposium on the public trust doctrine at Lewis & Clark Law School in Portland, Oregon. I am grateful to the scholars who helped push forward my thinking about the public trust doctrine at that gathering, to the Lewis & Clark law students who helped prepare that initial piece for publication, and especially to Matt Gallaway at Cambridge University Press for suggesting that I grow this account into a full book treatment. I am profoundly grateful to the academics, many of them my personal scholarly heroes, who offered meaningful guidance on drafts of this book, including Carol Rose, Richard Lazarus, Rick Frank, Robin Craig, Dave Owen, Alexandra Klass, and Karrigan Bork, and to Hap Dunning, Mike Blumm, and Bartshe Miller for comments on early components. I especially thank Geoff McQuilkin, Executive Director of the Mono Lake Committee, for keeping me updated on important Mono Basin happenings.

The book also incorporates material from several later law review articles: *From Mono Lake to the Atmospheric Trust: Navigating the Public and Private Interests in Public Trust Resource Commons*, 10 GEO. WASH. J. ENERGY & ENVTL. L. 39 (2019), which provided additional historical context, expanded legal analysis, and reporting on contemporary public trust developments; *A Short History of the Public Trust Doctrine and Its Intersection with Private Water Law*, 38 VA. ENVTL. L.J. 135 (2020), which took a much deeper dive into the historical roots of the doctrine and the conflict it creates with private water allocation laws; *Environmental Rights for the 21st Century: A Comprehensive Analysis of the Public Trust Doctrine and the Rights of Nature Movement*, 43 CARDOZO L.R. 2447 (2021) (with Holly Curry & Hayes Rule), which assessed the development of both the public trust doctrine and rights of nature movement across the nation and around the world; and *Public Trust*

Principles and Environmental Rights: The Hidden Duality of Climate Advocacy and the Atmospheric Trust, 49 HARV. ENVTL. L. REV. 225 (2025), which explored the confluence of public trust sovereign obligations and environmental rights, especially in the context of climate advocacy.

It also benefited from my work on several additional pieces, including *How the Successes and Failures of the Clean Water Act Fueled the Rise of the Public Trust Doctrine and Rights of Nature Movement*, 73 CASE WESTERN RES. L. REV. 475 (2022), which recognized how the Clean Water Act's failure to match protections for water quality with protections for water quantity has resulted in these competing legal approaches to protect ailing waterways; *Sackett v. EPA and the Regulatory, Property, and Human Rights Based Strategies for Protecting American Waterways*, 74 CASE WESTERN RES. L. REV. (2023), which assessed the likely impacts of a Supreme Court decision limiting the reach of the Clean Water Act on the dynamic competition among competing models of environmental protection; and my very first legal article, *Public Trust & Distrust: Theoretical Implications of the Public Trust Doctrine for Natural Resource Management*, 31 ENVTL. L. 477 (2001), which contrasted the public trust with other theoretical frameworks for natural resource management and environmental protection. I owe special thanks to the work of Joseph Sax and Richard Lazarus for inspiring that project, and to my academic mentors, Jim Salzman and Bob Percival, for encouraging me to publish it. I am also grateful to Mims Wood, Rick Frank, Jim Huffman, and Irma Russell for engaging with me on climate litigation and the atmospheric trust in Juliana v. United States: *Debating the Fundamentals of the Fundamental Right to a Sustainable Climate*, 45 FLA. ST. L. REV. ONLINE 1 (2018).

This book would not have been possible without the help of outstanding research assistants over the years, each of whom deserves personal recognition: Gabe Hinman, Ashley Garcia, Travis Voyles, Mallory Neumann, Jill Bowen, Ashley Englund, Amelia Ulmer, Holly Curry, Hayes Rule, Salo Garcia, Catherine Awasthi, Keeley Smith, and Nicola Strause. I offer profound thanks to Lindsay Peterson, Matt Henderson, and Molly Adamo, who helped me carry this enormous project across the finish line in its final years. The book is better for all of their contributions, in more places than I can count, and they offered precious intellectual company during the lonely journey of the writing process.

Having presented these works on many occasions over the years while simultaneously working on this manuscript, I am deeply thankful to the many scholars and students who contributed additional insights – including my research-assistants-turned-co-authors on the *Comprehensive Analysis* article, Holly Curry and Hayes Rule – and all the student law review editors who labored to ensure that my propositions were grounded. I am also indebted to my colleagues and fellow researchers at the Rachel Carson Center at Ludwig Maximillian University in Munich for their support and engagement during my 2019 research fellowship there, and to my colleagues at Florida State University for their generous support and suggestions over my various stages of writing. I will always be grateful to the Mono Lake District of the Inyo National Forest, the Mono Lake Committee, and the community of Lee Vining, CA for welcoming me home so many years ago, and inspiring the long professional journey that began with this story.

Finally, and most of all, I am ever grateful to my wide and wonderful family, my parents, Ned and Paula, my sister Caitlin, my son Dylan, my loving council of aunts and uncles, and especially to my beloved husband Elijah, for such steadfast love and support along this improbable journey.

About the Author

Erin Ryan is an internationally regarded expert in environmental and natural resources law, property and land use, federalism and multilevel governance, negotiation, and water law. She is the Elizabeth C. and Clyde W. Atkinson Professor and Associate Dean for Environmental Programs at the Florida State University College of Law, where she oversees the FSU Center for Environmental, Energy, and Land Use Law. In 2026, as this book goes to press, she returns to California to join the faculty at the University of Southern California Gould School of Law.

Ryan has presented widely in the United States, Europe, and Asia, including the Ninth Circuit Judicial Conference, the National Association of Attorneys General, the United States Forest Service, and the United Nations Institute for Training and Research. She has advised National Sea Grant multilevel governance studies involving Chesapeake Bay, provided federal legislative briefing on the public trust, and consulted with multiple institutions on developing sustainability programs. She has appeared in the Associated Press, Chicago Tribune, Foreign Policy, Huffington Post, London Financial Times, National Public Radio, Thomson-Reuters Beijing, and local NBC and CBS Television News. She is the author of over fifty scholarly works and twenty-five others, including FEDERALISM AND THE TUG OF WAR WITHIN (Oxford, 2012). She has lectured at leading universities and government agencies in China, India, Japan, Vietnam, Israel, England, Northern Ireland, Germany, the Netherlands, Spain, Greece, and Australia.

Ryan is a graduate of Harvard Law School, where she was an editor of the *Harvard Law Review* and a Hewlett Fellow at the Harvard Negotiation Research Project. She clerked for Judge James R. Browning of the US Court of Appeals for the Ninth Circuit before practicing environmental, land use, and local government law in San Francisco. She began her academic career at the College of William & Mary in 2004, joined the faculty at the Northwestern School of Law at Lewis & Clark College in 2011, moved to Florida State in 2015, and to the University of Southern California in 2026. Ryan served as a Fulbright Scholar in China, where she taught American law, studied Chinese governance, and lectured throughout the country – returning to teach and guest lecture in 2016 and 2025. In 2019, she was selected as a research fellow by the Rachel Carson Center for Environment and Society in Munich, Germany. In 2025, she was invited to join the Scientific Advisory Board for the Eurac Institute for Comparative Federalism in Bolzano, Italy.

Prior to law school, Ryan served as a US Forest Service ranger on the Mono Lake District of the Inyo National Forest, east of Yosemite National Park. She graduated from Harvard College with a degree in East Asian Languages and Civilizations and received a master's degree in Ethnomusicology from Wesleyan University.

How to Use This Book

This book is intended for a variety of audiences, each of whom might wish to engage with it differently. With that in mind, here is some advice for how different readers might want to approach its contents. To be sure, this book is written for everyone – in ordinary terms that should allow all kinds of readers to engage with the material in every chapter. At the same time, it is designed so that readers on a specific mission can engage with it selectively, charting a course based on what interests them most. The Preface and the Introduction are written for everyone, but after that, readers are free to choose their own adventure.

Readers interested in all legal aspects of the Mono Lake story may wish to begin with the history of the legal doctrines at its center, before proceeding through the Monospecific chapters in the first half of the book and then on to the second half, exploring its impact in the wider legal world. Readers with no special interest in the historical narrative of the Los Angeles Aqueduct, the Owens Valley saga, or the natural history of the Mono Basin may wish to skip Chapters 2 and 3 entirely, and potentially most of Chapter 4, which details the political mobilization to save Mono Lake that proceeded alongside the litigation.

In addition to the extensive legal history in Chapter 1, legal audiences will be especially interested in the analysis of the Mono Lake case and its aftermath in Chapters 5 and 6, respectively, and in Chapter 7's review of the legal impacts of Mono Lake precedent on related issues in California and other states. Those most interested in public trust principles and evolving conceptions of environmental rights will not want to miss further exposition of the doctrine in Chapter 8 (exploring its development across the United States), Chapter 9 (reviewing its role in climate advocacy), and Chapter 10 (exploring the adoption of public trust principles internationally and the simultaneous emergence of the global Rights of Nature movement). Those especially interested in the California public trust doctrine should also consult Part D of Chapter 4, which tracks the incremental development of older precedents that made the result at Mono Lake possible.

By contrast, those most interested in the historical saga of the Los Angeles Aqueduct and its impact on the adjacent communities can skip the legal history in

Chapter 1 and proceed from the Introduction directly to the narrative in Chapters 2–4, which tell the story of the early aqueduct and its impacts in the Owens Valley and Mono Basin. These readers can continue on to the story of the Mono Lake case in Chapter 5 and its aftermath in Chapter 6, and if they are not interested in the more general developments associated with public trust law after Mono Lake, they can skip over Chapters 7–10 to the concluding reflections on the Mono Lake story in the Conclusion.

Those interested in modern public trust developments and environmental law more broadly might wish to skim the public trust historical material in Chapter 1 for context before proceeding directly to the discussion of the Mono Lake case and its aftermath in Chapters 5 and 6. These readers may be interested in the case-specific doctrinal impacts reported in Chapter 7, but they will be especially interested in the wider public trust developments reported both domestically and internationally in Chapters 8–10. These include discussion in Chapter 8 of the proliferation of distinctive public trust approaches among American state law and the doctrinal intersections between the public trust and federal law; emerging models of "trust-rights" climate advocacy explored in Chapter 9; and discussion in Chapter 10 of the international development of (anthropocentric) public trust principles and the global rise of the Rights of Nature movement, a competing model of environmental rights founded on biocentric or ecocentric principles.

Finally, those interested solely in Mono Lake can proceed from the Introduction directly to Chapter 3, where the Mono Lake story begins. They will be interested in Chapter 4's review of the political mobilization to save Mono Lake, and in the analysis in Chapters 5 and 6 of the *Audubon Society* litigation and its aftermath. They may also be interested in the concluding reflections about the questions left open by the Mono Lake case in the Conclusion, pointing also to contemporaneous Mono Lake stories unfolding in other parts of the world, such as the Great Salt Lake in Utah, the Dead Sea and Sea of Galilee in the Middle East, and the Aral Sea in central Europe.

However you choose to engage this material, my hope is that the Mono Lake story will move you the way it has moved countless others around the globe – to appreciate the majesty of the natural world, and to shepherd human society toward a sustainable partnership within it.

Table of Cases

Adams v. Elliott, 174 So. 731 (Fla. 1937), 250, 260
Advocates Coalition for Development and Environment v. Attorney General, Misc. Cause No. 0100 of 2004 (July 11, 2005) (Uganda), 371, 387
Alec L. ex rel. Loorz v. McCarthy, 135 S. Ct. 774 (2014), 43
Alec L. ex rel. Loorz v. McCarthy, 561 Fed. App'x 7 (D.C. Cir. 2014), 15, 43, 48, 313
Alec L. ex rel. Loorz v. McCarthy, 574 U.S. 1047 (2014), 15, 277, 313
Alec L. v. Jackson, 863 F. Supp. 2d 11 (D.D.C. 2012), 312, 313
American & Ocean Ins. Co. v. 356 Bales of Cotton, 26 U.S. 511 (1828), 33
Apalachicola Land & Dev. Co. v. McRae, 98 So. 505 (Fla. 1923), 374
Ariz. Dep't of Water Res. v. McClennan, 360 P.3d 1023 (Ariz. 2015), 263
Arno v. Commonwealth, 931 N.E.2d 1 (Mass. 2010), 240
Arnold v. Mundy, 6 N.J.L. 1 (1821), 35, 36–37
Avenal v. State, 886 So. 2d 1085 (La. 2004), 271
Bd. of Trs. v. Webb, 618 So. 2d 1381 (Fla. Dist. Ct. App. 1993), 374
Berkeley v. Super. Ct., 606 P.2d 362 (Cal. 1980), 114, 115, 116, 122, 135
Betchart v. Dep't of Fish & Game, 205 Cal. Rptr. 135 (Cal. Ct. App. 1984), 48
Blades v. California, No. CGC11-510725 (Cal. Super. Ct. 2012), 312
Bohn v. Albertson, 238 P. 2d 128 (Cal. Ct. App. 1951), 112, 113
Bonelli Cattle Co. v. Arizona, 414 U.S. 313 (1973), 257
Bonser-Lain v. Texas Comm'n on Env't Quality, 438 S.W.3d 887 (Tex. App. 2014), 314
Bonser-Lain v. Texas Comm'n on Env't Quality, No. D-1-GN-11-002194, 2012 WL 2946041 (Tex. Dist. Ct. July 9, 2012), 314
Boone v. Kingsbury, 273 P. 797 (Cal. 1928), 115
Borough of Neptune City v. Borough of Avon-By-The-Sea, 294 A.2d 47 (N.J. 1972), 202, 254, 260, 427
Bos. Waterfront Dev. Corp. v. Commonwealth, 393 N.E.2d 356 (Mass. 1979), 241
Bowers v. Hardwick, 478 U.S. 186 (1986), 353
British Columbia v. Canadian Forest Products, (2004) 2 S.C.R. 74 (Can.), 378

Broward v. Mabry, 50 So. 826 (Fla. 1909), 374, 393
Brown v. the Board of Education, 347 U.S. 483 (1954), 296
Butler v. Att'y Gen., 80 N.E. 688 (Mass. 1907), 240
Butler v. Brewer, No. 1 CA-CV 12-0347 (Ariz. Ct. App. March 14, 2013), 314
Cal. Trout v. Super. Ct., 218 Cal. App. 3d. 187 (1990), 169
California ex rel. State Lands Comm'n v. United States, 805 F.2d 857 (9th Cir. 1986), 123, 163, 164
California Trout v. State Water Resource Control Board (Cal. Trout I) (CalTrout), 207 Cal. App. 3d 585 (1989), 166
CalTrout. See California Trout v. State Water Resource Control Board (Cal. Trout I) (CalTrout), 207 Cal. App. 3d 585 (1989)
Caminiti v. Boyle, 732 P.2d 989 (Wash. 1987), 153, 227, 262
Casitas Mun. Water Dist. v. United States, 102 FED. CL. 443 (2011), 272
Casitas Mun. Water Dist. v. United States, 543 F.3d 1276 (Fed. Cir. 2008), 56
Center for Biological Diversity v. FPL Group, 83 Cal. Rptr. 3d 588 (Cal. Ct. App. 2008), 215, 256, 260
Chernaik v. Brown, 475 P.3d 68 (Or. 2020), 312, 332
Chernaik v. Kitzhaber, 328 P.3d 799 (Or. Ct. App. 2014), 313
Chevron, U.S.A., Inc. v. Nat. Res. Def. Council, Inc., 467 U.S. 837 (1984), 435
Chong Yim v. City of Seattle, 451 P.3d 675 (Wash. 2019), 271
City of L.A. Dep't of Water & Power v. Nat'l Audubon Soc'y, 464 U.S. 977 (1983), 145, 267
City of Los Angeles v. Aitken, 52 P.2d 585 (Cal. 1935), 94, 114, 126
City of Los Angeles v. Bd. of Supervisors (Inyo Cnty. Super. Ct. 1991) (No. 12908), 191
City of Los Angeles v. Venice Peninsula Properties, 31 Cal. 3d 288 (1982), 282
City of Los Angeles v. Venice Peninsula Properties, 644 P.2d 792 (1982), 282
Clairison's CC v. MEC for Loc. Gov't Env't Affs. & Dev. Plan. & Bitou Mun., 2012 (3) SA 128 (CC) (S. Afr.), 373
Clean Air Council et al., v. Pennsylvania, No. 379 MD 2023 (Pa. Commw. Ct. 2023), 339
Cline v. Am. Aggregates Corp., 474 N.E. 2d 324 (Ohio 1984), 56
Cnty. of Inyo v. City of L.A., 61 Cal. App. 3d 91 (1976), 103
Cnty. of Inyo v. City of L.A., 71 Cal. App. 3d 185 (1977), 76
Cnty. of Inyo v. City of L.A., 124 Cal. App. 3d 1 (1981), 76
Cnty. of Inyo v. Yorty, 32 Cal. App. 3d 795 (1973), 76
Coastal Petrol. Co. v. Am. Cyanamid Co., 492 So. 2d 339 (Fla. 1986), 393
Coffin v. Left Hand Ditch. Co., 6 Colo. 443 (Colo. 1882), 54
Colo. Oil & Gas Conservation Comm'n v. Martinez, 433 P.3d 22 (Colo. 2019), 257, 261
Commonwealth v. Alger, 61 Mass. 53 (1851), 240
Corfield v. Coryell, 6 F. Cas. 546 (C.C.E.D. Pa. 1823), 12

Corner Post, Inc. v. Board of Governors of the Federal Reserve System, 603 U.S. 799 (2024), 359
Council of Organizations & Others for Educ. About Parochiaid v. State, 931 N.W.2d 65 (Mich. Ct. App. 2018), 243
Court on Its Own Motion v. Chandigarh Administration, CWP No. 18253 of 2009 (P&H H.C.) (2020), 387
Coyle v. Smith, 221 U.S. 559 (1911), 153, 276
CWC Fisheries, Inc. v. Bunker, 755 P.2d 1115 (Alaska 1988), 221
Dahlgren v. Los Angeles, No. 8092, slip op. (Mono Super. Ct. Aug. 17, 1985), 166, 169
Diamond Nat. Res. Prot. & Conservation Ass'n v. Diamond Valley Ranch, LLC, 511 P.3d 1003 (Nev. 2022), 233
Dobbs v. Jackson Women's Health Org., 597 U.S. 215 (2022), 434
Drewes Farms P'ship v. City of Toledo, 441 F. Supp. 3d 551 (N.D. Ohio 2020) (No. 19-cv-00434), 392, 393
East Cape May v. State Dep't of Env't Prot., 777 A.2d 1015 (N.J. Super. A.D. 2001), 153, 227, 262
EDF, Inc. v. East Bay Mun. Util. Dist., No. 425955, 1990 Lexis 7 (Alameda Cnty. Super. Ct. 1990), 213
Emma Johanna Kiehm, et al. v. State of Brandenburg, 306
Empire Water & Power Co. v. Cascade Town Co., 205 Fed. 123 (8th Cir. 1913), 57
Env't L. Found. v. State Water Res. Control Bd. (Scott River Case), 237 Cal. Rptr. 3d 393 (Cal. Ct. App. 2018), 15, 34, 48, 50, 56, 148, 217–20, 394
Env't Law Found. v. State Water Res. Control Bd., 26 Cal. App. 5th 844 (Cal. Ct. App. 2018), 149, 187, 282, 426, 427
Esplanade Props., LLC v. City of Seattle, 307 F.3d 978 (9th Cir. 2002), 267, 271
Ex parte Maier, 103 Cal. 476 (Cal. 1894), 216
Fafard v. Conservation Comm'n of Barnstable, 733 N.E.2d 66 (Mass. 2000), 255
Flast v. Cohen, 392 U.S. 83 (1968), 439
Fletcher v. Peck, 10 U.S. (6 Cranch) 87 (1810), 45
Florida v. Georgia, 138 S. Ct. 2502 (2018), 53, 54
Florida v. Georgia, 141 S. Ct. 1175 (2021), 53
Foster v. Wash. Dep't. of Ecology, 2016 WL 11359472 (Wash. Super. Ct. 2016), 313
Foster v. Washington Dep't of Ecology, 200 Wash. App. 1035, 2017 WL 3868481 (2017), 313, 314, 315, 318
Foster v. Washington Dep't of Ecology, No. 14-2-25295-1 SEA, 2015 WL 7721362 (Wash. Super. Ct. Nov. 19, 2015), 314, 315, 317
Franzini v. Layland, 97 N.W. 499 (Wis. 1903), 267
Fresh Air for the East Side, Inc. v. New York, No. E2022-000699 (Sup. Ct. Monroe Cty. Dec. 20, 2022), 335
Fresh Air for the Eastside, Inc. v. State of New York, No. 20-1234 (N.Y. App. Div. 4th, July 26, 2024), 339

Fresh Air for the Eastside, Inc. v. State of New York, No. E2022000699 (Sup. Ct. Monroe Cty. Jan. 28, 2022), 339

Fresh Air for the Eastside, Inc. v. Town of Perinton, No. E2021-008617 (Sup. Ct. Monroe Cty. Dec. 8, 2022), 335

Fresh Air for the Eastside, Inc. v. Waste Mgmt. of N.Y., No. 18-CV-06588-FPG-MJP (W.D.N.Y. Apr. 18, 2024), 339

Friends of the Earth v. Carey, 552 F.2d 25 (2d Cir. 1977), 6

Frothingham v. Mellon, 262 US 447 (1923), 439

Future Generations v. Ministry of Env't, (2018) 11001-22-03-000-2018-00319-01 (Colom.), 301

G. B. v. EPA, No. CV 23-10345-MWF (AGRX), 2024 WL 1601807 (C.D. Cal., May 8, 2024), 332

Gateview Ranch, Inc. v. Cannibal Outdoor Network, Inc., No. 01CV52 (Colo. Dist. Ct. Dec. 5, 2001), 259

Geer v. Connecticut, 161 U.S. 519 (1896), 216

Geiger v. Filor, 8 Fla. 325 (1859), 374

Gibbs v. Babbitt, 214 F.2d 483 (4th Cir. 2000), 7

Glass v. Goeckel, 703 N.W.2d 58 (Mich. 2005), 112, 202, 282

Golden Feather Cmty. Assn. v. Thermalito Irrigation Dist., 257 Cal. Rptr. 836 (Cal. Ct. App. 1989), 216

Gould v. Greylock Rsrv. Comm'n, 215 N.E.2d 114 (Mass. 1966), 255

Guilliams v. Beaver Lake Club, 175 P. 437 (Or. 1918), 260

Hambrick v. Healthcare Partners Med. Grp., Inc., 189 Cal. Rptr. 3d 31 (Cal. Ct. App. 2015), 216

Held v. Montana, 2024 MT 312 (Dec. 18, 2024), 285, 311, 336, 337

Held v. Montana, No. CDV-2020-307 (Mont. Dist. Ct. Aug. 14, 2023), 336, 337, 338

Held v. State, No. CDV-2020-307 (Mont. Dist. Ct. Aug. 4, 2021), 336

Held v. State of Montana, Cause No. CDV-2020–307, (Mont. 1st Jud. Dist. May 23, 2023), 257, 285, 337

Hill v. Warsewa, No. 20CA1780 (Colo. Ct. App. Jan. 27, 2022), 258

Honolulu et al. v. Sunoco, 344

HTF Devs. v. Minister of Env't Affs. and Tourism, 2006 (5) SA 512 (T) (S. Afr.), 373

Hughes v. Nelson, 399 S.E.2d 24 (S.C. Ct. App. 1990), 260, 265

Hughes v. Oklahoma, 441 U.S. 322 (1979), 216

Idaho Conservation League v. State, 911 P.2d 748 (Idaho 1995), 50, 153, 227

Idaho v. Coeur d'Alene Tribe, 521 U.S. 261 (1997), 277, 379

Illinois Central Railroad Co. v. Illinois, 146 U.S. 387 (1892), 14, 33, 35, 36, 42–48, 227, 240, 262, 268, 282, 293, 439, 442, 443

In re German Ditch & Reservoir Co., 139 P. 2 (Colo. 1914), 257

In re Haw. Elec. Light Co., Inc., 152 Haw. 352 (Haw. 2023), 341

In re Human Rights Case (Environmental Pollution in Balochistan), (1994) 46 PLD (SC) 102 (1992) (Pak.), 370

In re Powder River Drainage Area, 702 P.2d 948 (Mont. 1985), 221
In re United States, 895 F.3d 1101 (9th Cir. 2018), 321
In re Water Use Permit Applications (Waiahole Ditch), 9 P.3d 409 (Haw. 2000), 151, 153, 227, 246, 262, 271
In the Matter of Mono Lake Water Rights Cases. See Mono Lake case (*National Audubon Society v. Superior Court*) in Index
Inyo County v. Los Angeles Dep't of Water & Power, No. BCV-18–101260-TSC (Cal. App. Dep't Super. Ct. 2022), 195
Iowa Citizens for Cmty. Improvement v. State, 962 N.W.2d 780 (Iowa 2021), 315
Irwin v. Phillips, 5 Cal. 140 (Cal. 1855), 55
Jovenes v. Gobierno de Mexico, 304, 310
Juliana v. United States, 217 F. Supp. 3d 1224 (D. Or. 2016), 15, 31, 40, 276, 278, 302, 312, 318–33, 341, 379, 384, 407, 443
Juliana v. United States, 604 U.S. 645 (2025), 15, 31, 276, 278, 284, 310, 318, 330, 379, 384, 407, 430, 443
Juliana v. United States, 947 F.3d 1159 (9th Cir. 2020), 40, 278, 326
Juliana v. United States, 986 F.3d 1295 (9th Cir. 2021), 278
Juliana v. United States, Civ. No. 15-CV-01517-AA, 2023 WL 3750334 (D. Or. June 1, 2023), 278, 285, 294, 312, 320, 321, 323, 325, 327, 329, 334, 379
Juliana v. United States, No. 6:15-cv-01517-AA (D. Or. Mar. 9, 2021), 326
Juliana v. United States, No. 6:15-cv-01517-AA (June 8, 2021), 326
Juliana v. United States, No. 6:15-cv-01517-AA, 2018 WL 6303774 (2018), 326
Juliana v. United States, No. 6:15-CV-01517-AA, 2023 WL 9023339 (D. Or. Dec. 29, 2023), 294, 321, 323, 327, 328, 329
Juliana v. United States, No. 6:15-cv-01517-TC (D. Or. Aug. 12, 2015), 321
Juliana v. United States, No. 18-36082 (9th Cir. Feb. 26, 2019), 324
Juliana v. United States, No. 24-684, D.C. No. 6:15-cv-1517 (9th Cir. July 12, 2024), 330
Juliana v. United States, No. 24-684, D.C. No. 6:15-cv-1517, 2024 WL 5102489, (May 1, 2024), 15, 31, 276, 278, 284, 310, 318, 329, 330, 379, 384, 407, 430, 438, 443
Kain v. Mass. Dep't of Env't Protection, 49 N.E.3d 1124 (Mass. 2016), 312, 316
Kaiser Aetna v. United States, 444 U.S. 164 (1979), 268
Kaiser Steel Corp. v. W. S. Ranch Co., 391 U.S. 593 (1968), 120
Kanuk v. State, Dep't of Nat. Res., 335 P.3d 1088 (Ala. 2014), 314
Karnail Singh v. State of Haryana, 2019 SCC OnLine P&H 704 (India), 387, 404
Ker & Co. v. Couden, 223 U.S. 268 (1912), 374
Kootenai Environmental Alliance v. Panhandle Yacht Club, Inc., 671 P.2d 1085 (Idaho 1983), 151, 222
Kramer v. City of Lake Oswego, 395 P.3d 592 (Or. Ct. App. 2017), 282
Kramer v. City of Lake Oswego, 446 P.3d 1 (Or. 2019), 282
Kreuziger v. Milwaukee Cnty., 617 F. Supp. 3d 970 (E.D. Wis. 2022), 267
Krieter v. Chiles, 595 So. 2d 111 (Fla. 3d Dist. Ct. App. 1992), 250

La Rose v. Her Majesty the Queen, (2019) 2020 FC 1008 (Can.), 284, 304, 309, 310
La Rose v. His Majesty the King, (2023) 2023 FCA 241 (Can.), 310
Labrador Inuit Ass'n v. Newfoundland, (1997) 155 Nfld. & P.E.I.R. 93 (Can. Nfld. C.A.), 378
Lalit Miglani v. State of Uttarakhand, (2017) Writ Petition (PIL) No. 140 of 2015 (UTT H.C.) (India), 386
Lansing Sch. Educ. Ass'n v. Lansing Bd. of Educ., 792 N.W.2d 686 (2010), 243
Lawrence v. Clark Cnty., 254 P.3d 606 (Nev. 2011), 151, 153, 222, 227, 230, 232, 244, 262
Lawrence v. Texas, 539 U.S. 558 (2003), 353
Layla H. v. Commonwealth, No. CL22000632-00 (Va. Cir. Ct. Feb. 9, 2022), 340
Layla H. v. Commonwealth, No. CL22000632-00, (Cir. Ct. Richmond, Aug. 26, 2022), 340
Layla H. v. Virginia, No. 1639-22-2 (Va. Ct. App. Feb. 9, 2022), 339
Layla H. v. Virginia, No. 1639-22-2 (Va. Ct. App. June 25, 2024), 339
Lee v. Macomb Co. Bd. of Comm'rs, 629 N.W.2d 900 (Mich. 2001), 242, 243
Lessee v. Porter, 11 Ohio 138 (1841), 254
Light v. State Water Res. Control Bd., 173 Cal. Rptr. 3d 200 (Cal. Ct. App. 2014), 214, 218
Loper Bright Enterprises v. Raimondo, 144 S.Ct. 2244 (2024), 287, 348, 434, 435
Loper Bright Enterprises v. Raimondo, 603 U.S. 369 (2024), 358
Los Angeles Dep't of Water & Power v. County of Inyo, 67 Cal. App. 5th 1018 (Cal. Ct. App. 2021), 194, 195
Lowman v. Stafford, 226 Cal. App. 2d 31 (1964), 138, 226
Lucas v. South Carolina Coastal Council, 304 S.C. 376 (1991), 239, 268
Lucas v. South Carolina Coastal Council, 505 U.S. 1003 (1992), 201, 239, 268, 269
Lujan v. Defs. of Wildlife, 504 U.S. 555 (1992), 326, 333, 438, 439
Marbury v. Madison, 1 Cranch 137, 2 L.ED. 60 (1803), 437
Marbury v. Madison, 5 U.S. 137 (1803), 436
Marks v. Whitney, 491 P.2d 374 (Cal. 1971), 47, 113, 116, 135, 147, 202, 203, 260
Martin v. Waddell, 41 U.S. 367 (1842), 37–38, 41, 269
Mason v. Hoyle, 14 A. 786 (Conn. 1888), 51, 53
Massachusetts v. EPA, 549 U.S. 497 (2007), 10, 333, 433
Mathur v. Ontario, (2023) 2023 ONSC 2316 (Can.), 310
Matthews v. Bay Head Improvement Ass'n, 471 A.2d 355 (N.J. 1984), 47, 202, 255, 265, 282, 427, 431, 445
Mayor of Clifton v. Passaic Valley Water Comm'n, 557 A.2d 299 (N.J. 1989), 254, 394
Mbabzi v. Att'y Gen., Civil Suit No. 283 of 2012 (Uganda 2012), 301, 372
M.C. Mehta v. Kamal Nath, (1997) 1 S.C.C. 388 (1996) (India), 3, 28, 199, 367
McDonald v. City of Chicago, 561 U.S. 742 (2010), 294
McQueen v. S.C. Coastal Council, 580 S.E.2d 116 (S.C. 1995), 201
McQueen v. S.C. Coastal Council, 580 S.E.2d 116 (S.C. 2003), 271
Medlock v. S.C. Coastal Council, 346 S.E.2d 716 (S.C. 1986), 254

Merrill v. Ohio Dept. Nat. Res., 955 N.E.2d 935 (OH 2011), 254
Merrit v. Parker, 1 N.J.L. 460 (1795), 53
Metro. Manila Dev. Auth. v. Concerned Residents of Manila Bay, G.R. No. 171947-48, 574 S.C.R.A. 661 (Dec. 18, 2008) (Phil.), 366
M.I. Builders Priv. Ltd. v. Radhey Shayam Sahu, (1999) 6 SCC 464 (India), 367
Michigan Citizens for Water Conservation v. Nestle Waters N. Am. Inc., 709 N.W.2d 174 (Mich. Ct. App. 2005), 51, 242
Michigan Citizens for Water Conservation v. Nestle Waters N. Am. Inc., 737 N.W.2d 447 (Mich. 2007), 51, 242
Michigan Educ. Ass'n v. Superintendent of Pub. Instruction, 724 N.W.2d 478 (Mich. Ct. App. 2006), 242
Mineral Cnty. v. Dep't of Conservation & Nat. Res., 20 P.3d 800 (Nev. 2001), 151, 232, 260
Mineral Cnty. v. Lyon Cnty. (Walker Lake), 473 P.3d 418 (Nev. 2020), 50, 229–34, 244, 264
Minister of Water & Env't Affs. v. Really Useful Invs., 2017 (1) SA 505 (SCA) (S. Afr.), 373
Minors Oposa v. Factoran, G.R. No. 101083, 224 S.C.R.A. 792 (1993), 311, 366
Mod. Barber Colls. v. Cal. Emp. State Comm'n, 192 P.2d 916 (Cal. 1948), 138, 152, 226
Mohd. Salim v. State of Uttarakhand, (2017) Writ Petition (PIL) No. 126 of 2014 (UTT H.C.) (India), 386
Mono Cnty. v. Walker River Irrigation Dist., 2022 WL 314993 (D. Nev. 2022), 233
The Mono Lake Case. See Mono Lake case (*National Audubon Society v. Superior Court*) in Index
Mono Lake Committee v. City of Los Angeles, No. 8608 (Mono Super. Ct. Oct. 21, 1987), 166, 169
Myers v. United States, 272 U.S. 52 (1926), 5
Nat. Res. Def. Council. v. Train, 510 F.2d 692 (D.C. Cir. 1974), 441
Nat'l Ass'n of Home Builders v. Babbitt, 130 F.3d 1041 (D.C. Cir. 1997), 6
Nat'l Ass'n of Home Builders v. N.J. Dep't of Env't Prot., 64 F. Supp. 2d 354 (D.N.J. 1999), 271
Nat'l Audubon Soc'y v. Dep't of Water, 869 F.2d 1196 (9th Cir. 1988), 118, 119, 120, 137, 171
Nat'l Audubon Soc'y v. Dep't of Water, 869 F.2d 1206 (9th Cir. 1988), 145
Natalie R. v. State, 2025 UT 5 (Utah 2025), 339, 340
Natalie R. v. State, No. 220901658 (Utah Dist. Ct. Mar. 15, 2022), 340
Natalie R. v. Utah, No. 20230022-SC (Utah. Dist. Ct. Mar. 15, 2022), 340
National Audubon Society v. Superior Court (The Mono Lake Case), 658 P.2d 709 (Cal. 1983). See Mono Lake case (*National Audubon Society v. Superior Court*) in Index
Navahine v. Hawai'i Department of Transportation, No. 1CCV-22-0000631 (Haw. Cir. Ct. 2022), 337, 338, 351

Navahine v. Hawai'i Department of Transportation, No. 1CCV-22-0000631 (Haw. Cir. Ct. 2024), 285, 337
New York v. United States, 505 U.S. 144 (1992), 7
Newton v. MJK/BJK, LLC, 469 P.3d 23 (Idaho 2020), 228
Nollan v. California Coastal Commission, 483 U.S. 825 (1987), 272
Obergefell v. Hodges, 576 U.S. 644 (2015), 323, 353
Op. of the Justs. to the House of Representatives, 313 N.E.2d 561 (Mass. 1974), 255, 272
Op. of the Justs. to the Senate, 424 N.E.2d 1092 (Mass. 1981), 241, 255
Order Granting Summary Judgment, Colo. Oil & Gas Ass'n v. City of Fort Collins, No. 2013CV031385 (Colo. Dist. Ct. Aug. 7, 2014), 248
Order Granting Summary Judgment, Colo. Oil & Gas Ass'n v. City of Longmont, No. 2013CV63 (Colo. Dist. Ct. July 24, 2014), 248
Orion Corp. v. State, 747 P.2d 1062 (Wash. 1987), 271
Owsichek v. Guide Licensing & Control Bd., 763 P.2d 488 (Alaska 1988), 48
Pa. Env't Def. Found. v. Commonwealth, 161 A.3d 911 (Pa. 2017), 248, 255, 265
Pa. Gen. Energy Co. v. Grant Twp., 658 F. App'x. 37 (3d Cir. 2016), 391
Pa. Gen. Energy Co. v. Grant Twp., No. 14-209ERIE, 2017 WL 1215444 (W.D. Pa. Mar. 31, 2017), 390
Pa. Gen. Energy Co. v. Grant Twp., No. 20-cv-00351 (W.D. Pa. Dec. 9, 2020), 391
Pabai Pabai and Guy Kabai v Australia, VID622 (2021), 301
Palazzolo v. Rhode Island, 533 U.S. 606 (2001), 201, 269
Palazzolo v. State, No. WM 88–0297, 2005 WL 1645974 (R.I. Super. Ct. July 5, 2005), 271
Pandey v. India, (2019) No. 187/2017, 304, 309
Parks v. Cooper, 676 N.W.2d 823 (S.D. 2004), 221
Paul v. Virginia, 75 U.S. 168 (1869), 12
P.E.I. v. Canada, (2005) 256 Nfld. & P.E.I.R. 343 (Can. P.E.I. Sup. Ct.), 378
Penn Cent. Transp. Co. v. City of New York, 438 U.S. 104 (1978), 269
People ex rel. Baker v. Mack, 97 Cal. Rptr. 448 (Ct. App. 1971), 113, 114
People ex rel. Webb v. California Fish Co., 138 P. 79 (Cal. 1913), 112, 115
People v. Emmert, 597 P.2d 1025 (Colo. 1979), 257, 258, 261
Piper v. State, 480 P.3d 438 (Wash. Ct. App. 2021), 313, 315
Piper v. State, 497 P.3d 350 (Wash. 2021), 313, 315
Planned Parenthood v. Casey, 505 U.S. 833 (1992), 294
Platkin v. Exxon Mobil Corp., No. 22CV06733RKJBD, 2023 WL 4086353 (D.N.J. June 20, 2023), 252
Pollard v. Hagan, 44 U.S. 212 (1845), 38–40, 41, 240, 257, 268, 269, 276
Portland Fish Co. v. Benson, 108 P. 122 (Or. 1910), 256
PPL Montana, LLC v. Montana, 132 S. Ct. 1215 (2012), 48, 436
PPL Montana, LLC v. Montana, 565 U.S. 576 (2012), 239, 267, 277, 320, 378
Pub. Interest v. Hassell, 172 P.2d 356 (Ariz. Ct. App. 1991), 314

Pub. Interest v. Hassell, 837 P.2d 158 (Ariz. Ct. App. 1991), 221, 263, 331
Putah Creek Council v. Solano Cnty. Water Agency, No. 515766 (Solano Cnty. Super. Ct. 2002), 214
Puterman v. AG, PM 30, 7 (1962) (Isr.), 362, 370
Raines v. Byrd, 521 U.S. 811 (1997), 437
Raleigh Ave. Beach Assn. v. Atlantis Beach Club, Inc., 879 A.2d 112 (N.J. 2005), 202, 427
Ramchandra Simkhanda et. al v. Nepal Government, Office of the Prime Minister and Council of Ministers, 068WO-0597, Decision Number 10204 (2019) (Nepal), 368
Rapanos v. United States, 547 U.S. 715 (2006), 412
Regan v. Cherry Corp., 706 F. Supp. 145 (D.R.I. 1989), 441
Reno v. Flores, 507 U.S. 292 (1993), 294
Reynolds v. Florida, 316 So.3d 813 (Fla. Dist. Ct. App. 2021), 312
Reynolds v. Florida, No. 37 2018 CA 000819 (Fla. Cir. Ct. June 10, 2020), 312, 313
Rhode Island v. Atlantic Richfield Co., 357 F. Supp. 3d 129 (D.R.I. 2018), 251
Rhode Island v. Shell Oil Prod. Co., 35 F.4th 44 (1st Cir. 2022), 252, 265
Robinson Twp. v. Commonwealth, 83 A.3d 901 (Pa. 2013), 15, 199, 247, 249, 282, 390
Robinson v. Ariyoshi, 658 P.2d 287 (Haw. 1982), 246, 256
R.R. Comm'n. v. Pullman Co., 312 U.S. 496 (1941), 120
Rural Litigation and Entitlement Kendra, Dehradun v. State of Uttar Pradesh, 1985 AIR 652 (India), 367
R.W. Docks & Slips v. State Dep't of Nat. Res., 628 N.W.2d 781 (Wis. 2001), 267, 271
Sackett v. EPA, 598 U.S. 651 (2023), 7, 287, 358, 412, 434
Sagoonick v. Alaska II, No. 3AN-24- (Alaska Sup. Ct. May 22, 2024), 339, 349
Salt River Valley Water User's Assn. v. Kovacovich, 411 P.2d 201 (Ariz. Ct. App. 1966), 136
San Carlos Apache Tribe v. Super. Ct. ex rel. Cnty. of Maricopa, 972 P.2d 179 (Ariz. 1999), 262, 263, 314
San Diego Cnty. Archaeological Soc'y, Inc. v. Compadres, 81 Cal. App. 3d 923 (Ct. App. 1978), 282
San Diego Cnty. Archaeological Soc'y, Inc. v. Compadres, 146 Cal. Rptr. 786 (Cal. Ct. App. 1978), 203
Sanders-Reed v. Martinez, 350 P.3d 1221 (N.M. Ct. App. 2015), 314, 318
Save Mille Lacs Sportsfishing, Inc. v. Minn. Dep't of Natural Res., 859 N.W.2d 845 (Minn. Ct. App. 2015), 221
S.C. Coastal Conservation League v. Dep't of Health & Env't Control, 610 S.E.2d 482 (S.C. 2005), 201
Selkirk-Priest Basin Ass'n v. State ex rel. Andrus, 127 Idaho 239 (1995), 50, 153
Selkirk-Priest Basin Ass'n v. State ex rel. Andrus, 899 P.2d 949 (Idaho 1995), 227, 261, 263

Severance v. Patterson, 370 S.W.3d 705 (Tex. 2012), 272
Shailendra Prasad Ambedkar v. Office of Prime Minister et. al., Writ no: 077-WC-0099 (2021) (Nepal), 369
Shehla Zia v. WAPDA, (1994) 46 PLD (SC) 693 (Pak.), 370
Shively v. Bowlby, 152 U.S. 1 (1894), 36, 40, 47, 240, 268, 269, 321
Shokal v. Dunn, 707 P.2d 441 (Idaho 1985), 57
Shrestha v. Off. of the Prime Minister, (2018) 074-WO-0283 (Nepal), 284, 301, 304, 305, 369
Sierra Club v. City of Los Angeles et al., No. SICVCV-01–29768 (Cal. App. Dep't Super. Ct. June 24, 2005), 191
Sierra Club v. Env't Prot. Agency, 540 F.2d 1114 (D.C. Cir. 1976), 6
Sierra Club v. Morton, 405 U.S. 727 (1972), 288, 401, 416, 439
Sipriano v. Great Spring Waters of Am., 1 S.W.3d 75 (Tex. 1999), 56
The Slaughterhouse Cases, 83 US 36 (1873), 12
Solid Waste Agency of N. Cook Cnty. v. U.S. Army Corp of Engineers, 531 U.S. 159 (2001), 7, 412
State of California v. Superior Court (Fogerty), 29 Cal. 3d 240 (Cal. 1981), 115, 135
State v. Black River Phosphate Co., 13 So. 640 (Fla. 1893), 250
State v. Bunkowski, 503 P.2d 1231 (Nev. 1972), 244
State v. Cent. Vt. Ry., 571 A.2d 1128 (Vt. 1989), 221
State v. Chevron Corp., No. PC-2018–4716, 2023 WL 3274138 (R.I. Super. Ct. Apr. 28, 2023), 252, 265, 266
State v. Dickerson, 345 P.3d 447 (Or. 2015), 256
State v. Exxon Mobil Corp., 126 A.3d 266 (N.H. 2015), 251, 265
State v. Hess Corp., 20 A.3d 212 (N.H. 2011), 251, 266
State v. Super. Ct. (Lyon), 29 Cal. 3d 210 (Cal. 1981), 135
State v. Superior Court (Lyon), 625 P.2d 239 (Cal. 1981), 115, 116
State v. Valmont Plantations, 346 S.W.2d 853 (Tex. Civ. App. 1961), 33
State Water Res. Control Bd. Cases, 39 Cal. Rptr. 3d 189, 200–201 (Cal. Ct. App. 2006), 217
Stockman v. Leddy, 129 P. 220 (Colo. 1912), 257
Stop the Beach Renourishment, Inc. v. Fla. Dep't of Env't Prot., 560 U.S. 702 (2010), 160
Thomas v. Gouveia, 2008 (1) SA 392 (T) (S. Afr.), 373
Trepanier v. Cnty. of Volusia, 965 So. 2d 276 (2007), 245
Tulare Lake Basin Water Dist. v. United States, 49 Fed. Cl. 313 (2001), 56, 272
United Plainsmen Ass'n v. N.D. State Water Conservation Comm'n, 247 N.W.2d 457 (N.D. 1976), 150
United States v. 1.58 Acres of Land, 523 F. Supp. 120 (D. Mass. 1981), 241, 255
United States v. 32.42 Acres of Land, 683 F.3d 1030 (9th Cir. 2012), 225, 279
United States v. City & Cnty. of Denver, 656 P.2d 1 (Colo. 1982), 257
United States v. Dist. Court, 458 P.2d 760 (Colo. 1969), 258

United States v. Milner, 583 F.3d 1174 (9th Cir. 2009), 254
United States v. New Mexico, 438 U.S. 696 (1978), 58
United States v. Richardson, 418 U.S. 166 (1974), 437, 439
Urgenda Foundation v. Netherlands, (2015) HAZA C/09/00456689 (Neth.), 284, 301, 302–4, 318, 334, 340
U.S. v. Texas, 599 U. S. 650 (2023), 333
Utah v. United States, 403 U.S. 9 (1971), 258, 265
Uzuegbunam v. Preczewski, 592 U.S. 279 (2021), 327
Verein KlimaSeniorinnen Schweiz v. Switzerland, (2024) 53600/20 Eur. Ct. H.R., 304, 309
Walbridge v. Robinson, 125 P. 812 (Idaho 1912), 261, 263
Walton Cnty. v. Stop the Beach Renourishment, Inc., 998 So. 2d. 1102 (Fla. 2008), 245, 270, 271
Waweru v. Republic, (2006) 1 K.L.R. 677 (H.C.K.) (Kenya), 372
West Pakistan Salt Miners Union v. Director of Industries & Mineral Development, (1994) SCMR (SC) 2061 (Pak.), 370
West Virginia v. EPA, 142 S. Ct. 2587 (2022), 7, 10, 11, 313, 434
West Virginia v. EPA, 597 U.S. 697 (2022), 287, 288, 358
White v. Hughes, 190 So. 446 (Fla. 1939), 250, 260
Wilde Cypress Branch v. Beachline S. Residential, L.L.C., (Fla. 9th Cir. Ct. Apr. 26, 2021), 397
Wilde Cypress Branch v. Beachline S. Residential, L.L.C., No. 6D23-1412, 2023 WL 2580263 (Fla. 6th DCA 2023), 397
Wilson v. Pahrump Fair Water, LLC, 481 P.3d 853 (Nev. 2021), 233
Winters v. United States, 207 U.S. 564 (1908), 58
Zivotovsky v. Clinton, 556 U.S. 189 (2012), 347
Zobel v. Williams, 457 U.S. 55 (1982), 12

Table of Authorities

UNITED STATES CONSTITUTION
  amend. I, 5, 298
  amend. II, 343
  amend. IV, 5
  amend. IX, 322
  amend. I-X, 5
  amend. I-XXVII, 11
  amend. V, 266, 269
  amend. V, XIV, 7, 45
  amend. VI, 298
  amend. XIII, 5
  amend. XIV, §1, cl. 3, 322
  amend. XIV, §1, cl. 4, 322
  art. I, § 2, 5
  art. I, § 8, cl. 3, 6
  art. I, § 19, 8
  art. I-III, 5
  art. IV, § 2, 12
  art. IV, § 3, cl. 1, 153
  art. IV, § 4, 298
  art. V, 11
  art. IX, § 1, 8

UNITED STATES CODE
  5 U.S.C. § 702, 440
  15 U.S.C. § 2619, 111
  16 U.S.C. § 543, 92, 123
  16 U.S.C. § 583, 162
  16 U.S.C. § 1531 et seq., 4
  16 U.S.C. § 1540(g), 111, 440
  33 U.S.C. § 1251 et seq., 4
  33 U.S.C. § 1251(a), 411
  33 U.S.C. § 1342(a), 411
  33 U.S.C. § 1365(a), 111
  33 U.S.C. §§ 1251–1389, 411
  4 U.S.C. § 390h-11, 173, 179
  42 U.S.C. § 300j-8, 111
  42 U.S.C. § 421 et seq., 4
  42 U.S.C. § 4321, 351
  42 U.S.C. § 4321 et seq, 7
  42 U.S.C. § 6972, 111
  42 U.S.C. § 7401 et seq., 4
  42 U.S.C. § 7604, 440
  42 U.S.C. §§ 4321, 155
  42 U.S.C. §§ 7401–7671(q), 77
  42 U.S.C. § 11046, 111
  43 U.S.C. § 1301–1315, 276
  43 U.S.C. § 1311–1312, 277

FEDERAL STATUTES
  Administrative Procedures Act, 440
  Clean Water Act (CWA), 4, 9, 111, 411, 440
  Climate Change Act of 2008, 376
  Emergency Planning and Community Right to Know Act ("EPCRA"), 111
  Endangered Species Act ("ESA"), 4, 111, 417, 440
  Environment Protection Act of 2019, 305
  Environmental Protection Act of 1970, 48, 257
  Forest Act of 2019, 305
  Gaining Responsibility on Water Act of 2017, H.R. 23, 115th Cong. § 108(b), 220
  Gas and Oil Act, 247
  Inflation Reduction Act of 2002, 351, 357
  Lake Front Act of 1869, 44, 45
  National Environmental Policy Act of 1969 (NEPA), 4, 155, 366
  National Water Act of 1998, 373
  Natural Resources and Environmental Protection Act of 1994, 48, 242, 257
  Resources Conservation and Recovery Act ("RCRA"), 111, 339
  Safe Drinking Water Act ("SDWA"), 111
  Sustainable Groundwater Management Act, 149, 219
  Toxic Substances Control Act ("TSCA"), 111

CODE OF FEDERAL REGULATIONS
3 C.F.R. § 859, 351

U.S. STATE CONSTITUTIONS
Cal. Const.
  art. I, § 25, 126
  art. X, § 2, 58, 95, 127, 137, 168, 212, 259
  art. X, § 3, 127, 212, 252
  art. X, § 4, 127, 252
Colo. Const.
  art. IX, § 10, 258
  art. XVI, § 5, 55
  art. XVI, § 5–7, 258
  art. XXVII, § 1–3, 258
Fla. Const.
  art II, § 7, 20, 335
  art. X, § 11, 245, 250, 271, 393
Haw. Const.
  art IX, § 8, 335
  art. XI, § 1, 151, 246
  art. XI, § 11, 256
Ill. Const.
  art. XI, § 2, 335
Mass. Const.
  art. XCVII, 335
Minn. Const.
  art. II, § 2, 477
Mont. Const.
  art. IX, §1, 249, 335, 336
N.M. Const.
  art. XX, § 21, 318
N.Y. Const.
  art. I, § 19, 249, 285, 335
Pa. Const.
  art. I, § 27, 8, 27, 255, 341, 407
  art. I, § 27.58, 199
U.S. Const.
  art. IV, § 3, cl. 1, 276
Utah Const.
  art. XX, §1, 448
Virginia Const.
  art. XI, § 1, 261

STATE STATUTES
California Environmental Quality Act
  (CEQA), 9, 76, 103, 155, 156, 195
Cal. Pub. Res. Code
  § 2100, 9
  § 5045 et seq., 160
  § 5047, 164
  § 5048, 164
  § 6307, 128
  §§ 5045–5046, 164

§ 21000, 155
§ 21081, 156
Cal. Water Code
  § 102, 212, 253, 259
  § 104, 212, 253, 259
  § 106, 128
  § 1011, 136
  § 1201, 212, 253, 259
  § 1260, 181
  § 1727, 181
  §§ 10720–10737.8, 149
  § 85023, 127, 181, 212
California Wilderness Act of 1984, 162, 163
Cal.-Santa Monica, Cal., Mun. Code
  § 12.02.030(b), 391
Colo. Rev. Stat.
  § 18–4–504.5, 258
Fla. Stat.
  § 373.223, 245, 250
  § 403.412(9)(a), 396
Fla.-Orange, County, Fla,
  Charter art. VII, § 704.1(A)-(B), 396
Haw. Rev. Stat.
  § 174C-2(c), 246, 256
  § 174C-3, 246
  § 174C-49(a)(4), 246
Idaho Code
  § 58–1201, 151, 223
  § 58–1201–1203, 228, 250, 261, 263
  § 58–1201(4), (6), 153, 228, 261
  § 58–1203, 257, 264, 444
  § 58–1203 (1), 153, 228, 263
  § 58–1203 (3), 154, 228, 263
La. Civ. Code
  art. 450, 254
La. Stat.
  § 9:1101, 254
Mich. Comp. Laws
  § 324.1701(1), 48
  § 691.1202, 257
  § 691.1202(1), 48, 242, 257
Mich. Stat.
  § 324.1071(1), 242
  § 324.1704(2), 243
Michigan Environmental Protection Act of 1970, 242
Minn. Stat.
  § 116B.01, 242
  § 116B.01-.13, 243
  § 116B.03, 9
  § 116B.03(1), 243
  § 116D.01-.11, 243

Minnesota Environmental Rights Act, 9, 242
Mont. Code
  § 85-2-101(5), 57
Montana Environmental Protection Act, 336
N.J. Stat.
  § 58:11A-3(g), 254
Nev. Rev. Stat.
  § 533.025, 224
Ohio-Toledo, Ohio, Mun. Code ch. XVII,
  § 253, 392
  § 254(a)-(c), 392
  § 254(a), (d), 392
  § 257(a), 392
Pa. Const.
  art. I, § 27, 247
Pa.-Pittsburg, Pa., Code
  § 618.03, 390
S.C. Code
  § 49–1-10, 254
Utah Code
  § 23-21-4(1), 448
  § 65A-1-1(6), 448

STATE REGULATIONS
  Cal. Code Regs. tit. 14
    § 4752, 123
  Cal. Code Regs. tit. 23
    §§ 995–996, 187
    §995(b), 188
    §996, 359, 188
  Fish and Game Code
    § 5937, 166
    § 5946, 167, 168, 172
  Fla. Admin. Code
    r. 50-5.002, 312, 316, 317, 353

STATE EXECUTIVE ORDERS
  Mass. Exec. Order No. 569, 312, 315, 316
  Mass. Exec. Order No. 604, 316

INTERNATIONAL CONSTITUTIONS
  Brazil
    Constituição Federal [Constitution] 1988
      art. 20, 376
  Canada
    canadian charter of rights and freedoms
      § 7, 1982, 309

Ecuador
  Constitución De La Republica Del Ecuador
    [Constitution] 2008, 830, 831
    art. 71, 377, 381, 382
    art. 73, 382
India
  Constitution 1950
    art. 21, 367
Kenya
  Constitution 2010
    art. 42, 372
Nepal
  Constitution
    art. 30, 305
    art. 51(g), 305
Nigeria
  Constitution 1999
    ch. 2, § 20, 372
Pakistan
  Constitution 1973
    art. 9, 369, 370
Philippines
  Constitution 1987
    art. II, § 16, 366
South Africa
  Constitution 1996
    §11, 373
    §24, 373
    §27, 373
Uganda
  Constitution 1995
    art. 39, 371
    art. 237(2)(b), 371

INTERNATIONAL STATUTES
  Australia
    Yarra River Protection Act 2017, 385, 404
  New Zealand
    Te Awa Tupua (Whanganui River Claims Settlement) Act 2017, 384, 385, 403
  Scotland
    Land Reform (Scotland) Act 2003, 375
  South Africa
    National Water Act 36 of 1998, 373
  Uganda
    The Land Act, ch. 227, § 44 (2010), 371
    The Land Act, ch. 227, § 44(1) (1998), 371
    National Environmental Act, 2019, 388

Introduction

The Public Trust Doctrine and the Foundations of Environmental Governance

A. The Missing Constitutional Foundations of Environmental Law   4
B. The Public Trust as an Emerging Foundation for Environmental
   Governance   13
C. The Turning Point: Mono Lake and Beyond   16
D. Public Trust Principles and Environmental Rights   17
E. A Brief Synopsis of What Follows   21

This book explores the development of one of our oldest legal principles – the public trust doctrine – which comes down to the commonsense idea that some natural resources are so important to everyone that they cannot belong to just anyone, and so the government must therefore protect them for the benefit of all the people (who, in turn, can hold the government to account). The core public trust principle that flows from this idea partners an express government obligation to protect trust resources with an implied public right to the benefit of trust resources – and after the Mono Lake case, an implied *environmental* right. Centering on the birth of the modern doctrine at Mono Lake, the book examines how public trust principles have come to fill an important gap in environmental law – and perhaps even constitutional law – both in the United States and around the world.

Today, public trust principles in different legal settings create public rights and responsibilities with regard to designated natural resource commons, obligating the state to manage them in trust for the public. The original common law doctrine is thought to be among the oldest of the common law, with roots extending as far back as ancient Rome and early Britain, where it primarily protected public fishing and transportation values associated with navigable waterways.[1] Early on, the common law came to recognize that some natural resources – especially waterways – are so foundational to civilization that they cannot be owned by anyone in particular; instead, they must belong to everyone together. To prevent private expropriation or

---

[1] *See* J. INST. PROOEMIUM, 2.1.1. (T. Sandars trans., 4th ed. 1869) (translation from the INSTITUTES OF JUSTINIAN, by the Byzantine Emperor, Justinian I).

monopolization of these critical public commons, the sovereign – be it the Emperor, the King, or later, the elected legislative and executive branches of government – is entrusted to manage them on behalf of the public.[2]

Over these hundreds and even thousands of years, the doctrine has gradually transformed from an affirmation of sovereign authority over trust resources to a recognition of sovereign responsibility to protect them for present and future generations – historically to ensure public access, but increasingly for environmental reasons as well. Especially in recent decades, it has evolved substantially through U.S. common, constitutional, and statutory law to address a broader variety of natural resources, from waterways to wildlife, and a broader scope of public values associated with them, including ecological, recreational, scientific, and scenic values.[3] In many jurisdictions, the doctrine operates in constitutive terms – either as a quasi-constitutional or overtly constitutionalized constraint on sovereign authority that binds governmental discretion with regard to trust resources. In others, the doctrine remains a more fluid feature of common or statutory law, deployed in different circumstances for different legal purposes. In each of these contexts, the unifying public trust principle is the sovereign obligation to protect designated public natural resources, for the benefit of citizens who are entitled to hold the state to account.

As its primary example, the book shares the epic tale of the fall and rise of Mono Lake – the strange and beautiful Dead Sea of California – which fostered some of the most important environmental law developments of the last century,[4] and which has become a platform for some of the most potentially important developments in

---

[2] *See, e.g.*, Joseph Sax, *The Public Trust Doctrine in Natural Resource Law: Effective Judicial Intervention*, 68 MICH. L. REV. 471 (1970) (setting forth the seminal academic statement of the public trust doctrine as a modern legal tool to aid in the protection of natural resources); Michael C. Blumm, *Public Property and the Democratization of Western Water Law: A Modern View of the Public Trust Doctrine*, 19 ENV'T L. 573, 580 (1989) (discussing the public trust doctrine as "a democratizing force by (1) preventing monopolization of trust resources and (2) promoting natural resource decision making that involves and is accountable to the public").

[3] *See infra* Chapter 8 ("Beyond Mono Lake: The Development of the Public Trust across the United States"), Chapter 10 ("Environmental Rights Around the World: Public Trust Principles and the Rights of Nature Movement") (discussing the development of the doctrine domestically and internationally).

[4] *See, e.g.*, Michael Blumm & Thea Schwartz, *Mono Lake and the Evolving Public Trust in Western Water*, 37 ARIZ. L. REV. 701 (1995) (analyzing impacts of the *Mono Lake* case on subsequent cases and the evolving public trust doctrine nationwide); Craig Anthony Arnold, *Working out an Environmental Ethic: Anniversary Lessons from Mono Lake*, 4 WYO. L. REV. 1 (2004) (using the Mono Lake case study to suggest that politics and public participation are as critical as formal law to environmental successes); Craig Anthony Arnold & Leigh A. Jewell, *Litigation's Bounded Effectiveness and the Real Public Trust Doctrine: The Aftermath of the Mono Lake Case*, 8 HASTINGS W. NW. J. ENV'T L. & POL'Y 1, 4 (2001) (arguing that the *Mono Lake* case laid the foundation for a conception of the public trust that transcends the courtroom); Sherry A. Enzler, *How Law Mattered to the Mono Lake Ecosystem*, 35 WM. & MARY ENV'T L. & POL'Y REV. 413 (2011) (reviewing the significance of the *Mono Lake* case for public trust and environmental law at a systemic level).

the new century.[5] One of the all-time great stories of American environmental law, the Mono Lake epic recounts the protracted conflict over water between the City of Los Angeles and advocates for the Mono Basin, the eastern watershed of the high Sierra Nevada crest at Yosemite National Park, four hundred miles to the north. In 1983, in *National Audubon Society v. Superior Court*, the California Supreme Court took the first steps toward resolving that conflict by casting the public trust doctrine as an inalterable source of state obligation to protect the environmental values at stake in Mono Lake, in addition to such traditional trust values as public navigation.[6]

The Mono Lake conflict followed a century of California's efforts to cope with limited water resources in the face of compelling but conflicting demands, culminating in a historic legal decision that continues to influence related environmental dilemmas worldwide. The book explores the vivid backstory, unlikely journey, and lasting legacy of the California Supreme Court's famous decision in *National Audubon Society* – "the Mono Lake case" – which inspired a quiet revolution in public trust ideals that has expanded to other states and even nations as far distant as India.[7] Even today, in the fifth decade following the decision, the case remains the leading example of environmental public trust litigation in the United States, inspiring a new age of public trust advocacy that has extended well beyond navigable waterways to groundwater, wildlife, ecosystems, and even the global climate.

Yet the modern public trust is not limited to litigation. While environmental plaintiffs still apply the doctrine against the state as a sword in litigation, and states increasingly use the doctrine as a shield in litigation to defend their actions protecting trust resources, public trust principles are also implemented at all levels of government as a guiding principle and best management practice. Whether adopted constitutionally, by statute, or in administrative regulations, public trust principles help state actors methodically consider proposed actions before they are taken to ensure that they will not inadvertently or inappropriately harm jurisdictional trust resources.

Although public trust principles appear in legal systems across the world, they remain especially important in the United States, in part because they help fill a gap in the underlying principles supporting American environmental law. The United States was an early mover toward the modern norm of constitutional governance, but it is a relative latecomer to the importance of environmental

---

[5] *See, e.g.,* Chapter 9 ("Public Trust Principles, Environmental Rights, and Trust-Rights Climate Advocacy") (discussing atmospheric trust cases).
[6] Nat'l Audubon Soc'y v. Super. Ct. (The *Mono Lake* Case), 658 P.2d 709 (Cal. 1983).
[7] M.C. Mehta v. Kamal Nath, (1997) 1 S.C.C. 388 (1996) (India), in I UNITED NATIONS ENVIRONMENT PROJECT COMPENDIUM OF JUDICIAL DECISIONS IN MATTERS RELATED TO THE ENVIRONMENT, NATIONAL DECISIONS 259 (1998), www.asianjudges.org/wp-content/uploads/2013/10/Compendium_Judicial_Decisions_Nat_vi.pdf (discussing the role of the public trust doctrine in Indian law and quoting the California Supreme Court's description of the doctrine in *Mono Lake*).

governance. And while it has helped lead the development of environmental law through such groundbreaking statutes as the National Environmental Policy Act,[8] the Clean Air and Water Acts,[9] and the Endangered Species Act,[10] even these pioneering pieces of legislation have been challenged, both directly and through their implementing regulations, in ways that reflect their more attenuated constitutional grounding in comparison to alternative constitutional frameworks.[11] This attenuated support for U.S. environmental law reflects the contrasting governance concerns that prevailed at the time the Constitution was drafted. Its framers, mired in political contest over the nature of the unfolding American experiment, perceived the undue exercise of sovereign authority as the greatest potential threat, rather than the loss of environmental values in nature that perhaps only sovereign authority can protect.

Commencing the journey, this introductory chapter traces how the public trust doctrine has developed, in part, to buttress inherent weaknesses in the foundations of U.S. environmental law, providing additional support for environmental governance. It introduces the core public trust principle as a partnership between reciprocal principles of sovereign obligations and environmental rights, and how the Mono Lake case became an important inflection point in the development of the modern doctrine as a tool of environmental advocacy. It touches on the hopes and fears that ongoing doctrinal developments have engendered in proponents and skeptics, including an emerging generational divide between younger environmental advocates enthusiastic about its promise and older advocates leery of its potential to destabilize existing regulatory frameworks. It closes with a synopsis of the ten chapters that follow, fleshing out the full public trust saga in all the vivid detail it deserves.

A. THE MISSING CONSTITUTIONAL FOUNDATIONS OF ENVIRONMENTAL LAW

The American experiment of constitutional governance began with trial and error, but it set the global standard. In 1789, after a failed first try with the Articles of

---

[8] National Environmental Policy Act, 42 U.S.C. § 421 et seq. (1969).
[9] Clean Air Act, 42 U.S.C. § 7401 et seq. (1963); Clean Water Act, 33 U.S.C. § 1251 et seq. (1972).
[10] Endangered Species Act, 16 U.S.C. § 1531 et seq. (1973).
[11] Compare with Brazil's constitution, CONSTITUIÇÃO FEDERAL [C.F.] [CONSTITUTION] art. 225 (Braz.) ("All have the right to an ecologically balanced environment, which is an asset of common use and essential to a healthy quality of life, and both the Government and the community shall have the duty to defend and preserve it for present and future generations."). *See also* Ecuador's constitution CONSTITUCIÓN DE LA REPUBLICA DEL ECUADOR 2008 [C.P.] [CONSTITUTION] Oct. 20, 2008, art. 71 (Ecuador). The constitution refers to "[t]he unique and priceless natural assets of Ecuador includ[ing], among others, the physical, biological and geological formations whose value from the environmental, scientific, cultural, or landscape standpoint requires protection, conservation, recovery and promotion." *Id.* art. 404.

Confederation,[12] the framers of the American Constitution outlined a tripartite structure of government that diffused sovereign power among separately acting branches and guaranteed citizens a set of inalienable rights.[13] Enshrined in the Constitution's Bill of Rights, these famously included legal guarantees for freedom of speech and assembly,[14] and rights against cruel and unusual punishment.[15] But in the late eighteenth century, when open space was still plentiful, natural resources were bountiful, and the Industrial Revolution had not yet fully taken hold, environmental conflicts were not among the governance problems that worried the framers.[16] They were much more worried about the resurrection of a monarchy, and the potential for unchecked power to corrupt future leaders.[17]

The oldest written constitution still in force, the U.S. Constitution remains a landmark legal accomplishment, a bedrock for the distinctive American civilization that has followed, and inspiration for many of the most important developments in democratic governance worldwide.[18] Though it remains a work in progress,[19] it is an enduring source of American identity, culture, and aspiration that forever changed

---

[12] *See, e.g.*, Erin Ryan, Federalism and the Tug of War Within 70 (2012) (hereinafter Ryan, Tug of War) (discussing the failure of the Articles of Confederation because it failed to confer sufficient national power or structures of national government to overcome collective action problems among the new federation of states).

[13] U.S. Const. art. I-III; U.S. Const. amend. I-X; *see also* Ryan, Tug of War, *supra* note at 602–606.

[14] U.S. Const. amend. I.

[15] U.S. Const. amend. IV.

[16] *Cf.* Jack Lewis, *Looking Backward: A Historical Perspective on Environmental Regulations*, EPA J. (Mar. 1988), available at www.epa.gov/archive/epa/aboutepa/looking-backward-historical-perspective-environmental-regulations.html (discussing the paucity of environmental regulation at the time of the nation's founding in light of widespread fear of tyrannical governance and desire for economic development).

[17] *Id.*

[18] Christopher A. Suarez, *Democratic School Desegregation: Lessons from Election Law*, 119 Penn. State. L. Rev. 747, 757–58 (2015) (celebrating the court's embrace of the one person, one vote principle in electoral law.); David A.J. Richards, 32 Emory L.J. 405, 406 (1983) ("the idea of human rights lay behind the American innovation of judicial review: since human rights are not just the subject of political bargaining and compromise, countermajoritarian courts with the American power of judicial review are a natural institutional way to secure such rights from the incursions of the institutions based on majority rule."); Myers v. United States, 272 U.S. 52, 85 (1926) ("the separation of powers was adopted by the convention of 1787 not to promote efficiency but to preclude the exercise of arbitrary power.").

[19] The U.S. Constitution is not without its critics, or its flaws, for example, regarding the electoral college, the difficulty of amending it, and its original embrace of slavery. U.S. Const. art. I, § 2 (embracing slavery as a national institution), *repealed by* U.S. Const. amend. XIII; *see, e.g.*, David Shultz, *Voting Rights and the Unconstitutionality of the Electoral College Winner-Take-All Allocation*, 66 S.D. L. Rev. 457, 458 (2021) (arguing that "the winner-take-all allocation for awarding electoral votes" used in 48 states "disenfranchises voters"); Richard Albert, *The World's Most Difficult Constitution to Amend?*, 110 Cal. L. Rev. 2005, 2007 (2021) (arguing that the U.S. Constitution "may be the world's most difficult to amend."); Robert M. Cover, Justice Accused: Antislavery and the Judicial Process, 159–74 (1975) (critiquing the legal system's acquiescence to punishing the anti-slavery movement).

the world. Even so, it stands apart today for failing to definitively address the need for environmental regulation that many of the modern constitutions it helped inspire now do as a matter of course.[20]

The American Constitution pioneered individual rights and enumerated sovereign responsibilities, but no part speaks directly to the responsibility of environmental stewardship, or the various rights and duties that stewardship implies. While it sets forth the basic structure and functions of government, it elides the critical role government must play in protecting not only the human rights and relationships catalogued in its articles and amendments, but also the human relationship with the shared natural resources on which we all depend for life and livelihood.

Indeed, Americans are often surprised to learn that the most solid legal basis for our primary federal environmental laws – the Clean Air and Water Acts, the Endangered Species Act, and others curtailing pollution and harms to natural resources – are based not on any kind of constitutional environmental principle but instead on the Constitution's Commerce Clause, which empowers Congress to regulate market transactions across state, tribal, and international lines.[21] Since the modern environmental movement took form in the 1970s, opponents have challenged

---

[20] Sam Bookman, *Demystifying Environmental Constitutionalism*, 54 ENV'T L. 1, 9 (2023) ("Today, the constitutions of at least 141 UN member states expressly address environmental issues."); *see* Lael K. Weis, *Environmental Constitutionalism: Aspiration or Transformation?*, 16 INT'L J. CON. L. 863, 842 n. 34 (2018) ("Approximately two-thirds of national constitutions contain rights provision."); *see also* DAVID R. BOYD, THE ENVIRONMENTAL RIGHTS REVOLUTION: A GLOBAL STUDY OF CONSTITUTIONS, HUMAN RIGHTS, AND THE ENVIRONMENT 47–50 (2012) (outlining environmental rights provisions in constitutions worldwide); *see, e.g.*, BUNDESVERFASSUNG [BV] [CONSTITUTION] Apr. 18, 1999, SR 101, art. 74 (Switz.), www.constituteproject.org/constitution/Switzerland_2014 ("The Confederation shall legislate on the protection of the population and its natural environment against damage or nuisance."); CONSTITUCIÓN DE LA REPUBLICA DEL ECUADOR 2008 [C.P.] [CONSTITUTION] Oct. 20, 2008, art. 71 (Ecuador); Consolidated Version of the Treaty on the Functioning of the European Union art. 11, 191, 193, May 9, 2008, 2008 O.J. (C 115) 47 (establishing that the EU "shall contribute to pursuit of … preserving, protecting and improving the quality of the environment,"); *see also* James R. May & Erin Daley, *Vindicating Fundamental Rights Worldwide*, 11 OR. REV. INT'L L. 365, 407–33 (discussing the obstacles faced by American courts in vindicating environmental rights); *id.* at 366–72 (discussing the history of the evolution of international fundamental environmental rights).

[21] U.S. CONST. art. I, § 8, cl. 3; Friends of the Earth v. Carey, 552 F.2d 25, 37 (2d Cir. 1977) (noting that Congress enacted the Clean Air Act under the Commerce Clause); *accord* Sierra Club v. Env't Prot. Agency, 540 F.2d 1114, 1139 (D.C. Cir. 1976) ("Regulation of air pollution clearly is within the power of the federal government under the commerce clause."). The Commerce Clause has been used as the constitutional basis for environmental laws protecting air and water quality because, inter alia, these are channels of interstate commerce that Congress is authorized to regulate under the clause. Pollution and hazardous waste are also very often the product of activities in interstate commerce or were transported in interstate commerce. Even wildlife laws have been justified under the Commerce Clause because wildlife viewing and hunting are activities within the scope of interstate commerce. Nat'l Ass'n of Home Builders v. Babbitt, 130 F.3d 1041, 1057 (D.C. Cir. 1997) ("We hold that the section 9(a)(1) of the Endangered Species Act is within Congress' Commerce Clause power and that the Fish and Wildlife Service's application of the provision to the Delhi Sands Flower–Loving Fly was therefore constitutional.").

a number of these laws in court, sometimes successfully, for allegedly exceeding constitutional bounds.[22] Some of these challenges have attacked legislation directly and some have focused on their implementing regulations, often suggesting that environmental regulations exceed both statutory and constitutional authority.[23] In other cases, the Supreme Court has overturned environmental regulations it has concluded stray so close to the boundaries of constitutionally permissible authority that clearer congressional authorization is required.[24] Perhaps, the most successful federal environmental laws are those that create procedural rights and obligations,[25] such as the National Environmental Policy Act, requiring government actors to "look before they leap" on taking actions that could cause environmental harm,[26] and which follow from much clearer constitutional procedural traditions such as due process.[27] Laws that promise substantive environmental protection require more work to ground, at least federally.[28]

Other nations have taken a different approach. The Swiss Constitution, for example, explicitly authorizes legislation for "the protection of the population and its natural environment against damage or nuisance,"[29] removing some of the pragmatic hurdles that environmental governance has faced in the United States. The constitution of Nepal declares that "the State shall pursue … policies" that "protect, promote, and make environmentally friendly and sustainable use of natural resources."[30] In a less utilitarian commitment to environmental protection, Ecuador's constitution recognizes environmental rights directly in nature, declaring that "Pacha Mama" (Mother Earth) "has the right to integral respect for its existence and for the maintenance and

---

[22] See, e.g., New York v. United States, 505 U.S. 144 (1992) (challenging the Low Level Radioactive Waste Policy Act as violating the Tenth Amendment); Gibbs v. Babbitt, 214 F.2d 483, 497 (4th Cir. 2000) (upholding Endangered Species Act protection for red wolves against a challenge that it exceeded Commerce Clause authority on grounds of the regulations' substantial effect on interstate commerce via "tourism, scientific research, and other potential economic activities.").

[23] See, e.g., Solid Waste Agency of N. Cook Cnty. v. U.S. Army Corp of Engineers, 531 U.S. 159 (2001) (arguing that regulations implementing the Clean Water Act exceeded statutory authority and that reading the statute otherwise could put it in jeopardy of exceeding congressional authority under the Commerce Clause).

[24] See, e.g., West Virginia v. Env't Prot. Agency, 142 S. Ct. 2587 (2022) (overturning Clean Power Plan regulations designed to reduce greenhouse gas emissions under the Clean Air Act for this reason); Sackett v. Env't Prot. Agency, 598 U.S. 651 (2023) (overturning Clean Water Act regulations to protect wetlands without a continuous surface connection to conventionally navigable waterways for similar reasons).

[25] Dinah Shelton, *Developing Substantive Environmental Rights*, 1 J. Hum. Rts. & Env't 90–92 (2010).

[26] 42 U.S.C. § 4321 et seq.

[27] U.S. Const. amends. V, XIV.

[28] Shelton, *supra* note 25, at 90–99.

[29] Bundesverfassung [BV] [Constitution] Apr. 18, 1999, SR 101, art. 74 (Switz.), www.constituteproject.org/constitution/Switzerland_2014 ("The Confederation shall legislate on the protection of the population and its natural environment against damage or nuisance.").

[30] Constitution of Nepal, art. 51(g), https://lawcommission.gov.np/en/wp-content/uploads/2021/01/Constitution-of-Nepal.pdf.

regeneration of its life cycles, structure, functions and evolutionary processes," and that "[a]ll persons, communities, peoples and nations can call upon public authorities to enforce the rights of nature."[31] Many nations in the developing world, generally with newer constitutions, provide explicit constitutional protection for environmental values.[32] Nations in the European Union and other developed nations with older constitutions have often interpreted their own constitutional promises of fundamental rights or due process to include protection for environmental values.[33]

Most American state constitutions are modeled after the federal constitution, but some have departed from that model in adding environmental promises, often based on public trust principles emphasizing sovereign responsibility to protect environmental values for the benefit of the public. Some include constitutional language explicitly recognizing the rights of citizens to enjoy a healthy environment and establishing state responsibility to protect them. For example, the Pennsylvania Constitution asserts that citizens "have a right to clean air, pure water, and to the preservation of the natural, scenic, historic and esthetic values of the environment," and that "Pennsylvania's public natural resources are the common property of all the people, including generations yet to come."[34] It goes on to guarantee that "[a]s trustee of these resources, the Commonwealth shall conserve and maintain them for the benefit of all the people."[35] In 1972, Montanans added constitutional language affirming that "the state and each person shall maintain and improve a clean and healthful environment in Montana for present and future generations."[36] New York's constitution was amended in 2022 to promise "a right to clean air and water, and a healthful environment."[37]

---

[31] CONSTITUCIÓN DE LA REPUBLICA DEL ECUADOR 2008 [C.P.] [CONSTITUTION] Oct. 20, 2008, art. 71 (Ecuador). For further discussion of the constitutional adoption of environmental rights in Ecuador, see Chapter 10(B) ("The Public Trust Doctrine and Rights of Nature Movement").

[32] Specific examples are discussed in Chapter 10(B) ("The Public Trust Doctrine and Rights of Nature Movement"), including noteworthy examples from Brazil, Ecuador, Kenya, Nepal, Nigeria, and Pakistan, among others.

[33] BOYD, *supra* note 20, at 214 ("Western European nations without constitutional recognition of the right [to a healthy environment] have ratified the Aarhus Convention ... and are bound by the jurisprudence of the European Court of Human Rights, which recognizes the right to a healthy environment."); *id.* at 225–26 ("In Italy, there is no explicit constitutional right to a healthy environment. However, courts have interpreted the constitutional right to health as incorporating the right to live in a healthy environment."); Aarhus Convention on Access to Information, Public Participation in Decision-making and Access to Justice in Environmental Matters, art. 1 E.U., June 25, 1998, 2161 U.N.T.S 447 ("In order to contribute to the protection of the right of every person of present and future generations to live in an environment adequate to his or her health and well-being, each Party shall guarantee the rights of access to information, public participation in decision-making, and access to justice in environmental matters in accordance with the provisions of this Convention.").

[34] PA. CONST. art. I, § 27.

[35] *Id.*

[36] MONT. CONST. art. IX, § 1 ("the state and each person shall maintain and improve a clean and healthful environment in Montana for present and future generations").

[37] N.Y. CONST. art. I, § 19.

A. Missing Foundations of Environmental Law

Even without these constitutional provisions, American states have plenary authority to protect environmental values within them. Many have used it to enact meaningful environmental laws, including environmental procedural requirements, antipollution laws, land use planning mandates, and resource conservation laws.[38] Yet the natural resource commons most in need of protection – such as air, water, and biodiversity – very often defy jurisdictional boundaries, in that the benefits they confer and the harms we may cause them cross state lines.[39] Regulating water or air pollution in one state does no good when the waterway runs through multiple states and air pollutants travel on the wind, and wildlife roams freely.[40] Hazardous radioactive waste may require transport across multiple states or otherwise threaten shared resources.[41]

The special challenge of environmental law is that state laws often require federal coordination to be effective, while federal laws often rely on state implementation to be effective.[42] Similar dynamics unfold at every scale of governance – from the municipal to the international – although as regulatory scale increases, regulatory tools become even weaker, leaving international environmental law more aspirational than operational in many instances.[43] Moreover, even where they find solid legal foundation, both state and federal environmental laws struggle for efficacy in protecting public trust resources that are threatened for reasons other than pollution.[44]

For example, in the context of protecting American waterways, the closest thing to a unifying national strategy is the Clean Water Act. While it deserves enormous credit for reducing pollution into navigable waterways from many industrial and

---

[38] For example, the California Environmental Quality Act obligates the state "to provide a high-quality environment that at all times is healthful and pleasing to the senses and intellect," CAL. PUB. RES. CODE § 2100 (1970), and the Minnesota Environmental Rights Act authorizes citizen to sue "for the protection of the air, water, land, or other natural resources located within the state, whether publicly or privately owned, from pollution, impairment, or destruction." MINN. STAT. § 116B.03 (1971).

[39] See, e.g., RYAN, TUG OF WAR, supra note 12 at 145–80 (exploring the interjurisdictional nature of boundary-crossing environmental problems such as air and water pollution, hazardous waste management, and climate change).

[40] Id.

[41] Id.

[42] See RYAN, TUG OF WAR, supra note 12 at 378–79.

[43] See Erin Ryan, Environmental Federalism's Tug of War Within, in THE LAW AND POLICY OF ENVIRONMENTAL FEDERALISM (Kalyani Roberts, ed. 2015) at 377–79, 414 (discussing interjurisdictional environmental management challenges at the subnational level); L. Scambler, Despite Efforts, International Environmental Law is Aspirational Rather than Successful in Its Contribution to the Protection of the Global Environment and in the Fight against Climate Change, 9 PLYMOUTH L. & CRIM. JUSTICE REV. 66 (2017) (discussing the challenges of effective international environmental law).

[44] See Erin Ryan, How the Successes and Failures of the Clean Water Act Fueled the Rise of the Public Trust Doctrine and Rights of Nature Movement, 73 CASE W. RES. L. REV. 475 (2022) (noting the Clean Water Act's focus on protecting water quality provides few statutory tools to ensure sufficient water quantity in vulnerable waterways).

municipal pipes,⁴⁵ it has no means to protect vulnerable waterways from other kinds of harm, such as agricultural or nonpoint-source pollution – or even human actions that threaten their continued existence, by siphoning them down to dangerously low levels.⁴⁶ While the Clean Water Act regulates water quality, waterways across the world – like Mono Lake – are endangered by practices that threaten not just the quality but the quantity of water within them, often due to excessive water withdrawals under state laws.⁴⁷ The assertions of the Act that come closest to protecting waterways as *waterways* – regulations that prevent the destruction of wetlands – have repeatedly been challenged in court, sometimes successfully, for straying too close to the boundaries of authority conferred by the Commerce Clause.⁴⁸ Advocates defending waterways and other natural resources threatened by overuse have lamented the limits of the U.S. Constitution in failing to provide more straightforward authority for the kinds of regulations needed to protect them.⁴⁹

U.S. legal tools for protecting the atmospheric commons have fared even worse. The Clean Air Act is the recognized national strategy for regulating boundary-crossing air pollution, but the statute does not specifically address climate change, and efforts to deploy it in service of climate governance have met with stiff legal resistance. The Supreme Court did recognize a federal obligation to regulate greenhouse gas pollution under the Act in *Massachusetts v. EPA*,⁵⁰ and the Environmental Protection Agency (EPA) has interpreted parts of the statute authorizing the regulation of any air pollutant to support regulation of greenhouse gas pollution by cars and trucks.⁵¹ However, the Court's subsequent holding in *West Virginia v. EPA* clarified that more is needed from Congress before EPA may rely on some of its most

---

⁴⁵ The Clean Water Act was designed to limit this kind of "point-source" pollution, traceable to a discrete point of conveyance, but it has almost no tools to limit nonpoint source pollution, or the kind of overland pollution that arises when rain passes over pollutants accumulating on roads, yards, or agricultural fields. RYAN, TUG OF WAR, *supra* note 12 at 152.

⁴⁶ See Ryan, *How the Successes and Failures of the Clean Water Act Fueled the Rise of the Public Trust Doctrine and Rights of Nature Movement*, 73 CASE WESTERN RES. L. REV. 475, 481–83 (2022) (discussing the limits of the Clean Water Act).

⁴⁷ *Id.*

⁴⁸ Erin Ryan, *Federalism, Regulatory Architecture, and the Clean Water Rule: Seeking Consensus on the Waters of the United States*, 46 ENV'T L. 277, 289–97 (2016).

⁴⁹ Cf. James R. May, *The Case for Environmental Human Rights: Recognition, Implementation, and Outcomes*, 42 CARDOZO L. REV. 983 (2021) (detailing the history of failed attempts to constitutionally recognize a fundamental environmental right); *see generally* Robin Kundis Craig, *Should There Be a Constitutional Right to a Clean/Healthy Environment?*, 34 ENV'T L. REP. 11013, 11020–21 (2004).

⁵⁰ Massachusetts v. E.P.A., 549 U.S. 497 (2007).

⁵¹ See *Clean Air Act: A Summary of the Act and Its Major Requirements*, CONGRESSIONAL RESEARCH SERVICE (updated September 13, 2022), https://crsreports.congress.gov RL30853 (noting that Section 202 of the act "requires the EPA administrator to prescribe 'standards applicable to the emission of any air pollutant from any class or classes of new motor vehicles or new motor vehicle engines, which in his judgment cause, or contribute to, air pollution which may reasonably be anticipated to endanger public health or welfare,'" and that "[b]eginning in 2010, this language has been used to authorize standards for greenhouse gas (GHG) emissions from cars and trucks").

powerful statutory tools to regulate large-scale greenhouse gas emissions from fossil fuel burning power plants,[52] in a decision fraught with anxiety about various constitutional boundaries.[53] Of course, even robust climate governance at the national level cannot, on its own, solve the global problem of greenhouse gas pollution – but it would be significant, given that the United States is one of the world's largest greenhouse gas polluters.[54]

One potential solution is to amend the national constitution to provide the missing authority for environmental governance. Yet further revealing the price paid by early constitutional movers, who couldn't foresee this problem – and the lessons drawn by later constitutional drafters, who avoided it after the fact – the American Constitution is uniquely difficult to change.[55] This cumbersome process has been successfully invoked only twenty-seven times since the nation's founding, and only seven times in the last century.[56] Even aggressive campaigns to correct provisions arguably in conflict with core democratic principles in other parts of the Constitution, including amendments that would secure equal rights for women, have failed in recent decades.[57] Especially given the legislative paralysis of recent years, it seems unlikely that the Constitution will be amended any time soon to provide a stronger basis for environmental regulation.

Today, then, there are few uncontroversial choices for constitutionally grounding environmental rights or obligations on the scale needed to support meaningful climate governance. However, older jurisprudence suggests that there may have

---

[52] West Virginia v. EPA, 142 S. Ct. 2587, 2599, 2609, 2616 (2020).

[53] The majority's skepticism hinged, in part, on apparent concern that the agency's plan strayed too close to the limits of federal authority, barring it from interpreting its own statutory mandate as freely as it might have in more secure constitutional territory, at least without clearer legislative affirmation. *Id.* at 2620 (J. Gorsuch, concurring). Justice Gorsuch expressed this concern most directly in his concurring opinion, joined by Justice Alito, which explained that the major question doctrine under which the rule was invalidated "seeks to protect against 'unintentional, oblique, or otherwise unlikely' intrusions" on the areas of "self-government, equality, fair notice, federalism, and the separation of powers." *Id.*

[54] European Commission, *GHG Emissions for all World Countries*, https://edgar.jrc.ec.europa.eu/report_2024?vis=co2pop#emissions_table ("Per Capita Greenhouse Gas Emissions," 2023).

[55] Albert, *supra* note 19, at 2007 (arguing that the U.S. Constitution "may be the world's most difficult to amend."). It can be amended by either a two-thirds majority vote in both the House of Representatives and the Senate (and then ratified by three quarters of the state legislatures), or else by a constitutional convention called for by two-thirds of the State legislatures. U.S. CONST. art. V. In practice, a constitutional amendment has never been proposed by constitutional convention. *Constitutional Amendment Process*, NAT'L ARCHIVES, www.archives.gov/federal-register/constitution.

[56] U.S. CONST. amends. I-XXVII; *see also The Bill of Rights: A Transcription*, NAT'L ARCHIVES, www.archives.gov/founding-docs/bill-of-rights-transcript; *The Constitution: Amendments 11–27*, NAT'L ARCHIVES, www.archives.gov/founding-docs/amendments-11-27. The first ten amendments, comprising the Bill of Rights, were ratified at the same time in 1791. *Id.*

[57] *See* Equal Rights Amendment, H.R.J. Res. 208, 92d Cong., 1st Sess. (1971); S.J. Res. 8, 92d Cong., 1st Sess. (1971); *see also* H.R.J. Res. 681, 91st Cong. (1969) (calling for a direct popular vote in place of the electoral college, to align presidential elections with the one-person-one-vote premise on which American voting rights are founded).

once been a potential home for such rights in the Privileges and Immunities clause of Article IV,[58] which protects fundamental rights associated with citizenship,[59] including interstate comity and nondiscrimination,[60] the right to travel,[61] and potentially even the federal navigational servitude[62] – a federal mandate to preserve the navigability of public waterways against private encroachment[63] that is conceptually related to the public trust doctrine itself. The Clause was once thought to protect a set of interests ranging from life, liberty, and property to the pursuit of commercial advantage and even access to public resources.[64] If the Privileges and Immunities Clause was intended to protect citizens' rights to life, liberty, and property, could it offer protection for citizen's rights to a healthy environment and livable climate?

Dashing that hope as a matter of history, *The Slaughterhouse Cases* of 1873 reduced the potential importance of the Privileges and Immunities Clause to rights associated with interstate travel.[65] Yet even that right is conceptually related to the federal navigational servitude that is an expression of the core public trust principle

---

[58] U.S. Const. art. IV, sec. 2 ("The citizens of each state shall be entitled to all privileges and immunities of citizens in the several states.").

[59] *See generally* Stewart Jay, *Origins of the Privileges and Immunities of State Citizenship under Article IV*, 45 Loy. U. Chi. L.J. 1 (Fall 2013).

[60] *Id.* at 1, 8, 70.

[61] *See* Paul v. Virginia, 75 U.S. 168, 180 (1869) (defining the right to travel as "right of free ingress into other States, and egress from them."); Zobel v. Williams, 457 U.S. 55, 79–81 (1982) (O'Connor, J., concurring) (arguing that the right to interstate travel comes from the Privileges and Immunities Clause). *Cf.* Ilya Shapiro & Josh Blackman, *The Once and Future Privileges or Immunities Clause*, 26 Geo. Mason L. Rev. 1207, 1222–26 (2019) (discussing recognition of the right to travel under the Privileges or Immunities Clause of the Fourteenth Amendment).

[62] Today, we generally understand the federal navigational servitude as being rooted in Commerce Clause protection for the channels of interstate commerce, but it may once have been viewed as rooted in the right of travel protected by the Privileges and Immunities Clause. Early Supreme Court jurisprudence identifies "the right of a citizen of one state to pass through or to reside in any other state for purposes of trade agriculture professional pursuits or otherwise" as one of the key protections of the Privileges and Immunities clause, which could be construed to create a right of navigation. *See* Richard W. Bartke, *The Navigation Servitude and Just Compensation – Struggle for a Doctrine*, 48 Or. L. Rev. 1, 3 (1968).

[63] *See* Richard W. Bartke, *The Navigation Servitude and Just Compensation – Struggle for a Doctrine*, 48 Or. L. Rev. 1, 3 (December 1968). At least one scholar argues that the Federal Navigational Servitude should even be understood as an outgrowth of the Property Clause of the Constitution, art. IV, sec. 3, cl. 2. *See* Stewart Jay, *Origins of the Privileges and Immunities of State Citizenship under Article IV*, 45 Loy. U. Chi. L.J. 1, 6 (Fall 2013) (arguing that the Federal Navigation Servitude be understood as drawing support from the Property Clause to recognize federal proprietary interest in navigable waterways as "aggregates of rights, powers, privileges, and immunities").

[64] *See* Corfield v. Coryell, 6 F. Cas. 546, 552 (C.C.E.D. Pa. 1823) (explaining that the Clause protects such fundamental rights as "[p]rotection by the government; the enjoyment of life and liberty, with the right to acquire and possess property of every kind, and to pursue and obtain happiness and safety; subject nevertheless to such restraints as the government may justly prescribe for the general good of the whole").

[65] 83 US 36, 80 (1873) (holding that the Privileges and Immunities Clause protects citizen's rights by virtue of their U.S. citizenship, and not state citizenship, and defining those rights narrowly to exclude civil rights). *See also* Martin H. Redish & Brandon Johnson, *The Underused and Overused Privileges*

associated with the primary public commons that the Supreme Court has repeatedly affirmed receives protection under the common law public trust doctrine.[66] Modern scholarship suggests that there may even be interest among sitting members of the Supreme Court in reinvigorating the Privileges and Immunities Clause as a source of substantive rights.[67] It is thus possible that the Privileges and Immunities Clause could one day provide constitutional foundation for protecting additional rights, and perhaps even environmental rights – but there are no indications to expect that any time soon.

But what if there is already a source of underlying authority to help ground good environmental governance, not only procedurally but perhaps even substantively? A source that has been there all along, but that we are only just now rediscovering, or fully appreciating? While the public trust doctrine cannot single-handedly resolve this problem, the potential gap-filling importance of the doctrine – and the public trust principles that are an outgrowth of the original common law doctrine – is becoming increasingly evident.

B. THE PUBLIC TRUST AS AN EMERGING FOUNDATION FOR ENVIRONMENTAL GOVERNANCE

This book explores the development of the public trust doctrine and examines its potential for conferring additional structural support for environmental governance at the state and even federal level. It is a role of the doctrine that has long been overlooked, but one that has proved increasingly important in supporting environmental values beyond the focus of the federal Commerce Clause, and the many state constitutions modeled after the federal constitution. Charging the government with inalienable responsibility to care for designated public natural resources, the original common law doctrine provides an enduring source of sovereign obligation with quasi-constitutional elements, arguably constraining sovereign activity in the same way the written elements of a constitution do.[68]

---

and Immunities Clause, 99 B.U. L. REV. 1535, 1542, 1554 (2003) (discussing the jurisprudential evolution of the Clause).

[66] See *supra* notes 61–62 and accompanying text (discussing the federal navigational servitude) and *infra* notes 68–75 and accompanying text (discussing the common law public trust doctrine). *Cf.* William D. Araiza, *Democracy, Distrust, and the Public Trust: Process-Based Constitutional Theory, the Public Trust Doctrine and the Search for a Substantive Environmental Value*, 45 UCLA L. REV. 385, 409–10 (1997) (suggesting that the Privileges and Immunities Clause, inter alia, protects out-of-state citizens from discrimination by ensuring that their interests are "virtually represented" in the political process, and considering how the public trust doctrine can help hold the government accountable in resource management).

[67] Ilya Shapiro & Josh Blackman, *The Once and Future Privileges or Immunities Clause*, 26 GEO. MASON L. REV. 1207, 1228–31 (2019) (discussing Justice Thomas and Justice Kavanaugh's position that the Privileges or Immunities Clause is a potential path to substantive rights).

[68] *See* Chapter 7(C) ("Ordinary Common Law or Quasi-Constitutional?").

Public trust principles, passed down for millennia through multiple legal empires, have also been codified in state constitutions, statutes, and regulations.[69] In the United States, where the common law trust is considered a doctrine of state law, it can function to supplement other environmental regulation, but as noted, for natural resources that traverse state boundaries – such as navigable waterways, migratory wildlife, and atmospheric resources – state law may prove insufficient. For that reason, environmental advocates have sought to expand recognition for public trust principles in federal common and constitutional law.[70] Emerging movements for environmental rights, framed both as human rights and rights for nature directly, seek formal codification of related principles in constitutional and statutory contexts.[71]

Yet the story begins more than two thousand years earlier, when Roman common law recognized the doctrine as guaranteeing that the air, the sea, and the shores of the sea must forever remain the common property of all the people, guaranteeing open public access and preventing the destruction or private monopolization of these critical public natural resource commons.[72] The Roman doctrine was incorporated into early English common law and even the Magna Carta, which not only set the stage for the development of accountable democratic governance but also guaranteed sovereign protection for public rights of access to coastal and forest resources.[73] Eventually framed as a trust obligation for public benefit, the doctrine became part of American law when the early states seceded from the British Empire, borrowing their new legal codes from existing English common law.[74] The sovereign obligation to protect trust resources was recognized by the U.S. Supreme Court in application to navigable waterways, expanding its reach from coastal waters to the tens of thousands of miles of great rivers, streams, and lakes that traverse the great continent.[75] Waterways like the large inland salt sea draining the Yosemite high country at Mono Lake.

[69] *See* Chapter 1(A) ("Roots in Roman, English and Continental Law"); Chapter 8(A)(1) ("Vindicating Public Trust Principles Through Different Forms of Law").
[70] *See* Chapter 8(B) ("The Public Trust and Federal Law").
[71] *See* Chapter 10 (comparing the development of the public trust and rights of nature movements); *see also* David Takacs, *The Public Trust Doctrine, Environmental Human Rights, and the Future of Private Property*, 16 N.Y.U. ENV'T L.J. 711, 760 (2008). ("The Public Trust Doctrine stands for the proposition that some of nature's gifts inherently belong to all people, and the government must steward these to prevent both private arrogation of public resources and the 'tragedy of the commons' from unfettered public access to these shared resources. Environmental Human Rights represent a growing movement to codify this belief, to make positive law that firms up the philosophy promulgated for 1,500 or so years in the name of the Public Trust Doctrine.")
[72] J. INST. PROOEMIUM, 2.1.1. (T. Sandars trans., 4th ed. 1869); *see also* Chapter 1(A)(1) ("The Roman and Byzantine Empires: The Institutes of Justinian").
[73] Magna Carta, ch. 33 (Eng. 1215), www.bl.uk/collection-items/magna-carta-1215; Magna Carta, ch. 12 (Eng. 1217); *see also* Chapter 1(A)(2) ("Early English Law: The Magna Carta, Forest Charter, and Common Law").
[74] *See* Chapter 1(B) ("Reception in the United States").
[75] *See* Ill. Cent. R.R. Co. v. Illinois, 146 U.S. 387, 452 (1892); Chapter 1(B)(5) ("With Power Comes Responsibility: *Illinois Central Railroad Co. v. Illinois*").

B. The Public Trust as an Emerging Foundation

And there, at Mono Lake, the public trust doctrine would meet a critical inflection point, because it was in litigation over the fate of Mono Lake that the doctrine was most famously acknowledged as a quasi-constitutional sovereign obligation, a responsibility to account for environmental values that the state could not choose to ignore.[76] It was at Mono Lake that the public trust doctrine – long invoked to protect a suite of access rights associated with navigability to which environmental values were incidental[77] – was fully conceptualized as an obligation of environmental stewardship. And depending on how stewardship is itself conceptualized, perhaps even a vehicle for protecting public environmental rights.[78] In a decision that ultimately saved the lake from being drained away, the California Supreme Court held that the state could not simply ignore the environmental, scientific, scenic, and recreational values at Mono Lake when permitting water diversions that would destroy it.

Since then, the public trust doctrine has increasingly been deployed by plaintiffs, lawmakers, and citizens to protect environmental interests and resources that are otherwise underserved by American environmental (and constitutional) law, including the physical integrity of waterways, belowground aquifers, coastal resources, the atmospheric commons, and climate stability itself. Some of these efforts have proved successful,[79] though many have failed,[80] and the future remains uncertain.[81] There are clearly limits to what public trust advocacy can accomplish, especially in the absence of consensus over which resources are protected. Yet the intuitive force of the underlying legal command – sovereign stewardship of natural resource commons for the public – remains powerful in its simplicity.

---

[76] See Chapter 5 ("*National Audubon Society*: The 'Mono Lake Case'").

[77] See Chapter 1(B) ("Reception in the United States").

[78] See Chapters 9(A)(4) ("The Reciprocal Nature of Public Trust Principles and Environmental Rights") (framing the public trust as a doctrine of environmental rights) and 10(C) ("Comparing the Public Trust and Rights of Nature Movement") (comparing the public trust with an alternative conception of environmental rights).

[79] See, e.g., Env't L. Found. v. State Water Res. Control Bd. (*Scott River Case*), 237 Cal. Rptr. 3d 393 (Cal. Ct. App. 2018), *review denied* (Nov. 28, 2018) (extending the *Mono Lake* doctrine to protect groundwater); see Robinson Twp. v. Commonwealth, 83 A.3d 901 (Pa. 2013) (extending a constitutionalized version of the doctrine to protect against the harms of fracking); Rb. Den Haag 24 juni 2015, ECLI:NL:RBDHA:2015:7145 (Urgenda Found./Netherlands), at 32, https://elaw.org/system/files/urgenda_0.pdf (unofficial English translation) (applying public trust principles found in European Union law to require more effective climate governance).

[80] Alec L. *ex rel.* Loorz v. McCarthy, 561 Fed. App'x 7, 8 (D.C. Cir. 2014), *cert. denied*, 574 U.S. 1047 (2014) (rejecting an early atmospheric trust claim); Juliana v. United States, 217 F. Supp. 3d 1224, 1233 (D. Or. 2016) (arresting district court decision allowing the claim to go forward), *rev'd*, Juliana v. United States, No. 24-684, D.C. No. 6:15-cv-1517, 2024 WL 5102489, 2024 WL 5102489, (May 1, 2024) (dismissing the claim without leave to amend), *cert. denied*, 604 U.S. 645 (2025). For further discussion of successful and failed atmospheric trust cases, see Chapter 9(B) ("Trust-Rights Advocacy in Action: Atmospheric Trust & Climate Rights Litigation").

[81] See Chapter 9(C)(2) ("Heeding the Lessons of *Juliana*") (discussing newer trust-rights climate advocacy).

However these legal developments unfold, the power of the public trust as a defender of public environmental values emerged into global view through the Mono Lake story – a made-for-the-movies tale of how a ragtag coalition of locals, students, scientists, and birdwatchers deployed this thousand year-old idea in a wholly new way. There, they undertook a David-vs.-Goliath bid to save the Mono Basin, a remote and mysterious ecosystem just east of Yosemite National Park, from the thirst of Los Angeles, one of the largest, richest, and thirstiest cities in the world.

C. THE TURNING POINT: MONO LAKE AND BEYOND

The Mono Lake dispute pitted advocates for the Mono Basin ecosystem and its local community against proponents of the continued export of Mono Basin water to millions of thirsty Californians four hundred miles to the south.[82] The controversy itself spanned decades, but the story leading up to the litigation stretches back more than a hundred years, adding depth and dimension to the tale that is easily missed on a casual reading of the *Audubon Society* decision itself.[83] It is a case study on the challenges of, and possibilities for, balancing legitimate needs for public infrastructure and economic development with competing environmental values, all within systems of law that are still evolving to manage these conflicts. For the first time, the case plumbed the inexorable conflict that had long been developing between the public commons approach that underlies the public trust regulation of waterways and the privatization premise of the western prior appropriation doctrine of water allocation, which assigns perpetual rights to withdraw from a watercourse on a first-in-time basis.

Most important, the Mono Lake case demonstrates the evolution of the public trust doctrine from a justification for sovereign power over trust resources to a mandate for their protection. In this regard, the case presented the first opportunity for the highest court in the largest state in the land to consider the public trust doctrine as something more than ordinary common law. As framed by the California Supreme Court, the public trust doctrine functions as a quasi-constitutional foundation that creates sovereign obligations of stewardship – obligations that the sovereign cannot casually extinguish. It was this critical element that created the possibility,

---

[82] Nat'l Audubon Soc'y v. Super. Ct., 658 P.2d 709 (Cal. 1983).

[83] At this moment in time – recently commemorating the hundredth anniversary of the Los Angeles Aqueduct that would threaten the lake, and the thirtieth anniversary of the State Water Board's ultimate decision to save it – the Mono Lake story is especially worth revisiting. The Los Angeles Aqueduct formally opened in 1913. *Id.* at 713. The California Water Resources Control Board issued its decision implementing the state supreme court's decision in 1994. Mono Lake Basin Water Right Decision 1631, at 1, 6 (State of Cal. Water Res. Control Bd. Sep. 28, 1994), www.waterboards.ca.gov/waterrights/board_decisions/adopted_orders/decisions/d1600_d1649/wrd1631.pdf; *see also* Chapter 6(D) ("Decision 1631: Implementation by the Water Board") (reviewing this history).

in at least some jurisdictions, that the doctrine could provide needed infill for the underlying gap of support for environmental law.

After demonstrating this doctrinal potential for protecting environmental values underserved by existing legal infrastructure, the Mono Lake decision inspired environmental advocates around the country (and eventually the world) to expand public trust protections into new legal mechanisms, and to seek trust protection for other environmental resources and values, such as biodiversity, groundwater, ecosystems, the atmosphere, climate stability, and a healthy environment more generally. Today, the doctrine is frequently invoked in environmental conflicts, sometimes by private plaintiffs to compel states to do more to protect trust resources, and increasingly by states in defense of environmental regulations protecting trust resources against private constitutional takings claims. Although it has not thus far impacted courts, a vigorous scholarly debate asserts its rightful application as a principle that constrains not only state sovereign authority, but also federal authority.[84]

Some public trust lawsuits have pushed the boundaries of previously recognized law, such as the atmospheric trust plaintiffs' appeal to public trust principles in support of claims for meaningful climate governance.[85] Some innovative lawsuits have experimented with ways to partner public trust principles with other fundamental rights that stand on firmer constitutional ground, at both the state and federal levels.[86] American examples continue to provide inspiration for the adoption of public trust principles in foreign nations, even as the public trust provides a fascinating contrast for a simultaneously developing alternative premise for environmental law, the burgeoning Rights of Nature movement, which confers legal rights directly on nonhuman features of the natural environment.

Environmental theorists continue to search for sources of environmental rights on which to premise more effective environmental protection than our current governance models have been able to achieve. Yet the public trust doctrine – especially since the Mono Lake case – can itself be understood as a doctrine of public environmental rights. Somehow, it would seem, we just hadn't noticed it before now.

D. PUBLIC TRUST PRINCIPLES AND ENVIRONMENTAL RIGHTS

The public trust doctrine itself provides a basis for asserting environmental rights that could help buttress the inherent weaknesses of U.S. environmental law, especially when the trust is conceived as a constitutive element of sovereign authority.[87]

---

[84] *See* Chapter 8(B)(3) ("A Constitutive Constraint on Federal Authority?").
[85] *See* Chapter 9(B) ("Trust-Rights Advocacy in Action: Atmospheric Trust and Climate Rights Litigation").
[86] *Id.*
[87] *See* Chapter 8(B)(3) ("A Constitutive Constraint on Federal Authority?").

After all, the core public trust principle is really a pairing of two reciprocal, coequal elements – (1) a sovereign obligation to protect the environmental values of trust resources for the benefit of the public, and (2) the right of the public to benefit from the trust and hold the government to account for performance of its trust obligations.[88] Yet one does not exist without the other. They are mirror images, lacking genuine legal meaning without the partnership implied between them. And while different examples of public trust advocacy may emphasize one side of the coin over the other, as elaborated in Chapter 9, both are always in operation.[89] Even when the environmental advocacy focuses on the sovereign obligation element of the trust, it relies on the unspoken public right to invoke the sovereign obligation. Even when advocacy is premised on the environmental right, it implies the sovereign obligation to protect it.

In this regard, the public trust doctrine is, itself, a doctrine of environmental rights – perhaps even the original statement of environmental rights, at least within the western legal tradition. It stands for an ancient but evolving conception of partnered environmental rights and duties – a sovereign obligation that delimits governance, removing the government's option to destroy or allow these public natural resources to be destroyed, and reciprocally, an entitlement of the citizenry to the benefits of this stewardship obligation.

The big question, perhaps, is what these environmental rights entail.

Framing the rights conferred by the doctrine as legal entitlements to specific environmental goods – to a clean and healthful environment, for example – poses a conceptual hurdle in the United States, where positive rights are few and far between. In contrast to the more familiar framing of individual rights as negative rights, which constrain how the government engages with citizens, positive rights empower citizens to demand something affirmative from the government. While positive rights find reference in important sources of international human rights law,[90] American law generally regards them with suspicion. The U.S. Constitution does recognize a few positive rights, for example, the right to jury trial and legal representation in a criminal case,[91] and many U.S. states recognize a fundamental

---

[88] *See* Chapter 9(A)(4) ("Public Trust Principles and Environmental Rights in the Literature").

[89] *See* Chapter 9(B) ("Trust-Rights Advocacy in Action: Atmospheric Trust and Climate Rights Litigation").

[90] *See, e.g.,* U.N. UNIVERSAL DECLARATION OF HUMAN RIGHTS, art. 25, Dec. 8, 1948, G.A. Res. 217A (III), U.N. Doc. A/810 at 71 (1948) ("Everyone has the right to a standard of living adequate for the health and well-being of himself and of his family, including food, clothing, housing and medical care and necessary social services, and the right to security in the event of unemployment, sickness, disability, widowhood, old age or other lack of livelihood in circumstances beyond his control."); European Convention on Human Rights, art. 2, 8, EU, Sept. 3, 1953, CETS No. 213 (protecting, among others, broad conceptions of rights to life and human dignity).

[91] U.S. CONST. amend. VI. These positive rights are notably connected to circumstances in which the government has compelled an individual into legal process, somewhat bridging the divide between positive and negative rights. Then again, many negative rights arguably imply positive correlates

D. Public Trust Principles and Environmental Rights

right to free public education,[92] but most constitutional rights are framed as negative rights that constrain how the government can behave – such as rights against unreasonable search and seizure[93], cruel and unusual punishment,[94] or undue interference with the practice of religion.[95] Some invocation of public trust principles in support of environmental rights – for example, to climate stability – are framed as necessary for human survival,[96] yet the U.S. Constitution does not provide a positive right to food or medicine, even though they, too, are arguably necessary for survival.

Even so, several state constitutions arguably premised on public trust principles have done exactly that – for example, Montana's promise of "a clean and healthful environment,"[97] or New York's guarantee of "a right to clean air and water, and a healthful environment."[98] Moreover, environmental rights protected by the public trust doctrine, which poses a constraint on sovereign action, are just as naturally framed in terms of the negative rights that are commonplace in constitutional law. They constrain the government from authorizing or permitting the private expropriation of a public trust commons it holds in trust for the public. Pennsylvania overtly expresses both sides of this reciprocal coin in its constitution, which partners a guarantee that "[t]he people have a right to clean air, pure water, and to the preservation of the natural, scenic, historic, and esthetic values of the environment" with its affirmation that "Pennsylvania's public natural resources are the common property of all the people, including generations yet to come" and a sovereign commitment "as trustee of these resources [to] conserve and maintain them for the benefit of all the people."[99] Yet arguably, the two models would yield similar results, even if Pennsylvania had left out the overt statement of positive

---

for implementation. *See* Jean-François Akandji-Kombe, *Positive Obligations Under the European Convention on Human Rights*, DIRECTORATE GENERAL OF HUMAN RIGHTS COUNCIL OF EUROPE (2007), at 12–15 (discussing the necessary overlap between positive and negative obligations under the European Convention on Human Rights).

[92] *See* Trish Brennan-Gac, *Education Rights in the States*, 40 AMER. BAR ASSOC. No. 2 (April 1, 2014), www.americanbar.org/groups/crsj/publications/human_rights_magazine_home/2014_vol_40/vol_40_no_2_civil_rights/educational_rights_states/ (noting that many state constitutions recognize a fundamental right to education and that all states provide for compulsory free public education for children). *See also* U.N. UNIVERSAL DECLARATION OF HUMAN RIGHTS, art. 26, Dec. 8, 1948, G.A. Res. 217A (III), U.N. Doc. A/810 at 71 (1948) (recognizing rights to free elementary education).

[93] U.S. CONST. amend. IV.
[94] U.S. CONST. amend. VIII.
[95] U.S. CONST. amend. I.
[96] *See* Chapter 9(B)(2) ("The Atmospheric Trust Project in U.S. Law").
[97] MONT. CONST. art. IX. *See also* Chapter 9(C) ("Climate Claims on State Constitutional Grounds").
[98] N.Y. CONST. art. I, § 19.
[99] PA. CONST. § 27 ("The people have a right to clean air, pure water, and to the preservation of the natural, scenic, historic, and esthetic values of the environment. Pennsylvania's public natural resources are the common property of all the people, including generations yet to come. As trustee of these resources, the Commonwealth shall conserve and maintain them for the benefit of all the people.").

rights – as do still other state constitutions, which include only the statement of sovereign obligation.[100]

Environmental rights skeptics[101] may argue that the environmental dimensions of the trust are better framed as a mandate for environmental stewardship by the government, especially given the balancing act the Mono Lake case expressly required.[102] Yet that argument raises interesting questions about the meaningful distinction between environmental rights and stewardship obligations, if rights and duties are properly understood as reciprocal functions of one another.[103] Does a legal duty obligating one always imply a right held by another? At least one scholar has argued that human environmental rights necessarily imply a codification of public trust-themed sovereign management, arguing that "some of nature's gifts inherently belong to all people, and the government must steward these to prevent both private arrogation of public resources and the 'tragedy of the commons' [that could arise] from unfettered public access to these shared resources."[104]

If so, then what is the meaningful difference between environmental stewardship and environmental rights? Is a right wielded by individuals inadequate to protect future generations, as stewardship implies? But why cannot a public right encompass the interests of members both present and yet to come? Perhaps it has to do with the intersection between the environmental content of a stewardship obligation and the countervailing public interests with which it may collide. If that environmental content is framed as a right, does that imply that it will trump all other factors, including property rights, or even competing human rights? If framed instead as a stewardship obligation, does it automatically require a balancing among competing considerations in the overall calculus of the public benefit? Or would each of these conflicts arise under either frame of reference, requiring resolution on the basis of

---

[100] *See, e.g.,* FLA. CONST. art II, § 7 ("it shall be the policy of the state to conserve and protect its natural resources and scenic beauty."). *See also* Chapter 9(C) ("Climate Claims on State Constitutional Grounds") (discussing other examples).

[101] *See, e.g.,* Cynthia Giagnocavo & Howard Goldstein, *Law Reform or World Reform: The Problem of Environmental Rights*, 35 MCGILL L.J. 315 (1990); Mauricio Guim & Michael A. Livermore, *Where Nature's Rights Go Wrong*, 107 VA. L. REV. 1347 (2021); J.B. Ruhl, *The Metrics of Constitutional Amendments: And Why Proposed Environmental Quality Amendments Don't Measure Up*, 74 NOTRE DAME L. REV. 245, 252 (1999) ("Any [amendment] attempting to capture a normative statement about the environment and plug it into the United States Constitution is simply a bad idea."); Noah M. Sachs, *A Wrong Turn with the Rights of Nature Movement*, 36 GEO. ENV'T L. REV. 39 (2023) (critiquing the rights of nature movement).

[102] *See* Chapter 5(A)(5) ("The California Supreme Court's Decision") (describing the compromise the California Supreme Court required between the protection of public trust values and the need to also respect the state statutory system of water management); Chapter 6 (D)(1) ("Decision 1631: Implementation by the Water Board") (describing the Water Board's implementation of a compromise that protected the lake without prohibiting all water diversions).

[103] *See* Chapter 9(A)(4) ("The Reciprocal Nature of Sovereign Obligations and Environmental Rights"); *cf.* WESLEY NEWCOMB HOHFELD, FUNDAMENTAL LEGAL CONCEPTIONS AS APPLIED IN JUDICIAL REASONING, AND OTHER LEGAL ESSAYS 36–50 (Yale University Press 1919).

[104] *See* Takacs, *supra* note 71, at 760.

each individual case or controversy? Does it help to frame the trust as a right that belongs to the public at large, but which individuals vindicate as "private attorneys general" on behalf of the broader community?[105] What, if anything, distinguishes environmental rights from other kinds of rights?

Clearly, the provocative suggestions here raise important questions about the nature of public and private rights and their relationships to broader environmental values, some of which go beyond the scope of this book. The goal here is to provide a starting point for needed discussion of these issues, and likely not a finishing point. Yet whether framed as a doctrine of environmental rights or environmental stewardship, the public trust principles increasingly found in domestic and international jurisprudence provide compelling legal tools to secure legal protections for environmental values left vulnerable under conventional antipollution laws. Especially in the United States, where constitutional support for environmental law is complicated by features of omission and attenuation, the doctrine may provide environmental advocates – especially young advocates – the tools they feel they need to fight for their own futures, and for the future of nature itself.

That said, expansive public trust advocacy has also prompted concern among other advocates that it could undermine support for conventional environmental laws that have been far more effective in such contested realms as climate governance, displacing precision regulatory oversight with aspirational goals and vague legal demands.[106] Even if these reciprocal sovereign obligations and environmental rights are recognized, what exactly could their relatively vague directives deliver? Meanwhile, doctrinal opponents contend that these efforts are antidemocratic – dangerously empowering litigants over electorates and courts over legislatures, at a time when judicial power is already waxing.[107] In the ongoing struggle for good environmental governance, there is rarely a dull moment.

E. A BRIEF SYNOPSIS OF WHAT FOLLOWS

The Mono Lake case will turn fifty in the coming decade. After all these years, the Mono Lake story still prompts reflection about the way the public trust doctrine navigates complex conflicts between public and private rights in natural resource commons, from ancient protections for waterways to contested claims for atmospheric resources. It is a wonderful tale to tell, and as detailed in the Preface, it is also very dear to me personally – because it centers on the legal case that personally

---

[105] See Chapter 11(B)(4)(c) ("Citizen Suit Provisions and the Public Trust") (suggesting that the trust may be the original citizen suit provision of the common law, authorizing individuals to serve as "private attorneys general" to advocate for the diffuse public interest in cases where other factors may collude to subordinate it).
[106] See Chapter 9(C)(2) ("Heeding the Lessons of *Juliana*").
[107] See Chapter 9(D)(1) ("Separation of Powers Concerns"); Chapter 11(B)(4) ("Separation of Powers and the Antidemocratic Critique").

brought me into the law. During the aftermath of the California Supreme Court's decision, I lived and worked in the Mono Basin, serving as an interpretive ranger on the Mono Lake District of the Inyo National Forest, just east of Yosemite National Park. There, it was my job to share this story with the visiting public until it eventually inspired me to leave the Forest Service for law school, and eventually, an academic career – where it is now my job, and a great personal pleasure, to share a much fuller version of that story with you.

The chapters that follow plumb the story of the public trust doctrine from ancient Rome to the present day, pausing at length on the Mono Lake story that proved its environmental turning point, before turning to the ongoing development of public trust principles in environmental governance across the nation and the world.

Chapter 1 begins by introducing the main cast of characters in the Mono Lake story, starting with the two legal doctrines around which the conflict unfolds – the public trust doctrine that protects public rights in waterways and the prior appropriations doctrine that allocates private rights to the waters within them, set on an inexorable path of conflict. It traces the arc of public trust development from the time of the Roman Empire to the British Magna Carta, through early English common law to its reception in the new American states and by the U.S. Supreme Court, establishing the legal premise that the government holds certain natural resources in trust for the benefit of the public. Chief among them, navigable waterways like Mono Lake. It more briefly introduces the doctrines by which Americans assign legal rights for groups and individuals to take water out of these public waterways for private use, setting up the inevitable legal conflict that would unfold at Mono Lake.

Chapters 2 and 3 introduce the three places at the center of the drama – Los Angeles, the Owens Valley, and the Mono Lake Basin – in recounting the history of the Californian water struggles leading up to the Mono Lake case. Chapter 2 describes the path to the Los Angeles Aqueduct, a miracle of modern engineering that was nevertheless flawed by questionable dealings with local communities to acquire the needed land and water rights to build, as well as the catastrophic failure of the early St. Francis Dam that terrorized the downstream communities. It reviews how the aqueduct has forever changed the Owens Valley before extending even further north to the Mono Basin. Chapter 3 introduces the majestic Mono Basin, its unique ecosystem, indigenous inhabitants, and western settlers, and then recounts the serious environmental harms that befell the area following the arrival of the L.A. Aqueduct (and the departure of Mono Basin water).

Chapters 4 and 5 present the most famous arc of the made-for-the-movies Mono Lake story. Chapter 4 reviews the strategic mobilization of broader communities of interest to protect the failing lake, demonstrating the effective synergy between simultaneous legal and political processes in the overall effort to save the lake. It tells the story of how a loosely organized coalition of locals, scientists, birdwatchers, scholars, and advocates forged a rural–urban partnership around this new legal idea that would change history. Chapter 5 explores the Mono Lake case itself, analyzing the arguments

E. A Brief Synopsis of What Follows

that made it to the California Supreme Court, the court's disposition of them, and the significant doctrinal developments in its decision – affirming application of the doctrine to environmental values, extending its reach over expanses of watershed and time, and ensuring its durability against countervailing statutory claims.

Chapters 6 and 7 explore the aftermath of the Mono Lake case, both on the ground locally and in the wider world of legal ideas. Chapter 6 reviews the practical aftermath of the California Supreme Court's conclusion, including the establishment of surrounding state and national parklands, a series of buttressing litigation by CalTrout and other environmental plaintiffs, the Water Board's implementation of these judicial directives in the famous "Decision 1631," and Los Angeles' resulting embrace of conservation. It also updates the more recent state of affairs in both the Mono Basin and Owens River Valley.

Chapter 7 reviews the scholarly response to the Mono Lake decision, both praise and criticisms, from advocates for the environment, private property rights, and legal process. It reviews the impact of the *Mono Lake* doctrine on related public trust cases and executive actions in California and other states. The chapter also considers one of the most important legal issues raised by the Mono Lake case: the actual nature of the public trust as a legal doctrine. Is it a quasi-constitutional constraint limiting sovereign power to harm trust resources, overriding all but other constitutional guarantees? Or is it a feature of ordinary common law, which is easily abrogated by statute, or overridden by subsequent legislative or executive priorities in the moment? It then explores the contrasting interpretive approaches taken in three western states with similar water management challenges – California, Idaho, and Nevada.

Chapters 8, 9, and 10 explore the development of the public trust doctrine more broadly, domestically and internationally. Chapter 8 reviews the development of the doctrine and related public trust principles well beyond the shores of Mono Lake, analyzing its development across the United States along five central planes: (1) the different forms of law by which public trust principles operate; (2) the different natural resources protected by the doctrine; (3) the different societal values protected by the doctrine; (4) different legal theories about the nature of the doctrine; and (5) different legal remedies made available under the doctrine. It also assesses doctrinal intersections with federal law, discussing its role as a background principle in defending against Fifth Amendment takings challenges; reviewing a secret history of negotiations among U.S. Supreme Court justices to avoid ruling on the doctrine; and addressing whether the doctrine constrains federal as well as state authority.

Chapter 9 explores the potential evolution of the doctrine in application to air and atmospheric resources – one of the resources overtly designated for protection by the original Roman statement of the trust – and how the partnered public trust principles of sovereign obligations and public environmental rights are reflected in an emerging movement of global climate advocacy. The chapter describes an ongoing series of judicial and executive actions brought by environmental advocates worldwide, relying on these twin public trust principles in efforts to hold governments accountable for policies alleged to contribute to climate change. These lawsuits, the most successful of which have incorporated simultaneous constitutional claims, center on the idea that citizens have a right to insist that the government not be complicit in permissively enabling private polluters to expropriate the atmospheric commons for use as a carbon sink. Arrestingly, most of these claims have been brought by youth plaintiffs arguing that they represent the interests of future generations. These youth have achieved global awareness and admiration, though some older environmental advocates worry that their efforts could undermine the success of more established environmental laws, while others worry that they threaten the constitutional separation of powers that undergirds democracy.

Moving fully forward from the Mono Lake case and even the American public trust, Chapter 10 reviews the proliferation of public trust principles on all inhabited continents of the world, reporting on examples from Oceania, Asia, the Greater Middle East, Africa, Europe, South America, and North America. It also considers the coevolution of environmental doctrines worldwide that take alternative approaches to public commons and stewardship, such as ancient Ottoman law and the modern Rights of Nature movement. Chapter 10 especially contrasts the use of public trust principles for environmental protection with the simultaneously unfolding rights of nature model. In asserting rights for natural systems directly, rights of nature initiatives offer a biocentric alternative to the anthropocentrism of the public trust, which locates rights in human members of the public. After a brief review of developing rights of nature initiatives across the globe and in the United States, Chapter 10 considers the surprising ways in which these two philosophically dissimilar approaches showcase pragmatic overlap.

Finally, the Conclusion closes with reflections on the open questions the Mono Lake story leaves us to ponder about the public trust doctrine, including the force and flexibility of the doctrine, whose interests count when we talk about the "public" trust, and which to account for when balancing the competing considerations in public trust conflicts. It considers the ontological nature of the doctrine itself, and how the quasi-constitutional features of the doctrine intersect with other constitutional considerations, such as the separation of powers, jurisprudential standing limitations, and the institution of citizen suits. It considers the antidemocratic critique of the doctrine, and the wisdom of entrusting the judiciary with administration of the trust when judicial power is already on the rise. Finally, it reviews a set of Mono Lake stories unfolding in other parts of the world, including the Great Salt Lake in Utah, the Israeli Sea of Galilee, the Dead Sea between Israel and Jordan, and the Aral Sea in Kazhakhstan.

These contested issues are what make the public trust doctrine so fascinating, so powerful, and so critical as we confront a future of ongoing and inevitable conflicts over natural resource values, new and old. Our different answers to these concluding questions in each of the Mono Lake stories reviewed here (and countless others) prompt us to reflect on the role of the doctrine in helping us navigate the challenges of environmental governance in general.

1

The Historical Origins of the Modern Public Trust Doctrine

A. Roots in Roman, English, and Continental Law   28
   1. The Roman and Byzantine Empires: The Institutes of Justinian   30
   2. Early English Law: The Magna Carta, Forest Charter, and Common Law   31
   3. Early Spanish Law: *Las Siete Partidas*   33
   4. Critiquing the Conventional Account   34
B. Reception in the United States   35
   1. State Common Law: *Arnold v. Mundy*   36
   2. Affirmation by the U.S. Supreme Court: *Martin v. Waddell*   37
   3. The Public Trust on Equal Footing: *Pollard v. Hagan*   38
   4. The Definitive Supreme Court Statement: *Shively v. Bowlby*   40
   5. With Power Comes Responsibility: *Illinois Central Railroad Co. v. Illinois*   42
C. Conflicts with Water Allocation Law   48
   1. Riparian Rights   50
   2. Prior Appropriations   54
D. Setting the Stage for the Mono Lake Story   58

The Mono Lake story provides a paragon example of how the public trust doctrine serves as a guardian of environmental values. In the Mono Lake case, the California Supreme Court held that the doctrine required the state to safeguard the public trust values associated with the lake, including its ecological, scenic, and recreational importance. The case became an inspiration for environmental advocates across the nation and eventually the world, many of whom brought public trust litigation in their own efforts to protect threatened natural resources, while others sought to instantiate public trust principles into their own statutes and constitutions. The first half of this book tells the Mono Lake story in detail to showcase how the ancient public trust doctrine was reconceptualized in the modern era, perhaps more faithfully to its original Roman roots, as a device for protecting environmental rights and interests. The final chapters reveal how this reconceptualization has continued to evolve, especially in the absence of a clearer constitutional framework for protecting those interests.

But before delving into any good story, it is important to introduce the central cast of characters, the function of this chapter. And one unusual aspect of the Mono Lake saga is that two of the most important characters in that cast are neither people, nor cities, nor even geological formations on the land – they are laws. In the Mono Lake case, advocates invoked the public trust doctrine to protect public law interests in the environmental values of the waterway, defending them against private law claims to the actual water within it.[1] To understand how these public and private interests came into conflict at Mono Lake – and why they continue to harbor conflict across all arid lands – it is important to understand the different legal doctrines that govern different aspects of water governance in the United States. For this reason, the book begins with the law.

The public trust doctrine, the protagonist of much modern environmental advocacy in the United States, creates a set of public rights and responsibilities with regard to certain natural resource commons, obligating the state to manage them in trust for the public. As detailed in this chapter, it is thought to be among the oldest doctrines of the common law, with roots extending as far back as ancient Rome and early Britain, where it primarily protected public values of navigation, fisheries, and commerce associated with waterways.[2] Over these hundreds and even thousands of years, the common law came to recognize that some resources, such as navigable waters, are so critical that they cannot be owned by anyone in particular – instead, they must belong to everyone together.[3] To prevent private expropriation or monopolization of these critical public commons, the government – be it the Emperor, the King, or later, the elected executive and legislative branches – was entrusted to manage them on behalf of the public.[4]

In the last century, the doctrine has gradually transformed from an affirmation of sovereign authority over these resources to a recognition of sovereign

---

[1] Nat'l Audubon Soc'y v. Super. Ct. (*Mono Lake*), 658 P.2d 709, 726–27 (Cal. 1983).

[2] *See* J. INST. PROOEMIUM, 2.1.1. (T. Sandars trans., 4th ed. 1869) (translation from the INSTITUTES OF JUSTINIAN, by the Byzantine Emperor, Justinian I); *see also infra* Part A ("Roots in Early Roman and English Law").

[3] *See infra* Part A ("Roots in Early Roman and English Law").

[4] *See, e.g.*, Joseph Sax, *The Public Trust Doctrine in Natural Resource Law: Effective Judicial Intervention*, 68 MICH. L. REV. 471 (1970) (setting forth the seminal academic statement of the public trust doctrine as a modern legal tool to aid in the protection of natural resources); Jan S. Stevens, *The Public Trust: A Sovereign's Ancient Prerogative Becomes the People's Environmental Right*, 14 U.C. DAVIS L. REV. 195, 200 (1980) (arguing that the public trust is an inalienable aspect of sovereignty); Michael C. Blumm, *Public Property and the Democratization of Western Water Law: A Modern View of the Public Trust Doctrine*, 19 ENV'T L. 573, 580 (1989) [hereinafter Blumm, *A Modern View of the Public Trust Doctrine*] (discussing the public trust doctrine as "a democratizing force by (1) preventing monopolization of trust resources and (2) promoting natural resource decision making that involves and is accountable to the public").

responsibility to protect them for present and future generations.[5] Especially in recent decades, it has evolved substantially through U.S. common, constitutional, and statutory law to address a broader variety of natural resources and a broader scope of public values associated with them, including ecological, recreational, and scenic values.[6] Today, the doctrine is frequently invoked in natural resource management conflicts – some involving constitutional takings claims, and some of which push the boundaries of previously recognized environmental applications, such as the atmospheric trust movement's appeal to public trust principles in support of legal claims for meaningful climate governance.[7] State constitutions and other legal sources incorporating public trust principles are increasingly construed as a source of not only environmental obligations but also environmental rights.[8] Although it has not been matched in the courts, a vigorous scholarly debate asserts its rightful application not only to state sovereign authority but also to federal authority.[9]

The other main legal character in the Mono Lake story is the law of water allocation – and, in particular, the western water law doctrine of "prior appropriations" – which sets forth how much water individual users can take from a watercourse for their own private use. Under the traditional doctrine of prior appropriations, whoever is first to take water out of the watercourse and put it to beneficial use earns the right to continue taking the same amount of water for that same use, potentially indefinitely. That confers something like a private property right to the ongoing use of that water, even if it is coming from a public waterway protected by the public trust doctrine. Figuring out how these two legal rules should play nicely together has caused no small amount of heartache.

While Chapters 2–6 explore the legal dimensions of the Mono Lake story in more detail, this chapter introduces the law of the public trust and private water allocation to prepare readers for the tale that follows. It begins by introducing the public trust doctrine as a creature of common law, constitutional law, and perhaps as an underlying feature of sovereign authority more generally, potentially creating a set of related environmental rights. Part A introduces the historical origins of the doctrine, identifying the earliest statements of public trust principles in ancient Rome and early British law. Part B traces the formal reception of the doctrine in the United States through state and ultimately federal law, detailing the Supreme

---

[5] *See generally* Erin Ryan, *A Short History of the Public Trust Doctrine and Its Intersection with Private Water Law*, 38 VA. ENV'T L.J. 135 (2020) [hereinafter Ryan, *A Short History*]; *see* Erin Ryan, *From Mono Lake to the Atmospheric Trust: Navigating the Public and Private Interests in Public Trust Resource Commons*, 10 GEO. WASH. J. ENERGY & ENV'T L. 39, 64 (2019) [hereinafter Ryan, *From Mono Lake to the Atmospheric Trust*].
[6] *See* Chapter 8(A) ("The Planes of Public Trust Development across the United States").
[7] *See* Chapter 9 ("Public Trust Principles, Environmental Rights, and Trust Rights Climate Advocacy").
[8] *Id., see also* PA. CONST. ART. I, § 27 (setting forth both rights and obligations).
[9] *See* Chapter 8(B) ("The Public Trust and Federal Law").

Court's seminal decision in *Illinois Central Railroad*, which showcases the power of the doctrine to undo legislative action that would betray trust obligations.

Part C turns to the broad mechanics of water allocation law, setting up the potential for conflict with the public trust doctrine. It begins with a cursory review of the riparian rights doctrine of the eastern United States, inherited from British common law, and then explores the prior appropriations doctrine that developed later in the western states, and which has clashed notoriously with the public trust doctrine in so many western water conflicts. Part D reveals how the unresolved relationship between these doctrines creates ongoing friction in the legal regimes that follow them, setting the stage for the Mono Lake story that follows. Understanding the underlying conflicts of legal theory should enable us to better understand the core dilemmas within so many environmental disputes over water – and, ideally, help us resolve them.

A. ROOTS IN ROMAN, ENGLISH, AND CONTINENTAL LAW

Modern public trust principles, which assign state responsibility for natural resources held in trust for the public, are most commonly associated with American law.[10] American legal scholars have long debated the merits and the mechanics of the public trust doctrine, in a robust discourse that matches enthusiastic support[11] with deep

---

[10] *See, e.g.,* M. C. Mehta v. Kamal Nath, (1996) 1 SCC 388 (India) *in* 1 U.N. ENVIRONMENT PROGRAMME, COMPENDIUM OF JUDICIAL DECISIONS IN MATTERS RELATED TO ENVIRONMENT, NATIONAL DECISIONS 259 (1998) (referring to the California public trust doctrine, as expressed in Nat'l Audubon Soc'y v. Super. Ct., 658 P.2d 709 (Cal. 1983), in adopting similar public trust principles as a feature of Indian constitutional law); *see also* Alexandra B. Klass, *Modern Public Trust Principles: Recognizing Rights and Integrating Standards,* 82 NOTRE DAME L. REV. 699, 701 (2006) (discussing American versions of the public trust doctrine in general and referring to various expressions of the trust as "public trust principles").

[11] The list of scholarships sympathetic to the public trust doctrine is too long to capture in one footnote, but for a general overview, see MICHAEL BLUMM & MARY CHRISTINA WOOD, THE PUBLIC TRUST DOCTRINE IN ENVIRONMENTAL AND NATURAL RESOURCES LAW (2013); Ryan, *From Mono Lake to the Atmospheric Trust, supra* note 5; Erin Ryan, *The Public Trust Doctrine, Private Water Allocation, and Mono Lake: The Historic Saga of* National Audubon Society v. Superior Court, 45 ENV'T L. 561 (2015) [hereinafter Ryan, *The Historic Saga*]; Mary Turnipseed, Stephen E. Roady, Raphael Sagarin & Larry B. Crowder, *The Silver Anniversary of the United States' Exclusive Economic Zone: Twenty-Five Years of Ocean Use and Abuse, and the Possibility of a Blue Water Public Trust Doctrine,* 36 ECOLOGY L.Q. 1 (2009) (advocating that the public trust doctrine applies to federal fisheries management); Klass, *supra* note 10 (advocating an integrated approach to the public trust doctrine that includes common law, statutory, and constitutional bases); J. B. Ruhl & James Salzman, *Ecosystem Services and the Public Trust Doctrine: Working Change from Within,* 15 SE. ENV'T L.J. 223 (2006) (arguing for the protection of natural capital and ecosystem services through the public trust doctrine); Allan Kanner, *The Public Trust Doctrine, Parens Patriae, and the Attorney General as the Guardian of the State's Natural Resources,* 16 DUKE ENV'T L. & POL'Y F. 57 (2005) (advocating for the role of the public trust doctrine in contamination cleanups); Richard Roos-Collins, *A Plan to Restore the Public Trust Uses of Rivers and Creeks,* 83 TEX. L. REV. 1929 (2005) (advocating for the wider adoption of public trust principles in water rights regulation); Dale D. Goble, *Three Cases/Four*

concerns.¹² However, the central idea of the public trust has roots in some of the oldest doctrines of the common law and civil law traditions.¹³ Many accounts date its origins to early English or Spanish law, and some go all the way back to ancient Rome.¹⁴ Versions of the public trust doctrine now operate in every American state and many other nations,¹⁵ but the underlying theory evolved over a time horizon so

---

Tales: Commons, Capture, the Public Trust, and Property in Land, 35 ENV'T L. 807 (2005) (advocating for the role of the public trust doctrine in application to wildlife); William D. Araiza, *Democracy, Distrust, and the Public Trust: Process-based Constitutional Theory, the Public Trust Doctrine, and the Search for a Substantive Environmental Value*, 45 UCLA L. REV. 385 (1997) (identifying a foundation for the public trust doctrine in many state constitutions); Richard A. Epstein, *The Public Trust Doctrine*, 7 CATO J. 411, 422–26 (1987) (supporting the public trust doctrine from a libertarian, property rights perspective as a natural limitation on government power, comparable to restrictions on eminent domain); Charles F. Wilkinson, *The Public Trust Doctrine in Public Land Law*, 14 U.C. DAVIS L. REV. 269 (1980) (advocating for the use of public trust principles in judicial review of public land management decisions); Blumm, *A Modern View of the Public Trust Doctrine*, supra note 4, at 580. 19 ENV'T L. 573, 580; Joseph Sax, *The Public Trust Doctrine in Natural Resource Law: Effective Judicial Intervention*, 68 MICH. L. REV. 471 (1970) (setting forth the seminal academic statement of the public trust doctrine as a modern legal tool to aid in the protection of natural resources); *see also* Chapter 8(C)(3) ("A Constitutive Constraint on Federal Authority?") (discussing the public trust doctrine as a constitutive constraint).

¹² *See, e.g.*, Barton H. Thompson, Jr., *The Public Trust Doctrine: A Conservative Reconstruction and Defense*, 15 SE. ENV'T L.J. 47, 49 (2006) (suggesting reconstruction of the public trust doctrine in response to libertarian and property rights critiques); Randy T. Simmons, *Property and the Public Trust Doctrine*, PERC POLICY SERIES-39 (2007) (discussing the public trust doctrine as a threat to private property rights); Lloyd R. Cohen, *The Public Trust Doctrine: An Economic Perspective*, 29 CAL. W. L. REV. 239, 274–76 (1992) (criticizing the public trust doctrine's effects on private property rights); Richard Delgado, *Our Better Natures: A Revisionist View of Joseph Sax's Public Trust Theory of Environmental Protection, and Some Dark Thoughts on the Possibility of Law Reform*, 44 VAND. L. REV. 1209 (1991) (arguing that the doctrine is too weak to contend with broader environmental challenges); Barton H. Thompson, Jr., *Judicial Takings*, 76 VA. L. REV. 1449, 1532–33 (1990) (criticizing use of the doctrine to avoid just compensation for what otherwise looks like a taking); James L. Huffman, *A Fish Out of Water: The Public Trust in a Constitutional Democracy*, 19 ENV'T L. 527 (1989) (arguing that the doctrine lacks foundation in the police power and critiquing the judicial role under the doctrine as antidemocratic); Richard J. Lazarus, *Changing Conceptions of Property and Sovereignty in Natural Resources: Questioning the Public Trust Doctrine*, 71 IOWA L. REV. 631 (1986) (arguing that the property-based concepts of the doctrine are a problematic approach for accomplishing environmental protection in comparison with the stewardship approach of modern environmental statutory law); James L. Huffman, *Trusting the Public Interest to Judges: A Comment on the Public Trust Writings of Professors Sax, Wilkinson, Dunning and Johnson*, 63 DENV. U. L. REV. 565 (1986) (questioning the policy motives of pro-public trust scholarship).

¹³ *See, e.g.*, Sax, *supra* note 11 (laying the seminal academic foundations for the public trust doctrine as a tool to aid in the protection of natural resources and crediting its origins to early British and Roman law). *But see* James L. Huffman, *Speaking of Inconvenient Truths: A History of the Public Trust Doctrine*, 18 DUKE ENV'T L. & POL'Y F. 1, 20–23 (2007) (critiquing the conventional account of this history).

¹⁴ *See* Las Siete Partidas, P. III, tit. 28, laws III, IV, VI (embracing trust principles in Spain in the 1200s AD); J. INST. PROOEMIUM, *supra* note 2. *But see* J. B. Ruhl & Thomas McGinn, *The Roman Public Trust Doctrine: What Was It, and Does It Support an Atmospheric Trust*, 47 ECOLOGY L.Q. 117 (2020) (critiquing the standard account of the Justinian roots of the doctrine).

¹⁵ *See, e.g.*, Robin Kundis Craig, *A Comparative Guide to the Eastern Public Trust Doctrines: Classifications of States, Property Rights, and State Summaries*, 16 PENN. ST. ENV'T L. REV. 1 (2007)

long that it can be easy to miss the breadth of its historical reach. This chapter explores the historical development of the modern public trust doctrine, anchored with references to contemporaneous events to convey its remarkable journey through history.

1. The Roman and Byzantine Empires: The Institutes of Justinian

The earliest written accounts of public trust principles go astonishingly far back in time. For context, in the Sixth Century AD, King Arthur's victory in the battle of Mound Badon was slowing the Saxon conquest of England, and Yang Jian was reuniting China at the advent of the Sui Dynasty.[16] At about the same time, the Byzantine Emperor Justinian I set to work codifying Roman common law of the previous era, for the combined purpose of fortifying legal education and restating the law for enforcement purposes.[17] In the INSTITUTES OF JUSTINIAN, published in 533, he documented the *jus publicum*, a principle addressing the common ownership of certain natural resources:

> "By the law of nature these things are the common property to mankind—the air, running water, the sea, and consequently the shores of the sea."[18]

Thousands of years later, it is hard to know exactly how these principles helped govern the Roman Empire,[19] but this commanding early statement of public commons has echoed through common law jurisprudence ever since, in both judicial decisions and constitutional affirmations.[20] Analogous principles of public commons ownership, especially pertaining to waterways, also appear in civil law countries with legal codes that draw on ancient Roman law, including France, Spain, and other postcolonial nations with related legal systems.[21]

[hereinafter Craig, *Eastern Public Trust Doctrines*] (comparing eastern states' public trust doctrines); Robin Kundis Craig, *A Comparative Guide to the Western States' Public Trust Doctrines: Public Values, Private Rights, and the Evolution Toward an Ecological Public Trust*, 37 ECOLOGY L.Q. 53 (2010) [hereinafter Craig, *Western States' Public Trust Doctrines*] (comparing western states' public trust doctrines); Michael C. Blumm & Rachel D. Guthrie, *Internationalizing the Public Trust Doctrine: Natural Law and Constitutional and Statutory Approaches to Fulfilling the Saxion Vision*, 45 CAL. DAVIS L. REV. 742, 760 (2012) (reviewing the adoption of public trust principles internationally); *see also* Chapters 8 and 9 (discussing examples of public trust principles in operation around the nation and around the globe).

[16] *King Arthur*, ENCYCLOPAEDIA BRITANNICA, www.britannica.com/topic/King-Arthur (last visited Oct. 25, 2022) (noting that the battle at Mount Badon is believed to have taken place sometime that century); *Sui Dynasty*, ENCYCLOPAEDIA BRITANNICA, www.britannica.com/topic/Sui-dynasty (last visited Oct. 25, 2022) (noting that Yang Jian reunited China in 581).

[17] H. F. JOLOWICZ & BARRY NICHOLAS, HISTORICAL INTRODUCTION TO THE STUDY OF ROMAN LAW 492–93 (3d ed. 1972).

[18] *See* J. INST. PROOEMIUM, *supra* note 2.

[19] *See* Huffman, *Speaking of Inconvenient Truths*, *supra* note 13; Ruhl & McGinn, *supra* note 14.

[20] *See* Chapter 8 ("Beyond Mono Lake: The Evolving Public Trust Doctrine Across the U.S.") (tracing the evolution of the doctrine in the U.S. and international jurisdictions).

[21] *See, e.g.*, Glenn J. Macgrady, *The Navigability Concept in the Civil and Common Law: Historical Development, Current Importance, and Some Doctrines that Don't Hold Water*, 3 FLA. ST. U. L.

Recounting the Mono Lake story that serves as the central case study of this book offers rich opportunities to consider the intersection of public trust principles with water resources, which is fitting, because the doctrine is most often invoked to protect the environmental values in waterways. But before moving on, it is worth pausing to acknowledge the very first item in Justinian's list – "the air" – because that will become an important element in the modern developments reviewed toward the end of this book, now that advocates are deploying public trust principles to protect the atmospheric commons in the context of climate governance.[22]

2. Early English Law: The Magna Carta, Forest Charter, and Common Law

Some *jus publicum* principles were later incorporated into early English law, beginning with the Magna Carta. In 1215, a few decades before Marco Polo set sail for Asia and shortly after the sack of Constantinople during the Fourth Crusade,[23] King John of England issued the Magna Carta ("Great Charter"), promising his rebellious barons that he and all future sovereigns would operate within the rule of law.[24]

Although the Magna Carta was unsuccessful in the first instance, it eventually provided the foundations of the modern English legal system, and it is widely credited as a progenitor of Western democracy and constitutional law.[25] In addition to declaring the sovereign subject to the rule of law, the Magna Carta also set forth rights to speedy justice and trial by jury, and against unusual punishments.[26] It also incorporated into English law certain principles of Roman common law, including elements of the *jus publicum*. For example, chapter thirty-three of the Magna Carta required the removal of all weirs in the Thames and Medway Rivers "throughout the whole of England" that interfered with fishing or navigation.[27] The Magna

---

Rev. 513, 536–45 (1975) (reviewing Roman-inspired doctrines of public ownership over navigable waterways in Spain, France, and other civil law countries).

[22] *See, e.g.*, Juliana v. United States, 217 F. Supp. 3d 1224 (D. Or. 2016), *rev'd*, Juliana v. United States, No. 24–684, D.C. No. 6:15-cv-1517, 2024 WL 5102489, (May 1, 2024), *cert. denied*, 604 U.S. 645 (2025). This case is discussed further in Chapter 9(B)(4) ("*Juliana v. United States*").

[23] *Marco Polo*, Encyclopaedia Britannica, www.britannica.com/biography/Marco-Polo (last visited Oct. 25, 2022) (dating Marco Polo's eastern voyage as beginning in 1271); *Sack of Constantinople*, Encyclopaedia Britannica, www.britannica.com/event/Sack-of-Constantinople-1204 (last visited Oct. 25, 2022) (discussing the sack of Constantinople during the Fourth Crusade in 1204).

[24] *See* Andrew Blick, Beyond Magna Carta: A Constitution for the United Kingdom (2015).

[25] *See* Doris Mary Stenton, *Magna Carta*, Encyclopaedia Britannica, www.britannica.com/topic/Magna-Carta (last modified Mar. 16, 2020).

[26] Magna Carta, chs. 20, 39–40 (Eng. 1215), www.bl.uk/collection-items/magna-carta-1215.

[27] *Id.* at ch. 33; *see also* Michael C. Blumm & Courtney Engel, *Proprietary and Sovereign Public Trust Obligations: From Justinian and Hale to Lamprey and Oswego Lake*, 43 Vt. L. Rev. 1, 7 (2018). A weir is a barrier that crosses a river in order to alter its flow characteristics, usually changing the height of the water level, and often to control water flow into associated reservoirs, lakes, or ponds.

Carta, negotiated among a common pool of aristocrats, effectively decreed these navigable waters a public commons for these purposes.[28]

The Charter of the Forest, added to the Magna Carta in 1217 by King Henry III, further protected public rights to access natural resources on certain undeveloped royal lands (not just forests), and it remained in effect for centuries thereafter.[29] Re-establishing traditional rights of public commons that had been eroded by William the Conqueror, the Forest Charter promised that the King would not interfere with commoners' rights to graze animals, forage, plant crops, and collect lumber on open lands subject to Forest Law.[30] Notably, this law still governs the New Forest territory in southern England.[31] While these provisions do not necessarily follow from the Justinian references to common property in air, water, and coastlines, they do express an early affirmation of what would develop into more modern public trust principles of public rights in natural resource commons.

Early English common law also made reference to public trust principles in a series of cases and authorities affirming sovereign authority over submerged tidelands.[32] In 1611, the same year that Galileo first observed sunspots[33] and Shakespeare's *The Tempest* debuted,[34] the King's Bench held that while the beds of non-navigable waterways could be privately held, navigable waters were owned by the sovereign for public use.[35] Sir Matthew Hale, in his renowned 1670 Treatise on English Maritime Law, later described sovereign ownership of tidelands in an account of the three different kinds of coastal land: (1) that under the royal right (or police power), (2) that available for public navigational access, and (3) that which was privately owned.[36]

English law primarily applied the sovereign ownership principle to submerged lands beneath coastal tidelands, the navigable waterways of primary value there. American law would ultimately apply the doctrine to submerged lands beneath

---

[28] Blumm & Engel, *supra* note 27, at 7 (discussing the implementation of Justinian public trust principles in the Magna Carta).

[29] Magna Carta, ch. 12 (Eng. 1217). *See* Sarah Nield, *The New Forest: Ancient Forest and Modern Playground*, *in* 2 MODERN STUDIES IN PROPERTY LAW 287, 294 (Elizabeth Cooke ed., 2003); Anne Bottomley, *Beneath the City: The Forest! Civic Commons as Practice and Critique*, 5 BIRKBECK L. REV. 1, 2–3 (2018); Nicholas Robinson, *The Public Trust Doctrine in the 21st Century*, 10 GEO. WASH. J. ENERGY & ENV'T L. 83, 84–87 (2020).

[30] *See* Dr. John Langton, *The Charter of the Forest of King Henry III*, FORESTS AND CHASES OF ENG. AND WALES C. 1000 TO C. 1850, http://info.sjc.ox.ac.uk/forests/Carta.htm (last visited Aug. 8, 2018).

[31] *See* Nield, *supra* note 29, at 303.

[32] *See* Carol Rose, *The Comedy of the Commons: Custom, Commerce, and Inherently Public Property*, 53 U. CHI. L. REV. 711, 727–30 (1986).

[33] *Sunspot*, ENCYCLOPAEDIA BRITANNICA, www.britannica.com/science/sunspot (last visited Oct. 25, 2022).

[34] *The Tempest*, ENCYCLOPAEDIA BRITANNICA, www.britannica.com/topic/The-Tempest (last visited Oct. 24, 2022).

[35] The Royal Fishery of Banne (1611) 80 Eng. Rep. 540, 543 (KB).

[36] Matthew Hale, *A Treatise De Jure Maris et Brachiorum Ejusdem*, *reprinted in* STUART A. MOORE, A HISTORY OF THE FORESHORE AND THE LAW RELATING THERETO 370, 371–72 (1888).

all navigable waterways, including large watercourses to which there were no true analogs in Britain, such as America's Great Lakes and enormous river systems.[37] As detailed further in Part B, the doctrine made its first American appearances in key state court decisions during the early nineteenth century, and it was affirmed repeatedly by the U.S. Supreme Court by that century's end. While these decisions created uniquely American law going forward, they drew heavily on the historical roots of the doctrine in pre-American times.

3. *Early Spanish Law:* Las Siete Partidas

Alfonso X, the king of Castile and Leon from 1252 to 1284 A.D., was the great grandson of Holy Roman Emperor Frederick I.[38] His court scholars are credited with many sweeping works, including the Primera crónica general (a gleaning of historical facts from folklore and oral histories), the Gran e general estoria (a more comprehensive world history), and even the creation of the modern Castilian Spanish language.[39]

The Alfonso court also compiled a law code called Las Siete Partidas, which established a set of morals for both the king and his people.[40] The code drew heavily from Roman law – especially the Roman concept of *res communis*, which established the public right to access and use the sea.[41] The Alfonso court extended the res communis even further, though, by incorporating a public right to access and use the air, running water, seashore, and rainwater.[42] Las Siete Partidas was declared the law of all of Castile and Leon in 1348 after the death of King Alfonso.[43]

The application of Las Siete Partidas to the Spanish colonies was formalized in 1796, and the code was reaffirmed in every subsequent iteration of Spanish law.[44] The influences of Las Siete Partidas are still felt in the American states that were originally under Spanish or Mexican control, including Florida, California, and Texas.[45] The U.S. Supreme Court affirmed the continued validity of Spanish law in Florida following its acquisition from Spain.[46]

---

[37] *See* Ill. Cent. R.R. Co. v. Illinois, 146 U.S. 387, 453 (1892).
[38] *Alfonso X*, BRITANNICA, www.britannica.com/biography/Alfonso-X (last visited March 6, 2024).
[39] Id.
[40] Id.
[41] Michael Blumm, *Constitutionalizing the Public Trust Doctrine in Chile*, 52 ENV'T L. 649 (2022); Las Siete Partidas, P. III, tit. 28, laws III, IV, VI.
[42] Sources cited *id*.
[43] *Alfonso X*, BRITANNICA, www.britannica.com/biography/Alfonso-X (last visited March 6, 2024).
[44] John T. Vance, *The Old Spanish Code of "Las Siete Partidas" in Mexico*, 14 AM. BAR ASSOC. J. 4 219, 220–21 (1928).
[45] American & Ocean Ins. Co. v. 356 Bales of Cotton, 26 U.S. 511, 544 (1828); REPORT OF THE DEBATES IN THE CONVENTION OF CALIFORNIA ON THE FORMATION OF THE STATE CONSTITUTION IN SEPTEMBER AND OCTOBER, at 3 (J. Browne rptr. 1850); State v. Valmont Plantations, 346 S.W.2d 853, 855–56 (Tex. Civ. App. 1961).
[46] Ocean Ins. Co., 26 U.S. 511 (1828).

4. Critiquing the Conventional Account

While this account of the historical roots of the doctrine is frequently repeated in American jurisprudence and scholarship,[47] some regard the conventional account with skepticism.[48] A few scholars have debated the extent to which ancient legal practice does or should provide justification for the evolution of the modern public trust doctrine.[49] For example, Professor Jim Huffman has questioned whether the Magna Carta – designed to protect the property rights of English barons – can be a legitimate basis for a broad assertion of rights in the general public.[50] He further argues that the King's prerogatives under English common law did not include trust-like responsibilities to the public until well into the nineteenth century.[51] Professors J.B. Ruhl and Tom McGinn have scrutinized modern invocations of the Justinian *jus publicum*, especially by those who would apply it to protect the air commons in climate change litigation.[52] They worry that atmospheric trust advocates may overstate the environmental values associated with the historical premise, when the Roman public trust progenitor arose primarily to protect economic interests.[53] Nevertheless, they ultimately find more ancient Roman support for modern doctrinal elements than Huffman, and conclude that the public trust principle commonly credited to Justinian probably extends even further back in time.[54]

Although elements of the historical critique have merit, their arguments remain a footnote to the mainstream historical account.[55] Even Ruhl and McGinn, in the most rigorous interrogation of the Roman origin story to date, find support for the continuity of modern public trust principles all the way back to ancient common

---

[47] *See, e.g.*, Env't L. Found. v. State Water Res. Control Bd., 237 Cal. Rptr. 3d 393, 399 (Cal. Ct. App. 2018) ("From ancient Roman roots, the English common law has developed a doctrine enshrining humanity's entitlement to air and water as a public trust."); BLUMM & WOOD, *supra* note 11, at 57–82 (identifying the Roman roots of the public trust doctrine); Sax, *supra* note 11, at 475; Ewa M. Davison, *Enjoys Long Walks on the Beach: Washington's Public Trust Doctrine and the Right of Pedestrian Passage over Private Tidelands*, 81 WASH. L. REV. 813, 830–31 (2006) (invoking the Justinian roots of the public trust doctrine).

[48] For a fuller discussion on these scholars' critique of the conventional historical account, see Ryan, *A Short History*, *supra* note 5, at 146–49.

[49] *See* Huffman, *Speaking of Inconvenient Truths*, *supra* note 13, at 20–23; Bruce W. Frier, *The Roman Origins of the Public Trust Doctrine*, 32 J. ROMAN ARCHAEOLOGY 641, 643 (2019); *see also* Ryan, *A Short History*, *supra* note 5, at 146–49.

[50] *See* Huffman, *Speaking of Inconvenient Truths*, *supra* note 13, at 19–21.

[51] *Id.*

[52] Ruhl & McGinn, *supra* note 14.

[53] *Id.* at 167–71 ("[T]he surviving sources suggest to us that Roman policies are not linked, at least not in any obvious sense, to the protection of the environment. Instead, they are keyed to the exploitation of certain natural resources for economic motives.").

[54] *Id.* at 130, 163 (noting that "[t]he Institutes was an attempt to summarize and synthesize Roman law going back many centuries before its publication" and was "stitched together from excerpts drawn from the works of two juristic predecessors," Guis and Marcian); *see also* Frier, *supra* note 49.

[55] *See* Sax, *supra* note 11; Ruhl & McGinn, *supra* note 14.

law. And while Huffman is right that the Magna Carta was conceived as a political device by British nobles to protect their own aristocratic privileges, and not those of the general public – these unstately origins did not dull the worldwide inspiration that the Magna Carta would eventually provide for the development of universal civil rights. For the same reason, its aristocratic origins should not necessarily tarnish the force of this historical account on the development of more universal public rights in natural resources. The ideals set forth in the Forest Charter addendum to the Magna Carta, which unequivocally speak to commoners' rights in natural resources, may come even closer to the modern public trust principles that would ultimately evolve in the United States and elsewhere.[56]

In the end, whether or not critics like Huffman are right about this history, it is a story that American jurists have been telling for a very long time. As detailed in Part B, the American courts that adopted the public trust doctrine have been referring copiously (and perhaps even defensively) to its roots in both British and Roman law for two hundred years.[57] Regardless of its origins, the modern public trust doctrine finds its most important jurisprudential roots in the long chain of American judicial decisions and other sources that affirm its foundational role in American law.

B. RECEPTION IN THE UNITED STATES

The doctrine of sovereign authority over submerged lands was received in the United States through the individual states' reception of British common law and began making appearances in litigation within a few decades of the nation's founding. The emerging public trust doctrine established sovereign ownership over the submerged lands beneath navigable waterways, usually up to the mean high-water mark (the point representing the maximum rise of the waterbody at issue over the surrounding land).[58] In the expanding territory of the new United States, where the shores of the sea are matched by thousands of miles of navigable rivers and enormous freshwater lakes, the doctrine was expanded from the British focus on coastal tidelands to the resources associated with navigable waterways more generally.[59] The doctrine was first recognized by state courts during the early 1800s, not long

---

[56] See Robinson, *supra* note 29.
[57] See Part (A) ("Roots in Early Roman and English Law").
[58] The mean high-water mark (MHWM) is the primary tool for measuring the boundaries between public and private lands beneath navigable waterways, but some jurisdictions use other boundaries for certain waterways, such as the ordinary low water mark (OLWM) for non-tidal or littoral waterways, designating the lowest point of rise by the waterbody over its submerged lands. See Craig, *Eastern Public Trust Doctrines*, *supra* note 15, at 6. For example, the first case discussed below, *Arnold v. Mundy*, refers to the OLWM line. Some jurisdictions that adopted OLWM boundaries early in their history later changed to MHWM by statute. See Katrina M. Wyman & Nicholas R. Williams, *Migrating Boundaries*, 65 FLA. L. REV. 1957, 1964–65 (2013).
[59] See Ill. Cent. R.R. Co. v. Illinois, 146 U.S. 387, 453 (1892).

after Thomas Jefferson's tenure as the third president of the United States and Lewis and Clark's expedition of the western territories.[60] By the end of that century, the U.S. Supreme Court had affirmed it several times as an underlying feature of the American common law landscape.

This part reviews key moments in this early history of the American doctrine,[61] tracing its arrival in state courts in the early nineteenth century through the U.S. Supreme Court's seminal treatments of the doctrine near the turn of the twentieth century. These cases had consequential stakes, such as the rightful ownership of Chicago Harbor[62] and submerged lands on the Columbia River in Oregon.[63] Yet among the first cases to turn on the public trust doctrine had lesser stakes, a New Jersey dispute over the ownership of submerged oyster beds.

1. *State Common Law*: Arnold v. Mundy

In 1821, the former French Emperor Napoleon Bonaparte died in exile,[64] and the New Jersey Supreme Court became the first American court to discuss the sovereign ownership of submerged lands in *Arnold v. Mundy*, a case about who was entitled to harvest oysters from a riverbed.[65]

The plaintiff had purchased a farm alongside a navigable river, in which he planted oysters below the ordinary low-water mark[66] and staked off the bed.[67] When the defendant took oysters from this bed, the farmer argued that he was trespassing on submerged lands that had long been claimed and defended by his predecessors in title.[68] Although the farmer was able to show surveys proving the previous private claims to these submerged lands, and to prove that these predecessors in title really had driven would-be competitors away from them, the defendant argued that all

---

[60] *Thomas Jefferson*, ENCYCLOPAEDIA BRITANNICA, www.britannica.com/biography/Thomas-Jefferson (last visited Oct. 25, 2022) (dating Jefferson's presidency between 1801 and 1809); *Lewis and Clark Expedition*, ENCYCLOPAEDIA BRITANNICA, www.britannica.com/event/Lewis-and-Clark-Expedition (last visited Oct. 25, 2022) (dating Lewis and Clark's journey to find a route to the Pacific Ocean as beginning in 1804).

[61] For an even more thorough history of the early American doctrine, see generally Harrison C. Dunning, *The Public Right to Use Water in Place*, *in* WATERS AND WATER RIGHTS 28–1 to 33–22 (Amy C. Kelley ed., 2009).

[62] *See Ill. Cent.*, 146 U.S. 387.

[63] Shively v. Bowlby, 152 U.S. 1, 53–54 (1894).

[64] *Napoleon I*, ENCYCLOPAEDIA BRITANNICA, www.britannica.com/biography/Napoleon-I (last visited Oct. 25, 2022).

[65] Arnold v. Mundy, 6 N.J.L. 1 (1821).

[66] For discussion of mean high and ordinary low water marks, see generally Huffman, *Speaking of Inconvenient Truths*, *supra* note 13, at 18–27. It is noteworthy that the oyster bed here was below the ordinary low water mark, indicating that it would meet the requirements of public ownership under either measuring approach.

[67] *Arnold*, 6 N.J.L. at 9–10, 65–66.

[68] *Id.* at 9, 66.

citizens of New Jersey had a common right to take oysters from a navigable river where oysters would grow naturally.[69]

Writing for the court, Chief Justice Kirkpatrick determined that the farmer could only prevail in his suit if he had proper title to the oyster bed[70] – but that this farmer could not do so, because his private claim extended only to the landward side of the water's edge.[71] The Chief Justice held that the land beneath navigable waterways[72] is common property,[73] and that proprietors have no more power than the English Crown to convert lands beneath them into private property.[74] Referencing Justinian, the Chief Justice characterized common property as "the air, the running water, the sea, the fish, and the wild beasts," and held that title to these were in the sovereign, to "be held, protected, and regulated for the common use and benefit."[75] Writing with strong tones of judicial gravity, he concluded:

> The sovereign power itself, therefore, cannot, consistently with the principles of the law of nature and the constitution of a well ordered society, make a direct and absolute grant of the waters of the state, divesting all the citizens of their common right. It would be a grievance which never could be long borne by a free people.[76]

With these words, he became the first American jurist to tie the public commons element of the public trust doctrine to the orderly functioning of democracy. Not long thereafter, in 1842, the U.S. Supreme Court approved the reasoning of *Arnold v. Mundy* in a similar case about the ownership of submerged oyster beds, *Martin v. Waddell*.[77]

2. Affirmation by the U.S. Supreme Court: Martin v. Waddell

The United States Supreme Court first formally invoked the public trust doctrine in 1842, the same year that the Chinese and British Empires ended the First Opium

---

[69] *Id.* at 66.
[70] *Id.* at 11–14.
[71] *Id.* at 67.
[72] *Id.* at 12 (specifying "the navigable rivers, where the tide ebbs and flows, the ports, the bays, the coasts of the sea, including both the water and the land under the water, for the purposes of passing and repassing, navigation, fishing, fowling, sustenance, and all the other uses of the water and its products").
[73] *Id.* at 71–72.
[74] *Id.* at 78 (indicating that any grants purporting to convey this common property were therefore null and void).
[75] *Id.* at 71.
[76] *Id.* at 78.
[77] Martin v. Waddell, 41 U.S. 367, 410 (1842) ("[W]hen the Revolution took place, the people of each state became themselves sovereign; and in that character hold the absolute right to all their navigable waters and the soils under them for their own common use, subject only to the rights since surrendered by the Constitution to the general government."); *see also id.* at 409 ("The country mentioned in the letters patent, was held by the king in his public and regal character as the representative of the nation, and in trust for them.").

War.[78] In *Martin v. Waddell*, the Supreme Court affirmed the sovereign ownership of navigable waters and their submerged resources in another dispute over oyster beds.[79] Here, the plaintiff claimed ownership of tidelands whose chain of title traced back to a grant to the Duke of York from King Charles of England, made to facilitate the establishment of the early American colonies.[80] Yet the Court held that the plaintiff proprietors could not prevail, because even a royal grant was subject to public trust rights of common fishery for the common people.[81] In affirming the public trust principles of sovereign ownership of navigable waters and the submerged resources therein,[82] the Court referenced the presence of the doctrine in English law as far back as the Magna Carta.[83] Three years later, the Supreme Court applied the same principles in a more consequential case resolving a dispute over the ownership of submerged lands in Alabama and Georgia.[84]

3. *The Public Trust on Equal Footing:* Pollard v. Hagan

In 1845, the year Texas was admitted as the 45th U.S. state and Henry David Thoreau took up residence at Walden Pond,[85] the Supreme Court considered the relationship between the public trust and equal footing doctrines. In *Pollard v. Hagan*, the Court rejected an argument that territory in Alabama that had originally been ceded by Spain should not be subject to the public trust doctrine,[86] partnering the common law concept of sovereign ownership with the federal constitutional doctrine of

---

[78] *Opium Wars*, ENCYCLOPAEDIA BRITANNICA, www.britannica.com/topic/Opium-Wars#ref1262803 (last visited Oct. 25, 2022).

[79] *Martin*, 41 U.S. 367, 417–18.

[80] *Id.* at 407–18.

[81] *Id.* at 416–18.

[82] *Id.* at 418. The court concludes that the former proprietors had no right to alienate the submerged land as private property in conflict with the people's rights to common fisheries. The original royal charters to the Duke of York, later surrendered to these proprietors, conferred the same powers as those held by the Crown, which protected common rights of fishery absent clear contrary language (not evident here) to convert the land under navigable waters to private property. *See id.* at 413–14.

[83] *Id.* at 368, 413–14 ("The lands under the navigable waters within the limits of the charter passed to the grantee, as one of the royalties incident to the powers of government; and were to be held by him, in the same manner, and for the same purposes, that the navigable waters of England and the soils under them are held by the Crown.... The policy of England since the Magna Carta (for the last six hundred years), has been carefully preserved – to secure the common right of piscary for the benefit of the public.... [I]t would require very plain language in these letters-patent [to the Duke of York] to persuade [the Court] that the public and common right of fishery in navigable waters, which has been so long and so carefully guarded in England, and which was preserved in every other colony founded on the Atlantic borders, was intended, in this one instance, to be taken away.").

[84] Pollard v. Hagan, 44 U.S. 212 (1845).

[85] *Texas*, ENCYCLOPAEDIA BRITANNICA, www.britannica.com/place/Texas-state (last visited Oct. 25, 2022); *Walden Pond*, ENCYCLOPAEDIA BRITANNICA, www.britannica.com/place/Walden-Pond (last visited Oct. 25, 2022).

[86] *Pollard*, 44 U.S. at 228–29.

B. Reception in the United States

"equal footing" between the states.[87] The equal footing doctrine holds that all states in the union, regardless of the timing and circumstances of their entry, possess the same sovereign rights and responsibilities as the original thirteen states, including those regarding submerged lands.[88]

In this case, the issue turned on whether the common law public trust doctrine would apply in Alabama, a state whose territory had come into the United States by Treaty with the King of Spain, a non-common law sovereign. The plaintiff claimed ownership by a U.S. Patent to submerged land under the Mobile River, which had originally been ceded to the United States by Spain under the 1819 Adams-Onis Treaty, also known as the Florida Treaty.[89]

In his appeal, the plaintiff argued that because the land had been conveyed to the U.S. by Spain, and not England, the fuller powers of the Spanish Crown over navigable waters should govern his ownership rights.[90] The Spanish Crown had held full title to these submerged lands without the encumbering public trust obligations of British common law. By his reasoning, those were the unencumbered rights that had been conveyed to the United States, which later conveyed those same unencumbered rights to him.

In a critical moment for the American public trust doctrine, the Court rejected this argument. Instead, it determined that when Alabama was admitted to the Union, it entered on "equal footing" with neighboring states, such as Georgia, and thereby succeeded to all the same rights of sovereignty, jurisdiction, and eminent domain as these other states.[91] The Court explained that the U.S. had not succeeded to the specific rights the King of Spain had held previously, but came into possession of the new territory subject to the institutions and laws of its own government.[92] The court held that the land under navigable waters was reserved to the states, that new states have the same sovereignty and rights over navigable waters as did the original states, and that the United States did not have the power to grant the lands claimed by the plaintiff.[93]

---

[87] *Id.* at 222–23.
[88] *Id.* at 222 ("The manner in which the new States were to be admitted into the union, according to the Ordinance of 1787, as expressed therein, is as follows: 'And whenever any of the said states shall have sixty thousand free inhabitants therein, such state shall be admitted by its delegates into the Congress of the United States, on an equal footing with the original States in all respects whatever.'").
[89] *Id.* at 225. When the case went to trial, the jury was instructed – consistent with the public trust doctrine – that if they believed the land was below the high-water mark at the time Alabama was admitted to the union, then the patent was void and the plaintiff had no title. When the jury found against the plaintiff, he appealed on grounds that they had been improperly instructed.
[90] *Id.*
[91] *Id.* at 223, 228–29.
[92] *Id.* at 225 ("It cannot be admitted that the King of Spain could, by treaty or otherwise, impart to the United States any of his royal prerogatives; and much less can it be admitted that they have capacity to receive or power to exercise them. Every nation acquiring territory, by treaty or otherwise, must hold it subject to the constitution and laws of its own government, and not according to those of the government ceding it.").
[93] *Id.* at 230.

Pollard v. Hagan is an especially important case because it sheds light on some of the questions that continue to preoccupy public trust jurisprudence today. By establishing that all lands passing into U.S. possession are encumbered by the public trust regardless of their source, it lends credence to contemporary arguments that the public trust doctrine constrains federal as well as state sovereign management of public trust resources.[94] After all, if all submerged lands within the United States are subject to the trust regardless of what sovereign possessed them beforehand, what distinguishes submerged lands under federal jurisdiction? Some scholars also read the case to suggest that the doctrine has quasi-constitutional features, drawing from a well of constitutive authority that departs from more ordinary doctrines of law. Accordingly, some argue that *Pollard* reveals the constitutional dimensions of the doctrine as an attribute of sovereignty that transcends mere common law status.[95] Others have argued that the public trust doctrine expresses a fiduciary aspect of the constitutional equal footing doctrine.[96]

4. *The Definitive Supreme Court Statement:* Shively v. Bowlby

By the late nineteenth century, it was well established among American courts that the state holds navigable waterways in trust for the public.[97] In 1894, the same year Thomas Edison and William K. L. Dickson obtained the first copyright for a motion picture film in the U.S.,[98] the Supreme Court made its most definitive statement of the public trust doctrine as an attribute of sovereign authority in *Shively v. Bowlby*, a case quieting title to submerged lands beneath a state-sanctioned wharf on the Columbia River in Oregon.[99]

The case resolved a dispute over the ownership of submerged lands along the Columbia River near its delta into the Pacific, in what would eventually become the city of Astoria, Oregon.[100] The defendant's riverbed claim was challenged in a complicated fact pattern involving a countervailing claim by successors in title

---

[94] *See* Part (C) ("Conflicts with Water Allocation Law"). *See generally* Juliana v. United States, 217 F. Supp. 3d 1224, 1234 (D. Or. 2016), *rev'd*, 947 F.3d 1159 (9th Cir. 2020).

[95] Harrison C. Dunning, *The Public Trust: A Fundamental Doctrine of American Property Law*, 19 ENV'T L. 515, 516–524 (1989). *But see* James R. Rasband, *The Disregarded Common Parentage of the Equal Footing and Public Trust Doctrines*, 32 LAND & WATER L. REV. 1 (1997) (arguing that both the equal footing doctrine and public trust doctrine should be understood as flip sides of the same federal common law coin). For further discussion of the relationship between the equal footing doctrine and the public trust doctrine, see Chapter 8(B)(3) ("A Constitutive Constraint on Federal Authority?") (exploring the quasi-constitutional nature of the doctrine).

[96] *See generally* Michael C. Blumm, Harrison C. Dunning & Scott W. Reed, *Renouncing the Public Trust Doctrine: An Assessment of the Validity of Idaho House Bill 794*, 24 ECOLOGY L.Q. 461 (1997).

[97] *See* Blumm, *A Modern View of the Public Trust Doctrine*, *supra* note 4, at 580.

[98] *Edison Kinetoscopic Record of a Sneeze*, January 7, 1894, LIBR. OF CONG., www.loc.gov/item/00694192/ (last visited Feb. 27, 2023).

[99] Shively v. Bowlby, 152 U.S. 1, 53–54 (1894).

[100] *Id.* at 7, 9.

who had built a wharf on the same land.[101] The original claimant had taken title under a grant from the U.S. Congress to U.S. territorial lands before Oregon had become a state, and the case turned on whether that grant had conveyed not only the uplands, but also the submerged lands below the mean high-water mark.[102]

In a meticulous exposition, the Court traced how the doctrine of public rights in submerged lands had progressed from English common law into the original thirteen states and those that had followed, identifying the overwhelming majority that had explicitly adopted the public trust. Citing both *Martin v. Waddell* and *Pollard v. Hagan*, the Court once again affirmed that submerged lands had been held by the English king for the benefit of the public,[103] that those rights became vested in the original states after the American Revolution,[104] and that all U.S. territory ever after would be subject to the same public trust limitations on submerged lands.[105] The Court held that whenever territory came into the U.S. by whatever means, the same public ownership of submerged lands below the mean high-water mark passed to the federal government, held in trust for the new states that would be carved from this territory.[106]

As new states entered the Union, they therefore did so on equal footing with the original states, holding the same rights and responsibilities in submerged lands.[107] While Congress could have conveyed title to submerged territorial land before statehood, it could only have done so for appropriate public purposes, and did not do so by general law.[108] Otherwise, sovereign grants of riparian and littoral lands to private owners remain subject to the paramount right of navigation inherent in the public.[109]

Having traced the full history of the doctrine from British law through the American Revolution and forward since then, the Court concluded that the disputed lands near the Columbia River Delta "include[] no title or right in the land below high-water mark; and the statutes of Oregon, under which the defendants in error hold, are a constitutional and legal exercise by the state of Oregon of its dominion over the lands under navigable waters."[110] In so holding, the U.S. Supreme Court formally ratified, then and forever, the general provenance of American

---

[101] *Id.*
[102] *Id.* at 52–55, 57.
[103] *Id.* at 48–49.
[104] *Id.* at 14–15, 57.
[105] *Shively*, 152 U.S. at 58.
[106] *Id.* at 57.
[107] *Id.* at 49, 57.
[108] *Id.* at 58.
[109] *Id.* at 52, 57–58.
[110] *Id.* at 58. The force of its exposition immediately before this holding, summarizing its exhaustive analysis, is worth quoting at length:

> Lands under tidewaters are incapable of cultivation or improvement in the manner of lands above high-water mark. They are of great value to the public for the purposes of commerce, navigation, and fishery. Their improvement by individuals, when permitted, is incidental or subordinate to

lands submerged in navigable waters (below the mean high-water mark) as owned by the sovereign and held in trust for the benefit of the public.

5. *With Power Comes Responsibility*: Illinois Central Railroad Co. v. Illinois

Although *Shively v. Bowlby* was the U.S. Supreme Court's most definitive treatment of the public trust doctrine, its most famous statement of the doctrine arose in *Illinois Central Railroad Co. v. Illinois*, a decision issued two years earlier.[111] In 1892, the same year Sir Arthur Conan Doyle published *The Adventures of Sherlock Holmes*,[112] the Supreme Court provided a crisp statement of the traditional American public trust doctrine that is routinely quoted by the cases that have followed:

> [T]he State holds the title to the lands under the navigable waters ... in trust for the people of the state, that they may enjoy the navigation of the waters, carry on commerce over them, and have liberty of fishing therein, freed from the obstruction or interference of private parties.[113]

> the public use and right. Therefore, the title and the control of them are vested in the sovereign, for the benefit of the whole people.
>
> At common law, the title and the dominion in lands flowed by the tide were in the king for the benefit of the nation. Upon the settlement of the colonies, like rights passed to the grantees in the royal charters, in trust for the communities to be established. Upon the American Revolution, these rights, charged with a like trust, were vested in the original states within their respective borders, subject to the rights surrendered by the constitution to the United States.
>
> Upon the acquisition of a territory by the United States, whether by cession from one of the states, or by treaty with a foreign country, or by discovery and settlement, the same title and dominion passed to the United States, for the benefit of the whole people, and in trust for the several states to be ultimately created out of the territory.
>
> The new states admitted into the Union since the adoption of the constitution have the same rights as the original states in the tidewaters, and in the lands under them, within their respective jurisdictions. The title and rights of riparian or littoral proprietors in the soil below high-water mark, therefore, are governed by the laws of the several states, subject to the rights granted to the United States by the constitution.
>
> The United States, while they hold the country as a territory, having all the powers both of national and of municipal government, may grant, for appropriate purposes, titles or rights in the soil below high-water mark of tidewaters. But they have never done so by general laws, and, unless in some case of international duty or public exigency, have acted upon the policy, as most in accordance with the interest of the people and with the object for which the territories were acquired, of leaving the administration and disposition of the sovereign rights in navigable waters, and in the soil under them, to the control of the states, respectively, when organized and admitted into the Union.
>
> Grants by [C]ongress of portions of the public lands within a territory to settlers thereon, though bordering on or bounded by navigable waters, convey, of their own force, no title or right below high-water mark, and do not impair the title and dominion of the future state, when created, but leave the question of the use of the shores by the owners of uplands to the sovereign control of each state, subject only to the rights vested by the constitution in the United States.

[111] *Shively*, 152 U.S. at 58.
[112] *The Adventures of Sherlock Holmes*, ENCYCLOPAEDIA BRITANNICA, www.britannica.com/topic/The-Adventures-of-Sherlock-Holmes-by-Conan-Doyle (last visited Oct. 25, 2022).
[113] Ill. Cent. R.R. Co. v. Illinois, 146 U.S. 387, 452 (1892).

B. Reception in the United States

Yet note how the theme of state ownership of trust resources is limited by the fact that the state only holds title *in trust* for the public. With great power comes great responsibility.

The public trust's doctrinal infrastructure shows that it doesn't just protect the public nature of these common resources, it also assigns responsibility for their protection, specifically, to the government. Analogizing to the property law construct of the legal "trust," the government (acting as trustee) is responsible for protecting the resource (or trust *res*) for the public benefit.[114] With very narrow exceptions,[115] the trustee can neither alienate the trust resource nor allow its destruction.[116] This means that, when it is acting as trustee, the government does not own trust resources in the same way that it owns more ordinary public lands under its jurisdiction. Instead, it holds the resource "in trust" for the real legal owner – the public it serves. Some scholars have described the difference as one between state "sovereign" and "proprietary" ownership, in which resources held as sovereign property are subject to the trust, while those subject to proprietary ownership may be alienated by the state on terms more like ordinary private property.[117]

The public is the ultimate beneficiary of the trust, and as in conventional trust relationships, the public can hold the government accountable for failure to manage trust resources in accordance with its responsibility as trustee.[118] If they feel the government is failing its obligations as trustee, citizens can usually seek to enforce their rights in court.[119] In this critically important way, the public trust doctrine acts not just as a *grant* of sovereign authority with regard to trust resources, but also as a *limit* on sovereign authority with regard to the same resources, constraining what the government can and cannot do to ensure against private expropriation and monopolization.[120]

---

[114] *See, e.g.*, Richard M. Frank, *The Public Trust Doctrine: Assessing Its Recent Past and Charting Its Future*, 45 U.C. DAVIS L. REV. 665, 667 (2012) ("Simply stated, however, the doctrine provides that certain natural resources are held by the government in a special status – in 'trust' – for current and future generations.").

[115] *See, e.g., Ill. Cent.*, 146 U.S. at 453 (approving limited dispositions of trust resources to private parties to improve navigation or when discrete parcels can be disposed of without impairing the public interest in the remaining trust resource); *see also* Michael C. Blumm, *The Public Trust Doctrine and Private Property: The Accommodation Principle*, 27 PACE ENV'T L. REV. 649, 660–62 (2010) (discussing the *Illinois Central* exception, "authoriz[ing] privatization of trust resources when 1) the conveyance furthered public purposes, and 2) there was no substantial effect on remaining trust resources").

[116] Frank, *supra* note 114, at 667 ("Government officials may neither alienate those resources into private ownership nor permit their injury or destruction.").

[117] *See* DAVID C. SLADE ET AL., PUTTING THE PUBLIC TRUST DOCTRINE TO WORK 6–8 (1997) (describing the distinction between the *jus privatum* element of public land, which the state may convey to a private interest, and the *jus publicum* element, which it may not).

[118] *See* Sax, *supra* note 13, at 473 (describing how citizens have brought lawsuits to enforce the trust obligations of the state).

[119] *Id.*

[120] *See* Brief for Law Professors et al. as Amici Curiae in Support of Granting Writ of Certiorari at 1–2, 7, Alec L. *ex rel.* Loorz v. McCarthy, 561 F. App'x 7 (D.C. Cir. 2014) (No. 14–405), *cert. denied*, 135 S. Ct. 774 (2014) (discussing the public trust doctrine as an attribute of sovereignty).

In *Illinois Central*, the Court not only affirmed sovereign authority over submerged lands, it also clarified the nature of the sovereign's obligations to the public as trustee of those lands.[121] And indeed, the facts of the *Illinois Central* case demonstrate just how powerful that public trust obligation can be.

To give a sense of the enormous power packed by this seemingly simple doctrine, consider the striking facts of the case. This nineteenth century legal mêlée followed a fraught moment in Illinois history, when, in 1869, the state legislature conveyed the better part of Chicago Harbor – the most valuable submerged lands in all of Lake Michigan – to the Illinois Central Railroad, a private company.[122] After a series of complicated transactions in which the legislature granted Illinois Central rights to construct infrastructure along the dry and wet sides of the lakeshore,[123] the legislature enacted the Lake Front Act of 1869,[124] which conveyed ownership rights in perpetuity to the railroad.[125] To accomplish this, the legislature had to first override a gubernatorial veto, by which the governor of Illinois had attempted to prevent the conveyance.[126]

Whether the legislative grant was an example of flagrant government corruption or a well-intended plan to spur economic development,[127] the people of Illinois were not delighted.[128] Public reaction ranged from dubious to furious.[129] While some hoped that associated economic development would eventually confer public benefits, the gift smacked of political patronage and cronyism, and it generated considerable outrage.[130] When both the *Chicago Tribune* and the *Chicago Times* condemned

---

[121] Ryan, *The Historic Saga*, *supra* note 11, at 568.

[122] Ill. Cent. R.R. Co. v. Illinois, 146 U.S. 387, 438–39 (1892) (describing "a grant by the State in 1869 of its right and title to the submerged lands, constituting the bed of Lake Michigan.").

[123] Joseph D. Kearney & Thomas W. Merrill, *The Origins of the American Public Trust Doctrine: What Really Happened in Illinois Central*, 71 U. CHI. L. REV. 799, 818–23 (2004) (discussing the railroad's improvements to the lakeshore); *see also* Crystal S. Chase, *The Illinois Central Public Trust Decision and Federal Common Law: An Unconventional View*, 16 HASTINGS W.-NW. J. ENV'T L. & POL'Y 113, 126 (2010).

[124] *See* Kearney & Merrill, *supra* note 123, at 860–77 (discussing the enactment of the Lake Front Act of 1869); *see also* H.R. Journal, 26th Cong., at 239–40 (Ill. 1869) (noting the Senate's passage of the House's version of the bill, enacting the Act).

[125] *See* Kearney & Merrill, *supra* note 123, at 800–801 (describing the Lake Front Act, by which the state legislature "awarded the Illinois Central both a portion of the lakeshore for a new depot and over one thousand acres of submerged land for the development of an outer harbor for Chicago"). Professors Kearney and Merrill explain that "[t]he practical effect of the Lake Front Act, in terms of the market for harbor facilities in Chicago, was to authorize the creation of a large, privately owned harbor facility in the lake." *Id.* at 881.

[126] *Id.* at 874–75.

[127] *See* Sax, *supra* note 13, at 490 (arguing that the conveyance could not be justified by any public benefit); Kearney & Merrill, *supra* note 123, at 893 ("[A]lthough the documentary record from 1869 cannot be said definitely to establish … corrupt means … it probably leans in that direction.").

[128] *See* Kearney & Merrill, *supra* note 123, at 840–42, 875–76 (describing public outrage over the conveyance).

[129] *Id.*

[130] *Id.*

B. Reception in the United States

the conveyance, legislative support for the deal began to collapse, and the Illinois House and Senate created committees to investigate the possibility of corruption.[131]

When the legislative session finally turned over, the new legislature – responding to this significant public pressure – attempted to undo what the previous legislature had wrought.[132] In 1873, legislators sought to reestablish public control over the full harbor by repealing the original conveyance.[133] Ten years later, when the railroad continued to assume a proprietary posture toward the harbor, the state sued for declaratory relief to establish public ownership of the lakebed.[134] Now Illinois Central was the outraged party, and it fiercely resisted the state's claim.

In court, the railroad argued that the new legislature could not repeal the Chicago Harbor conveyance made by the prior legislature.[135] It argued that these submerged lands were now its private property, conveyed by the Lake Front Act of 1869,[136] and that the state lacked authority to reclaim property that had already passed in a fully executed conveyance.[137] As the railroad argued, the state could not formally convey a thing of such value and then just take it back, as if the conveyance had never happened![138] The Supreme Court had previously recognized that an otherwise valid private real estate contract made in reliance on a state law remained in effect even after the legislature had repealed the law, offering some support for the railroad's argument.[139]

Of course, even if the legislative grant were sound, it is worth noting that in actuality, the state *could* have just taken it back – though not as if the conveyance had never happened. The state's power of eminent domain would have allowed it to reclaim the property for public use, so long as it paid just compensation to the railroad.[140] "While" other scholars have written about *Illinois Central* as though the most important issue in the litigation was the state's liability for an uncompensated taking[141] – a legal issue in which the public trust doctrine might also play a role[142] – that claim

---

[131] Id. at 889–90, 908–909 (describing legislative committees created to investigate potential corruption).
[132] See id. at 911 (indicating the legislative turnover that followed); Ill. Cent. R.R. Co. v. Illinois, 146 U.S. 387, 449 (1892) ("On the 15th of April, 1873, the legislature of Illinois repealed the act.").
[133] Ill. Cent., 146 U.S. at 449.
[134] Id. at 439.
[135] Id. at 438–39.
[136] Id. at 450.
[137] Id. at 450–51 ("[The Act] is treated by the counsel of the company as an *absolute* conveyance to it of title to the submerged lands, giving it as full and complete power to use and dispose of the same ... and not as a license to use the lands subject to revocation by the state." (emphasis added)).
[138] As my students have often remarked, the Railroad's claim would have been well understood by any toddler under the hallowed doctrine of "No Backsies!"
[139] Fletcher v. Peck, 10 U.S. (6 Cranch) 87, 113–14 (1810).
[140] See U.S. Const. amend. V.
[141] See, e.g., Epstein, supra note 11, at 422; Cohen, supra note 12, at 246.
[142] See, e.g., Erin Ryan, Palazzolo, The Public Trust, and the Property Owner's Reasonable Expectations: Takings and the South Carolina Marsh Island Bridge Debate, 15 Se. Env't L.J. 121, 137–40 (2006) (discussing use of the public trust doctrine to defend takings claims by defusing the reasonableness of claimants' expectations).

was not a subject of the actual litigation.[143] Instead, Illinois Central staked its most important claim on the power of the original legislative grant and the lack of state authority to undo it (together with subsidiary claims for rights incident to its ownership of riparian lands and a later claim that the repeal interfered with rights under its original charter).[144]

Nevertheless, the state had a formidable response, deploying public trust principles as a novel legal shield. Illinois argued that its power to undo a fully executed conveyance was immaterial under the circumstances.[145] Conceding that there might have been a legal problem if there really had been a legal gift, the state argued that in this case, there was not an actual problem, because – thanks to the public trust doctrine – there had not been any actual gift.[146] Even if it looked as though the previous legislature had conveyed the bed of Chicago Harbor to the railroad, in fact, no such thing had happened.[147] The bed of Chicago Harbor was subject to the public trust doctrine – held by the state in trust for the public – and therefore, as a matter of law, could not be alienated away.[148]

The state argued that the previous legislature had lacked the power to make a gift of lands encumbered by the public trust.[149] Such an act would be *ultra vires* – literally, beyond the authority of the state – at least without taking more heroic measures to clarify why such an unusual conveyance was in accord with its public trust obligations.[150] As a result, there was no actual gift, and accordingly no harm in repealing it, and therefore, no legal foul.

Accepting this argument, the Supreme Court affirmed that the operation of the public trust doctrine had prevented the legislature from ever alienating the harbor in the first place.[151] The railroad had never been the actual owner of the submerged lands, and so its legal claims ended there. In this way, Illinois was able to successfully

---

[143] See Kearney & Merrill, *supra* note 123, at 811 n.54 (explaining this popular misconception).
[144] Ill. Cent. R.R. Co. v. Illinois, 146 U.S. 387, 438–39 (1892) (stating the railroad's claims).
[145] *Id.*
[146] *Id.*
[147] *See id.*
[148] *See id.* at 453–54 ("The trust devolving upon the State for the public, and which can only be discharged by the management and control of property in which the public has an interest, cannot be relinquished by a transfer of the property. The control of the State for the purposes of the trust can never be lost.").
[149] *See id.*
[150] *Id.* at 455–56 ("The ownership of the navigable waters of the harbor and of the lands under them is a subject of public concern to the whole people of the State. The trust with which they are held, therefore, is governmental and cannot be alienated, except in those instances ... of parcels used in the improvement of the interest thus held, or when parcels can be disposed of without detriment to the public interest in the lands and waters remaining.").
[151] *Id.* at 453. Of note, Justice Field explained that the trust extended to Chicago Harbor because it was "a subject of public concern to the whole people," leaving open the possibility, embraced by later scholars and litigants, that the same rationale should apply to other commons resources also vulnerable to monopolization. *Id.* at 455; *see also* BLUMM & WOOD, *supra* note 11, at 72–73 (discussing *Illinois Central* and various scholars' interpretations of the case).

B. Reception in the United States

reestablish public ownership of Chicago Harbor on the grounds that the public trust doctrine acted as a limit on the state's legal ability to casually convey trust lands.[152]

More importantly, *Illinois Central* demonstrated that the public trust doctrine functions not only as a grant of affirmative state authority over submerged lands, but also as a limit on state authority with regard to the management of those lands. This is because the state is required to manage them as trustee for the public benefit.[153] The public, as the beneficiary of this trust relationship, is entitled to call the state to account for errant management choices in the courts. If members of the public believe the state has failed its obligations as trustee, they can pursue their legal claim under the public trust doctrine in court.

The premise affirmed in *Illinois Central* provided critical impetus for the development of the common law public trust in nearly all of the United States.[154] Today, the common law public trust doctrine offers meaningful protection of navigable waterways as public commons in nearly every state.[155] Over the years, as plaintiffs across the country have litigated to vindicate and define public trust obligations, the doctrine has developed differently from one state to the next.[156] Some states protect different resources under the doctrine and some assign different levels of protection to trust resources,[157] but at a minimum, most share the common principle of sovereign authority over lands beneath navigable waters held in trust for the public.[158] Following the Mono Lake *National Audubon Society* decision and the cases that paved its way in California law, the doctrine has become increasingly associated not only with the protection of such traditional uses as boating, commerce, fishing, and swimming, but with environmental protection as well.[159] In some jurisdictions,

---

[152] See *Ill. Cent.*, 146 U.S. at 453, 463.

[153] Shively v. Bowlby, 152 U.S. 1, 57 (1894) (holding that the "title and the control of [submerged lands] are vested in the sovereign, for the benefit of the whole people"). *See supra* notes 97–111 and accompanying text (quoting *Shively* more fully and discussing its significance).

[154] See Kearney & Merrill, *supra* note 123, at 802–803 (outlining the history of the case in light of its importance in modern public trust theory).

[155] *See generally* Craig, *Eastern Public Trust Doctrines*, *supra* note 15 (comparing eastern states' public trust doctrines); Craig, *Western States' Public Trust Doctrines*, *supra* note 15 (comparing western states' public trust doctrines); ALEXANDRA B. KLASS & LING-YEE HUANG, RESTORING THE TRUST: WATER RESOURCES AND THE PUBLIC TRUST DOCTRINE, A MANUAL FOR ADVOCATES 21–24 (2009) (comparing the sources of various states' public trust doctrines); MICHAEL C. BLUMM ET AL., THE PUBLIC TRUST DOCTRINE IN FORTY-FIVE STATES (2014), http://papers.ssrn.com/sol3/papers.cfm?abstract_id=2235329 (analyzing the public trust doctrines of 45 states); LING-YEE HUANG, CTR. FOR PROGRESSIVE REFORM, RESTORING THE TRUST: AN INDEX OF STATE CONSTITUTIONAL AND STATUTORY PROVISIONS AND CASES ON WATER RESOURCES AND THE PUBLIC TRUST DOCTRINE (2009), https://papers.ssrn.com/sol3/papers.cfm?abstract_id=1478512.

[156] See sources cited *supra* note 155.

[157] See sources cited *supra* note 155. For example, most states protect public access to submerged lands below the high-water mark, but New Jersey protects access to dry sand beaches as well. Matthews v. Bay Head Imp. Ass'n., 471 A.2d 355, 363 (N.J. 1984).

[158] See sources cited *supra* note 155.

[159] *See, e.g.*, Marks v. Whitney, 491 P.2d 374, 380 (Cal. 1971) (finding increasing recognition that one of the most important uses of tidelands protected by the doctrine is "the preservation of those lands in

the public trust doctrine has also been applied to protect other resources, including groundwater, wildlife, and atmospheric resources.[160]

The common law public trust doctrine continues to play an important role in the regulation of public waterways, but the trust concept has also developed independently through state constitutional law. As addressed in Chapters 8 and 9, public trust principles have been incorporated into a number of U.S. state constitutions, even where the doctrine is also part of that state's common law.[161] Constitutionalized versions of the doctrine thus expand recognition for new public trust values beyond those traditionally protected at common law. Operating as a matter of common or constitutional law, American case law has generally presumed that the public trust doctrine is a feature of state law,[162] although this state law owes a substantial debt to the early federal jurisprudence on state sovereign ownership reported earlier. Nevertheless, points of intersection between the public trust doctrine and important areas of federal law continue to emerge, especially its role as a background principle of law in constitutional takings analysis, and in ongoing debate over the extent to which it should operate as a constitutive constraint on sovereign authority more generally (including federal authority).

C. CONFLICTS WITH WATER ALLOCATION LAW

So far, this chapter has introduced the public trust doctrine as a public commons-based theory of rights and responsibilities with regard to natural resource commons, especially waterways.[163] However, there is a countervailing body of law that we must

---

their natural state, so that they may serve as ecological units for scientific study, as open space, and as environments which provide food and habitat for birds and marine life, and which favorably affect the scenery and climate of the area"); Nat'l Audubon Soc'y v. Super. Ct., 658 P.2d 709 (Cal. 1983) (affirming the application of the public trust doctrine to protect the environmental values at Mono Lake).

[160] *See, e.g.*, Env't Law Found. v. State Water Res. Control Bd., 237 Cal. Rptr. 3d 393 (Cal. Ct. App. 2018) (following the Mono Lake rule in applying the public trust doctrine to protect the non-navigable groundwater tributaries of a navigable waterway); Owsichek v. Guide Licensing & Control Bd., 763 P.2d 488, 495 (Alaska 1988) ("[C]ommon law principles incorporated in the common use clause impose upon the state a trust duty to manage the fish, wildlife and water resources of the state for the benefit of all the people."); Betchart v. Dep't of Fish & Game, 205 Cal. Rptr. 135 (Cal. Ct. App. 1984) ("California wildlife is publicly owned and is not held by owners of private land where wildlife is present."); Environmental Protection Act of 1970, MICH. COMP. LAWS ANN. § 691.1202(1) (West 1970) (extending the public trust, via statute, to authorize legal actions "for the protection of the air" in addition to water and other natural resources) (repealed and replaced by the Natural Resources and Environmental Protection Act, MICH. COMP. LAWS § 324.1701(1) (1994)).

[161] *See infra* Chapter 8 ("Beyond Mono Lake: The Development of the Public Trust across the United States") and Chapter 9 ("Public Trust Principles, Environmental Rights, and Trust Rights Climate Advocacy"); *see also* Barton H. Thompson, Jr., *Environmental Policy and State Constitutions: The Potential Role of Substantive Guidance*, 27 RUTGERS L.J. 863, 866 (1996).

[162] Alec L. ex rel. Loorz v. McCarthy, 561 F. App'x 7, 8 (D.C. Cir. 2014); *see also* PPL Montana, LLC v. Montana, 132 S. Ct. 1215, 1235 (2012) (indirect support in dicta).

[163] For analysis of other public commons arguably subject to the public trust, see BLUMM & WOOD, *supra* note 11, discussing wildlife; *id.* at 195–232, parks and public lands; *id.* at 233–256, atmospheric

C. Conflicts with Water Allocation Law

also contend with to understand the regulation of waterways in the United States, and it follows a wholly different theoretical model. This is the law of private water allocation, known more simply in the United States as "water law," and it tells us who gets to use the water within these watercourses and for what purposes.

Water law regulates the private benefits that individuals and others can receive from public water commons. Deciding how much water can be withdrawn from a waterway is just as important to the maintenance of public environmental values as the public trust doctrine (and in many cases, arguably more so), but historically, water law has been more focused on promoting economic development through the allocation and protection of private rights in water resources. Water laws grant discrete rights for the use or extraction of freshwater, including both surface and groundwater sources. This enables families, farms, and businesses to claim water for household, agricultural, and industrial purposes. Water laws also enable cities, towns, and irrigation districts to claim water that they then make available to residents and commercial entities for the same uses through distribution networks within their jurisdictions.

Like the public trust doctrine, there is much regional variation in American water law. Water allocation is a feature of state law, and though there are many differences between the states, there are two main models for allocating water rights: (1) the riparian rights approach followed in most eastern states, under which all users must share, and (2) the prior appropriations approach preferred in most western states, in which the first to claim water has a superior right to later-comers.[164] In a smaller "hybrid" category, a few states incorporate elements of both systems.[165] The eastern approach establishes correlative rights in a common pool framework, but the western approach comes closer to a privatization model, allowing users to claim an entitlement to water from which they can exclude later-comers, no matter how compelling their need.[166]

The looming problem should be obvious by now, especially in the western United States: while the public trust doctrine follows a public commons model, the prior appropriations doctrine follows a privatization model – and yet the water governed under both laws is *the very same water*. The water to which individuals and other entities can obtain private rights of use under water allocation doctrines is the exact same water that makes up the waterways protected by the public trust doctrine. If all available water in the watercourse is allocated to private appropriators, then

---

resources; *id.* at 349–64, ocean resources; *id.* at 365–67, electromagnetic spectrum; *id.* at 386–91, cultural property; *id.* at 392–96, and others.

[164] *See* Christine Klein, Mary Jane Angelo & Richard Hamann, *Modernizing Water Law: The Example of Florida*, 61 FLA. L. REV. 403, 406–407 (2009) (contrasting eastern and western water law).

[165] California, Kansas, Mississippi, Nebraska, North Dakota, Oklahoma, Oregon, South Dakota, Texas, and Washington have a hybrid system. STEPHEN HODGSON, DEV. L. SERV., FAO LEGAL OFF., FAO LEGIS. STUDY 92: MODERN WATER RIGHTS THEORY AND PRACTICE 13 n.2 (2006).

[166] Klein et al., *supra* note 164, at 406–409.

there will no longer be a watercourse for protection under the public trust doctrine. Indeed, the two bodies of law – the public trust doctrine and the law of private water allocation – are doctrinally orthogonal, with no intentional points of overlap. In one of the more serious follies of American legal evolution, each developed independently of the other, as though they have no substantive relationship at all.[167]

This part introduces these two approaches to water allocation, touching on the eastern riparian rights approach before focusing on the western approach of prior appropriations that is poised for more serious conflict with the public trust doctrine. It shows why these two bodies of laws were inevitably destined to collide, as they have done so famously in epic western water battles such as the Mono Lake and Scott River cases in California, the legislative-judicial showdown in Idaho, the Walker Lake Basin dispute in Nevada, and the *Waiahole Ditch* case in Hawaii.[168]

1. *Riparian Rights*

Eastern states generally follow the riparian rights doctrine inherited from British common law, which historically assigned interdependent rights for reasonable use of water resources among all the landowners along a watercourse.[169] In riparianism, the "reasonableness" of use is contextual, determined by the total set of individual demands on the available resource.[170]

The riparian rights approach treats the waterway as a common pool resource in which authorized users hold correlative rights, because the scope of every right to withdraw is dependent on the scope of all others. As a rule, everybody has to share.[171] At common law, authorization to use the waterway was based on the possession of riparian land bounding the watercourse. Today, many riparian jurisdictions have modernized the doctrine to de-privilege riparian ownership, allowing water to be exported from the riparian tract and treating all users under the same rubric for

---

[167] See Ryan, *From Mono Lake to the Atmospheric Trust, supra* note 5, at 47.
[168] Nat'l Audubon Soc'y v. Super. Ct. of Alpine Cnty., 658 P.2d 709 (Cal. 1983); Env't L. Found. v. State Water Res. Control Bd., 237 Cal. Rptr. 3d 393 (Cal. Ct. App. 2018) (the Scott River case); Selkirk-Priest Basin Ass'n v. State *ex rel.* Andrus, 127 Idaho 239, 240 (1995) (suggesting that the public trust doctrine might be used to constrain harm from logging activities to an impacted water body); Idaho Conservation League v. State, 911 P.2d 748 (Idaho 1995) (declining intervention by environmental groups to raise public trust issues where state ownership was not at issue, but suggesting in dicta that the public trust doctrine could take precedence over vested water rights); Mineral Cnty. v. Lyon Cnty. (*Walker Lake*), 473 P.3d 418 (Nev. 2020) (the Walker Lake case); *In re* Water Use Permit Applications (*Waiahole Ditch*), 9 P.3d 409, 445 (Haw. 2000) (holding that the state water code "does not supplant the protections of the public trust doctrine"); *see also* Chapter 5 ("*National Audubon Society*: The 'Mono Lake Case'"); Chapter 7(B)(1)(c) ("The Scott River Case"); Chapter 7(C)(2) ("The Idaho Approach") (discussing Idaho's legislative abrogation of the common law doctrine); Chapter 7(C)(3) ("Nevada: Mixed Messages in the Walker Lake Basin").
[169] See Klein et al., *supra* note 164, at 406.
[170] *Id.* at 407.
[171] *Id.*

assigning claims.[172] Yet under both the modern and traditional approach, all rights of use are coupled with a duty not to unreasonably harm other rights-holders by overdrawing or otherwise compromising the resource.

By establishing correlative rights in a shared resource with liability to other users for unreasonable harm, riparianism incorporates elements of tort law within a framework bearing resemblance to the public commons model that animates the public trust.[173] These laws treat the water subject to allocation as a public commons or a common pool, establishing interdependent rights wherein every user's rights are limited by the legitimate needs of all other users.[174] For example, in 1888, as Susan B. Anthony was organizing for women's suffrage,[175] the Connecticut Supreme Court enjoined one mill owner from impounding a stream to the detriment of other downstream mill operators in *Mason v. Hoyle*.[176] Emphasizing the reciprocal nature of rights and duties among riparian claimants, the court articulated the five core principles for "reasonably" allocating water under the common law "reasonable use" doctrine of riparian rights:

(1) All riparians have an equal opportunity to use the stream;
(2) No owner may use his own property so as to injure another;
(3) Adjudicators should consider the character and capacity of the stream;
(4) The burden of foreseeable shortages should be allocated fairly among all riparians; and
(5) Customary practices provide a foundation for evaluating "reasonableness."[177]

Modern riparianism jurisdictions continue to apply the correlative spirit of reasonable use riparianism in considering the interests of all claimants on a waterway before assigning definitive rights to any, and they increasingly consider the environmental values of healthy stream ecosystems as well. For example, in 2005, in *Michigan Citizens for Water Conservation v. Nestle Waters North America*, the Michigan Court of Appeals enjoined some – but not all – of the Nestle Corporation's claims to withdraw water from a stream that also served boating, swimming, fishing, wildlife, and aesthetic purposes.[178] The case highlights the responsibility of a

---

[172] *Id.* at 411–12 (discussing the elimination by regulated riparianism of the common law riparian ownership criteria).
[173] Professor Christine Klein has characterized the model as based in tort, because users are prohibited from inflicting unreasonable harm on one another by their use of the shared water resource. Klein et al., *supra* note 164, at 406.
[174] *Id.* at 406–407.
[175] *International Council of Women*, ENCYCLOPAEDIA BRITANNICA, www.britannica.com/topic/International-Council-of-Women (last visited Sept. 24, 2019) (explaining that in 1888, Susan B. Anthony organized the International Council of Women to fight for suffrage).
[176] Mason v. Hoyle, 14 A. 786 (Conn. 1888).
[177] *Id.* at 788–90.
[178] Mich. Citizens for Water Conservation v. Nestlé Waters N. Am., 709 N.W. 2d 174, 194–95, 208 (Mich. Ct. App. 2005).

riparian rights state to fairly allocate water to preserve as many different uses of a waterway as possible.

One advantage of the riparian rights system, especially after de-privileging riparian ownership, is that it puts the needs of all claimants on relatively equal footing – every riparian claim is as important as any other. Local Michigan residents could challenge lucrative diversions by the Nestle Corporation, and the concerns of mill owners harmed by upstream impoundments were not foreclosed if their mills were established later in time. Still, a resulting disadvantage is that the pure common law system creates enormous uncertainty about the scope of any user's rights because new claims along the waterway will always require a new analysis of the resulting web of interdependent rights. The workability of riparian rights hinged on the assumption, generally true in Britain and the early eastern American states, that there would usually be enough water to go around.[179] As water resources have come under the pressure of increasing population and development in the east, many states have therefore adopted statutory systems of "regulated riparianism." These systems partner elements of the original correlative rights framework with a permit-based system that preserves the riparian "reasonableness" inquiry with greater security of right over set periods of time.[180]

Because riparian rights are premised on a theory of waterways as commons resources, conflicts with the public trust doctrine – which also presumes that waterways are public commons – have been relatively modest thus far. Riparianism also includes features that, at least historically, have been more friendly to environmental and distributive justice concerns than the western appropriations doctrine. Conceptualizing water as a resource that everyone must share, riparianism requires a balancing of equities during water emergencies,[181] requiring all users to proportionally "share the shortage" during times of drought or emergency. In addition, riparianism has always protected uses that leave water in the stream (as for fishing, swimming, and boating), on par with uses that extract water from the stream (as for irrigation or manufacturing). For this reason, riparian rights have historically afforded more protection for such environmental concerns as ecological values, habitat, and the scenic and recreational values associated with instream flow and intact stream systems.[182]

Indeed, under the original "natural flow doctrine" of riparian rights that American states initially inherited from England, rights to withdraw were limited

---

[179] See Klein et al., *supra* note 164, at 429; T. E. Lauer, *The Common Law Background of the Riparian Doctrine*, 28 MO. L. REV. 60, 64 (1963).

[180] See sources cited *supra* note 179 (discussing Florida's model of regulatory riparianism). See generally REGULATED RIPARIAN MODEL WATER CODE (AMERICAN SOC'Y OF CIVIL ENG'RS 2004).

[181] In the traditional common law doctrine, water was shared equally by all riparian landowners. See RESTATEMENT (SECOND) OF TORTS § 858 cmt. a., illus. 1 (AM. LAW INST. 1979). In states that adopt regulated riparianism statutes, most privileges associated with riparian ownership are eliminated. See Klein et al., *supra* note 164, at 411–12.

[182] See Klein et al., *supra* note 164, at 410–11.

by the requirement that the stream retain enough water to approximate its "natural flow."[183] Under "natural flow" riparian rights, instream uses like fishing, swimming, and boating were favored over extractive uses, and waterways were necessarily protected from overdraft in ways that benefited their associated ecological, recreational, and aesthetic values. However, by mandating unimpeded flows in waterways, the natural flow doctrine substantially inhibited economic development and was eventually replaced by the modern "reasonable use doctrine" of riparian rights.[184] The reasonable use doctrine limits users from depleting streamflow only relative to the needs of other users, thus enabling fuller depletion if extractors' claims outweigh those for instream use.[185]

The shift from "natural flow" to "reasonable use" riparianism represents a rare example from water law in which the original common law doctrine is more environmentally protective than the modern trend. It stands in opposition to the historical arc of the public trust doctrine described in this chapter, in which environmental values have received increasingly more doctrinal protection over time – and it is noteworthy that the contrast may not be accidental. As water allocation law became less environmentally protective over time, perhaps more responsibility for maintaining the health of the waterway was effectively shifted to the state's obligations under the public trust doctrine.

In any event, as demands on the water resource intensify even in the comparatively wet eastern states, riparianism is coming under more and more of the same environmental pressures as appropriative rights regimes. Without additional regulation, traditional riparianism could provoke a tragedy-of-the-commons race to withdraw, with no absolute requirement to leave flow instream independent of claimed uses. Exactly such a dilemma is now playing out in the Apalachicola-Chattahoochee-Flint river basin dispute among Georgia, Alabama, and Florida, where growing withdrawals by Atlanta and other upstream users have so depleted river flows that it has decimated the oyster fishery at the river system's delta in Apalachicola Bay on the northern Gulf Coast.[186] In the most recent development of a decades-long dispute, the Supreme Court overruled Florida's exceptions to the Special Master's Report and dismissed the case in a unanimous opinion.[187]

For this and other reasons, riparian rights states shifting from the pure common law system to statutory systems of regulated riparianism generally add protections for instream uses, environmental values, distributive justice, and other concerns

---

[183] *See, e.g.*, Merrit v. Parker, 1 N.J.L. 460 (1795).
[184] *See, e.g.*, Mason v. Hoyle, 14 A. 786 (Conn. 1888).
[185] *Id.*
[186] Florida v. Georgia, 138 S. Ct. 2502 (2018).
[187] *See* Florida v. Georgia, 141 S. Ct. 1175 (2021); *see also* Florida v. Georgia, SCOTUSBLOG, www.scotusblog.com/case-files/cases/florida-v-georgia-2/ (last visited Feb. 8, 2023) (outlining the full case history); Florida v. Georgia, 138 S. Ct. 2502, 2509–10 (2018) (describing the long dispute between Florida and Georgia).

that are not necessarily addressed by the common law.[188] These protective measures will hopefully forestall the tragedy of the commons that the traditional doctrine could enable. Even so, increasing water scarcity issues in the east suggest that the potential for conflicts between riparian rights and the public trust doctrine that have remained dormant until now could materialize at some future point.[189]

2. *Prior Appropriations*

The doctrine of prior appropriations, adopted in arid western states where water scarcity is the defining feature, works very differently. Following the "first-come, first-claimed" rule of resource allocation that nineteenth century miners brought with them as they pushed westward, this doctrine establishes first-in-time rights to appropriate water for exclusive private use.[190] Under the traditional common law approach, the first user to take water out of a watercourse and put it to "beneficial use" (domestic or economically productive use) creates a perpetual right to continue taking the same amount for the same use.[191] That right of appropriation can be asserted against any conflicting needs by those who come later – including the general public.[192] There is no formal obligation to share or proportionally curtail use during times of shortage.

Moreover, instream uses such as fishing, navigation, and related environmental values received no protection at common law, because appropriative rights could be substantiated only by withdrawal.[193] For example, in the 1882 case of *Coffin v. Left Hand Ditch*, the first case to formally apply the new doctrine of appropriative rights, the Colorado Supreme Court affirmed the rights of an irrigator removing water from the stream over the claims of a downstream riparian farmer who had long benefited from the stream without specifically diverting it.[194] In the same year that western outlaw Jesse James was brought to justice,[195] the Colorado high court brought justice for the irrigator that had first removed water from the watercourse, protecting his right to continue appropriating that water for his own purposes without regard to the needs of the downstream user who had failed to perfect an appropriative claim.[196]

---

[188] *See* Klein et al., *supra* note 164 (discussing Florida's model of regulatory riparianism).

[189] *See, e.g.*, Florida v. Georgia, 138 S. Ct. 2502 (remanding to the special master a dispute between three riparian rights jurisdictions, Florida, Alabama, and Georgia, over Atlanta's depletion of the Apalachicola-Chattahoochee-Flint River system to the point of leaving insufficient water to sustain the fishing industry at the river's terminus in Florida's Apalachicola Bay).

[190] Klein et al., *supra* note 164, at 406 ("[T]he arid western states historically have followed the prior appropriation doctrine, protecting the right to use water according to temporal priority of use.").

[191] *Id.* at 408–09.

[192] *See id.*

[193] *Id.* at 215–18.

[194] Coffin v. Left Hand Ditch. Co., 6 Colo. 443 (Colo. 1882).

[195] *Jesse James and Frank James*, Encyclopedia Britannica, www.britannica.com/biography/Jesse-James-and-Frank-James (last visited Sept. 24, 2019).

[196] *Coffin*, 6 Colo. at 447.

C. Conflicts with Water Allocation Law

Water rights administration under the traditional prior appropriations doctrine had the advantage of being relatively simple, especially in comparison to riparianism. There was no need for a contextual determination of reasonableness, or to repeatedly account for all the needs that might be asserted along a watercourse. In the world of appropriative rights, it was understood from the start that there would not be sufficient water in the stream to satisfy everyone's needs. First-in-time rights were adopted and then entrenched to encourage the settlement and economic development of the arid west, ensuring rewards to those who had invested in anticipation of continued access to the water resources they had been first to identify.[197] Waterways were still public commons,[198] but once use rights were assigned, they operated independently of one another – at least to the extent that earlier claims would not be diminished by the demands of later-comers.[199]

Appropriative rights are not correlative, but assigning them on the basis of temporal priority nevertheless creates elaborate webs of interrelated claims along a watercourse. Long-established uses are always satisfied before newer uses, whether they are upstream, downstream, more or less geographically or economically sensible, or of lower or higher social value. But the ordering of different uses from the top to the bottom of the stream creates multiple points of intersection that tie one use to another.[200] Some uses are purely extractive, while others, such as irrigation or hydropower generation, return some or all of their flow back to the watercourse. These "return flows" are then available for junior claimants downstream from the point of reintroduction (upstream claimants, even those more senior in time, are obviously out of luck), so return flows are assiduously calculated, reclaimed, and jealously guarded.[201] An inefficient alfalfa farm in place before an upstream hospital was built will always be able to satisfy its claim before the hospital can draw any water, but whatever water returns to the stream after irrigating the alfalfa will be available to a downstream factory that came later still ... and so the web extends.

For this reason, even seemingly exclusive western water rights can be as interdependent as riparian rights. Rights are interrelated because water in a stream cycles through multiple uses along its journey through the watershed, with the sequence of claims depending not only on the temporal priority of users, but also the nature of their use, how much is returned, and their positions along the watercourse. Many prior appropriation states similarly imposed first-in-time rules for allocating

---

[197] NAT'L RES. COUNCIL, WATER TRANSFER IN THE WEST: EFFICIENCY, EQUITY, AND THE ENVIRONMENT 70–71 (1992), https://doi.org/10.17226/1803.
[198] See, e.g., COLO. CONST. art. XVI, § 5 (declaring that all waters in the state belong to the public).
[199] Klein, supra note 164, at 408.
[200] See, e.g., Irwin v. Phillips, 5 Cal. 140, 147 (Cal. 1855) (involving the overlapping nature of appropriative rights).
[201] See Steven E. Clyde, *Marketplace Reallocation in the Colorado River Basin: Better Utilization of the West's Scarce Water Resources*, 28 J. LAND RES. & ENV'T L. 49, 57 (2008) (explaining the importance of the historic right to return flows).

groundwater – often without appreciating the hydrological relationship between surface and groundwater resources – further intertwining appropriative claims.[202] Making changes within these webs is accordingly very difficult, because altering the nature, amount, or positioning of any one use will likely affect the availability of water claimed by other appropriators on the stream.[203] And when their entitlements to continue diverting water have been challenged, appropriators have defended their claims vigorously, sometimes with the full force of constitutional protection for private property.[204]

In contrast to the riparian rights common-pool approach, then, the prior appropriation doctrine takes a privatization approach to resource allocation – the very opposite of the public commons approach implied by the public trust doctrine.[205] Whoever is first to put water to beneficial use can claim the right to continue doing so, potentially indefinitely, and excluding all others.[206] Not only does the doctrine reward early movers, granting them a protectable right to exclude those who seek to establish claims afterward, it rewards those who take full possession of the water – literally removing it from the waterway, leaving nothing behind for other uses. As noted, a common law appropriator had to actually withdraw water from the stream to perfect a claim; appropriative rights were not available for instream uses such as fishing, swimming, wildlife, or aesthetic purposes. And because any water that remains or returns to the stream after use is subject to subsequent claims enforceable by other users, the prior appropriation doctrine creates powerful incentives to use as much as possible, as early as possible – and if you don't want to be subject to someone else's future demands, with as little return to the common pool as possible.

---

[202] *See, e.g.*, Env't Law Found. v. State Water Res. Control Bd., 237 Cal. Rptr. 3d 393 (Cal. Ct. App. 2018) (applying the public trust doctrine to curtail groundwater withdrawals that were affecting the surface water resources of the Scott River in California). The law of groundwater withdrawals has historically been treated separately from the law of surface water withdrawals, having developed awkwardly before science demonstrated that proximate ground and surface waters are usually hydrologically connected. In some states, water law has evolved to account for this relationship while, in others, ground and surface water remain separately allocated. *Compare* Cline v. Am. Aggregates Corp., 474 N.E. 2d 324 (Ohio 1984) (rationalizing groundwater allocation with surface water allocation doctrines under the Restatement's Reasonable Use doctrine), *with* Sipriano v. Great Spring Waters of Am., 1 S.W.3d 75 (Tex. 1999) (affirming that Texas groundwater is allocated under the rule of capture, even though surface water is allocated by prior appropriation, and one who captures groundwater may directly interfere with a prior appropriative right to impacted surface waters).

[203] BARTON H. THOMPSON, JR. ET AL., LEGAL CONTROL OF WATER RESOURCES: CASES AND MATERIALS 224–27 (5th ed. 2013) (discussing the requirements for maintaining a permit).

[204] *See, e.g.*, Tulare Lake Basin v. United States, 49 Fed. Cl. 313 (Fed. Cl. 2001) (holding that efforts to protect species under the Endangered Species Act constitute a taking of property in violation of the Fifth Amendment); Casitas Mun. Water Dist. v. United States, 543 F.3d 1276 (Fed. Cir. 2008) (a government-ordered water diversion to protect an endangered fish species under the ESA may be a physical taking under the Fifth Amendment, requiring government compensation to holders of private water rights).

[205] Ryan, *The Historic Saga*, *supra* note 11, at 576–77.

[206] Klein et al., *supra* note 164, at 408–409.

C. Conflicts with Water Allocation Law

Some water dependent users and communities have learned this lesson the hard way. In 1913, for example, as the first coast-to-coast highway was paved,[207] a small Colorado town sued to prevent a hydroelectric power company from diverting the entirety of a stream that had long cascaded over a beautiful waterfall through the heart of the town, forming the basis of its tourism and resort-based economy.[208] But in *Empire Water & Power v. Cascade Town*, the Eighth Circuit applied the prior appropriation doctrine to hold that only the power company had a protectable water right because only the power company had made an actual withdrawal from the stream.[209] The town had been relying on the water for economic purposes even longer, but only by leaving it instream.[210] Thus, the power company could continue to divert water to its reservoir for economic uses, even though doing so would fully dewater the Cascade Creek Canyon waterfalls and destroy the longstanding economic mainstay of the town.[211]

Just as many riparian rights states are shifting away from the common law and toward a model of regulated riparianism, most western states have adopted a regulatory overlay on top of the common law doctrine of prior appropriations. While these states preserve the temporal priority at the heart of the common law system, most users beyond a threshold must now seek state recognition of their rights in an administrative permit.[212] Permits are subject to licensing requirements that supplement the common law approach with new statutory criteria, including a public interest analysis that requires consideration of factors beyond pure temporal priority before new rights may be assigned.[213] Beginning in the 1970s, most western states have also provided greater statutory protections for instream flow values – some even approximating public trust values[214] – in an attempt to mitigate the enormous pressure to withdraw from the stream in order to receive a legally protected water right.[215]

In this respect, eastern and western states may be converging on a modern regulatory permit system with a bit more in common than previous generations. A handful

---

[207] All Things Considered, *America's First Transcontinental Highway Turns 100*, NAT'L PUB. RADIO (Oct. 31, 2013), www.npr.org/2013/10/31/242129231/americas-first-transcontinental-highway-turns-100.
[208] Empire Water & Power Co. v. Cascade Town Co., 205 Fed. 123 (8th Cir. 1913).
[209] *Id.* at 128–29.
[210] *Id.*
[211] *Id.*
[212] *See, e.g.*, N.D. STATE WATER COMM'N, NORTH DAKOTA'S WATER PERMITTING PROCESS (Jan. 2018), www.swc.nd.gov/pdfs/water_permitting_process.pdf; MONT. CODE ANN. § 85-2-101(5) (West 1997) (establishing a permit system for obtaining water rights for new or additional water developments); *Water Appropriations Permit Program*, MINN. DEP'T OF NAT. RES., www.dnr.state.mn.us/waters/watermgmt_section/appropriations/index.html (last visited Oct. 30, 2022).
[213] *See, e.g.*, Shokal v. Dunn, 707 P.2d 441, 448–50 (Idaho 1985) (analyzing the public interest requirements that "appear frequently in the statutes of the prior appropriation states of the West").
[214] *See e.g.*, Steven M. Smith, *Instream Flow Right within Proper Appropriation Doctrine: Insights from Colorado*, 59 NAT. RES. J. 1, 192 (discussing how the Colorado Conservation Board appropriates "instream water rights on behalf of the public to 'preserve the natural environment to a reasonable degree.'").
[215] THOMPSON ET AL., *supra* note 203, at 215–16.

of states, including California, allocate water under both riparian and appropriative rights regimes simultaneously, adding further complexity to an already complicated field.[216] And today, water rights in all states are also subject to various forms of federal regulation, and occasionally to the federal reservation of water for public and tribal lands (if, following the rule of temporal priority, the federal lands were reserved for these purposes before later assertions of private rights).[217] However, commentators have pointed out that the later protections introduced to western water law can be of limited value in a system that continues to be defined by temporal priority.[218] In most respects, the heart of the western water law analysis remains the traditional rules of prior appropriations.[219] Very few states treat appropriations for instream flow the same way they do conventional appropriations; for example, only three states allow private parties to hold them.[220]

D. SETTING THE STAGE FOR THE MONO LAKE STORY

Understanding the history of the public trust doctrine provides important foundation for using the doctrine today to respond to contemporary environmental conflicts and – better still – prevent them in the first place. It also enables us to better analyze the unresolved relationship between the public trust doctrine and adjacent doctrines of private water allocation – riparian rights and prior appropriations – that complicates modern water management in the United States. This chapter has

---

[216] In California, the owners of land abutting watercourses hold some traditional riparian rights, which coexist with the more abundant appropriative rights that are unconnected to riparian land ownership but subject to similar requirements of reasonable and beneficial use. *See* THOMPSON ET AL., *supra* note 203, at 200 (discussing California's hybrid system of water law); *see also* CAL. CONST. art. X, § 2 (confirming the protection of riparian rights and discussing the requirement of beneficial use). However, prior appropriations remains the defining doctrinal approach in the state. *See* THOMPSON ET AL., *supra* note 203, at 208 (explaining how the doctrines interact with one another in California); *see also* John Franklin Smith, *The Public Trust Doctrine and* National Audubon Society v. Superior Court: *A Hard Case Makes Bad Law or the Consistent Evolution of California Water Rights*, 6 GLENDALE L. REV. 201, 207–209 (1984) (outlining the history of California's dual water rights system).

[217] *See Winters v. United States*, 207 U.S. 564 (1908) (creating the doctrine of federal reserved water rights, which implies such water rights as needed to fulfill the purpose of federal reservations of land, here Indian reservations, with priority established as of the date of the reservation); *United States v. New Mexico*, 438 U.S. 696 (1978) (applying the doctrine to other federal public lands); *see also* PETER FOLGER ET AL., CONG. RSCH. SERV., R45259, THE FEDERAL ROLE IN GROUNDWATER SUPPLY 3–6 (2018).

[218] THOMPSON ET AL., *supra* note 203, at 215–16.

[219] *See, e.g.*, Norman K. Johnson & Charles T. DuMars, *A Survey of the Evolution of Western Water Law in Response to Changing Economic and Public Interest Demands*, 29 NAT. RES. J. 347, 367–71 (1989) (considering ramifications of the public trust doctrine for the future of western, prior appropriations-based water law).

[220] THOMPSON ET AL., *supra* note 203, at 216 (noting that while most states now allow some sort of appropriation to protect instream flows, only Alaska, Arizona, and Nevada allow private entities to claim them).

D. Setting the Stage for the Mono Lake Story

traced the development of public trust principles from the progenitors of western law to the early United States, and outlined the basic principles of American water law, bringing us to the historical edge of the conflict that would arise at Mono Lake, where the doctrine would evolve more clearly from an affirmation of sovereign authority over public natural resource commons to a recognition of sovereign responsibility to protect them for present and future generations.

Even as the doctrine requires the state to protect navigable waterways in trust for the public, however, the doctrines of private water allocation – especially western prior appropriations – govern how the state gives away the waters within them. And unlike the correlative, indeterminate rights associated with eastern riparian rights, the perpetual, excludable use-rights associated with the western prior appropriations system are theoretically absolute. A conflict between the public trust doctrine and private water allocation law was perhaps inevitable, especially in the arid West, because states there apply a privatization model to allocating rights to take water from waterways at the very same time that they apply a public commons approach to protect the underlying waterways. That inevitable conflict exploded most dramatically in eastern California, right in the path of the upper Los Angeles Aqueduct.

2

Building the Los Angeles Aqueduct

A.	Water Scarcity in Los Angeles	61
B.	The Early 1900s: Tapping the Owens River Valley	63
	1. The Owens Valley	64
	2. A Self-Powering Design	67
	3. Prospecting in the San Fernando Valley	68
	4. The Miracle of Modern Engineering	69
	5. Acquiring the Owens Valley Water Rights	70
C.	An Alternative Account of the Owens Valley Water Transfer	73
D.	After the Aqueduct	75
	1. The Local Consequences of Withdrawals	75
	2. The St. Francis Dam	78
	3. Reprise: The Oroville Dam	81

The Mono Lake case[1] reached the California Supreme Court in the early 1980s, but the crisis that led to the case began almost a century earlier, when the growing City of Los Angeles first began to run out of water. Moving water to Los Angeles, California's most populous and economically dynamic city, has been a state priority since the turn of the twentieth century.

This chapter explores the California water struggles that led to the construction of the Los Angeles Aqueduct and ultimately to the Mono Lake litigation. It reviews the history of water exports from the Owens Valley in the early 1900s, and the devastating effects on the local community and ecology – prompting the decline of its once thriving agricultural economy and an open rebellion by Owens Valley farmers. It then recounts the St. Francis Dam disaster of 1928, which terrified the population and tempered the judgement of regional managers about the safety risks of large-scale water projects near population centers, further prompting water speculation in more remote areas of the state.

---

[1] Nat'l Audubon Soc'y v. Superior Court, 658 P.2d 709 (Cal. 1983).

As advocates across the globe increasingly turn to the public trust doctrine to protect environmental values associated with water, the St. Francis Dam disaster serves as a sobering reminder of the consequences associated with the mismanagement of water resources. The loss of life in that infamous disaster testifies to just how high the stakes are in efforts to manage the water dilemmas that continue to bedevil California and other arid lands. And it underscores the problem at the heart of the Mono Lake story: water is life – but for whom?

A. WATER SCARCITY IN LOS ANGELES

The Mono Lake story begins in the early city of Los Angeles, where potable water has long been considered "wet gold." An aerial tour of California quickly shows why that is.

Los Angeles lies in the arid bottom of the state, far from the many mountain rivers that furnish northern Californians with more abundant water resources. Although the city hugs the southern California coast, the climate is dry and surface water is scarce.[2] It is California's largest city, the second largest in the United States (second only to New York), and the second most populated desert city on Earth (second only to Cairo, Egypt).[3] Its vast numbers were drawn by the promise of oil and agricultural resources, mild weather, and a deepwater harbor enabling ready commercial access to other ports across the Pacific.[4] Some ten million people now live in Los Angeles County, the greater Los Angeles metropolitan area.[5] However, the Los Angeles River, the main regional source of surface water, has about enough water to support a population of about 100,000, or at most two,[6] and in the decades surrounding the

---

[2] HILDA BLANCO ET AL., U.S.C. CENTER FOR SUSTAINABLE CITIES, WATER SUPPLY SCARCITY IN SOUTHERN CALIFORNIA: ASSESSING WATER DISTRICT LEVEL STRATEGIES vii, xiv (2012), http://sustainablecities.usc.edu/quicklinks/H%20Blanco%20WSSC%20Exec%20Summary%2012%20 2012.pdf.

[3] See MARC REISNER, CADILLAC DESERT: THE AMERICAN WEST AND ITS DISAPPEARING WATER 105 (1986) (comparing L.A. and Cairo); see also Erin Ryan, The Public Trust Doctrine, Private Water Allocation, and Mono Lake: The Historic Saga of National Audubon Society v. Superior Court, 45 ENV'T L. 561, 578 (2015) [hereinafter Ryan, The Historic Saga].

[4] See DAVID KIPEN, CALIFORNIA IN THE 1930S: THE WPA GUIDE TO THE GOLDEN STATE 59 (2013) (describing successful efforts to increase immigration to the city of Los Angeles in the late nineteenth century).

[5] U.S. Census Bureau, State & County QuickFacts: Los Angeles County, California, http://quickfacts .census.gov/qfd/states/06/06037.html (last visited Sept. 18, 2022).

[6] See DAVID CARLE, WATER AND THE CALIFORNIA DREAM: HISTORIC CHOICES FOR SHAPING THE FUTURE 82 (2016) (noting Mulholland's admonition that the city population of 200,000 around the turn of the twentieth century was already twice what local water supplies could sustain); Kai Ryssdal, The Aqueduct That Gave Rise to Los Angeles, MARKETPLACE (AM. PUB. MEDIA), Mar. 31, 2015, www.marketplace.org/topics/sustainability/big-book/aqueduct-gave-rise-los-angeles ("As early as 1894, the city faced severe water shortages. Engineers estimated that natural sources serving the Los Angeles basin could support a population of 200,000 or so, in typical years."); REISNER, supra note 3, at 55, 61–63 (describing the Los Angeles River as the first local source of water and how reliance on it became untenable as the population grew).

turn of the twentieth century, the city's population had already quadrupled to surpass 200,000.[7]

At first, the growing city of Los Angeles was able to slake its thirst by pumping available groundwater resources.[8] Users tapped the Los Angeles aquifer not far beneath the surface, a saturated layer of gravel and silt that channels stormwater runoff from the coast range through the soils below the San Fernando and San Gabriel valleys and out to the Pacific.[9] By the end of the nineteenth century, however, when both the surface and groundwater reserves of the region had been exhausted, state and city leaders realized that they were going to have to find water elsewhere to sustain the growing metropolis.[10] Repatriating water from elsewhere to the city of Los Angeles became one of California's highest priorities, but the geography of the state made this no small task.

The map of California readily shows where the water is available, and where it is not.[11] Vibrant blue lines crisscrossing the north reveal where the naturally occurring streams are, mostly draining snowmelt and runoff from the vast Cascades and Sierra Nevada mountain ranges.[12] Further south, toward Los Angeles, large natural drainages like these mostly disappear from the surface.[13] Today, even the L.A. River runs mostly underground, fully channelized, out of sight and generally out of mind. Even where it is above ground, it is almost entirely encased in concrete – a drainage ditch remnant of the alluvial river it once was. However, three snaking aqueducts converge at the city, delivering redirected water from distant lands to the large population centers in and around Los Angeles.[14] It is an especially impressive feat, given that the Los Angeles Basin is surrounded by ocean on one side and mountains on all others.[15]

---

[7] PBS, *One Sky Above Us*, NEW PERSPECTIVES ON THE WEST, Episode Eight: 1887–1914 (2001), www.pbs.org/weta/thewest/program/episodes/eight/takeit.htm.

[8] *See* REISNER, *supra* note 3, at 61–64 (describing Los Angeles' water sources in the late nineteenth century).

[9] D.J. Waldie, *Beneath Our Feet: Water and Politics in Southeast L.A.*, KCET, Sep. 2, 2016, www.kcet.org/shows/lost-la/beneath-our-feet-water-and-politics-in-southeastla#:~:text=Artesian%20well%20in%20northern%20Long,that%20flowed%20like%20this%20one (last visited Oct. 21, 2022).

[10] REISNER, *supra* note 3, at 62 ("By 1900, Los Angeles' population had gone over 100,000; it doubled again within four years. During the same period, the city experienced its first severe drought.... In late 1904, the newly created Los Angeles Department of Water and Power issued its first public report. 'The time has come,' it said, 'when we shall have to supplement the supply from some other source.'").

[11] *See California: Physical Features*, CAL. STATE UNIV., NORTHRIDGE, www.csun.edu/~cfe/maps/CA_Physical.pdf (last visited Sept. 18, 2022).

[12] *Id.*

[13] *See CNRFC Interactive Map Interface: Rivers*, CAL. NEV. RIVER FORECAST CTR., www.cnrfc.noaa.gov (last visited Sept. 18, 2022).

[14] *See Los Angeles Depends on Imported Water*, SIERRA CLUB, https://angeles2.sierraclub.org/los_angeles_depends_imported_water (last visited Sept. 18, 2022) (explaining that aqueduct construction continued through the twentieth century and currently sources from the Colorado River and two Northern California locations).

[15] *Current Research Projects: Neogene Tectonics of Southern California*, UNIV. OF HOUSTON: EARTH & ATMOSPHERIC SCI., fig. 1, www.uh.edu/nsm/earth-atmospheric/people/faculty/tom-bjorklund/Bjorklund-Research-Project-1-June-2016.pdf (last visited Sept. 18, 2022) (showing the Los Angeles Basin bordered by the Santa Monica Mountains, San Gabriel Mountains, Santa Ana Mountains, and the Pacific Ocean).

Water now arrives in Los Angeles from the Colorado River Aqueduct, which brings water from Rocky Mountain states to the east,[16] and from the California Aqueduct, which taps the wetter, western slope of the Sierra Nevada Range and the agricultural Central Valley to the northwest.[17] Yet even before these were built, imported water first began arriving through the Los Angeles Aqueduct that reaches almost due north, improbably delivering it from the eastern midsection of the state, near the bend at the Nevada state line.[18] Today, it extends 400 miles north of the city, past the Tehachapi Mountains and along the Eastern Sierra Nevada to the Mono Basin, which is nestled beside the high Sierra peaks of Yosemite National Park, some 250 miles east of San Francisco.[19] Of these great western water projects, the Los Angeles Aqueduct is the oldest, the most colorful historically, and doubtlessly the most notorious of the three[20] – and with it begins our story.

B. THE EARLY 1900S: TAPPING THE OWENS RIVER VALLEY

The L.A. Aqueduct now ends at Mono Lake, but that wasn't always so. The first place the city looked to for water was the Owens Valley, an unlikely oasis in the southern California desert, roughly halfway between L.A. and Mono Lake. The first few chapters of this story center on the Owens Valley and the devastating impacts that water diversions posed for the local environment and economy over the first half of the twentieth century.

When water consumption began to exceed the locally available supply in Los Angeles, local leaders struggled with the challenge of finding water elsewhere. The need was laid especially bare in the summer of 1904, when daily water consumption exceeded reservoir inflows by four million gallons a day, for ten straight days.[21] As William Mulholland, head of city water resources, warned an anxious crowd at the time: "If Los Angeles runs out of water for one week, the city within a year will not have a population of 100,000 people. A city quickly finds its level, and that level is its

---

[16] *See* Sierra Club, *supra* note 14 (noting that the Colorado River Aqueduct supplies water to L.A.).
[17] *See California Aqueduct East Branch*, CTR. FOR LAND USE INTERPRETATION, http://clui.org/ludb/site/california-aqueduct-east-branch (last visited Sept. 18, 2022) (explaining that the California Aqueduct brings water south to the agricultural industry of the Central Valley and Los Angeles).
[18] Sierra Club, *supra* note 14.
[19] *See* Louis Sahagun, *"There It Is – Take It": A Story of Marvel and Controversy*, L.A. TIMES, Oct. 28, 2013, http://graphics.latimes.com/me-aqueduct/ (describing the path and history of the Los Angeles Aqueduct).
[20] *First Owens River – Los Angeles Aqueduct*, AM. SOC. OF ENG'R, www.asce.org/about-civil-engineering/history-and-heritage/historic-landmarks/first-owens-river-los-angeles-aqueduct (last visited Sept. 18, 2022).
[21] *Biographical Information: Joseph Barlow Lippincott*, OWENS VALLEY HISTORY, www.owensvalleyhistory.com/stories3/lippincott_biography.pdf (extracted from the "Memoir" on Lippincott prepared by Kenneth Q. Volk and Edgar Alan Rowe that appeared in 108 TRANSACTIONS OF THE AMERICAN SOCIETY OF CIVIL ENGINEERS 1543–50 (1943)).

water supply!"[22] In 1905, from the pages of the Los Angeles Times, he would again admonish the city of the urgency of finding new supply, warning that "[i]f you don't get the water now, you'll never need it," because "[t]he dead never get thirsty."[23]

Angelenos were listening. As they began imagining the civic and economic consequences that would befall the unfolding development of the southwest if new water supplies were not located, city, state, and even federal leaders leapt into action. Several public figures became especially important to the story, starting with Fred Eaton, the former city mayor, and Bill Mulholland, whom he appointed superintendant and chief engineer of the new Los Angeles Water Department (which would later become known as the Department of Water and Power, or "DWP").[24] Mulholland quickly invited the supervising engineer for the U.S. Reclamation Service's Pacific Coast Region, Joseph Lippincott, to the Board of Engineers considering alternatives for the water project, and eventually lured him away from the Reclamation Service to join him as Assistant Chief Engineer on building the aqueduct.[25]

Working together, the three bucked a number of more modest proposals to execute an elaborate plan to import water from a distant part of the state that was, ironically, itself a desert.[26] Their unlikely target was the sparsely populated Owens Valley, 233 miles north of the city.[27]

1. *The Owens Valley*

The arid but enchanting Owens Valley is a large, long, and narrow canyon in eastern California that lies between two mountain ranges – the Sierra Nevada to the west and the White and Inyo Mountains to the east.[28] The valley extends both north and south of Bishop, California – the largest population center in Inyo County with a present population of about 3,500 people. It sits at the transition zone between the Great Basin desert to the east and the Mojave desert to the south, sandwiched between the highest and lowest points in the continental United States. In Death Valley, just east of the Owens Valley, Badwater Basin plumbs to 282 feet below sea level, while Mount Whitney on its western boundary soars to 14,505 feet (and just 85 miles from Badwater).[29]

---

[22] JOHN RUSSELL MCCARTHY, WATER: THE STORY OF BILL MULLHOLLAND 31 (1937); *see also* CARLE, *supra* note 6, at 82.
[23] CARLE, *supra* note 6, at 82 (quoting Mulholland's words in an August 18, 1905, article in the Los Angeles Times).
[24] REISNER, *supra* note 3, at 61–65, 91.
[25] *Biographical Information: Lippincott, supra* note 21.
[26] REISNER, *supra* note 3, at 61–65, 97.
[27] *Id.* at 61–63.
[28] *Id.* at 59.
[29] *See Badwater Basin*, NAT'L PARK SERV., www.nps.gov/places/badwater-basin.htm (last visited Sept. 9, 2022); *see also* Stewart Green, *Mount Whitney: Highest Mountain in California*, ABOUT.COM, http://climbing.about.com/od/mountainclimbing/a/MtWhitneyFacts.htm (last updated Apr. 12, 2019).

B. The Early 1900s: Tapping the Owens River Valley

The climate is accordingly very arid, and yet the valley is a catchment for snowmelt from the high mountain ranges on either side.[30] Rain and snow intercepted at elevations between 10,000 and 14,000 feet drain into the improbably robust Owens River that runs the length between them.[31] That is to say, it was robust at the beginning of this story. In the early days of the twentieth century, the Owens River was an extraordinarily life-productive river running through the desert, supporting both a rich array of wildlife that thronged to its waters and a rich agricultural community that was able to thrive amidst the otherwise punishing environment.[32] Even today, the Owens remains a flourishing river oasis above the diversion dam that would eventually shunt its waters toward Los Angeles.[33]

Back then, the Owens River drained into a large salt lake at its terminus – the Lake formerly known as Owens. Owens Lake was a terminal lake, which means that water flowed into the basin of surrounding land through the river but had no opportunity to flow out, collecting instead at the base of an upslope in the land at the southern end.[34] In a terminal lake, water departs the system only through surface evaporation, but that process leaves behind the trace minerals dissolved in the incoming river water, which gradually leaches them out of the surrounding rocks and soils as it passes through.[35] Over thousands of years, the accumulated minerals left behind as water evaporated from the lake's surface made Owens Lake a saltwater body, by essentially the same process that makes the planet's oceans saline.[36] Except that Owens Lake, at least before the coming of the aqueduct, was about twice as salty as the sea.[37]

---

[30] See REISNER, *supra* note 3, at 61–63 (explaining that the few rivers draining from the arid East Slope of the Sierra Nevada range are generally small; however, the Owens River, flanked by two mountain ranges, is the exception).

[31] See *Evaluation of the Hydrologic System and Selected Water-Management Alternatives in the Owens Valley, California*, CAL. WATER SCI. CTR., http://ca.water.usgs.gov/owens/report/hydro_system_2surface.html (last visited Sept. 18, 2022) (explaining that precipitation runoff from the Sierra Nevada feeds into the Owens River).

[32] REISNER, *supra* note 3, at 61.

[33] And one where I still fondly remember getting hypothermia while attempting to inner tube it one sunny day in July! Some years later, beginning in the 2000s, restoration efforts have apparently resurrected some of the Owens River below the dam. See Louis Sahagun, *Tule Vegetation Infests Lower Owens River*, L.A. TIMES, July 7, 2006, http://articles.latimes.com./2011/jul/25/local/la-me-tules-20110725 [hereinafter *Tule Vegetation*] (reporting that restoration efforts, which began in 2006, have brought water and wildlife back to the Owens River).

[34] REISNER, *supra* note 3, at 63.

[35] CAL. DEP'T OF WATER RESOURCES, THE IMPORTANCE OF THE SALTON SEA AND OTHER TERMINAL LAKES IN SUPPORTING BIRDS OF THE PACIFIC FLYWAY 1, www.water.ca.gov/saltonsea/historicalcalendar/docs/TerminalLakes.pdf (describing the geologic processes that intensify salinity in terminal lakes with freshwater tributaries).

[36] See *id*.

[37] David B. Herbst & Michael Prather, *Owens Lake – From Dustbowl to Mosaic of Salt Water Habitats*, LAKELINE 34, 35 (Fall 2014), www.nalms.org/wp-content/uploads/LakeLine/34-3/Articles/34-3-9.pdf (noting that samples taken in 1886, during a time of little change in lake volume, showed a salinity level of 72.7 grams per liter, compared to the ocean's average salinity of 35 grams per liter).

The Owens River and its delta at Owens Lake were a critical part of the regional ecosystem, because they combined fresh and saltwater resources in a high desert environment where water was otherwise scarce.[38] Countless birds journeying along the Pacific Flyway would congregate at Owens Lake to feed and water themselves, desperate for respite after traversing countless miles of barren land.[39] Residents recalling Owens Valley life before the aqueduct said that the sky would become so black with birds during migration season that it was sometimes hard to see sky between them.[40] On visiting Owens Lake in 1917, before the impacts of the aqueduct were felt, the famous naturalist Joseph Grinnell described the conflagration of birdlife in his field notes:

> Great numbers of water birds are in sight along the shore – Avocets, Phalaropes and Ducks. Large flocks of shorebirds in flight over the water in the distance, wheeling about show en masse, now silvery now dark, against the gray-blue of the water. There must literally be thousands of birds within sight of this spot. En route around the south end of Owens Lake to Olancha saw water birds almost continuously.... The shore shallows are thronged with water birds. Avocets predominate; I estimated one bird every four feet of shoreline, which would make 1,300 per mile![41]

The Owens Valley was thus a treasured oasis in the high California desert, but for the very same reasons, it offered Los Angeles the promise of urgently needed water, and a seemingly bountiful supply. In 1876, while conducting topographic and geologic surveys of eastern California, Lieutenant George M. Wheeler was astonished by the volume of water that the Owens River regularly furnished to Owens Lake.[42] Based on the equilibrium between input and evaporation indicated by seasonally stable lake levels, he imagined the enormous inflow needed to offset the voluminous evaporation that would have taken place under such hot and dry conditions and over a hundred square miles of surface:

> The Owens Lake has no outlet and is fed by the Owens River ... as the level of the lake remains constant, there must be a perfect equilibrium between the amount of evaporation and the incoming water. The lake having 110 square miles surface, an evaporation of 4.6 feet per year would suffice to swallow up the annual volume of Owens River. Those who cannot appreciate the amount of evaporation have invented the hypothesis of a subterranean outlet, as in the case of Great Salt Lake in Utah.[43]

But no such subterranean outlet existed, as demonstrated by what would befall the lake when the surface water was eventually diverted by Los Angeles. Indeed, we

---

[38] *Important Bird Areas – Owens River*, AUDUBON SOC'Y, www.audubon.org/important-bird-areas/owens-river (last visited Sept. 18, 2022).
[39] *Id.*
[40] *See, e.g.*, Herbst & Prather, *supra* note 37, at 35 (quoting Joseph Grinnell).
[41] *See id.* at 35–36 (fully quoting Grinell).
[42] *Id.* at 34 (quoting Wheeler).
[43] *Id.*

B. *The Early 1900s: Tapping the Owens River Valley*

already know the end of this story: the Owens River would soon thereafter be redirected, and the Owens Lake would quickly evaporate away, taking with it the rich environmental and agricultural bounty it had once supported.

And yet the story between that point and these origins is still surprising. After all, the Owens Valley is hundreds of miles from the city, and there are no fewer than two mountain ranges in between. There was closer and easier water to be had, including yet untapped groundwater resources from aquifers and artesian springs in the greater Los Angeles vicinity.[44] Exploiting these sources would have been faster, easier, and cheaper – at least in the short term. So why on earth would Los Angeles seek water two hundred miles north to the Owens Valley when there was more accessible water closer to home?

2. *A Self-Powering Design*

Eaton, Mulholland, and Lippincott's team considered seven potential sources for water imports, many of them closer and more easily accessible with a lower initial outlay.[45] However, regional planners were concerned that exploiting groundwater resources closer to the city would curtail desired development of the surrounding metropolitan areas.[46] Yet there was another reason city leaders were drawn to the Owens Valley – one that had to do with the literal relationship between water and power. Over time, the other potential sources would have required the use of substantial energy to continuously pump water toward Los Angeles. Even artesian wells that produce without assistance in the present would eventually require expensive pumps, after withdrawals reduced pressure in the aquifer.[47] Moreover, the city had already learned – the hard way – that groundwater resources are not infinite, and civic planners worried that these sources would ultimately tap out.

By contrast, the Owens River would provide a heartily renewable flow, as demonstrated by the Owens Lake's stalwart resistance to the punishing evaporation of the Mojave desert. And while the Owens Valley lies hundreds of miles away, it rests at an altitude of 4,000 feet above sea level.[48] Those 4,000 feet of elevation gain would make all the difference to the engineering project: The elevation gain provided enough potential energy to pipe water downhill toward Los Angeles – even over the two intervening mountain ranges – without any additional power source, enabling a completely gravity-powered design.[49] Gravity, in the end, was the force that not only

---

[44] *Biographical Information: Lippincott, supra* note 21.
[45] *Id.*
[46] *Id.*
[47] *Id.*
[48] Sahagun, *Tule Vegetation, supra* note 33 (reporting that restoration efforts, which began in 2006, have brought water and wildlife back to the Owens River).
[49] *Id.*

brought the river water down from the surrounding mountains to the Owens Valley – it would literally power the transfer of the same river back over the same mountains, and then some, into Los Angeles basin, two hundred and thirty-three miles away.

3. Prospecting in the San Fernando Valley

Gravity highlights one important relationship between water and power in California, but every Californian knows there are others of near equal force, and with more political significance. There was another important reason that the Owens Valley plan was so attractive to city leadership, one having less to do with civil engineering and more to do with conventional pocket-lining. As chronicled more fully in *Cadillac Desert*[50] and the classic movie *Chinatown*,[51] the additional value that attracted them so forcefully was in the place that lies between the Owens Valley and Los Angeles. If you check that California map, you'll see that it is none other than the San Fernando Valley.

Today, the San Fernando Valley is about 260 square miles of pricey southern California real estate, with prime access to both Los Angeles and the Pacific coast.[52] Bounded by the Santa Monica and San Gabriel Mountains, among others, it includes such posh communities as Burbank and Glendale and, in its unincorporated area adjacent to Hollywood, Universal Studios. From the higher points in San Fernando parks and neighborhoods, you can see the skyscrapers of downtown Los Angeles. It is the valley from which the Valley Girl got her name, and from which most generations that have followed inherited her accent.[53] Indeed, we can proudly thank the San Fernando Valley for seeding the filler word "like" into virtually every third sentence that Americans would speak thereafter.

However, when Eaton, Mulholland, and Lipincott were masterminding the plan – before the aqueduct was constructed and the lands surrounding Los Angeles were even drier than the city – the San Fernando Valley was open, empty, economically worthless land.[54] There was little there, because there was so little water. At the time, the best anyone could do with the land was dry wheat farming. Yet proponents of the new aqueduct realized that moving water from the Owens Valley down to Los Angeles meant that this worthless, barren land would soon host a steady flow of cool mountain water – and that it would not be worthless for long.[55] Many leaders privy

---

[50] REISNER, *supra* note 3, at 73–75; CADILLAC DESERT: THE AMERICAN WEST AND ITS DISAPPEARING WATER AND THE TRANSFORMATION OF NATURE (Columbia TriStar Television 1997).
[51] CHINATOWN (Paramount Pictures 1974).
[52] JOEL KOTKIN & ERIKA OZUNA, THE CHANGING FACE OF THE SAN FERNANDO VALLEY 8 (2002), http://publicpolicy.pepperdine.edu/davenport-institute/content/reports/changing-face.pdf.
[53] VALLEY GIRL (Atlantic Ent. Group & Valley 9000 Prod. 1983).
[54] REISNER, *supra* note 3, at 75.
[55] Id. at 76–77.

to the plan quietly bought land in the San Fernando Valley on the cheap before aqueduct plans were made public.[56] Trading on their inside knowledge of what was to come, these self-dealing leaders became overnight real estate moguls when the water rolled through.[57]

4. The Miracle of Modern Engineering

Construction began on the aqueduct in 1905. The gravity-propelled design, spanning hundreds of miles and two mountain ranges, was considered a miracle of modern engineering on par with the Panama Canal.[58] The early project included more than fifty miles of open canals, nearly one hundred miles of covered conduits, about another fifty miles of tunnels, and some twelve miles of steel tubes perilously escorting the flow across plunging mountain canyons.[59] To begin the long journey of this water south to Los Angeles, engineers moved the entire Owens River out of its natural bed.[60] This they accomplished by constructing a full-length diversion dam at Aberdeen, a tiny hamlet just north of the Inyo County seat in Independence, California.[61]

That simple dam at Aberdeen changed everything for the Owens Valley. After the dam went in, if you stood at the diversion point and looked upstream to the north, you would see the Owens river flowing toward you – down its naturally arching alluvial channel, lined by point bars, willows, and other riparian vegetation that slows the water and creates cozy pockets of fish and wildlife habitat. Then the river would reach the diversion dam, where the entire flow was shunted abruptly sideways into a narrow concrete channel, where it gathered speed along its journey to Los Angeles. The water moves quickly over that concrete bed, suddenly devoid of contact with the natural world of which it was so recently a part. And if you looked downstream from the diversion dam, as I did in the 1990s, you would look out over an empty riverbed, where the water had stopped flowing almost a century earlier. By then, it was filled with tangled brush and overgrowth, but it was still a gaping, ancient riverbed – with no river in it.

New efforts to restore dewatered portions of the Lower Owens have been underway since 2006,[62] but the old Aberdeen diversion dam still marks the beginning of

---

[56] Id. at 78–79 (describing the syndicate of investors that purchased an option on the Porter Land and Water Company, which owned the greater part of the San Fernando Valley).

[57] Id.

[58] Eric Malnic, The Aqueduct: DWP Smooths Out Rough Edges on the 74-Year-Old Engineering Marvel, L.A. TIMES, Oct. 18, 1987, http://articles.latimes.com/1987-10-18/local/me-15046_1_los-angeles-river.

[59] BD. OF PUB. SERV. COMM'RS OF THE CITY OF L.A., CONSTRUCTION OF THE LOS ANGELES AQUEDUCT FINAL REPORT 271 (1916).

[60] See Henry H. Thomas, Construction – River Diversion, http://community.dur.ac.uk/~desowww4/cal/dams/cons/conss2.htm (last updated Aug. 30, 2007).

[61] See Malnic, supra note 58 (discussing the diversion dam thirty miles south of Bishop, California).

[62] Lower Owens River Project, INYO CNTY. WATER DEP'T www.inyowater.org/projects/lorp/ (last visited Sept. 18, 2022) (describing efforts to restore a dewatered 62-mile stretch of the Lower Owens

the original Los Angeles Aqueduct. For many miles below that point, the aqueduct snakes across the desert, crosses mountain and valley, and finally rolls down the California Coast Range into the Los Angeles Basin – by this point in a giant concrete tube.[63] Symbolically completing its journey, some of that water finally flows into the reflecting pool in front of DWP headquarters, where Chief Bill Mulholland was once king.[64]

5. Acquiring the Owens Valley Water Rights

The aqueduct may have been a miracle of modern engineering but, to be sure, that wasn't the only puzzle that city leaders had to resolve – there was also the legal puzzle. Our earlier discussion of private water law alludes to the other hurdle Los Angeles had to overcome before the aqueduct could begin delivering water from afar. And though it seemed more easily handled at first, it became the thornier problem over time.

The problem was how to deal with the existing water users who were already putting Owens River water to beneficial use, mostly for local agricultural purposes.[65] Under both riparian rights and prior appropriations doctrine, Los Angeles could not just take an entire river out of its bed, leaving established downstream users in the lurch.[66] Landowners all along the river held riparian rights, and many more Owens Valley residents had additional rights to withdraw from the river that were protected under the doctrine of prior appropriations.[67] Under California water law, Los Angeles couldn't just start exporting water south, no matter how many thirsty residents were waiting for it; the city had to get in line.[68]

River below the diversion dam). For more information on Owens Valley restoration projects, see the Memorandum of Understanding Between L.A. Dep't of Water and Power, the Cnty. of Inyo, Cal. Dep't of Fish and Wildlife, Cal. State Lands Cmm'n, the Sierra Club, and the Owens Valley Comm., www.inyowater.org/LORP/DOCUMENTS/1997MOU.pdf.

[63] See Malnic, *supra* note 58.

[64] See Andrea Ford, *Recycling Water: Environment: Bicyclists Are Carrying L.A. Water to Mono Lake in a Symbolic Effort to 'Rehydrate' It. They Also Call Attention to DWP Vote that May Reward Conservationists*, L.A. TIMES, Sep. 1, 1992, http://articles.latimes.com/1992-09-01/local/me-6794_1_mono-lake (last visited Oct. 21, 2022) (describing an event in which ninety cyclists carried bottles of water from DWP's reflecting pool 350 miles north to symbolically repatriate it to Mono Lake).

[65] See REISNER, *supra* note 3 (discussing how water rights were necessary for the Owens Valley Project).

[66] See Chapter 1(C) ("Conflicts with Water Allocation Law") (discussing the doctrines of prior appropriations and riparian rights, and the current doctrine for California water law); *see also* GARY LIBECAP: OWENS VALLEY REVISITED: A REASSESSMENT OF THE WEST'S FIRST GREAT WATER TRANSFER 9–11 (Stanford Economics and Finance 2007) (summarizing the relevant water rights systems at play, including appropriative rights, riparian rights, and groundwater rights).

[67] See A.P. Night Wire, *Ranch Men in Favor of City Offer*. OWENS VALLEY HISTORY, www.owensvalleyhistory.com/ov_aqueduct/page20c.html (last visited Oct. 22, 2022) (discussing how Los Angeles officials had to buy land and water rights in the Owens Valley).

[68] See Chapter 1(C) ("Conflicts with Water Allocation Law") (discussing the law of prior appropriations).

B. The Early 1900s: Tapping the Owens River Valley

Even more problematic, the agricultural use that Owens Valley farmers were making was intrinsically more generous to the community. Agricultural water use often forms part of a cycle, or a circle of recycling, in which upstream users withdraw water to irrigate crops that is largely returned back to the original water source through ground seepage. These irrigation "return flows" become available for future use either by downstream users directly, or by replenishing the underlying aquifer from which groundwater is then available. In this way, Owens River water was being recycled through multiple in-basin uses and instream flows within the watershed, and in relatively stable equilibrium with climatic conditions.

Los Angeles' intended use would be very different. The plan was not to sprinkle the water over crops, or even to send it south through a riverbed that would maintain hydrological connections to flowing groundwater beneath. The water was moved into a concrete ditch with the sole purpose of getting as much of it south as possible, without interruption. Exporting the water this way would yield return flows to neither the river nor the underlying aquifer, interrupting the entire web of uses and appropriations, and making LA's claim more vulnerable to challenge. Los Angeles' change in use could also set the city to the back of the line, making it the junior appropriator within the overall system and further complicating its desired yield. How the city resolved these issues became one of the seamier aspects of the aqueduct's history.

The only solution was for Los Angeles to acquire the appropriative and riparian rights it needed from existing Owens Valley farmers – and to iron out the problems of intersecting rights and priority in time, the city would have to buy up most if not all of the rights. But imagine, for a moment, the complications of trying to buy an entire town's worth of riparian land and water rights, in an agricultural community no less. Imagine the likely reaction of most local farmers – presumably fond of the local community, the neighbors, and their families – to such a proposal. Perhaps the farmer is even ready to retire from farming, and the land is already on the market. And suppose the City of Los Angeles approaches with a generous offer to buy the farm and all associated water rights, so that it can send that water south and extinguish the community forever. How many farmers in this position would have accepted that offer?

The city leaders charged with executing the plan predicted, almost certainly accurately, that few of them would. They surmised that most Owens Valley farmers would be hesitant to extinguish their communities, no matter the payout.[69] Accordingly, they concluded that the best approach was simply to keep the details of their intentions quiet. Assessing that the community was unlikely to just hand all the water over when Los Angeles announced its interest, they decided to trick the

---

[69] Local rebellions following the onset of water exports from the valley suggest that this perception was accurate. *See* Malnic, *supra* note 58.

locals into giving up these coveted water rights.[70] Essentially, when Los Angeles representatives went looking to buy, they pretended to be farmers.

City agents operating undercover posed as regular farmers acquiring land and water rights to continue farming Owens Valley lands just as the previous rights-holders had been doing.[71] They covered up or conveniently left out that they were buying on behalf of Los Angeles, as well as any mention of their true intentions for the water.[72] At the same time, Joseph Lippincott and other champions of the aqueduct were quietly convincing the U.S. Reclamation Service to scuttle existing plans to build a new water project in the Owens Valley that would have benefited the regional agricultural economy.[73] By the time local residents figured out what was happening, it was too late to stop it.[74]

Working undercover this way, Los Angeles gradually bought up most of the farmland and associated water rights in the Owens Valley. When it was too late to stop the plan, the city erected the Aberdeen dam and started diverting all available surface water south to Los Angeles.[75] When the city needed still more water, it began pumping groundwater below its landholdings in the valley and sent that south as well.[76] Before the local community had really figured out what was afoot, the vast majority of the region's water was being redirected to Los Angeles, and the Owen Valley was effectively divested of its water.[77]

The consequences that followed for the Owens Valley were staggering. After acquiring the bulk of all water rights in the valley, the Los Angeles Aqueduct began operations in 1913.[78] The Aberdeen diversion dam was completed and water began moving south, nourishing the burgeoning metropolis but depleting the ancient watershed – and fomenting the environmental catastrophe and social rebellion that would follow (described below in Part D). At the gathering to celebrate the first Owens River water that rolled through the aqueduct into Los Angeles, Chief Engineer William Mulholland famously told the assembled crowd: "There it is. Take it."[79] And while the Owens Valley communities ranted

---

[70] Id.
[71] REISNER, *supra* note 3, at 65, 70.
[72] See Malnic, *supra* note 58 (discussing how city officials began to quietly buy up water rights).
[73] REISNER, *supra* note 3, at 78 (discussing how the Bureau of Reclamation project in Owens Valley complicated the Los Angeles Aqueduct project); *see also* Malnic, *supra* note 58 ("[O]thers successfully lobbied Congress and President Theodore Roosevelt to abandon plans for a federal reclamation and irrigation project there.").
[74] See, e.g., REISNER, *supra* note 3, at 86–87 (discussing how farmers who did not originally sell out were eventually forced to do so).
[75] Malnic, *supra* note 58.
[76] Id.
[77] Id. ("Despite the outrage of Owens Valley farmers and the furor over Gen. Otis' potential profits, Los Angeles voters turned out on June 12, 1907, to approve construction bonds by a margin of 10 to 1. Federal approval for the municipal project was won in Congress two weeks later.").
[78] Sahagun, *Tule Vegetation, supra* note 33.
[79] REISNER, *supra* note 3, at 89.

against the injustice of their loss, greater Los Angeles took Mulholland's offer, and it has never looked back.

C. AN ALTERNATIVE ACCOUNT OF THE OWENS VALLEY WATER TRANSFER

Before cataloging the harms to the Owens Valley that followed Mulholland's fateful invitation, it is worth considering an alternative account of this crucial moment in California history by academic economist Gary Libecap. In 2007, Professor Libecap published a very different take on the early history of the Los Angeles Aqueduct in the Owens Valley that puts these water transfers in a more favorable light.[80]

While acknowledging the conventional narrative that appears in both the academic literature and the popular press – in which L.A. devastates the Owens Valley community by secretly obtaining its water rights through questionable means[81] – Professor Libecap argues that, in fact, the Owens Valley farmers were never tricked,[82] there was no theft by savvy Angelenos,[83] and the transfers were almost certainly justified by sound economic analysis.[84] Although Los Angeles did receive the lion's share of benefit from these transfers, Libecap maintains that the farmers who transferred their rights were still made better off than they would otherwise have been, because the agricultural community would have eventually declined for unrelated economic reasons even without these water transfers.[85]

Professor Libecap employs rigorous economic analysis to refute the principal narrative that casts the small Owens Valley community as hapless victims of an aggressive big city. He argues that complex problems of bilateral monopoly, monopsony, third-party impacts, and other economic factors conspired to complicate the bargaining in this case, distorting the way that normal market forces would have produced an efficient exchange in simpler economic contexts.[86] These are problems that threaten bargaining over large-scale water transfers endemically, corresponding with limited-participant markets and the difficulty of moving water resources over great distances.[87] He essentially argues that if not for the strategy Los Angeles employed, these valuable transfers may not have been possible, even though they produced the maximum social benefit for the state. Libecap maintains that Los

---

[80] LIBECAP, *supra* note 66.
[81] *Id.* at 12–25.
[82] *Id.* at 32–65, 148.
[83] *Id.* at 99–114, 148.
[84] *Id.* at 26–28, 99–114.
[85] *Id.* at 96–98.
[86] LIBECAP, *supra* note 66, at 67–98.
[87] *See* Barton H. Thompson, *Institutional Perspectives on Water Policy and Markets*, 81 Cal. L. Rev. 673, 689–94 (1993) (discussing the unique characteristics of water markets and the institutions that have developed to serve them).

Angeles behaved responsibly in these difficult bargaining circumstances by internalizing most of the externalities caused by the transfers by purchasing all affected properties, even those that didn't furnish much water to the aqueduct but would have been hurt by the city's diversions.[88]

It bears mention that a less generous interpretation of the city's move to purchase properties that didn't furnish much water for diversion is that the city bought out all members of the community who would have had standing to challenge those diversions in court. It may bear further mention that while Libecap may be right that the city attempted to internalize externalities by purchasing all properties (or at least protecting itself from judicial intervention this way), it is harder to see how the city attempted to internalize any of the environmental externalities of the transfers, or made any attempt to remedy the harms to impacted members of the community without standing to sue. Even today, as discussed further below, Owens Valley community members continue to battle the city for relief from the ongoing environmental problems associated with the dewatering of the lower Owens River and Owens Lake.

Libecap nevertheless contends that the mischaracterization of these historical events has seriously harmed the development of water markets that many economists believe are the only hope for rationalizing access to scarce water resources in the arid West.[89] Where appropriative rights are the primary rule of allocation, priority in time commands more respect than any other basis for distributing life-sustaining water, allowing senior agricultural interests to outweigh the countervailing needs of the vastly larger numbers people in growing urban areas with more junior water rights, if any. Libecap is not alone in arguing that water markets would facilitate the needed transfer of water from low-value agricultural uses with temporal priority to higher-value urban uses that, according to conventional utilitarian economics, should rationally take place.[90] Even conventional environmental organizations have made similar arguments.[91] The overall argument for facilitating low-to-high-value water transfers cannot be casually dismissed.

However, even Libecap acknowledges that the related problems of environmental degradation and other third-party impacts of the transfers were what made the Owens Valley story so controversial.[92] He notes that these environmental and indirect impacts must be properly compensated in order for future such water transfers to be more welcome,[93] and proposes potential means of renegotiating water allocation in light of environmental harms not foreseen at the time of the initial licensing,

---

[88] LIBECAP, *supra* note 66, at 4.
[89] *Id.* at 2, 150–51.
[90] *Id.* at 2, 150–51; *see generally* Thompson, *supra* note 87; Thomas J. Graff & David Yardaes, *Reforming Western Water Policy: Markets and Regulation*, 12 NAT. RES. & ENV'T 165 (1998).
[91] *See, e.g., Better Access. Healthier Environment. Prosperous Communities: Recommended Reforms for the California Water Market*, ENV'T DEF. FUND (2016).
[92] LIBECAP, *supra* note 66, at 2–3.
[93] *Id.* at 2–3.

including bond funding to acquire rights back from Los Angeles, or eminent domain.[94] He critiques the bargaining strategy that was used, and the resolution reached, both of which have done damage to the future of needed water transfers.[95] Libecap is especially critical of how the public trust principles articulated in the eventual Mono Lake litigation now pose what he considers an inefficient drag on water markets and interbasin transfers,[96] arguing that a negotiated transfer of water rights back to the public from Los Angeles would have been a more efficient, less costly, and less controversial alternative than the judicial affirmation of the role of the public trust doctrine in mediating such decisions.[97]

That said, it remains unclear how financial compensation could have remedied the sort of environmental harms that continue to cripple the Owens Valley, beginning as soon as the aqueduct went online.

D. AFTER THE AQUEDUCT

Whatever economic wisdom the original Owens Valley water transfers may or may not have held, the environmental consequences that followed are unambiguous.

1. The Local Consequences of Withdrawals

As demand for water in Los Angeles continued to grow, so did exports from the Owens Valley. Eventually, the city took not only the surface water of the Owens River, but also the groundwater from the Owens Valley aquifer, extracted by pumps on the land that the city had purchased to acquire associated water rights.[98] With the disappearance of the river, and the loss of agricultural uses that had once returned so much water to the ground through irrigation, the local aquifer was rapidly depleted.[99] Unsurprisingly, the consequences of removing the entire water supply were severe. Once-thriving farm communities were devastated, and the irrigated agricultural economy has never recovered.[100]

Still, the Owens Valley farmers did not go down quietly. They did not appreciate the less-than-forthright approach the city had taken in acquiring land and water rights.[101] They felt swindled, and not just out of a few dollars, acres of land, or gallons of water per day – they felt robbed of their community, their homes, and their

---

[94] Id. at 148–51.
[95] Id.
[96] Id. at 150–54.
[97] Id. at 145–53.
[98] See LIBECAP, supra note 66, at 100–01 (discussing how DWP "sank wells and began depauperating the aquifer" and that Los Angeles refused to limit its groundwater pumping).
[99] Id. at 100.
[100] Sahagun, Tule Vegetation, supra note 33.
[101] See id. (explaining that tensions were high between Los Angeles and the Owens Valley, and that the aquifer was dynamited over a dozen times in the 1920s in citizen rebellions).

very way of life.[102] In several incidents of open rebellion, angry farmers famously dynamited the aqueduct and released water back into the valley.[103] Headline-making drama ensued, and the National Guard was called in to restore order.[104]

The farmers' desperate stand drew attention from around the world, with newspaper coverage effectively depicting the Owens Valley farmers as tiny Davids pounding on the toe of the Goliath-like City of Los Angeles.[105] Nobody really expected them to prevail, and they didn't – but vulnerable areas of the aqueduct have remained under guard or behind barbed wire ever since.[106] Especially after additional bombings in the mid 1970s,[107] high fences and locked gates prevent public access and interference.[108] It's hard to get physically close – so people went to the courts. Litigation against Los Angeles in the 1970s claimed DWP operations were harming the environment of Owens Valley and that the California Environmental Quality Act required preparation of an Environmental Impact Report (EIR).[109] The court ordered the city to prepare an EIR – but, in the years after, Los Angeles did not satisfy the order, and the court continually directed further steps to be taken to comply.[110] By 1984, both sides agreed to stop litigating and began cooperative studies and development of a groundwater management plan.[111] The agreement was approved by a court and a draft EIR was released in 1990.[112]

At the end of the day, however, Los Angeles secured the water rights it sought, the Owens River was diverted, and water effectively disappeared from the lower Owens Valley, south of the diversion dam.[113] The most obvious local casualty was Owens Lake, the large but shallow salt lake at the bottom of the now-empty river.[114]

---

[102] See Scott Harrison, *Dynamite Attacks on the Los Angeles Aqueduct*, L.A. TIMES, Feb. 6, 2013, http://fraiework.latimes.com/2013/02/06/los-angeles-aqueduct-2/#/0 (describing incidents at the Alabama Gates and No Name Canyon, among others).

[103] *See id.*

[104] *Id.*

[105] *Cf.* REISNER, *supra* note 3, at 97 (discussing public sympathy for Owens Valley farmers).

[106] *See, e.g.,* Los Angeles Department of Water and Power, *A Legacy of Safe-Keeping*, INTAKE, Nov. 2013, at 53–54, www.laaqueduct100.com/wp-content/uploads/LAA100Issue.pdf.

[107] Harrison, *supra* note 102; *see also* Louis Sahagun, *Los Angeles Aqueduct Bomber Reveals His Story*, L.A. TIMES, Oct. 30, 2013, www.latimes.com/local/la-me-c1-aqueduct-bomber-20131030-dto-html story.html#axzz2jDMnv8Wo (describing the 1976 bombing of an aqueduct gate).

[108] *See* Elson Trinidad, *A Self-Guided Tour of the Los Angeles Aqueduct*, KCET, Nov. 4, 2013, www.kcet.org/news/redefine/revisit/commentary/concrete-and-chaparral/a-self-guided-tour-of-the-los-angeles-aqueduct.html (describing water pumps surrounded by high chain link fences).

[109] Cnty. of Inyo v. Yorty, 32 Cal. App. 3d 795 (1973); Appendix R. Legal History of the Mono Lake Controversy, Mono Basin Research, pg. R-10, www.monobasinresearch.org/images/mbeir/dappendix/app-r-text.pdf.

[110] Cnty. of Inyo v. City of L.A., 71 Cal. App. 3d 185 (1977); Cnty. of Inyo v. City of L.A., 124 Cal. App. 3d 1 (1981); Appendix R. Legal History of the Mono Lake Controversy, *supra* note 109.

[111] Appendix R. Legal History of the Mono Lake Controversy, *supra* note 109.

[112] *Id.*

[113] *See* REISNER, *supra* note 3, at 72.

[114] *See* Sahagun, *Tule Vegetation*, *supra* note 33.

D. After the Aqueduct

The great waterway simply evaporated without replenishment, until all that was left were the dusty, dried up minerals that had been accumulating over thousands of years.[115] Today, there is an expansive salt sump where the majestic Owens Lake once anchored the valley and its wildlife, including vast populations of migratory birds that no longer appear.[116] Where there had once been an enormous black-with-birds desert oasis, there was now just a giant, white, empty salt flat – ugly, foul-smelling, and with nothing to offer the people or the wildlife that once depended on it.[117] We now call it "Owens Dry Lake."[118]

Since then, the Owens Dry Lake wasteland has become an urgent problem for the valley, and not just because it is ugly and barren. The Owens Valley tragedy is compounded by the fact that the exposed lakebed is composed of fine alkali salts that are toxic to breathe. The valley happens to rest at the base of the tallest mountain in the lower forty-eight states – the Sierra Nevada's Mount Whitney, looming more than 10,000 feet above the valley floor at 14,500 feet above sea level.[119] Ferocious winds whip off the nearly vertical escarpment of the Eastern Sierra near Mount Whitney, picking up dust and salt from the bed of Owens Dry Lake and churning it into chronic regional dust storms that can be choking to inhale.[120]

Yet Owens Valley dust storms are even more threatening than the average dust storm. To make matters even worse, this dust is carcinogenic. The fine-particle alkali salts that compose the dust are so small that they pass through the membranes of the human respiratory system and are associated with asthma, other respiratory ailments, and even cancer.[121] Today, the Owens Valley still suffers from decimating air pollution which regularly violates Clean Air Act[122] standards for ambient air quality.[123] In fact, the region often ranks as the most polluted place in the United States by particulate matter standards.[124]

---

[115] *See* Marith C. Reheis, *Dust Deposition Downwind of Owens (Dry) Lake, 1991–1994 – Preliminary Findings*, 102 J. GEOPHYSICAL RES. (ATMOSPHERES) 25999–26008 (1997) (describing the post-aqueduct deposits of minerals accumulated in Owens Lake over thousands of years).
[116] *Id.*
[117] Siegler, *Owens Valley Salty as Los Angeles Water Battle Flows into Court*, NAT'L PUB. RADIO (Mar. 11, 2013), www.npr.org/2013/03/11/173463688/owens-valley-salty-as-los-angeles-water-battle-flows-into-court.
[118] *See, e.g.*, Reheis, *supra* note 115 (describing Owens Lake in a dust disposition study as the "Owens (dry) Lake").
[119] *See* Stewart Green, *Mount Whitney: Highest Mountain in California*, ABOUT.COM, http://climbing.about.com/od/mountainclimbing/a/MtWhitneyFacts.htm (last visited Sept. 18, 2022).
[120] MARITH REHEIS ET AL., POTENTIAL HEALTH HAZARDS OF OWENS LAKE DUST? (2003), https://geochange.er.usgs.gov/sw/impacts/geology/owens/.
[121] SARAH KITTLE, GREAT BASIN UNIFIED AIR POLLUTION CONTROL DIST., SURVEY OF REPORTED HEALTH EFFECTS OF OWENS LAKE PARTICULATE MATTER (Jan. 14, 2000), https://gbuapcd.org/District/Background/ReferenceLibrary/pmHealthEffects.html.
[122] 42 U.S.C. §§ 7401–7671(q) (2012).
[123] *Owens Valley, CA Particulate Matter Plan*, U.S. ENV'T PROT. AGENCY, https://19january2017snapshot.epa.gov/www3/region9/air/owens/index.html (last updated Feb. 14, 2017) (describing Owens Lake as "the nation's worst particulate air pollution problem").
[124] *Id.*

The results of the aqueduct for the lower Owens Valley were nothing short of tragic. Not only did it destroy the original farming communities, it made people sick. With no water, limited economic potential, and now elevated health risks, the Owens Valley stagnated.[125] Driving around these parts in the mid 1990s (with car windows rolled up) yielded sad sights amidst otherwise stunning vistas. In the worst hit areas, there were many abandoned structures, and few children. You might have seen a couple of older people unwilling to leave their abandoned towns, sitting vacantly on the porches of distressed homes that looked a lot like the empty ones next door.

In the late 1990s, Los Angeles began flooding more than 100 square miles of dry lake bed with billions of gallons of water to keep the dust from becoming airborne, responding to deep public concern over adverse health impacts, environmental litigation, and state and federal laws requiring better management of the air quality hazard.[126] In late 2014, the city reached an agreement with the Great Basin Unified Air Pollution Control District enabling it to manage the lakebed hazard with a new method that consumes far less water.[127] Under this agreement, tractors will till the moist lakebed to create basketball-sized dirt clods that can contain the toxic dust for years before breaking down, at which point the process will be repeated.[128]

2. The St. Francis Dam

The devastation of the Owens Valley is not the only tragic chapter in the saga of the early days of the aqueduct. There is also the story of the St. Francis Dam.

To enable the aqueduct to deliver a steady flow of water to Los Angeles year round, engineers constructed a series of reservoirs along the aqueduct to store additional supply during the wet season, for gradual release during the dry season or other emergency circumstances.[129] When the aqueduct was first constructed, one such dam was built at San Francisquito Canyon,[130] a promising narrows located near the bottom of the aqueduct system, about forty miles north of Los Angeles near present

---

[125] Richard L. Forstall, *California: Population of Counties by Decennial Census: 1900 to 1990*, U.S. CENSUS BUREAU (Mar. 27, 1995) (showing population growth from 11,684 in 1960 to 18,281 in 1990), www2.census.gov/library/publications/decennial/1990/population-of-states-and-counties-us-1790-1990/population-of-states-and-counties-of-the-united-states-1790-1990.pdf; *State and County QuickFacts: Inyo County*, U.S. CENSUS BUREAU, www.census.gov/quickfacts/fact/table/inyocountycalifornia/HCN010217 (last visited Sept. 18, 2022) (showing current population of 18,970).

[126] *See* Louis Sahagun, *New Dust-Busting Method Ends L.A.'s Longtime Feud with Owens Valley*, L.A. TIMES, Nov. 14, 2014, www.latimes.com/science/la-me-1115-owens-20141115-story.html (describing new and former methods of containing lakebed dust).

[127] *Id.*

[128] *Id.* (noting that the new method saves enough water to supply 150,000 Los Angeles residents per year).

[129] *See* REISNER, *supra* note 3, at 87–88.

[130] *Id.* at 101. The St. Francis Dam was constructed in part to ensure supply if seismic activity along the San Andreas fault disrupted the aqueduct. *See* Kevin Roderick, *Dam Disaster Killed 450, Broke Mulholland*, L.A. TIMES, Oct. 12, 1999, http://articles.latimes.com/1999/oct/12/local/me-21385.

D. After the Aqueduct 79

day Santa Clarita.[131] A photo of the dam when it was completed in 1926 shows a sturdy, shining component of the overall miracle of modern engineering.[132]

Yet a photo of the same dam two years later shows nothing more than a single spire of concrete between gaping voids on either side, like a single front tooth in a baby's mouth.[133] It took just a few hours for that transition to take place, in the dead of night. As news reports described this awful moment in California history, the dam gave way shortly after midnight on March 12, 1928:

> [I]n an instant 38,000 acre feet, totaling 12,000,000,000 gallons, of stored water was rushing on its mad race to the sea.... What little warning there was of the wall of water that swept the floor of the valley was insufficient to give any of the inhabitants of the upper part of the canyon time to flee its fury. Caught in the swirl of the raging flood, the hundreds of ranch houses that once dotted the canyon were crushed like egg shells and their inhabitants, in most instances, swept to their doom.[134]

Raging floodwaters swept through the Santa Clara Valley toward the Pacific for more than fifty miles, devastating some sixty-five miles of valley before reaching the ocean between Oxnard and Ventura.[135] The peak surge was estimated to be nearly eighty feet high.[136] When it reached Santa Paula, forty-two miles south of the dam, the water was estimated to be twenty-five feet deep.[137] Almost everything in its path was destroyed: ten bridges, twelve hundred homes, railways, power lines, orchards, and livestock.[138] The flood carried away entire towns, wreaking "unthinkable carnage" along the way.[139]

By the time it was over, parts of Ventura County lay under seventy feet of mud and debris. Over 450 people were killed, including half the student body at a local elementary school, hundreds of DWP workers sleeping in a nearby work camp, and many migrant farmworkers camping in the valley and swept out to sea.[140] Damages

---

[131] *See* Michael E. Martinet, *Section 6: Flooding Hazards in the City of Downey*, in CITY OF DOWNEY NATURAL HAZARDS MITIGATION PLAN 11, Section VI (Emergency Planning Consultants ed. 2004), www.yumpu.com/en/document/view/36375896/section-6-flooding-hazards-in-the-city-of-downey (quoting a contemporaneous report of the disaster).

[132] *See* Scott Harrison, *St. Francis Dam Collapse*, L.A. TIMES, Mar. 12, 2013, www.latimes.com/visuals/photography/la-me-fw-archives-the-1928-st-francis-dam-collapse-20180206-htmlstory.html.

[133] *Id.*

[134] Special to the New York Times, *274 Perish, 700 Missing in Torrent Loosed by Bursting California Dam; Flood Engulfs Victims as They Sleep*, N.Y. TIMES, Mar. 14, 1928, at 1. Note that this article appears to misstate the date of the incident as March 13, 1928, and most other sources report the date as March 12, 1928. *See, e.g.*, Martinet, *supra* note 131; Harrison, *supra* note 132; Roderick, *supra* note 130.

[135] *See* Roderick, *supra* note 130.

[136] *Id.* (describing a wall of water ten stories high).

[137] *See* Martinet, *supra* note 131 (quoting a contemporaneous report of the disaster).

[138] *See id.*; Harrison, *supra* note 132; Roderick, *supra* note 130 (describing the devastation).

[139] *See* Roderick, *supra* note 130.

[140] *Id.*

topped $20 million at the time,[141] valued at well over $250 million today.[142] Even now, it is considered one of the worst civil engineering failures in American history.[143]

The spectacular failure of the St. Francis Dam terrified Californians. Modern engineering suddenly seemed less miraculous, and more dangerous. Angelenos who had once celebrated William Mulholland turned against him, and he went from being a local celebrity to a pariah, seemingly overnight.[144] The surrounding community rebuilt and eventually removed all evidence of the dam, as though hoping to erase the memory of the horror that had unfolded there.[145] Today, if you try to seek out where the dam had been, you can't really find it; there is only an ordinary canyon, rich with greenery, and not even a memorial.[146]

One hundred years later, as this book goes to press, plans to create a St. Francis Dam Memorial may finally be underway, but only long after the fear factor has dissipated.[147] Nevertheless, perhaps the fear factor is still warranted.

---

[141] Jan Silver Maguire, *Water Triumphs and Tragedies*, 77 AQUEDUCT MAG. (2006), www.mwdh2o.com/Aqueduct/may_06/article_03_01.html.

[142] The actual figure in 2015 U.S. dollars is $273,341,520. *See* Consumer Price Index Inflation Calculator, U.S. BUREAU OF LABOR STATS., http://data.bls.gov/cgi-bin/cpicalc.pl (last visited Sept. 18, 2022).

[143] *See* Roderick, *supra* note 130. The coroner's inquest into the dam's failure found that the dam failed because it was built on top of a rock type called red Sespe conglomerate, which disintegrates when exposed to water. Alan Pollock, M.D., *St. Francis Dam: Too Big Not to Fail*, SCVHISTORY.COM (MARCH-APR. 2010), https://scvhistory.com/scvhistory/pollacko310dam.htm. Mulholland took personal responsibility for the deadly decision to build on top of this type of rock. *Id.* However, sixty-four years later, geological engineer Dr. J. David Rogers published a series of papers finding that the actual cause of the dam's failure was that the eastern abutment was anchored to an ancient Paleolithic landslide – and this Mulholland did not know. *Id.* When the ancient landslide became saturated with water, it resulted in the collapse of the dam. *Id.* Rogers also noted that the dam was constructed in such a way that when the collapse occurred, it resulted in "hydraulic uplift": the force of the water caused the dam structure to lift upward and tilt downstream, allowing the water to flow quickly past the structure. *Id.* Engineers can prevent hydraulic uplift by building uplift relief walls at the base of the dam. *Id.* In the case of the St. Francis Dam, only the center portion of the dam had these uplift relief walls. *Id.* The center portion of the dam remained standing after the collapse. *Id.* Ultimately, Rogers concluded that Mulholland should not have borne personal responsibility for the dam's failure; the effects of hydraulic uplift were not well understood at the time of the collapse. *Id.* Rogers acknowledges that Mulholland should have hired outside consultants and, but concludes that the greatest contributor to the collapse was the general lack of knowledge of proper dam construction in the civil engineering field at the time. *Id.*

[144] *See* REISNER, *supra* note 3, at 102–103 (describing the decline of Mulholland's reputation).

[145] *See* Hadley Meares, *The Flood: St. Francis Dam Disaster, William Mulholland, and the Casualties of L.A. Imperialism*, KCET, July 26, 2013, www.kcet.org/socal/departures/columns/lost-landmarks/the-flood-st-francis-dam-disaster-william-mulholland-and-the-casualties-of-la-imperialism.html.

[146] A former student of mine who grew up near the former dam site told me that she was baffled by the lack of local lore and remembrances about the disaster, noting that there was a small plaque somewhere in town mentioning what had happened, but nothing at the actual site of the disaster. *See also id.* ("We were passing the former site of the St. Francis Dam, but we couldn't tell where it had been, so effective had nature been in reclaiming its land.").

[147] *See* Tom Kisken, *Trump's Signature Means St. Francis Dam Memorial Is Coming*, VENTURA CNTY. STAR, Mar. 16, 2019 (reporting on 2019 legislation that would create a national memorial at the dam

3. Reprise: The Oroville Dam

Hiding the history of the St. Francis dam disaster may not be helpful for Californians and others who may thereby be doomed to repeat it.[148]

In fact, a chilling coda to the St. Francis Dam story threatened to unfold ninety years later in Oroville, California, about seventy miles north of the state capital in Sacramento. The community sits just downstream from Oroville Dam, which holds back 3.5 million acre-feet of water in Lake Oroville.[149] Oroville Dam is the nation's tallest dam at 770 feet, about 44 taller than the Hoover Dam.[150] Lake Oroville is one of California's largest man-made lakes, but more importantly, it is considered the linchpin of California's public water delivery system, providing water for both Central Valley agriculture and Southern California domestic and commercial use.[151] Reminiscent of the St. Francis Dam tragedy, the Oroville Dam's close proximity to large population centers, including Sacramento and Chico, threaten the possibility of serious harm when failing infrastructure are combined with unpredictable weather.[152]

This scenario nearly came to pass on February 12, 2017, when state officials terrified the region by ordering the evacuation of 200,000 downstream residents when the security of the dam was in question.[153] While the edifice of the dam itself had remained secure, significant erosion had damaged the dam's main spillway and surrounding soils.[154] Record-setting rainfall had placed the emergency spillway into use for first time since the dam was completed almost fifty years prior.[155] While the California Department of Water Resources was able to prevent major flooding,

---

site off San Francisquito Canyon Road, north of Santa Clarita, if funds are successfully raised by a nonprofit foundation).

[148] For a searching look at the risks of building significant infrastructure on the fault lines and saturated subsoil typical in California, see MARC REISNER, A DANGEROUS PLACE (2003).

[149] Samantha Schmidt, Derek Hawkins & Kristine Phillips, *188,000 evacuated as California's massive Oroville Dam threatens catastrophic floods*, WASH. POST, Feb. 13, 2017, www.washingtonpost.com/news/morning-mix/wp/2017/02/13/not-a-drill-thousands-evacuated-in-calif-as-oroville-dam-threatens-to-flood/?utm_term=.0c1a7abad29f.

[150] *Id.* The Hoover Dam, straddling the border between Nevada and Arizona, was completed in 1936. California fought hard for rights to access some of the water it stored. *Id.* A few years after the dam's completion, the Metropolitan Water District of Southern California built a 200 mile aqueduct siphoning water from Hoover Dam to Los Angeles. REISNER, A DANGEROUS PLACE, *supra* note 148, at 54.

[151] Schmidt, Hawkins & Phillips, *supra* note 149.

[152] The Oroville Dam was an extremely expensive project – valued at nearly $15 billion in 1999 dollars – but was pushed through by then-governor Pat Brown. REISNER, A DANGEROUS PLACE *supra* note 148, at 55. Brown stated that one of his primary reasons for prioritizing the dam's construction was he "didn't want all those people moving to northern California." *Id.* at 56.

[153] Henry Fountain, K.K. Rebecca Lai & Tim Wallace, *What Happened at the Oroville Dam*, N.Y. TIMES, Feb. 13, 2017, www.nytimes.com/interactive/2017/02/13/us/oroville-dam.html?_r=0; Schmidt, Hawkins & Phillips, *supra* note 149.

[154] *Id.*

[155] *Id.*

the potential failure of such a massive water infrastructure project almost one hundred years after the St. Francis Dam failure resurrected debate over dam-dependent approaches to comprehensive water management and flood protection,[156] with some heralding less dangerous approaches that might prove more resilient in the face of climate-related stress and uncertainty.[157]

But back in the late 1920s, even as public sentiment turned against Mulholland after the failure of the St. Francis Dam, Angelenos still jealously coveted the water he had brought to them.[158] In the 1930s, as the city's thirst continued to grow, engineers continued to look to other remote sources. And there in the distance – just another hundred miles north of the Owens River headwaters and an additional 2,000 feet up – was the Mono Lake Basin.

---

[156] Christopher Cadelago & Jim Miller, *Trump approves funds for California relief, including $274 million for Oroville Dam*, SACRAMENTO BEE, Apr. 2, 2017, www.sacbee.com/news/politics-government/capitol-alert/article142272894.html; Jennie Blevins & Kyra Gottesman, *Oroville Dam crisis 5 years later: The evacuation and events that sent 180,000 people fleeing*, ENTERPRISE-RECORD, Feb. 12, 2022, https://chicoer.com/2022/02/12/oroville-dam-crisis-5-years-later-the-evacuation-and-events-that-sent-180000-people-fleeing/.

[157] *See, e.g.*, Adam Nagourney & Henry Fountain, *Oroville Is a Warning for California Dams, as Climate Change Adds Stress*, N.Y. TIMES, Feb. 13, 2017, www.nytimes.com/2017/02/14/us/oroville-dam-climate-change-california.html; Lauren Sommer, *Where Levees Fail In California, Nature Can Step In To Nurture Rivers*, NAT'L PUB. RADIO, Mar. 29, 2017, www.npr.org/2017/03/29/521939643/where-levees-fail-in-california-nature-can-step-in-to-nurture-rivers.

[158] *See* REISNER, *supra* note 3, at 107.

3

The Mono Basin Extension

A.	The Mono Lake Basin	84
	1. The Mono Lake Ecosystem	85
	2. The Indigenous People of the Mono Basin	88
	3. European Settlement of the Basin	89
	4. The Modern Mono Basin Economy	91
B.	Acquiring the Mono Basin Water Rights	93
	1. 1940: The Mono Basin Extension	93
	2. 1970: The Second Barrel	96
C.	The Impacts of Water Exports on the Basin	97

Some forty years after the aqueduct first began tapping the Owens Valley, Los Angeles leaders realized that the growing city needed still more water. They also realized that there was a wealth of additional, unappropriated water in the next watershed up from the Owens Valley, just two hundred miles to the north – the Mono Lake Basin.

This chapter explores the extension of the aqueduct to the Mono Basin in 1940 and the acceleration of exports from the Mono Basin after the Second Barrel was built in 1970. It begins by introducing the extraordinary features of the Mono Lake ecosystem itself – the trillions of brine shrimp, clouds of alkali flies, and millions of migratory birds that depend on a hypersaline sea suspended in a high-desert basin marked by dormant volcanism, geothermal activity, and limestone tufa towers rising from calcium laden springs entering Mono's carbonate-rich waters. It also reviews the human communities of the Basin, including the indigenous Mono Lake Kootzaduka'a people and the European settlement that followed the California Gold Rush.

Finally, it explores the human and environmental consequences that followed Los Angeles's acquisition of rights to take water from the Basin, setting the stage for the legal controversy that would follow.

A. THE MONO LAKE BASIN

Mono Lake lies in a high desert basin just east of the Sierra crest – the peaks of the mountains that divide Yosemite National Park on the west from the Mono Basin and the Inyo National Forest on the east.[1] Mono Lake is the eastern watershed of the Yosemite highlands, draining the eastern flanks of mountains that rise up to 14,000 feet into the air and then plunge more than 7,000 feet to their eastern base.[2] Surrounded by mountains in three of four directions, it is a staggeringly beautiful and occasionally otherworldly place – pierced by volcanic islands and geothermal activity, and adorned with limestone towers of tufa that grow where calcium-rich underground springs meet the carbonate-rich waters of the lake.[3]

To call Mono a lake is almost a misnomer; it is more of an inland sea. At around seventy square miles in surface area, it is twice the size of the County of San Francisco, five times deeper than the Great Salt Lake in Utah, and three times saltier than the Pacific ocean.[4] It averages about fifty feet deep but runs as deep as 159 feet where its western shores approach the Sierra.[5] Like Owens Lake, Mono is a saltwater terminal lake, which means that water flows in, but has no way of leaving the basin except by evaporation.[6] The lake collects snowmelt from the five freshwater creeks that flow into the basin, carrying in trace elements and minerals leached from the surrounding mountains and deserts. And unlike Owens Lake, whose geological age could be counted in thousands of years, Mono Lake's age is estimated at between one and three million years old – roughly tied with Lake Tahoe as the oldest continuous lake in North America.[7] For those millions of years, waters laced with trace elements have flowed into the basin and then evaporated off the surface, leaving the minerals behind to form a hypersaline body

---

[1] See Louis Sahagun, *"There It Is – Take It": A Story of Marvel and Controversy*, L.A. TIMES (Oct. 28, 2013), http://graphics.latimes.com/me-aqueduct/; Mono Basin National Forest Scenic Area, USDA & FS www.fs.usda.gov/detail/inyo/specialplaces/?cid=stelprdb5129903 (last visited Sept. 26, 2022).

[2] See JOHN HART, STORM OVER MONO: THE MONO LAKE BATTLE AND THE CALIFORNIA WATER FUTURE 5–7 (1996).

[3] See generally Natural History, MONO LAKE COMM., www.monolake.org/learn/aboutmonolake/naturalhistory/ [hereinafter *Mono Lake Facts*] (last visited Oct. 21, 2022) (listing attributes and statistics about Mono Lake); see also HART, supra note 2, at 20–21 (describing the formation of tufa).

[4] Compare *Mono Lake Facts*, supra note 3, with QuickFacts San Francisco County, California, U.S. CENSUS BUREAU, www.census.gov/quickfacts/fact/table/sanfranciscocountycalifornia/PST045217 (last visited Sept. 27, 2022) (noting San Francisco County's land area is 46.87 square miles); Physical Characteristics of Great Salt Lake, LEARN.GENETICS, http://learn.genetics.utah.edu/content/gsl/physical_char/ (last visited Sept. 27, 2022) (comparing the depths of the Great Salt Lake and Mono Lake); see also HART, supra note 2, at 5–7.

[5] *Mono Lake Facts*, supra note 3.

[6] CAL. DEP'T OF WATER RES., THE IMPORTANCE OF THE SALTON SEA AND OTHER TERMINAL LAKES IN SUPPORTING BIRDS OF THE PACIFIC FLYWAY 1 (2004), https://nrm.dfg.ca.gov/FileHandler.ashx?DocumentID=9123.

[7] See HART, supra note 2, at 5–7; Tahoe Fun Facts, TAHOE FUND, www.tahoefund.org/about-tahoe/tahoe-fun-facts/ (last visited Sept. 27, 2022).

three times saltier than the oceans, and nearly as saline as parts of the Great Salt Lake in Utah.[8]

The water is so alkaline that fish cannot survive there.[9] Nevertheless, the lake is home to a thriving ecosystem based on a unique species of brine shrimp and the alkali fly that breeds at its shores, a dietary staple of the Mono Lake Kootzaduka'a people who still live there.[10] Mark Twain didn't care much for the place, referring to it disparagingly as the Dead Sea of California.[11] But many who live, work, and visit there consider Mono Lake a magical place, because of its rugged natural beauty, its unique ecosystem, the unusual scientific research conducted there, and the local cultures and communities that have lived beside it over history.

1. *The Mono Lake Ecosystem*

The basis of the simple Mono Lake ecosystem is the benthic algae in the lake, which support both the alkali fly and brine shrimp populations that, in turn, support the rest of the food chain.[12] The species of brine shrimp in the lake are unique to Mono Lake, and they are rather small – no bigger than the size of a clipped fingernail.[13] Yet there are estimated to be as many as three to four trillion of them in the lake.[14] If I were to scoop a coffee cup of water out of the lake – as I did every day on countless South Tufa tours as a Mono Lake ranger with the Forest Service – I could have ten or twenty in my cup.

These shrimp don't hold much appeal to the human palate, but the tiny pupae of the alkali flies are rich in fat, protein, and flavor – a tiny cocoon that bursts on the tongue with the distinct taste of salt and butter. They were a dietary staple of the

---

[8] *See* HART, *supra* note 2, at 5–7, 198 (listing Mono as three times saltier than the ocean); World's Saltiest Bodies of Water, WORLD ATLAS, www.worldatlas.com/articles/the-world-s-most-saline-bodies-of-water.html (last visited Sept. 27, 2022) (noting salinity ranges of the Pacific Ocean at 3.5 percent, Mono Lake at 5–9.9 percent, and the Great Salt Lake at 5–27 percent); *Physical Characteristics of Great Salt Lake*, *supra* note 4 (describing the Great Salt Lake as 3.5 times saltier than the ocean).

[9] *See* HART, *supra* note 2, at 16.

[10] Nat'l Audubon Soc'y v. Super. Ct., 658 P.2d 709, 726–27 (Cal. 1983); Brine Shrimp: Mono Lake's Unique Species, MONO LAKE COMM., www.monolake.org/about/ecoshrimp [hereinafter *Mono Lake Brine Shrimp*] (last visited Sept. 27, 2022); *Mono Lake Facts*, *supra* note 3; Kutzadika'a People, MONO LAKE COMM., www.monolake.org/learn/aboutmonolake/humanhistory/kutzadikaapeople/ [hereinafter *Mono Basin Kutzadika'a*] (last visited Sept. 22, 2022). In 2024, the tribe formalized a new preferred spelling for its name, "Kootzaduka'a". *Mono Lake Kootzaduka'a Tribe Formalizes Preferred Spelling*, Mono Lake Committee News (Nov. 15, 2024), https://www.monolake.org/today/mono-lake-kootzadukaa-tribe-formalizes-preferred-spelling/; Mono Lake Kootzaduka'a Tribe, *The Website of the Mono Lake Kootzaduka'a Tribe of California and Nevada*, https://monolaketribe.us (last visited Dec. 6, 2025). Thanks to the tribe and to Caelen McQuilken for guidance on these updates.

[11] MARK TWAIN, ROUGHING IT 243, 245 (Harriet Elinor Smith & Edgar Marquess Branch eds., 3d ed. 2011).

[12] *Nat'l Audubon Soc'y*, 658 P.2d at 711; *Mono Lake Facts*, *supra* note 3.

[13] *Mono Lake Brine Shrimp*, *supra* note 10.

[14] *Id.*

local indigenous people – cooked with other foods or snacked on like popcorn – and a coveted item of trade that made Mono Lake famous among regional indigenous tribes.[15] When I introduced the delicacy to Mono Lake visitors on my ranger tours, I mostly plucked them from the undersides of submerged rocks or debris in the lake, and there was almost always a prepubescent boy or girl eager to be the first to eat the prepubescent bug. After they invariably exclaimed "like butter!", virtually everyone on the tour wanted to try one. Fortunately, in the right season, a healthy Mono Lake provides enough for everyone to enjoy.

From the perspective of a hungry bird, then, Mono Lake is a giant bowl of shrimp soup, deliciously garnished with alkali flies. For that reason, Mono Lake holds an even more important position along the Pacific Flyway than Owens Lake held. Birds arriving from as far north as the Arctic Circle en route to points as far south as the tip of Argentina use Mono Lake as a critical resting place to gorge their body weights back up to full strength before resuming their journeys over the vast desert.[16] Hundreds of species of migratory birds visit the lake regularly, including flocks of grebes, phalaropes, plovers, and sandpipers that occasionally constitute substantial percentages of their world populations.[17] Mono Lake is also a primary breeding ground for California gulls, providing a first home to more than 85 percent of the state's population.[18] Year after year, they return to breed on Negit Island, the small black cinder cone in the middle of the lake, where they are safe from predation by coyotes and other local predators reluctant to swim in Mono's punishingly alkaline waters.[19]

In fact, Negit and Paoha, the white island beside it, are the newest members of the youngest volcanic range in North America, the Mono Craters.[20] Reaching as high as 9,000 feet, the Mono Craters extend from the south shore of the lake, through the islands in the middle, all the way to Black Point, a long-exposed underwater volcano that bites into the lake's northwest shore.[21] Paoha heaved above the surface of the lake

---

[15] DAVID CARLE, MONO LAKE VIEWPOINT 30 (Artemisia Press 1992).

[16] Kevin Neal, *The Los Angeles Aqueduct and the Owens and Mono Lakes*, THE MANDALA PROJECTS, http://mandalaprojects.com/ice/ice-cases/mono.htm (last visited Sept. 27, 2022) (explaining Mono Lake's importance to migratory bird routes from the Arctic Circle to South America); Birds of the Basin: The Migratory Millions of Mono, MONO LAKE COMM., www.monolake.org/about/ecobirds [hereinafter *Mono Lake Bird Facts*] (last visited Sept. 27, 2022).

[17] *Mono Lake Facts*, *supra* note 3; *Mono Lake Bird Facts*, *supra* note 16.

[18] *Mono Lake Facts*, *supra* note 3.

[19] *Id.*; *Mono Lake Bird Facts*, *supra* note 16. See also HART, *supra* note 2, at 16–17. In recent years, however, an explosive growth of invasive weeds on Negit Island is threatening nesting birds. See Louis Sahagun, *Nonnative Weeds Are Engulfing the Ancient Breeding Grounds of Mono Lake's California Gulls*, L.A. TIMES (Dec. 17, 2019), www.latimes.com/california/story/2019-12-17/weeds-pushing-california-gulls-out-breeding-grounds-mono-lake.

[20] Renee Murdock, *Mono Basin Volcanism*, (June 17, 2004), https://sierra.sitehost.iu.edu/papers/2004/murdock.pdf.

[21] Shaped by Fire and Ice: Young Volcanic Activity and Glaciation, MONO LAKE COMM., www.monolake.org/learn/aboutmonolake/naturalhistory/geology/ (last visited Sept. 27, 2022); *see also* HART, *supra* note 2, at 13–14.

without exploding only three hundred years ago, and hot springs and fumaroles continue to mark its cracked, lakebed surface.[22] Mono Lake has been a destination for scientific research into underwater volcanism because it is safer and easier to explore than some of the more active underwater volcanoes in Hawaii.[23]

In 2010, Mono Lake briefly made international scientific news, when NASA scientists announced that they had discovered there the first known species of life on earth that exchanged arsenic for phosphorous in its chemical profile.[24] These scientists had been studying bacteria from the bottom of Mono Lake as part of a research effort to imagine how life might evolve on other planets.[25] Their discovery of the Mono Lake GFAJ-1 arsenic bacteria was initially an exciting development, indicating that life in stressed environments might make creative use of a normally poisonous element as a basic chemical building block.[26] However, later research failed to replicate these findings,[27] and the scientific implications of Mono Lake's unique chemistry remain unresolved. In the meanwhile, NASA's interest in the Mono Basin for this kind of research provides further testimony to the unique otherworldly qualities of the place.

In 2024, the unusual chemistry of the lake revealed a more durable scientific discovery by a group of biologists from U.C.-Berkeley, who found within its briny waters a unique species of choanoflagellates – microscopic, single-celled organisms that form large colonies, propelled in unison by individual flagellum, hosting a shared bacterial microbiome within their hollow core.[28] Occupying a niche near the bottom of the evolutionary chain, choanoflagellates are believed to be the closest living relative of animals.[29] Colonies like the ones found at Mono Lake, just visible to the naked eye, are providing scientists with a model of how the leap to multicellular life was made, helping us understand how animals branched off the tree of life some 650 million years ago.[30] In honor of their home, the new species was christened "Barroeca monosierra."[31]

---

[22] Lucas Hatcher, *The Geology and Biology of Mono Lake*, https://sierra.sitehost.iu.edu/papers/2013/hatcher.html (last visited Sept. 27, 2022).

[23] See, e.g., Current Research, MONO BASIN CLEARINGHOUSE www.monobasinresearch.org/research/index.php (last visited Sept. 27, 2022) (listing ongoing scientific studies in the Mono Basin).

[24] Discovery of "Arsenic-Bug" Expands Definition of Life, NASA SCIENCE (Dec. 2, 2010), http://science.nasa.gov/science-news/science-at-nasa/2010/02dec_monolake/.

[25] See id.

[26] Id.

[27] Richard A. Lovett, *Arsenic-Life Discovery Debunked – but "Alien" Organism Still Odd*, NAT'L GEOGRAPHIC (July 10, 2012), www.nationalgeographic.com/science/article/120709-arsenic-space-nasa-science-felisa-wolfe-simon.

[28] Robert Sanders, *Creature the Size of a Dust Grain Found Hiding in California's Mono Lake*, U.C. BERKELEY NEWS (Aug. 22, 2024), https://news.berkeley.edu/2024/08/22/creature-the-size-of-a-dust-grain-found-hiding-in-californias-mono-lake/ (last visited Sep. 7, 2024).

[29] Id.

[30] Id.

[31] Id.

Finally, the five freshwater creeks of the Mono Basin that feed the lake with snowmelt from the eastern slope of the Sierra are, themselves, an important part of the local ecology. They provide rich regional fisheries, critical riparian habitat in an otherwise high desert environment, and irreplaceable cultural and sustenance values for the local people.[32]

2. The Indigenous People of the Mono Basin

Mono Lake's fascinating natural history is coupled with its compelling cultural history. It is the ancestral homeland to the southernmost branch of the indigenous Northern Paiute tribe known as the Mono Lake Kootzaduka'a, who have lived there for thousands of years, despite substantial land loss to western settlers.[33] The Kootzaduka'a famously harvest the Mono Lake alkali fly pupae as a staple of their diet, collecting them in large conical woven baskets that they use to skim the flies off the surface of the water.[34] The Kootzaduka'a refer to the alkali flies as "kootsavi," and "Kootzaduka'a" roughly translates as "the eaters of the flies." In the language of the Yokuts, a neighboring tribe to the west, the Kootzaduka'a were known as the "Mono" people.[35] European Americans would come to know the region by the Yokut word for it, rather than the Kootzaduka'a, because they came to the Mono Basin through Yokut territory on the western side of Yosemite.[36]

Traditionally, the Kootzaduka'a shifted seasonally through the different parts of the Mono region where food sources were prevalent at different times of year - food sources that remain culturally important today.[37] In the autumn, they camped in the northern and eastern hills, surviving on the rich stores of pinyon pine nuts.[38] Following the pine nut harvest, they hunted rabbits and pronghorn antelope for food and skins.[39] In the winter, they retreated to the milder, lower valleys east of the lake, surviving on their stores, until they returned in the spring and summer seasons to camp along Rush Creek and Mono's other freshwater feeder streams.[40] There, they harvested kootsavi from the lake and moth larvae from the surrounding Jeffrey pine

---

[32] Mono Basin Creeks: Rush, Parker, Walker, Lee Vining, Mill, MONO BASIN CLEARINGHOUSE, www.monobasinresearch.org/timelines/streams.php (last visited Sept. 27, 2022).

[33] HART, supra note 2, at 22–24 (describing the traditional lifestyle and culture of the Kootzaduka'a); Rep. Cook Seeks Recognition for Mono Lake Kutzadikaa Tribe, MAMMOTH TIMES (Sept. 17, 2020), https://infoweb-newsbank-com.eu1.proxy.openathens.net/apps/news/document-view?p=AWNB&t=pubname%3AMTMM%21Mammoth%2BTimes%2B%2528CA%2529&sort=YMD_date%3AD&fld-base-0=alltext&maxresults=20&val-base-0=Rep.%20Cook%20seeks%20recognition%20for%20Mono%20Lake%20Kutzadikaa%20Tribe&fld-nav-1=YMD_date&val-nav-1=2019%20-%202021&docref=news/17D93A979DA1A9B0.

[34] HART, supra note 2, at 22–24; see also CARLE, supra note 15; Mono Lake Brine Shrimp, supra note 10; Alkali Flies, MONO LAKE COMM., www.monolake.org/about/ecoflies (last visited Sept. 27, 2022).

[35] See CARLE, supra note 15.

[36] Id.

[37] See Mono Basin Kutzadika'a, supra note 10.

[38] Id.

[39] Id.

[40] Id.

forests, gathered roots and berries, and hunted waterfowl and seasonal game.[41] It is estimated that nearly 200 Kootzaduka'a were living in the Mono Basin when the first European Americans arrived.[42]

The Kootzaduka'a have long advocated for the preservation of the lake that is so central to their culture, and they have been steadily seeking federal recognition for their tribe and their lands since the 1970s.[43] In 2002, the Lee Vining Indian and Community Center opened just west of the lake, providing resources to support the Mono Lake Kootzaduka'a Indian Community Cultural Preservation Association.[44] In 2020, Mono County Rep. Paul Cook introduced a bill to Congress to recognize their claims, followed by a similar bill by Rep. Kevin Kiley in 2025. In 2020, Cook argued that the Kootzaduka'a "were not the beneficiary of the treaty process, and they remained landless and without federal protection in the wake of the California Gold Rush and other encroachments into their ancestral lands," but that despite these challenges, they "have remained politically and culturally distinct, living continuously near Mono Lake since time immemorial."[45]

Charlotte Lange, the leader of the Mono Lake Kootzaduka'a Tribe, responded to the effort with a mix of gratitude, frustration, and resolve: "The Mono Lake Kootzaduka'a Tribe has been enduring the process of recognition for decades. It saddens my heart to hear our elders say, 'I won't see it in my lifetime.' My grandfather fought for the tribe and his strength keeps my dedication to follow in his path."[46] She and her fellow tribe members continue to advocate for their cause, though at the time this book goes to press, neither bill has been acted on.

3. *European Settlement of the Basin*

Indeed, it was the California Gold Rush that brought the first European Americans to the Mono Basin. In the early 1850s, a group organized by United States Army Lieutenant Tredwell Moore were reportedly the first westerners to arrive at Mono Lake.[47] They encountered the Basin from the west while pursuing Chief Tenaya and several men from the Awahnichi tribe across the Sierra Nevada, near what is now Yosemite National Park.[48]

---

[41] *Id.*

[42] *Id.*

[43] *See* MAMMOTH TIMES, *supra* note 33 (reporting on efforts by Mono County's congressional representative to extend federal recognition to the tribe); H.R.5820 – Mono Lake Kootzaduka'a Tribe Recognition Act (introduced Oct. 24, 2025 to 119th Congress (2025–26)), https://www.congress.gov/bill/119th-congress/house-bill/5820/text/ih (more recent effort, sponsored by Rep. Kevin Kiley).

[44] *Mono Basin Kutzadika'a, supra* note 10.

[45] MAMMOTH TIMES, *supra* note 33.

[46] *Id.*

[47] Pioneers & Miners, MONO LAKE COMM., www.monolake.org/about/prospectors (last visited Oct. 21, 2022); Historical Landmarks in the Mono Basin, MONO BASIN CLEARINGHOUSE, www.monobasinresearch.org/historical/landmarks.php (last visited Oct. 21, 2022).

[48] *See Historical Landmarks in the Mono Basin, supra* note 47.

Two of Moore's prospectors were brothers Leroy and Thomas Vining, both former Texas Rangers and veterans of the Mexican War.[49] As Mono Lake ranger David Carle tells the story in his written account, the Vining brothers headed to California after the war ended to seek their fortunes in gold.[50] They eventually reached Sonora, where they were soon indicted for murder, along with ten other men, after a man was killed and several others wounded in a mine uprising.[51] Most of the accused fled to evade capture, and not long after that, the Vining brothers arrived in the Mono Basin.[52]

Leroy Vining never did find his fortune in gold, but he did find another way to profit from the Gold Rush.[53] There were no minerals of value in the Mono Basin, even though a successful mine exploded just north of the Mono Basin at Bodie, which would come to host a boomtown population of 10,000 miners at its height.[54] But Vining recognized the value of the Jeffrey pine forests to the south of the lake, as well as the navigational value of the lake for transporting goods north to the successful gold mine at Bodie. Perhaps most importantly, he recognized the invaluable freshwater resources in the basin, which, among other things, enabled small-scale agriculture. He established a ranch and a sawmill along one of Mono Lake's feeder creeks, hosting travelers, transporting logs for construction at Bodie, and growing vegetables for miners weary of the monotony of pork and beans.[55]

That creek, Lee Vining Creek, would eventually come to bear his name, as would the small town settlement that grew up around his ranch. But he would never live to know it, as the town was named in his honor only after his accidental death from a gunshot wound to the groin.[56] No one is completely clear on how it happened, but one account suggests that Vining, who enjoyed carrying a small Deringer pistol in his front pocket, may have shot himself while drinking in a saloon in Aurora.[57] When the gun went off, Vining and all the customers fled the saloon, and Vining was later found dead on the street, having bled to death from the wound.[58]

Today, Bodie is no more than a ghost town, though strikingly preserved by the desert climate as a California state park, remembering the many such Gold Rush boom towns that had been. By contrast, Lee Vining continues to sport a year-round population and has developed into an international tourist destination, especially for nature enthusiasts. Tourists come from all over the world to visit the lake itself

---

[49] David Carle, *Ghosts, Sagebrush and the History of Lee Vining*, THE SHEET (Sept. 24, 2012), https://thesheetnews.com/2012/09/24/ghosts-sagebrush-and-the-history-of-lee-vining/.
[50] *Id.*
[51] *Id.* (discussing the Holden Garden Riot).
[52] *Id.*
[53] *See Pioneers & Miners, supra* note 47.
[54] HART, *supra* 2, at 24–25.
[55] Mono Basin History Overview, MONO BASIN HIST. MUSEUM, www.monobasinhistory.org/history (last visited Sept. 27, 2022).
[56] *See Pioneers & Miners, supra* note 47.
[57] *Id.*
[58] *Id.*

and the Great Basin desert to the east, Yosemite National Park and the surrounding Sierra wilderness areas to the west, the Mammoth Mountain ski area and the Long Valley Caldera to the south, and Lake Tahoe and Reno, Nevada to the north.[59]

4. The Modern Mono Basin Economy

Most of the people who now call the Mono Basin home live in the tiny hamlet of Lee Vining, still nestled at 6,781 feet alongside the western shore of the lake at the base of the Inyo-Sierra Crest.[60] With the three mountain passes leading into the town from the north, west, and south closed more than half the year, only 315 people made it their year-round home when I lived there in the mid 1990s. When the local 1950s-style burger stand in the center of town, the "Mono Cone," opened for business at the start of the summer season, it was the equivalent of a local holiday.

There are limited economic opportunities in the Mono Basin. When I lived there, the holy grail of Lee Vining residence was a year-round job with benefits (rather than, say, a seasonal job with the June and Mammoth Lake ski resorts in towns further south), and they were few and far between. As in most towns, Lee Vining residents work for the public schools, the local electric utility, the state highway department, one or two small stores and restaurants, and a few gas stations and hotels. Other employment comes from the three primary sources of local industry, all drawing on the bounty of unique natural resources in the area.

The first source of industry is the local volcanic range. The Mono Craters are a rich source of pumice – a commercially valuable lightweight volcanic rock used in landscaping, gardens, and foot stones – and there is a productive pumice mine to the south of Mono Lake.[61] There is also a brine shrimp processing plant on the west side of the lake, which harvests Mono Lake brine shrimp as commercial fish food.[62] In the days of the Gold Rush, the Jeffrey pine forests southeast of the Mono Lake were harvested for timber to build Bodie, and the lake was used to transport building materials.[63] There are still one or two sheep ranches in the area.

---

[59] *See, e.g.*, Robert Reid, *Top 10 US Travel Destinations for 2013*, LONELY PLANET (Dec. 25, 2012), www.lonelyplanet.com/articles/top-10-us-travel-destinations-for-2013 (describing points of interest in the Eastern Sierra region of California); *see also* Mammoth Facts: Town of Mammoth Lakes Fact Sheet, TOWN OF MAMMOTH LAKES, www.townofmammothlakes.ca.gov/DocumentCenter/View/571/Mammoth-Facts (last visited Sept. 27, 2022) (noting the nearby town of Mammoth Lakes receives an average of 2.8 million visitors every year).

[60] *See* Lee Vining, California, CITY-DATA.COM, www.city-data.com/city/Lee-Vining-California.html (last visited Oct. 21, 2022).

[61] *See* U.S. Pumice Mine and Mill (U.S. Pumice & Supply Co.), Panum Crater, Mono Craters, Mono Co., California, USA, MINDAT.ORG, www.mindat.org/loc-83387.html (last visited Oct. 21, 2022).

[62] Nat'l Audubon Soc'y v. Super. Ct., 658 P.2d 709, 726–27 (Cal. 1983); *Mono Lake Brine Shrimp, supra* note 10 ("A small portion of Mono Lake brine shrimp are harvested by the High Sierra Brine Shrimp company and are processed to sell as food for tropical fish or commercial prawns.").

[63] HART, *supra* note 2, at 24–25 (describing the construction of Bodie).

Today, however, the largest regional industry is provided by the national and state public lands in the area, which draw hundreds of thousands of visitors from all around the world.[64] Most of the area has been designated for protection within the Inyo National Forest as the Mono Basin National Forest Scenic Area, the first National Forest lands set aside by Congress with a conservation management directive.[65] Since then, several others have been designated, including the Columbia River Gorge National Forest Scenic Area in Oregon.[66] Parts of the basin have also been set aside as the Mono Lake Tufa State Natural Reserve, a California State Park.[67] Mono County maintains a municipal park on the north shore of the lake, and other basin lands are separately conserved by private parties.[68] Visitors to the area hike, fish, camp, canoe, climb, ski, bird watch, photograph, and otherwise enjoy the ample natural amenities – and, seasonally, fill the local restaurants, hotels, and shops.[69]

The Mono Basin is well-loved by naturalists, scientists, recreationalists, local tribes, other local residents, and visitors from around the world. For these reasons, the Mono Basin was once considered for designation within the National Park Service as a National Monument or an annex to Yosemite, but the idea could not survive local opposition because it would have required the discontinuation of all commercial extraction, including the local pumice mine and brine shrimp plant.[70] Even so, I was unofficially told, Yosemite Park managers still itch to acquire Lee Vining Canyon – the beautiful passageway along Highway 120 that dives from the eastern tip of Yosemite over Tioga Pass at 10,000 feet, and then extends nail-bitingly along granite cliffs past alpine Saddlebag and Ellery lakes, unfolding into the rolling meadows and canyons of the upper Mono Basin glacial moraines.[71]

Strikingly, the United States Census reported that the population had dwindled from 315 in 1990 to 222 by 2010, and to 217 by 2020 – a loss of nearly a third of the

---

[64] See Peter Fimrite, *Mono Lake Efforts May Be Undone by Park Closures*, SF GATE (July 24, 2011), www.sfgate.com/green/article/Mono-Lake-efforts-may-be-undone-by-park-closures-2353453.php (describing Lee Vining as a "community that relies on the 271,000 annual visitors who come to the area solely because of [Mono Lake]").

[65] See 16 U.S.C. § 543 (2012).

[66] U.S. GEN. ACCT. OFF., NATIONAL FORESTS: SPECIAL RECREATION AREAS NOT MEETING ESTABLISHED OBJECTIVES 9 (1990), www.gao.gov/assets/150/148579.pdf.

[67] Mono Lake Tufa State Natural Reserve, CAL. DEP'T OF PARKS & RECREATION www.parks.ca.gov/?page_id=514 (last visited Sept. 27, 2022).

[68] HART, *supra* note 2, at 7. See also Press Release, Eastern Sierra Land Trust, Permanent Protection of Mono Lake Scenic Vista Draws Applause, www.eslt.org/wp-content/uploads/2017/03/Yednock-Press-Release.pdf (last visited Feb. 13, 2023) (describing the donation of a 480-acre conservation easement in Mono Basin).

[69] Activities, MONO LAKE COMM., www.monolake.org/visit/activities (last visited Sept. 27, 2022).

[70] See HART, *supra* note 2, at 92 (discussing efforts to designate the Mono Basin as a National Monument); *see also* Author communications with U.S. Forest Service supervisors (1996–1998) (on file with author).

[71] Author communications with U.S. Forest Service supervisors (1996–1998) (on file with author).

population over the two intervening decades.[72] This may be related to a budgetary decision by the U.S. Forest Service to close the year-round Mono Basin Scenic Area Visitor Center, where interpretive rangers like me once introduced the cultural and natural history of the area to visitors from around the world. The loss of the Visitor Center may have reduced the number of tourists visiting the area, spending fewer of the tourist dollars that supported the small local hospitality industry, which had offered employment to additional local and seasonal residents. It may also be related to the closure of the Mono Craters pumice mine, which employed local residents independently of the tourist economy.

B. ACQUIRING THE MONO BASIN WATER RIGHTS

It was in the post-Gold Rush, prestate and national conservation days that Los Angeles arrived in the 1930s, looking to expand supply for the aqueduct. The freshwater creeks of the Mono Basin would provide ample supply and, like the Owens Valley, all by gravity-powered conveyance. Indeed, the Mono Basin lies at an even higher elevation than the Owens Valley, with corresponding advantages. As an added benefit, it was estimated that diverting the Mono creeks through the Owens River Gorge would enable the city to generate some 268 million kilowatt hours of power annually – more than offsetting the 186 million kilowatt hours it would ultimately take to bring water to the city from the Colorado River each year.[73] With all this in mind, the city concluded that it should acquire rights to divert from Mono Lake's feeder creeks, just as it had done to acquire the waters of Owens River – but this time, Los Angeles took a different approach.

1. *1940: The Mono Basin Extension*

In many respects, the Mono Basin Extension was an easier project than the original Owens Valley aqueduct had been. Most of the flow in the freshwater Mono Basin creeks had never been privately appropriated,[74] so from the perspective of California water allocation law, it was there for Los Angeles' taking. The traditional approach assigned no protectable rights to instream flows, so the fact that this snowmelt had long been preserving the Mono Lake ecosystem had no legal force under the doctrine of prior appropriations.[75]

---

[72] Lee Vining CDP, California, U.S. CENSUS BUREAU, https://data.census.gov/cedsci/profile?g=1600000US0640998 (last visited Sept. 27, 2022).
[73] GARY D. LIBECAP, OWENS VALLEY REVISITED: A REASSESSMENT OF THE WEST'S FIRST GREAT WATER TRANSFER 133 (2007).
[74] *See* Nat'l Audubon Soc'y v. Super. Ct., 658 P.2d 709, 711 (Cal. 1983) (explaining that the five freshwater streams had historically been Mono Lake's main source of water prior to being appropriated by the city's Department of Water and Power).
[75] *See* Chapter 1(C)(2) ("Prior Appropriations") (discussing the law of prior appropriations).

In addition, the Mono Basin was never as developed as the Owens Valley had been, so there were fewer prior rights holders to contend with. Most preexisting claims were riparian rights associated with adjacent real property, so the city simply sought to purchase the land.[76] The aqueduct had now been operating for decades, so there was neither mystery nor chicanery about the process. When Los Angeles came looking for land and water rights in the Mono Basin, nobody pretended to be a farmer. Instead, the city simply offered to buy riparian land and water rights, underscored by an open threat of condemnation if offers were refused.[77] In fact, most owners sold willingly, although a few holdouts had to concede or lower their asking prices after the city brought consolidated eminent domain proceedings against all Basin landowners.[78]

Nevertheless, creating the Mono Basin Extension introduced one new challenge. California water law had developed over the intervening decades, so this time, Los Angeles had to do more to secure its rights before it could begin withdrawals. In 1913, California enacted the Water Commission Act, which required permits for all newly asserted rights to unappropriated waters and all transfers of previously acquired water rights.[79] All rights acquired before 1914 were grandfathered into the system, and as Los Angeles had secured rights to Owens Valley water before the Los Angeles Aqueduct opened in 1913, it had avoided the formal permitting process.[80]

However, the law now required Los Angeles to establish its rights to previously unappropriated Mono Basin waters by permit.[81] It also needed permits to transfer the preexisting rights it acquired for new, out-of-basin purposes.[82] Under the appropriative system, a user can't just take existing water rights and do something wholly different with them – creating new patterns of return flow and other potentially negative impacts on downstream riparians and appropriators.[83] The California State Water Resources Control Board (Water Board) must first verify that the new purpose

---

[76] See HART, *supra* note 2, at 39–40 (describing how Los Angeles acquired land and water rights); *see also* City of Los Angeles v. Aitken, 52 P.2d 585 (Cal. Dist. Ct. App.1935) (litigating just compensation for the related condemnation of Mono Basin property).

[77] HART, *supra* note 2, at 38–39. *See also* Andrew H. Sawyer, Changing Landscape and Evolving Law: Lessons from Mono Lake on Takings and the Public Trust, 50 OKLA. L. REV. 311, 323–24 (1997) (describing methods of water rights acquisition by the Los Angeles Department of Water and Power); LIBECAP, *supra* note 73, at 132–44 (reporting in detail on the acquisition of the Mono Basin water rights). Professor Libecap provides an account of the negotiations between Los Angeles and Owens Valley farmers that casts the city in a more favorable light.

[78] *Aitken*, 52 P.2d at 585 (consolidated condemnation proceedings for Mono Basin property); *see also* LIBECAP, *supra* note 73, at 133–34 (describing the *Aitken* litigation).

[79] See Brian E. Gray, The Modern Era in California Water Law, 45 HASTINGS L.J. 249, 273–75 (1994).

[80] *Id.* at 274–75.

[81] See William R. Attwater & James Markle, Overview of California Water Rights and Water Quality Law, 19 PAC. L.J. 957, 972–73 (1988) (noting that the Water Commission Act required permits to establish new rights in previously unappropriated water).

[82] *See id.*

[83] *See* Chapter 1(C)(2) ("Prior Appropriations") (discussing the law of prior appropriations).

is an eligible beneficial use, and then it has to figure out where the appropriation will lie in the chain of temporal priority.[84]

When Los Angeles had acquired all the necessary rights from previous owners and sought permission from the state to begin diverting water to the aqueduct, water agency personnel were openly troubled about the decision.[85] Staff at the Division of Water Resources (the predecessor to the State Water Rights Board and modern-day Water Board) worried aloud about the impacts these exports would have on the local community and environment.[86] They recalled what happened to the Owens Valley. They knew what similar diversions would mean for the Mono Basin, and it clearly alarmed them. They had no desire to be responsible for turning Mono Lake into another Owen's Dry Lake. Yet without clearer means of constitutional or statutory protection for environmental values, the Division saw no avenue to prevent it.

Agency staff determined that their hands were effectively tied by California water law.[87] California water policy made clear that the task of the agency was to ensure that water was put to beneficial use,[88] and domestic and municipal uses by state residents are the highest of all beneficial uses.[89] "[T]here is apparently nothing that this office can do to prevent it," lamented agency staff.[90] Los Angeles was among the state's largest and most economically important cities,[91] and it sought this water for the most beneficial of possible uses. "This office therefore has no alternative but to dismiss all protests based upon the possible lowering of the water level in Mono Lake," they reluctantly reasoned.[92] The city's agreement to provide a regional fish hatchery also helped persuade the Water Board to allow it to effectively dewater four of the Mono Basin's five main tributary streams below aqueduct diversion dams.[93]

---

[84] *See id.*
[85] *See* Nat'l Audubon Soc'y v. Super. Ct., 658 P.2d 709, 713–14 (Cal. 1983) (discussing the 1940 Water Board decision, which found that "it had to grant the application notwithstanding the harm to public trust uses of Mono Lake").
[86] *Id.* at 714.
[87] *See id.* at 713–14 (discussing the Water Board's finding that it was required to prioritize domestic use above all others).
[88] CAL. CONST. art. X, § 2. ("[T]he general welfare requires that the water resources of the State be put to beneficial use to the fullest extent of which they are capable.").
[89] *See Nat'l Audubon Soc'y*, 658 P.2d at 713–14.
[90] *Id.* at 714.
[91] *See* HART, *supra* note 2, at 31. *See also* Cynthia L. Koehler, Water Rights and the Public Trust Doctrine: Resolution of the Mono Lake Controversy, 22 ECOLOGY L.Q. 541, 577–82 (1995) (describing Los Angeles's potential for growth and success as a prime acquirer of land and water rights of the Mono Basin).
[92] *Nat'l Audubon Soc'y*, 658 P.2d at 714.
[93] LIBECAP, *supra* note 73, at 135–37 (reporting on the Hot Creek fish hatchery agreement). As reported further in Chapter 7 ("The *Mono Lake* Doctrine"), 1953 legislation would later require greater protection for fish habitat that would have changed the city's rights to withdraw, but they remained governed by the 1940s Hot Creek agreement until it was eventually undone by the Mono Lake litigation of the 1970s and 1980s. *Id.*

In 1940, the permits were granted.[94] The Division of Water Resources granted the City of Los Angeles permission to appropriate almost the complete flow of four of the five streams that supply water into Mono Lake.[95] Immediately after receiving these rights, the Department of Water and Power (DWP) erected the infrastructure to divert approximately half of the flow of the four streams into the existing Owens Valley aqueduct.[96] With the opening of a sluice, the Los Angeles Aqueduct formally reached the Mono Basin.[97] It began shunting water from the four creeks south into the upper Owens River, where it could continue through the established pathway to Los Angeles.[98] A new reservoir, Crowley Lake, was built just north of where the Owens River passes through the elongated canyon of the Owens River Gorge.[99]

However, the original infrastructure lacked the capacity to take the entirety of streamflow in the Mono Basin, so the original appropriation didn't include all the available fresh water supply.[100] There were additional engineering complications to overcome – most notably, the Mono Crater volcanic range that extended south from Mono Lake along the path the water would take to reach Crowley. To complete the aqueduct, engineers had to tunnel through eleven miles of dormant volcanoes, and the local lore is that the project had lost a man per mile as workers encountered steam vents and toxic gases – just another indication of how valuable this water was considered to be.[101] So valuable, in fact, that thirty years later, they built a second aqueduct.

2. 1970: *The Second Barrel*

As demand for water in Los Angeles continued to grow (and the legal availability of water from the Colorado River began to shrink[102]), the city realized that it could export even more water from the Mono Basin, if only the system could be modified to accommodate additional flow.[103] To make that happen, DWP essentially built a second aqueduct, resulting in the diversion of nearly all flow in the four intercepted streams.[104]

---

[94] Nat'l Audubon Soc'y, 658 P.2d at 711.
[95] Craig Anthony Arnold, Working out an Environmental Ethic: Anniversary Lessons from Mono Lake, 4 WYO. L. REV. 1, 13 (2004).
[96] Id.
[97] Nat'l Audubon Soc'y, 658 P.2d at 711 (describing how Mono Lake receives water from its feeder streams, of which four out of five were appropriated by Los Angeles).
[98] Id. at 711, 713.
[99] See HART, supra note 2, at 34, 42, 137 (discussing the creation of Crowley Lake, also known as the "Long Valley reservoir").
[100] LIBECAP, supra note 73, at 134 (reporting on this history and noting that LA's failure to fully appropriate stream flows in the Basin became the weakness that allowed Mono Lake advocates to later challenge LA's claims).
[101] See HART, supra note 2, at 43 (discussing the tunnel); TIMOTHY TIERNEY, GEOLOGY OF THE MONO BASIN 51 (2d ed. 2000) (noting the eleven deaths).
[102] Arnold, supra note 95, at 13–14.
[103] HART, supra note 2, at 56.
[104] Id. at 56–57; see also Arnold, supra note 95, at 13–14.

The second barrel increased the capacity of the original system by roughly 50 percent, laying an additional, parallel channel where needed to accommodate increased flow.[105] Following the logic of the original 1940 permits, the Water Board affirmed permission for the additional exports in 1970.[106] By this time, Los Angeles was importing about 100,000 acre-feet of water per year from the Mono Basin, comprising between 15 and 20 percent of its total water supply[107] – supplemented by the California and Colorado River aqueducts that were also in place by that time. In 1974, the Water Board quietly converted the interim permits into permanent permission.[108]

C. THE IMPACTS OF WATER EXPORTS ON THE BASIN

Mono Lake had been slowly declining ever since the arrival of the aqueduct, but when the Second Barrel was installed in 1971, the lake began to decline much more quickly.[109] In 1962, the lake had already lost twenty-five vertical feet from its original elevation before diversions began in the 1940s.[110] After the Second Barrel went in, the lake lost nearly as much height in half the time. By the time of the litigation that followed in the early 1980s, the lake had lost forty-five vertical feet and half of its entire volume to water exports through the aqueduct.[111]

As the lake declined, the famous Mono Lake tufa towers, which develop beneath the surface, became increasingly visible.[112] These otherworldly geologic structures form at the mouth of underground springs, where calcium-rich fresh water meets the carbonates suspended in the alkaline lake water, and gradually precipitate out as calcium carbonate – limestone – in stalagmite-like towers that grow only as high as the water level.[113] As the lake receded, the decline could be marked by how much tufa had become exposed above the surface. One famous cluster of human-height tufa towers near the north shore became known as the "Benchmark" tufa,

---

[105] Nat'l Audubon Soc'y v. Super. Ct., 658 P.2d 709, 714 (Cal. 1983).
[106] The Los Angeles Aqueduct formally opened in 1913. Id. at 713. The California Water Resources Control Board issued its decision implementing the state supreme court's decision in 1994. In the Matter of Amendment of the City of Los Angeles' Water Right Licenses for Diversion of Water from Streams Tributary to Mono Lake (Water Licenses 10191 and 10192, Applications 8042 and 8043) City of Los Angeles, Licensee, 1994 WL 758358, 1, 6 (Cal. State Water Res. Control Bd. 1994) [hereinafter Decision 1631]. *See also* Chapters 2(B) ("The Early 1900s: Tapping the Owens River Valley") and 7(C) ("Ordinary Common Law or Quasi-Constitutional?") (reviewing this history).
[107] Id. ("Annual Mono Basin exports increased to an average of 102,000 acre-feet per year through 1981."); *Nat'l Audubon Soc'y*, 658 P.2d at 714. *See also* HART, *supra* note 2, at 76; WILLIAM L. KAHRL, WATER AND POWER 433 (1983).
[108] JUDITH A. LAYZER, *Making History in the Mono Basin*, *in* NATURAL EXPERIMENTS 233, 237 (2008).
[109] Erin Ryan, *The Public Trust Doctrine, Private Water Allocation, and Mono Lake: The Historic Saga of National Audubon Society v. Superior Court*, 45 ENV'T L. 561, 590, 592–93 (2015) [hereinafter Ryan, *The Historic Saga*].
[110] *See* HART, *supra* note 2, at 49, 51.
[111] *Mono Lake Facts*, *supra* note 3.
[112] *See* HART, *supra* note 2, at 50–51.
[113] Id.

because they provided a useful visual benchmark of Mono Lake's disappearance.[114] In 1962, when the lake had lost twenty-five vertical feet, the tops of the Benchmark Tufa were just beginning to appear over the surface. By 1968, they were exposed at the base, on a tiny island of "relicted" (exposed) lakebed near the water's edge. By 1995, after twenty years of augmented exports through the Second Barrel, the Benchmark Tufa would stand bone dry, a mile from the new shoreline of the shrunken lake.[115]

The falling lake level also caused formidable air quality problems for the region, as lakebed that had been submerged for millennia became increasingly exposed, and the tiny hazardous particulates that had collected at the bottom became airborne in the fierce eastern Sierra Nevada winds.[116] The bed of Mono Lake is similar to the toxic salt flats that were exposed after Owens Lake was drained, except that Mono Lake is much more alkaline because it has been accumulating mineral deposits for exponentially more time.

Satellite photos from 1968 show the pronounced ring of white, exposed alkali flats that encircled the lake like a ring of bathtub soap scum after the first two decades of water diversions – a ring that appeared to double in size by 1983, after the Second Barrel had gone in.[117] Like Owens Lake, Mono Lake sits at the base of a dramatic 10,000-foot escarpment along the Eastern Sierra, where high winds ricochet off the mountainsides and churn exposed salts into airborne, cancer-causing dust storms. Pollution hadn't yet reached the critical levels recorded in the Owens Valley, but Mono is so much more saline than Owens that the potential public health implications were concerning.[118] As detailed further in Chapter 5, the Mono Basin National Forest Scenic Area that Congress would eventually establish – for its extraordinary scenic, ecological, and recreational values – would periodically violate Clean Air Act particulate standards, testifying to the local peril.[119]

At the same time, the decreasing amount of water in Mono Lake caused enormous problems for its ecosystem. When the lake lost half its water volume to unreplenished evaporation, that caused the salinity of the remaining lake water to double.[120] The sharply increased salinity placed stress on the brine shrimp, who had long thrived in the lake.[121] Their reproductive rate slowed down, threatening the simple Mono Lake ecosystem and portending impacts for the millions of birds

---

[114] Id.
[115] See Ryan, The Historic Saga, supra note 109, at 600.
[116] See HART, supra note 2, at 52–54.
[117] See image from L.A. Dep't of Water & Power (1962) (on file with author).
[118] Michael Blumm & Thea Schwartz, Mono Lake and the Evolving Public Trust in Western Water, 37 ARIZ. L. REV. 701 (1995) (describing Mono Lake's unique level of salinity).
[119] HART, supra note 2, at 154–55.
[120] Id. at 69.
[121] My own memory is that some began to change color, turning slightly reddish, possibly indicating parasitic infections to which they had become more vulnerable under stress.

C. The Impacts of Water Exports on the Basin

who came to the lake for nourishment during their long migratory journeys.[122] Negit Island, the small black volcano that had been the historic breeding ground for California gulls, became bridged to the north shore, exposing the gulls to the coyotes that regularly decimated the new chick populations.[123] The National Guard attempted to breach the land bridge with dynamite to help the gulls – twice – but it failed both times.[124] The mountain creeks were desiccated below the diversion points, destroying critical freshwater fisheries and riparian habitat.[125]

By 1979, the Mono Lake feeder streams were providing up to 20 percent of Los Angeles' municipal water supply, and negative impacts in and around the lake were accelerating.[126] As the lake dropped, its surface area shrunk to one-third of its pre-diversion size.[127] Between 1940 and 1970, Los Angeles had diverted an average of 57,067 acre-feet of water per year from the Mono Basin, causing the lake to drop an average of 1.1 feet per year.[128] Between 1970 and 1980, construction of the Second Barrel enabled DWP to almost double diversions to an average of 99,580 acre-feet per year.[129] Over the forty-year span from 1940 to 1980, these diversions caused Mono Lake to decrease in area from 85 square miles to 60.3 square miles, and its surface level dropped from 6,416 feet above sea level to 6,373 feet above sea level.[130] In 1985, the New York Times reported that diversions were supplying about 17 percent of Los Angeles' water, which had lowered the lake's elevation by 43 feet from 1941 to 1981.[131] Between 1982 and 1984, exceedingly wet winters gave the lake a reprieve to rejuvenate, raising the lake level to 6,379 feet above sea level – but even that was thirty-eight feet lower than its pre-diversion level in 1941.[132]

By the mid 1970s, the disappearing lake, struggling wildlife, declining air quality, and other threats to the region had reached a tipping point. The environmental problems that accompanied Mono Lake's decline created serious challenges for the local community, including economic losses, threats to public health, and general impacts to quality of life.[133] Gradually at first, but with accelerating pace, people began to act. As it became increasingly clear that the Mono Basin ecosystem – and

---

[122] See HART, *supra* note 2, at 69 (discussing shrimp reproductive issues).

[123] *Id.* at 72, 88.

[124] See *id.* (describing attempts to breach the Negit land bridge in 1978 and 1979).

[125] *Id.* at 54–56; Blumm & Schwartz, *supra* note 118, at 717–18.

[126] Arnold, *supra* note 95, at 13; KAHRL, *supra* note 107. See also E-mail from Bartshe Miller, Education Director, Mono Lake Committee, to Mallory Neumann, Research Assistant to Dean Erin Ryan (Oct. 19, 2017, 02:38 EST) (on file with author) (noting that the amount of water diverted to Los Angeles was not precisely fixed but confirming that the range 12–20 percent would be generally correct).

[127] Nat'l Audubon Soc'y v. Super. Ct., 658 P.2d 709, 711 (Cal. 1983).

[128] *Id.* at 714.

[129] *Id.*

[130] *Id.*

[131] Concern Voiced on Shrinking California Lake, N.Y. TIMES (Sept. 29, 1985) www.nytimes.com/1985/09/29/us/concern-voiced-on-shrinking-california-lake.html.

[132] Arnold, *supra* note 95, at 14.

[133] Ryan, *The Historic Saga*, *supra* note 109, at 597–98.

all the communities that depend upon it – were on the brink of collapse, a concerned group of scientists, environmentalists, landowners, and other local citizens decided to fight back. As detailed in Chapter 5, they banded together to form a local grassroots advocacy group – the Mono Lake Committee – to campaign for the protection and restoration of Mono Lake, ideally without transferring the same environmental problems to another remote watershed.[134] This unlikely coalition of resistance gathered force, hailing from very different corners of the community, but joined with one goal in mind: to Save Mono Lake.

The Mono Lake Committee would operate on many levels to save the lake, and one of the avenues they pursued was the litigation detailed in Chapter 5, which would change not only the fate of Mono Lake, but the force of the public trust doctrine worldwide. Ultimately, the Mono Lake advocates would center their lawsuit on an idea inspired by an academic article, authored in 1970 by law professor Joseph Sax.[135] In the pages of the Michigan Law Review, Joe Sax was the first to recognize that the public trust doctrine could require the protection of environmental values associated with navigable waterways[136] (and his later scholarship would recognize it as a potential source of environmental rights).[137] His foundational insight – that state sovereign authority over navigable waterways could also imply sovereign responsibility for environmental protection – was entirely new at the time, but it would soon change the landscape of natural resource management and water governance in California, and beyond.

Translating that insight into actual governance required a journey of many steps, taken by many individuals throughout the political process, but it started – as good ideas so often do – with a handful of creative and ambitious young people.

---

[134] Saving Mono Lake, MONO LAKE COMM., www.monolake.org/learn/aboutmonolake/savingmonolake/ (last visited Sept. 27, 2022).

[135] Joseph Sax, The Public Trust Doctrine in Natural Resource Law: Effective Judicial Intervention, 68 MICH. L. REV. 471 (1970).

[136] Id. I always make this point when teaching the Mono Lake case to law review editors – and especially the most beleaguered ones – to remind them that what they are doing really is important, because law review articles really can change the world!

[137] Joseph L. Sax, The Search for Environmental Rights, 6 J. LAND USE & ENV'T L. 93, 93 (1990); see also Chapter 10(B)(3)(a) ("Philosophical Duality or False Dichotomy?") (discussing Sax's later arguments about the public trust doctrine as a source of environmental rights).

4

Saving Mono Lake

The Political Mobilization

A. For the Love of Place: Science Begets Activism   102
B. A Coalition of Resistance: The Mono Lake Committee Forms   105
C. The Rural–Urban Partnership: MLC Reaches Out to Angelenos   108
D. Joseph Sax and the Power of a Good Idea   110
E. The Path to Litigation   116

As environmental devastation in the Mono Basin gathered speed, local resistance gathered force.[1] Students and scientists who studied the unique geologic and biological resources in the area raised the alarm of impending ecologic collapse.[2] Residents feared both for their health and their livelihoods, as water exports eroded the lake at the center of their increasingly public lands-based tourist economy.[3] Gradually, a coalition of locals, students, scientists, birders, fishers, hunters, lawyers, politicians, and government agency staff coalesced around the idea that something had to be done.[4]

This chapter explores how that unlikely coalition joined together to mobilize political support for limiting water exports to preserve Mono Lake. While the precedent set by the Mono Lake litigation often garners the most attention, that decision would not have been possible without the political advocacy that preceded and simultaneously accompanied it.[5] This chapter reviews the origins of the Mono Lake

---

[1] For a beautiful and more detailed narrative of the roots of the advocacy movement at Mono Lake, see generally JOHN HART, STORM OVER MONO (Univ. of Cal. Press, 1996).
[2] *Id.* at 61–63 (describing how scientists of various fields demonstrated concern for Mono Lake).
[3] *Id.* at 52–54, 58–59 (discussing the dust storms and the increased tourism in the valley).
[4] For the most thorough historical account of scientific, political, and legal advocacy at Mono Lake, see generally HART, *supra* note 1. For a discussion of the different advocates on the eve of litigation, see *id.* at 61–83. For a description of the legal research produced by Professor Harrison Dunning's pivotal public trust doctrine conference in 1980 at U.C. Davis, see *id.* at 101.
[5] See generally Craig Anthony Arnold & Leigh A. Jewel, *Litigation's Bounded Effectiveness and the Real Public Trust Doctrine: The Aftermath of the Mono Lake Case*, 14 HASTINGS W. NW. J. ENV'T L. & POL'Y 1177 (2008); Craig Anthony Arnold, *Working out an Environmental Ethic: Anniversary Lessons from Mono Lake*, 4 WYO. L. REV. 14 (2004) [hereinafter *Working out an Environmental Ethic*].

advocacy movement, the founding of the Mono Lake Committee, and the strategic legal and political choices that Mono Lake's advocates made in laying the necessary foundation for the California Supreme Court's famous decision.

As legal advocates mulled and then initiated litigation to protect the Mono Basin, political advocates worked diligently to generate public interest in the issue and engage the political process by other means. The Mono Lake Committee launched a statewide campaign to "Save Mono Lake," peppering California with awareness-raising and bumper stickers,[6] while simultaneously cultivating relationships with the Los Angelenos who relied directly on exported Mono Basin water.[7] Committee volunteers strategically focused on L.A. communities of color, rather than easier-sold environmentalists in the Bay Area.[8] They made it their project to connect with inner-city community groups, even creating an outdoor education program that brought local children to the Mono Basin to see for themselves where their water came from, and why they should care about it.[9] This political groundwork created the local support that would later facilitate compliance with the mandates resulting from judicial and agency process.[10]

Finally, the campaign to save Mono Lake drew inspiration from a good idea, published by a legal scholar and championed by a student several years later and thousands of miles away. When other sources of environmental law proved unavailing, the advocates turned to the public trust doctrine for help – buttressed by previous trust litigation incrementally establishing the precedent that would enable the California high court's decision in the case that would follow. In the end, the combined strategy of public education, political pressure, and strategic litigation shifted public attitudes in favor of environmental protection at Mono Lake, enabling not only favorable treatment in court but ultimately compliance with judicially and agency mandated remedies.[11] In recounting that history, this chapter follows the progression of the public trust idea along its journey to the Mono Lake decision, buoyed by the political groundswell alongside it.

A. FOR THE LOVE OF PLACE: SCIENCE BEGETS ACTIVISM

The eclectic group who would lead the campaign to Save Mono Lake shared more differences than they held in common, but they were touchingly united by a

---

[6] Jane Kay, *It's Rising and Healthy: Three Decades Ago, a Bunch of College Students Reported on and Worried About the Fate of Mono Lake. This Month, They Celebrated Its Recovery.*, SF GATE (July 29, 2006), www.sfgate.com/green/article/it-s-rising-and-healthy-three-decades-ago-a-2515840.php.

[7] Kevin Roderick, *SELLING A LAKE: Tenacious Mono Backers Use Sophisticated Tactics to Beat DWP to its Knees*, L.A. TIMES (Sept. 24, 1989), www.latimes.com/archives/la-xpm-1989-09-24-mn-277-story.html.

[8] Judith A. Layzer, *Making History in the Mono Basin*, in NATURAL EXPERIMENTS: ECOSYSTEM-BASED MANAGEMENT AND THE ENVIRONMENT 239 (2008).

[9] See id.

[10] Id.

[11] See generally id. at 233–66.

common theme: true love. Each of them, in various ways and under different circumstances, had fallen head over heels in love with the Mono Basin. (Indeed, it is a feeling that most of us who have lived in the Basin know all too well.[12])

Kenneth Lajoie, a geology graduate student at UC Berkeley, fell in love with the Mono Basin while conducting research there for his doctoral dissertation.[13] In 1974, he formed a Mono Lake Task Force through the regional Sierra Club to advocate for halting the stream diversions that were drawing down Mono Lake.[14] The Task Force drew participation from a number of concerned lake advocates, including a young college student by the name of Tim Such (who would play a key role later on in the story).[15] At the time, Inyo County was already suing Los Angeles over groundwater withdrawals from the Owens Valley, and Lajoie was successful in persuading the County (and ultimately a reviewing court) that a full accounting of Los Angeles' water exports should also address withdrawals in the Mono Basin.[16]

At around the same time, a young ornithologist by the name of David Gaines was falling in love with Mono Lake while performing a biological inventory of Mono County for the California Natural Areas Coordinating Council.[17] In 1975, Gaines spent a year researching birds at Mono Lake while shifting between professional responsibilities at UC Davis and Stanford.[18] Gaines, who originally hailed from Los Angeles, must have been aware of his various connections with Mono Lake.[19] In 1976, he helped form the Mono Basin Research Group after he and a few friends secured a federal research grant for scientific study in the Mono Basin.[20] As the senior member of the group, he helped oversee a team of twelve undergraduate researchers documenting the regional ecology and, eventually, the declining environmental conditions there.[21]

In researching area wildlife, the team performed the first ever Bird Census at Mono Lake, which provided official documentation of the critical habitat the Lake

---

[12] See, e.g., ERIN RYAN, Sierra Stars, on THE ERIN RYAN COLLECTION, VOL 3: BOOTLEGS (WW&C Publishing, 1996), https://archive.org/details/TheErinRyanCollectionVolume3Bootlegs/3-11SierraStars.mp3 (Track 11, a love song to the Mono Basin).

[13] HART, supra note 1, at 62–63.

[14] Id.

[15] See Chapter 4(E) ("The Path to Litigation").

[16] HART, supra note 1, at 62–63. Antonio "Tony" Rossman, then special counsel to Inyo County, agreed to include discussion of the effects of Mono Basin water diversions in the lawsuit. Id. See also Cnty. of Inyo v. City of L.A., 61 Cal. App. 3d 91, 93–94 (1976) (requiring Los Angeles to prepare an environmental impact report in compliance with the California Environmental Quality Act because the proposed extraction increase was a "project" under the meaning of the Act and indicating that all related water withdrawals should be analyzed together).

[17] HART, supra note 1, at 66; Arnold, Working out an Environmental Ethic, supra note 5, at 14.

[18] HART, supra note 1, at 66.

[19] Cf. id. at 77–78.

[20] Id. at 66.

[21] Id.

provided for countless individuals and species of migratory birds.[22] Among other discoveries, they found that Negit Island, the black cindercone near the north shore of the lake, was home to the second largest known breeding colony of *Larus californicus*, or California Gulls, in the world.[23]

Yet assessing the importance of the lake to these bird populations forced the researchers to consider what would happen if the Lake continued to decline. For example, a spit of land was becoming gradually exposed between the north shore and Negit Island, bringing the California Gull nesting area within perilous reach of predation by coyotes. In 1976, the emerging land bridge was under a mere three feet of water at the deepest point.[24] Just as budding ornithologist David Winkler was falling in love with Mono Lake's *Larus californicus* population, he realized that in just a few years it would be decimated by predators, potentially irrevocably.[25]

Moreover, as Mono Lake continued to evaporate without replenishment by its diverted feeder streams, it left behind increasing concentrations of dissolved minerals.[26] The increasing salinity of the lake water threatened the populations of alkali flies and brine shrimp near the base of the Mono Basin food chain, threatening migratory birds and other wildlife populations.[27] After falling in love with Mono Lake's unique species of brine shrimp, Gayle Dana would become the preeminent expert on *Artemia monica*, while David Herbst's love story led him to become a world expert on the *Ephydra hians* alkali flies that fringe the Mono Lake shallows.[28] To assess the impacts of continued water diversions, the researchers scientifically projected the likely course of the lake's decline and how this would affect the chemistry of the water, the topography of the basin, the fortitude of the wildlife, and the sustainability of the overall ecosystem.[29]

In the end, David Winkler authored the resulting research project, which reported on the sobering effects of Los Angeles' diversions on Mono Lake[30] and provided a galvanizing force for the opposition.[31] If Los Angeles continued to export 100,000 acre-feet of water from the Mono Basin creeks annually, the Lake was expected to lose another forty-three vertical feet and twenty square miles of surface area over

---

[22] *Id.* at 67–68.
[23] *Id.* at 68. Only the breeding colony at the Great Salt Lake in Utah was larger. *Id.*
[24] HART, *supra* note 1, at 68.
[25] *Id.*
[26] DAVID W. WINKLER, JEFFERSON B. BURCH, & DAVID B. HERBST, AN ECOLOGICAL STUDY OF MONO LAKE, CALIFORNIA 2–3 (Inst. of Ecology Publication, No. 12 Univ. of Cali. Davis) (1977 www.monobasinresearch.org/onlinereports/1976study/ecologicalstudyofmonolake.pdf.),
[27] *Id.*
[28] HART, *supra* note 1, at 70–71.
[29] *Id.* at 68–70.
[30] WINKLER, BURCH & HERBST, *supra* note 26.
[31] *See The Origin of the Mono Lake Committee*, MONO LAKE COMM., www.monolake.org/whatwedo/aboutus/missionandhistory/ (last visited Oct. 11, 2022) [hereinafter *MLC History*] ("[The] report drew attention to the potentially catastrophic ecological impacts of Mono Lake's falling level….").

the next eighty to one-hundred years.³² The skyrocketing salinity in the seepage that would continue to pool in the bottom of the Basin would prove unadaptable for native plants and wildlife, and unwelcoming to colonization by others.³³ The forecast predicted that Mono Lake would eventually reach equilibrium as a lifeless, hypersaline sump at the center of a vast and toxic salt plains created by the formerly submerged lakebed.³⁴

The gravity of their report left Gaines, Winkler, and the other individual researchers with a great personal dilemma. As John Hart poignantly recounts this moment in STORM OVER MONO: "One night, staring into a campfire at the Simis Ranch, the Ecological Study group realized that they were on the hook. Their study done, they decided, they could not walk away ... [t]hey would have to make an attempt to save Mono Lake."³⁵ Hart goes on to recount that none of the young scientists was eager to mastermind the revolution that was needed, so they turned, one after another, to existing environmental organizations looking for help.³⁶ All were sympathetic, but none could commit to spearheading the effort.³⁷ Still, the young researchers could not just walk away. By now, each of them had fallen too hopelessly in love.

B. A COALITION OF RESISTANCE: THE MONO LAKE COMMITTEE FORMS

If Mono Lake was to be salvaged, then, it would be left to these advocates to do the heavy lifting. In 1978, David Gaines and David Winkler organized the Mono Lake Committee, an ad hoc grassroots organization committed to saving Mono Lake.³⁸ In the end, it was David Gaines who stepped up to lead.³⁹ He received initial support from the Santa Monica Bay *Audubon Society*, which provided him with early organizational and practical assistance on structuring a formal NGO, but the Mono Lake Committee would soon operate independently.⁴⁰ Together with a handful of other Mono Lake activists, David Gaines and his wife, Sally, launched a David-vs.-Goliath battle to save Mono Lake from disappearing into Los Angeles taps.

When Los Angeles water use fell 19 percent in response to a drought between 1976 and 1977, the positive effect on lake levels made the Committee realized that this was more than the amount of conservation needed to save Mono Lake.⁴¹ Their message

---

[32] Nat'l Audubon Soc'y v. Super. Ct., 658 P.2d 709, 715 (Cal. 1983).
[33] HART, *supra* note 1, at 68–70.
[34] *See Nat'l Audubon Soc'y*, 658 P.2d at 715 (noting that forecasters predicted the lake would stabilize at 6,330 feet, with a surface area of approximately 38 square miles).
[35] HART, *supra* note 1, at 70.
[36] *Id.* at 72.
[37] *Id.*
[38] *Id.* at 71; *see MLC History, supra* note 31.
[39] HART, *supra* note 1, at 72.
[40] *Id.*
[41] *Id.* at 76.

evolved to one of water conservation as the tool to prevent ecological catastrophe. David became so passionate about the cause that he left his teaching job at UC Davis to advocate full time for Mono Lake, lecturing at Sierra Club meetings, *National Audubon Society* chapters, and Lion's Clubs statewide about the declining ecological health of the Basin and the damage being wrought by ongoing diversions to L.A.[42]

The early committee may have operated on a shoestring budget from the proverbial kitchen table, but the group distinguished itself early on by hewing closely to clear principles. They called for the minimum necessary to accomplish their task, and no more. They avoided posturing and attempted to engage in principled problem solving whenever possible. Notably, the Committee's platform called for the restoration of Mono Lake to its 1976 surface elevation, and not to its original surface elevation before water diversions had already lowered the lake by more than thirty vertical feet.[43] The Committee didn't even call for an end to all diversions, as Kenneth Lajoie's Sierra Club group had done – they conscientiously asked only for the minimum necessary to save the lake.[44]

In setting this target, they rejected the learned counsel of more experienced negotiators, who uniformly advised them to ask for more than what they wanted, so that they would have something to concede at the bargaining table.[45] But the fledgling Committee chose their comparatively modest target on principled grounds. Their demand was based in sound science, and science is not something over which one bargains. Instead of playing a game in which you start high and end low, they reasoned, they would start with the right answer – the only right answer – and just stay there forever. This was the level necessary to sustain the Mono Lake ecosystem. That was the best and, indeed, the only justification for their ask.[46]

They were equally principled in their insistence that saving Mono Lake not come at the expense of another watershed elsewhere, and that part of the solution to the Mono Lake problem had to involve helping Los Angelenos adjust to a reduction in their overall water supply.[47] It would have been easier to rescue Mono Lake from the perils of water diversions that would simply be offloaded to another distant watershed, or to leave it to L.A. to solve their water deficit independently, but this they were unwilling to do. They stuck to this principle of a unified solution, even when it was costly for them and politically expedient shortcuts were tempting. For example, in 1979, Assemblyman Norman Waters would call for a halt to streamflow diversions until the surface returned to 6,390 feet, but the Mono Lake Committee

---

[42] Id. at 77; Arnold, *Working out an Environmental Ethic*, supra note 5, at 14.
[43] See HART, *supra* note 1, at 74.
[44] Id.
[45] Id.
[46] Oral communications with author in mid 1990s, Mono Lake Committee staff. *Cf.* HART *supra* note 1, at 74 (describing Sally Gaines' memories of this time); *id.* at 76 (noting that the Committee asked only for the minimum necessary to accomplish their goal).
[47] HART, *supra* note 1, at 76.

would not endorse his proposal because it did not outline any solution to the problem of meeting Los Angeles's resulting need for new water supply.[48]

In 1977, as Committee efforts were getting underway, David Winkler finally walked to Negit Island over the fully emerged land bridge, prompting him to pour his own efforts into saving the California Gull population that he loved.[49] With the help of the *Audubon Society's* Western Regional Office, he lobbied the State of California and the federal Bureau of Land Management for a bold, if temporary, solution to the land bridge problem: dynamite.[50] On March 17 and March 18, 1978, twenty members of the California National Guard blasted a moat across the Negit landbridge using helicopters and high explosives.[51] Nevertheless, coyotes eventually reached Mono Lake breeding islands the following year,[52] and in April of 1979, a second attempt was made to breach the land bridge.[53] The California Department of Fish & Game estimated that fifty million people watched the blasting on the news, but the attempt failed to produce a moat (as most of the detritus simply fell back into position along the bridge), and 75 percent of the gull population failed to nest that year.[54] Similar attempts at a chain-link fence across the landbridge proved no more effective at preventing coyotes from reaching the breeding gulls.[55]

Meanwhile, David and Sally Gaines tirelessly traveled the state, raising awareness about the Mono Lake situation with "schools, conservation groups, legislators, and anyone who would listen"[56] – although they were especially sure to spend time in the two cities with the most influence over Mono Lake's future: Sacramento, the state capital, and Los Angeles.[57] The Mono Lake Committee opened a headquarters and visitor center in Lee Vining near the western shore of the lake and the eastern entrance to Yosemite National Park, where they welcomed the public to learn about the vulnerable environmental resources at stake in the Mono Basin.[58] They began producing T-shirts and bumper stickers emblazoned with "Save Mono Lake" and "I Save Water for Mono Lake," and later "Restore Mono Lake" (and eventually "Long Live Mono Lake"), partnering their intensive campaign to educate the public about the Mono Basin ecosystem with a simple declarative message to which Californians everywhere could lend their support.[59]

---

[48] *Id.* at 84.
[49] *Id.* at 71.
[50] *Id.* at 72–73.
[51] *Id.* at 72–74.
[52] Arnold, *Working out an Environmental Ethic*, *supra* note 5, at 14.
[53] Hart, *supra* note 1, at 88.
[54] *Id.*
[55] *Id.*
[56] *See* MLC History, *supra* note 31.
[57] Hart, *supra* note 1, at 77.
[58] Arnold, *Working out an Environmental Ethic*, *supra* note 5, at 14.
[59] *See* Arnold & Jewel, *supra* note 5, at 16.

All of these efforts helped focus public attention on the problems at Mono Lake. Between 1978 and 1979, the issue received widespread media coverage, appearing in *Smithsonian, Sports Illustrated, National Geographic, Audubon*, and *Outside*, and it even received coverage in German press.[60] (The latter drew a surprising number of German tourists to the Mono Basin, and the rangers often remarked on how much better informed they were about Mono Lake than the average American.) By January of 1979, representatives from all Audubon chapters in California met and chose the plight of Mono Lake as their issue of highest concern.[61] Audubon directors agreed to campaign actively for lake protection, and for the next fifteen years, they fundraised specifically for efforts to protect Mono Lake.[62]

The Committee headquarters eventually attracted a dedicated staff of (mostly) volunteers. They began offering interpretive tours of the lake by foot and canoe, selling books, and producing publications and informational resources (and eventually a website) to provide information about Mono Lake and their fight for its survival. They offered presentations, slide shows, school visits, and other educational programs and activities inviting all Californians to form a personal relationship with the place the Committee was working so hard to protect – a relationship that would inspire visitors, too, to want to Save Mono Lake.

But they also worked hard to establish a presence in parts of the state where residents may have never seen Mono Lake, and especially in southern California areas where residents depended on exported water. Wherever they went, they brought the same message with them, inviting urban and suburban Californians to care about Mono Lake, even if they might never see the lake in person. The tireless and passionate advocacy of the Mono Lake Committee ultimately gained them 20,000 dues-paying members, and far more sympathizers bearing "Save Mono Lake" bumper stickers.[63]

C. THE RURAL–URBAN PARTNERSHIP: MLC REACHES OUT TO ANGELENOS

Despite its humble origins as a grassroots organization, the Mono Lake Committee deployed a sophisticated campaign to build public support for protecting the Mono Basin. The group focused its efforts on the communities of color in Los Angeles who would be directly impacted by a change in water policy, rather than friendlier

---

[60] HART, *supra* note 1, at 79.
[61] *Id.* at 81.
[62] *Id.*
[63] *See Saving Mono Lake*, MONO LAKE COMM., www.monolake.org/learn/aboutmonolake/savingmonolake/ (last visited Feb. 23, 2025) [https://perma.cc/ZJ5R-KMBD]. ("As the Mono Lake Committee got organized, they built their grassroots origins, eventually growing to 20,000 members strong."); *see also* Layzer, *supra* note 8, at 241 (discussing the "Save Mono Lake" bumper sticker campaign).

C. The Rural–Urban Partnership

environmentalists in the San Francisco Bay Area.[64] Even though San Francisco is much closer to the west than Los Angeles is to the south, Committee organizers understood that proximity was not the issue – they had to follow the water. To build support for reduced diversions, they needed to connect with actual people who relied on that water and persuade those people to care enough to consider a change. But they also understood that they could not just lecture these communities about the importance of water conservation and environmental values. They needed to understand what was important to these people first and then look for bridges between these environmental and social justice concerns.

Presaging the environmental justice critique by decades, they worked to educate themselves about the plight of poor urbanites in Los Angeles who relied on Mono Basin water, and to seek solutions that would partner protection for remote watersheds with strategies to meet the water needs of dense urban communities.[65] They joined forces with Mothers of East Los Angeles and other L.A. community organizations to connect environmental issues with broader social justice advocacy, promoting water conservation while advocating for public support to enable poor families to acquire water conserving household technologies, such as low-flush toilets and faucets, which would both reduce pressure on the lake and help low-income families minimize the expense of costly water bills.[66] They launched an Outdoor Experiences educational program for inner city youth from Los Angeles, bringing them to the Mono Basin for a camp-like experience to help them understand not only where their water came from, but also their own relationships to the natural world and the ecological processes with which their lives in urban Los Angeles are nevertheless intertwined.[67]

But the campaign extended beyond Lee Vining and Los Angeles. While it built thick public support for saving Mono Lake, the Committee also tirelessly advocated policy solutions, winning over allies in the state legislature and executive agencies. An Interagency Task Force of state and federal environmental agencies concluded that diversions would need to be reduced to 15,000 acre-feet per year to stabilize the lake,[68] and the Committee convinced their allies to introduce legislation requiring those reductions, though it was never enacted.[69] Still, statewide public sentiment began shifting in their favor. Vehicles all over California began sporting "Save

---

[64] Layzer, *supra* note 8, at 239 (noting that the Committee "set up an office in the city and began hosting programs aimed at urban residents ... emphasiz[ing] their willingness to help L.A. find ways to replace lost Mono Basin water").

[65] HART, *supra* note 1, at 39–40.

[66] Id.

[67] Id. at 40.

[68] INTERAGENCY TASK FORCE ON MONO LAKE, REPORT OF INTERAGENCY TASK FORCE ON MONO LAKE 1–2 (1979); *see also* HART, *supra* note 1, at 88 (describing the report of the Task Force).

[69] HART, *supra* note 1, at 84, 88–89. Earlier legislation inspired by the Owens Valley conflict imposed tighter controls on some out-of-basin water exports, but Los Angeles Aqueduct exports were not subject to these restrictions. *See* GARY LIBECAP, OWENS VALLEY REVISITED: A REASSESSMENT

Mono Lake" bumper stickers.[70] The *National Audubon Society* expressed interest in helping the fledgling Mono Lake Committee bring a lawsuit, and the advocates continued brainstorming legal theories that might support their cause of action.[71]

These community outreach efforts were important both because they engaged community members in organizing on behalf of conservation at the front end of the struggle, but also because they likely facilitated the ultimate acceptance by Los Angeles city leaders of the Water Board's decision to reduce the water it could take from Mono Lake when it eventually applied the Supreme Court's ruling in favor of greater conservation. The political groundwork that lake advocates so carefully laid in Los Angeles would ultimately provide critical strategic foundation for compliance with the result after the legal decisions came down.

D. JOSEPH SAX AND THE POWER OF A GOOD IDEA

Even before the Second Barrel was put into place, however, another important development was occurring that would later play a critical role in the Mono Lake story. In 1970, Professor Joseph Sax published a law review article entitled *The Public Trust Doctrine in Natural Resource Law: Effective Judicial Intervention*.[72] In his article – one of those rare academic works that literally changes the world – he noted:

> Private citizens, no longer willing to accede to the efforts of administrative agencies to protect the public interest, have begun to take the initiative themselves. One dramatic result is a proliferation of lawsuits in which citizens, demanding judicial recognition of their rights as members of the public, sue the very governmental agencies which are supposed to be protecting the public interest.[73]

Sax warned that inconsistent legislative and administrative responses to environmental problems were compelling private citizens to court to protect threatened environmental values, all of them searching for some broad legal theory that would facilitate effective judicial intervention.[74] Framing that search as the subject of his article, he concluded that "[o]f all the concepts known to American law, only

---

OF THE WEST'S FIRST GREAT WATER TRANSFER 16 (Stanford Economics and Finance 2007) (describing California's 1943 Area of Origin Law).

[70] Indeed, in driving back and forth between the Mono Basin and the east coast, I saw them on highways all over the country, in states as far distant as South Dakota (at Wall Drug) and Massachusetts. Kay, *supra* note 6 (reporting on the distribution of Mono Lake bumper stickers).

[71] *See MLC History*, *supra* note 31 (discussing two lawsuits brought by the Mono Lake Committee and the National Audubon Society).

[72] *See generally* Joseph Sax, *The Public Trust Doctrine in Natural Resource Law: Effective Judicial Intervention*, 68 MICH. L. REV. 471 (1970).

[73] *Id.* at 473.

[74] *Id.* at 474 (noting that plaintiffs' diverse legal theories "range[d] from grandiose constitutional claims of the right to a decent environment to simple assertions that an administrator committed a procedural error.").

D. Joseph Sax and the Power of a Good Idea

the public trust doctrine seems to have the breadth and substantive content which might make it useful as a tool of general application for citizens seeking to develop a comprehensive legal approach to resource management problems."[75]

Professor Sax recounted the conventional common law history of the doctrine, noting that the concept of the public trust had received attention in Roman and English law with respect to "the nature of property rights in rivers, the sea, and the seashore."[76] He emphasized that "certain interests, such as navigation and fishing, were sought to be preserved for the benefit of the public; accordingly, property used for those purposes was distinguished from general public property which the sovereign could routinely grant to private owners."[77] He noted that "it was understood that in certain common properties – such as the seashore, highways, and running water – 'perpetual use was dedicated to the public,'" but observed remaining uncertainty on the extent to which members of the public could legally enforce the doctrine to prevent infringement of these interests "against a recalcitrant government."[78]

Worrying that legislatures are susceptible to capture by industry that would monopolize and degrade commonly held natural resources, Sax contended that the doctrine must enable judicial access to "promote equality of political power for a disorganized and diffuse majority."[79] He saw the doctrine as providing critical tools for regular people to protect their interests in commonly held natural resources by invoking judicial oversight. As plaintiffs in an ordinary court of law, ordinary citizens could leverage judicial review to check potentially shortsighted decision-making by political branches over natural resources that belong to all. In this way, the public trust doctrine operates as the original "citizen-suit" environmental law, on which citizen-suit provisions in the federal Clean Air and Water Acts[80] and other emerging environmental statutes[81] were modeled.

Sax further argued that public trust obligations should not be limited in application to navigable waters but should be extended to "a wide range of situations in

---

[75] *Id.* Sax also considered a framework of environmental rights, but suggested that the public trust doctrine was preferable because environmental rights claims were overly ambitious and received inconsistent judicial response. Sax, *The Public Trust Doctrine in Natural Resource Law*, 68 Mich. L. Rev. 471, at 474. For a more thorough comparison of rights of nature and public trust doctrine, see Chapter 10(B)(3) ("Comparing the Public Trust and Rights of Nature").
[76] *See* Sax, *supra* note 72, at 475.
[77] *Id.*
[78] *Id.*
[79] *Id.* at 560.
[80] The Clean Water Act ("CWA") authorizes "any citizen" to commence a civil action "on his own behalf" against an alleged violator. 33 U.S.C. § 1365(a). The Clean Air Act ("CAA") authorizes "any person" to commence a civil action "on his own behalf" against an alleged violator. 33 U.S.C. § 1365(a).
[81] The Federal Safe Drinking Water Act ("SDWA"), 42 U.S.C. § 300j-8, the Endangered Species Act ("ESA"), 16 U.S.C. § 1540(g), the Toxic Substances Control Act ("TSCA"), 15 U.S.C. § 2619, the Resources Conservation and Recovery Act ("RCRA"), 42 U.S.C. § 6972, and the Emergency Planning and Community Right to Know Act ("EPCRA"), 42 U.S.C. § 11046 also include citizen suit provisions.

which diffuse public interests need protection against tightly organized groups with clear and immediate goals."[82] He concluded with the admonition that while the public trust doctrine could provide grounds for a comprehensive approach to natural resource management, it would require three interpretive criteria: (1) it must contain some concept of a legal right in the general public; (2) it must be enforceable against the government; and (3) it must be capable of an interpretation consistent with contemporary concerns for environmental quality.[83] Professor Sax would later suggest that public trust obligations could even be understood as the basis for environmental rights.[84] His scholarship initially made slow ripples in the legal literature, but these ripples would eventually build into a tsunami – a quiet revolution in how we think about environmental rights and obligations in natural resources.

The full power of the public trust in natural resource management began to show in a series of legal actions in California that would eventually bear directly on the Mono Lake case. This litigation indicates a final realm of strategic support for the Mono Lake decision that deserves acknowledgment here, because the suit to save Mono Lake was not brought in a legal vacuum. Advocates laid foundation for the Mono Lake case by bringing preliminary litigation to create the precedent that would enable the high court to reach the legal conclusions it did in the Mono Lake case. And according to former members of the California Attorney General's Office of Legal Counsel, they were not brought by accident.[85] They were brought by plaintiffs and lawyers both in and out of government who understood what was necessary to get to the result they hoped to see in the Mono Lake case and others like it.

Some of the most important precedent protecting public trust interests in California waterways was created long before Joseph Sax's article was published, and before anyone was thinking specifically about Mono Lake. For example, in 1913, in *People ex rel. Webb v. California Fish Co.*, the California Supreme Court held that when the government conveys submerged lands to private parties, those lands remained subject to the public trust.[86] The case established the concept of the public trust as a set of obligations to the public on submerged lands that can overlay otherwise private rights.[87] In 1951, in *Bohn v. Albertson*, the Court of Appeal

---

[82] Sax, *supra* note 72, at 556.
[83] *Id.* at 556.
[84] Joseph L. Sax, *The Search for Environmental Rights*, 6 J. LAND USE & ENV'T L. 93, 93 (1990); *see also* Chapter 10(B)(3)(a) ("Philosophical Duality or False Dichotomy?") (discussing Sax's later arguments about the public trust doctrine as a source of environmental rights).
[85] Email from Richard Frank, Professor of Env't Pract., Dir., Cali. L. & Pol'y Ctr. Sch. of L., Univ. of Cali. Davis to author, (Feb. 7, 2018, 02:40 EST) (on file with author). Details were further confirmed in oral communications prior and subsequent to this email.
[86] People ex rel. Webb v. Cali. Fish Co., 138 P. 79 (Cal. 1913).
[87] This is sometimes characterized as the divisible *jus publicum* and *jus privatum* in waterfront property in which the state retains the jus publicum rights of public navigation, fishing, and swimming over lands for which other elements are conveyed to a private owner. *See, e.g.*, Glass v. Goeckel, 703 N.W. 2d 58 (Mich. 2005) (contrasting the jus publicum and jus privatum).

D. Joseph Sax and the Power of a Good Idea

of California for the First Appellate District affirmed the paramount nature of the public trust rights of navigation and fishing in holding that even previously non-navigable waters would be subject to these rights if they later became navigable by sustained geomorphological changes (in this case, avulsive flooding by the San Joaquin River).[88]

By the 1970s, however, the ripples of Sax's article were beginning to widen, and the significance of the public trust doctrine to the future of Mono Lake was becoming apparent. The Mono Lake case itself rested directly on the shoulders of a 1971 California Supreme Court case, *Marks v. Whitney*, which first recognized environmental values as within the scope of the public trust.[89] A groundbreaking decision, *Marks v. Whitney* expanded recognition of values protected in public trust waterways from the traditional values of navigation, fishing, and commerce to include those associated with wildlife habitat, nature study, and aesthetic beauty.[90]

Remembering *Marks v. Whitney*, former California Deputy Attorney General Richard (Rick) Frank reports that his office filed an amicus brief with the California Supreme Court that relied heavily on Joe Sax's seminal article, and that the California Supreme Court relied heavily on that amicus brief and the Sax article to articulate "how the ancient public trust doctrine could and should be applied as a cornerstone principle of modern California environmental law."[91] The *Marks* dispute addressed mostly private interests between private Tomales Bay shoreline owners, so even though it would eventually have enormous significance for beloved public trust resources like Mono Lake, it did not attract a lot of public attention at the time. But the lawyers involved recognized its significance and, according to Rick Frank, some were already thinking about Mono Lake.[92]

In the same year, in *People ex rel. Baker v. Mack*, the California Court of Appeal for the Third District clarified that the rule for navigability is the suitability of the water for public use such as boating, swimming, fishing, hunting, and all recreational purposes.[93] As the Mono Lake rangers would routinely tell our visitors, during the California Gold Rush era, Mono Lake had been used for commercial transport of logs from the Jeffrey Pine forest south of the lake to build residential and commercial infrastructure in the Bodie boomtown north of the lake. For that reason, it has

---

[88] Bohn v. Albertson, 238 P. 2d 128, 140–41 (Cal. Ct. App. 1951) (holding that the waters of Frank's Tract, which had previously been non-navigable, became subject to the right of public navigation and fishing due to the sustained flooding of the tract by the San Joaquin River). The court clarified that the owner of the tract in question could reclaim the land, but so long as it remained submerged by navigable waters, the tract was subject to the usual public rights associated with navigability. *Id.*

[89] Marks v. Whitney, 491 P.2d 374 (Cal. 1971).

[90] *Id.* at 256–60 ("[T]he state is not burdened with an outmoded classification favoring one mode of utilization over another ... the preservation of those lands in their natural state, so they may serve as ecological united for scientific study ... which favorably affect the scenery and climate of the area.").

[91] Email from Richard Frank, *supra* note 85.

[92] *Id.*

[93] People ex rel. Baker v. Mack, 97 Cal. Rptr. 448 (Ct. App. 1971).

long been recognized as a commercially navigable water.[94] But if there were ever any doubt that Mono Lake was a navigable waterway for the purposes of the public trust, *Baker v. Mack* cleared it, as the lake was then regularly used for recreational boating.

A decade later, even as the Mono Lake case progressed through the courts, public trust advocates continued to lay foundation for that decision in an important set of cases that further entrenched the power of the public trust doctrine in California. In 1980, the California Supreme Court decided *Berkeley v. Superior Court*, a case with unavoidable parallels to the U.S. Supreme Court's famous decision in *Illinois Central* a century earlier.[95] The case involved tidelands along the City of Berkeley's waterfront that the State of California had patented to a private railroad company under an 1870 statute, at about the same time that Chicago Harbor had been conveyed to Illinois Central.[96] The Berkeley tidelands constituted 77 percent of the city's waterfront along San Francisco Bay,[97] and previous precedent had assumed they had been granted in fee simple.[98] Representing the California State Lands Commission, the State Attorney General sued to establish the reserved public trust rights in those tidelands.

The California high court clarified that those patents, though given private effect above the waterline, indeed remained impressed with their original public trust obligations for public commerce, navigation, fishing, and related uses below the mean high water mark.[99] The court affirmed the principle that public trust protections remained intact on submerged lands conveyed to private parties as an easement in favor of the public, and that any statute purporting to abandon the public trust must be "strictly construed."[100] As the court instructed, "the intent to abandon must be clearly expressed or necessarily implied; and if any interpretation of the statute is reasonably possible which would retain the public's interest in tidelands, the court must give the statute such an interpretation."[101] The case signaled how seriously the State of California would take its obligations as trustee for the public interest under the public trust doctrine.

While the *Berkeley* case concerned the nature of public rights in the space between the mean high and low tide lines of coastal property, the 1981 case of

---

[94] City of Los Angeles v. Aitken, 52 P.2d 585, 588 (Cal. 1935) (referencing the commercial use of Mono Lake to transport property as a factor in determining that Mono Lake is a navigable lake).

[95] Berkeley v. Super. Ct., 606 P.2d 362, 369 (Cal. 1980); *see* Chapter 1(B)(5) ("With Power Comes Responsibility: *Illinois Central Railroad Co. v. Illinois*").

[96] *Id.*

[97] *Id.* at 364.

[98] *Id.* at 363.

[99] *Berkeley*, 606 P.2d at 369. The Court decided to balance the interests of the public against those of the landowners to hold that the submerged lands subject to tidal action are subject to the public trust but properties that were filled that are not subject to tidal action are free from the trust. *Id.* at 535.

[100] *Id.*

[101] *Id.*

D. Joseph Sax and the Power of a Good Idea 115

State v. Superior Court (*Lyon*) drew the same conclusions with regard to the space between the high and low water mark of navigable freshwater lakes and streams[102] – waterways more like those in the Mono Basin.

In the *Lyon* case, plaintiffs owned 800 acres of mostly submerged marshland along Clear Lake, under grants that did not specify the waterward boundary.[103] When the owner sought a permit to develop them, the Fish and Game Commission declined it on grounds that the State had retained the submerged lands below the high water mark, and that they were subject to the public trust.[104] The plaintiff argued that at statehood, California had acquired ownership of submerged lands in nontidal navigable waterways only to the low water mark,[105] but the Court disagreed.[106] While conceding that the legislature could specifically grant these lands to private parties under some circumstances,[107] it affirmed that in general, and in this case, the mean high water mark sets the boundary between state and private ownership, for both tidal and nontidal waterways.[108] The decision ensured that public trust protections would apply to more, rather than fewer, wetlands at the margins between public and private property at waterways.

Recalling this litigation from the perspective of the California Attorney General's Office, Rick Frank reported that the next step was to apply the public trust doctrine explicitly to California's inland navigable waterways. He recalls:

> We did so in two cases, involving Lake Tahoe and Clear Lake in California. In those 1981 California Supreme Court decisions, the Court expressly embraced our position that the public trust doctrine fully applies to the beds and banks of all navigable inland lakes and rivers in California, which the Lands Commission has quantified as involving about 4,000 linear miles of river and lake shoreline.[109]

In *State v. Superior Court of Placer County* (*Fogerty*), the court considered the ownership rights in land between the high and low water marks of Lake Tahoe.[110] When pollution-targeting regulations prevented plaintiff property owners from further developing the shorezone, they sued for inverse condemnation (among other things),[111] arguing

---

[102] State v. Super. Ct. (Lyon), 625 P.2d 239, 241 (Cal. 1981).
[103] *Id.* at 241–42.
[104] *Id.*
[105] *Id.* at 243.
[106] *Id.* at 246.
[107] *See, e.g.*, Boone v. Kingsbury, 273 P. 797, 814–15 (Cal. 1928) (holding that the state may only alienate the trust when used in promoting the public interest or when doing so would not impair the public's interest); City of Berkeley v. Super. Ct., 606 P.2d 362, 379 (Cal. 1980) (holding that the legislature must clearly express an intent to abandon the public trust, and if there is any reasonably possible interpretation retaining the trust, a court must construe the statute in that manner); People v. California Fish Co., 138 P. 79, 87–88 (Cal. 1913).
[108] *Lyon*, 625 P.2d at 225.
[109] Email from Richard Frank, *supra* note 85.
[110] *Lyon*, 625 P.2d at 257.
[111] *Id.*

that existing regulations were enough to protect the public interest in the lake from overuse.[112] However, the court held that the State was not estopped from asserting the rights of the public in those lands when other pollution regulation was insufficient to protect the public trust resource from harm.[113] The court further held that landowners who had previously built docks, piers, and other structures could continue to use them unless the State determines that their existence is inconsistent with the reasonable needs of the trust.[114] In the other case, *State v. Superior Court (Lyon)*, the California high court held that private landowners could utilize the land between the low and high water marks of Clear Lake, but only in a manner compatible with the public trust.[115]

In different ways, each of these cases strengthened the developing public trust doctrine in California. The Berkeley waterfront and Clear Lake cases affirmed that public trust protections would be meaningfully enforced. Even when waterfront lands are granted to private holders, public trust protection of submerged lands to the mean high water mark would remain unless the legislature specifically finds otherwise, and only under specific circumstances that offset the loss in public trust benefits.[116] So the public trust protections associated with Mono Basin resources were durable, and they would be meaningfully enforced, even after long periods of time, and contrary reliance by competing private interests (such as Los Angeles' interests in water exports since the licensing of diversions to the L.A. aqueduct). The Lake Tahoe case demonstrated the power of public trust protections, affirming that the State has the power and obligation to protect public trust resources from undue harm, even that resulting from legitimate neighboring private uses – such as, for example, harm to the Mono Basin from water exports to the L.A. aqueduct. And of course, *Marks v. Whitney* applied the public trust doctrine to modern environmental values for the first time, opening the door for the role it would play at Mono Lake and similarly situated watersheds across California.

E. THE PATH TO LITIGATION

In 1974, five years after publication of Joseph Sax's seminar article, college student Tim Such – that young member of Kenneth Lajoie's early Mono Lake Task Force – read the article while researching a project on the Mono Basin Extension for his Environmental Studies class at UC Berkeley.[117] After researching the law of all fifty

---

[112] *Id.* at 260.
[113] *Id.* at 259–60. The other issue in the case was whether the boundary between public and private ownership should be determined by lake Tahoe's current condition or its natural level that existed prior to the construction of a dam built in 1870, which raised the lake level. The Court held that the last natural level (the level before the dam was built) was an inappropriate measure. *Id.* at 259–62.
[114] *Id.* at 261.
[115] *Lyon*, 625 P.2d 239 (Cal. 1981).
[116] *See* Berkeley v. Super. Ct., 606 P.2d 362, 369 (Cal. 1980).
[117] HART, *supra* note 1, at 61.

E. The Path to Litigation

states, Mexico, England, the Roman Empire, the California state constitution, international treaties protecting migratory birds, and an alliance with the Kootzaduka'a Paiute Tribe, he concluded that the public trust doctrine as Sax described it was the most promising legal tool for forestalling further environmental harm in the Mono Basin.[118]

When Such joined the Mono Lake Committee a few years later, the advocates were struggling to find a way to protect the lake by legal means. New federal and state environmental laws protecting clean air and water were of no help, as this was not a problem of pollution. But Such shared his conviction that the public trust doctrine he had read about in Sax's article could help save Mono Lake.[119] In October of 1978, as the momentum toward litigation gathered force, Such successfully pitched the concept of seeking protection for Mono Lake under the public trust doctrine to an elite California law firm, Morrison & Foerster.[120] To assist in their representation, Such began working for Morrison & Foerster as an investigator.[121] The firm agreed to bring the Mono Lake litigation on a pro bono basis,[122] committing to contribute $250,000 in uncompensated legal assistance.[123]

By this time, as described in Chapter 3, Los Angeles was drawing almost 20 percent of its water from four out of five of the Mono Lake feeder streams, and the ecological impacts on the Mono Basin were acute.[124] The lake had lost over forty vertical feet – to 6,376 feet above sea level, down from its pre-diversion level of 6,417 feet – and it had lost nearly one-third of its surface area, from eighty-five to sixty square miles.[125] Between 1940 and 1970, when Los Angeles diverted an average of 57,067 acre-feet of water per year, the lake dropped an average of 1.1 feet each year.[126] But after the Second Barrel was constructed in 1970, Los Angeles began diverting almost twice as much water, averaging 99,580 acre-feet per year.[127]

---

[118] *Id.* at 64.
[119] *Id.* at 62–64 (discussing Tim Such); *see also* Arnold, *Working out an Environmental Ethic*, *supra* note 5, at 15.
[120] HART, *supra* note 1, at 62–63.
[121] *Id.* at 82.
[122] *Id.* at 81.
[123] *Id.* at 82.
[124] The New York Times reported in 1985 that diversions supplied about 17 percent of Los Angeles' water, lowering the lake's elevation by 43 feet from 1941 to 1981. *Concern Voiced on Shrinking California Lake*, THE N.Y. TIMES (Sept. 29, 1985), www.nytimes.com/1985/09/29/us/concern-voiced-on-shrinking-california-lake.html.
[125] "Between 1970 and 1980, the city diverted an average of 99,580 acre-feet per year from the Mono Basin. By October of 1979, the lake had shrunk from its pre-diversion area of 85 square miles to an area of 60.3 square miles." Nat'l Audubon Soc'y v. Super. Ct., 658 P.2d 709, 714 (Cal. 1983); E-mail from Bartshé Miller, Educ. Dir., Mono Lake Comm., to author (Oct. 19, 2017, 02:38 EST) (on file with author).
[126] *Nat'l Audubon Soc'y*, 658 P.2d at 714.
[127] Arnold, *Working out an Environmental Ethic*, *supra* note 5, at 14; *see also* E-mail from Bartshé Miller, *supra* note 125 (The amount of water diverted to Los Angeles was not precisely fixed. Miller confirmed that the range (12–20 percent) would be generally correct).

On May 5, 1979, as ecological catastrophe loomed nearer, representatives from the Mono Lake Committee, the *National Audubon Society*, and the Los Angeles Department of Water and Power ("DWP") met in departmental offices to discuss the issue and explore the possibilities for resolving the crisis unfolding at Mono Lake.[128] The environmental groups proposed several compromises to protect the Mono Basin while still enabling the city to take reduced diversions, but DWP, as the Department is locally known, quickly rejected them.[129]

One week later, on May 12, the Mono Lake Committee, the *National Audubon Society*, and a third group, Friends of the Earth, filed suit against DWP in the Mono County Courthouse in Bridgeport, alleging a series of claims involving the public trust doctrine, violations of state constitutional provisions involving public waterways, and common law nuisance.[130] But it would take more than a year of complex procedural litigation to determine who should be involved in the lawsuit, where it should be heard, and by whom.

Soon after the case was filed in 1979, DWP sought a change of venue to another district, because it feared it would face local bias if the trial took place in Bridgeport, the county seat for Mono County.[131] The case was then shifted to Alpine County, landing before Judge Hilary Cook.[132] In February of 1980, DWP filed a cross-complaint to establish its water rights against other potential claimants in the Mono Basin, naming 117 additional parties with land holdings in the Mono Basin, including the State of California, the federal government, June Lake and Lee Vining Public Utility Districts, and private landowners.[133] DWP argued that water diversions by these other parties were also contributing to the lake's decline.[134] The plaintiffs responded that their collective diversions were small in comparison to those by DWP and therefore had negligible impacts,[135] but Judge Cook allowed the

---

[128] HART, *supra* note 1, at 83.
[129] Arnold, *Working out an Environmental Ethic*, *supra* note 5, at 15–16.
[130] Nat'l Audubon Soc'y v. Dep't of Water, 869 F.2d 1196, 1198 (9th Cir. 1988) (describing the original *Audubon Society* complaint, which is not available electronically, in later federal litigation); *see also* Chapter 5(A)(3) ("The Legal Arguments").
[131] HART, *supra* note 1, at 83. The Mono Lake Committee Newsletter stated that the Los Angeles Department of Water & Power was "unwilling to try the case in Mono County," and so it was transferred to Alpine County. David Gaines, THE MONO LAKE COMM., Fall 1979 Vol. 2 No. 2, at 11.
[132] *Id.*
[133] *Nat'l Audubon Soc'y v. Dep't of Water*, 869 F.2d at 1199 (explaining that DWP's cross-complaint in the original case contained four counts: "The first count sought adjudication of Basin water rights as to all appropriators; the second sought to quiet title to those rights. These two causes named 117 [listed] cross-defendants.... The third cause of action sought a declaration that, to the extent that the United States has jurisdiction over California's exercise of its navigation trust, Congress has consented to the impairment of the navigable waters of Mono Lake. Finally, DWP asserted that any nuisance at Mono Lake is attributable to the owner of the newly exposed lakebed and sought a declaration that conditions at the Lake resulted from a valid exercise of the police power by the State of California.").
[134] David Gaines, THE MONO LAKE COMM., Winter 1980 Vol. 2 No. 3, at 10.
[135] *Id.*

E. The Path to Litigation

new parties to be joined to the lawsuit.[136] The case now included the U.S. Bureau of Reclamation, the agency then responsible for managing the federal lands surrounding Mono Lake, and the California State Attorney General's Office, defending the interests of the State.[137]

This initially felt like a loss for the Mono Lake advocates, but litigation, as does the rest of life, involves unexpected twists and turns. Whenever a case in state court includes a federal party or question of federal law, that suit becomes eligible for "removal" to federal court, meaning that the case is transferred from supervision under the state judicial process to supervision under the federal judiciary. In April of 1980, the United States removed the case to federal court because DWP's cross-complaint had now involved federal agencies. The case was transferred once again, this time landing before U.S. District Court Judge Lawrence Karlton.[138]

Both parties suspected Judge Karlton of sympathizing with environmental causes,[139] so DWP then fought to remand the case back to state court on grounds that only one of its arguments implicated the federal agencies,[140] while the Mono Lake advocates fought to keep the case in front of him.[141] In a high-stakes game of pretrial motion racquetball, DWP tried to get back into state court by amending its cross-complaint to drop the cause of action involving the federal agencies, coupling its petition for remand with a request that the federal court duly abstain from interpreting an open question of state law.[142] To counter this attempt to remand the case back to state court, the Mono Lake plaintiffs sought to amend their complaint to include federal common law nuisance claims for air and water pollution.[143] Judge Karlton generously granted both requests – allowing DWP to drop its federally relevant claim while also allowing the plaintiffs to add their federal claim – thus keeping the claim in federal court.[144]

At this point, the California State Attorney General's Office, intervening on behalf of the State, sided with DWP on the question of the remand. Although many of the lawyers in that office were sympathetic with the plaintiffs' public trust argument,[145] the State's attorneys are always protective of state legal jurisdiction, especially when in competition with federal courts. For that reason, the State filed a motion asking Judge Karlton to refer the case back to the Alpine County Superior Court, on

---

[136] *Id.*
[137] *Nat'l Audubon Soc'y v. Dep't of Water*, 869 F.2d at 1199.
[138] HART, *supra* note 1, at 90.
[139] David Gaines, THE MONO LAKE COMM., Fall 1980 Vol. 3 No. 2, at 13.
[140] *Nat'l Audubon Soc'y v. Dep't of Water*, 869 F.2d at 1199.
[141] Gaines, *supra* note 139, at 13; HART, *supra* note 1, at 90.
[142] *Nat'l Audubon Soc'y v. Dep't of Water*, 869 F.2d at 1199.
[143] *Id.*; Gaines, *supra* note 139, at 13 (noting that the plaintiffs' petition also sought to separate the trials of the original complaint from the cross-complaint that added the 117 new parties).
[144] *Nat'l Audubon Soc'y v. Dep't of Water*, 869 F.2d at 1200.
[145] Telephone interview with Roderick Walston, March 2, 2018, 4 pm EST/1 pm PST (notes on file with author).

grounds that the real legal issues under consideration were novel matters of state law that had never been ruled on by any California court.[146] In their motion, the state attorneys suggested that Judge Karlton certify the two main legal questions raised by the case for resolution by the state courts: the relationship between the public trust doctrine and prior appropriations doctrine, and whether the plaintiffs would have to pursue additional administrative remedies with the Water Board before getting their day in court.[147]

By now, the case had grown in both size and complexity, raising unresolved questions of state law that federal courts are loathe to decide in the first instance. Following legal abstention doctrines that instruct federal courts to step aside on such matters, Judge Karlton agreed with the State's arguments and stayed the federal proceedings to enable the California courts to interpret these matters under state law.[148] Accepting the State's suggestion, he sent the parties back to state court specifically to answer the two questions critical to proper resolution of the dispute: (1) what was the nature of the legal relationship between the public trust doctrine and the California system of water rights, and (2) whether the plaintiffs must exhaust administrative remedies before seeking judicial relief.[149] He did not let go of the federal case entirely, but he allowed the separation of the federal nuisance claim from the state public trust and administrative law issues, pausing further federal proceedings pending the resolution of these state law questions.[150]

The plaintiffs immediately refiled in state court, landing back in Alpine County Superior Court, once again before Judge Cook.[151] Though DWP had been trying to get out of Judge Karlton's court, it objected to the form of the abstention and tried to file an interlocutory appeal with the U.S. Court of Appeals for the Ninth Circuit, but the petition was denied.[152] DWP was perhaps lucky to have failed, however,

---

[146] Id.
[147] Id.
[148] Nat'l Audubon Soc'y v. Super. Ct., 658 P.2d 709, 716–18 & n. 12 (Cal. 1983) (describing Judge Karlton's decision to stay federal proceedings in accordance with abstention doctrine following R.R. Comm'n. v. Pullman Co., 312 U.S. 496 (1941) and Kaiser Steel Corp. v. W. S. Ranch Co., 391 U.S. 593 (1968)).
[149] Nat'l Audubon Soc'y v. Super. Ct., 658 P.2d 709, 717 (Cal. 1983).
[150] *Nat'l Audubon Soc'y v. Dep't of Water*, 869 F.2d at 1199 (describing this result, and noting the court's ruling that "it would retain jurisdiction over the case during the pendency of the state action"). Eventually, the parties returned to federal court to finish the federal litigation, in which the Ninth Circuit ruled against the federal nuisance claims. Id. at 1206 (holding that the federal common law nuisance claim based on water pollution was preempted by the Clean Water Act, declining to recognize the federal common law nuisance claim based on air pollution because the case did not involve federal rights or obligations or an interstate dispute unsuitable for the application of state law, and declining to decide whether the air pollution claim was preempted by the Clean Air Act).
[151] *Nat'l Audubon Soc'y v. Super. Ct.*, 658 P.2d at 717. DWP objected and sought leave to file an interlocutory appeal with the U.S. Court of Appeals for the Ninth Circuit, but the Ninth Circuit denied the petition.
[152] Id. at n.13. In the later *Nat'l Audubon Soc'y* proceedings, DWP would further object that the state court's action, filed after Judge Karlton's abstention order, sought an advisory opinion beyond the jurisdiction of the California courts – raising further novel issues at the intersection of state and

E. The Path to Litigation

because in September of 1981, Judge Cook found against the plaintiffs on both issues.¹⁵³ He concluded that the plaintiffs should have taken the case to the State Water Resources Control Board to exhaust administrative remedies before filing litigation in court, and that in any event, the public trust doctrine did not provide an independent basis for challenging DWP's diversions.¹⁵⁴ In a ruling strongly favoring DWP, Judge Cook held that the doctrine had been subsumed within the state system for allocating water rights, obviating any objections to Los Angeles' licenses for violating the public trust.¹⁵⁵

The plaintiffs nevertheless persisted, challenging these rulings on appeal. But time was of the essence, as the lake continued to draw down. Rather than following the normal chain of appeals through intermediate state courts, the plaintiffs used a rarely deployed petition for writ of mandate to appeal directly to the California Supreme Court.¹⁵⁶ The California high court accepted the case for its 1982 calendar.¹⁵⁷ On May 3, 1982, oral arguments were heard, and the court would ponder the case for the next nine months.¹⁵⁸

As the litigation wound its way along this journey, the battle to save Mono Lake waged on in the political context. On September 9, 1979, as the case was just gathering steam, a crowd of about 250 locals, visitors, biologists, birders, and photographers gathered at Mono Lake to demonstrate their support for the plaintiffs.¹⁵⁹ On August 27, 1980, a few months after the case was filed, a bikeathon of Mono Lake supporters famously carried water from the reflecting pool at DWP's headquarters over two mountain ranges and for hundreds of miles back to Mono Lake, where they poured the water back into the lake as part of a publicly heralded "rehydration ceremony."¹⁶⁰ On November 27, the Point Reyes Bird Observatory hosted birdathons in support of the effort to save Mono Lake.¹⁶¹

---

federal procedural law. *Id.* at n.14. The California Supreme Court briefly puzzled over the implications of this claim before rejecting the notion that it should refuse to cooperate with federal abstention and thereby compel the federal courts to decide unsettled questions of California law. *Id.*

¹⁵³ *Id.* at 425; DAVID GAINES, THE MONO LAKE COMM., Autumn 1981 Vol. 4 No. 2, at 7–8.
¹⁵⁴ *Nat'l Audubon Soc'y*, 658 P.2d at 712.
¹⁵⁵ HART, *supra* note 1, at 98.
¹⁵⁶ *Nat'l Audubon Soc'y*, 658 P.2d at 712.
¹⁵⁷ *Id.* Former Assistant State Attorney General Roderick Walston, who litigated the case as an intervenor on behalf of the state, recalls advising the plaintiffs to follow this strategy: "I recommended to them that there was a mechanism to bypass the court of appeal and get right to the Supreme Court without having to go through all the intermediate levels – they should petition for a writ of mandate." Telephone interview with Roderick Walston, March 2, 2018, 4 pm EST/1 pm PST (notes on file with author). From his point of view, the case was going to be appealed through the appellate and supreme court anyway, so it was in everyone's interest to save two years and get the case straight to the high court. *Id.* As he recalled, "The [state supreme court] almost never takes them, but I had a good feeling that they would be interested in this one, and they were." *Id.*
¹⁵⁸ HART, *supra* note 1, at 99.
¹⁵⁹ *Id.* at 1.
¹⁶⁰ *Id.* at 89–90.
¹⁶¹ *Id.* at 89.

Following the California Supreme Court's decision earlier that year in *Berkeley v. Superior Court* and the other strategic litigation discussed earlier,[162] scholarly attention to the doctrine continued to increase, further galvanizing the movement. In 1980, as the litigation unfolded, a group of legal scholars gathered to apply Sax's theory to Mono Lake in a series of published legal research produced for Professor Harrison Dunning's Public Trust Doctrine conference at U.C. Davis,[163] providing legal insight on which the California Supreme Court would rely in the famous Mono Lake decision that followed. In November of the same year, the Mono Lake Committee asked President Jimmy Carter to declare the federal Bureau of Land Management lands surrounding Mono Lake a National Monument to facilitate its protection, but he declined.[164]

In January of 1981, California state senator John Garamendi, a Democratic representing two Bay Area counties, introduced a bill in Sacramento to protect the state-owned lands around Mono Lake.[165] In June, a few months later, Congressman Norman Shumway, a Republican representing California's 14th District in the U.S. House of Representatives, attempted unsuccessfully to revive the National Monument plan in a bill formally proposing the Mono Lake National Monument.[166] DWP opposed the proposal, recognizing that national recognition would only intensify pressure to reduce water diversions, and it unsuccessfully countered with an application to the Reagan Administration for 23,850 acres of federal land around the lake.[167] Under federal law, this would have opened further possibilities for L.A. to claim adjacent lands from the public domain at $1.25 per acre, a move that Congressman Shumway opposed with additional proposed legislation.[168]

Congressmen Shumway and Richard Lehman introduced two other bills in February 1982[169] and January 1983[170] before Congressman John Seiberling

---

[162] *See supra* notes 89–116 and accompanying text (describing the strategic litigation that paved the way for the California Supreme Court's decision in *Audubon Society*)

[163] *See* HART, *supra* note 1, at 101 (describing the California high court's reliance on the scholarship resulting from the U.C. Davis symposium).

[164] *Id.* at 92.

[165] *Id.*

[166] "A bill to establish the Mono Lake National Monument in the State of California, and for other purposes." H.R. 4057, 97th Cong. (1981–1982), www.congress.gov/bill/97th-congress/house-bill/4057?s=2&r=40.

[167] HART, *supra* note 1, at 92; *see also* Mono Scenic Area Advances in Senate, 6 THE MONO LAKE NEWSLETTER 6 (Winter 1984), www.monolake.org/wp-content/uploads/2020/09/1984-Winter-Mono-Lake-Newsletter.pdf (suggesting that the eventual creation of a Mono Scenic Area would prohibit the sale to Los Angeles of land for $1.25 an acre, repealing a 1936 "special interest" law).

[168] HART, *supra* note 1, at 92; *see also* "A bill to amend certain provisions of law relating to the disposition of public lands in Mono County, California, and for other purposes." H.R. 4056, 97th Cong. (1981–1982), www.congress.gov/bill/97th-congress/house-bill/4056 (a bill, introduced by Congressman Shumway with no further action, that aimed to block the DWP's land grab attempt and repeal the 1936 law that authorized the sale of federal land in Mono County to LA for $1.25 an acre).

[169] "A bill to establish the Mono Lake National Monument in the State of California, and for other purposes." H.R. 5424, 97th Cong. (1981–1982), www.congress.gov/bill/97th-congress/house-bill/5424 (died in House Interior and Insular Affairs Subcommittee on Public Lands and National Parks).

[170] *Id.*

cosponsored a bill in June 1983 to retain the proposed protected area within the National Forest system, rather than transferring it to the National Park System as a National Monument, changing the name from Mono Lake National Monument to Mono Basin National Scenic Area.[171] Ultimately, the Mono Basin National Scenic Area was created, which became the first National Forest lands set aside by Congress with a conservation management directive.[172]

Meanwhile, conservation efforts continued at the State level. In September of 1981, Governor Jerry Brown signed into law the bill that California Senator Garamendi had initially proposed, creating the Mono Lake Tufa State Reserve to protect the state-owned lands immediately surrounding Mono Lake.[173] The following year, the state park was formalized.[174] Even so, almost none of the infant gulls born at Mono Lake that year survived to adulthood, as the land bridge exposed by the declining lake level finally enabled Basin coyotes to access Negit Island and decimate the breeding colony.[175] A picture of the Mono Lake tufa towers exposed by the declining lake was featured on the cover of *Life* Magazine.[176]

On July 6, 1982, a few months after oral arguments in the Mono Lake case (but still many before the final decision would come), Los Angeles Mayor Tom Bradley announced that Los Angeles would reduce water diversions enough to halt the decline of Mono Lake.[177] The Mayor, then running for governor, portrayed this as a significant policy change, and the Mono Lake advocates made "a considered decision to play along," hoping that by praising the city's actions, they could induce similar behavior in the future.[178] However, the reality was that the winter of 1981–1982 was incredibly wet, creating a snowpack that sent more water into the Mono Lake creeks the next summer than the aqueduct could handle.[179] As John Hart memorably describes it, "Nature had done what lobbying could not."[180]

---

[171] "A bill to establish the Mono Basin National Forest in the State of California, and for other purposes." H.R. 3356, 98th Cong. (1983–1984), www.congress.gov/bill/98th-congress/house-bill/3356?s=5&r=67 (died in Subcommittee on Energy and the Environment); Norman Shumway, *The National Monument Legislation*, 4 THE MONO LAKE NEWSLETTER 5 (Spring 1982), www.monolake.org/wp-content/uploads/2020/09/1984-Winter-Mono-Lake-Newsletter.pdf.
[172] *See* 16 U.S.C. § 543 (1984).
[173] HART, *supra* note 1, at 92; *see also* CAL. CODE REGS. tit. 14, § 4752 (listing the Mono Lake Tufa State Reserve).
[174] The state established the Mono Lake Tufa State Reserve in January 1982. Around the same time, California and the Federal Government were engaged in a legal battle over the boundaries of the state's ownership of lands surrounding Mono Lake. *See* Cal. ex rel. State Lands Comm'n v. United States, 805 F.2d 857, 859 (9th Cir. 1986). For more on this state-federal dispute over the lands surrounding Mono Lake, *see* Chapter 6 ("In the Wake of *Audubon*: The Legal and Political Aftermath").
[175] Arnold, *Working out an Environmental* Ethic, *supra* note 5, at 14.
[176] HART, *supra* note 1, at 80.
[177] *Id.* at 100.
[178] *Id.*
[179] *Id.*
[180] *Id.*

The next few winters were equally generous, but everyone knows that wet seasons come and go in California. Dry seasons to come loomed large, and so all eyes remained fixed on the pondering justices of the California Supreme Court. The decision that would result owes a deep debt to the thoughtful and committed political organizing that preceded it – and it would require ongoing support from the same communities of interest to ensure its implementation afterward. The moral here is that the Mono Lake story is *not* a story just about litigation – it has required, and continues to require, enormous effort from committed individuals far from any courthouse.

Yet the impacts of a judicial decision can be felt many thousands of miles from where it is authored, and they can live on for generations to come, even after living memory of the groundwork has faded. The Mono Lake case, unpacked in Chapter 5, offers a prime example.

5

National Audubon Society

The "Mono Lake Case"

A. The Historic Mono Lake Case: *Audubon Society v. Superior Court*   126
    1. The Pleadings   126
    2. The Players   128
    3. Settlement Negotiations   132
    4. The Legal Arguments   133
        a. The Mono Lake Plaintiffs   134
        b. The Los Angeles Defendants   136
        c. The State of California   138
        d. The Bottom Line   140
    5. The California Supreme Court's Decision   141
B. Unpacking the *Mono Lake* Decision: Legal Elements and Innovations   146
    1. Environmental Public Trust Values   146
    2. Application to Non-Navigable Tributaries   147
    3. Duty of Ongoing Supervision   149
    4. The Nature of the Public Trust Doctrine   152
    5. A Substantive or Procedural Doctrine?   155

This chapter discusses the landmark Mono Lake litigation that finally reached the California Supreme Court, *National Audubon Society v. Superior Court*, after so many years of hardship, political groundwork, and legal preparation. This is the case that turned the tide for the survival of Mono Lake, through public trust reasoning that would go on to foment a quiet revolution in environmental law. Before long, the decision would inspire related environmental advocacy in distant states and nations the world over – but that movement began with this striking courtroom drama, protecting an ancient and remote saline lake against the thirst of one of the largest and most powerful cities in the United States.

The first half of the chapter reviews the basic elements of the litigation, introducing the parties, their commanding legal avatars, and their overall positions in the lawsuit before unpacking the specific arguments that reached the California Supreme

Court. It reviews the lake advocates' argument that the public trust values at Mono Lake obligated sovereign protection, Los Angeles's defense that the public trust had been abrogated by its licenses to take water under the statutory prior appropriations doctrine, and the State of California's intervening contention that both parties were wrong for different reasons. Then it turns to the justices' landmark public trust ruling and its legal significance, attempting to balance so many competing considerations.

The second half highlights the most important doctrinal features of the decision, including the court's affirmation that environmental values are protected by the public trust doctrine, its application of the doctrine to the upper reaches of the watershed, its assertion that public trust obligations extend over time, and its understanding of the legal nature of the doctrine itself. In casting the doctrine as a nonwaivable sovereign obligation to protect environmental values of trust resources for future generations, the decision set the stage for recognition of the doctrine as a framework for environmental rights. The chapter closes with consideration of whether the California doctrine confers more procedural or substantive protection.

A. THE HISTORIC MONO LAKE CASE: *AUDUBON SOCIETY V. SUPERIOR COURT*

This part briefly introduces the pleadings and parties to the litigation and the colorful individuals representing them before plunging more fully into the complex legal arguments made in court.

1. *The Pleadings*

In 1979, when the *National Audubon Society* and Mono Lake Committee filed their lawsuit in Mono County court, nobody knew if the novel public trust idea they advanced would even make it to the courtroom – so to play it safe, they raised a number of claims simultaneously. The lake advocates alleged that Los Angeles' diversions violated the public trust doctrine, but also that they constituted a common law nuisance and violated portions of the California Constitution protecting navigable waterways.[1] To support their state constitutional argument, they primarily relied on Article X, Section 2, limiting appropriative water rights to reasonable and beneficial uses.[2] Even so, multiple provisions provided support for their claims, including the state constitutional right to fish,[3] restrictions on the alienation of

---

[1] See Nat'l Audubon Soc'y v. Super. Ct., 658 P.2d 709, 716 (Cal. 1983) ("[P]laintiffs filed suit for injunctive and declaratory relief in the Superior Court for Mono County on May 21, 1979."). Mono Lake had been previously established as a navigable waterway in an earlier takings case. City of L.A. v. Aitken, 52 P.2d 585, 588 (Cal. 1935) ("There can be no doubt that Mono Lake is a navigable body of water.").

[2] See Nat'l Audubon Soc'y, 658 P.2d at 725.

[3] CAL. CONST. art. I, § 25 ("The people shall have the right to fish upon and from the public lands of the State and in the waters thereof, excepting upon lands set aside for fish hatcheries, and no land owned by the State shall ever be sold or transferred without reserving in the people the absolute right

tidelands,[4] and public rights to access navigable waters.[5] Of note, the public trust principles the plaintiffs advocated for would eventually be added to California's State Water Code, but only decades later in 2009 – a result of the decision in this case, and not something the Mono Lake advocates could rely on during the litigation itself.[6]

With so much at stake, Los Angeles tenaciously defended the legality of the diversions under California statutory and constitutional law.[7] As discussed further below, the city argued that the California Constitution provides ambiguous guidance, recognizing that

> because of the conditions prevailing in this State[,] the general welfare requires that the water resources of the State be put to beneficial use to the fullest extent of which they are capable, and that the waste or unreasonable use or unreasonable method of use of water be prevented, and that the conservation of such waters be exercised with a view to the reasonable and beneficial use thereof in the interest of the people and for the public welfare.[8]

Los Angeles maintained that the highest beneficial use of the water was for the domestic and municipal purposes to which it was being diverted through the aqueduct,

---

to fish thereupon; and no law shall ever be passed making it a crime for the people to enter upon the public lands within this State for the purpose of fishing in any water containing fish that have been planted therein by the State; provided, that the legislature may by statute, provide for the season when and the conditions under which the different species of fish may be taken.").

[4] CAL. CONST. art. X, § 3 ("All tidelands within two miles of any incorporated city, city and county, or town in this State, and fronting on the water of any harbor, estuary, bay, or inlet used for the purposes of navigation, shall be withheld from grant or sale to private persons, partnerships, or corporations; provided, however, that any such tidelands, reserved to the State solely for street purposes, which the Legislature finds and declares are not used for navigation purposes and are not necessary for such purposes may be sold to any town, city, county, city and county, municipal corporations, private persons, partnerships or corporations subject to such conditions as the Legislature determines are necessary to be imposed in connection with any such sales in order to protect the public interest.").

[5] CAL. CONST. art. X, § 4 ("No individual, partnership, or corporation, claiming or possessing the frontage or tidal lands of a harbor, bay, inlet, estuary, or other navigable water in this State, shall be permitted to exclude the right of way to such water whenever it is required for any public purpose, nor to destroy or obstruct the free navigation of such water; and the Legislature shall enact such laws as will give the most liberal construction to this provision, so that access to the navigable waters of this State shall be always attainable for the people thereof.").

[6] CAL. WATER CODE § 85023 (2009) ("The longstanding constitutional principle of reasonable use and the public trust doctrine shall be the foundation of state water management policy and are particularly important and applicable to the Delta.").

[7] Nat'l Audubon Soc'y, 658 P.2d at 727.

[8] CAL. CONST. art. X, § 2 (the same provision continues: "The right to water or to the use or flow of water in or from any natural stream or water course in this State is and shall be limited to such water as shall be reasonably required for the beneficial use to be served, and such right does not and shall not extend to the waste or unreasonable use or unreasonable method of use or unreasonable method of diversion of water. Riparian rights in a stream or water course attach to, but to no more than so much of the flow thereof as may be required or used consistently with this section, for the purposes for which such lands are, or may be made adaptable, in view of such reasonable and beneficial uses; provided, however, that nothing herein contained shall be construed as depriving any riparian owner of the reasonable use of water of the stream to which the owner's land is riparian under reasonable methods of diversion and use, or as depriving any appropriator of water to which the appropriator is lawfully entitled.").

pointing to the state water code's affirmation that domestic use and irrigation are the highest beneficial uses when allocating state waters,[9] and other statutory law enabling the state to release itself from public trust obligations in certain circumstances.[10]

Los Angeles received support from the State of California for the outcome it sought, but under an entirely different legal theory of how the public trust doctrine should operate (and one that maximized state autonomy to determine what best serves the public interest).[11] The State agreed that the city's diversion permits should be honored – not because the public trust had been subsumed by state water law, but because it was satisfied when the Water Board determined that the public interest was best served by sending Mono Lake water southward.[12] To bring closure and finality to these issues, Los Angeles took the additional step of moving to adjudicate *all* water rights in the Mono Basin – effectively joining all private, state, and federal landholders in a suit that would ultimately proceed all the way to the highest court in the land.[13] Which means that by the time the case was heard, there were a lot of players on the field.

2. The Players

A lot of people were concerned about what would happen to Mono Lake. Even more were concerned about the implications of the different legal arguments being advanced. The parties to the resulting litigation included local residents; state landowners; environmental nongovernmental organizations (NGOs) at various levels of geographical scale; government agencies at various levels of jurisdiction responsible for impacted land, water, wildlife, and air resources; and of course, the Los Angeles Department of Water and Power (DWP). Today, the attorneys representing these various parties read like a "Who's Who" of regional experts and environmental scholars, indicating the level of talent operating in that courtroom – and perhaps how the experience of participating in this momentous litigation impacted individual careers.

As a practical matter, the Mono Lake Committee coordinated efforts on behalf of the plaintiffs from Lee Vining, where they remain a Mono Basin watchdog and

---

[9] CAL. WATER CODE § 106 (1943).
[10] *See* CAL. PUB. RES. CODE § 6307 (2005) (specifying conditions under which the California State Lands Commission may enter an exchange freeing the State's interest in public trust lands while imposing the public trust on the lands or interests received in the exchange); *Nat'l Audubon Soc'y*, 658 P.2d at 713–14.
[11] *Nat'l Audubon Soc'y*, 658 P.2d at 723 ("noting that in the State's view, '"trust uses' encompass all public uses, so that in practical effect the doctrine would impose no restrictions on the state's ability to allocate trust property"").
[12] Telephone Interview with Roderick E. Walston, former Assistant State Attorney General, State of California, (Mar. 2, 2018) (explaining that the state intervened to take a middle ground position. National Audubon Society went too far, because it's not illegal to divert if it's under a permit – its only illegal if it violates the beneficial use doctrine under const. art. 10. But L.A. was also wrong because even under a permit, there is no vested water rights if the use violates the constitutional standard).
[13] *Nat'l Audubon Soc'y*, 658 P.2d at 716, 727.

advocacy group today.[14] Committee founders David and Sally Gaines remained essential players, raising awareness about the issues through all available channels while leading the charge to "Save Mono Lake" through litigation and other means.[15] Practical and levelheaded, Sally managed the administrative details while the more romantic David dedicated himself to evangelizing for the cause, inspiring audiences across the state.[16] In addition to the local and national chapters of the *Audubon Society*, the Mono Lake advocates were joined by several other environmental NGOs, including Friends of the Earth, the Sierra Club Legal Defense Fund, and CalTrout.[17]

The plaintiffs were primarily represented by Bruce Dodge, a widely respected partner at the San Francisco epicenter of Morrison & Foerster, whose first legal victory was to convince the large, corporate law firm to represent the lake advocates pro bono.[18] Known as an engaging and effective attorney, Dodge relied on straightforward arguments, controlled irritation, humor, and commonsense to capture the courtroom with what others characterized as "real honesty and fairness in the practice of law."[19] Dodge was joined by Sanford Skaggs of Palmer Brown Madden, and Maria Rivera, then of Van Voorhis & Skaggs,[20] who would later become a state judge. Other attorneys who wrote in support of the plaintiffs as amici curiae ("friends of the court") included notable state environmental attorneys Antonio "Tony" Rossman, who would later go on to advise the United Nations Food and Agriculture Organization as a consultant on water resource law,[21] and Clement Shute, Jr., who was recognized by the California State Bar in 2015 with a Lifetime Achievement Award for his contributions to environmental law.[22]

---

[14] In the Matter of Amend. of L.A.'s Water Right Licenses, 1994 WL 758358, at *6 (Cal. State Water Res. Control Bd. Sept. 28, 1994) [hereinafter Decision 1631]; *see also Saving Mono Lake*, MONO LAKE COMM., www.monolake.org/learn/aboutmonolake/savingmonolake/ (last visited Sept. 27, 2022) [https://perma.cc/ZJ5R-KMBD] [hereinafter *Saving Mono Lake*] (describing the mission of the organization as a non-profit citizens group dedicated to protecting and restoring the Mono Basin ecosystem, educating the public about Mono Lake and the impacts on the environment of excessive water use, and promoting cooperative solutions that protect Mono Lake and meet real water needs without transferring environmental problems to other areas).

[15] See *infra*, Chapter 5 (discussing their pre-litigation advocacy); *see also* JOHN HART, STORM OVER MONO 78–79 (Univ. of Cal. Press 1996).

[16] HART, *supra* note 15, at 78–79 (Univ. of Cal. Press 1996).

[17] Decision 1631, *supra* note 12, at 7, 19.

[18] See *Nat'l Audubon Soc'y*, 658 P.2d at 709; HART, *supra* note 15, at 81–82; *Defender of the Trust Award*, MONO LAKE COMM., www.monolake.org/whatwedo/aboutus/eventsandawards/dtaward/ (last visited May 21, 2024) (discussing Dodge's role in securing affordable legal assistance for the litigation).

[19] HART, *supra* note 15, at 172.

[20] *Nat'l Audubon Soc'y.*, 658 P.2d at 709.

[21] Tony Rossman, AUBURN ENDURANCE CAP., https://auburnendurancecapital.org/endurance-sports-auburn-ca/the-committee/central-square-endurance-zone/tony-rossman/.

[22] *Our Founders*, SHUTE MIHALY & WEINBERGER LLP, www.smwlaw.com/our-founders/ (highlighting Shute's career in environmental law). *Nat'l Audubon Soc'y.*, 658 P.2d at 709. Attorneys Robin Pulich and Frank Lowe also submitted amici briefs in support of the plaintiffs. *Id.*

The DWP, of course, defended the city's exports.[23] Operating as the institutional voice on the matter of Mono Lake, Assistant General Manager Duane L. Georgeson[24] famously summarized the department's position as: "We bureaucrats at the Department are charged with maintaining, protecting, sustaining, and defending these large municipal assets."[25] Although cordial with Mono Lake Committee representatives, he was regarded as an obstacle to conservation and remained deeply skeptical of the movement to save the lake, warning that the Committee would stop all water diversion from the Mono Basin if it could.[26]

Adolph Moskovitz, a name partner with the firm of Kronick, Moskovitz, Tiedemann, & Girard, served as the principal defense attorney on behalf of Los Angeles, together with a team of municipal attorneys under the direction of City Attorney Ira Reiner, who went on to establish the Los Angeles County Environmental Crimes Strike Force during his time as District Attorney for Los Angeles.[27] A formidable attorney, Moskovitz relentlessly defended the positions he represented, at times producing comedic banter with the bench (including his memorable Mono Lake oral argument, in which his casted broken middle finger comically appeared to "flip off" the justices of the California Supreme Court).[28] Other attorneys appeared separately in defense of DWP's position on behalf of state water contractors, including Richard Gill, Anthony Alexander, and Arthur Littleworth, a renowned water law expert who would later coauthor the pinnacle book on California water law and serve as special master for a United States Supreme Court case dealing with river flows.[29] Amici writers in support of DWP's position included Anne Schneider, the first female partner at her law firm and a future leading voice in western water law.[30]

Yet as noted, the principals were hardly the only ones interested in the outcome of this case. The State of California supported DWP's position while emphasizing

---

[23] Nat'l Audubon Soc'y., 658 P.2d at 727.

[24] HART, supra note 15, at 144.

[25] Interview by Dick Nelson with Duane L. Georgeson, Assistant General Manager, L.A. Dep't of Water and Power, in L.A., Cal. (July 1, 1998).

[26] Id.

[27] Id. Reiner was joined in his representation by Assistant City Attorneys Edward Ferrell and Kenneth Downey. Nat'l Audubon Soc'y, 658 P.2d at 709.

[28] Symposium, Introduction and Dedication, 57 HASTINGS L.J. 1237, 1238–39 (2006). Participants recalled a particularly memorable example during oral argument before the California Supreme Court, at a time when Moskovitz wore a cast on his broken middle finger, holding it in perpetual extension. As Moskovitz staunchly defended the position that LA's water rights were set in stone no matter the consequences against open skepticism from the justices, he appeared to reciprocate the hostility when his gesturing appeared to give them 'the finger.'

[29] Nat'l Audubon Soc'y, 658 P.2d at 709; Gail Wesson, Leading Water-Rights Expert Arthur Littleworth Dies, UC RIVERSIDE NEWS (Nov. 3, 2021), https://news.ucr.edu/articles/2021/11/03/leading-water-rights-expert-arthur-littleworth-dies (Littleworth's book, California Water, was originally published in 1995 and updated in 2008).

[30] Symposium, Introduction and Dedication, 57 HASTINGS L.J. 1237, 1238–39 (2006); The Anne J. Schneider Lecture Series, ELLISON SCHNEIDER HARRIS DONLAN, https://eslawfirm.com/water/AJS-Lecture-Series.

the flexibility of the State to act in pursuit of any public interest without violating its public trust responsibilities.[31] California was officially represented by Attorney General George Deukmejian and a collection of his deputies.[32] Deukmejian was a dedicated and influential political leader who would later go on to serve two terms as Governor of California,[33] but Deputy Attorney General Roderick "Rod" Walston became the principal architect of the state's legal position, and later wrote about it in a *University of Wyoming Law Journal*.[34] In his subsequent writings about the litigation, Walston would characterize the proceedings as a battle between environmental idealists who did not understand the complexities of California water law and water experts wholly unconcerned by the environmental impacts of California water policy. In this regard, his contribution to the litigation could be seen as middle ground advocacy that considered the interests on all sides with fuller appreciation for the complexity of California Water Law.[35]

The United States also appeared, represented by a gaggle of federal lawyers from the U.S. Attorney General's Office and the Department of Justice,[36] including Carol Dinkins and Donald Ayer, each of whom would later serve as Deputy Attorney General of the United States (Dinkins as the first woman to do so);[37] Stuart Somach, one of the most highly respected water law attorneys in the Western United States, who would later argue before the U.S. Supreme Court, testify before Congress, and brief the President on water law matters;[38] and Richard Lazarus, who would go on to become a leading scholar of environmental law as a professor at Harvard Law School.[39] Independent amici were provided by San Francisco City Attorney George Agnost and his Deputy City Attorney, McMorris Dow, and by commercial litigators

---

[31] *Nat'l Audubon Soc'y*, 658 P.2d at 723 ("Since the public trust doctrine does not prevent the state from choosing between trust uses, the Attorney General of California, seeking to maximize state power under the trust, argues for a broad concept of trust uses. In his view, 'trust uses' encompass all public uses, so that in practical effect the doctrine would impose no restrictions on the state's ability to allocate trust property." (citation omitted)).

[32] Other state lawyers included John Bury, Tom Gilfoy, Philip Walsh, Jennifer Moran, and Elizabeth Bigman. *Id.*

[33] Honorary Degrees, George Deukmejian, THE CALIFORNIA STATE UNIVERSITY, www.calstate.edu/impact-of-the-csu/alumni/Honorary-Degrees/Pages/george-deukmejian.aspx.

[34] Roderick Walston, *The Public Trust and Water Rights*: National Audubon Society v. Superior Court, 22 LAND & WATER L. REV. 701 (1987).

[35] Roderick Walston Interview, *supra* note 12.

[36] *Nat'l Audubon Soc'y*, 658 P.2d at 710. Other federal lawyers included Francisco Goldsherry, Mary Beth Uitti, and Jaques Gelin. *Id.*

[37] *Deputy Attorney General: Carol E. Dinkins*, U.S. DEP'T OF JUST., www.justice.gov/dag/bio/deputy-attorney-general-carol-e-dinkins (last updated Feb. 29, 2024) (Dinkins served as Deputy Attorney General from 1984–1985); *Deputy Attorney General: Donald B. Ayer*, U.S. DEP'T OF JUST., www.justice.gov/dag/bio/deputy-attorney-general-donald-b-ayer (last updated Feb. 29, 2024) (Ayer served as the Deputy Attorney general from 1989–1990).

[38] Joe Mullich, *Thicker Than Water: Stuart Somach is in Water Law for the Long Haul*, SUPER LAWS., www.superlawyers.com/articles/california/thicker-than-water/ (discussing the highlights of Somach's career in water law) (last visited June 26, 2023).

[39] *Faculty: Richard J. Lazarus*, HARV. L. SCHOOL, https://hls.harvard.edu/faculty/richard-j-lazarus/.

Jerome Falk and Brian Gray, the latter of whom would go on to teach water law at UC-San Francisco.[40]

The full list of state and federal agencies represented by these attorneys included the U.S. Forest Service and Bureau of Land Management (with responsibility for managing lands in and around the Mono Basin),[41] the U.S. Fish and Wildlife Service (with interests in the Mono Basin creeks and fisheries), the California Department of Fish and Game (concerned with wildlife impacts), the California Department of Parks and Recreation (responsible for the Mono Lake Tufa State Natural Reserve), the State Lands Commission (responsible for state land resources), the California Great Basin Unified Air Pollution Control District (charged with managing compliance with the Clean Air Act and other air quality controls), and the State Water Resources Control Board (the Water Board) itself.[42] Some of these parties were intervenors, and some were drawn into the suit by DWP's 1980 cross-complaint.[43] Everyone was watching the case closely.

3. Settlement Negotiations

As noted in Chapter 4, extensive negotiations preceded the California Supreme Court's disposition of the case, in which lawmakers and others tried and failed to persuade the disputants to reach a compromise.[44] Sizeable state and federal grants were offered to help Los Angeles adopt water conservation technologies that might reduce its need for water imports,[45] but the city was loathe to give any ground on its claims for imported water. Los Angeles commanded one of the largest metropolitan areas in the country, but its continued existence hinged on access to imported water. City leaders likely worried that conceding any water in the Mono Basin might redound negatively to other claims.[46] Moreover, under the "use it or lose it" principle of appropriative water law, any sustained failure by Los Angeles to exercise those water rights could result in their legal forfeiture forever.[47]

---

[40] *People: Brian E. Gray*, U.C. L. S.F., www.uclawsf.edu/people/brian-e-gray/.

[41] For the argument that the federal government might also have challenged diversions on the basis of the riparian rights associated with its ownership of Mono Basin public lands, see Richard P. Shanahan, *The Application of California Riparian Water Rights Doctrine to Federal Lands in the Mono Lake Basin*, 34 HASTINGS L. J. 1293, 1296 (1983).

[42] Decision 1631, *supra* note 12, at *11.

[43] *See* Chapter 4(E) ("The Path to Litigation").

[44] HART, *supra* note 15, at 85, 88.

[45] *Id.* at 88 ("The state and federal governments would pay two-thirds of the cost of replacement water for the first two years ....").

[46] E-mail from Geoff McQuilkin, Exec. Dir. of the Mono Lake Comm., to Erin Ryan, Elizabeth C. & Clyde W. Atkinson Professor and Assoc. Dean for Env't Programs, Fla. St. U. Coll. Of L. (Apr. 26, 2015, 11:29 am) (on file with author). *See also* HART, *supra* note 15, at 88–89, 168–70 (discussing the city's reluctance to engage in any activity that might undermine its appropriative rights); *id.* at 83 (describing a failed settlement conference among the parties in which the DWP representative pledged the city's resolve to protect its appropriative rights by warning the Mono Lake advocates that "[t]he last lawsuit we had like this took forty-three years.... Fortunately, we're young.").

[47] *See* Chapter 1(C)(2) ("Prior Appropriations") (discussing the law of prior appropriations).

A. *The Historic Mono Lake Case*

Meanwhile, the Interagency Task Force had determined that 6,388 feet above sea level was the minimum water level required in Mono Lake to forestall ecological collapse and prevent further degradation of air resources.[48] Although the Mono Lake advocates did not insist that the lake be returned to its pre-diversion level of 6,417 feet, they refused to consider any proposal that would not protect the lake at the 6,388-foot level.[49] Geoff McQuilkin, a later executive director of the Mono Lake Committee, would later explain to me that David and Sally Gaines had been counseled by negotiation experts to open with a more extreme demand that would provide them with bargaining room to make concessions during negotiations with the city.[50] But the Committee pointedly rejected this conventional negotiating tactic for a position that was unimpeachably grounded in the science, choosing the level that the Task Force had established as the minimum necessary to ensure the stability of the ecosystem and the public health of surrounding communities.[51]

"We were twenty-year-old idealists," recalled Sally Gaines, "and we were going to do things differently."[52] "Why play games?" they reasoned: "We weren't going to bluff; we were just going to start with what the science said was necessary, and then stay there forever."[53]

According to Water Chief Paul Lane, "forever" was on everyone's mind during the period preceding the litigation. At a pretrial conference contemplating the last chance for settlement, Lane commented to Bruce Dodge, "The last lawsuit we had like this took forty-three years." In his characteristically crisp response, Dodge remarked, "Fortunately, we're young."[54]

4. *The Legal Arguments*

As negotiations failed to resolve the dispute, Mono Lake continued to decline, and the case quickly proceeded through all levels of the judicial system to the California Supreme Court.[55] In their original complaint filed in Mono County, the plaintiffs

---

[48] *See* HART, *supra* note 15, at 85, 88 (discussing the Mono Lake Committee's and Interagency Task Force's insistence on restoring the lake level to 6,388 feet, depending on how the lake level would be defined).

[49] *See id.* at 85 (discussing negotiations between the Mono Lake Committee, the Interagency Task Force, and the City of Los Angeles).

[50] Geoff McQuilkin, Exec. Dir. of the Mono Lake Comm., Oral Communication (July 1996); Geoff McQuilkin, Exec. Dir. of the Mono Lake Comm., Oral Communication (May 2001).

[51] *Id. See also* Decision 1631, *supra* note 12, at *6 (describing the long-term goal of returning the lake to a level that would protect the various public trust resources at issue).

[52] HART, *supra* note 15, at 75.

[53] Geoff McQuilkin, Exec. Dir. of the Mono Lake Comm., Oral Communication (July 1996); Geoff McQuilkin, Exec. Dir. of the Mono Lake Comm., Oral Communication (May 2001); *see also Saving Mono Lake*, *supra* note 14 (noting that Martha Davis and the other Mono Lake Committee leaders "decided to ask for exactly what they wanted, instead of asking for more and then compromising down to the true goal.").

[54] HART, *supra* note 15, at 83.

[55] *See* Chapter 4(E) ("The Path to Litigation") (reviewing the procedural history of the case and discussing how it arrived at the Supreme Court without proceeding through all the usual stages of

had asserted multiple claims, including violation of the public trust doctrine and an action to establish public trust rights in the Mono Basin waters, violations of state constitutional provisions prohibiting gifts of state assets and the obstruction of navigable waterways, and public and private nuisance claims relating to air and water pollution from the mud and dust exposed by the lake's recession.[56] Yet by the time the plaintiffs reached the high court, their claim had been pared down to the barebones question of how the public trust doctrine would operate on these facts.

a. The Mono Lake Plaintiffs

Before the high court, the Mono Lake advocates made a simple claim that threatened to undermine a century's worth of seemingly settled California water law. Following Tim Such's recommendation and channeling the insights of Professor Sax and the U.C. Davis conference scholars,[57] the plaintiffs argued that allowing the destruction of Mono Lake through continued water diversions was impermissible, notwithstanding that these diversions were pursuant to state-approved appropriations – because doing so violated state obligations under the public trust doctrine. California, they claimed, could not allow Los Angeles to continue water exports that were destroying Mono Lake, a navigable water held by the State in trust for the people.[58]

Although the city claimed appropriative rights to this water, the plaintiffs countered that these rights had been illegally granted in violation of the public trust

---

review). As detailed there, when federal agencies became involved in the litigation, the case was removed to federal district court, which abstained on the novel issues of state law and remanded back to state court. *See* Nat'l Audubon Soc'y v. Dep't of Water & Power of L.A., 496 F. Supp. 499 (E.D. Cal. 1980); Nat'l Audubon Soc'y v. Super. Ct., 658 P.2d 709, 712 (Cal. 1983) (describing the federal district court's request "that the state courts determine the relationship between the public trust doctrine and the water rights system"); *see also Political & Legal Chronology*, MONO BASIN CLEARINGHOUSE, www.monobasinresearch.org/timelines/polchr.php [https://perma.cc/FY7A-8U94] [hereinafter *Mono Chronology*] (describing the history of the various lawsuits taking place at Mono Lake).

[56] A later Ninth Circuit review of related federal claims summarized the original complaint, which is not accessible electronically: "Audubon's original complaint, filed in the Superior Court for Mono County, asserted: 1) violation of the public trust; 2) violation of California Constitution article XVI, section 6 (prohibiting a gift by the state of a state asset); 3) a quiet title action to establish public trust rights in the waters of the Mono Basin; 4) public and private nuisance (from mud and dust created by reliction); and 5) violation of California Constitution article X, section 4 (prohibiting obstruction of navigable waters)." Nat'l Audubon Soc'y v. Dept. of Water, 869 F.2d 1196, 1198–99 (9th Cir. 1988).

[57] *See* Chapter 4(D) ("Joseph Sax and The Power of a Good Idea") & Chapter 4(E) ("The Path to Litigation") (recounting how a college student first suggested the public trust doctrine argument that drove the litigation, based on a law review article by Professor Joseph Sax, and the subsequent conference at U.C. Davis exploring the idea).

[58] *See Nat'l Audubon Soc'y*, 658 P.2d at 712 (describing plaintiffs' theory that "the shores, bed and waters of Mono Lake are protected by a public trust" and that diversions that fail to consider the public trust "may result in needless destruction of [public trust] values"); *see also* sources cited *supra* notes 3–6 (describing significant constitutional and statutory provisions referencing the public trust doctrine).

doctrine, which prevents the state from alienating or allowing the casual destruction of navigable waterways. As discussed in Chapter 4, the importance of the public trust doctrine had been repeatedly recognized by the California Supreme Court,[59] and the plaintiffs argued that the state's obligations as trustee must take precedence over Los Angeles' claims for water.

They maintained that the State had first failed its trust obligations all the way back in 1940, when the State Water Board first granted Los Angeles permission to divert from the Mono Basin creeks.[60] These licenses were granted in violation of the trust, they explained, because the Water Board's decision failed to account for the State's obligation to prevent foreseeable harms to Mono Lake's ecologic, scenic, and recreational values.[61] They argued that the current rate of exports would result in a lake level decrease of at least 50 feet and that the lake could even dry up entirely.[62] They pointed to the Board's own written record of its concerns at the time, in which members had wrung their hands about the apparent fact that there was nothing they could do to prevent the same tragedy that had devastated Owens Lake from being repeated at Mono Lake.[63] To the plaintiffs, these writings demonstrated that the Board had either failed to consider the state's obligations under the public trust doctrine to protect the lake, or if it had considered them, it had ignored them.[64]

Instead, the plaintiffs argued, the public trust doctrine both empowered and obligated the Water Board to prevent exports that would destroy the lake, not permit them. Mono Lake was held by the state in trust for the public, and no organ of the state could give away its water if that would result in the destruction of the resource.[65] Although they didn't mention the older case, the argument, in essence, was that it

---

[59] See, e.g., State of California v. Superior Court (Fogerty), 29 Cal. 3d 240, 247 (Cal. 1981) (applying the public trust doctrine to "all the navigable lakes and rivers in California"); State v. Super. Ct. (Lyon), 29 Cal. 3d 210, 227 (Cal. 1981) (same); City of Berkeley v. Superior Court, 606 P.2d 362, 364 (1980) (characterizing the public trust right as "illimitable and unrestrainable and incapable of individual exclusive appropriation") (internal quotation marks omitted); Marks v. Whitney, 491 P.2d 374, 378 (1971) (recognizing the public trust doctrine as a matter "of great public importance").

[60] See Nat'l Audubon Soc'y, 658 P.2d at 728–29 (noting that the rights had been acquired "in 1940 from a water board which believed it lacked both the power and the duty to protect the Mono Lake environment" and that DWP "continues to exercise those rights in apparent disregard for the resulting damage to ... Mono Lake").

[61] Id.

[62] Id. at 715; cf. infra text accompanying note 46 (describing DWP's more optimistic projections for future lake level and volume).

[63] Nat'l Audubon Soc'y, 658 P.2d at 714 (noting that "[i]t is indeed unfortunate that the City's proposed development will result in decreasing the aesthetic advantages of Mono Basin but there is apparently nothing that this office can do to prevent it") (emphasis in opinion); see also Decision 1631, supra note 12, at *1 (noting the Water Board's conclusion that the Water Code "required issuance of the permits despite anticipated damage to Mono Lake and other natural resources").

[64] See Nat'l Audubon Soc'y, 658 P.2d at 712–14 (noting plaintiffs' public trust violation cause of action and DWP's determination not to consider the public trust in its 1940 decision).

[65] Id. at 712 (summarizing the state's public trust duty and synthesizing the doctrine with the prior appropriations doctrine).

was no more permissible for California to give away Mono Lake's waters than it was for Illinois to give away Chicago Harbor in the famous *Illinois Central* case a hundred years earlier – which the Supreme Court had pointedly affirmed the State could *not* do.[66] As an implied limit on state sovereign authority, the doctrine must therefore trump whatever appropriative rights the state might purport to grant in dereliction of its duty as trustee. For that reason, the Water Board, acting for the State of California, lacked authority to permit Los Angeles to destroy the lake by draining it away – just as the legislature in Illinois lacked authority to convey away the bed of Chicago Harbor. The plaintiffs also argued that Los Angeles's harmful diversions should be considered an unreasonable use under applicable state water law.[67]

b. The Los Angeles Defendants

Los Angeles had a lot at stake, and it ferociously defended the lawsuit. City leaders realized that if they lost, they not only stood to lose up to 20 percent of their already strained water supplies; the negative precedent the case could create might threaten their ability to import other critical water supplies from other distant, out-of-basin locations.[68] From their perspective, Los Angeles had complied with both the letter and the spirit of California water law, which has always sought to facilitate municipal access to water resources for beneficial use in urban areas.[69] They were even reluctant to implement the water conservation efforts urged by the Mono Lake advocates and incentivized by offers of state and federal funding.[70] The "use-it-or-lose-it" prior appropriations regime would have contributed to this reluctance because a user who manages to conserve water risks forfeiture of their rights to use that water in the future.[71]

According to Los Angeles, the plaintiffs had it all wrong, on both the facts and the law. DWP predicted that the rate of exports would lead to a lake level decrease of no

---

[66] *See id.* at 721 (discussing *Illinois Central* and applying its rule of law); *see also* Chapter 1(B)(5) ("With Power Comes Responsibility: *Illinois Central Railroad Co. v. Illinois*") (discussing *Illinois Central*, the seminal U.S. Supreme Court case establishing that the public trust doctrine prevented the state from alienating Chicago Harbor to a private railroad).

[67] *See Nat'l Audubon Soc'y*, 658 P.2d at 718 (discussing defendant's attempt to require plaintiffs to exhaust administrative remedies before the Water Board for claims "based on asserted unreasonable or nonbeneficial use of appropriated water").

[68] *Id.* at 715.

[69] *Id.* at 724–26.

[70] HART, *supra* note 15, at 85, 88.

[71] *See* Chapter 1(C)(2) ("Prior Appropriations") (discussing the doctrine of prior appropriations); *see, e.g., Salt River Valley Water User's Assn. v. Kovacovich*, 411 P.2d 201, 203–04 (Ariz. Ct. App. 1966) (concluding that an irrigator who implemented water conserving technology was not entitled to the conserved water under his appropriative right). Today, most prior appropriation states have amended their water laws to provide greater incentives for water users to conserve and protect them against forfeiture. For example, California now entitles those who conserve water to use, sell, or lease conserved water yielded by these efforts. CAL. WATER CODE § 1011.

more than forty-three feet over a period of 80–100 years, and that the lake level would stabilize during this time.[72] Moreover, the city was hardly violating the public trust doctrine, which protects only navigable waterways, because the city was drawing water not from the hypersaline lake but from Mono's non-navigable feeder creeks.[73] Above all, Los Angeles argued, the public trust was the wrong doctrine to focus on. The dispositive law was the statutory water law of prior appropriations, with which the city had diligently complied in seeking and perfecting the Mono Basin diversion permits. The California constitution affirms that water should be put to beneficial use,[74] and much of this water was going to the highest recognized form of beneficial use – domestic use by the citizens of Los Angeles.[75] (This, they would have argued, was hardly comparable to giving away the bed of Chicago Harbor!)

DWP thus vigorously defended Los Angeles's rights to export Mono Basin water on grounds that the licenses were fully consistent with the clearly articulated California water law principles of prior appropriations and beneficial use.[76] DWP pointed to the vast legal and physical infrastructure by which water is moved all over the State of California, from watersheds with more to watersheds with less.[77] This elaborate network of water transfers is formalized by the system of licenses that confer the appropriative rights on which cities like Los Angeles have long relied – a concern also raised by the State Attorney General's Office.[78] DWP also argued that the plaintiffs were not entitled to judicial relief because they had not exhausted administrative remedies available to resolve water rights disputes through the State Water Board.[79] In the early stages of litigation, DWP had already filed cross-complaints against other Mono Basin landowners to clarify water rights and potential contributions to the alleged harms.[80] Finally, the city's arguments suggested the possibility of

---

[72] *Nat'l Audubon Soc'y*, 658 P.2d at 715; *cf. supra* text accompanying note 33 (describing the plaintiffs' prediction of exports' impact on lake level and stability).

[73] *Nat'l Audubon Soc'y*, 658 P.2d at 716, 727. Domestic use, they would have argued, was hardly comparable to giving away the bed of the Chicago Harbor.

[74] CAL. CONST. art. X, § 2 ("[I]n this State the general welfare requires that the water resources of the State be put to beneficial use to the fullest extent of which they are capable, and that the waste or unreasonable use or unreasonable method of use of water be prevented, and that the conservation of such waters is to be exercised with a view to the reasonable and beneficial use thereof in the interest of the people and for the public welfare.").

[75] *Nat'l Audubon Soc'y*, 658 P.2d at 713.

[76] *Id.* at 727 (noting defendant's argument that the public trust had been subsumed into the prior appropriation system, giving it "a vested right in perpetuity to take water without concern for the consequences to the trust").

[77] *Id.* at 727–28 (discussing California's historical reliance on water diversions out of stream).

[78] *Id.* at 727 (discussing the Water Board's power to "grant usufructuary licenses that will permit an appropriator to take water from flowing streams and use that water in a distant part of the state"). *See also* Roderick Walston Interview, *supra* note 12 (discussing state concerns).

[79] *Nat'l Audubon Soc'y*, 658 P.2d at 718.

[80] Nat'l Audubon Soc'y v. Dep't of Water, 869 F.2d 1196, 1198–99 (9th Cir. 1988) (in a separate decision resolving later federal claims, describing the four counts of DWP's original cross-complaint, which had sought adjudication of Mono Basin water rights and to quiet title to those rights, as well as

a future claim for an unconstitutional taking of its property rights if the State moved to interfere with its licenses to divert Mono Basin water[81] (a claim that it would eventually, but unsuccessfully, raise on appeal[82]).

Yet even if none of that were enough, the city argued that the plaintiffs could not rely on the public trust doctrine to interfere with its appropriative water rights because of the customary relationship between statutory and common law. Los Angeles contended that the California Water Code, incorporating the prior appropriations doctrine by statute, should be construed to override the public trust doctrine.[83] It reasoned that the well-developed body of statutory water law in California had effectively subsumed and displaced the common law public trust doctrine.[84] After all, that is how the legal system normally works: judicially interpreted common law doctrines fill jurisprudential gaps until the legislature passes a relevant statute, which abrogates conflicting common law precedents.[85] This is ordinarily what happens whenever statutes contradict prior common law – as they have in vast areas of tort, contract, and criminal law.[86]

c. The State of California

Meanwhile, the State of California, represented by the Attorney General's Office, appeared in support of Los Angeles' position on preserving its rights to divert water from the Mono Basin – but it offered a third, independent legal view that partially overlapped with the plaintiffs' public trust argument. The State agreed with the plaintiffs' position that the public trust doctrine must be taken into account, but it separately argued for a wider interpretation of "public uses" under the doctrine.[87] Noting the State's heavy responsibility to ensure scarce water supplies across its large

---

declaratory relief that DWP had permission to impair navigation on Mono Lake and was not responsible for alleged nuisances, and that "conditions at the Lake resulted from a valid exercise of the police power by the State of California"); see also Chapter 4(E) ("The Path to Litigation").

[81] In its own *Audubon Society* decision, the California Supreme Court responded preemptively to this suggestion by noting that, despite DWP's argument that the prior appropriations doctrine creates a vested right to the Mono Lake diversions, DWP cannot eschew its obligations to the public trust and use of the public trust doctrine does not "constitute[] a taking of property for which compensation was required." *Nat'l Audubon Soc'y*, 658 P.2d at 723.

[82] *See* Timothy J. Conway, National Audubon Society v. Superior Court: *The Expanding Public Trust Doctrine*, 14 ENV'T L. 617 (1984) (discussing the city's appeal to the U.S. Supreme Court, which the Court declined to take).

[83] *Nat'l Audubon Soc'y*, 658 P.2d at 716, 727.

[84] *Id.*

[85] *See* Lowman v. Stafford, 226 Cal. App. 2d 31, 38–39 (1964) ("[T]he law itself, as a rule of conduct, may be changed at will by the Legislature subject only to constitutional provision.") (citations omitted).

[86] *See, e.g.*, 58 CAL. JURIS. 3D *Effects of Statutes on Common Law* § 6 (2023) ("The legislature is at liberty to change any rule of the common law and thereby prevent it from being the rule of decision in this state."); Mod. Barber Colls. v. Cal. Emp. State Comm'n, 192 P.2d 916, 920 (Cal. 1948) (noting that the legislature may "create new rights or provide that rights which have previously existed shall no longer arise, and it has full power to regulate and circumscribe the methods and means of enjoying those rights").

[87] *Nat'l Audubon Soc'y*, 658 P.2d at 723.

and arid territory, the State Attorney General urged the court to adopt a "broad concept" of permissible trust uses, in which the doctrine would encompass *all* potential public uses – including the supply of drinking water for Los Angeles.[88]

The Attorney General emphasized that although the State was in fact bound by the public trust doctrine in administering trust resources, its trust obligations would be satisfied by any course of action it chose that somehow advanced the public interest.[89] So long as the public benefited from state action in some way – or in legal terms, so long as the state was acting within its police powers to protect the public health, safety, and welfare – then it could not be held to have violated the public trust doctrine, even if the result of that action was to damage the underlying trust resource.[90] This would effectively tether the public trust analysis to the "beneficial use" standard embedded in state water allocation law and enshrined in related parts of the California Constitution.[91]

The interpretation advanced by the Attorney General would have affirmed the importance of the public trust doctrine as a source of state authority, while simultaneously limiting it as a source of state obligation toward the environmental stewardship of trust resources – a responsibility to protect them as *waterways*, and not just as sources of water for export and other potential uses. But even within the State Attorney General's Office, there was substantial controversy over how to respond to the case.

Assistant Attorney General Rod Walston recalled the most contentious and dramatic meetings he ever experienced while in office, which occurred over a heated two hours early in the litigation. Some state attorneys wanted to support the plaintiffs' position that any diversion impairing public trust uses was illegal, while others opposed it because the entire state water system relies on moving water around, and, as he explained, "if this principle were adopted, then the entire state water apparatus is illegal." Walston explained that their argument would invalidate the Los Angeles Aqueduct, the California Aqueduct, and the Colorado River Aqueduct. "People responsible for delivering that water should be very concerned about this case, and we must ensure that the State Water Project is not undermined."

However, he recalls that the State Water Board was generally sympathetic to the plaintiffs, as was the popular state governor, Jerry Brown, who had weighed in on

---

[88] Id.; see also Roderick Walston Interview, *supra* note 12 (describing the concerns the state of California raised as an intervenor in the suit).

[89] Nat'l Audubon Soc'y, 658 P.2d at 723–24 (rejecting the state's argument that "the state could grant tidelands free of the trust merely because the grant served some public purpose....").

[90] Roderick Walston, *The Public Trust and Water Rights*: National Audubon Society v. Superior Court, 22 LAND & WATER L. REV. 701, 714–19 (1987); Roderick Walston Interview, *supra* note 12 (in which Walston argued that despite conceptual differences, there is no practical difference between the beneficial use standard he argued for under the state constitution and the one the State adopted under the public trust doctrine.)

[91] Nat'l Audubon Soc'y, 658 P.2d at 723. See also Chapter 1(C)(2) ("Prior Appropriations") (discussing the beneficial use standard).

the issue in support of the public trust argument. "Everyone else was pounding on me from every direction in opposition to my hesitation: it was worse than a Supreme Court argument, because then there are only nine opposing you, and here there were twenty-five!"[92]

Many years later, while interviewing Rod Walston about these fractious debates within state government over the issue, I asked what his opponents in that heated room must have been thinking. Why did this argument make sense to them, when it made no sense to him? He explained his understanding in stark, simple terms: "These folks were not lawyers, and they hadn't thought it through."[93] Even the lawyers – including Bruce Dodge, he observed – hadn't thought through all the ramifications.[94] The strong *Audubon Society* view on the public trust doctrine was romantic, he said, but its proponents had never practiced water law, and they hadn't worked through the actual consequences of such a decision for the State's ability to provide the needed water resources on which the modern California economy and populace depended.[95]

As for the other personnel within his own agency, who did understand the stakes and were still sympathetic to the lake advocates position – well, he explained, they just thought Los Angeles didn't need so much water, and that Mono Lake should be protected.

d. The Bottom Line

In a nutshell then, the Mono Lake advocates claimed that diverting water to the detriment of a public trust resource violated state obligations, while Los Angeles maintained that the city had vested rights to export the water on the basis of its permits, regardless of this harm (and the State argued that providing city residents with needed water resources satisfied its public trust obligation). The plaintiffs essentially argued that the common law public trust doctrine, in defining a core requirement of state sovereign ownership of waterways, should trump any contrary claims under the statutory law of prior applications – while the defendants argued that the prior appropriations doctrine, an overriding act of statutory law, should trump the common law public trust (and the State argued that both its statutory and trust obligations were satisfied by the same act of providing Los Angeles with water).[96] The parties deadlocked over the seemingly irreconcilable issue of which rule of law reigns supreme. Meanwhile, the State maintained that the lake advocates' argument went too far, because it would cripple the State's ability to provide water to its largest

---

[92] Roderick Walston Interview, *supra* note 12.
[93] *Id.*
[94] *Id.*
[95] *Id.*
[96] *See* Nat'l Audubon Soc'y, 658 P.2d at 713–14, 718.

A. The Historic Mono Lake Case

urban municipalities, while Los Angeles's argument also went too far, because in its view, there could be no vested right – even under a valid permit – if the challenged use violates the California Constitution's beneficial use standard in Article X.[97]

Indeed, reviewing the two doctrines in isolation reveals a set of legal principles that seem hard to reconcile; neither so much as acknowledges the other. The court openly acknowledged that "the two systems of legal thought have been on a collision course," and that it was time to resolve the issue.[98] This, then, was the critical question of first impression that the *Mono Lake* case presented to the justices of the California Supreme Court: what is the relationship between the public trust doctrine and the law of appropriative water rights? When they point in opposite directions, which do we follow? Which trumps the other?

In its ultimate decision, the high state court famously declined to choose. Instead, it affirmed that both doctrines remain bedrock principles within California law, and that neither displaces the other.[99]

5. The California Supreme Court's Decision

In a highly anticipated decision, the California Supreme Court issued a complex opinion that both affirmed and disappointed the central arguments made by both principals. The prior appropriations statute does not foreclose the common law public trust doctrine,[100] it concluded, but neither did the public trust doctrine determine the future of California's massive and entrenched water works.[101] The Attorney General's Office was correct that protecting Mono Lake could not be the only meaningful state obligation, but neither could those other obligations excuse the state for allowing the annihilation of this treasured public trust resource. Solomon-like in his opinion for the court, Justice Allen Broussard announced that neither of the two sets of law at issue can be understood to trump the other, and that the state must somehow find an accommodation between them.[102] He emphasized that it is the obligation of the state to navigate the requirements of both – and that here, this state obligation had been failed.[103]

Justice Broussard's conclusions about the relationship between the public trust doctrine and statutory system of water law was joined by every member of an illustrious bench – Chief Justice Rose Bird, the first female member of the California Supreme Court and the first woman appointed as Chief Justice; Justice Stanley

---

[97] Roderick Walston Interview, *supra* note 12.
[98] *Nat'l Audubon Soc'y*, 658 P.2d at 712, 727.
[99] *Id.* at 727.
[100] *Id.* at 712.
[101] *Id.* at 712, 727.
[102] *Id.* at 716, 727.
[103] *Id.* at 712 (conceiving of California water law as "an integration including both the public trust doctrine and the board-administered appropriative rights system").

Mosk, the longest serving justice in the history of the court; Justice Cruz Reynoso, the first Latino member of the court; and Justice Otto Kaus, who had emigrated to California from Austria as his family fled the Nazis.[104] Justice Broussard – the first Black president of the California Judges Association, who put himself through school selling shoes and working in a cannery[105] – even won agreement on these points from his most staunchly conservative colleague, Justice Frank Richardson, who was elevated to the court by Governor Ronald Reagan and famous for his frequent and eloquent dissents in favor of judicial restraint.[106] Yet even Justice Richardson concurred in all but the final part of the decision, raising the separate procedural question of whether the court should share jurisdiction with the agency.[107]

On this point, the majority affirmed its concurrent jurisdiction with the Water Board to administer the public trust doctrine with regard to water rights, and it thereby approved the plaintiffs' ability to seek judicial relief without first exhausting administrative remedies.[108] Justice Richardson dissented on this point, emphasizing the importance of judicial modesty,[109] and his dissent was partnered with a separate concurrence by Justice Kaus, expressing sympathy his concerns while emphasizing why it should not apply in this case, given unique historical factors and the reasonable reliance interests of the plaintiffs.[110]

---

[104] *Nat'l Audubon Soc'y*, 658 P.2d *at* 733 (listing the concurring members of the majority opinion); *id.* at 733 (Richardson, J., concurring and dissenting) ("I concur with parts 1 through 4 of the majority opinion and with its analysis of the relationship between the public trust doctrine and the water rights system in this state."). For personal details about the members of the Court, see the online biographical materials curated by the California Supreme Court Historical Society, *California Supreme Court Justices*, at www.cschs.org/history/california-supreme-court-justices/.

[105] *In Memoriam – Allen E. Broussard: A California Supreme Court Justice Looks at Law and Society, 1964–1996*, Regional Oral History Office, Bancroft Library, University of California (1997), available by California Supreme Court Historical Society at www.cschs.org/history/california-supreme-court-justices/allen-e-broussard/.

[106] William Gallagher, Justice Frank K. Richardson, CAL. SUP. CT. HISTORICAL SOC'Y NEWSLETTER, Vol. II, No. 2 (1993), pp. 129–31, reprinted at www.cschs.org/wp-content/uploads/2022/03/Legal-Hist-1994-Yearbook-Oral-History-Justice-Richardson.pdf (noting that the justice is "best remembered for his role as a staunch judicial conservative on a decidedly liberal court").

[107] *Nat'l Audubon Soc'y*, 658 P.2d at 734 (Richardson, J., concurring and dissenting) ("The majority's suggestion that various statutory provisions contemplate the exercise of concurrent jurisdiction in cases of this kind is unconvincing.").

[108] *Id.* at 730–32. *See also id.* at 731–32 (finding that the California Water Code "impl[ies] that the superior court has concurrent original jurisdiction in suits to determine water rights.... The court ... need not ... invest the time required to acquire the skills and knowledge the board already possesses. When the case raises issues which should be considered by the board, the court may refer the case to the board. Thus the courts, through the exercise of sound discretion and the use of their reference powers, can substantially eliminate the danger that litigation will bypass the board's expert knowledge and frustrate its duty of comprehensive planning.").

[109] *Id.* at 733 (Richardson, J., dissenting) (concurring with the majority's analysis of the relationship between the public trust doctrine and the water rights system in California, but dissenting from the holding that the courts and the Water Board have concurrent jurisdiction in such cases).

[110] *Id.* at 733 (Kaus, J., concurring) (expressing sympathy for Justice Richardson's concern, but concluding that it should not apply in this case).

A. The Historic Mono Lake Case   143

Having established its jurisdiction to decide the matter, the majority proceeded to invalidate Los Angeles's decades-old old licenses and remand them back to the Water Board for reconsideration in light of its decision – directing the Board to balance the city's need for diversions from Mono Lake against the State's independent legal obligation to protect the scenic, ecological, and recreational values in the Mono Basin.[111] Reports that Justice Broussard had been heavily influenced by the public trust scholarship produced by the UC Davis symposium on the Mono Lake case[112] appear confirmed by frequent citations in his opinion, revealing the unusual intellectual dimensions of the case and the ongoing importance of legal scholarship to the development of the doctrine.[113]

The court also summarily dispensed with the possibility that Los Angeles might respond to a subsequent move by Water Board to curtail its diversions with a lawsuit contending such limitations would constitute a taking of property rights in violation of the Fifth Amendment. Noting that the issue had never been properly raised or considered, the court rejected the premise of such a suit by concluding that no vested rights barred its treatment of the issues now,[114] especially given the declaration in Article 10, § 2 of the California Constitution that water is always state property.[115] Responding to Adolf Moskovitz's invocation of the takings issue, Justice Frank Richardson memorably suggested that the opposite might be true: "It seems to me, Mr. Moskovitz, that if the City of L.A. wants to take the water supply and damage the public trust in Mono Lake, then they ought to pay the people of California for that privilege."[116]

Detailed further in the fuller legal analysis below, the court's most significant holding – that the prior appropriations doctrine did not abrogate California's public trust – was cause for celebration among the Mono Lake advocates.[117] The court rejected Los Angeles' argument that the common law trust had been displaced by statutory water allocation law, and it declined the Attorney General's invitation to interpret trust uses to incorporate any potential state interest recognized under the beneficial use standard. The majority warned that if it were to follow this suggestion, "in practical effect the doctrine would impose no restrictions on the state's ability to allocate trust property."[118] Instead, it emphasized that the public trust doctrine

---

[111] *Id.* at 728–29.
[112] E-mail from Harrison Dunning, Professor L. Emeritus, UC Davis, to Erin Ryan, Professor of L., Fla. State Univ. Coll. of L. (Mar. 1, 2015, 5:29 PM) (sharing anecdotal reports years after the case that a close friend of Justice Broussard's had indicated that "the articles from the conference had a big influence on the court").
[113] *See Nat'l Audubon Soc'y*, 658 P.2d at 709–32 (producing some eleven references to works in the symposium).
[114] *Id.* at 728–29; *see also* Chapter 5(B)(3) ("Duty of Ongoing Supervision").
[115] *Nat'l Audubon Soc'y*, 658 P.2d at 724–25.
[116] Brian Gray, Symposium, *Introduction and Dedication*, 57 HASTINGS L.J. 1237, 1238–39 (2006).
[117] *Nat'l Audubon Soc'y*, 658 P.2d at 712.
[118] *Id.* at 723.

protects "in stream" uses, not those that may be served by taking the water off-tract and out of basin.[119] The decision reinforced the public trust as not only a doctrine of state power but also a doctrine of state obligation – framing a duty "to protect the people's common heritage" in state waterways and to specific trust "uses and activities in the vicinity" of the water.[120]

Even so, the court also declined the invitation to exalt the public trust above all other considerations, including Los Angeles's legitimate need for water. Even as it refused to conflate public trust uses with beneficial uses, it heeded warnings by the Attorney General's Office that the entrenched legal and mechanical infrastructure constructed to move water resources around California could not be wished away, nor should it.[121] The court's decision acknowledged that the State's most populous areas have long depended on the appropriation of water from remote locations, often to the detriment of the basin of origin.[122] Water permitting laws govern established legal relationships, and the court could not casually dismiss the appropriative rights upon which holders, especially major metropolitan areas, had come to rely.[123] Though affirming that the instream values advocates heralded at Mono Lake are considered beneficial uses in California,[124] the court allowed that there may be times when the public interest in diversions outweighs the public values protected by the trust.[125]

Nevertheless, the court reconfirmed that the public trust doctrine remains the law of the land, and for that reason, the state may not casually ignore the legal obligations the doctrine imposes for the protections of navigable waterways.[126] Under circumstances like these, the court recognized that a navigable waterway cannot be meaningfully separated from the non-navigable tributaries that maintain it.[127] The state decision to permit out-of-basin diversions from the Mono Basin Creeks was properly subject to the constraints of the trust, and the court found that the Water Board had patently failed to consider the public trust implications of its licensing decisions in 1940[128] and 1970.[129] "Before state courts and agencies approve water diversions," warned the majority, "they should consider the effect of such diversions upon interests protected by the public trust, and attempt, so far as feasible, to avoid or minimize any harm to those interests."[130] In this regard, even as it heeded the

---

[119] Id. at 722–24.
[120] Id. at 723–24.
[121] Id. at 712, 727.
[122] Id. at 728–29.
[123] Nat'l Audubon Soc'y, 658 P.2d at 712.
[124] Id. at 726.
[125] Id. at 712, 727.
[126] Id. at 712.
[127] Id.
[128] Id. (finding the State's actions wanting because "[a]pproval of such diversion without considering public trust values ... may result in needless destruction of those values").
[129] Nat'l Audubon Soc'y, 658 P.2d at 714, 728–29.
[130] Id. at 712.

A. The Historic Mono Lake Case

Attorney General's warning that the State must be empowered to provide for the public welfare by shifting water out of basin, it rejected the State's bid for plenary power to decide such matters without regard to the environmental values at stake.[131]

Los Angeles appealed the case to the Supreme Court of the United States, arguing first that California had misinterpreted the public trust doctrine, which it framed as a doctrine of federal law, and second, that the court's decision had effected an unconstitutional taking by depriving Los Angeles of vested property rights without due process of law.[132] The United States, an additional defendant in the suit, argued that the petition did not present a proper issue for Supreme Court review, because the public trust doctrine was a matter of state law rather than federal law and opposed the takings claim.[133] The United States Supreme Court ultimately denied the petition, leaving the California Supreme Court's decision to stand.[134] As detailed in Chapter 8, the Supreme Court would come closer to considering the public trust doctrine in more detail about a decade later, only to avoid the issue once again,[135] leaving it entirely to the states. With the resolution of the state law claims in the original *Audubon Society* suit, the parties returned to federal court to finish litigating the federal common law air and water pollution nuisance claims, but the Ninth Circuit dismissed these claims.[136] That left several of the more important innovations introduced by the *Mono Lake* decision to become even more important legal elements, inviting the more detailed analysis that follows.

---

[131] Roderick Walston Interview, *supra* note 12. Walston noted that the California Supreme Court eventually adopted something close to the middle position the State had advocated, except that instead of tethering its analysis to Article X, as the State had recommended, it relied on the public trust doctrine itself (noting in a footnote that it did not have to reach the constitutional issue). *Id. See also* Nat'l Audubon Soc'y, 658 P.2d at 728 n.28 (noting that "[i]n view of our reliance on the public trust doctrine as a basis for reconsideration of DWP's usufructuary rights, we need not resolve that controversy," referring to the State's Article X, Section 2 argument).

[132] Petition for Writ of Certiorari, City of L.A. Dep't of Water & Power v. Nat'l Audubon Soc'y, 464 U.S. 977 (1983) (No. 83-300). *See also* Andrew H. Sawyer, *Changing Landscapes and Evolving Law: Lessons from Mono Lake on Takings and the Public Trust*, 50 OKLA. L. REV. 311, 317–18 (1997) (discussing the petition for certiorari).

[133] *See* sources cited *supra* note 131; *see also* Conway, *supra* note 56, at 634 n.108 (discussing opposition of the Department of Interior's Regional Solicitor). Conway explains that the United States argued against the takings claim "[o]ver the strenuous objections of the Department of Interior's Regional Solicitor for California ... [who] asserted that the case was ripe for review because the state court's ruling fundamentally changed the nature of Los Angeles's water rights. Despite his objections, the Solicitor's Office felt that the case was not ripe because no allocation of water has yet been determined ...." *Id.*

[134] GARY LIBECAP, OWENS VALLEY REVISITED: A REASSESSMENT OF THE WEST'S FIRST GREAT WATER TRANSFER 141 (2007) (reporting on the denial of Los Angeles's petition for certiorari).

[135] *See* Chapter 8(B)(2) ("The Secret Supreme Court Public Trust Debate").

[136] Nat'l Audubon Soc'y v. Dep't of Water, 869 F.2d 1206 (9th Cir. 1988) (holding that the federal common law nuisance claim based on water pollution was preempted by the Clean Water Act, declining to recognize the federal common law nuisance claim based on air pollution because the case did not involve federal rights or obligations or an interstate dispute unsuitable for the application of state law, and declining to decide whether the air pollution claim was preempted by the Clean Air Act).

B. UNPACKING THE *MONO LAKE* DECISION: LEGAL ELEMENTS AND INNOVATIONS

The reactions to the Mono Lake decision in political, legal, and scholarly circles was swift and passionate, as reviewed further in Chapter 6. But first, we pause to consider the most important legal ramifications of the decision for public trust conflicts even beyond Mono Lake itself.

The *Mono Lake* case not only saved Mono Lake, it established several important legal principles, interpreting the scope of the public trust doctrine in California and influencing its development in other states (and even other nations).[137] As noted earlier, its central jurisprudential contribution was the affirmation that – at least in California[138] – the common law trust had not been preempted by statutory and constitutional provisions establishing the prior appropriations doctrine and state water permitting program. The public trust doctrine thus continues to exert force independently from the statutory laws of private water allocation, and water planners must accommodate the interests protected by each. The court also took the opportunity to reiterate that public trust resources are not causally alienable by the state, which remains bound by trust principles in its responsibilities as trustee over the disposition of trust resources.[139]

Yet in addition to clarifying the relationship between the public trust and prior appropriation doctrines, the decision yielded several important points of public trust law, expanding doctrinal protections to environmental values, non-navigable tributaries, and even the operation of these principles over time. The case also signals important implications for the ongoing theoretical debate about the legal nature of the public trust doctrine itself.

1. *Environmental Public Trust Values*

The legal principle for which the *Mono Lake* case is most often celebrated is the recognition that the public trust doctrine protects not only the navigation and fishing values traditionally associated with the common law doctrine but also the ecological, scenic, and recreational values at stake at Mono Lake.[140] The Mono Basin

---

[137] *See* Chapters 7 ("The *Mono Lake* Doctrine") and 8 ("The Development of the Public Trust across the United States") (reviewing the development of the doctrine nationally and internationally).

[138] *See* Chapter 7 ("The *Mono Lake* Doctrine") (discussing jurisdictional differences between the states). Although the California court's interpretation is limited to California law, most states have reached similar conclusions, including Hawaii and Pennsylvania. *Id.* However, the Idaho legislature has taken its state's doctrine down a markedly different legal pathway. *Id.*

[139] Nat'l Audubon Soc'y v. Superior Ct., 658 P.2d 709, 723 (Cal. 1983) (responding to the California Attorney General's effort to "maximize state power under the trust" by broadly construing trust purposes to include any public use).

[140] As discussed in Chapter 4(D), the public trust analysis in the Mono Lake case is complemented by several additional cases that helped lay political foundation for the role of the doctrine in California

B. Unpacking the Mono Lake Decision

makes a great poster child for this proposition because it is such a visually stunning place, with a unique and life-productive ecosystem, attracting hundreds of thousands of recreational visitors each year. When I would give the daily South Tufa tour along the southwest shore as a Mono Lake ranger, we casually extolled the decision for its famous extension of public trust principles to include these more modern environmental values as though the *Mono Lake* case had invented the idea. Only later, in law school, would I learn that this was a bit of a local conceit; while the *Mono Lake* case made it famous, that expansion was really established by another case more than ten years earlier.

In this regard, *Mono Lake* is really just riding the coattails of a slightly earlier California case, *Marks v. Whitney*, a 1971 decision in which the California Supreme Court first allowed for consideration of environmental values.[141] The *Marks* court affirmed the flexibility of the public trust doctrine to encompass changing public needs in trust resources, including ecological, open space, habitat, scenery, and scientific values.[142] However, *Marks* addressed a comparatively dry set of facts, adjudicating the conflicting rights of private parties over the construction of a wharf in trust-protected tidelands.[143] By comparison, the compelling facts of the *Mono Lake* case, together with the force of the more photogenic environmental values at risk there, have made it the more popular standard-bearer for the expansion. As the later comer to the scene, *Mono* effectively stole *Marks'* rightful thunder. Regardless, the use of the public trust doctrine to protect the vulnerable water, air, wildlife, scenic, scientific, and recreational values of the Mono Basin remains the best-known feature of the Mono Lake story.

2. Application to Non-Navigable Tributaries

More concretely, the *Mono Lake* case extended public trust protections from the navigable waterway itself to include the non-navigable tributaries on which it relies

---

water law, including disputes over the American River and Putah Creek. *See, e.g.*, Stuart L. Somach, *The American River Decision: Balancing Instream Protection with Other Competing Beneficial Uses*, 1 RIVERS 251, 258–60 (1990) (discussing use of the doctrine in an unpublished Alameda County Court decision that led the state agency to relocate its exercise of rights from the Folsom South Canal upstream of Sacramento to Freeport downstream in order to preserve instream flow through the intervening channel); Joseph Sax, *Bringing an Ecological Perspective to Natural Resources Law: Fulfilling the Promise of the Public Trust*, in Nat. Res. Pol'y & Law: Trends and Directions 152–60 (Lawrence J. MacDonnell & Sarah F. Bates, eds. 1993) (discussing the same Alameda County case); Michael C. Blumm, *Public Property and the Democratization of Western Water Law: A Modern View of the Public Trust Doctrine*, 19 ENV'T L. 573, 591 (1989); Richard M. Frank, *The Public Trust Doctrine: Assessing Its Recent Past and Charting Its Future*, 45 U.C. DAVIS L. REV. 665, 670 (2012); Conway, *supra* note 56, at 631.

[141] Marks v. Whitney, 491 P.2d 374, 380 (Cal. 1971) (expanding public trust protections to ecological, habitat, open space, climatic, and scenic values).

[142] *Id.*

[143] *Id.* at 377.

hydrologically.[144] Nobody questioned that Mono Lake itself, spanning 45,000 acres and reaching depths of hundreds of feet, is a navigable waterway.[145] It has been commercially navigated since the time of the California Gold Rush, when it was used to transport logs from the Jeffrey pine forest south of the lake to Bodie, one of the principal Gold Rush boom towns north of the Basin.[146] Yet Los Angeles was not diverting water directly from Mono Lake, whose salty waters are notoriously nonpotable – rather, the aqueduct diverts from the freshwater Mono Basin creeks that channel snowmelt from the Sierra Nevada mountains into the lake, continuously replenishing the waterway against continuous evaporation. These steep, rocky creeks were nowhere near navigable at the points of diversion.[147] Los Angeles attempted to leverage this distinction, arguing that the public trust protects *only* navigable waterways. It was a viable argument, as the question had not been addressed before then.

However, the court recognized the hydrological relationship between the lake and its tributaries to construe them as one for the purpose of doctrinal protection,[148] holding that the essential tributaries of a navigable waterway must also be protected if the alternative would result in the destruction of the protected waterway. As the court reasoned, protection of the public trust values at Mono Lake had to include protection of its tributaries, without which the navigable waterway itself would inexorably disappear.

This legal recognition of the critical hydrological relationship between protected navigable waterways and their tributaries continues to play a pivotal role in the unfolding power of the public trust doctrine to protect California waterways. Most recently, this element of *Mono Lake* precedent proved foundational in a public trust decision extending the non-navigable tributary rule to groundwater, where harm to the groundwater tributaries of a navigable water threaten the public trust values of the waterway itself.[149] The Scott River in Northern California is a navigable river substantially fed by groundwater sources, and the river has seriously declined as these sources are increasingly exploited, mostly for agricultural use.[150] The plaintiffs in the *Scott River* case sought to extend the *Mono Lake* rule to groundwater on exactly the same theory – that even though groundwater tributaries are non-navigable, withdrawals must be limited to protect the navigable waterway that depends on them.

In 2018, the California Court of Appeal affirmed that the State has the authority and obligation under the public trust doctrine to regulate extractions of groundwater

---

[144] Nat'l Audubon Soc'y, 658 P.2d at 720–21.
[145] HART, *supra* note 15, at 24–25.
[146] *See* Chapter 3(A) ("The Mono Lake Basin") (describing human history at Mono Lake); *see also* HART, *supra* note 15, at 24–25.
[147] Nat'l Audubon Soc'y, 658 P.2d at 709, 720–21.
[148] *Id.*
[149] Env't L. Found. v. State Water Res. Control Bd. (*Scott River Case*), 237 Cal. Rptr. 3d 393, 401–03 (Cal. Ct. App. 2018), *review denied* (Nov. 28, 2018) (for further discussion of this case, see Chapter 7(B)(1)(c) ("The Scott River Case and Extension to Groundwater")).
[150] *Scott River Case*, 237 Cal. Rptr. 3d at 397.

that affect public trust uses in the Scott River.[151] The decision was heralded by environmentalists, who have long urged that water law better account for the interdependence of ground and surface water resources.[152] Yet it was equally decried by advocates for property rights holders, including the farmers and ranchers who had been withdrawing groundwater that was the subject of this litigation for commercial purposes.[153] Later that year, when the defendant county appealed this decision to the California Supreme Court, the high court denied review, making the Court of Appeal's decision the final word in the case.[154]

3. Duty of Ongoing Supervision

While these are all important features of the *Mono Lake* decision, its potentially widest-reaching element was its characterization of the State's public trust responsibilities over time.[155] Setting off alarm bells for water managers throughout the Western United States, the California Supreme Court articulated a state duty of ongoing oversight for public trust resources.[156] The court clarified that the public trust doctrine not only requires the state to protect trust resources as much as feasible when allocating water or otherwise managing trust resources, but also imposes on the state a *continuing duty* to supervise trust resources – long after any given management decision is made.[157]

Conceptually, this element of the decision – the *Mono Lake* doctrine of ongoing oversight – was necessary to overcome the time lag between Los Angeles' original water licenses in 1940 and the filing of the *Mono Lake* litigation forty years later.[158] It was the ongoing oversight doctrine that empowered (and obligated) the state to

---

[151] *Id.* at 401–03.
[152] *See* Richard Frank, *California Court Finds Public Trust Doctrine Applies to State Groundwater Resources*, LEGALPLANET (Aug. 29, 2018), legal-planet.org/2018/08/29/california-court-finds-public-trust-doctrine-applies-to-state-groundwater-resources/ [https://perma.cc/C2VP-N3ZL] (reporting that the court declared that "California's powerful public trust doctrine applies to at least some of the state's overtaxed groundwater resources ... [and] rejects the argument that California's Sustainable Groundwater Management Act displaces the public trust doctrine's applicability to groundwater resources").
[153] Jeremy Talcott, *Should the Public Trust Doctrine Be Expanded to the Use of Groundwater?*, PAC. LEGAL FOUND. (Aug. 10, 2017), https://pacificlegal.org/public-trust-doctrine-expanded-use-groundwater/ ("We ask the Court of Appeal to overturn this ... decision, which expanded public trust considerations to permits issued for the use of groundwater.").
[154] Order Denying Petition for Review, Env't L. Found. v. State Water Res. Control Bd., No. S251849 (Cal. Nov. 28, 2018). Since then, much ink has been spilled over the implications of the decision for California water law and how it may affect the development and review of groundwater sustainability plans under California's 2014 Sustainable Groundwater Management Act. Sustainable Groundwater Management Act, CAL. WATER CODE §§ 10720 – 10737.8, added by Stats. 204, c. 346 (S.B. 1168, eff. Jan 1, 2015).
[155] *See* Nat'l Audubon Soc'y v. Superior Ct., 658 P.2d 709, 709 (Cal. 1983).
[156] *Id.* at 727.
[157] *Id.* at 728.
[158] *Id.* at 728–29.

revisit its decision to approve Mono Basin water exports a half century earlier, when that decision had failed to take account of public trust obligations. *Mono Lake* was not the first case to apply the doctrine in the context of water rights – it followed a recent North Dakota case requiring consideration of the impacts of a new consumptive permit on existing and future supply[159] – but it was the first to do so retroactively. In its decision, the California high court held that there is no statute of limitations on public trust claims; the state has an ongoing duty to supervise public trust resources and consider its responsibilities under the doctrine.[160]

This new understanding of the doctrine had potentially staggering consequences. By implication, it meant that the state might have to revisit its Mono Lake diversion decision again in another forty years' time – or sooner than that, or later – as circumstances evolve. But of course, a state duty to revisit past allocation decisions that are compromising trust values in the present has ramifications far beyond the Mono Basin. It could require the state to revisit any past decision involving a navigable waterway for the same reason, or if new circumstances significantly alter the calculus underlying any past decision. At least in theory, all water allocation or management decisions impacting public trust waterways could be up for renegotiation, as would be all future decisions. And not just in California, but in other western states influenced by California law.

The potential ramifications of the public trust duty of ongoing supervision sent shock waves through the American West, where diverters feared what this could mean for the certainty of their rights and infrastructure.[161] Throughout the arid western states, large volumes of water are transported long distances in just the way the Los Angeles aqueduct exports it from the Mono Basin.[162] Urban and agricultural development all over the arid west has depended on the ability to shift water from wetter to drier parts.[163] If this new doctrine of ongoing oversight were widely applied, all of those water licenses would suddenly become very uncertain. The prospect of revisiting management decisions made without consideration of public trust values threatened to upend many seemingly settled allocation plans because before the *Mono Lake* case called attention to them, public trust issues were unlikely to have been raised during the decision-making process.[164] If public trust values were being affected in ways that had not been anticipated when those licenses were initially

---

[159] United Plainsmen Ass'n v. N.D. State Water Conservation Comm'n, 247 N.W.2d 457, 463 (N.D. 1976).
[160] *Nat'l Audubon Soc'y*, 658 P.2d at 727–28, 732.
[161] See LIBECAP, *supra* note 134, at 144 ("Moreover, the notoriety of the Mono Lake situation and the nature of the judicial opinions rendered in regard to it potentially had very profound implications for the security of water rights and actions to be taken to respond to changing water values and externalities throughout the West.").
[162] *See generally* MARC REISNER, CADILLAC DESERT: THE AMERICAN WEST AND ITS DISAPPEARING WATER 12 (1993) (noting that water from Colorado River canyons is moved to meet demand in Phoenix and Palm Springs).
[163] *See id.*
[164] *Nat'l Audubon Soc'y*, 658 P.2d at 728.

B. Unpacking the Mono Lake Decision

granted, then all the appropriative rights on which remote uses had developed in reliance would be up for renegotiation. The doctrine of continuing oversight quickly became an extremely controversial element of the decision.[165]

Perhaps for the same reason, it is also a doctrinal element of the case that has rarely been adopted outside of California. One exception is Hawaii, where the state Supreme Court has also held that private allocation decisions do not displace the trust,[166] though it is a riparian state operating under a wholly different set of legal and hydrological constraints, with a constitutionally incorporated trust.[167] Beyond Hawaii, however, no western state has formally adopted the California requirement of ongoing oversight. The closest a prior appropriations state has come to embracing the *Mono Lake* doctrine of ongoing oversight is in Nevada, where two concurring justices once suggested an important role for the public trust doctrine in a water rights case, although their analysis did not become part of the majority opinion[168] (and as discussed in Chapter 7, subsequent caselaw has probably obviated these moves[169]). Also, as discussed further below, at least one state has gone out of its way to ensure that it does not follow in California's footsteps after Mono Lake. After several Idaho cases signaled approval of this feature of the California public trust,[170] they were pointedly overruled by the state legislature.[171]

Even within California, where the doctrine remains good law, the ongoing oversight doctrine has had a very limited impact on previously established water rights outside of the Mono Basin – though it does play an important role in prospective administrative decision-making.[172] In a quantitative study of freshwater public trust litigation in California since *Mono Lake*, Professor David Owen concludes that outside of the Mono Basin, the doctrine has exerted almost no force on existing

---

[165] *See* LIBECAP, *supra* note 134, at 151–53 (critiquing the Mono Lake decision's impact on prior appropriations systems by creating uncertainty, undermining property rights, and compromising economic efficiency); Barton H. Thompson, Jr., *Judicial Takings*, 76 VA. L. REV. 1449, 1533 (1990) (noting how Mono Lake "surprised many people and was certainly a deviation from most water lawyers' expectations").

[166] In re Water Use Permit Applications (Waiahole Ditch), 9 P.3d 409, 445 (Haw. 2000) (holding that the state water code "does not supplant the protections of the public trust doctrine").

[167] *See* HAW. CONST. art. XI, § 1.

[168] Mineral Cnty. v. Dep't of Conservation & Nat. Res., 20 P.3d 800, 807 (Nev. 2001) (Rose, J., concurring) (arguing that the Court should affirm the existence and role of Nevada's public trust doctrine); *see also* Lawrence v. Clark Cnty., 254 P.3d 606, 617 (Nev. 2011) (adopting the public trust doctrine expressly but in a case that did not address water rights).

[169] *See* Chapter 7(C)(3) ("Nevada: Mixed Messages in the Walker Lake Basin").

[170] *See, e.g.*, Kootenai Env't Alliance v. Panhandle Yacht Club, 671 P.2d 1085, 1094, 1096 (Idaho 1983) (adopting the "California rule" but finding that the land grant at issue did not violate it).

[171] *See* Idaho Code § 58–1201 (1996); *see also* Chapter 7(C)(2) ("Idaho: Legislative Repudiation of the Constitutive Constraint") (discussing Idaho's legislative abrogation of the common law doctrine).

[172] *See generally* David Owen, *The Mono Lake Case, the Public Trust Doctrine, and the Administrative State*, 45 U.C. DAVIS L. REV. 1099 (2012) (noting that, despite this potential, the doctrine has not upended many established water rights). Depending on the final outcome of the *Scott River* litigation, however, the doctrine may yet be extended to previously asserted groundwater rights. *See generally Scott River Case*, *supra* note 105.

patterns of water use, even when serious interference with trust values are manifest.[173] He concludes that effects of the doctrine are inextricably intertwined with the force of other environmental laws, which are often more responsible for substantive results, almost exclusively at the administrative level, and most often with regard to prospective uses of water, rather than existing rights.[174]

4. The Nature of the Public Trust Doctrine

As noted, the court concluded that California's statutorily adopted prior appropriations doctrine did not abrogate its common law public trust doctrine, and that neither legal precept necessarily trumps the other.[175] Both sets of legal requirements must be considered together and perhaps balanced against one another when the state makes management decisions about water resources, like Mono Lake, subject to the public trust.[176] Yet this grand gesture of legal compromise highlights a singular feature of the public trust doctrine and how it departs from the usual legal norms. Because at first blush, Los Angeles' argument on this point seems correct – normally, statutory law *does* trump the common law.[177] As an intervenor in the lawsuit, the California State Attorney General's office had similar concerns when it urged the court to tether its analysis not to the public trust doctrine but to the beneficial use standard embedded in Article X of the California Constitution.[178]

This seemingly paradoxical result makes sense, however, if the public trust doctrine originated as a constitutive obligation regarding the management of public commons water resources, rather than an ordinary common law doctrine subject to statutory override. If the public trust doctrine serves to both grant and limit sovereign authority – granting the sovereign ownership of these resources but obligating it to manage them in trust for the public – then it would be self-defeating to allow the state to abolish that limit legislatively. Some have argued that this gives the doctrine a quasi-constitutional foundation, an underlying legal constraint that statutory law can build upon but not undermine, which makes it inherently different from more conventional, garden-variety common law doctrines.[179] Others have argued

---

[173] Owen, *supra* note 128, at 1122–23.
[174] See id. at 1135–36.
[175] Nat'l Audubon Soc'y v. Super. Ct., 658 P.2d 709, 727 (Cal. 1983).
[176] Id.
[177] See, e.g., *Effects of Statutes on Common Law*, *supra* note 60; Mod. Barber Colls. v. Cal. Emp. State Comm'n, 192 P.2d 916, 920 (Cal. 1948) (noting that the legislature may "create new rights or provide that rights which have previously existed shall no longer arise, and it has full power to regulate and circumscribe the methods and means of enjoying those rights").
[178] Roderick Walston Interview, *supra* note 12 (describing the concerns the state of California raised as an intervenor in the suit).
[179] See, e.g., Jan S. Stevens, *The Public Trust: A Sovereign's Ancient Prerogative Becomes the People's Environmental Right*, 14 U.C. DAVIS L. REV. 195, 200 (1980) (arguing the same); see also Michael Blumm & Mary Christina Wood, "*No Ordinary Lawsuit*": *Climate Change, Due Process, and the*

B. *Unpacking the* Mono Lake *Decision*

that this interpretation of the public trust doctrine is a necessary implication of the Equal Footing doctrine,[180] which is also recognized as a principle of U.S. constitutional law[181] – even though, like the words "public trust," the words "equal footing" appear nowhere in the U.S. Constitution.

Indeed, while many American jurisdictions have followed California's model,[182] at least one American state – Idaho – has taken a markedly different approach, prompting both political and scholarly controversy.[183] As detailed further in Chapter 7, after the Idaho Supreme Court issued a series of public trust decisions converging on the California Supreme Court's interpretation in *Mono Lake*,[184] the state legislature enacted a statute that expressly foreclosed this interpretive path.[185] The legislation declared that the public trust doctrine did limit the State's ability to alienate title to the beds of navigable waters, but that it had little impact beyond that,[186]

Public Trust Doctrine, 67 Am. U. L. Rev. 1, 43–44 (2017) (arguing that the public trust doctrine is "an inherent constitutional limit on sovereignty"); Michael C. Blumm, Harrison C. Dunning & Scott W. Reed, *Renouncing the Public Trust Doctrine: An Assessment of the Validity of Idaho House Bill 794*, 24 Ecology L.Q. 461 (1997).

[180] *See, e.g.*, Michael Blumm & Lynn Schaffer, *The Federal Public Trust Doctrine: Misinterpreting Justice Kennedy and Illinois Central Railroad*, 45 Env't L. 257, 400–01 (2015); James R. Rasband, *The Disregarded Common Parentage of the Equal Footing and Public Trust Doctrines*, 32 Land & Water L. Rev. 1 (1997); Harrison C. Dunning, *The Public Trust: A Fundamental Doctrine of American Property Law*, 19 Env't L. 515, 524 (1989).

[181] U.S. Const. art. IV, § 3, cl. 1; *see also* Coyle v. Smith, 221 U.S. 559, 566 (1911) (interpreting the equal footing clause in reference to sovereign ownership of submerged lands).

[182] *See, e.g.*, Lawrence v. Clark Cnty., 254 P.3d 606, 613 (Nev. 2011) ("The final underpinning of our formal adoption of the public trust doctrine arises from the inherent limitations on the state's sovereign power."); In re Water Use Permit Applications (Waiahole Ditch), 9 P.3d 409, 445 (Haw. 2000) ("[H]istory and precedent have established the public trust as an inherent attribute of sovereign authority."); East Cape May v. State Dep't of Env't Prot., 777 A.2d 1015, 1034 (N.J. Super. A.D. 2001) (noting that "tidally-flowed land has always been subject to the public trust doctrine … [which] provides that the sovereign never waives its right to regulate the use of public trust property"); Caminiti v. Boyle, 732 P.2d 989, 994 (1987) ("The state can no more convey or give away this jus publicum interest than it can 'abdicate its police powers in the administration of government and the preservation of the peace.'"); *see also* Chapter 7(C)(1) ("California: A Constitutive Constraint").

[183] James M. Kearney, *Recent Statute: Closing the Floodgates? Idaho's Statutory Limitation on the Public Trust Doctrine*, 34 Idaho L. Rev. 91, 94 (1997); Blumm, Dunning & Reed, *supra* note 135, at 472 (noting that the new statute "was the legislature's response to judicial public trust declarations" in a series of Idaho Supreme Court cases).

[184] *See, e.g.*, Selkirk-Priest Basin Ass'n v. State *ex rel*. Andrus, 127 Idaho 239, 240 (1995) (suggesting that the public trust doctrine might be used to constrain harm from logging activities to an impacted water body); Idaho Conservation League v. State, 911 P.2d 748 (Idaho 1995) (declining intervention by environmental groups to raise public trust issues where state ownership was not at issue, but suggesting in dicta that the public trust doctrine could take precedence over vested water rights); *see also* Kearney, *supra* note 139 at 95–96 (discussing the reaction of the legislature to these cases).

[185] Idaho Code §§ 58–1201–58–1203 (1996); *see also* Chapter 7(C)(2) ("Idaho: Legislative Repudiation of the Constitutive Constraint").

[186] *See* Idaho Code §§ 58–1201(4), (6) (defining the public trust doctrine as guiding alienation of the title of the beds of navigable waters and clarifying that the purpose of the act is to define limits on the public trust doctrine); *id.* at § 58–1203(1) (limits the public trust doctrine to "solely a limitation on the power of the state to alienate or encumber the title to the beds of navigable waters").

preventing the doctrine from impacting the allocation of prior appropriative water rights or state decisions about the commercial, agricultural, or recreational uses of public trust waterways.[187]

While many observers contend that the Idaho statute represented an illegitimate legislative move,[188] in fairness, that depends on the nature of the doctrine at its core. If the public trust doctrine does include a constitutive limit on sovereign authority over natural resource public commons, then yes – the Idaho legislature's move to abrogate this limit was *ultra vires*, or beyond its legitimate authority. That view is reflected in the California approach, mirrored in other states with strong common law doctrines, such as Hawaii, New Jersey, and Washington, and those with express constitutional trusts, such as Pennsylvania.[189] But the Idaho legislature treated the doctrine as just another conventional expression of ordinary state authority, which is normally subject to legislative change. The Idaho example poses a strong challenge to the constitutive public trust model, indicating both the variability of the doctrine among U.S. jurisdictions and also this critical underlying theoretical dilemma.

As discussed at length in Chapter 7, the contest between the California and Idaho models is significant, because it reveals precisely this unresolved theoretical question at the heart of the public trust doctrine. Is it an inviolate element of sovereign authority that cannot be cavalierly extinguished? Or is it an example of conventional police power, the more ordinary well of state authority through which it acts to protect the public, which is always subject to legislative modification? The contrary approaches taken by these states pose a thorny jurisprudential problem because they stake out mutually exclusive interpretations of the nature of the public trust doctrine: either the doctrine has always been a malleable expression of conventional state authority, or it is a less negotiable constraint on sovereign power that was never ripe for renegotiation.[190]

This disjuncture begs the question: which is the correct approach? To varying degrees, debate over the contours of public trust governance continues to unfold in centers of judicial, legislative, and executive decision-making across the nation,[191] demonstrating that the project of interpreting the public trust remains a work in progress to which we are all bearing witness. But more importantly, at least for the purposes of the central story here, what did all this mean for Mono Lake?

---

[187] *Id.* at § 58–1203(3) (does not limit the state to authorize public and private use or alienation of title to the beds of navigable waters if the state board of land commissioners determines that it is in accordance with Idaho statutes and constitution and for the purposes of navigation, commerce, recreation, agriculture, mining, forestry, or other uses).

[188] *See, e.g.,* Kearney, *supra* note 139, at 94; Blumm, Dunning & Reed, *supra* note 135, at 472.

[189] *See* Chapter 8(A) ("The Planes of Public Trust Development across the United States") (discussing the public trust doctrine in these states).

[190] *See* Chapter 7(C) ("Ordinary Common Law or Quasi-Constitutional?").

[191] *See* Chapter 8 ("Beyond Mono Lake: The Development of the Public Trust Doctrine across the United States").

5. A Substantive or Procedural Doctrine?

The California Supreme Court's decision in 1983 was both a turning point in the history of the evolving American public trust doctrine and a turning point for the protection of Mono Lake. But from the latter perspective, it was a starting point, and hardly a finish line. What did that decision actually mean for the falling lake level and failing ecology? What did it actually mandate legally? What, if anything, would it require anyone to actually *do*, or *not* do?

It is important to acknowledge that as momentous as the decision may have seemed, the court did not provide much guidance about *how*, exactly, the state should proceed in balancing the protection of public trust values at Mono Lake with the legitimate needs for water in Los Angeles. Essentially, the court affirmed that these are both legitimate, if incommensurate interests, and that the state is obliged to consider all of them in managing the wet gold of its scarce water resources. But was there more? Analytically, one can reasonably ask whether the decision creates a mere procedural requirement – a command to think carefully before deciding to compromise trust values, such as the "look before you leap" analysis required by the National Environmental Policy Act (NEPA)[192] or its state equivalents[193] that require the government to assess possible environmental impacts before taking potentially harmful action – or an enforceable substantive command to protect trust values when harm is imminent. The procedural requirement is clear, as the decision was premised on the state's failure to consider public trust obligations at Mono Lake in the original licensing decision. But was there also more than that?

The decision is so understated on this point that it takes a careful review to locate it, but in fact, the court did articulate a cognizable, if modest, substantive component: to protect public trust values as much as – well, as much as possible.[194] Its specific choice of word was "feasible" – in its direction that state courts and agencies approving water diversions should "consider the effect of such diversions upon interests protected by the public trust, *and attempt, so far as feasible, to avoid or minimize any harm to those interests.*"[195]

Requiring the state to avoid harming trust values as much as is "feasible" leaves an awful lot to state discretion, but it does imbue a substantive dimension to California's public trust doctrine that distinguishes it from the purely procedural requirements of, for example, the NEPA – which requires only that agencies look before they leap, regardless of what that look tells them about the likely environmental outcomes.[196]

---

[192] National Environmental Policy Act of 1969 (NEPA), 42 U.S.C. §§ 4321.
[193] *See, e.g.*, California Environmental Quality Act, CAL. PUB. RES. CODE § 21000 (1970) (setting forth a state analog to the federal National Environmental Policy Act subjecting state action to look-before-you-leap environmental analysis).
[194] Nat'l Audubon Soc'y v. Super. Ct., 658 P.2d 709, 728 (Cal. 1983).
[195] *Id.* at 728 (emphasis added).
[196] *See* National Environmental Policy Act §§ 4321–4370.

Such breadth of discretion begs questions about whether the California court's command has any real bite, but the language does provide both a moral impetus for state action and a legal hook for public and judicial oversight.

As described earlier, on these particular facts, the court agreed with the plaintiffs that the State could not allow the Mono Lake tributaries to be diverted to the extinguishment of its public trust values without meaningfully considering what possibilities existed to avoid that. While affirming that Southern California's legitimate water needs remain protected by appropriations law – and that the State retains the power to prioritize other public purposes even if appropriated diversions harm public trust values – it also concluded that such appropriative rights are always subject to the state's ongoing duty to supervise the impact of diversions on the navigational and environmental values associated with trust resources.[197]

The decision thus makes clear that the State may not rely on past decisions as determinative without seriously assessing their current and future consequences, and that the Water Board must protect trust values as much as is *feasible* – perhaps appropriately punting the determination to the agency experts who can best engage in the kinds of research and public participation necessary to evaluate what is "feasible" under the given circumstances.

And punt it did, because the decision itself does not provide very much guidance about what "feasible" actually means. Would the Water Board have satisfied the court's command had it considered the issues and simply decided to renew Los Angeles's rights to divert as before? So long as it produced a solid enough record of the evidence to withstand the traditional "arbitrary and capricious" standard of judicial review for agency decision-making, a sympathetic court might have affirmed the agency's action against subsequent challenge. On the other hand, we now know that this almost certainly should *not* have satisfied the command to protect as much as is feasible, because more really *was* feasible. At least with the benefit of hindsight we have seen that much more protection was possible, once Los Angeles undertook the serious water conservation measures detailed in Chapter 6. Does it all just come down to what kind of record the agency produces, how hard a look the overseeing court takes, and perhaps how good everyone is at predicting the future at the moment of decision?

In the end, the decision raises questions as big as those it answers. The requirement to protect trust resources at some level clearly deviates from NEPA's purely procedural requirement, but it remains notably unclear what kind of substantive obligation is left. In keeping with California legal tradition, perhaps the State's public trust obligations come closer to the command of California's own version of NEPA, the California Environmental Quality Act[198] – which disallows approval of an unmitigated environmentally harmful project only if the state formally

---

[197] *Nat'l Audubon Soc'y*, 658 P.2d at 727.
[198] CAL. PUB. RES. CODE § 21081 (2007).

B. Unpacking the Mono Lake Decision

explains the overriding public considerations that outweigh the project's significant impacts.[199] Either way, in implementing a doctrine that stakes its methodology on judicial discretion to oversee political decision-making, a lot hinges on both judicial and political discretion. Like most environmental governance, the task is distinguished by its complexity.

* * *

And so it was that on February 17, 1983, the California Supreme Court held that the public trust doctrine obligated good faith efforts by the State to protect Mono Lake, and accordingly, that Los Angeles's water rights must be reconsidered in light of these public trust obligations. The news was met with celebration by Mono Lake advocates around the state, the nation, and even the world. It was a dramatic legal moment, but it was hardly the end of the legal drama in the Mono Basin. There was still much to be done to save the lake.

The decision left a lot to the uncertain judicial, administrative, and political processes that would follow. Over the next ten years, a series of additional cases were brought in court and ultimately consolidated to become part of the Water Board's fateful decision-making, all while big state and federal moves were made to protect the Mono Basin lands surrounding the lake, as well as the water security of millions of Angelenos.

In the meanwhile, though the public trust doctrine was cast more as a vehicle for environmental protection than a guarantor of environmental rights, the decision's emphasis on the state's duty of ongoing trust supervision made clear that the beneficiaries of the public trust include future generations. And in casting the doctrine as a nonwaivable sovereign obligation to protect environmental values for these future generations – all entitled to the benefit of the trust and to hold the state to account – it set the stage for modern recognition of the doctrine as a set of reciprocal rights and duties, or a framework for environmental rights.

---

[199] *Id.*

6

In the Wake of *Audubon*

The Legal and Political Aftermath

A.	Protecting the Mono Basin Land	159
	1. The Mono Lake Tufa State Natural Reserve	159
	2. The Mono Basin National Forest Scenic Area	161
B.	Other Mono Lake Litigation	165
	1. *Dahlgren*	165
	2. *CalTrout*	166
	3. *In the Matter of Mono Lake Water Rights*	169
C.	State and Federal Funding for Water Conservation	172
D.	Decision 1631: Implementation by the Water Board	174
	1. A New Lake Level Target: 6,392'	174
	2. Los Angeles Turns a New Page	177
E.	A Reprieve for Mono Lake?	181
	1. Mono Lake after Decision 1631	182
	2. Owens Valley after *Audubon*	189

Even though the California Supreme Court's 1983 decision in *Audubon Society* was the seminal step toward the protection of Mono Lake, it was only the first step – and an uncertain one at best. It required the Water Board to consider the public trust values in the Mono Basin before adjudicating Los Angeles's permits, but it did not specify how to balance the competing interests at stake. Moreover, it was not the only means by which advocates sought to protect the lake and its failing ecosystem. Various proposals to conserve Mono basin lands and fund water conservation projects were generated in the policymaking spheres, and a series of additional cases were brought by environmentalists, hunters, and fishers, all adding legal force to the California Supreme Court's command to take seriously the State's obligation to protect the Mono Basin environment.

In the immediate aftermath of *Audubon Society*, Congress established the Mono Basin National Forest Scenic Area – the first of an entirely new form of federally designated conservation lands – in an effort to further protect the scenic, ecological, and recreational features of the Basin. Additional litigation further expanded protections for environmental values at Mono Lake, including the less famous sibling litigation to *Audubon Society*, the *CalTrout* series. Yet the legal fate of Mono Lake would be uncertain for at least another decade, as all stakeholders awaited the Water Board's decision reconfiguring Los Angeles' water rights in light of all these judicial actions.

This chapter addresses the legal aftermath of the *Audubon Society* decision, proceeding simultaneously along judicial, legislative, administrative, and political pathways. It reviews the creation of the Mono Basin National Forest Scenic Area to protect the resources of the Basin without imposing the specific constraints of National Park Service management. It traces the complex web of the later *CalTrout* litigation over Mono Basin creeks that put further pressure on water allocation plans. It recounts how the Water Board ultimately interpreted and implemented the results of all this litigation in Decision 1631, the historic legal moment that would actually ensure more water for Mono Lake, and the efforts to brainstorm additional sources of water supply for Los Angeles.

Finally, it addresses the important choices that Los Angeles made in its response to these legal outcomes – brave decisions that changed the direction of subsequent efforts to restore Mono Lake. These shifts, following new preferences voiced by Angelenos, highlight the force and persuasiveness of the underlying public trust principle expressed in *Audubon Society* and honored by Decision 1631. The chapter closes with an update on the status of ongoing efforts to protect both the Mono Basin and the Owens Valley.

A. PROTECTING THE MONO BASIN LAND

While the judicial activity focused on protecting the waters of the Mono Basin, other advocacy centered on protecting the Mono Basin Lands, achieving legislative protection at the state and federal levels for surrounding lands and waters in the Mono Lake Tufa State Natural Reserve and the Mono Basin National Forest Scenic Area.

1. *The Mono Lake Tufa State Natural Reserve*

Alongside the drama in court, the protection of natural resource values in the Mono Basin continued along a parallel political track – the movements to protect both the Mono Lake Basin as a federally protected National Monument and the state lands immediately surrounding Mono Lake as a state park.

It may seem an unusual arrangement – a state park alongside a surrounding federal "park" – but the reason for these fragmented state and federal conservation lands relates back to the very doctrine at the center of the Mono Lake story: the public trust doctrine. Mono Lake is a navigable waterway, and so by operation of the public trust doctrine described in Chapter 1, the lake and submerged lands beneath it have been owned by the State in trust for the public ever since California became a state.[1] Under the common law doctrines of reliction, accretion, and avulsion, the artificial (and relatively sudden) exposure of the formerly submerged lakebed (the ring of land between the pre-diversion 6,417' lake level and the post-diversion lowered shoreline) was believed to belong to the State, and so the exposed tufa towers and immediate lakefront territory were sheltered as state lands.[2] As a result, prior to the 1986 litigation between the California State Land Commission and the United States discussed later, one could visit Mono Lake only by passing through the surrounding federal lands, but one could only reach Mono Lake itself by entering the State Park that completely encircled it.[3] That litigation would eventually alter this configuration.[4]

In any event, creating the Mono Lake Tufa State Natural Reserve was the comparatively easy part. Californians and others fell in love with the unique and bizarrely beautiful groves of limestone tufa towers that became exposed at the edge of the lake (especially at the mouths of the Mono Basin feeder creeks, where underground springs pump calcium-laden spring water into the carbonate-rich lake water).[5] These tufa towers were beautiful to behold and vulnerable to destruction, so Mono Lake advocates sought their formal protection as conservation lands of some kind. In response, lawmakers considered a variety of alternatives to facilitate public enjoyment of the area while conserving the fragile resources there and educating the public about the environmental values at Mono Lake.

In 1981, even as the *Audubon Society* litigation was unfolding, California lawmakers passed a bill, signed into law shortly thereafter by Governor Jerry Brown, to protect Mono Lake and its exposed lakebed as a component of the California State Park system.[6] In 1982, the Mono Lake Tufa State Natural Reserve was established, encompassing the lake and the tightly surrounding ring of "relicted land" that had been underwater before the aqueduct had begun to draw the lake level down. In fact, Mono Lake sits at the interesting nexus of all three levels of municipal, state, and federal conservation lands management – completed by the municipal Mono Lake County park on the northwest side of the lake, where mostly local residents enjoy the Mono County-administered boardwalk, picnic area, playground, and

---

[1] See Chapter 1 ("The Historical Origins of the Modern Public Trust Doctrine") (explaining the mechanics of the doctrine).
[2] See, e.g., Stop the Beach Renourishment, Inc. v. Fla. Dep't of Env't Prot., 560 U.S. 702, 709–11 (2010) (explaining operation of the avulsion/accretion doctrines).
[3] MONO LAKE TUFA STATE NATURAL RESERVE MONO BASIN NATIONAL FOREST SCENIC AREA, CAL. STATE PARKS (rev. ed. 2018), www.parks.ca.gov/pages/514/files/MonoLakeFinalWebLayout 2018.pdf.
[4] See Chapter 6(A)(2) ("The Mono Basin National Forest Scenic Area") (discussing *California ex rel. State Lands Commission v. United States*).
[5] See Chapter 3(A) ("The Mono Lake Basin").
[6] CAL. PUB. RES. CODE § 5045 et seq. (2021); *see also* State Senator Dan O'Keefe, *Mono Lake: A Land Worth Saving*, 4 MONO LAKE NEWSL. 1, 4 (Winter 1982), at www.monolake.org/wp-content/uploads/2020/09/1982-Winter-Mono-Lake-Newsletter.pdf.

interpretive materials.[7] In 2011, together with one quarter of the California Park System, the Reserve was selected for closure due to budget cuts.[8] The park narrowly survived the planned closure when the Mono Lake Committee and the Foundation for the adjacent Bodie State Park were able to raise the needed funds by initiating a parking fee at the Old Marina port of access along Mono Lake's western shore.[9]

2. The Mono Basin National Forest Scenic Area

Protecting the surrounding federal lands for conservation purposes proved more difficult. At the time, National Monuments were exclusively managed by the National Park Service, under implementing laws that disallowed any form of extractive activity in the conservation area – extractive activity like the commercial harvest of Mono Lake brine shrimp for fish food, or the commercial harvest of volcanic pumice from the surrounding Mono Craters for gardening and industrial purposes. These were ongoing economic activities in the Basin, and so there was opposition.

On March 29, 1982, shortly after the creation of the Mono Lake Tufa State Natural Reserve, Congressman Richard Lehman, an outdoorsman dedicated to environmental protection and water policy,[10] replaced Norman Shumway in the U.S. House of Representatives, and he took on the role of advocating for the creation of a National Monument at Mono Lake.[11] He authored legislation to confer Monument status on the selected lands, but in a novel political move, instead of advocating for National Park Service administration, he advocated that the Monument be administered by the U.S. Forest Service which already managed adjacent lands within the Inyo National Forest.[12] Although the proposal did not directly affect Los Angeles' water diversions, the city was deeply worried about the indirect effect that establishing such a monument might have in subsequent litigation.[13] DWP's Duane Georgeson expressed concern that the bill would strain the city's position, balancing its long-standing water rights against the State's public

---

[7] *Mono Lake County Park Mono Lake Tufa State Natural Reserve*, OUTDOOR PROJECT, www.outdoorproject.com/united-states/california/mono-lake-county-park (last visited Feb. 14, 2025).

[8] *State Announces Closure of Mono Lake State Park*, MONO LAKE COMM., www.monolake.org/today/state-announces-closure-of-mono-lake-state-park/ (last visited May 13, 2011).

[9] *#1: The Mono Lake Tufa State Natural Reserve is Open!*, MONO LAKE COMM., www.monolake.org/today/1-the-mono-lake-tufa-state-natural-reserve-is-open (last visited Dec. 31, 2011).

[10] *See Elections and the Environment*, L.A. TIMES, Nov. 20, 1986, at C4; Editorial, *Wilderness Breakthrough*, L.A. TIMES, May 7, 1984, at C6 (reporting on other examples of Lehman's environmental advocacy).

[11] JOHN HART, STORM OVER MONO 103 (Univ. of Cal. Press, 1996).

[12] *A bill to establish the Mono Lake National Monument in the State of California, and for other purposes*, H.R. 1341 98th Congress (1983–1984).

[13] HART, *supra* note 11, at 104.

trust obligations set forth in *Audubon Society*.[14] Georgeson urged that "[i]f there must be a Mono Lake reserve, the establishment law should proclaim 'the intent of Congress that ... export continue.'"[15]

Just over a year later, on September 28, 1984, the California Wilderness Act was signed into law by President Reagan, establishing (among other things) the "Mono Basin National Forest Scenic Area."[16] The Mono Basin was the first of a wholly new designation of federal conservation lands, the "Scenic Area," which would eventually include the much larger Columbia River Gorge National Scenic Area in Oregon and Washington, designated in 1986, and a handful of others, including the 2019 Alabama Hills, a few hundred miles south in the Eastern Sierra.

The placement of the Scenic Area within the National Forest System, and not the adjacent Yosemite National Park, was a highly salient factor in the legislation. Ushering in this new form of public land, the National Forest Scenic Area was designed to enable National Park-like protections for natural treasures in the area to coexist with the extractive uses of other area resources, such as hunting and mining, that are allowed within National Forests but not National Parks.[17] When I worked there, it was well-known among the Mono Lake rangers that Yosemite National Park had long hoped to annex Lee Vining Canyon, the exquisitely glaciated canyon that extends downward from the 10,000' Tioga Pass marking the Park's eastern boundary all the way down to the western shore of Mono Lake, almost four thousand vertical feet below – and perhaps even Mono Lake itself. Designating the new protected lands within the Inyo National Forest rather than Yosemite National Park helped overcome local resistance to what many feared would be more restrictive federal regulation of their longstanding extractive uses.[18] (And indeed, working as a Mono Lake ranger, I learned to tag downed deer and toured my fair share of mining interests and timber sales, all uses that would have been prohibited in a National Park.)

The California Wilderness Act authorized the federal government to acquire the lands and interests within the designated boundaries of the new Scenic Area, defined in the statute as "the Mono Basin within and adjacent to the Inyo National Forest," and to administer it as a separate unit within the Inyo National Forest in accordance with the National Forest System rules and regulations.[19] Certain parcels

---

[14] Id.
[15] Id.
[16] California Wilderness Act of 1984, Pub. L. No. 98–425, 98 Stat. 1619.
[17] See 16 U.S.C. § 583.
[18] *History of the Mono Lake Committee*, MONO LAKE COMM., www.monolake.org/whatwedo/aboutus/missionandhistory/ (last visited Oct. 18, 2022); E-mail from Bartshé, Educ. Dir., Mono Lake Comm., to Erin Ryan, Professor of L., Fla. State Univ. Coll. of L. (Oct. 19, 2017, 2:38 AM) (on file with author). (The U.S. Forest Service designation is like a "watered-down National Monument/Park" that enables multiple uses (hunting, mining, etc.) to continue with the "park-like protections." The U.S. Forest Service designation was because it is a "multiple-use agency" and helped to assuage local resistance to the National Park Service, which is viewed as "overly restrictive").
[19] California Wilderness Act of 1984, 98 Stat. 1619; E-mail from Bartshé Miller, *supra* note 18.

A. Protecting the Mono Basin Land

that had formerly been administered by the Bureau of Land Management were added to the Inyo National Forest and became administered by the Forest Service.[20] The limestone-studded Mono Lake Tufa State Natural Reserve, the narrow ring of relicted land exposed by the retreating shoreline of the lake since diversions began, remained under management by the California Department of Parks and Recreation – but its boundaries eventually became a subject of contention.

The federal government owned the Mono Basin uplands that had been gradually exposed over thousands of years since the last ice age, comprising some 70 percent of the Basin, but a debate arose over the proper boundaries between the state and federal territory.[21] In 1986, the U.S. Ninth Circuit of Appeals ultimately resolved the issue in *California* ex rel. *State Lands Commission v. United States*, concluding that the federal government held legitimate title to the 12,000 acres of exposed lakebed around Mono Lake that would become an essential part of the Scenic Area.[22] The court applied the common law doctrines of accretion, avulsion, and reliction, affirming that state ownership of submerged lands held in public trust is bounded by the mean high water mark and that state ownership follows this boundary line even as it slowly shifts over time through gradual natural changes. However, if the waterline is dramatically shifted by a sudden, avulsive change, then the boundary of state ownership remains the original, pre-avulsion waterline. California had argued that Mono Lake's receding waterline was avulsive and should not dislodge its ownership of formerly submerged lakebed, but the court found that the State had gradually lost ownership of the exposed lakebed because the recession of Mono Lake had been slow and imperceptible.[23] The exposed lands were incorporated into the larger reserve of protected federal lands in the Mono Basin.

In the end, the Scenic Area included 118,000 acres of land and water, with substantial tracts of land on all sides of the lake, including the range of Mono Craters volcanoes that extend southward of the lake.[24] The Act provided that the Scenic Area be managed to protect the geologic, ecologic, and cultural resources within the Scenic Area with as little interference with existing grazing permits, mining claims, and water rights as possible.[25] The law was carefully drafted to ensure that it did not

---

[20] See California Wilderness Act of 1984, 98 Stat. 1619; E-mail from Bartshé Miller, *supra* note 18.
[21] See California *ex rel.* State Lands Comm'n v. United States, 805 F.2d 857, 859–61 (9th Cir. 1986).
[22] *Id.* at 859; *see also* JUDITH A. LAYZER, *Making History in the Mono Basin*, *in* NATURAL EXPERIMENTS 233, 242 (Mass. Inst. of Tech., 2008) (describing the litigation).
[23] *California* ex rel. *State Lands Comm'n*, 805 F.2d at 863 ("Federal law defines a reliction as previously submerged land which becomes exposed by the gradual recession of water"). California attempted to characterize the lake's recession as an "intentional uncovering," which might have triggered different law assigning land deliberately exposed by a reclamation project to the State, *id.* at 864, but the court rejected that argument and affirmed Judge Lawrence Karlton's finding that the United States owned title to the exposed lakebed. *Id.* at 866.
[24] See California Wilderness Act of 1984 §§ 301–304.
[25] See *id.* § 304.

affect the water rights claimed by Los Angeles one way or the other,[26] and to step carefully around the open issue of relicted lands ownership while the *State Lands Commission* case was still being litigated, a process that took another few years.[27]

Today, the public lands around Mono Lake are managed cooperatively by California State Parks and the U.S. Forest Service.[28] While the Ninth Circuit determined that the exposed lakebed remains in federal ownership, the 1989 *Mono Basin National Forest Scenic Area Comprehensive Management Plan* clarifies that the "[r]elicted lands are jointly managed by the Forest Service and the State Department of Parks and Recreation through a Memorandum of Understanding."[29] The State park was established in 1982,[30] two years after it brought suit against the federal government to establish ownership of these lands, but four years before losing the case.[31] By the time the Ninth Circuit concluded that the recessional lands were federal, California had already been managing them as a park for four years. With shared management goals, the state and federal government reached an agreement to manage these lands cooperatively, and state and federal Mono Lake rangers now work side by side to protect them.

The National Forest Scenic Area and State Natural Reserve were successful at preserving the lands of the basin and increasing attention to the natural treasures at Mono Lake.[32] In addition to curious Californians, these public lands would be visited by tourists from around the country and even the world – especially German environmentalists who flocked to the Mono Basin after learning about Mono Lake from environmental reporting in their own national press. Even so, as much as the *Audubon Society* decision and the creation of these conservation areas were victories for the lake advocates, they had no bearing on the actual allocation of Mono Basin water. As John Hart memorably observes in his famous account of the Mono Lake story, STORM OVER MONO, Los Angeles had still not "budge[d] an inch, or a gallon" on "the essential point."[33] Even after all these successes, Mono Lake still

---

[26] HART, *supra* note 11, at 107.
[27] *See* CAL. PUB. RES. CODE § 5047 (2021).
[28] CAL. PUB. RES. CODE §§ 5045–5046 (2021); *see also* BOATING AND CAMPING REGULATIONS, U.S. FOREST SERV. 2 (rev. ed. 2010), www.fs.usda.gov/sites/nfs/files/legacy-media/inyo/MB%20ROG%20Mono%20Lake%20Boating.pdf (indicating this cooperation on the federal end by saying, "[t]he U.S. Forest Service and the Mono Lake Tufa State Reserve would like to welcome you to Mono Lake").
[29] Dennis W. Martin & Bill Bramlette, *Mono Basin National Forest Scenic Area Comprehensive Management Plan*, U.S. DEP'T OF AGRIC. 13 (1989), www.monobasinresearch.org/images/legal/scenicareacmp.pdf [www.perma.cc/GTS9-MKL5]; *see also id.* at 30–1.
[30] CAL. STATE PARKS, MONO LAKE TUFA STATE NATURAL RESERVE: MONO BASIN NATIONAL FOREST SCENIC AREA 5 (rev. ed. 2015), www.parks.ca.gov/pages/514/files/MonoLakeFinalWebLayout2015.pdf [www.perma.cc/NK3V-T2V2].
[31] California *ex rel.* State Lands Comm'n v. United States, 805 F.2d 857, 857 (9th Cir. 1986). It is possible that the State was seeking to strengthen its claim on the land by establishing the park.
[32] *See, e.g.*, CAL PUB. RES. CODE § 5048 (2021) (describing the enforcement mechanisms for protecting the Mono Lake Basin and Mono Lake tufa from damage).
[33] HART, *supra* note 11, at 107.

had no more guaranteed water supply than it had since the second barrel had gone in, which was to say – none at all.[34]

B. OTHER MONO LAKE LITIGATION

1. Dahlgren

As the fight for Mono Lake continued, a flurry of additional Mono Basin litigation followed the 1983 *Audubon Society* decision.[35] Lake advocates immediately asked federal court Judge Lawrence Karlton for an injunction ordering DWP to release enough water into the lake to keep the surface at 6,378 feet above sea level.[36] DWP and the State of California, under the leadership of newly elected Governor George Deukmejian[37] – the former State Attorney General during the *Audubon Society* litigation – requested that the case be sent back to state court for resolution, since the *Audubon* decision did not dictate a specific outcome or impose specific limits on the city's diversions.[38]

Lake advocates resisted sending the case back to state court in favor of remaining in Judge Karlton's environmentally sympathetic courtroom, as well as to avoid a judge or Water Board adjudicator appointed by Governor Deukmejian.[39] Yet despite his support for DWP's interests as Attorney General, Deukmejian was expressing support for the protection of Mono Lake by 1984, particularly in his endorsement of the Mono Basin National Forest Scenic Area legislation.[40] In 1986, the Mono Lake Committee, now headed by Executive Director Martha Davis, filed additional litigation to prevent

---

[34] *Id.*
[35] *See generally* JONES & STOKES ASSOC.'S, DRAFT ENVIRONMENTAL IMPACT REPORT FOR THE REVIEW OF MONO BASIN WATER RIGHTS OF THE CITY OF LOS ANGELES app. R, at R-2 to -4 (1993) [hereinafter EIR APPENDIX], www.monobasinresearch.org/images/mbeir/dappendix/app-r-text.pdf [www.perma.cc/LX5Z-STQE] (describing the litigation filed in the overall legal controversy). For an excellent exposition of the timeline of the litigation described in this chapter, see also Richard Roos-Collins, *The Mono Lake Cases*, *in* 4 RIVERS 328, 328–36 (A. Dan Turlock ed., 1993).
[36] HART, *supra* note 11, at 102.
[37] HART, *supra* note 11, at 103–104.
[38] *Id.* at 102; *see also Political and Legal Chronology*, MONO BASIN CLEARINGHOUSE, www.monobasinresearch.org/timelines/polchr.php (last visited Feb. 15, 2025) [www.perma.cc/FY7A-8U94] [hereinafter *Mono Chronology*] (last visited Oct. 11, 2022) (1984-Rush Creek Lawsuit); EIR Appendix, *supra* note 35, at R-5.
[39] HART, *supra* note 11, at 103–104. Concerns about Deukmejian's appointees may have been warranted, given his open zeal for the power of making appointments. When asked why he ran for governor he replied, "Attorneys General don't appoint judges – Governors do." *California Gov. George Deukmejian*, NAT'L GOVERNORS ASS'N, www.nga.org/governor/george-deukmejian/ (last visited August 15, 2024). By the end of his term he had appointed over 1,000 judges. *Id.*
[40] *Scenic Area Wins Wilson, Deukmejian Support*, THE MONO LAKE NEWSLETTER (Mono Lake Committee, Lee Vining, CA), Spring 1984, at 4, 4 (explaining that Governor George Deukmejian endorsed the Mono Basin National Forest Scenic Area legislation because it would "recognize the beauty and uniqueness of Mono Lake, and allow us to continue effective management of natural resources in this region") (internal quotations omitted).

DWP from shutting off flows to the Lake from Lee Vining Creek, one of its main feeder creeks, citing the State's public trust obligations recognized in *Audubon Society*.[41] The Mono County Superior Court would eventually grant a temporary restraining order requiring DWP to release flows until the case was tried.[42]

Even before that, within a year of the Lake advocates' victory in *Audubon Society*, sportfishing advocates filed an additional lawsuit against the State that would become critical in the fight for Mono Lake, on grounds unrelated to the public trust issues raised in *Audubon Society*. In the earliest iteration, *Dahlgren v. Los Angeles*, these sportfishing plaintiffs claimed that the Water Board had issued diversion licenses to Los Angeles in violation of Section 5937 of the Fish and Game Code, which prohibits the dewatering of creeks below dams.[43] *Audubon Society* and the Mono Lake Committee, represented by Bruce Dodge and Palmer Madden, joined Dahlgren in support of the plaintiffs as "friends of the court," adding the argument that the Mono Basin streams and fish within were also public trust resources requiring protection.[44] In response, the Inyo County Superior Court issued a temporary restraining order that required the release of water into Rush Creek, one of Mono's main feeder creeks, until the State completed a joint study on how much water could be diverted to sustain the fishery.[45]

2. CalTrout

Before the Water Board could respond to the court's relicensing directive in *Audubon Society* or *Dahlgren*, it was sued once again by Mono Lake advocates, again led by the sportfishing plaintiffs and this time joined by the Mono Lake Committee and National *Audubon Society*, seeking to modify DWP's later diversion licenses on additional statutory grounds.[46] In *California Trout v. State Water Resource Control Board*, which would become famous in Mono Lake circles as the pivotal "*CalTrout*" litigation, the environmental plaintiffs argued that the 1974 diversion licenses violated the requirements of a related part of the California Fish and Game Code, which requires that certain dam operators ensure that sufficient water remains instream to preserve fish in good condition.[47] DWP defended its diversions on grounds that this provision did not apply to licenses allowing the appropriation of

---

[41] Mono Lake Comm. v. Los Angeles, No. 8608 (Mono Super. Ct. Oct. 21, 1987); *see also* EIR APPENDIX *supra* note 35, at R-8; *Mono Chronology*, *supra* note 38 (1986-Lee Vining Creek Lawsuit).
[42] *See Mono Chronology*, *supra* note 38.
[43] Dahlgren v. Los Angeles, No. 8092, slip op. (Mono Super. Ct. Aug. 17, 1985) (order granting preliminary injunction); *see also* HART, *supra* note 11, at 109–11, 116–17 (discussing the *Dahlgren* litigation); LAYZER, *supra* note 22, at 242 (discussing *Dahlgren*).
[44] HART, *supra* note 11, at 115.
[45] *See* EIR APPENDIX, *supra* note 35, at R-7 to -8; *Mono Chronology*, *supra* note 38; *see also* LAYZER, *supra* note 22, at 242.
[46] Cal. Trout, Inc. v. State Water Res. Control Bd. (*Cal. Trout I*), 207 Cal. App. 3d 585, 592 (1989).
[47] *Id.*

B. Other Mono Lake Litigation

all available waters of a stream, which implicitly authorize the destruction of aquatic resources formerly within the stream.[48]

The lower court sided with DWP at trial,[49] but the California Court of Appeal reversed, finding that the trial court had inaccurately interpreted the relevant provision of the state Fish and Game Code, Section 5946.[50] Rejecting the lower court's reasoning, the appellate court held that the amount of water that could be appropriated was limited by the plain language of Section 5946, which mandates that certain dams allow sufficient water to pass through a fishway at all times to keep the fish below the dam in good condition.[51] It concluded that all permits issued after 1953, when Section 5946 was adopted – including DWP's later licenses for the Second Barrel – require full compliance with this mandate.[52] The licenses DWP had been issued in 1974 were thus properly subject to this requirement, and therefore in clear violation of the law.[53]

Los Angeles also contended that the rights in question were protected because they were grandfathered into the 1940 permits that predated the 1953 change in Fish & Game law.[54] The City argued that their 1970s era licenses should withstand scrutiny under the more protective fish and game law, not only because the pre-1953 licenses anticipated the construction of future infrastructure to claim all available water sources, but because the original 1940 water licenses implicitly treated the creation of the Hot Creek trout hatchery in the Mammoth Lakes basin, just south of the Mono Basin, in trade for the lost fish habitat around Mono Lake.[55]

However, the Court of Appeal determined that the Fish and Game code did not retroactively alter any rights that DWP claimed it had acquired prior to the effective

---

[48] Id. at 598.
[49] Id. at 592. ("The trial court denied the petitions on the view that Section 5946 does not apply to the appropriation of water by diversion from dams constructed, as in this case, before September 9, 1953.").
[50] Id. (discussing Fish & Game Code § 5946, which applies § 5937 to dams in certain regions of the state).
[51] Id. at 599. The court held that the text facially applied to licenses issued after the specified date regardless of whether it was based upon a permit issued prior to that date, id., and that the trial court had incorrectly limited § 5946 in concluding that it only applied to the appropriation of water obtained by diversion from dams constructed after the effective date of the §5946, id. at 604. The appeals court concluded that no legitimate reading of the statute supported DWP's contention that it could not apply to licensing stemming from permits issued before the law's effective date. Id. at 606.
[52] Cal. Trout, 207 Cal. App. 3d at 599. The court held that the text facially applied to licenses issued after the specified date regardless of whether it was based upon a permit issued prior to that date, id., and that the trial court had incorrectly limited § 5946 in concluding that it only applied to the appropriation of water obtained by diversion from dams constructed after the effective date of the § 5946. Id. at 604. The appeals court concluded that no legitimate reading of the statute supported DWP's contention that it could not apply to licensing stemming from permits issued before the law's effective date. Id. at 606.
[53] Id. at 603–06.
[54] Id. at 603.
[55] Id. at 608; see also GARY LIBECAP, OWENS VALLEY REVISITED: A REASSESSMENT OF THE WEST'S FIRST GREAT WATER TRANSFER 141–42 (Stan. Univ. Press 2007) (describing the reformation of diversion licenses that the City argued had been grandfathered out of the post-1953 requirements under the original 1940 permits and the fish hatchery agreement).

date of these statutory provisions.[56] The court concluded that the projects contemplated by DWP's earlier permits, even those issued prior to 1953, could not have accomplished a vested water right under California's prior appropriations doctrine before the actual completion of the project, long after the relevant code had gone into effect.[57] Because appropriative rights cannot vest before water is actually put to a specific beneficial use, and no new water had been put to a formal beneficial use until completion of the project, the permit thus could not have created a cognizable water right before that time, and thus was not protected by appropriations law until twenty years after the statute went into effect in 1953.[58] Under the settled principles of the prior appropriations doctrine, the court therefore held that DWP could not assert appropriative rights beyond the fishery protections of Section 5946 on the basis of permits issued prior to the effective date of the statute for water projects that were not completed until long afterward.[59]

The Court of Appeal also rejected another key argument DWP had made, which was that these Fish and Game Code protections for fish habitat violated the state constitution itself.[60] Article X, Section 2 of the California Constitution provides that water rights "shall not extend to the waste or unreasonable use or unreasonable method of use or unreasonable method of diversion of water."[61] DWP had argued that the legislature cannot impose a categorical priority for one use of water over another, because the reasonableness inquiry embedded in state constitutional language requires a comparison of alternative uses – an essentially adjudicative question that cannot be constrained by a fixed, statutory rule.[62] However, the appellate court found that the legislature can indeed make rules concerning what uses of water are reasonable, so long as those rules are not themselves unreasonable.[63] It concluded that Section 5946's requirement of minimal in-stream flows to preserve fish was not itself unreasonable.[64]

The *CalTrout* decision required the Water Board to attach conditions to the 1974 licenses in accordance with the opinion,[65] and additionally ordered it to incorporate

---

[56] *Cal. Trout*, 207 Cal. App. 3d 585, 608–09.
[57] *Id.* at 612.
[58] *Id.*
[59] *Id.* at 617.
[60] *Id.* at 622.
[61] *Id.*
[62] *Cal. Trout*, 207 Cal. App. 3d 585, at 622.
[63] *Id.*
[64] *Id.*
[65] *Id.* at 632–33 ("The judgements of dismissal of the petitions for writs of mandate are reversed. The trial court shall issue appropriate writs, commanding the Water Board to exercise its ministerial duty to attach the conditions required by Section 5946 to licenses 10191 and 10192 as that section is construed in this opinion."). In 1990, the appellate court entered another decision that specified the conditional language to the city's licenses: "In accordance with the requirements of Fish and Game Code Section 5946, this license is conditioned upon full compliance with Section 5937 of the Fish and Game Code. The licensee shall release sufficient water into the stream from its dams to reestablish and maintain

these concerns into its reconsideration of Los Angeles' permits to export from the Mono Basin under the *Audubon Society* ruling.[66] Where the *Audubon Society* case turned on abstract theoretical principles, the *CalTrout* litigation took place in the deep weeds of statutory and administrative law, and the resulting judicial relief was also less theoretical and subject to interpretation. The court's order to the Water Board was much more specific than *Audubon Society*, mandating a change in DWP's licenses that would require that actual, untheoretical water be returned to the Mono Basin Creeks (and, thereby, to Mono Lake). In this regard, the *CalTrout* decision was every bit as critical as the *Audubon Society* decision in determining the outcome at Mono Lake, and arguably more so in terms of its ultimate impact on stream restoration requirements.

3. In the Matter of Mono Lake Water Rights

The California Court of Appeal remanded the *CalTrout* questions back to the El Dorado County Superior Court for reconsideration in light of its holdings. On March 23, 1989, the Judicial Council had already consolidated the legal issues raised by the *National Audubon Society v. Superior Court*, *Dahlgren v. City of Los Angeles*, and *Mono Lake Committee v. City of Los Angeles* cases into a single legal proceeding, known thereafter as *In the Matter of Mono Lake Water Rights Cases*.[67] The matter was assigned to Judge Terrence Finney of the El Dorado County Superior Court, a jurist so respected by the Judicial Council that they often sought him out for complex cases, including the Mono Lake case.[68] From here, the already confusing flurry of litigation became even more so.

At around the same time, alleging that the Water Board was dragging its feet, the Mono Lake advocates in *CalTrout I* petitioned the appellate court to compel the Water Board to condition licenses 10191 and 10192 by the provisions of Section

---

the fisheries which existed in them prior to its diversion." Cal. Trout v. Super. Ct., 218 Cal. App. 3d. 187, 198 (1990); State of Cal. Water Res. Control Bd., Mono Lake Basin Water Right Decision 1631 (Sept. 28, 1994), at 9, www.waterboards.ca.gov/waterrights/board_decisions/adopted_orders/decisions/d1600_d1649/wrd1631.pdf [hereinafter Decision 1631].

[66] *Cal. Trout*, 207 Cal. App. at 632–33.

[67] In re Mono Lake Water Rights Cases (El Dorado Cnty., Super. Ct. Coordinated Proc. Nos. 2284 & 2288). The injunctions referenced *infra* notes 74, 75, 82, and 83, as well as the State Water Board's order Decision 1631, *supra* note 65, were the outcomes of the consolidated action. "Los Angeles and the conservation organization that brought the Mono Lake Cases agreed not to appeal the ... order." Roos-Collins, *supra* note 35, at 335–36.

[68] See LAYZER, *supra* note 22, at 246 (describing the consolidation of water rights issues in the three cases); Paula Peterson, *Public Memorial for Judge Terrence Finney in South Lake Tahoe Friday*, SOUTH TAHOE NOW (Jan. 3, 2019, 10:58 AM), www.southtahoenow.com/story/01/03/2019/public-memorial-judge-terrence-finney-south-lake-tahoe-friday [www.perma.cc/8ADA-DGR7] ("Judge Finney was so well regarded that the Judicial Council sought him out for some complex criminal case assignments throughout the years. However, the biggest case of his career, and, one of his favorites, was the renowned Mono Lake case, to which he was assigned by the chief justice of the California Supreme Court").

5946.[69] In what came to be known as *CalTrout II*, the appellate court did command the Water Board to amend its licenses, but it sent the issue back to the trial court to "specify the standard for compliance with Section 5946 and direct DWP to adhere to that standard, pending modification of the licenses by the Water Board to specify precise flow rates."[70] A few months after the first set of Mono Lake cases were consolidated, Judge Finney ordered that *CalTrout* also be consolidated with the other three and issued a stay on further litigation on the merits of any of the coordinated cases until the Water Board completed its reevaluation of Los Angeles' water rights. The waves of litigation that followed included all the Mono Lake water cases (pursuant to *National Audubon*) and all the tributary fisheries cases (pursuant to both *CalTrout I* and *CalTrout II*.)

All of these lawsuits sought various forms of relief to protect Mono Lake and its surrounding ecosystem, including the riparian habitat associated with its feeder creeks and the wildlife that depended on it. They sought the establishment of a minimum water level for Mono Lake and that minimum instream flows be established for Rush Creek and Lee Vining Creek, the two major tributaries of the lake intercepted by the Los Angeles Aqueduct. They asked the Court to require the Water Board to amend DWP's water licenses to require these minimum levels and flows. Judge Finney quickly determined that all claims would have to wait for the scientifically informed administrative process that was already underway to complete its work, relying on the Water Board's Mono Basin Work Plan, which called for the preparation of a formal Environmental Impact Report and reevaluation of DWP's licenses by December 1992.[71]

Judge Finney then made a series of critical rulings that protected Mono Lake from irretrievable decline while awaiting the Water Board's results. On August 22, 1989, one week before staying the proceedings, at the repeated request of Bruce Dodge,[72] Judge Finney granted a preliminary injunction that prohibited DWP from taking any further action that would cause Mono Lake to fall below 6,377' through March of 1990, the remainder of that annual wet cycle.[73] Yet by winter, it became clear that to protect the lake from disaster, it was not enough to make *no* changes to the current plan – for Mono Lake to even reach that critical ecological threshold, DWP would have to stop taking any water at all. On December 6, 1989, Judge Finney issued a temporary restraining order requiring DWP to release diverted water from the aqueduct system into Mono Lake to maintain its surface above that same critical level.[74]

In his December order, Judge Finney granted a preliminary injunction in accordance with the previous August 22, 1989 injunction requiring minimum stream

---

[69] *Cal. Trout*, 218 Cal. App. 3d at 194–95.
[70] *Id.* at 212.
[71] EIR Appendix, *supra* note 35, at R-9.
[72] HART, *supra* note 11, at 132.
[73] EIR Appendix, *supra* note 35, at R-8 to -9.
[74] *See id.* at R-9.

B. Other Mono Lake Litigation

flows through the Rush Creek and Lee Vining Creek tributaries of the lake, on which aqueduct infrastructure had been placed to intercept Sierra meltwater on its way to the lake.[75] DWP was required to allow sufficient water past its diversion facilities to maintain the level of Mono Lake at 6,377 feet pending the conclusion of the scientific studies required by the Water Board's environmental assessment.[76] Eventually, Judge Finney would also order the warring parties to begin working together on plans to restore the damaged Mono Lake streams, helping to transform, very gradually, relationships of deep distrust between the bitterly opposed litigants into platforms for collaboration.[77]

The Mono Lake advocates didn't always win. While waiting for meaningful results from the Water Board, environmental plaintiffs tried additional legal strategies that didn't pan out – for example, a 1989 attempt by the *National Audubon Society* to sue Los Angeles for harming Mono Lake under a theory of common law nuisance.[78] The doctrine of common law nuisance, which is probably as old as the common law public trust doctrine, curtails uses of property that interfere with neighboring uses or harm the public as a whole. Here, the plaintiffs claimed that Los Angeles' diversions were effectively polluting Mono Lake and thus harming the public environmental values there (and nearly all other uses). However, as noted in Chapter 5, judicial common law is usually overridden when the legislative enacts a contrary statute, or purposefully preempts it by enacting a more purposeful means of regulating the same harm. In this case, the court held that the management of water pollution under the federal Clean Water Act had preempted the regulatory field, thus foreclosing the nuisance lawsuit.[79]

The tide eventually began to turn after the Mono Lake advocates' success in *CalTrout*. On April 4, 1990, pursuant to the *CalTrout* appellate court's command, the Water Board made its first move, amending DWP's licenses to divert from the Mono Basin to include the required language regarding fish protection flows under the Fish and Game Code Section 5946.[80] Two months later, in June 1990, Judge

---

[75] *Id*.

[76] *See id*. ("The order required that water be released through the diversion facilities into Rush Creek at a rate between 85 and 100 cubic feet per second and into Lee Vining Creek at 60 cubic feet per second [or the rate of inflow into the diversion facility, if that is less]").

[77] *See* LAYZER, *supra* note 22, at 247 (describing Judge Finney's orders requiring a minimum flow schedule to increase flows in Rush Creek and Lee Vining Creek until studies ordered in 1986 were completed, ordering the parties to plan for stream restoration together, and affirming the injunction preventing DWP from taking water out of the mono Basin before the lake level reached 6,377').

[78] Nat'l Audubon Soc'y v. Dep't of Water, 869 F.2d 1196 (9th Cir. 1989).

[79] *Id*. (holding that the Federal Water Pollution Control Act ("FWPCA") preempted the federal common law nuisance action against DWP for polluting Mono Lake's water); *see also* Beverly Saxon, National Audubon Society v. Department of Water: *The Ninth Circuit Disallows Federal Common Law Nuisance Claim for Mono Lake Water and Air Pollution*, 20 GOLDEN GATE U. L. REV. 209, 214 (1990).

[80] In the Matter of Licensed Applications 8042 & 8043, Order 90–3 Amending Licenses, State Water Res. Control. Bd. (1990).

Finney entered a preliminary injunction that established interim flow rates for the diverted Mono Lake tributaries.[81] This interim streamflow order compelled DWP to release approximately 60,000 acre-feet of water down Mono Lake tributaries annually. For the first time since the litigation began, a meaningful amount of water was being redirected back toward the Lake.

For perspective, an acre-foot of water is about 326,000 gallons – enough water to cover one acre of land (about the size of a football field) one foot deep. Still, it was a fraction of the amount of water that used to flow through the Mono Basin Creeks into the lake before the aqueduct.[82] These new requirements superseded Judge Finney's prior preliminary injunctions requiring lower minimum flows while awaiting further judicial and administrative process. One year later, on April 17, 1991, recognizing that the 60,000 acre-feet required by the earlier injunction was insufficient to sustain Mono Lake at 6,377, Judge Finney issued a further preliminary injunction requiring DWP to allow whatever flow was necessary past its diversion facilities to maintain the level of Mono Lake at or above 6,377 feet – trying to hold the lake's forecasted ecological collapse off long enough to allow the Water Board to do its work.[83]

C. STATE AND FEDERAL FUNDING FOR WATER CONSERVATION

Even as these judicial battles played out and the Water Board struggled with its task of finding the appropriate equipoise of so many conflicting interests, Mono Lake continued to preoccupy the political sphere. As the agency pored over the scientific inquiry, public hearings, and policy research that would culminate in its 1994 decision, legislators and advocates worked to facilitate a positive resolution to the conflict by not only protecting Mono Lake, but also working to help Los Angeles resolve its water needs. Growing state and national recognition of the problem gradually inspired federal, state, and municipal actors to begin collaborating on strategies to reduce the underlying causes of the water conflict by developing new sources of water for Los Angeles – ideally, through the recycling and conservation of existing sources.

California State Assemblyman Phil Isenberg, characterized by California Chief Justice Patricia Guerrero as a "champion for the people of California," led

---

[81] EIR APPENDIX, supra note 35, at R-9; see also Mono Chronology, supra note 38 (1990–Coordinated Proceedings). This preliminary injunction is another outcome of the *In the Matter of Mono Lake Water Rights* consolidated cases, separate from the injunctions issued in 1989 which *required* the flow of water. See *supra* note 75 and accompanying text. This preliminary injunction *established* the flows.

[82] For an overview of data analyzing the flows and levels of Mono Lake before and after the diversions, see David W. Winkler, *An Ecological Study of Mono Lake, California*, 12 INST. OF ECOLOGY PUBL'N U.C. DAVIS 13 (June 1977), www.monobasinresearch.org/onlinereports/1976study/ecologicalstudyofmonolake.pdf.

[83] See *Mono Chronology*, supra note 38 ("After a 40-day evidentiary hearing, Judge Finney granted MLC's and NAS's motion renewing the preliminary injunction which required that Mono Lake be maintained at an elevation of 6,377 feet until the completion of the SWRCB process to amend the DWP licenses and until all legal appeals of that decision are exhausted.")

C. State and Federal Funding for Water Conservation 173

the charge.[84] In 1989, he shepherded a state law, AB 444, from proposal to passage, securing legislative authorization of some $60 million for projects to restore Mono Lake and resolve the regional water crisis, including $36 million in a special Environmental Water Account to help Los Angeles develop alternative sources of water.[85] However, the law required that the city and environmentalists agree on plans, and the authorized funds lay deadlocked while DWP and Mono Lake activists argued over how to use them while fighting their ongoing battles in court.

In December of 1993, on the eve of the Water Board's decision (and after the *CalTrout* litigation revealed further weaknesses in DWP's water licenses), Los Angeles Councilwoman Ruth Galanter was finally able to broker a deal to break the impasse. If DWP would relinquish its claim to at least 41,000 acre-feet per year of Mono Basin water, then all parties would agree to release the $36 million held in the Environmental Water Account for an East Valley Reclamation Project.[86] The Reclamation Project would enable Los Angeles to begin developing alternative means of satisfying water demand through recycling programs, better using the water it already had, without having to identify new sources of supply. It was a wise compromise, and an extremely significant one, because it was the first time the city of Los Angeles had ever voluntarily relinquished appropriative water rights in favor of an alternative source.[87]

Of note, a year earlier, in 1992, Congress had also authorized federal funds for reclamation of 120,000 acre-feet of water for Los Angeles, in an exchange designed to offset reduced diversions from Mono Lake. This was twice the amount of water that Judge Finney had ordered Los Angeles to give up from the Mono Lake creeks in his 1990 preliminary injunction to preserve minimum stream flows after the *CalTrout* litigation. It would certainly have eased Los Angeles' painful transition, but it would also have represented a concession the city was not ready to make. It would take the parties four more years to move forward on this possibility,[88] but these unfolding opportunities began to grease the path toward potential cooperation in the future – a potentiality that was about to become very important.

---

[84] Merrill Balassone, *California Courts Newsroom*, CHIEF JUSTICE ISSUES STATEMENT ON PASSING OF PHIL ISENBERG, www.newsroom.courts.ca.gov/news/chief-justice-issues-statement-passing-phil-isenberg (last visited Oct. 27, 2023).

[85] Water conservation and water quality, A.B. No. 444 (1989), www.leginfo.legislature.ca.gov/faces/bill TextClient.xhtml?bill_id=198919900AB444.

[86] Marla Cone, *DWP Agrees to Take Less Mono Lake Water: Resources: City Plans to Make up Loss in Reclamation Effort. Environmentalists Hail the Landmark Accord*, L.A. TIMES, (Dec. 14, 1993) www.latimes.com/archives/la-xpm-1993-12-14-mn-1847-story.html (last visited October 2, 2025).

[87] LAYZER, *supra* note 22, at 252.

[88] Craig Anthony Arnold, *Working Out an Environmental Ethic: Anniversary Lessons from Mono Lake*, 4 WYO. L. REV. 1, 17 (2004); *see* 4 U.S.C. § 390h-11; H.R. Conf. Rep. No. 102–1016 at 183 (1992), www.congress.gov/bill/102nd-congress/house-bill/429/text (authorizes water reclamation and reuse projects to treat 120,000 acre-feet per year of effluent from the city and county of Los Angeles to provide new water supplies for industrial, environmental, and other purposes to reduce demand for imported water).

D. DECISION 1631: IMPLEMENTATION BY THE WATER BOARD

After the Supreme Court's 1983 *Audubon Society* decision and the subsequent *CalTrout* litigation required revisitation of L.A.'s water rights in the Mono Basin, the Water Board went to work assessing the proper balance between each of the competing demands for Mono Basin water – and for the next ten years, everyone paying attention awaited that decision with bated breath. While the foregoing judicial decisions set forth the relevant rules of law, everyone understood that it would be the Water Board's decision implementing these rules that would determine the actual fate of Mono Lake, as well as the available means to satisfy Los Angeles' water needs. The Water Board understood this as well, so it took its time – producing a decision only after ten solid years of scientific research, stakeholder consultation, evidentiary hearings, public input, and a full Environmental Impact Report providing a critical set of data to support the decision that would follow.[89]

Following that decade of exhaustive administrative process, the agency eventually approved a new, more limited schedule of diversion licenses for the city that would allow Los Angeles to continue taking water from the Mono Basin – but *only* if critical public trust values at Mono Lake remained protected. In 1994, it released its 200-page directive, a set of conclusions and instructions that would become known as Decision 1631.

1. *A New Lake Level Target: 6,392'*

While Decision 1631 followed substantial independent inquiry, many elements reflected a proposal originally submitted by an Interagency Task Force that had been endorsed by the Mono Lake advocates but opposed by Los Angeles.[90] Water exports to Los Angeles would be curtailed as needed to enable Mono Lake to rise to the level of 6,392 feet above sea level, presumably over the next twenty years, and then allowed more permissively after this target was achieved.[91] Export limitations were carefully staged: diversions would be eliminated entirely while the lake rose from the pre-litigation low of 6,372' to a preliminary threshold of 6,377' and, after that, they would be permitted on a limited, graduated basis, carefully designed to achieve and maintain the ecologically sound lake management level.[92] Decision 1631 also included requirements for restoration of the desiccated Mono Basin creeks

---

[89] FINAL ENVIRONMENTAL IMPACT REPORT FOR THE REVIEW OF MONO BASIN WATER RIGHTS AND THE CITY OF LOS ANGELES, CAL. STATE WATER RES. BD. (1994), www.monobasinresearch.org/onlinereports/feir1.php.

[90] *See* HART, *supra* note 11, at 88–89 (discussing DWP's refusal to adopt the Interagency Task Force plan that offered state and federal money to cover the majority of the cost of replacement water for the first two years after adoption).

[91] Decision 1631, *supra* note 65, at 101–02.

[92] *Id.* at 97–98.

D. Decision 1631: Implementation by the Water Board

and minimum instream flows going forward, and it designated Mono Lake as an Outstanding National Resource Water.[93]

The Water Board chose 6,392' as the recovery target because the best available science indicated that this lake level would resolve the most serious threats to the public trust values in the Mono Basin.[94] It would stabilize salinity at a level that would allow the fragile Mono Lake ecosystem to recover, supporting the brine shrimp and alkali fly populations at the base of the food web.[95] The breeding grounds of the California Gulls and migratory bird nesting habitat would be protected, as would fisheries and riparian habitat associated with the desiccated Mono Basin creeks (although some waterfowl areas would be forsaken).[96] It would cover the most hazardous salt flats, limiting toxic dust storms and thus protecting public health.[97]

Significantly, it would also protect the scenic and recreational values of Mono Lake,[98] and with it, the local communities and economies that depend on it.[99] The lake level would rise enough to protect the fragile ecosystem and public health, but it would remain low enough to allow the public to continue enjoying the geologically fascinating and visually stunning tufa towers exposed at the lake's margins, which had become iconic throughout the world (and were now protected by the California Mono Lake Tufa State Reserve). Finally, it would allow Los Angeles to resume and continue exporting Mono Basin water, but only after designated benchmarks and recovery levels were met and maintained.[100] Once Mono Lake reached the designated maintenance level of 6,392, the city could increase diversions to a little over thirty thousand acre-feet per year, so long as the lake level remained stable.[101] If the lake maintained or exceeded the target level, exports could theoretically increase.[102]

---

[93] *Id.* at *2, *21, *40–41 (requiring Los Angeles to prepare stream restoration plans); *see generally* Cynthia L. Koehler, *Water Rights and the Public Trust Doctrine: Resolution of the Mono Lake Controversy*, 22 ECOLOGY L.Q. 541, 577–83 (1995) (reviewing the historical buildup to *Audubon Society* and critiquing the positive and negative aspects of the Water Board's resulting Decision 1631).

[94] Decision 1631, *supra* note 65, at *50–98.

[95] *Id.* at *50.

[96] *Id.* at *96–97.

[97] *Id.* at *82, *93.

[98] Notably, the designated lake level would leave some of the relicted lands tufa towers exposed, a source of beauty and fascination for area visitors. "Relicted lands" refers to the formerly submerged lakebed that has been exposed by water diversions. *See id.* at *82.

[99] *Id.* at *86.

[100] Decision 1631, *supra* note 65, at *97–98. Decision 1631 articulated a complicated series of interim benchmarks and recovery levels with corresponding permissible diversions. Exports were initially prohibited until the lake level reached the first benchmark, after which reduced exports would be permitted until the next benchmark was reached, and so on. *See id.*

[101] *Id.* at 2 ("Once the water level of 6,391 feet is reached, it is expected that Los Angeles will be able to export approximately 30.8 thousand acre-feet of water per year from the Mono Basin." *Id.*)

[102] *Id.* at *98 (explaining that as the water level rises, the amount "in excess of the amount needed to maintain the required fishery protection flows" will also increase, leading to an increased volume of water available for export).

The decision was, in every respect, a compromise plan – not unlike the Supreme Court's decision in *Audubon Society* itself. Indeed, almost poetically, the plan to achieve 6,392 would raise the lake approximately twenty vertical feet from its post-diversion low of 6,372 feet but leave it twenty-five feet below its pre-diversion level of 6,417 feet – roughly in the middle. It would bring salinity levels to a more ecologically sustainable level, but it would leave critical waterfowl habitat un-remediated. It would rewater the most hazardous relicted lands most likely to contribute to particulate pollution in the Basin, but vast expanses of Mono Lake's bathtub ring of exposed salt flats would remain. And of course, several decades later, it's worth noting that the 6,392' target has still not been achieved; in recent the lake currently averages around 6,378.7 feet of elevation, not quite halfway toward the original 6,392' goal.[103] Unfortunately, California's ongoing water woes and unpredictable weather patterns cast doubt on when, if ever, that goal will be met.

Decision 1631 marked a true turning point for the Mono Lake story – but an equally significant moment would follow immediately thereafter, as the City of Los Angeles carefully calculated its reaction to the decision.

Over the decade stakeholders had waited for the Water Board's decision, everyone knew that asking Los Angeles to give up any claim to water the city had relied on would be an extremely painful loss.[104] Los Angeles had fought the *Audubon Society* lawsuit with all its might, because nothing made the city more vulnerable than the threat of lost access to water. Moreover, the underlying reasoning in the *Audubon* decision would leave the city not only vulnerable to losing water from the Mono Basin, but potentially much more, because so much of its supply was imported from distant watersheds.[105]

For that reason, when the Water Board ruled that the city would have to stop exporting all Mono Basin water until interim benchmarks were met, many perceived the decision *not* as an epic compromise between the interests of both sides, but as a brutal loss for Los Angeles. The big question on everyone's mind was whether the city would appeal the Water Board's decision.[106] Many observers fully expected that it would.

An appeal would have brought many more years of litigation and even more serious environmental impacts for the Mono Basin during the interim. Had Los

---

[103] *See Mono Lake Levels 1979-Present*, MONO BASIN CLEARINGHOUSE, www.monobasinresearch.org/data/levelmonthly.php (hereinafter *Mono Lake Levels*) (last visited Oct. 11, 2022) [www.perma.cc/V57V-45QZ] [hereinafter *Mono Lake Levels*].

[104] *See* LIBECAP, *supra* note 55, at 151–53 (critiquing the Mono Lake decision's impact on prior appropriations systems by creating uncertainty, undermining property rights, and compromising economic efficiency); Barton H. Thompson, Jr., *Judicial Takings*, 76 VA. L. REV. 1449, 1533 (1990) (noting how Mono Lake "surprised many people and was certainly a deviation from most water lawyers' expectations").

[105] *See* LIBECAP, *supra* note 55, at 151–53.

[106] *Cf.* Eric Brazil, *Environmentalists Hail Ruling on Mono Lake Water Use: L.A. Won't Appeal Decision Cutting Draw*, S.F. EXAM'R, Sept. 28, 1994, at A-6 (discussing the decision).

Angeles sought judicial review of the Water Board's decision, the consequences for Mono Lake and its ecosystem could have been devastating, and the ongoing litigation would have been both expensive and polarizing. Even so, Los Angeles now faced the added strain from the mandate for restoration work on the streams and lake-fringing wetlands. The city had fought the underlying litigation so bitterly that an equally vigorous appeal seemed inevitable – and in fact, an appeal was initiated.[107]

Yet in a remarkable turnaround, the city changed course. Much like the citizens in the *Illinois Central Railroad* story who forced a change in their legislators' conveyance of Chicago Harbor,[108] the people of Los Angeles voted in new city leadership, who took office with a new platform and a new approach: conservation.

2. Los Angeles Turns a New Page

Whether Mono Lake will continue to recover partly depends on climatic conditions beyond human control, but it will also depend on decision making in Los Angeles, at levels both political and personal. Choices made in the wake of Decision 1631 offer reasons to be hopeful.

One of the best chapters of the Mono Lake story is how the city of Los Angeles reacted to the various losses it encountered between *Audubon Society* and Decision 1631. While those losses pale in comparison to what the Owens Valley has lost – and those losses the Mono Basin is still trying to avoid – it is worth acknowledging that Los Angeles also lost a good deal over the foregoing course of events. It lost in court, multiple times. It lost water rights it had believed were settled decades earlier, and it lost any sense of security that its current rights are fully vested. It also lost access to a fair amount of water – between 12 and 20 percent of its total supply. That's a lot, for any community.

To avoid these painful losses, the city had fought hard to prevail on the legal issues, fearful of weakening its access to critical water imports on which it had come to rely. It dragged its feet on offers of state and federal funds to experiment with water recycling and other technology that might enable it to use and import less water, fearful that a decision to forgo any of its hard-fought rights to water would subject them to forfeiture or abandonment under the use-it-or-lose-it features of the prior appropriations doctrine.[109] But after investing so much energy in fighting an ultimately losing battle, the city finally turned to a new page after the Water Board's decision. The city embraced a wholly new approach to its ongoing problem of water

---

[107] HART, *supra* note 11, at 174–75.
[108] *See* Chapter 1(B)(5) ("With Power Comes Responsibility") (discussing *Illinois Central Railroad Co. v. Illinois*, 146 U.S. 387 (1892)).
[109] *See* HART, *supra* note 11, at 88–89 (discussing DWP's refusal to adopt the Interagency Task Force plan that offered state and federal money to cover the majority of the cost of replacement water for the first two years after adoption).

insecurity – conservation – an approach that has spawned dividends as issues of water security loom increasingly larger throughout the arid west.

After Decision 1631, Los Angeles made two critical decisions. First, and perhaps most importantly, the city decided not to appeal the Water Board's decision. Even though a significant portion of the city's water supply was at stake, equally significant support for restoration of Mono Lake had developed among city residents. Participants in the process had fully expected an appeal, and DWP's lead attorney had already made it clear that he planned to file a petition for a writ of mandate to overturn the decision.[110] However, the political mobilization to Save Mono Lake had landed, and the political winds shifted accordingly. Martha Davis, Mono Lake's new champion as the Executive Director of the Mono Lake Committee, reacted swiftly to the city's lingering concerns.

Davis organized a private meeting with DWP leadership in which she persuaded them to forgo further litigation with a promise that the Mono Lake Committee would help secure outside funding for restoration work.[111] Mayor Richard Riordan, who shared Davis' desire to resolve conflict with consideration for all interests,[112] pulled the plug on the appeal, deciding that the city would offer no further challenge to the Water Board's conclusions.[113] A city official would later explain that the mayor wanted to engage a more forward-thinking environmental policy, and the decision to accept the Water Board's new allocation was consistent with this new ethic.[114] In addition, the Mono Lake Committee worked hard to generate ideas and funding to help Los Angeles gracefully absorb the loss of Mono Basin water, and not just replace it with harmful exports from other vulnerable watersheds.[115]

Los Angeles' second critical decision was to fully embrace the conservation alternative.[116] Rather than carrying on the same old battle, the city took advantage of its own infrastructural expertise, citizen initiative, and those now available sources of state and federal funding to embrace water conservation and recycling as a means of coping with reduced supply.[117]

---

[110] Telephone interview with Roderick Walston, former Assistant State Attorney General (March 2, 2018), (notes on his recollections from the litigation and its aftermath are on file with author).

[111] HART, *supra* note 11, at 174.

[112] See *id.* at 169 ("Riordan ... brought to the job an executive's virtues: dislike of waste and unresolved conflict...."); *id* at 177 ("Davis's goal is what she calls 'closure': reaching a solution that will stick because it is accepted by all.").

[113] See *id.* at 174.

[114] Cal. State Water Res. Control Bd., *Mono Lake @ 20: Past, Present, Future Part 2*, YOUTUBE (Nov. 17, 2014), www.youtube.com/watch?v=rRqAPJ_Fb2A&t=644s (address of David Cobb, National Director of Civic Affairs, HDR Inc., at the UC Berkeley Mono Lake Symposium).

[115] *Id.*

[116] See HART, *supra* note 11, at 169–70.

[117] See *supra* note 85 and accompanying text (discussing legislative authorization of $60 million for projects to restore Mono Lake and resolve the regional water crisis, including the designation of $36 million for a special Environmental Water Account to help Los Angeles develop alternative sources of water).

D. Decision 1631: Implementation by the Water Board

The city began to cooperate with the Mono Basin advocates they'd been fighting in court, resolving to work together toward increased water conservation in the Los Angeles basin and restoration of the deteriorated resources of the Mono Basin.[118] Instead of appealing Decision 1631, they took advantage of the state and federal grants that had been first offered in 1989 and 1992 to implement large-scale water conservation projects.[119] When Los Angeles finally agreed with environmentalists to build a $50 million water reclamation plant with the federal funding that Congress had authorized in 1992, in one bold move, the city obviated the need for almost half of the water it had been diverting from the Mono Basin.[120] This project greatly eased the burden of Decision 1631's curtailment of supply from Mono Lake.[121]

The city also embarked on a campaign to encourage demand-side conservation efforts by individuals and other users. Through a series of programmatic initiatives – from facilitating industrial recycling to subsidizing low-flow installations – the city made remarkable progress reducing its water use. Springing into a new phase of action, the city experimented with infrastructural improvements, new methods of municipal and highway barrier management, and grassroots campaigns for household water-saving devices.[122] The city pushed forward with the use of recycled water for irrigation and industrial purposes.[123] It sponsored neighborhood drives to trade in old toilets for low-flush models.[124] "Save Mono Lake" bumper stickers gave way to "I Save Water for Mono Lake" bumper stickers, which appeared throughout the city and even the state.

In the end, by effectively deploying these strategies to reduce its own demand, Los Angeles was able to offset *all* the water it had lost from the Mono Basin through conservation alone, without having to tap new remote sources.[125] And this makes the Mono Lake story one of the very rare cases in environmental law with a happy ending for both sides in the dispute. Angelenos had access to the water they needed, Mono Lake had a chance to recover, and no other ecosystems were put at risk in its place.

The credit for this achievement accrues to the collaboration of many different individual players, from engaged members of the public to actors across all levels

---

[118] *See id.*
[119] *See* Chapter 6(C) ("State and Federal Funding for Water Conservation") (discussing the state and federal funds); *see also* HART, *supra* note 11, at 148–49.
[120] Arnold, *supra* note 88, at 18; *see* 4 U.S.C. § 390h-11; H.R. Conf. Rep. No. 102–1016, *supra* note 88, at 183 (authorizes water reclamation and reuse projects to treat 120,000 acre-feet per year of effluent from the city and county of Los Angeles to provide new water supplies for industrial, environmental, and other purposes to reduce demand for imported water).
[121] Arnold, *supra* note 88, at 22.
[122] HART, *supra* note 11, at 148–49.
[123] *Id.* at 148.
[124] *Id.* at 149.
[125] *Compare id.* at 76 (noting that Mono Lake provided 12 percent of Los Angeles' water supply), *with Natural History*, MONO LAKE COMM., www.monolake.org/learn/aboutmonolake/naturalhistory/ (last visited Oct. 6, 2022) (noting that Los Angeles conservation efforts have more than replaced water no longer diverted from Mono Lake).

of government – but many of these very players have offered special praise for the talented negotiation and tireless problem-solving that Martha Davis brought to the conflict in her work on behalf of the Mono Lake Committee. Through a series of carefully managed confidential meetings with environmentalists, state officials, and city leadership over the course of a decade, Davis positioned the Committee as a moderate consensus-builder, willing to compromise with the opposition on all but the most vitally important issues.[126] Mayor Riordan pointedly described Davis in one word – "persistent," adding that it was a quality worthy of his admiration.[127] Indeed, her diplomatic persistence helped spark a revolution in California water conservation.

Los Angeles remains at the forefront of water conservation efforts and has become a leader nationwide.[128] Although the population has grown substantially in the decades since, municipal water use has remained flat.[129] This decrease in per capita water use is partly attributable to municipal restrictions, such as an unprecedented set that went into effect in June 2022.[130] Under these new restrictions, for example, residents within the boundaries of DWP's jurisdiction are limited to two days per week for lawn watering, either at 8 minutes per station per day, or two 15 minute-cycles per watering day if the sprinklers are fitted with water-conserving nozzles.[131] The city may have earned scorn for its water management approach at the beginning of the twentieth century, but it deserves credit for the changed approach it has undertaken at the beginning of the twenty-first century. Even so, the work of "saving Mono Lake" continued.

---

[126] HART, *supra* note 11, at 177.

[127] *Id.*

[128] *See* Jacques Leslie, Opinion, *Los Angeles, City of Water*, N.Y. TIMES (Dec. 6, 2014), www.nyti .ms/1u55oyO (noting that Los Angeles has become "a leader in sustainable water management, a pioneer in big-city use of cost-effective, environmentally beneficial water conservation, collection and reuse technologies").

[129] *See Replacement Water: Helping Los Angeles Find Better Solutions*, MONO LAKE COMM., www .monolake.org/mlc/altwater (last visited Apr. 17, 2015) ("[D]espite growth of a million people between 1975 and 2005, LA's water usage (of about 600,000 AF/yr) had not changed."); *Urban Water Use Data*, PAC. INST, www.pacinst.org/gpcd/table/ (last visited Feb. 7, 2025) [www.perma.cc/4524-QD62] (reporting Los Angeles Department of Water and Power water usage from June 2015-present). Angelenos' per capita usage continued to drop during the 2022 drought, reportedly to 111 gallons per person per day. *Los Angeles Sets Record-Low Water Usage for 3rd Straight Month*, LOS ANGELES DAILY NEWS (Sep. 13, 2022), www.dailynews.com/2022/09/13/la-city-sets-record-low-water-usage-for-3rd-straight-month/ [www.perma.cc/Y4PT-JYKK].

[130] *See* Hayley Smith, *Unprecedented Water Restrictions Hit Southern California Today: What they mean to you*, L.A. TIMES (June 1, 2022), www.latimes.com/california/story/2022-06-01/southern-california-new-drought-rules-june-2022; *see also* Chapter 6(E)(2) ("Mono Lake After Decision 1631") (discussing the concurrent statewide water use regulations. In most cases, California residents were instructed to follow both state and local regulations. *Water Conservation Emergency Regulations*, STATE WATER RES. CONTROL BD., www.waterboards.ca.gov/water_issues/programs/conservation_portal/regs/emergency_regulation.html (last visited Feb. 7, 2025) [www.perma.cc/N27T-VJJX].

[131] *Water Conservation Emergency Regulations*, *supra* note 130; *id*. While municipalities were given discretion to implement supply cuts through whatever means they saw fit, most opted to regulate outdoor watering, which accounts for nearly half of all urban water use. Smith, *supra* note 130.

E. A REPRIEVE FOR MONO LAKE?

In October of 1998, and with agreement by all legal stakeholders, the Water Board issued final orders regarding its Mono Basin Restoration Plan, supplementing Decision 1631 with an implementing order that established stream and waterfowl habitat restoration plans. The new order was designed to effectuate the requirements of Decision 1631 with specific ecosystem restoration measures and monitoring requirements, and it effectively ended the courts' jurisdiction over the Mono Lake controversy.[132] By that time, Los Angeles and the Mono Lake advocates had already been cooperating to restore the damaged Mono Basin streams that had been desiccated by years of dewatering and then cut through with floodwater releases that destroyed the natural meanders and slower channels that create habitat for riparian plant and animal species. Volunteers were planting trees along the creeks and hosting inner city Los Angeles teens on summer retreats to learn about the environment on which their city depends.

Eleven years later, in 2009, the California Water Code was amended to formalize the importance of the public trust doctrine as a matter of statutory and administrative law. Language was added to Section 85023 to clarify that the public trust doctrine was as much a foundation of California water law as the doctrine of reasonable and beneficial use, declaring that "The longstanding constitutional principle of reasonable use *and the public trust doctrine* shall be the foundation of state water management policy...."[133] By that time, public trust considerations had already been formalized in the Water Board's own implementing regulations, requiring assessment for impacts to protected public trust values before new water licenses were granted.[134]

In the late 1990s, when the Mono Lake litigation was all over, the Mono Basin Restoration Plan had been released, and Decision 1631 was well under implementation, I left the Mono Basin to attend law school, inspired by the very legal events it had been part of my job to explain to the public. When I left, the physical results of these decisions were all visible to the naked eye. The land bridge joining Mono Lake's north shore to the gull rookery on Negit Island was receding underwater. As the lake gradually reclaimed its formerly exposed bed, the rangers had to pull up

---

[132] Arnold, *supra* note 88, at 23; *see* Cone, *supra* note 86.
[133] CAL. WATER CODE § 85023 (emphasis added).
[134] CAL. WATER CODE § 1260 (2024) (requiring new water license applicants to submit "[a]ll data and information reasonably available to applicant or that can be obtained from the Department of Fish and Game concerning the extent, if any, to which fish and wildlife would be affected by the appropriation, and a statement of any measures proposed to be taken for the protection of fish and wildlife in connection with the appropriation"; CAL. WATER CODE § 1727 (requiring applicants for temporary water transfers to establish that "[t]he proposed temporary change would not unreasonably affect fish, wildlife, or other instream beneficial uses 2024"); *see also* Dave Owen, *The Mono Lake Case, the Public Trust Doctrine, and the Administrative State*, U.C. DAVIS L. REV. 1099, 1147–48.

leg after leg of the old boardwalks that once extended public trails over the relicted lands to the receded water's edge. The toxic dust devils were less intense and less frequent. The lake level had risen about ten feet to 6,382 feet in the first five years after the decision, moving in exactly the right direction and raising high hopes all around.[135]

And then – suddenly and sadly – it stopped.

Climate patterns have shifted in California – as elsewhere – leading to reduced snowmelt in the creeks.[136] The drought that hit California in the 2000s intensified to epic levels in the 2010s.[137] Precipitation has not been following the modeled average conditions that Decision 1631 relied on, and so the lake did not reach 6,392 feet in 2015, as the Water Board had projected.[138] Even though Los Angeles has remained on a curtailed schedule of diversions, the lake level has hovered around 6,382 feet since 1998, suspended at halfway to the compromise point – and in 2014, for the first time in decades, it declined below 6,380.[139] The lake remained low until 2017, when it began to rise and fall, but since October of 2022, as this book goes to press, the lake level has remained below 6,380.[140]

The final parts of this chapter provide the most recent updates on the still unfolding Mono Lake story and its neglected older-sibling saga, unfolding in the Owens Valley.

1. *Mono Lake after Decision 1631*

In 2015, California suffered from a record-setting drought after four consecutive years in which precipitation fell below normal while temperatures hovered above normal.[141]

---

[135] See *Mono Lake Levels*, *supra* note 103.
[136] See, e.g., *Monthly Weather Summaries for Lee Vining, CA*, MONO BASIN CLEARINGHOUSE, www .monobasinresearch.org/data/weather.php (last visited Feb. 23, 2025) [www.perma.cc/A9JF-HDDG] (noting average temperatures in Lee Vining and providing precipitation data).
[137] Kyle Kim & Thomas Suh Lauder, *163 Drought Maps Reveal Just How Thirsty California Has Become*, L.A. TIMES (Feb. 27, 2015), www.latimes.com/science/la-me-g-california-drought-map-htmlstory .html [www.perma.cc/NX47-Y7RM] (showing the severity of the California drought with map infographic).
[138] See *Mono Lake Levels*, *supra* note 103 (providing recent sub-6,392-foot water levels). In fact, with the lake level below 6,380 feet as of April 1, 2015, Los Angeles will be required to dramatically curtail exports again. Geoff McQuilkin, *Lake Level Means Reduced Water Exports to LA, More Protection for Mono Lake*, MONOLOGUE, April 1, 2015, www.monolake.org/today/2015/04/01/april-1-lake-level-means-reduced-water-exports-to-la-more-protection-for-mono-lake/ [www.perma.cc/RN4A-MZH3] [hereinafter McQuilkin, *Lake Level Means Reduced Water Exports*] (noting that the lake has declined to a level at which water exports to Los Angeles are automatically reduced by 70 percent to 4,500 acre-feet of export annually).
[139] See *Mono Lake Levels*, *supra* note 103.
[140] Id.
[141] Bartshé Miller, *Mono Lake Mired in Drought*, MONO LAKE NEWSL. (June 9, 2015), www.monolake .org/today/mono-lake-mired-in-drought/ [https://perma.cc/R7FY-GQCU] [hereinafter Miller, *Mono Lake Mired in Drought*].

Mono Lake lost five feet of elevation, the land bridge between Negit Island and the mainland gained ground, and air quality declined as regular Eastern Sierra winds blew toxic alkali dust off the newly reexposed lakebed.[142] For the first time since the Water Board's decision in 1994, Mono Lake declined below the specific legal threshold it had established to trigger significant export reductions to Los Angeles.[143]

To comply with the Water Board's carefully designed protections for Mono Lake, DWP and the Mono Lake Committee jointly measure the water level every year on April 1st.[144] According to Decision 1631, if the lake falls to below 6,380 feet, as measured on April 1 of any year, then allowable exports to Los Angeles must be reduced by 70 percent of its usual allocation.[145] When the lake falls to below 6,377 feet, as measured or projected on April 1, then Los Angeles may no longer export any water from the Mono Basin.[146]

On April 1, 2015, staff from the Mono Lake Committee and DWP measured the water level and found it at 6379.01'.[147] This level, just below the 6,380' requirement, automatically triggered the required 70 percent reduction in water exports.[148] Exports were accordingly reduced from 16,000 acre-feet to 4,500 acre-feet of water until the lake rose to, or above, the threshold on a future April 1st.[149] Fortunately for everyone, the lake level had not reached the 6377' threshold, which would have cut off DWP's ability to export any water from Mono Lake.[150] Still even this small decrease represented a 1.8 percent reduction in Los Angeles' overall water supply,[151] a noticeable loss during a drought that had already strained all sources of supply.

During the drought of 2014 and 2015, California Governor Jerry Brown – the same Jerry Brown who, as Governor twenty-five years earlier, signed the bill creating the California Mono Lake Tufa Natural State Reserve[152] – implemented a host of water conservation efforts to reduce consumption, both to protect waterways and ensure that citizens' critical water needs would be met.[153] On January 17, 2014, he declared a State of Emergency over the severe drought conditions.[154] By Executive Order, he imposed restrictions to achieve a 25 percent reduction in urban use of potable water sources through February 28, 2016, created partnerships with local agencies to replace lawns and turf with drought tolerant landscapes, and implemented a variety

---

[142] *Id.*
[143] *Id.*
[144] *Id.*
[145] Decision 1631, *supra* note 65, at *156.
[146] *Id.*
[147] Miller, *Mono Lake Mired in Drought, supra* note 141.
[148] McQuilkin, *Lake Level Means Reduced Water Exports, supra* note 138.
[149] Miller, *Mono Lake Mired in Drought, supra* note 141.
[150] *Id.*
[151] *Id.*
[152] *See supra* text accompanying note 6–7.
[153] Exec. Order No. B-29-15, Exec. Dep't State of Cal. (Apr. 1, 2015), [www.perma.cc/X7SY-FHYD].
[154] *Id.*

of other strategies, including appliance rebate programs to encourage more household water conservation.[155]

At the time, the Mono Lake Committee credited the *Audubon Society*, *CalTrout*, and Decision 1631 legal protections enacted two decades earlier for Mono Lake's ability to withstand the drought.[156] But it was still uncertain whether winter snowfall would bring Mono Lake levels up again or drop them below the 6,377' threshold[157] the following April, triggering a complete prohibition on water exports.[158] In the fall of 2015, the lake level had dropped another foot down to 6,378', just a foot over the threshold.[159] The Mono Lake Committee reported that Basin exports could also be halted if projections show the lake level decreasing beyond the 6,377' threshold at "any time during the runoff year of April 1 through March 31," even before the formal April 1st measurement.[160] The looming question was what would happen if the Mono Lake Committee and DWP's projections differed.[161] The issue was debated, but an answer was never required, as subsequent weather events brought the lake level above the critical lower threshold.[162]

In January 2016, the lake level was measured at 6,377.9'.[163] The following month, the lake level rose to 6,378.0' and continued to rise until July 2016, when it was measured at 6378.3'.[164] After another wet winter, in July 2017, the lake rose almost two feet to 6380.2', finally exceeding the upper threshold.[165] However, the 70 percent reduction in water exports remained in place until the required annual measurement was made the following April 1st,[166] because Decision 1631 allows DWP to resume annual exports of 16,000 acre-feet per year only when the lake exceeds the upper threshold on the official measurement date. On April 1, 2018, the lake was

---

[155] *Id.*
[156] Geoff McQuilkin, *New Twists as Mono Lake's Level Falls: Spotlight on Lake Level Forecasting in 2016*, Mono Lake Newsl., www.monolake.org/today/new-twists-as-mono-lakes-level-falls-spotlight-on-lake-level-forecasting-in-2016/ (last visited Oct. 29, 2015) [www.perma.cc/B2QY-KC6N] [hereinafter McQuilkin, *New Twists*].
[157] *Id.*
[158] *Id.*; Louis Sahagun, *Mono Lake's Ecological Crisis Is a Blow to Wildlife, L.A. Water Supply*, L.A. Times, www.latimes.com/science/la-me-mono-drought-20150625-story.html [https://perma.cc/3SLH-CH5N] (last visited Jun. 24, 2015).
[159] McQuilkin, *New Twists*, *supra* note 156.
[160] *Id.*
[161] *Id.*
[162] Louis Sahagún, *Once Teetering, Mono Lake Is Revived by Heavy Rains, Snow*, L.A. Times, www.latimes.com/local/california/la-me-mono-lake-storm-20170109-story.html (last visited Jan. 10, 2017, 8:00 AM) [www.perma.cc/WV4R-KS45]; *see also* Geoff McQuilkin, *Record Winter Snowpack Melt Underway*, 3 Mono Lake Newsl., www.monolake.org/today/record-winter-snowpack-melt-underway/ (last visited May 23, 2017) [www.perma.cc/WV4R-KS45].
[163] *See Mono Lake Levels*, *supra* note 103.
[164] *Id.*
[165] *Id.*
[166] E-mail from Bartshé Miller, Educ. Dir., Mono Lake Comm., to Mallory Neuman, Rsch. Assistant (Oct. 28, 2017, 8:24 PM) (on file with author).

E. A Reprieve for Mono Lake?

officially and jointly measured by DWP and the Committee at 6,381.86',[167] enabling DWP to resume exports of up to 16,000 acre-feet of water that year.[168]

Nevertheless – and in a true watershed moment for Mono Lake – late in 2021, the State Water Board imposed important new constraints on Los Angeles' water rights in the Mono Basin,[169] designed to help restore damage to the 20 miles of streams, forests, and fisheries downstream from the Los Angeles Aqueduct diversion dams.[170] These new requirements ended the diversion of Walker and Parker creeks into the aqueduct, modernized the Grant River Dam, and established an ongoing process for science-based adaptive management of annual flow patterns, including the required delivery of instream water flows to Rush and Lee Vining creeks that mimic the natural pattern of annual snowmelt.[171]

The 28th anniversary of Decision 1631 was celebrated in September 2022.[172] Yet Mono Lake has still not reached its stabilization target, rising only 25 percent of the way by volume to the prescribed 6,392 management level.[173] At no point since the decision has the lake come even within ten feet of this target. When Decision 1631 was taken in 1994, the Water Board had expected Mono Lake to reach the mandated level by 2014, at which point Los Angeles' allowable diversions would be reconsidered.[174] In 2014, when the lake had still not reached the target level, that expectation was extended to 2020.[175] This followed five years of drought, which had dropped the lake level by seven feet and triggered an emergency hearing

---

[167] Arya Degenhardt, *Official April 1 Mono Lake Level: 6381.86 Feet*, MONO LAKE COMM. (Apr. 2, 2018), www.monolake.org/today/official-april-1-mono-lake-level-6381-86-feet/ (last visited Oct. 2, 2025).

[168] *Id.*

[169] In the Matter of Licenses 10191 & 10192, Order WR 2021-0086 Exec, State Water Res. Control Bd. (2021), www.perma.cc/LYY6-66DZ.

[170] *Id.*; Arya Degenhardt, *State Water Board Launches New Era of Restoration at Mono Lake*, MONO LAKE COMM., www.monolake.org/today/state-water-board-launches-new-era-of-stream-restoration-at-mono-lake/ (last visited October 2, 2021) [www.perma.cc/RD3V-ED9E].

[171] *Mono Lake Basin*, CAL. WATER BDS., www.waterboards.ca.gov/waterrights/water_issues/programs/mono_lake/ (last visited Oct. 25, 2025) ("Background" tab) ("The amended water right licenses issued by Order WR 2021-0086 incorporate the provisions of the 2013 Mono Lake Basin Restoration Settlement Agreement and combine into a single document all prior terms and conditions imposed by the State Water Board in past orders and Decision 1631. Order WR 2021-0086 approves major changes to the Mono Lake Stream Restoration Program, including a requirement for LADWP to modify Grant Lake Dam by constructing an outlet structure capable of releasing the higher peak flows required in certain year-types to benefit the environment. The new Stream Ecosystem Flow regime is aimed at accelerating ecosystem recovery processes that will benefit the trout fishery and riparian habitats of Rush, Lee Vining, Walker, and Parker creeks."); *see also* Degenhardt, *State Water Board Launches New Era*, *supra* note 170.

[172] Arya Degenhardt, *Happy Save Mono Lake Day!*, MONO LAKE COMM., www.monolake.org/today/happy-save-mono-lake-day/ (last visited Sept. 28, 2022) [www.perma.cc/3ZND-6NR9].

[173] *Id.*

[174] Geoffrey McQuilkin, *Raising Mono Lake Requires a New Plan*, MONO LAKE COMM. (May 26, 2022), www.monolake.org/today/raising-mono-lake-requires-a-new-plan/ [www.perma.cc/VG4Q-VLJL] [hereinafter McQuilkin, *Raising Mono Lake*].

[175] *Id.*

requirement in 2020.[176], DWP maintained that "more water restrictions are not the answer,"[177] because the city's diversions have only "a negligible impact on the lake's decline" in comparison to climate change and related drought.[178]

Even so, the prescribed annual reading on April 1, 2022, showed the lake at 6,379.92 feet above sea level,[179] which triggered a restriction in DWP's exports.[180] For the following twelve months, stream diversions were limited not to exceed a total of 4,500 acre-feet,[181] substantially down from the 16,000 acre-feet DWP could divert over the previous year.[182] However, DWP was separately able to export more than 5,000 acre-feet annually of Mono Basin groundwater through the Mono Craters Tunnel, which exports both surface and groundwater to the Los Angeles Aqueduct intake at the headwaters of the Owens River.[183] But groundwater exports still impact the lake level, because they decrease the amount of water that will pass from the Mono Lake tributaries into the lake itself. As of 2023, the annual reading showed the lake at 6,379.99 feet above sea level.[184]

Indeed, the impacts and extent of groundwater exports allowable at each stage of the lake recovery process was not considered in Decision 1631.[185] Sadly, this is consistent with the failure to consider the hydrologic relationship between surface and groundwater diversions in most state water allocation laws until fairly recently. The Mono Lake Committee reports that, at present, nobody monitors the collection of Mono Basin groundwater through the Mono Craters Tunnel, nor is it subject to any

---

[176] *Id.*

[177] Elin Ljung, *San Francisco Chronicle Covers Mono Lake's Low Level*, MONO LAKE COMM., www.monolake.org/today/san-francisco-chronicle-covers-mono-lakes-low-level/ (last visited July 23, 2022) [www.perma.cc/S2MS-S2CF].

[178] *Id.* (quoting an email to The Chronicle by Paul Liu, DWP's managing water utility engineer).

[179] McQuilkin, *Raising Mono Lake*, *supra* note 174. The 2023 reading was 6,379.99 feet. Were the reading 6,380.00 (a difference of 0.01 feet), DWP would have been able to export 16,000 acre-feet of water in the next runoff year, as opposed to the current limit of 4,500 acre-feet per year. The Mono Lake Committee expressed relief that the lake did not exceed the 6,380.00 feet mark, because it means more of an opportunity for the lake to grow without diversions quadrupling. Geoff McQuilkin, *By Smallest of Margins Mono Lake Avoids Water Diversions Quadrupling*, MONO LAKE COMM., www.monolake.org/today/by-smallest-of-margins-mono-lake-avoids-water-diversions-quadrupling/ (last visited Apr. 1, 2023) [https://perma.cc/S2MS-S2CF].

[180] *Id.*

[181] *Id.*

[182] *Id.*

[183] *Id.*; Geoffrey McQuilkin, *Groundwater Exports Benefit Los Angeles; Impact Mono Lake*, MONO LAKE COMM., www.monolake.org/today/groundwater-exports-benefit-los-angeles-impact-mono-lake/ (last visited March 18, 2022) [www.perma.cc/YUK8-S3Y4] [hereinafter *Groundwater Exports Benefit Los Angeles*].

[184] Arya Degenhardt, *The 2023 Mono Lake Level Forecast*, MONO LAKE COMM., www.monolake.org/today/the-2023-mono-lake-level-forecast/#:~:text=At%20the%20end%20of%20last,feet%20on%20April%201%2C%202023 (last visited May 24, 2023) [www.perma.cc/Y3W7-EZ6V] ("At the end of last year Mono Lake had fallen to 6378.4 feet above sea level due to very dry weather and dry runoff conditions. Winter precipitation was abundant and then raised the lake to 6379.99 feet on April 1, 2023.").

[185] *See generally* Decision 1631, *supra* note 65.

E. A Reprieve for Mono Lake?

legal constraints: "No agency or court requires reporting on groundwater capture, oversees its volume, nor mandates mitigation of its impacts."[186] In fact, this critique continues, "it appears that the Mono Craters Tunnel is the largest unregulated, unreported, and unmitigated source of water entering the Los Angeles Aqueduct."[187] Yet as discussed further in Chapter 7, the California Court of Appeal decision in the Scott River case, one of the most important progeny of the Mono Lake case itself, casts doubt as to whether unregulated groundwater exports in the Mono Basin are legally appropriate.[188]

Unfortunately, Mono Lake is unlikely to benefit from favorable weather trends in the coming years. Despite seasonal deluges of heavy precipitation and improved technology,[189] the record drought California is experiencing is expected to be long and to intensify over the next century, largely due to climate change.[190] In response to acute periods of drought in 2021 and 2022, the State undertook a number of interim and long term regulatory actions to control commercial and residential water usage, including the Governor's proclamation of a drought state of emergency and two emergency regulations promulgated by the Water Board.[191]

---

[186] McQuilkin, *Groundwater Exports Benefit Los Angeles*, supra note 183.

[187] *Id.*

[188] Env't Law Found. v. State Water Res. Control Bd., 26 Cal. App. 5th 844, 851 (Cal. Ct. App. 2018); Chapter 7(B)(1)(c) ("The Scott River Case") (discussing the *Scott River* litigation).

[189] The atmospheric river event, which began in late December 2022 and lasted until mid-January 2023, released a huge amount of precipitation in California. *See* Joel Lisonbee, Britt Parker, Adam Lang, Elizabeth Ossowski, Andrea Bair, Alan Haynes, Robin Fox, Paul Miller, Joe Casola, Ryan Andrews, Mike Anderson, Karin Bumbaco, Erica Fleishman, Roger Gorke, David Hoekema, Julie Kalansky, Larry O'Neill, Jonathan Rutz, Erinanne Saffell & David Simeral, *A Series of Atmospheric Rivers Have Hit Parts of the West. What Does This Mean for Drought?*, NAT'L INTEGRATED DROUGHT INFO. SYS. www.drought.gov/drought-status-updates/special-edition-drought-status-update-western-united-states-2023-01-24 (last visited Jan. 24, 2023), [www.perma.cc/4SGV-SZ29]; *see also* Elin Ljung, *A Glimpse at the Amazing New Snow at Mono Lake*, MONO LAKE COMM., www.monolake.org/today/a-glimpse-at-the-amazing-new-snow-at-mono-lake/ (last visited Jan. 13, 2023) [www.perma.cc/NQS9-M7QF] (noting that precipitation from the atmospheric river raised the Mono Lake water level by 0.77 feet between January 2, 2023 and January 13, 2023; *Stormwater Capture Swells during Season's Biggest Rainstorm, Accumulating 10.6 Billion Gallons – Enough Water to Serve 139,000 Households*, L.A. DEP'T OF WATER & POWER, www.ladwpnews.com/stormwater-capture-swells-during-seasons-biggest-rainstorm-accumulating-10-6-billion-gallons-enough-water-to-serve-139000-households/ (last visited Jan. 11, 2023), [https://perma.cc/C45M-4XCT] (noting that investments in stormwater capture technology have helped to recharge groundwater supply).

[190] Henry Fountain, *Will Storms End California's Drought? That May Be the Wrong Question*, N.Y. TIMES, www.nytimes.com/2023/01/11/climate/california-drought-rain.html?action=click&pgtype=Article&state=default&module=styln-california-storm&variant=show&region=MAIN_CONTENT_1&block=storyline_top_links_recirc (last visited Jan. 11, 2023).

[191] Governor Gavin Newsom proclaimed a drought state of emergency on October 19, 2021, ongoing as this publication goes to press. *Water Conservation Emergency Regulations*, STATE WATER BDS., www.waterboards.ca.gov/water_issues/programs/conservation_portal/regs/emergency_regulation.html (last visited Oct. 18, 2022). Under authority granted to it by Governor Newsom, the California State Water Board enacted an emergency regulation on January 18, 2022, followed by a second, stricter emergency regulation on June 10, 2022. CAL. CODE REGS. tit. 23, §§ 995–996 (2022). The regulations primarily regulate outdoor watering uses. *See id.*

The Water Board's regulations, promulgated in response to the declared state of emergency, demonstrate the tools and limits of demand-side limitations. The first round targeted consumers, prohibiting such activities as excessive watering of outdoor landscapes; use of hoses to wash cars (unless fitted with a shutoff nozzle); watering sidewalks, driveways, buildings, structures, patios, and parking lots; use of water for street cleaning or construction site preparation; decorative fountains; the filling of decorative lakes or ponds (excepting those with recirculation pumps and that replace only evaporative losses); and the irrigation of turf and ornamental landscapes within 48 hours of measurable rainfall and on public street medians.[192] The second round of emergency regulations targeted water suppliers directly, requiring most urban suppliers to implement all "Level 2" demand-reduction actions under their required Water Shortage Contingency Plans.[193] These regulations were lifted in June 2023,[194] before a series of "atmospheric river" rain events poured out over California in 2024,[195] but new regulations continue to issue as conditions evolve.[196]

Yet conditions are not evolving favorably for Mono Lake. Based on current computer modelling technology, Mono Lake advocates contend that the lake will not be able to reach the target sustainable level within the next thirty years if present diversion patterns continue.[197] The snowpack remained below-average in the first three years following 2020, at 37 percent of the recorded average in 2022 alone.[198] The lake level has slowly but steadily declined over these same years.[199] The trend has not been as bad as it was during the 2012–2016 drought, but "consecutive years of well-below-average winter precipitation have been more frequent" since the drought.[200] If exports are reduced by 50 percent, the computer model projects that the lake will rise but still not be able to reach the target level over the next thirty years.[201] According to the model, Mono Lake could reach the target if stream diversions are paused entirely over the next thirty years.[202]

---

[192] CAL. CODE REGS. tit. 23, §995(b) (2022).
[193] CAL. CODE REGS. tit. 23, § 996 (2022).
[194] *Water Conservation Emergency Regulations*, *supra* note 433 (noting that emergency regulations expire one year after their effective dates and stating that "[t]he requirement for urban water suppliers to implement demand-reduction actions that correspond to at least Level 2 of their water shortage contingency plans has not been in effect since June 5, 2023").
[195] *Atmospheric River Impacts in California*, NAT'L WEATHER SERV., www.weather.gov/mtr/AtmosphericRiver-February_3–5_2024 (last visited Apr. 10, 2025) [www.perma.cc/L4EN-4AZQ].
[196] *See, e.g.*, CAL. CODE REGS. tit. 23, §996 (2022) (amended) (prohibiting the use of potable water for non-functional turf irrigation in commercial, industrial, and institutional areas, with exceptions for tree health and safety needs; instituting fines of up to $500 per day for violations).
[197] McQuilkin, *Raising Mono Lake*, *supra* note 174.
[198] Bartshé Miller, *Drought Worsens at Mono Lake*, MONO LAKE COMM., www.monolake.org/today/drought-worsens-at-mono-lake/ (last visited Jun. 1, 2022) [www.perma.cc/B8VV-N2KN] [hereinafter Miller, *Drought Worsens at Mono Lake*].
[199] The yearly measurements of Mono Lake's surface level (measured in feet above sea level) are as follows: 2019: 6382.6'; 2020: 6381.5'; 2021: 6379.9'; 2022: 6378.7'. *See Mono Lake Levels*, *supra* note 103.
[200] Miller, *Drought Worsens at Mono Lake*, *supra* note 197.
[201] McQuilkin, *Raising Mono Lake*, *supra* note 174.
[202] *See id.*

E. A Reprieve for Mono Lake? 189

And then, in a late 2025 surprise – as this book was already in press – Los Angeles city leaders recognized that a different path was possible. The city approved plans to double the capacity of previously planned water reclamation facilities by the end of 2027, announcing that the new supply would alleviate the need to withdraw further water from the Basin except in emergency circumstances.[203] President Richard Katz of the L.A. Board of Water and Power Commissioners called the decision "a solution with lots of winners," noting that once the recycled water starts flowing, "we won't need Mono Lake water to meet the supplies in L.A."[204] The announcement is a stunning turnaround from the city's recent posture – once again reflecting strong local concern for Mono Basin protection and for the state's public trust obligations. If action is taken to implement this announcement, the city will deserve enormous credit for its vision and courage in retreating from Mono Basin water at a time all western cities are straining under increasing conditions of water scarcity.

But first, the water license annual diversion rules must be updated, requiring another potentially contentious Water Board hearing. Even if the proposal comes to fruition, diversions will continue until the facility is completed, and Mono Lake recovery afterward will still take many years. Los Angeles has not abandoned its water rights there, preserving the possibility of resuming diversions for emergency circumstances – which seem likely. For all these reasons, environmental conditions in the basin will remain tenuous for some time. Even so, this is the best harbinger for the recovery of Mono Lake since the California Supreme Court decided *Audubon Society* and the Water Board issued Decision 1631, and lake supporters rejoiced. The Executive Director of the Mono Lake Committee quickly sent out the message: "We're doing it!"

Sadly, things have not gone as well for the Owens Valley.

2. Owens Valley after Audubon

Before leaving the epic saga of the Los Angeles Aqueduct, it is also worth noting the story that has continued to unfold in the Owens Valley since the Mono Lake litigation and

---

[203] See Ian James, *Los Angeles Will Nearly Double Recycled Water for 500,000 Residents*, L.A. TIMES (Oct. 31, 2025), www.latimes.com/environment/story/2025-10-31/los-angeles-wastewater-recycling (last visited Nov. 2, 2025) ("In a plan that will reverberate more than 300 miles north at Mono Lake, Los Angeles city leaders have decided to nearly double the wastewater that will be transformed into drinking water at the Donald C. Tillman Water Reclamation Plant in Van Nuys. Instead of treating 25 million gallons per day as originally planned, the L.A. Board of Water and Power Commissioners voted to purify 45 million gallons, enough water for 500,000 people. Board President Richard Katz said this will enable the city to stop taking water from Sierra streams that feed Mono Lake – a major shift that will address long-standing demands by environmentalists, who criticize L.A. for failing to allow the lake to rise to a healthy level.").
[204] *Id.*

Decision 1631. As described in Chapter 3, the lower leg of the Los Angeles Aqueduct first began shifting water south to L.A. from the Owens Valley well over a 100 years ago, leading to the desiccation of Owens Lake and the lower Owens River and incalculable harm to the Owens Valley ecosystem and regional agricultural community. Los Angeles' permissions to divert water from the Owens Valley were entrenched much earlier in state history, before many subsequent environmental and administrative constraints were put in place.[205] There was no corresponding *Audubon Society* case, rallying the greater public to protect the Owens Valley. Most of the damage was done long before the actual *Audubon Society* decision established guidelines for state decision making on water exports that might have produced a different result there.

However, the successes of the later Mono Basin advocates inspired activism in the Owens Valley as well, where local advocates have been tirelessly campaigning for their own environmental justice. In 1983, loosely modeled after the Mono Lake Committee, concerned Inyo County residents formed the Owens Valley Committee to oppose a joint water management plan that county supervisors had been poised to form with DWP.[206] Concerned that the plan favored DWP's interests over Owens Valley interests, the Committee rallied public opposition through educational outreach, public speaking engagements, telephonic surveys, and newspaper editorials and advertisements critiquing the proposed terms.[207] The Committee sought "just and sustainable management of Owens Valley land and water resources," envisioning "a valley in which existing open space is protected, historic land use sustained, and depleted groundwater and surface flows restored as Los Angeles phases out its dependence on Owens Valley Water."[208]

Eight years later, the Mono Lake plaintiffs had prevailed in *Audubon Society*, *CalTrout*, and many of the other legal decisions requiring DWP to do more to protect Mono Lake – some of which, by extension, also required better protection for other waterways implicated for compliance with the fish protections litigated in *CalTrout*, including stretches of the Owens River.[209] In this context, DWP finally agreed to do more to protect the Lower Owens Valley in Inyo County

---

[205] For a comprehensive timeline of Owens Valley water history between 1902 and 2008, see *Owens Valley Water History (Chronology)*, INYO CNTY. WATER DEP'T, www.inyowater.org/documents/reports/owens-valley-water-history-chronology/ (last visited Oct. 11, 2022).

[206] *About OVC*, OWENS VALLEY COMM., www.owensvalley.org/about-ovc/ (last visited Oct. 11, 2022) [https://perma.cc/2GQW-93TL]; Greg James, Former Director of the Inyo Cty. Water Dep't., "Owens Valley History 101," transcript available at: www.thereitistakeit.org/owens-valley-water-history-101by-greg-james-former-director-of-the-inyo-county-water-dept/ (last visited March 22, 2016), [https://perma.cc/5WYG-QAV6] (reporting on the plans of the Owens Lake Committee to follow the example of the Mono Lake Committee.)

[207] *About OVC*, *supra* note 208.

[208] *Id.*

[209] *See* Karrigan S. Bork, et al., *The Rebirth of California Fish & Game Code Section 5937: Water for Fish*, 45 U.C. DAVIS L. REV. 809, 848 at n.181, 884–85 (discussing the applicability of the *CalTrout* ruling to stretches of the Owens River that had also been dewatered by DWP).

as well, in a 1991 Long Term Water Agreement that displaced the earlier water management plan.²¹⁰

The Owens Valley Committee supported the Inyo-Los Angeles Long Term Water Agreement, but it argued that the supporting environmental assessment had been inadequate.²¹¹ Related litigation and six years of subsequent negotiation resulted in a 1997 Memorandum of Understanding (MOU) to remedy the deficient environmental impact report, and a Lower Owens River Project to restore parts of the Owens Valley.²¹² The Committee then shifted its focus to ensuring that the mitigations in the MOU were properly implemented, which would eventually require three separate lawsuits to compel DWP to implement the Lower Owens River Project according to the terms of the 1991 Long Term Water Agreement and the 1997 MOU.²¹³

Of note, Los Angeles seemed more amenable to the concerns of the Owens Valley Committee in the immediate wake of the Mono Lake litigation and Decision 1631, when it committed to environmental remediation and future harm avoidance in the Long-Term Water Agreement and the Lower Owens River Project. However, for whatever reasons, the city's priorities appeared to shift in the years that would follow. Conflict escalated between the Owens Valley advocates and DWP, which appeared to stall and/or backpedal on some of these commitments, fighting vigorously against additional air pollution requirements imposed by state environmental agencies.

In 2005, the Committee and the Sierra Club jointly sued DWP for failing to draft the Lower Owens River Project Ecosystem Management Plan envisioned by the 1997 MOU.²¹⁴ In the suit, they asked the court to sanction DWP for delaying the re-watering of sixty-two miles of dry Lower Owens River under the 1991 Long-term Water Agreement.²¹⁵ On July 24, 2005, Inyo County Superior Court Judge Lee Cooper ruled against DWP, holding that it could not export from the Owens Valley until a list of conditions was met. He ordered that initial flows be released into the lower Owens River by January 25, 2007, and that full flows must begin by six months afterward.²¹⁶ He also ordered DWP to spread 16,294 acre-feet of water for groundwater recharge to the local water table, and he imposed $5,000 per day fines until

---

²¹⁰ Stipulation and Order for Judgment at 17–18, City of Los Angeles v. Bd. of Supervisors (Inyo Cnty. Super. Ct. 1991) (No. 12908), www.inyowater.org/wpcontent/uploads/legacy/Water_Resources/long_term_water_agreement.pdf; Louis Sahagún, *Eastern Sierra's Lower Owens River Is Ripe for a Recreational Rebirth*, L.A. TIMES (Oct. 5, 2013), www.latimes.com/local/la-me-1006-owens-river-20131006-story.html [www.perma.cc/K7L7-Y9SY] [hereinafter Sahagún, Eastern Sierra's Lower Owens River].

²¹¹ *About OVC, supra* note 208.

²¹² *Id*; Memorandum of Understanding, City of Los Angeles Department of Water and Power-County of Inyo (Feb. 1997) www.inyowater.org/wp-content/uploads/legacy/Water_Resources/mou/default.html (last visited Oct. 28, 2022).

²¹³ *Id*.

²¹⁴ Sierra Club v. City of Los Angeles et al., No. SICVCV-01-29768 (Cal. App. Dep't Super. Ct. June 24, 2005).

²¹⁵ *Id*. at 2–3.

²¹⁶ Order Re: Defendants' Violations of Court Orders at 4, *id*.

the projects were completed.[217] In September of 2008, the Committee and Sierra Club filed a second lawsuit to compel acceptable management plans for the Lower Owens River Project, which were still outstanding.[218]

Soon thereafter, state environmental agencies acted to better protect public health in the Owens Valley, launching further conflict with DWP. In 2012, the Great Basin Unified Air Pollution Control District, the regional state agency tasked with protecting air quality along the central Eastern Sierra, ordered DWP to control sources of toxic air pollution from additional miles of the exposed Owens Dry Lake bed.[219] DWP sued to challenge the agency's order, which would have cost $400 million to satisfy,[220] alleging that the order created "excessive and unreasonable demands."[221] That November, the statewide California Air Resources Board reviewed the regional agency's air pollution control measures and found them both reasonable and legally required.[222] DWP lost its case in state court, and the Kern County Superior Court required it to pay the legal expenses the Great Basin District had incurred in defending its rules.[223]

While the state court case was still pending, DWP filed a corresponding suit against the Great Basin District in federal court[224] with support from the Los Angeles City Council, Mayor Villaraigosa, and Los Angeles business groups.[225] However, the U.S. Department of Justice, the U.S. Environmental Protection Agency, and the California Attorney General's Office all opposed the lawsuit, supporting the Great Basin District regulations.[226] On May 2, 2013, the U.S. District Court for the Eastern District of California dismissed DWP's lawsuit, settling the matter.[227]

---

[217] *Id.* at 3–4; Louis Sahagan, *DWP Told to Restore Part of River*, L.A. TIMES, www.inyowater.org/wp-content/uploads/2013/04/LA-Times-article.pdf (last visited Jul. 26, 2005).

[218] Carla Scheidlinger, *President's Message*, The Rainshadow 2 (Summer 2009) Volume 5, Number 1, OWENS VALLEY COMM.

[219] The Times Editorial Board, *100 Years Later, The Dust Settles in the Owens Valley*, L.A. TIMES, www.latimes.com/opinion/editorials/la-ed-owens-valley-settlement-20141116-story.html (last visited Nov. 16, 2014).

[220] *Id.*

[221] Jim Newton, *Newton: Owens Valley Dust-Up*, L.A. TIMES, www.articles.latimes.com/2012/nov/19/opinion/la-oe-newton-column-owens-valley-20121119 (last visited Nov. 19, 2012).

[222] *LADWP Loses Federal Cases*, SIERRA WAVE MEDIA, www.sierrawave.net/loses-federal-case/ (last visited May 2, 2013); *Current Owens Valley Water Issues*, The Rainshadow 2 (Spring/Summer 2013) Volume 8, Number 1, OWENS VALLEY COMM., www.owensvalley.org/wp-content/uploads/2015/10/Rainshadow_spring-summer-2013_v4.pdf ("DWP has filed a State lawsuit challenging the California Air Resources Board decision to uphold Great Basin's 2011 order for DWP to control dust on additional 2.9 square miles of lake bed.").

[223] Molly Peterson, *LADWP on the Hook for Regulators' Legal Expenses Related to Owens Lake*, 89.3KPCC, www.scpr.org/blogs/environment/2012/12/18/11608/ladwp-hook-regulators-legal-expenses-related-owens/ (last visited Dec. 18, 2012); *Current Owens Valley Water Issues, supra* note 221.

[224] SIERRA WAVE MEDIA, *supra* note 221 (reporting that the case "attempted to prevent the District from enforcing state laws that require the LADWP to control the air pollution caused by its water diversions in the Eastern Sierra").

[225] *Id.*

[226] *Id.*

[227] *Current Owens Valley Water Issues, supra* note 221; SIERRA WAVE MEDIA, *supra* note 221.

E. A Reprieve for Mono Lake?   193

At this point, after fifteen years of litigation, DWP finally redirected aqueduct infrastructure to restore water flows to the Lower Owens River.[228] It was (quite literally) a watershed moment for the Owens River and the Owens Valley, which had been deprived of its normal flow since the earliest days of aqueduct history. For the first time in a hundred years, water flowed through the gapingly empty riverbed – an enormous chasm that had become so choked with dryland vegetation by the 1990s that it was nearly invisible to the naked eye. The *Los Angeles Times* reported that the Inyo County Water Department and L.A. River Expeditions were jointly considering use of the Lower Owens River as a potential site for public recreation.[229] Even so, flow was legally required only for the Owens Valley agricultural irrigation season.[230] The southbound aqueduct ran dry for six months but resumed delivery in 2015, when the irrigation season requirements had ended.[231]

The following year, in 2014, DWP and the Great Basin District agreed to try a method for suppressing airborne dust from dry Owens Lake that would hopefully contain the toxic alkali particulates by means other than resubmerging the dry lake bed.[232] Instead of flooding it with water, DWP would employ tractors to till the lake bed into clods of dirt that would ideally hold the toxic dust for years before breaking down, and the process would be repeated as needed to secure the dust on the ground.[233] The same agreement funded a new Owens Lake Scientific Advisory Panel, established by the National Academies of Sciences, which would assess the effectiveness of these dust control efforts over time.[234] Six years later, in 2020, the panel published its findings regarding the effectiveness of various dust management strategies.[235] After analyzing a range of Dust Control Measures,[236] it found that while many reduced PM10 concentrations, none achieved the targeted levels of dust control without substantial application of water, and only the shallow flooding technique consistently provided the desired wildlife habitat.[237]

Even after the formation of the Advisory Panel, distrust continued to brew between the city and the Owens Lake Committee. In November of 2014, the Owens Valley Committee and the Sierra Club conducted a public records request

---

[228] Sahagun, *Eastern Sierra, supra* note 209.
[229] *Id.*
[230] *L.A. Aqueduct Flows After Dam Supplying Owens Valley is Dismembered*, THE WEATHER CHANNEL, www.weather.com/news/news/los-angeles-aqueduct-flows-toward-city (last visited Oct. 28, 2015).
[231] *Id.*
[232] Louis Sahagun, *New Dust-Busting Method Ends L.A.'s Longtime Feud with Owens Valley*, L.A. TIMES, www.latimes.com/science/la-me-1115-owens-20141115-story.html (last visited Nov. 14, 2014).
[233] *Id.*
[234] *Id.* Great Basin Unified Air Pollution Control District, *Owens Lake Scientific Advisory Panel*, www.gbuapcd.org/OwensLake/OLSAP/ (last visited Aug. 18, 2024).
[235] National Academies of Sciences, Engineering, and Medicine, EFFECTIVENESS AND IMPACTS OF DUST CONTROL MEASURES FOR OWENS LAKE 4 (Nat'l Acad. Press 2020).
[236] *Id.*
[237] *Id.* The report states that some control measures show promise if hybridized with other control measures. *Id.*

to gather information about ranch leases to determine whether DWP was acting consistently with the Long Term Water Agreement, but DWP was not quick to respond.[238] In April of 2015, the Committee requested electronic map information and collection data for all wells and measuring stations in the Owens Valley, but when DWP responded in June, it withheld the geographical information system map information under a public records exemption.[239] The Committee then opposed DWP's plans to construct an industrial-scale solar energy facility in the Owens Valley.[240]

In 2016, the city attempted to reduce tensions with Owens Valley communities when it constructed the 700-acre, $4.6 million Owens Lake Trails recreational project, intended as a destination for hikers, bird watchers, community gatherings, and wedding ceremonies.[241] As part of the massive $305 million dust-mitigation effort to cover the Owens Dry Lake alkali flats, the State Lands Commission had also required Los Angeles to enhance wildlife habitat and increase visitor access to the area, inspiring the project.[242] Scenic gravel trails emanate from a public plaza with interactive artwork, curved granite walls resembling the wings of shorebirds, and stone and earth sculptures invoking whitecaps on water.[243] Perry Cardoza, the project architect, framed it as an "olive branch" from Los Angeles to the Owens Valley amid the century-long conflict, but the *Los Angeles Times* reported that locals remained generally skeptical at the time.[244]

Perhaps crystallizing that skepticism, the most recent move in the ongoing Owens Valley conflict has been an attempt by the local community to repossess Los Angeles' Owens Valley property and associated water rights through eminent domain.[245] Following the saga described in Chapter 3, Los Angeles emerged owning one quarter of the Owens Valley floor, including some land that Inyo County leases back from the city for use as a local landfill.[246] In 2016, Los Angeles had surprised Inyo County with a fourfold rent increase of more than $20,000 annually and the addition of a termination clause that allowed DWP to terminate the agreement with 180 days of notice for any

---

[238] *The People Need to Know: Wringing Public Records from DWP*, The Rainshadow 5 (2015 Annual Edition), Volume 10, Number 1, THE OWENS VALLEY COMM., www.owensvalley.org/wp-content/uploads/fall-2015.pdf.

[239] *Id.*

[240] *About OVC*, *supra* note 208.

[241] Louis Sahagun, *Is it an Olive Branch or 'Crazy'? Owens Valley is Skeptical of Angelenos Bearing Gifts*, L.A. TIMES, www.latimes.com/local/california/la-me-adv-owens-art-controversy-20160426-story.html (last visited Apr. 25, 2016).

[242] *Id.*

[243] *Id.*

[244] *Id.*

[245] *See* Los Angeles Dep't of Water & Power v. County of Inyo, 67 Cal. App. 5th 1018 (Cal. Ct. App. 2021); Louis Sahagun, *L.A. Took Their Water and Land a Century Ago. Now the Owens Valley is Fighting Back*, L.A. TIMES, www.latimes.com/local/california/la-me-owens-valley-eminent-domain-20170712-story.html (last visited Jul. 13, 2017).

[246] Sahagun, *L.A. Took Their Water*, *supra* note 244.

reason.[247] Inyo County found itself over a barrel, pressured to accept the unfavorable terms because the state agency that regulates landfills would not offer the legal permission to continue operating until a new lease was in place, and the County could not be without a solid waste facility without violating other laws and obligations.[248]

After 100 years of conflict with Los Angeles, this was, perhaps, the last straw for Inyo County. The landfill lease dispute prompted Inyo County to initiate legal proceedings to acquire full ownership of these lands using its power of eminent domain, announcing plans to use the targeted 200 acres for local public purposes of landfill, park lands, ranch lands, and commerce.[249] Based on a county appraisal, Inyo County offered $522,000 for the land and associated water rights.[250] The city rejected the county's offer and filed suit against the county first, alleging violations of the California Environmental Quality Act (CEQA) for initiating these moves without first conducting the required environmental assessments and for violating the Long Term Water Agreement.[251]

In 2021, Inyo County initiated its own lawsuit to reclaim its land and water rights at the three landfill sites leased from DWP.[252] But in *Los Angeles Dep't of Water & Power v. County of Inyo*, the trial court, affirmed by the California Court of Appeal, ruled for Los Angeles,[253] ordering Inyo County to cease its efforts because its proposals did not comply with the CEQA, as alleged by the city.[254] On appeal, the county argued that it should be considered exempt from CEQA because its proposal concerned existing landfills[255] and that DWP should not prevail for such technical violations as failure to exhaust administrative remedies,[256] but its arguments fell flat.[257] As this book goes to press, Los Angeles and the Owens Valley continue to

---

[247] *Id.*
[248] *Id.*
[249] *Id.*
[250] *Id.*
[251] *See* Deb Murphy, *LADWP, Inyo County Dispute on County Landfills*, SIERRA WAVE MEDIA, www.sierrawave.net/ladwp-inyo-continue-dispute-county-landfills/ (last visited Feb. 19, 2018), (noting that Los Angeles explained that the time period to object to Inyo County's action was expiring and the county would not extend the deadline).
[252] *County of Inyo*, 67 Cal. App. 5th.
[253] *Id.*
[254] *Id.* at 1018, 1025. The court determined that (1) Inyo County's description of the activities constituting its project was too narrow and thus did not comply with the California Environmental Quality Act (CEQA) and (2) that the project, once properly defined, was not exempt from CEQA's requirements. *Id.* at 1024–25. On appeal, Inyo County argued that LADWP did not exhaust administrative remedies because it did not raise the alleged CEQA violations during the County's administrative proceedings. *Id.* at 1033–34. The Court of Appeals concluded that because the County did not give LADWP notice that CEQA issues would be discussed at the first hearing, LADWP could not be expected to raise CEQA issues at this time. *Id.* at 1034.
[255] *Id.* at 1035, 1041.
[256] *Id.* at 1033–34.
[257] *Id.* at 1025. A nearly identical suit was filed in California state court at the same time. In the state court case, the Superior Court of California granted summary judgment in favor of LADWP on May 19, 2022. Inyo County v. Los Angeles Dep't of Water & Power, No. BCV-18-101260-TSC (Cal. App. Dep't Super. Ct. 2022).

fight out the battle that has lasted a century so far, with little indication that it will be over soon.

This latest iteration demonstrates why that battle has been so long, so fierce, and so unrelenting. The county is suing to recover sovereignty over lost land, as well as the autonomy over its destiny that ownership of that land represents. The local indigenous tribe, the Owens Valley Paiute, continues to fight with the city to recover lost land and water rights that it has been seeking to recover for well over a century.[258] For its part, Los Angeles doesn't seem to care very much about the land itself – after all, it had long ago leased some of that land back to Inyo County for use as a garbage dump. What Los Angeles cares about – what it has always cared about in the Owens Valley – is the water rights attached to that land. Now more than ever, that water is wet gold, more valuable even than land. As we begin to reconceptualize climatic drought as climate change induced aridification, the same is increasingly true all over the West.

---

[258] See Teresa Cotsirilos, *In California, a Native People Fight to Recover Their Stolen Waters*, FOOD & ENVT. REPORTING NETWORK (May 16, 2024), www.thefern.org/2024/05/in-california-a-native-people-fight-to-recover-their-stolen-waters/ (reporting on efforts by the tribe to recover land and water rights for over 170 years).

7

The *Mono Lake* Doctrine

A. Public Trust and Distrust: The Scholarly Discourse Erupts — 198
   1. The Property Rights Critique — 201
   2. The Legal Process Critique — 204
   3. The Environmental Critique — 207
B. The *Mono Lake* Doctrine Develops — 211
   1. Impacts of the Mono Lake Case in California — 211
      a. Legislative and Executive Impacts — 212
      b. Judicial Impacts — 213
      c. The *Scott River Case* and Extension to Groundwater — 217
   2. Impacts of the Mono Lake Case in Other States — 220
C. Ordinary Common Law or Quasi-Constitutional? — 223
   1. California: A Constitutive Constraint — 225
   2. Idaho: Legislative Repudiation of the Constitutive Constraint — 227
   3. Nevada: Mixed Messages in the Walker Lake Basin — 229

The California Supreme Court's affirmation of public trust principles in its Mono Lake decision – coupled with meaningful implementation by the Water Board in its Decision 1631 reconfiguration of Los Angeles's water rights – was a game changer for Mono Lake, the public trust doctrine, and more broadly, environmental law. Suddenly, plaintiffs all over the state, and then other states – and eventually the globe – saw a potential new tool for protecting vulnerable natural resource commons that had previously seemed destined for demise. Transitioning from a social movement to a legal precedent, the "Mono Lake case" became known in legal circles as either *National Audubon Society v. Superior Court* or, more concisely, as *Mono Lake*.

Almost immediately, the scholarly discourse erupted – in both praise and fear of the possibilities opened up by the new strands of legal reasoning in the case. The *Mono Lake* doctrine quickly rippled through the California legal system, with implications for both judicial and administrative decision-making. Not long afterward, the case began to influence the law in other states as well. Citations to the case appeared in judicial proceedings in both state and federal courts. The influence of the decision was felt in legislative, administrative, and even constitutional matters. In California, in a case protecting the Scott River, the *Mono Lake* doctrine was extended to cover even groundwater tributaries of navigable trust resources. In other states, as addressed further in Chapter 8, the doctrine would apply to resources beyond waterways. It became increasingly possible to understand the doctrine as a statement of environmental rights.

This chapter explores the impacts of the *Mono Lake* doctrine beyond Mono Lake. Its dramatic entrance to the scholarly discourse drew much praise, but it also prompted criticism by property rights advocates, those concerned about its implications for the constitutional separation of powers, and even from some environmentalists concerned that it inserted property concepts into a realm of environmental protection where a stewardship approach would be preferable. The chapter explores the journey of the *Mono Lake* doctrine through California law and beyond, with special focus on the contrasting paths taken in two neighboring states, Nevada and Idaho. Idaho, fearful of the environmental protection prioritized at Mono Lake, controversially rejected the majority view of the doctrine as a quasi-constitutional constraint. Nevada, already bound by a quasi-constitutional trust, sought a different approach to preserve appropriative water rights.

A. PUBLIC TRUST AND DISTRUST: THE SCHOLARLY DISCOURSE ERUPTS

The Mono Lake litigation was followed by a surge of interest in the use of the public trust doctrine for environmental advocacy.[1] Litigants sought to expand its application to other water issues[2] and other public commons also subject to private

---

[1] See, e.g., Carol Rose, *The Comedy of the Commons: Custom, Commerce, and Inherently Public Property*, 53 U. CHI. L. REV. 711, 711 (1986) (recognizing the inevitable conflict between the public trust and private property rights and considering what type of property can be considered inherently public); Michael C. Blumm, *Public Property and the Democratization of Western Water Law: A Modern View of the Public Trust Doctrine*, 19 ENV'T L. 573, 579 (1989) (characterizing the public trust doctrine as "chameleon-like" in its ability to shape itself to different contexts); Richard M. Frank, *The Public Trust Doctrine: Assessing Its Recent Past and Charting Its Future*, 45 U.C. DAVIS L. REV. 665, 667, 671–73 (2012) (analyzing the past and future of the public trust and the various resources subject to the trust); Allison Rieser, *Ecological Preservation as a Public Property Right: An Emerging Doctrine in Search of a Theory*, 15 HARV. ENV'T L. REV. 393, 403–406 (1991) (discussing the significance of the *Mono Lake* case in recognizing the preservation of ecological function as a trust value and proposing additional theoretical support for the move).

[2] See, e.g., Ralph W. Johnson, *Water Pollution and the Public Trust Doctrine*, 19 ENV'T L. 485, 486–88 (1989) (suggesting innovative application of the trust to nonpoint pollution sources left largely unregulated by the Clean Water Act); Danielle Spiegel, *Can the Public Trust Doctrine Save Western Groundwater?*, 18 N.Y.U. ENV'T L.J. 412, 414 (2010) (analyzing the public trust's extension to groundwater and concluding that western states where depletion is most problematic are least likely to do so); Carol Necole Brown, *Drinking from a Deep Well: The Public Trust Doctrine and Western Water*

appropriation,[3] while states such as Pennsylvania constitutionalized broader versions of the trust that extend to additional natural resources.[4] Directly inspired by the *Mono Lake* doctrine, India incorporated the public trust doctrine into its own constitutional order, as discussed further in Chapter 10.[5] The doctrine achieved instant notoriety among environmentalists, property rights advocates, and legal academics researching these fields.

Environmentalists hailed the doctrine as a means of preserving ecological treasures that might otherwise be lost.[6] Some began looking for opportunities to

---

Law, 34 FLA. ST. U. L. REV. 1, 2 (2006) (advocating for expansion of public trust doctrine to preempt prior appropriations in western states where water scarcity issues loom); Joseph L. Sax, *The Constitution, Property Rights and the Future of Water Law*, 61 U. COLO. L. REV. 257, 257–59 (1990) (discussing the future of water law and the takings law ramifications of government-mandated restoration of instream flows from appropriations right-holders); Sam Brandao, *Louisiana's Mono Lake: The Public Trust Doctrine and Oil Company Liability for Louisiana's Vanishing Wetlands*, 86 TUL. L. REV. 759, 761–62 (2012) (comparing Louisiana's public trust doctrine to that of California following *Mono Lake*, and arguing for its expansion to better protect Louisiana's coastal wetlands).

[3] *See, e.g.*, Michael C. Blumm & Aurora Paulsen, *The Public Trust in Wildlife*, 2013 UTAH L. REV. 1437, 1440–41 (2013) (arguing that the public trust should be integrated into state wildlife protection law); Alexandra B. Klass, *Renewable Energy and the Public Trust Doctrine*, 45 U.C. DAVIS L. REV. 1021, 1026 (2012) (considering use of the doctrine within the field of renewable energy law); Robin K. Craig, *Adapting to Climate Change: The Potential Role of State Common-Law Public Trust Doctrines*, 34 VT. L. REV. 781, 781 (2010) (arguing that the doctrine could provide "legal support for adaptive management-based climate change adaptation regimes"); David D. Caron, *Time and the Public Trust Doctrine: Law's Knowledge of Climate Change*, 35 U. HAW. L. REV. 441, 442–43 (2013) (advocating that the doctrine be used to prevent sea level rise in the context of climate change); *see also* Irma S. Russell, *A Common Tragedy: The Breach of Promises to Benefit the Public Commons and the Enforceability Problem*, 11 TEX. WESLEYAN L. REV. 557, 558, 560–61 (2005) (suggesting contract law as a solution to the difficulty of enforcing legislation designed to protect ublic commons).

[4] *See* PA. CONST. art. I, § 27.58; Robinson Twp. v. Commonwealth, 83 A.3d 901, 919–20 (Pa. 2013) (discussing the Pennsylvania Environmental Rights Amendment); John C. Dernbach, *The Potential Meanings of a Constitutional Public Trust*, 45 ENV'T L. 257, 469–73 (2015); *see also* RESTORING THE TRUST: AN INDEX OF STATE CONSTITUTIONAL AND STATUTORY PROVISIONS AND CASES ON WATER RESOURCES AND THE PUBLIC TRUST DOCTRINE, CTR. FOR PROGRESSIVE REFORM (Sept. 2009), www.progressivereform.net/articles/PubTrust_State_table_2009.pdf (listing state-by-state public trust surveys by Craig, Klass, & Blumm); William D. Araiza, *Democracy, Distrust, and the Public Trust: Process-Based Constitutional Theory, the Public Trust Doctrine, and the Search for a Substantive Environmental Value*, 45 UCLA L. REV. 385, 394–95 (noting that many state constitutions have developed a conception of the public trust that is based on a more substantive commitment to preservation than most common law analogues); Jeffrey S. Silvyn, *Protecting Public Trust Values in California's Waters: The Constitutional Alternative*, 10 UCLA J. ENV'T L. & POL'Y 355, 356–57, 373 (1992) (comparing California's common law and constitutional public trust rights and concluding that the latter is more expansive).

[5] M.C. Mehta v. Kamal Nath, (1997) 1 S.C.C. 388 (1996) (India), in I UNITED NATIONS ENVIRONMENT PROJECT COMPENDIUM OF JUDICIAL DECISIONS IN MATTERS RELATED TO THE ENVIRONMENT, NATIONAL DECISIONS 259 (1998), www.wedocs.unep.org/handle/20.500.11822/25379 (discussing the role of the public trust doctrine in Indian law and quoting the California Supreme Court's description of the doctrine in the *Mono Lake* case).

[6] *See, e.g.*, Blumm, *supra* note 1, at 579 (characterizing the public trust doctrine as "chameleon-like" in its ability to shape itself to different contexts); Jan S. Stevens, *The Public Trust and In-Stream Uses*,

apply the public trust concept in other realms of natural resources management.[7] Environmental scholars hailed the Mono Lake story and its aftermath as a role model for collaborative environmental management to which other stakeholders in environmental conflicts could aspire.[8] They emphasized the role of executive agencies in administering the trust,[9] and began exploring the role of the doctrine in defending takings challenges to regulations that protect trust resources.[10]

Nevertheless, the rapid rise of the doctrine as a tool of environmental advocacy spawned alarm among competing constituencies, especially property rights

---

19 ENV'T L. 605, 621 (1989) (concluding that the public trust and prior appropriations doctrines were intertwined long before *Mono Lake* and other cases, and arguing that the public trust is an inalienable attribute of sovereignty); Kevin M. Raymond, *Protecting the People's Waters: The California Supreme Court Recognizes Two Remedies to Safeguard Public Trust Interests in Water* – National Audubon Society v. Superior Court, 33 Cal. 3d 419, 658 P.2d 709, 189 Cal. Rptr. 346, cert. denied, 104 S. Ct. 413 (1983), 59 WASH. L. REV. 357, 357–58 (1984) (examining the administrative and judicial remedies available for public trust violations in California after the case); Brian E. Gray, *Ensuring the Public Trust*, 45 U.C. DAVIS L. REV. 973, 975, 979, 997 (2012) (describing the author's work with the San Francisco City Attorney's office on an amicus brief for the plaintiffs, and arguing that one especially significant aspect of the case is the court's recognition of an environmental baseline in the management of public resources); *see also* Craig Anthony Arnold, *Working out an Environmental Ethic: Anniversary Lessons from Mono Lake*, 4 WYO. L. REV. 1, 2 (2004) (celebrating *Mono Lake* as an environmental achievement); Sherry A. Enzler, *How Law Mattered to the Mono Lake Ecosystem*, 35 WM & MARY ENV'T L. & POL'Y REV. 413, 456–501 (2011) (reviewing the significance of the *Mono Lake* case for public trust and environmental law at the systemic level).

[7] *See* Chapter 8(A) ("The Planes of Public Trust Development across the United States"). *See generally* Rieser, *supra* note 1 (advocating for the expansion of the public trust doctrine beyond navigable waterways based on the macro-economic value of ecological preservation).

[8] JUDITH A. LAYZER, *Making History in the Mono Basin*, *in* NATURAL EXPERIMENTS 233, 237 (Mass. Inst. of Tech., 2008).

[9] *See, e.g.*, Ronald B. Robie, *Effective Implementation of the Public Trust Doctrine in California Water Resources Decision-Making: A View from the Bench*, 45 U.C. DAVIS L. REV. 1155, 1157 (2012) (reflecting on the impact of the case thirty years later and concluding that protection of the public trust should primarily rest with administrative actors); Dave Owen, *The* Mono Lake Case, *the Public Trust Doctrine, and the Administrative State*, 45 U.C. DAVIS L. REV. 1099, 1104–05 (2012) (considering the administrative ramifications of the case and its impacts on the California water board); Gregory S. Weber, *Articulating the Public Trust: Text, Near-Text and Context*, 27 ARIZ. ST. L.J. 1155, 1159 (1995) (examining the judicial, legislative, and administrative development of the public trust doctrine in California after the case).

[10] *See* J. Peter Byrne, *The Public Trust Doctrine, Legislation, and Green Property: A Future Convergence?*, 45 U.C. DAVIS L. REV. 915, 916 (2012) (suggesting that the doctrine be used as a defense to innovative regulatory takings claims and to "sustain environmental legislation against judicial hostility"); John D. Echeverria, *The Public Trust Doctrine as a Background Principles Defense in Takings Litigation*, 45 U.C. DAVIS L. REV. 931, 931–34 (2012) (analyzing use of the doctrine as a takings defense in light of two California cases that did not allow it); Erin Ryan, *Palazzolo, The Public Trust, and the Property Owner's Reasonable Expectations: Takings and the South Carolina Marsh Island Bridge Debate*, 15 SE. ENV'T L.J. 121, 123 (2006) (analyzing how the public trust doctrine operates as a background principle of law that can constrain the reasonable expectations of a property owner alleging a taking). *But see* Barton H. Thompson, Jr., *Judicial Takings*, 76 VA. L. REV. 1449, 1532–33 (1990) (criticizing use of the doctrine to avoid just compensation for what otherwise looks like a taking). For full discussion of the use of the doctrine in takings litigation, *see* Chapter 8(B)(1) ("The Doctrine as a Background Principle in Takings Claims").

advocates, and even among competing environmental advocates.[11] This part briefly addresses the distrust that emerged around the idea of the public trust, focusing on concerns about property rights, legal process, and the development of environmental law. Advocates for private property rights feared the erosive potential of the doctrine, legal process critics feared its empowerment of judicial decision making, and early environmental critics had hoped that environmental protection norms would take root in administrative law responsibilities more aligned with the principles of stewardship than the dominion of ownership.

1. The Property Rights Critique

Perhaps the most immediate concerns were those raised by advocates for private property rights, alarmed that expansive use of the doctrine would result in the confiscation of private rights found to be in tension with public trust values.[12] These critics were leery of how quickly the modern doctrine had developed, and they warned that it would effectively put a fist on the scale on the side of public interests at the expense of private interests in resources held protected by the trust. They worried about the trajectory of a doctrine that suddenly seemed so malleable, encompassing new values as they became recognized – especially if previous allocations of rights could be revisited after long periods of time, as they were at Mono Lake.[13]

Conflicts between public and private rights have manifested over water rights,[14] waterfront and wetland development,[15] the regulation of private activity on

---

[11] See Chapter 6(B) ("Other Mono Lake Litigation") (discussing various critiques of the public trust doctrine).

[12] See James L. Huffman, *A Fish out of Water: The Public Trust Doctrine in a Constitutional Democracy*, 19 ENV'T L. 527, 533 (1989) (identifying the doctrine as a creature of property law that has been distorted by the courts beyond its proper boundaries); Barton H. Thompson, Jr., *The Public Trust Doctrine: A Conservative Reconstruction and Defense*, 15 SE. ENV'T L.J. 47, 49 (2006) (suggesting reconstruction of the public trust doctrine in response to libertarian and property rights critiques); Lloyd R. Cohen, *The Public Trust Doctrine: An Economic Perspective*, 29 CAL. W. L. REV. 239, 274–76 (1992) (criticizing the public trust doctrine's effects on private property rights); *see also* Rose, *supra* note 1, at 711–13, 717 (recognizing the inevitable conflict between the public trust and private property rights and considering what type of property can, under competing notions of public trust, be considered inherently public). *But see* Richard A. Epstein, *The Public Trust Doctrine*, 7 CATO J. 411, 428–30 (1987) (analyzing the public trust doctrine from a similarly libertarian, property rights perspective, but supporting it as a natural limitation on government power, comparable to restrictions on eminent domain).

[13] See Thompson, *supra* note 12, at 48–49.

[14] See, e.g., Nat'l Audubon Soc'y v. Super. Ct. of Alpine Cnty., 658 P.2d 709 (Cal. 1983) (discussing public and private rights over water).

[15] See, e.g., Palazzolo v. Rhode Island, 533 U.S. 606, 611 (2001) (resolving takings claim related to waterfront development, in part, on public trust grounds); *see also* Lucas v. S.C. Coastal Council, 505 U.S. 1003 (1992); McQueen v. S.C. Coastal Council, 580 S.E.2d 116 (S.C. 1995); S.C. Coastal Conservation League v. Dep't of Health & Env't Control, 610 S.E.2d 482 (S.C. 2005).

submerged lands,[16] and beach and lakefront access.[17] For example, in one of the more controversial early extensions of the doctrine, the New Jersey Supreme Court held that the doctrine protected public passage over private beachfront property if needed for public access to the ocean.[18] Like the California Supreme Court had concluded in *Marks v. Whitney* and affirmed in *Audubon Society*, the New Jersey Supreme Court stressed that the doctrine must be construed flexibly, to respond to changing societal needs.[19]

When courts administering the trust emphasize its flexibility to adapt to changing public needs,[20] the champions of private property rights are uneasy.[21] Without a clear limit on how far the public trust doctrine may intrude on seemingly settled private rights, they worry about its potential as an unlimited tool of legal opportunism that, caricatured, could theoretically eat everything in its path.[22]

The property rights critique asks what, then, is the limiting principle?[23] Whenever the public decides it wants something new in a trust resource, does that mean private interests must yield, no matter how well established?[24] Especially in California, where the *Audubon Society* decision establishes an ongoing duty of supervision, the state can theoretically revisit water licenses at any time (although, as Professor Dave

---

[16] *See, e.g.*, Marks v. Whitney, 491 P.2d 374, 380 (Cal. 1971) (discussing regulation of private activity on submerged lands).

[17] *See e.g.*, Matthews v. Bay Head Improvement Ass'n, 471 A.2d 355, 355-56 (N.J. 1984) (discussing private and public activity on beachfront property); Glass v. Goeckel, 703 N.W.2d 58 (Mich. 2005) (discussing private and public rights on lakefront property).

[18] *Matthews*, 471 A.2d at 363 ("In order to exercise these rights guaranteed by the public trust doctrine, the public must have access to municipally-owned dry sand areas as well as the foreshore. The extension of the public trust doctrine to include municipally-owned dry sand areas was necessitated by our conclusion that enjoyment of rights in the foreshore is inseparable from use of dry sand beaches.") *see also* Borough of Neptune City v. Borough of Avon-by-the-Sea, 294 A.2d 47, 51 (N.J. 1972) (first finding public rights of access in dry sand uplands from submerged trust lands); Raleigh Ave. Beach Assn. v. Atlantis Beach Club, Inc., 879 A.2d 112 (N.J. 2005) (extending the *Matthews* doctrine to fully private dry sand beaches).

[19] *Matthews*, 471 A.2d at 365.

[20] *See, e.g., id.*; Nat'l Audubon Soc'y v. Super. Ct. of Alpine Cnty., 658 P.2d 709, 719 (Cal. 1983) (discussing public and private rights over water).

[21] *See* Thompson, *supra* note 12, at 48-49 (discussing concerns among conservatives about judicial interpretations of the public trust doctrine); Thompson, *supra* note 10, at 1478 (discussing concerns among property owners about possible takings under the public trust doctrine).

[22] Thompson, *supra* note 10, at 1478, 1507-08, 1520, 1532-33. *But see* Michael C. Blumm, *The Public Trust Doctrine and Private Property: The Accommodation Principle*, 27 PACE ENV'T L. REV. 649, 654 (2010) (arguing that there is no inherent conflict between private property and the public trust doctrine). *See also* Thompson, *supra* note 12, at 48-49.

[23] *See, e.g.*, Thompson, *supra* note 10 at 1478 (discussing the belief that property is determined politically with no objective principle); Joseph D. Kearney & Thomas W. Merrill, *The Origins of What Really Happened in Illinois Central*, 71 U. CHI. L. REV. 799, 929-30 (2004) (arguing for limited application and worrying about unclear boundaries). *But see* Epstein, *supra* note 12, at 428-29 (arguing that the sweep of the doctrine, as he construes it, "should be broad indeed").

[24] *Cf.* JOSEPH WILLIAM SINGER, PROPERTY LAW: RULES, POLICIES, AND PRACTICES 62-63, 65 (2010) (discussing how far the public trust doctrine will go and querying whether it might require the public to give up public use rights as an incident to public enjoyment of trust resources).

Owen has noted, this has never actually happened).²⁵ Analyzing the doctrine from a law and economics perspective, Professor Lloyd Cohen criticized it as "a piece of disingenuous gimmickry" destined to undermine property rights.²⁶

Professor Gary Libecap has especially critiqued the rule for impeding economically efficient interbasin transfers and frustrating the development of water markets.²⁷ In a thorough review of the Owens Valley saga, Libecap reports in detail on the events at Mono Lake and critiques the judicial resolution of those matters as an ultimately inefficient way of resolving the overall western water crisis.²⁸ From an economic perspective, he argues that the public trust doctrine deployed at Mono Lake has imposed an inefficient drag on water transfers and water markets that are the best available tool for reallocating scarce water resources from lower to higher value uses in the American West. He contends that a negotiated transfer of rights back to the state from DWP would have been the more efficient, less costly, and ultimately less controversial resolution,²⁹ offering potential suggestions for how water allocations might be renegotiated in light of later, unforeseen environmental harms, including eminent domain and/or bond funding to acquire the desired rights back from DWP.³⁰ He critiques the bargaining strategy employed during the Mono Lake affair and the resolution reached, both of which, he argues, have done damage to the future of needed water transfers.³¹

Even so, it's worth noting that even the California courts have never given the developing public trust doctrine a blank check against property rights, even after the California Supreme Court first affirmed its application to environmental values in *Marks v. Whitney*.³² For example, in *San Diego County Archaeological Society v. Compadres*, the California Court of Appeal held that the doctrine did not apply to archaeological artifacts found on private property, because the state did not own the underlying land.³³ The Society had sued to stop a private company from grading parts of a 20-acre plot that contained a significant archaeological site, asking that the artifacts "be declared a part of the public trust of which [the private company] is the public trustee."³⁴

---

²⁵ Owen, *supra* note 9, at 1132–33.
²⁶ Cohen, *supra* note 12, at 276. Professor Gary Libecap has critiqued the rule for impeding economically efficient interbasin transfers and frustrating the development of water markets. *See* GARY LIBECAP, OWENS VALLEY REVISITED: A REASSESSMENT OF THE WEST'S FIRST GREAT WATER TRANSFER 151–53 (2007).
²⁷ LIBECAP, *supra* note 26.
²⁸ *Id.* at 145–53.
²⁹ *Id.*
³⁰ *Id.* at 148–51.
³¹ *Id.* at 150–54.
³² Marks v. Whitney, 491 P.2d 374 (Cal. 1971).
³³ San Diego Cnty. Archaeological Soc'y, Inc. v. Compadres, 146 Cal. Rptr. 786, 788–89 (Cal. Ct. App. 1978).
³⁴ *Id.* at 787 (also alleging that the company was purposefully trying to destroy the site to circumvent the requirements of the California Environmental Quality Act).

The Society argued that the doctrine should be extended to artifacts on private property because they are "intrinsically important to every citizen and should be freely available, are particularly 'a gift of nature' and should be preserved, and are such that adaptation to private use is inappropriate."[35] However, the court declined both to extend the public trust doctrine to archeological artifacts on private property and to confer trustee obligations on private owners, on grounds that the doctrine had traditionally only applied to limited types of real property to which the state held title, or public lands that should rightfully be available to all.[36] The appellate court had the last word in this case, decided a few years before the state supreme court heard *Audubon Society*, but the latter did not displace its holding. *San Diego County Archaeological Society* thus appears to provide at least one answer to the property rights critique as to how far the public trust doctrine may intrude upon private rights: even in California, the limiting principle is that trust resource must be public in nature.

2. The Legal Process Critique

Another critique arises from those concerned with the legal process ramifications of the public trust doctrine.[37] These scholars worry about the separation of powers implication of a doctrine that allows the judiciary to second-guess legislative and executive decision-making. They view judicial encroachment on policy decisions with skepticism, given that the judiciary is "the least democratic branch," in comparison with the others that are more directly beholden to electing constituents. Legal process critics are troubled by the idea that unelected judges could countermand the popular will. To these champions of the political branches, the public trust doctrine seems not only antidemocratic but potentially destabilizing to the rule of law.[38]

The concern that the doctrine empowers judicial decision making at the expense of political decision making is not without foundation. After all, as demonstrated in *Audubon Society*, the doctrine expressly enables the judiciary to countermand legislative and executive decisions, here the administrative issuance of water licenses conferring statutory rights under the prior appropriation doctrine. These political branch actors are conventionally considered to be more responsive to voter preferences as expressed through elections, although the conventional wisdom is less fitting in the context of state government, where many state judges are also elected, and many administrative agency personnel are insulated from elections. Yet even in states where judges are elected, legal process critics worry that their decisions could maintain precedential value long after a judge leaves office.[39]

---

[35] *Id.* at 788.
[36] *Id.* at 788–89.
[37] *See, e.g.*, Thompson, *supra* note 12, at 48–49; Araiza, *supra* note 4, at 432.
[38] *See* Huffman, *supra* note 12, at 533.
[39] *Id.*

A. Public Trust and Distrust

Public trust supporters argue that the role of judicial review is among the greatest strengths of the doctrine, enforcing necessary checks and balances among the three branches of government.[40] Indeed, a defining feature of the common law doctrine is that it empowers ordinary citizens to seek redress for public trust violations in court. For trust supporters, the separation-of-powers critique – that the doctrine overpowers the judiciary at the expense of legislative policymaking – is overblown, not only because it discounts the way that judicial review further empowers democratic participation, but also because the law of trusts has always been interpreted and enforced by courts.[41]

If the trust analogy holds, goes this reasoning, then who better than judges to oversee the public beneficiary's interest in trust resources against self-serving or neglectful management by the legislative trustee? The government is always under a duty to protect the public; it is the foundational purpose of government, and the charge that underlies the very police power from which government generally operates. Government decisions faithfully made under the police power generally get a lot of judicial discretion, but some public trust obligations are less open to interpretation, such as the extremely high bar it sets for alienation of trust assets. Courts may be the best venue for evaluating government decisions that may transgress the acceptable margins of interpretation.

Embracing this counterargument, Professor Mary Wood makes the fully reverse legal process critique – that the public trust doctrine is a necessary corrective for the failure of modern environmental law, which she traces to the public-choice related failures of political process that have overly empowered the executive and legislative branches at the expense of the judiciary.[42] She argues that the recent shift toward statutory environmental law – which she argues is excessively influenced by industry during rulemaking, implementation, and enforcement – has foreclosed public oversight through common law judicial process,[43] leading to the failure of environmental governance to protect natural resources and facilitating the catastrophic pollution of wider trust resources, such as the original Justinian air commons.[44] She argues that agencies should be afforded less deference, so that they can be held more accountable for their choices in court.[45]

---

[40] See, e.g., Blumm, *supra* note 1, at 580 (arguing that the public trust doctrine compensates for defects in the democratic process).

[41] *Cf.* Charles Wilkinson, *The Headwaters of the Public Trust: Some Thoughts on the Source and Scope of the Traditional Doctrine*, 19 ENV'T L. 425, 470 (1989) (in discussing the legal process critique, observing: "Then, as now, judges can be expected to employ old and honored notions of trusteeship in order to fulfill the interests and the expectations of the public.").

[42] MARY CHRISTINA WOOD, NATURE'S TRUST: ENVIRONMENTAL LAW FOR A NEW ECOLOGICAL AGE 19 (Cambridge Univ. Press, 2014).

[43] *Id.* at 52–53.

[44] *Id.* at 13.

[45] *Id.* at 235.

Nevertheless, traditional legal process critics argue that the doctrine provides insufficient guidance to decision makers from all branches of government,[46] and that the judiciary – potentially prone to abstraction and elitism[47] – will not be as responsive to the public as regularly elected legislators.[48] Voicing this critique, Professor William Araiza argues that the doctrine violates democratic principles,[49] while Professor James Huffman argues that it has been distorted by the courts beyond its appropriate boundaries, threatening both liberty and democracy.[50] Others worry about the implications of the doctrine for upending the role of law in protecting settled expectations more generally.[51] Professor Buzz Thompson evocatively summarizes the general distrust of the public trust doctrine among political conservatives for this reason:

> To environmentalists and public-access supporters, the public trust doctrine appears to provide a relatively malleable legal tool to address a variety of issues involving the use and protection of waterways, beaches, and perhaps other important lands and resources.... These environmental advantages, however, are conservative anathema. To many conservatives, the public trust doctrine is an anchorless doctrine that is anti-democratic and an easy way to evade critically important property protections.[52]

Concerns about the malleability of the doctrine tap into age-old anxieties about the evolving nature of the common law – pitting the need for flexibility to meet changing public interests against the need for certainty to establish order and expectations.[53] The *Mono Lake* doctrine of ongoing oversight stands squarely on the side of flexibility at the cost of certainty[54] – but popular resistance to that idea may also explain why it has been so seldom used, even in California.[55] Apparently, even the courts and agencies from which the modern public trust doctrine evolved have perceived the limitations of public distrust if too much is asked of it.

---

[46] Araiza, *supra* note 4, at 386, 407–19 (comparing the public trust and equal protection doctrines and concluding that a process justified public trust fails to provide a comparable substantive principle for limiting an "extraordinarily broad scope for judicial review").

[47] *See, e.g.*, Thompson, *supra* note 10, at 1507–08, 1532–33.

[48] *See, e.g.*, Huffman, *supra* note 12, at 533; *see also* Cohen, *supra* note 12, at 271–72.

[49] Araiza, *supra* note 4, at 432.

[50] *See* Huffman, *supra* note 12, at 533.

[51] *See, e.g.*, Ryan, *supra* note 10, at 130–31 (discussing concerns by coastal landowners that the administration of public trust principles would frustrate their expectations).

[52] *See* Thompson, *supra* note 12, at 48–49.

[53] *See generally* John F. Smith, *The Public Trust Doctrine and* National Audubon Society v. Superior Court: *A Hard Case Makes Bad Law or the Consistent Evolution of California Water Rights*, 6 GLENDALE L. REV. 201 (1984) (defending *Mono Lake* against critiques during its immediate aftermath).

[54] *See, e.g.*, Nat'l Audubon Soc'y v. Super. Ct. of Alpine Cnty., 658 P.2d 709, 721 (Cal. 1983) (emphasizing that appropriative rights are nonvested, and subject to the state's continuing oversight).

[55] BARTON H. THOMPSON, JR. ET AL., LEGAL CONTROL OF WATER RESOURCES: CASES AND MATERIALS 224–27 (5th ed. 2013) (noting that the *Nat'l Audubon Soc'y* duty of ongoing oversight generated concern among water planners but never amounted to many changes in allocations).

The separation-of-powers critique receives additional consideration in Chapter 9's exploration of the atmospheric trust project,[56] but the new debate surrounding the atmospheric trust is an extension of the long-standing discourse that either critiques or praises the doctrine as a check on the political branches. With special attention to the intersection between these issues and the rise of judicial power during the Roberts Court era, the Conclusion further dissects the antidemocratic critique, ultimately analogizing between public trust claims and the citizen suits authorized by many environmental statutes.[57]

3. The Environmental Critique

From the perspective of advancing environmental protection, the Mono Lake story paints a heroic portrait of the public trust doctrine. After the Mono Lake litigation, the doctrine emerged as a darling of the wider environmentalist community – the unlikely savior of a treasured place against the forces of those with far greater power. Many celebrated the David-and-Goliath result, in which a ragtag collection of local scientists and bird watchers organized around a kitchen table somehow defeated one of the largest and most powerful cities in the world. Professor Judith Layzer celebrated the Mono Lake story as a successful example that not only avoided environmental catastrophe but also used an ecosystem-wide adaptive management approach to restore the natural processes that enable the entire system to thrive.[58]

However, even within the environmental community, not everyone was so enamored with the case. While most environmentalists continue to support use of the public trust doctrine, the *Audubon Society* decision also produced an environmental critique.[59] Leading that charge forty years ago was Professor Richard Lazarus, who participated in the Mono Lake litigation as a young attorney with the U.S. Department of Justice and is now a leading environmental law scholar at Harvard

---

[56] *See* Chapter 9(D)(1) ("Separation of Powers Concerns") (discussing critiques of the atmospheric trust litigation on these grounds).

[57] *See* Concluding Chapter (B)(4) ("Separation of Powers and the Antidemocratic Critique").

[58] Layzer, *supra* note 8.

[59] *See, e.g.*, Erin Ryan, Public Trust and Distrust: Theoretical Implications of the Public Trust Doctrine for Natural Resource Management, 31 Env't L. 477, 492–93 (2001) [hereinafter Public Trust and Distrust] (citing Telephone Interview with Richard J. Lazarus, Professor of Law, Georgetown University (May 3, 2000) [hereinafter Lazarus Interview]) (Professor Lazarus notes that he prefers "that environmental matters be decided by the executive or legislative branches over the judiciary; he favors 'getting it in the regs,' or sending it through the administrative or legislative process over trusting the protection of a natural resource to the discretion of an unaccountable judge who may know nothing about ecological science." Id. at 492.); Erin Ryan, *The Public Trust Doctrine, Private Water Allocation, and Mono Lake: The Historic Saga of* National Audubon Society v. Superior Court, 45 Env't L. 561, 620–21 (2015); Richard J. Lazarus, *Changing Conceptions of Property and Sovereignty in Natural Resources: Questioning the Public Trust Doctrine*, 71 Iowa L. Rev. 631, 715–16 (1986); Araiza, *supra* note 4, at 387–89.

Law School.[60] He famously criticized the environmentalist embrace of the doctrine, arguing that it would take the burgeoning environmental law movement – which had come of age barely ten years earlier over the 1970s – in the entirely wrong direction.[61]

Environmental critics were skeptical that the doctrine, with its roots in property law, would provide the best legal tools to support the unfolding environmental law movement.[62] They worried that it was a mistake to embrace the vocabulary of "property" to accomplish the stewardship-oriented goals that they saw as the proper focus of environmental law. As Lazarus explained after the Mono Lake litigation, the public trust doctrine relies on public ownership and oversight of natural resources to effectuate environmental protection – emphasizing property law concepts such as ownership, trustees, and beneficiaries[63] – but owners can be fickle and shortsighted, and public participation requirements are content-neutral.[64] The trust may prohibit private monopoly, but if public opinion swings away from environmental protection at a critical moment, competing concerns may prevail.[65] The same public owners advocating for environmental protection one day may find themselves longing for cheaper fuels the next.

Recognizing that the doctrine isn't invariably "green," these "green dissenters"[66] would have preferred that the legal protection of natural resources be established according to stewardship concepts with a more explicit commitment to environmental protection. Just as the *Audubon Society* case was filed, executive agencies were being given new roles of responsibility for administering the major federal environmental statutes of the 1970s.[67] Instead of infusing environmental law with property concepts, Lazarus maintained that environmental law should embrace the approaches taken by these new statutory accomplishments, such as the National Environmental Policy Act (NEPA), the Clean Air and Water Acts, and the emerging principles of administrative law.[68] Grounding environmental law in the ethics of stewardship, rather than the dominion of ownership, would oblige the state to protect valued resources independently from the whimsical impulses of owners, public or otherwise.[69]

---

[60] See, e.g., Ryan, *Public Trust and Distrust, supra* note 59, at 492–93 (citing to Lazarus Interview).
[61] Lazarus, *supra* note 59, at 715–16.
[62] See, e.g., *id.*; Araiza, *supra* note 4, at 387–88.
[63] Lazarus, *supra* note 59, at 648, 642–43.
[64] See, e.g., *id.* at 715–16 (discussing public trust and shifts in notions of private property).
[65] See, e.g., Araiza, *supra* note 4, at 432 (criticizing the doctrine's reliance on process over a substantive commitment to environmental protection). *But see* Arnold, *supra* note 6, at 39, 41 (using *Nat'l Audubon Soc'y* to suggest that politics and public participation are as critical to environmental protection as formal environmental law).
[66] See Ryan, *Public Trust and Distrust, supra* note 59, at 493 (citing to Lazarus Interview) (discussing the "green dissent" by environmentalists objecting to use of the doctrine for environmental protection in lieu of conventional environmental statutory and administrative law); Lazarus, *supra* note 59, at 696.
[67] See Lazarus, *supra* note 59, at 681 n.308, 684.
[68] *Id.* at 665, 698–702.
[69] *Id.* at 681 n.308, 684.

A. Public Trust and Distrust

Concerns over sidelining the emerging environmental stewardship model with a model of environmental law premised on ownership are compelling. Centering legal protections around stewardship principles would avoid tragic results if the public suddenly decided that it would be more valuable to, say, "pave paradise and put up a parking lot."[70] That said, when the public trust doctrine obligates the protection of environmental values and its public beneficiaries include future generations, as it was framed at Mono Lake, then the stewardship and ownership models begin to converge. If future generations are equally entitled to the ecological, scenic, and recreational values of public trust resources, then the state would violate its obligations under either approach if it were to "pave paradise," or destroy them for unrelated short term benefits.

Yet Lazarus also worried that the newfound celebrity of the public trust doctrine might distract the progress of environmental law toward effectuating resource protection through these more concrete state and federal mandates, memorably arguing that it was a "romantic step backward toward a bygone era at a time when we face modern problems that demand candid and honest debate on the merits."[71] Later, Professor William Araiza argued that a substantive commitment to environmental values would be preferable to the untethered political process implied by public trust adjudication.[72] After all, even the *Audubon Society* decision did not require the absolute protection of Mono Lake; it simply required that the Water Board think carefully about it.[73] In scholarship sympathetic to environmentalists' turn to the public trust doctrine as a tool of advocacy, he notes that states that have constitutionalized the doctrine – such as the Pennsylvania and Hawaii examples introduced in Chapter 2 – often do better at providing the missing principled constraints of the common law doctrine.[74]

On the other hand, scholars such as Professor Carol Rose have argued that recognizing the significance of public property on par with private property is a critical component of the larger project of environmental protection.[75] Professor Mike Blumm argues that public trust and private property coexist according to principles

---

[70] Joni Mitchell, Blue (A&M Studios 1971).
[71] Lazarus, *supra* note 59 at 715–16. *But see* Albert C. Lin, *Public Trust and Public Nuisance: Common Law Peas in a Pod?*, 45 U.C. Davis L. Rev. 1075, 1097 (2012) (distinguishing the public trust doctrine and common law nuisance as elements of property and tort law respectively, and answering Lazarus's arguments that the public trust should be superseded by nuisance law with his conclusion that the two fill distinct roles).
[72] Araiza, *supra* note 4, at 386; *see also* William D. Araiza, *The Public Trust Doctrine as an Interpretive Canon*, 45 U.C. Davis L. Rev. 693, 697 (2012) (suggesting the public trust doctrine be interpreted as a canon of construction, establishing a background principle against which legislation and administrative actions are construed, rather than as an independent legal principle).
[73] Nat'l Audubon Soc'y v. Super. Ct. of Alpine Cnty., 658 P.2d 709, 712, 727 (Cal. 1983).
[74] Araiza, *supra* note 4, at 386 (arguing that state constitutions provide the missing commitment to stewardship principles through provisions more directly requiring environmental protection).
[75] Rose, *supra* note 1, at 711.

of accommodation[76] and that the doctrine prevents the monopolization of critical natural resources into the hands of any single private owner.[77] I have argued that the environmental protection of natural resource commons is threatened by overly protecting impacted private property rights without similarly protecting impacted public property rights – a strategy that requires the recognition of the property held by the public on par with property held by private individuals.[78] After all, property law is already competing directly with environmental protection in Fifth Amendment takings cases routinely filed against environmental law at all levels of government[79] – so the question isn't *whether* environmental law will engage with property concepts, only how it will.

Most urgently of all, Professor Mary Wood relies on the public property framework in her "Nature's Trust" imperative that we recognize and enforce the pivotal role government plays as trustee of natural resources.[80] She contends that we must enforce an unwavering fiduciary duty of government oversight of these ecological assets to reverse the ongoing destruction of public natural resources that represents a clear violation of the trust.[81] To demonstrate its gross dereliction of this duty, she points to the government's failure to take on the epidemic of greenhouse gas pollution contributing to climate change.[82] She casts the protection of the public trust in nature as a model of legal responsibility at a time when environmental law is otherwise failing to address the world's most urgent crises.[83]

Perhaps ironically, given so much scholarly celebration and critique, Professor Dave Owen has observed that the most forceful elements of the *Mono Lake* doctrine – the ongoing supervisory duty and the ability to retrospectively reform existing water rights – have never really amounted to much outside of California, or even outside of Mono Basin, other than through prospective administrative regulation.[84] Still, other scholars continue to try and push the doctrine forward in judicial and administrative proceedings. Professor Blumm, in addition to his copious scholarship on the doctrine,[85] has attempted to push the doctrine forward

---

[76] Blumm, *supra* note 22, at 658–59.
[77] *See generally* Michael C. Blumm & Aurora Paulsen, *The Public Trust as an Antimonopoly Doctrine*, 44 BOS. COLL. ENV'T AFFS. L. REV. 1 (2017).
[78] *See, e.g.,* Erin Ryan, *Public Commons, Privatization, and the Takingsification of Environmental Law*, 171 U. PENN. L. REV. 617 (2023) (describing how the environmental protection may be threatened by overly protecting private property rights in natural resource commons without similarly protecting public property rights in natural resource commons).
[79] *See id.* at 640–46.
[80] WOOD, *supra* note 42, at 125.
[81] *Id.* at 167–68.
[82] *Id.* at 168.
[83] *Id.* at 337–38.
[84] Owen, *supra* note 9, at 1132–33.
[85] *See, e.g.,* sources cited *supra* notes 1, 3, 4, 22, 77; Michael C. Blumm & Zach Schwartz, *The Public Trust Doctrine Fifty Years after Sax and Some Thoughts on Its Future*, 44 PUB. LAND & RES. L. REV. 1 (2021).

through impact litigation to help develop missing material through common law processes.[86] Professor Alexandra Klass has argued that environmental protection requires a mutually reinforcing relationship between the mechanisms of the common law doctrine and the substantive environmental protection provisions contained in state statutes and constitutions.[87] She argues that integrating statutory and regulatory standards would remedy the environmental critique and allow the "environmental common law" of the judicial doctrine and the more specific statutory frameworks to work side by side, rather than forcing an "either/or" approach.[88]

Accordingly, not everybody loves the public trust doctrine as it stands, nor does everyone cheer where it may be headed – but everyone seems to have a strong opinion, at least among those paying attention. These critiques and counterarguments warrant consideration, especially as new developments push the doctrine into territory not previously recognized under U.S. law.

B. THE *MONO LAKE* DOCTRINE DEVELOPS

After the Mono Lake litigation, the public trust doctrine continued to develop rapidly, in widening circles of jurisdiction that started with the State of California. Yet the *Mono Lake* doctrine influenced the development of public trust principles in other states across the nation, and, as discussed in Chapter 9, even other nations of the world. As discussed in Chapter 8, it has also impacted the development of federal law, especially regarding its role as a potential defense in takings challenges against environmental and access regulations protecting trust resources and, perhaps more uncertainly, its role as an agent of legal change in the contested arena of climate governance.

This part traces the immediate impacts of the *Audubon Society* decision in California and a few neighboring states, setting up the more holistic exploration of the development of public trust principles across the United States, within federal law, and internationally in the chapters that follow.

1. *Impacts of the Mono Lake Case in California*

In California, the public trust doctrine has continued to unfold through judicial, legislative, and administrative contexts. The legislature eventually adopted the doctrine as part of the state Water Code, while litigants have attempted to extend the doctrine to apply to related natural resources held in trust for the public – with

---

[86] Ryan Roberts & Michael C. Blumm, *Oregon's Amphibious Public Trust Doctrine: The Oswego Lake Decision*, 50 ENV'T L. 1227, 1281–82 (2020).

[87] Alexandra B. Klass, *Modern Public Trust Principles: Recognizing Rights and Integrating Standards*, 82 NOTRE DAME L. REV. 699, 748 (2006).

[88] *Id.* at 744.

more robust successes in some areas (such as groundwater) than others (such as recreational reservoirs). This section discusses the still unfolding impacts of the *Mono Lake* doctrine in California, all the way up to efforts to repeal it as a matter of federal law in Congress.

a. Legislative and Executive Impacts

In addition to the common law roots of the doctrine, public trust principles have been codified in California both constitutionally and statutorily.[89] While the public trust doctrine had been added to the California constitution seven years prior to the *Audubon Society* decision, the provisions took on added importance in the Mono Lake litigation. Article X, Section 2 of the California Constitution requires the preservation of water resources for the public welfare and in the public interest,[90] while Section 3 codifies the doctrine in application to the sale or grant of tidelands.[91] The doctrine also appears in provisions of the California Water Code, a set of statutes adopted in 1943, a few years after state approval of DWP's original licenses to divert from Mono Lake. The Water Code declares that "all water within the state is the property of the people of the State,"[92] designates the responsibility to the state to determine the appropriate uses of available water resources,[93] and specifies that all unappropriated water will be considered the "public water of the State."[94] After the *Audubon Society* decision, litigants were inspired to explore the boundaries of these provisions.

After the Mono Lake litigation, the most significant implementation of the California public trust may be taking place at the behest of the legislature, rather than the courts, and implemented at the level of administrative law.[95] Twenty-six years after the case affirmed the doctrine as a matter of state common law, the legislature formally instantiated it as a matter of state statute. In perhaps the most important post-Mono development for the California public trust doctrine itself, the California Water Code was amended in 2009 to require public trust analysis in all water management decisions statewide.[96]

As part of the Sacramento-San Joaquin Delta Reform Act enacted that year, the California legislature formally adopted the public trust doctrine as a foundational consideration in all state water management decisions, together with the doctrine of reasonable use, with special significance for unfolding water management dilemmas

---

[89] CAL. CONST. art. X, §§ 2, 3.
[90] *Id.* art. X, § 2.
[91] *Id.* art. X, § 3.
[92] CAL. WATER CODE § 102.
[93] *Id.* § 104.
[94] *Id.* § 1201.
[95] Owen, *supra* note 9, at 1104–05.
[96] CAL. WATER CODE § 85023.

B. *The* Mono Lake *Doctrine Develops*

in the Sacramento and San Joaquin River Valley Delta Area. The new law declares that: "The longstanding constitutional principle of reasonable use and the public trust doctrine shall be the foundation of state water management policy and are particularly important and applicable to the Delta."[97]

As a result, the state executive agencies that administer the Water Code and its associated regulations, primarily the State Water Resources Control Board, are legally bound to perform the analysis the Mono Lake plaintiffs fought so hard to achieve in the *Audubon Society* case: the agency must consider the impacts of water allocation and other management decisions on public trust resources throughout the state. Notably, the legislatively mandated trust analysis defeats some of the scholarly concerns raised in the legal process critique by reducing the potential for separation of powers conflicts when courts independently question legislative choices under the doctrine.[98]

b. Judicial Impacts

Both before and after passage of the Delta Reform Act, California litigants have continued to explore the boundaries of the *Mono Lake* doctrine through the courts, meeting with different levels of success in different contexts. The judicial impacts of the Mono Lake litigation became visible in California fairly quickly. For example, even before the Water Board finally acted to protect Mono Lake, the Mono Lake cases had already inspired related litigation regarding the American River and Putah Creek, both of which relied on the Mono Lake decisions for resolution.

In the late 1980s, as instream flows waned in the American River, environmental plaintiffs challenged rights held by the East Bay Municipal District (EBMUD) to divert 150,000 acre-feet annually from the Folsom South Canal.[99] The American River runs for thirty miles from the Sierra Nevada mountains southwest toward downtown Sacramento, where it joins the Sacramento River. The Environmental Defense Fund and local plaintiffs challenged EBMUD's diversions on grounds that the reduced flows that resulted were damaging fisheries, recreation, ecological values, and other public trust values associated with the lower American River.[100] In 1990, citing *Audubon Society*, the reviewing court applied a balancing test to weigh the diversion and public trust interests at issue.[101] The court ultimately upheld EBMUD's diversion rights, but mirroring the Water Board's solution at Mono Lake, it required that specified minimum instream flows be maintained on the river to protect the public trust values at risk.[102]

---

[97] *Id.*
[98] *See supra* notes 37–55 and accompanying text.
[99] EDF, Inc. v. East Bay Mun. Util. Dist., No. 425955, 1990 Lexis 7, *1 (Alameda Cnty. Super. Ct. 1990).
[100] *Id.*
[101] *Id.* at *43.
[102] *Id.* at *172–76.

On the other side of Sacramento, a related dispute over Putah Creek arose at around the same time, although it took much longer to resolve. Another tributary of the Sacramento River, Putah Creek is a significant watercourse in Northern California that runs for eighty-five miles from the Coast Range east to Lake Solano, forming the boundary between Yolo and Solano Counties. Due to both diversions and drought in the late 1980s, the majority of Putah Creek ran dry – prompting a regional movement to reduce water diversions to save the creek and its watershed.[103] In 1989, conservationists hoping to protect the creek's wetlands formed the Putah Creek Council and sought to purchase water rights from the Bureau of Reclamation to augment instream flow.[104] However, the Solano County Water Agency intervened to prevent it, based on its prior contracts with the Bureau for diversions to supply water to cities and irrigation districts in Solano County.[105]

The Council, later joined by U.C.-Davis and the city of Davis itself, filed suit against Solano County's Water Agency and Irrigation District, alleging violations of both the public trust doctrine and the California Fish and Game Code – modeling their claims on both legal prongs of the Mono Lake litigation strategy.[106] In 1996, the trial court issued a permanent injunction requiring the Water Agency to maintain minimum flows in the creek to protect fish and flow.[107] In 2000, while awaiting appeal, the parties reached a settlement in the Putah Creek Accord, and then successfully petitioned the trial court to amend its original order to reflect these terms.[108]

An important judicial extension of the doctrine also took place in 2014, when the California Court of Appeal for the First Appellate District held that the public trust doctrine applied to both appropriative water rights and riparian water rights, even though *Audubon Society* had only considered the public trust doctrine in relation to permitted appropriative water rights.[109] The case, *Light v. State Water Resources Control Board*, arose after scientists had determined that stranded salmon in the Russian River stream system of Northwestern California were dying because of abrupt declines in the water level due to artificial withdrawals. To protect the stream system and its fisheries, the State Water Board required that grape growers reduce

---

[103] Sylvia Wright, *Settlement Reached in Long-Running Putah Creek Water Dispute*, UC DAVIS NEWS, www.ucdavis.edu/news/settlement-reached-long-running-putah-creek-water-dispute (last visited May 24, 2000).

[104] Chapter 3: A Creek in Court, PUTAH CREEK LEGACY, www.putahcreeklegacy.com/chapter-three-creek-in-court.html (last visited Sept. 30, 2024) [hereinafter: A Creek in Court].

[105] *Id.*; *see also* Sylvia Wright, *supra* note 102.

[106] *See* A Creek in Court, *supra* note 103 (discussing both the public trust and Fish and Game Code Section 5937 claims).

[107] *See* A Creek in Court, *supra* note 103; *see also* Second Amended Judgment at 2, Putah Creek Council v. Solano Cnty. Water Agency, No. 515766 (Solano Cnty. Super. Ct. 2002).

[108] Second Amended Judgment at 2–10, Putah Creek Council v. Solano Cnty. Water Agency, No. 515766 (Solano Cnty. Super. Ct. 2002).

[109] Light v. State Water Res. Control Bd., 173 Cal. Rptr. 3d 200, 217–20 (Cal. Ct. App. 2014).

B. *The* Mono Lake *Doctrine Develops*

water diversions used for crop-sprinkling frost protection,[110] but some riparian diverters and early appropriators challenged the Board's authority to regulate them, because their water diversions did not require Board-issued permits.[111]

The court concluded that public rights in the public trust waterways authorized the Board's regulation even in these contexts.[112] The appellate court cited the California Supreme Court's determination in *Audubon Society* that "no party can acquire a vested right to appropriate water in a manner harmful to public trust interests and the state has 'an affirmative duty' to take the public trust into account in regulating water use by protecting public trust uses whenever feasible."[113] Conceding that the decision at Mono Lake considered the doctrine only in relation to permitted appropriative water rights, the *Light* court concluded that "subsequent decisions have assumed the doctrine applies as well in the context of riparian and pre-1914 appropriator rights,"[114] effectively holding that all categories of water rights affecting navigable waters are subject to the public trust doctrine.

A few years earlier, in 2008, the same court boldly extended the *Mono Lake* doctrine from protecting the public trust in navigable waterways to protecting the public trust in wildlife, even though all previous California public trust cases involved waterways. In *Center for Biological Diversity v. FPL Group*, environmental advocates challenged the operation of wind turbines in the Altamont Pass area, just east of the San Francisco Bay Area, on grounds that they injure and kill raptors and other birds.[115] The plaintiffs succeeded in securing the court's holding that wildlife is a public trust resource belonging to all the people of the state, and that the doctrine requires public agencies to consider wildlife preservation when making decisions that could impact species.[116] It also affirmed that members of the public have standing to enforce the public trust protections over wildlife in court.[117] Nevertheless, the court upheld the lower court's dismissal of the suit against the private owners and operators of the turbines, clarifying that the proper target of suit is the public agency with permitting authority.[118] Of note, although state ownership

---

[110] *Id.* at 206–207. The regulation prohibited as unreasonable any water uses inconsistent with the programs that are formulated and approved by the local supervisory board, though it delegated oversight to local governing bodies comprised of the diverting growers themselves, a separate subject of legal challenge. *Id.* at 205.

[111] *Id.* at 205–206.

[112] *Id.*

[113] *Id.* at 218–19.

[114] *Id.*

[115] Ctr. for Biological Diversity, Inc. v. FPL Grp., Inc., 83 Cal. Rptr. 3d 588 (Cal. Ct. App. 2008), *as modified on denial of reh'g* (Oct. 9, 2008).

[116] *Id.* at 599 ("Thus, whatever its historical derivation, it is clear that the public trust doctrine encompasses the protection of undomesticated birds and wildlife. They are natural resources of inestimable value to the community as a whole. Their protection and preservation are a public interest that is now recognized in numerous state and federal statutory provisions.").

[117] *Id.* at 600.

[118] *Id.* at 603.

of wildlife in trust for the public is long established,[119] few (if any) other courts have extended the public trust doctrine recognized at Mono Lake to wildlife – and while *Center for Biological Diversity* has never been overturned, there have been no reported decisions in California applying its holding to issues regarding the public trust since then.[120]

On other occasions, the California courts of appeal have flatly declined to extend the doctrine. Twenty years earlier, in 1989 – even before Decision 1631 had formally concluded the *Mono Lake* litigation – the California Court of Appeal for the Third Appellate District rejected an attempt to use the public trust doctrine to compel appropriators of water from a non-navigable stream to continue diverting (but forgo use of the diverted water) to maintain an artificial reservoir for public recreational uses.[121]

In *Golden Feather Community Association v. Thermalito Irrigation District*, a nonprofit community association and the owners and residents of nearby property sued an irrigation district that impounded the waters of a creek behind a dam to create a reservoir.[122] The plaintiffs argued that the District had violated the public trust doctrine when it reduced the water in the reservoir, harming the fishery and other recreational uses. Alleging that defendants were planning to build a hydroelectric project below the dam that would lower the reservoir's level and destroy current fishing, wildlife, and recreational uses, they asked the court to declare that the public trust doctrine required maintenance of the reservoir with a minimum level of water to sustain public health, fishing, wildlife, aesthetic, and recreational uses.[123]

However, the court distinguished these facts from those at issue at Mono Lake. It concluded that the question whether the public trust doctrine extended to the protection of non-navigable waterways was not squarely addressed by *Audubon Society*, which had applied public trust protections only to the non-navigable *tributaries* of a navigable waterway.[124] Noting that the plaintiffs here had conceded that the artificial reservoir was not itself a navigable waterway, and that they had not asserted that the diversions harmed trust resources in a navigable waterway, the court declined to extend the doctrine to non-navigable waterways in the abstract.[125]

---

[119] *See, e.g., ex parte* Maier, 103 Cal. 476, 483 (Cal. 1894) ("The wild game within a state belongs to the people in their collective, sovereign capacity; it is not the subject of private ownership, except in so far as the people may elect to make it so; and they may, if they see fit, absolutely prohibit the taking of it, or any traffic or commerce in it, if deemed necessary for its protection or preservation, or the public good."); Geer v. Connecticut, 161 U.S. 519, 527, 529 (1896), *overruled by* Hughes v. Oklahoma, 441 U.S. 322 (1979) (describing "[t]he common ownership, and its resulting responsibility in the state [over] animals ferae nature").

[120] *But see* Hambrick v. Healthcare Partners Med. Grp., Inc., 189 Cal. Rptr. 3d 31 (Cal. Ct. App. 2015) (following *Ctr. for Biological Diversity* on procedural grounds).

[121] Golden Feather Cmty. Assn. v. Thermalito Irrigation Dist., 257 Cal. Rptr. 836, 837 (Cal. Ct. App. 1989).

[122] *Id.* at 838.

[123] *Id.*

[124] *Id.* at 841.

[125] *Id.*

B. *The* Mono Lake *Doctrine Develops*　　　217

   The same court, in 2006, took a narrow view of the *Mono Lake* doctrine in resolving a complex set of eight cases challenging the State Water Resources Control Board's plans for meeting the water quality objectives in the Water Quality Control Plan for the Bay Delta.[126] In its decision, it upheld the Board's plans against alleged violations of the public trust doctrine, holding that the Board had the discretion to balance public trust uses with other beneficial uses of water unrelated to the public trust.[127] Citing the *Audubon Society* decision, the court held that the Board may, in determining whether protection of values such as fish and wildlife is "feasible," consider whether protecting such values would be "consistent with the public interest," which may also include the pumping and diversion of water for other reasonable domestic and commercial uses.[128]

   That said, a decade later, the very same court of appeal issued the most important judicial extension of the *Audubon Society* decision in California when it applied the logic of the *Mono Lake* doctrine's protection of non-navigable tributaries of navigable waterways to groundwater resources that supply surface water to waterways subject to the trust. Just as the Mono Lake plaintiffs had argued that the doctrine be extended to Mono's non-navigable tributaries to protect the trust values of the navigable lake, plaintiffs in an analogous case involving the groundwater tributaries of the Scott River argued that the doctrine protects the non-navigable tributaries of a river that is demonstrably dependent on groundwater recharge.[129] When the California Court of Appeal for the Third Appellate District agreed (and the California Supreme Court declined to overturn its ruling),[130] the case became one of the first American decisions to protect groundwater resources under the public trust doctrine.

c. The *Scott River Case* and Extension to Groundwater

Located in Siskiyou County at the very roof of Northern California, just below the Oregon border, the Scott River is famous for hosting regionally important runs of salmon and steelhead trout. A navigable tributary of the larger Klamath River

---

[126] The case arose out of an omnibus water rights proceeding before the State Water Resources Control Board, where it allocated responsibility among various water rights holders for meeting the flow-dependent water quality objectives in the Water Quality Control Plan for the Bay-Delta. Much of the responsibility was allocated to the United States Bureau of Reclamation's Central Valley Project and the California Department of Water Resources State Water Project. The Board had decided to conditionally grant the Bureau and the Department the right to use each other's pumping plants to export the water in Decision 1641, in which the Board allowed the Bureau to add fish and wildlife enhancement as an authorized purpose of use of water and allowed the addition of lands not previously included in the permit (subject to mitigation requirements). State Water Res. Control Bd. Cases, 39 Cal. Rptr. 3d 189, 200–201 (Cal. Ct. App. 2006).
[127] *Id.* at 322–23.
[128] *Id.* at 272.
[129] Env't L. Found. v. State Water Res. Control Bd. (*Scott River Case*), 237 Cal. Rptr. 3d 393 (Cal. Ct. App. 2018), *rev. denied* (Nov. 28, 2018).
[130] *Id.*

system, the lower reaches of the Scott River derive the majority of its flow from groundwater, along well-established hydrologic pathways.[131] But as locally permitted groundwater withdrawals increased, long portions of the river run dry in the summer.[132] Many years of agricultural groundwater withdrawals had been depleting the river when plaintiffs finally brought suit to protect it.[133] In litigation widely known as the *Scott River* case, the plaintiffs sought to extend the logic of the Mono Lake decision to this unfamiliar yet parallel context, in which the public trust values associated with the navigable Scott River were pitted against established appropriative rights to pump non-navigable tributary groundwater for agricultural use.[134]

The plaintiffs argued that the state must curtail groundwater pumping to satisfy its public trust obligations to protect the Scott River – even though groundwater had never before been considered within reach of the public trust doctrine.[135] The lower court followed the *Audubon Society* precedent to conclude that diverting essential hydrologically connected groundwater tributaries is analogous to diverting essential non-navigable tributaries.[136] Concluding that the trust applies to protect the Scott River, the court held that it therefore obligated the state to protect the "public's right to use the Scott River for trust purposes, including fishing, rafting, and boating," and "to use, enjoy and preserve the Scott River in its natural state and as a habitat for fish" if "the extraction of groundwater near the Scott River adversely affects those rights...."[137]

The lower court also sided with the plaintiffs on whether the Water Board has the authority and duty under the doctrine to regulate extractions of groundwater that affect public trust uses in the Scott River, holding that the courts have construed the California Water Code to "vest in the Board broad adjudicatory and regulatory power and suggest the Board's regulatory authority is coincident with that of the Legislature," and that "given the Board's broad authority to administer the state's water resources, it is but a short step to the conclusion that the Board has the authority to administer the public trust on behalf of the state."[138]

---

[131] *Id; see also* Marcus Griswold, *Scott River Decision Gives Californians One More Tool to Keep Water in Streams*, SWITCHBOARD NAT. RES. DEF. COUNCIL STAFF BLOG (Aug. 25, 2025); https://web.archive.org/web/20140831230532/www.switchboard.nrdc.org/blogs/mgriswold/scott_river_decision_gives_cal.html (snapshot of www.switchboard.nrdc.org/blogs/mgriswold/scott_river_decision_gives_cal.html last captured Aug. 31, 2014).

[132] Order after Hearing on Cross Motions for Judgment on the Pleadings at 3, *Scott River Case*, 237 Cal. Rptr. 3d 393 (Cal. Sacramento Cnty. Ct. July 15, 2014) (No. 34-2010-80000583).

[133] *Id.*

[134] *Id.* at 4–5.

[135] *See id.* at 2 (characterizing application of public trust doctrine to groundwater as an "issue of first impression"); *see also* Frank, *supra* note 1, at 675–76 (discussing application of public trust doctrine to groundwater in Hawaii, Vermont, and California).

[136] *See* Order After Hearing on Cross Motions for Judgment on the Pleadings, *supra* note 132, at 9–10.

[137] *Id.* at 9.

[138] *Id.* at 13 (citing Light v. State Water Res. Control Bd. 173 Cal. Rptr. 3d 200, 215–16 (Cal. Ct. App. 2014)); *Scott River Case*, 237 Cal. Rptr. 3d 393, 399 (Cal. Ct. App. 2018) (citation omitted); *see also* Gabriel

In 2018, the California Court of Appeals affirmed, holding that the public trust doctrine does protect the Scott River from the diversion of groundwater tributaries, notwithstanding claimed statutory rights to the water.[139] When the California Supreme Court declined the defendants' petition for review, that made the Third District Court of Appeal's decision final, and its novel reasoning applying the trust to groundwater tributaries was left to stand.[140]

The Court of Appeal anchored its reasoning in the *Audubon Society* decision protecting Mono Lake, declaring that "[t]he analysis begins and ends with whether the challenged activity harms a navigable waterway and thereby violates the public trust."[141] It held that the state may not forsake its obligation to protect a critical public trust commons by allowing private expropriation, by whatever means.[142] Drawing on many of the landmark public trust decisions reviewed in Chapter 1, it concluded:

> What *Illinois Central* was on the national level in the 19th century, *National Audubon* was to California in the 20th century – a monumental decision enforcing, indeed expanding, the right of the public to benefit from state-owned navigable waterways and the duty of the state to protect the public's "common heritage" in its water. We reject the County's effort to diminish the importance of the opinion, including its mistaken labeling of its central holdings as dicta. To the contrary, *National Audubon* is binding precedent, factually analogous, precisely on point, and indeed dispositive of the threshold question in this appeal: does the public trust doctrine apply to the extraction of groundwater that adversely impacts the Scott River, a navigable waterway?[143]

The court also rejected the defendant's argument that the state Sustainable Groundwater Management Act preempts or fulfills counties' fiduciary duties to independently consider the public trust in groundwater management decisions.[144]

The widely anticipated decision was the first time that an appellate court in the continental United States applied the public trust doctrine to the administration of groundwater,[145] charging counties and other state subdivisions with the fiduciary

---

Neves, *Judgment for Environmental Law Foundation's Lawsuit against Siskiyou County Affirmed*, LEGAL NEWSLINE, www.legalnewsline.com/stories/511555484-judgment-for-environmental-law-foundation-s-lawsuit-against-siskiyou-county-affirmed (last visited Sept. 10, 2018).

[139] *Scott River Case*, 237 Cal. Rptr. 3d at 402 ("[T]he water subject to the trust is the Scott River, a navigable waterway … '[and] the public trust doctrine applies if extraction of groundwater adversely impacts a navigable waterway to which the public trust doctrine does apply.'").

[140] Order Denying Petition for Review, *Scott River Case*, 237 Cal. Rptr. 2d 393 (Cal. Nov. 28, 2018) (No. S251849).

[141] *Scott River Case*, 237 Cal. Rptr. 3d at 403 (with the court adding that "the dispositive issue is not the source of the activity, or whether the water that is diverted or extracted is itself subject to the public trust, but whether the challenged activity allegedly harms a navigable waterway").

[142] *Id.* at 408–411.

[143] *Id.* at 401.

[144] *Id.* at 409.

[145] *See* Chapter 8 ("The Development of the Public Trust across the United States") (Hawaii is the only state that already applies the trust to all groundwater resources in the state, whether or not they are tributaries of navigable waterways).

duty to consider public trust values before authorizing groundwater wells that could adversely impact trust resources.[146] Environmental advocates were elated when the California Supreme Court declined to revisit the decision, apparently settling the matter at least with regard to the Scott River. Nevertheless, disputes over the public trust treatment of groundwater more generally, which is also heavily regulated by statute in California, are likely to continue.

The extension of the *Mono Lake* doctrine in the *Center for Biological Diversity* and *Scott River* cases, among other developments, prompted growing anxiety among appropriative rights holders who worried that their uses may be curtailed for public trust purposes. Reflecting the concerns of the property rights critique,[147] at least one California lawmaker attempted to overturn the *Mono Lake* doctrine of the California public trust as a matter of federal law. In 2017, Congressman David Valadao introduced the "Gaining Responsibility on Water Act"[148] to the 115th Congress, an elaborate bill consolidating several earlier attempts to weaken environmental regulations and federal reserved water rights to facilitate access by other users to scarce water resources. Among many other extended titles, the bill tucked in the following provision: "Nor shall the State of California ... restrict the exercise of any water right obtained pursuant to State law ... in order to protect, enhance, or restore under the Public Trust Doctrine any public trust value."[149] The bill was passed by the U.S. House of Representatives and read twice in the U.S. Senate before it was referred to the Committee on Energy and Natural Resources, where it appeared to have stalled.[150]

2. Impacts of the Mono Lake Case in Other States

The surge of environmental advocacy following the Mono Lake litigation prompted public trust conversations around the country.[151] While *Audubon Society* became the law of the land in California, it inspired judicial consideration of the *Mono Lake* doctrine throughout the United States, with some following California's lead, others adopting parts (but not all) of the *Mono Lake* doctrine, and a few rejecting

---

[146] *Third Appellate District Extends Public Trust Doctrine to Groundwater, Finding that Counties Have a Duty to Administer the Trust in Issuing Ministerial Well Permits*, DOWNEY BRAND, www.downeybrand.com/legal-alerts/third-appellate-district-extends-public-trust-doctrine-to-groundwater-finding-that-counties-have-a-duty-to-administer-the-trust-in-issuing-ministerial-well-permits/ (last visited Sept. 7, 2018).

[147] *See supra* notes 12–36 and accompanying text.

[148] Gaining Responsibility on Water Act of 2017, H.R. 23, 115th Cong. § 108(b) (2017).

[149] *Id.*

[150] 115 Cong. Rec. S4053 (daily ed. July 17, 2017); *see also H.R.23–Gaining Responsibility on Water Act of 2017*, CONGRESS.GOV, www.congress.gov/bill/115th-congress/house-bill/23/all-actions?overview=closed#tabs (stating that committee referral is the latest procedural update for the bill).

[151] For a fuller treatment of the development of the public trust doctrine throughout the country, see Chapter 8(A) ("The Planes of Public Trust Development across the United States").

it outright. While Chapter 8 describes the general development of the public trust doctrine across the nation, this section describes the treatment by other state courts of the specific *Audubon Society* decision itself.

Following the precedent set at Mono Lake, for example, the Supreme Court of Alaska relied on *Audubon Society* to determine that the private rights conveyed in state tidelands grants remain subject to public trust rights of use for navigation, commerce, and fishing.[152] The Arizona Court of Appeals relied on the case to invalidate an Arizona statute that relinquished the state's interest in title to riverbed lands, noting that thirty-eight other states had concluded that the land beneath navigable waterways was held in trust for the public by the state.[153] Similarly, the Montana Supreme Court held that title to submerged school trust lands remained vested in the State even after their transfer,[154] citing *Audubon Society* for the proposition that interests acquired in lands subject to the public trust remain subject to the requirements of the trust.[155] The Vermont Supreme Court relied on *Audubon Society* to support its holding that the public trust doctrine is not static but evolves to meet changing conditions and needs of the public,[156] and that as administrator of the trust, the state maintains ongoing authority to enforce the trust, even to revoke previously granted rights on lands mistakenly believed free of the trust.[157]

Other courts have adopted some important aspects of the *Mono Lake* doctrine while distinguishing others. For example, the Minnesota Court of Appeals touted *Audubon Society* as a significant application of the public trust doctrine but distinguished Minnesota law, which did not recognize doctrinal protection for the fish resource.[158] The Supreme Court of South Dakota relied on *Audubon Society* for the proposition that the public trust doctrine exists independently from state statutes and cannot be legislatively abrogated,[159] but it determined that even though the water in

---

[152] CWC Fisheries, Inc. v. Bunker, 755 P.2d 1115, 1118 (Alaska 1988) (following the California approach set forth in Nat'l Audubon Soc'y that "[t]he grantee may 'assert a vested right to the servient estate (the right of use subject to the trust)'" (quoting Nat'l Audubon Soc'y v. Super. Ct. of Alpine Cnty., 658 P.2d 709, 723 (Cal. 1983))).

[153] Ariz. Ctr. for L. in Pub. Interest v. Hassell, 837 P.2d 158 (Ariz. Ct. App. 1991) (court considered the validity of an Arizona statute that relinquished title to the beds of watercourses and held that it was invalid because it violated the public trust doctrine).

[154] *In re* Powder River Drainage Area, 702 P.2d 948, 950, 957 (Mont. 1985).

[155] *Id.* at 956–57.

[156] State v. Cent. Vt. Ry., 571 A.2d 1128, 1136 (Vt. 1989).

[157] *Id.* The court determined that a railroad company did not hold title to a 1.1 mile-long strip of filled lands adjacent to the waterfront free of the public trust, and that the lands may only be used for purposes approved by the legislature as public trust uses. *Id.* at 1136–37.

[158] Save Mille Lacs Sportsfishing, Inc. v. Minn. Dep't of Natural Res., 859 N.W.2d 845, 851 (Minn. Ct. App. 2015) (upholding a fishing regulation on Mille Lacs Lake despite challenges that it allowed extraction of the fish resource that was inconsistent with the public trust doctrine).

[159] Parks v. Cooper, 676 N.W.2d 823, 824–25 (S.D. 2004) (concluding that the statutory Water Resources Act did not override the public trust doctrine). However, the court also held that while the state must hold lake water in the trust for the public, the decision of what is considered a "beneficial use" of that water remains a legislative choice. *Id.* at 841.

lakes is public, submerged lake beds may be privately owned.[160] The Supreme Court of Nevada cited *Audubon Society* in expressly adopting the public trust doctrine after many years during which the question was unsettled in Nevada,[161] though as detailed further below, it has enforced the constraints of the doctrine with much less vigor.

Still other states have simply rejected the *Mono Lake* doctrine outright. In an opinion issued by the North Dakota Attorney General, *Audubon Society* was used to distinguish between California's public trust doctrine and North Dakota's. The opinion contrasted the ongoing duty of supervision that the California public trust doctrine imposes on the state, set forth in *Audubon Society* as an obligation to continually review vested water rights for needed adjustment,[162] from the less demanding doctrine articulated by North Dakota courts, which had imposed no such obligations.[163] The Attorney General determined that the State Engineer was not required to limit water resources appropriated under existing water permits.[164]

Yet no state has rejected the *Mono Lake* doctrine as pointedly as Idaho did, opening an especially interesting conversation about the nature of the public trust doctrine itself. When the Idaho Supreme Court made early moves embracing the *Mono Lake* doctrine in *Kootenai Environmental Alliance v. Panhandle Yacht Club*,[165] legislators were not pleased. Fearing that the court would soon adopt the California approach in full, the Idaho Legislature took an approach that the courts in California, Nevada, and South Dakota had all suggested would be *ultra vires*, or beyond the available sovereign authority of the state. It enacted a new statute foreclosing this judicial path, declaring a much more limited version of the doctrine than the court had seen fit to recognize – effectively abrogating these features of the common law public trust doctrine legislatively.

In *Kootenai Environmental Alliance*, the Idaho Supreme Court reviewed the evolution of the public trust doctrine in Massachusetts, Wisconsin, and California in considering whether the doctrine precluded the Idaho Department of Lands from granting a lease to a private entity for the construction, maintenance, and use of private docking facilities on the bed of a navigable lake.[166] In reviewing California law, the court cited *Audubon Society* for the proposition that statutes alienating public trust resources are subject to the requirements of the public trust doctrine, which

---

[160] *Id.* at 837–38.
[161] Lawrence v. Clark Cnty., 254 P.3d 606 (Nev. 2011) (adopting the public trust doctrine in a case considering whether state-owned land that was once submerged under the Colorado River could be freely transferred).
[162] Letter Opinion No. 2006-L-23, 2006 N.D. AG LEXIS 35, 14–15 (Aug. 16, 2006) (Attorney General stating that the public trust doctrine in North Dakota did not require the State Engineer to limit water appropriated under existing permits).
[163] *Id.* at 15.
[164] *Id.* at 1.
[165] Kootenai Env't All., Inc. v. Panhandle Yacht Club, Inc., 671 P.2d 1085 (Idaho 1983).
[166] *Id.* at 1087 (holding that a permit to build private docking facilities on the bay of a navigable lake did not violate the public trust doctrine).

takes precedence over vested water rights.[167] The court determined that the grant of trust property for sailboat slips did not violate the trust, but that it nevertheless remains subject to the trust.[168] Moreover, it adopted the *Mono Lake* doctrine of ongoing supervision, emphasizing that the state may yet determine in the future if the conveyance is no longer compatible with the requirements of the public trust.[169] In response, and as discussed further in Part C(2) below, the Idaho legislature statutorily overrode the state supreme court's decision, limiting the doctrine only to protecting the state-owned beds of navigable waterways from alienation.[170]

In so doing, the Idaho legislature chose a markedly different legal interpretation of the nature of the public trust doctrine from the states its supreme court had reviewed, with important implications for the future of the doctrine and the protections it offers trust resources. Led by California, these other states had interpreted the trust's prohibitions as a limit on sovereign decision-making that the sovereign itself cannot change, either by judicial or legislative means. This construction sees the doctrine as a quasi-constitutional rule – one that constitutes the very legal framework in which other policy decisions can be made. The Idaho Supreme Court appeared poised to follow that approach when the Idaho Legislature abruptly charted a different course, treating the doctrine like an ordinary common law rule, subject to modification – or even elimination – by the sitting legislature.

A critical difference in the application of the public trust doctrine from state to state boils down to one determining factor – whether the doctrine should be treated as common law or constitutive in nature. The following part discusses the important question of law these contrasting decisions raise for the future.

C. ORDINARY COMMON LAW OR QUASI-CONSTITUTIONAL?

The *Audubon Society* Mono Lake case and its progeny express a powerful view of the public trust doctrine at the level of legal theory. These cases suggest that the public trust doctrine is not simply an ordinary common law rule, but something much more powerful. They suggest that it is a background principle of law that cannot be withdrawn by the sovereign authority it is designed to constrain, and in that regard, it is made of similar stuff as constitutional rules. Constitutional rules are beyond the authority of the courts or legislature to modify through ordinary processes because they are the rules within which all other rules can be made. The *Mono Lake* doctrine suggests that the public trust is a similarly quasi-constitutional doctrine, or at least a constitutive one, which cannot be so easily limited by the very forces of government it was created to delimit.

---

[167] *Id.* at 1094.
[168] *Id.*
[169] *Id.*
[170] IDAHO CODE ANN. § 58-1201.

The legal nature of the public trust doctrine has been a subject of academic debate. While some would treat it as an ordinary doctrine of the common law, others, including Professors Jan Stevens and Charles Wilkinson, have long argued that it is best understood as a quasi-constitutional or constitutive limit on state sovereign authority[171] – and perhaps sovereign authority in general.[172] A constitutive limit is an inherent limit built into the fabric of sovereign authority, such that it cannot be extinguished through the normal judicial or legislative processes that curtail the exercise of sovereign power. Common law doctrines can ordinarily be rejected by later courts or displaced by contrary legislative statute, but state supreme courts in California, Hawaii, Nevada, and elsewhere have determined that the public trust cannot be so casually eliminated because it is a built-in constraint on sovereign authority.[173] As Professor Gerald Torres and Nathan Bellinger have written:

> While some rights are created by government, others – often the most important pre-existing rights – are inherent to humankind and merely secured by government.

---

[171] *See, e.g.*, Stevens, *supra* note 6, at 609 (arguing that the public trust is an inalienable attribute of state sovereignty); *see also* Jan S. Stevens, *The Public Trust: A Sovereign's Ancient Prerogative Becomes the People's Environmental Right*, 14 U.C. DAVIS L. REV. 195, 200 (1980) (suggesting that the inalienable nature of the trust is rooted in the Magna Carta which established that the King held navigable waters in trust for the people in his sovereign capacity. This concept was retained in American colonies. Then, following the American Revolution, the absolute right to the navigable waters of each state was transferred to the people as sovereign); Wilkinson, *supra* note 41 (stating that "[t]he standards for the trust ... are best understood ... as a matter of federal mandate, either by way of congressional preemption or constitutional law," but that "the constitutional rationale is more consonant with the whole body of law.").

[172] *See, e.g.*, Joseph Regalia, *A New Water Law Vista: Rooting the Public Trust Doctrine in the Courts*, 108 KY. L.J. 1, 6 (2020) ("Not only should litigants be able to argue for an expansion of trust duties in state courts under state constitutions, they should also be able to argue for this expansion in federal courts under the U.S. Constitution."); Michael Blumm & Mary C. Wood, *"No Ordinary Lawsuit": Climate Change, Due Process, and the Public Trust Doctrine*, 67 AM. U.L. REV. 1, 43–44 (2017) (arguing that the public trust doctrine is "an inherent constitutional limit on sovereignty"); Michael Blumm & Lynn Schaffer, *The Federal Public Trust Doctrine. Misinterpreting Justice Kennedy and* Illinois Central Railroad, 45 ENV'T L. 257, 400–401 (2015) (arguing that the public trust doctrine is an inherent limit on both state and federal sovereign authority, and that *Illinois Central* represents an application of the Tenth Amendment's reserved powers doctrine); Gerald Torres & Nathan Bellinger, *The Public Trust: The Law's DNA*, 4 WAKE FOREST J.L. & POL'Y 281, 288 (2014) (arguing that the public trust doctrine is an implied limit on federal authority because it "is the chalkboard on which the Constitution is written"); Crystal S. Chase, *The Illinois Central Public Trust Decision and Federal Common Law: An Unconventional View*, 16 HASTINGS W.-NW. J. ENV'T L. & POL'Y 113, 137–42 (2010) (arguing that the *Illinois Central* public trust doctrine is grounded in federal common law, and that the federal common law reading confers continuing legitimacy on the decision, even after the 1938 *Erie Railroad* decision limited the reach of federal common law); Wilkinson, *supra* note 41, at 453, 458, 461–62 (arguing that the Supreme Court's *Illinois Central* decision was "premised on federal law" and that the public trust doctrine is therefore a feature of both federal and state law because states manage trust lands within a federally imposed limit that prevents them from abdicating their responsibility as trustees). *But see* Charles F. Wilkinson, *The Public Trust Doctrine in Public Land Law*, 14 U.C. DAVIS L. REV. 269, 273–74, 278 (1980) (arguing for a public trust responsibility in the federal administration of federal public lands, but that this trust responsibility arises from a different source from the state-constraining public trust in submerged lands).

[173] *See* Chapter 8(A)(4) ("Different Legal Theories about the Nature of the Doctrine"); Chapter 8(B)(3) ("A Constitutive Constraint on Sovereign Authority?").

C. Ordinary Common Law or Quasi-Constitutional?

The public trust doctrine is one of these inherent rights that predates the United States Constitution. As such, we suggest that the public trust doctrine is the chalkboard on which the Constitution is written. When one writes something on a chalkboard, we see the meaning of the writing, but we commonly forget that there is still a chalkboard that created the space for the writing. We recognize that meaning comes from what is actually written, but there could be no such conveyance of meaning without the chalkboard as a foundation. After all, the Constitution was not written on a blank slate but was written with certain principles and rights in mind. As the chalkboard on which the Constitution was written, the public trust doctrine provides the background and context for the Constitution.[174]

Some scholars have even argued that this interpretation of the public trust doctrine is a necessary implication of the Equal Footing doctrine (holding that each state be treated on equal footing with all others) – a well recognized principle of U.S. constitutional law, even though, like the words "public trust," the words "equal footing" appear nowhere in the U.S. Constitution.[175] Indeed, in 2012, the State of California argued (unsuccessfully) to the Ninth Circuit that the public trust was such an essential aspect of state sovereignty that even federal power under the Supremacy Clause should not be able to displace it in favor of a private grantee.[176]

Unresolved questions about the fundamental nature of the public trust doctrine and its relationship with conflicting statutory systems, especially regarding water allocation, have set in motion a series of inevitable collisions, which continue to unfold across the American West even now. The following section explores how that conflict has been managed in three different western prior appropriation states: California, Idaho, and Nevada.

1. *California: A Constitutive Constraint*

As detailed at length in Chapter 5, the *Audubon Society* decision framed the public trust as a doctrine with constitutive features, because in contrast to conventional common law, it withstood ordinary processes of legislative abrogation.[177] While the

---

[174] Torres & Bellinger, *supra* note 172, at 288.
[175] Harrison C. Dunning, *The Public Trust: A Fundamental Doctrine of American Property Law*, 19 Env't L. 515, 524 (1989).
[176] United States v. 32.42 Acres of Land, 683 F.3d 1030 (9th Cir. 2012). When the United States Navy sought to extinguish California's public trust rights in land taken by eminent domain, the California State Lands Commission did not dispute the U.S.'s power to take and use the land, but disputed its ability to then transfer the filled land to a private party. *Id.* Citing *Illinois Central* and *Nat'l Audubon Soc'y*, California argued (unsuccessfully) that the public trust was an aspect of state sovereignty beyond federal power to extinguish, urging the court to determine that its public trust rights were not extinguished when the parcel was taken but instead that the public trust rights were "quiescent" and without effect until the United States attempted to transfer the property to a private party. *Id.*
[177] *See* Part (A)(1) ("The Property Rights Critique") and Part (C) ("Ordinary Common Law or Quasi-Constitutional?").

California Supreme Court's decision there emphasized the importance of balancing the values served by both the common law public trust and the statutory system of water allocation, it affirmed that the public trust doctrine (1) protects environmental values associated with trust resources; (2) applies to the non-navigable tributaries of trust resources; (3) creates an ongoing duty of state supervision; (4) constrains state authority to license water rights in derogation of trust values; and most important for the present conversation, and (5) was neither abrogated by nor subsumed into California's statutory system of prior appropriation law.[178]

In disputes like the Mono Lake and subsequent Scott River[179] cases, the litigants holding private rights under state water allocation laws argued that statutorily based water rights should trump whatever values the public trust doctrine protects because, after all, that is normally how the common law works.[180] Judge-made common law is used to resolve disputes that have not been directly regulated by statute, but common law is easily overridden when the legislature enacts a contrary directive.[181] However, *Audubon Society* and its progeny established that, at least in states following the California approach, the public trust doctrine was not displaced by the prior appropriations doctrine, leaving the state obligated to protect trust values as much as possible while also maintaining its statutory water allocation system.[182]

The California approach casts the public trust doctrine as a constitutive grant of partnered authority and obligation regarding the management of public commons water resources, because it grants sovereign ownership of trust resources while obligating the sovereign to manage them in trust for the public.[183] Because the California doctrine imposes a constraint on sovereign authority in addition to its sovereign grant, it stands to reason that the public trust cannot be abrogated by simple statute.[184] This approach has an undeniable internal logic, because permitting the state to use its legislative authority to abolish a foundational constraint on its authority would undermine the very purpose of the doctrine in protecting public

---

[178] For a full discussion of the *Mono Lake* decision, see Chapter 5 ("*National Audubon Society*: The 'Mono Lake Case'").

[179] See *supra* notes 129–149 and accompanying text.

[180] 58 CAL. JURIS. 3D, *Effects of Statutes on Common Law* § 6 (2023) ("The legislature is at liberty to change any rule of the common law and thereby prevent it from being the rule of decision in this state."); Mod. Barber Colls. v. Cal. Emp. State Comm'n, 192 P.2d 916, 920 (Cal. 1948) (noting that the legislature may "create new rights or provide that rights which have previously existed shall no longer arise, and it has full power to regulate and circumscribe the methods and means of enjoying those rights").

[181] See Lowman v. Stafford, 226 Cal. App. 2d 31, 38–39 (1964) ("[T]he law itself, as a rule of conduct, may be changed at will by the Legislature subject only to constitutional provision.") (internal citations omitted).

[182] Nat'l Audubon Soc'y v. Super. Ct. of Alpine Cnty., 658 P.2d 709, 728 (Cal. 1983).

[183] See Chapter 8(B)(3) ("A Constitutive Constraint on Sovereign Authority?").

[184] *But see* Chapter 2 n. 98 and accompanying text (discussing the narrow exceptions to the general public trust constraints stated in *Illinois Central*).

C. Ordinary Common Law or Quasi-Constitutional?

commons.[185] A constraint on legislative authority that the legislature can easily legislate its way out of is no constraint at all. (Still, there are some acknowledged exceptions to this limit, as detailed in the original *Illinois Central* decision,[186] which allow "privatization of trust resources when (1) the conveyance further[s] public purposes and (2) there [is] no substantial effect on remaining trust resources."[187])

Most American jurisdictions that have addressed the issue have followed the California approach set forth in *Audubon Society*,[188] including Hawaii,[189] New Jersey,[190] and Washington,[191] and those with express constitutional trusts, such as Pennsylvania.[192] Even so, as noted earlier, Idaho has specifically rejected it.[193]

2. Idaho: Legislative Repudiation of the Constitutive Constraint

In the decade after the Mono Lake litigation, the Idaho State Supreme Court decided several public trust cases converging on California's approach[194] when the state legislature intervened with a statute that expressly foreclosed the court's

---

[185] *See, e.g.*, Blumm & Wood, *supra* note 172, at 43–44 (arguing that the public trust doctrine is "an inherent constitutional limit on sovereignty"); Michael C. Blumm, Harrison C. Dunning & Scott W. Reed, *Renouncing the Public Trust Doctrine: An Assessment of the Validity of Idaho House Bill 794*, 24 ECOLOGY L.Q. 461 (1997).

[186] In *Illinois Central*, the Court approved limited dispositions of trust resources to private parties to improve navigation or when discrete parcels could be disposed of without impairing the public interest in the remaining trust resource. Ill. Cent. R. Co. v. Illinois, 146 U.S. 387, 453 (1982) *see also* Chapter 1(B)(5) ("With Power Comes Responsibility") (discussing the case in detail).

[187] Blumm, *supra* note 22, at 660–62 (discussing the *Illinois Central* exception).

[188] *See, e.g.*, Lawrence v. Clark Cnty., 254 P.3d 606, 613 (Nev. 2011) ("The final underpinning of our formal adoption of the public trust doctrine arises from the inherent limitations on the state's sovereign power.").

[189] *See In re* Water Use Permit Applications for the Waiahole Ditch, 9 P.3d 409, 432 (Haw. 2000) ("[H]istory and precedent have established the public trust as an inherent attribute of sovereign authority.").

[190] *See* E. Cape May v. State Dept. of Env't Prot., 777 A.2d 1015, 1034 (N.J. Super. Ct. App. Div. 2001) (noting that "tidally-flowed land has always been subject to the public trust doctrine ... [which] provides that the sovereign never waives its right to regulate the use of public trust property").

[191] *See* Caminiti v. Boyle, 732 P.2d 989, 994 (Wash. 1987) ("The state can no more convey or give away this jus publicum interest than it can 'abdicate its police powers in the administration of government and the preservation of the peace.'").

[192] *See supra* note 4 and accompanying text (discussing the Environmental Rights Amendment to the Pennsylvania State Constitution).

[193] This move by Idaho prompted considerable scholarly controversy on this issue. *See* James M. Kearney, *Recent Statute: Closing the Floodgates? Idaho's Statutory Limitation on the Public Trust Doctrine*, 34 IDAHO L. REV. 91, 94 (1997); Blumm et al., *supra* note 185, at 472 (noting that the new statute "was the legislature's response to judicial public trust declarations" in a series of Idaho Supreme Court cases).

[194] *See* Selkirk-Priest Basin Ass'n, Inc. v. State *ex rel.* Andrus, 899 P.2d 949, 950 (Idaho 1995) (suggesting that the public trust doctrine might be used to constrain harm from logging activities to an impacted water body); Idaho Conservation League v. State, 911 P.2d 748 (Idaho 1995) (declining intervention by environmental groups to raise public trust issues where state ownership was not at issue, but suggesting in dicta that the public trust doctrine could take precedence over vested water rights); *see also* Kearney, *supra* note 193, at 95–96 (discussing these cases and the legislature's reaction).

apparent interpretive path.[195] The legislation was designed specifically to clarify the scope of the public trust doctrine, with the apparent target audience of the state's supreme court justices.[196] While it acknowledged that the doctrine prevents the state from alienating title to submerged lands,[197] the legislation specified that the doctrine will not impact the allocation of prior appropriative water rights or other state decisions about the use of public trust waterways for commercial, agricultural, or recreational uses.[198] In other words, the state legislature formally rejected the California approach before the state supreme court could fully articulate it. As a result, and in contrast to California and the other states that follow similar principles, in Idaho, the prior appropriation doctrine *does* trump the public trust doctrine.[199]

Environmental scholars quickly condemned the Idaho statute as illegitimate,[200] but the legitimacy of the statute really depends on the underlying nature of the public trust doctrine. If the doctrine includes a constitutive limit on sovereign authority over natural resource public commons, as the California approach understands it, then the Idaho legislature's move to abrogate that limit would indeed exceed the scope of legislative authority at its disposal. Yet the Idaho legislature treated the doctrine as an ordinary exercise of state authority to protect the public health, safety, and welfare – the conventional reservoir of police power authority that is normally subject to legislative adjustment. The contest between the California and Idaho approaches is symptomatic of the variability of the doctrine among U.S. jurisdictions, but more importantly, it exposes this core underlying dilemma of legal theory.

Is the public trust doctrine a constitutive element of sovereign authority that cannot be casually dissolved by the one wielding that sovereign authority at any given moment in time? Or is it an expression of the state's conventional police power to protect the public welfare, which can always be revisited by future legislative decision-makers? If we assume that the public trust doctrine in every state evolved from a single, unified principle, then the contrary approaches taken by these states pose a thorny legal problem, because it would seem that they cannot both be right. Either the doctrine originated as a modifiable expression of conventional state authority, or it has always been a less negotiable constraint on sovereign power.[201]

---

[195] IDAHO CODE tit. 58, ch. 12 §§ 58-1201-1203 (1996).
[196] *Id.* at § 58-1201(4) (clarifying that the purpose of the act is to define limits on the public trust doctrine).
[197] *Id.* at § 58-1201(6) (defining the public trust doctrine as guiding alienation of the title of the beds of navigable waters); *id.* at § 58-1203(1) (limiting the doctrine to "solely a limitation on the power of the state to alienate or encumber the title to the beds of navigable waters").
[198] *Id.* at § 58-1203(3) (clarifying that the doctrine does not limit the state to authorize public and private use of submerged lands, or even alienation of title to them, if the state land commission determines that it is in accordance with Idaho statutes and constitution and for the purposes of navigation, commerce, recreation, agriculture, mining, forestry, or other uses).
[199] In Idaho, in contrast to most other states, the public trust doctrine has been construed to not allow a private cause of action. Newton v. MJK/BJK, LLC, 469 P.3d 23, 29 (Idaho 2020).
[200] *See, e.g.*, Kearney, *supra* note 193, at 94; Blumm et al., *supra* note 185, at 472.
[201] If there is one, an alternative explanation would probably require the operation of something like the controversial "Constitutional Moments" higher lawmaking hypothesis offered by Professor Bruce

C. Ordinary Common Law or Quasi-Constitutional?

If California is right, then unlike the conventional common law, the public trust doctrine represents a quasi-constitutional limit on sovereign authority that cannot be so easily legislated away. But if Idaho is right, then the doctrine is just another common law rule that is forever subject to new sovereign consensus. Neither of these principles can reduce to the other without constitutional change. The Idaho approach could not legitimately evolve from the California model, nor could the California approach evolve from the Idaho model – because either path threatens conventional rule of law principles. At least in the United States, sovereign authority cannot free itself of constitutional constraints, nor does ordinary common law assume constitutive status through conventional common law processes.[202]

At the level of legal theory, then, the California and Idaho approaches are mutually exclusive, and neither can reduce to the other without constitutional change. But if both states cannot be right about the underlying theory of the public trust, then which one got it wrong – California, or Idaho?

It bears noting that even now, we may not know the end of the story. In Idaho, the last serious move was made by the legislature, in a separation-of-powers struggle for interpretive supremacy that could yet be revisited in court. A plaintiff with standing could still challenge the legality of the Idaho statute as *ultra vires* – just like the statute in *Illinois Central* – and the high court could decide to hear the case, although that seems both judicially and politically unlikely at this point in time. And in California, though the *Mono Lake* doctrine authorizes the unsettling of appropriative rights, that power has been virtually unused outside the Mono Basin, manifesting today much more powerfully in prospective administrative process than retrospective adjudication.[203]

In the meanwhile, other states managing the same conflict between the public trust and prior appropriations doctrines continue to wrestle with the dilemma in new contexts. In fact, another western state neighboring both California and Idaho subsequently weighed in with a decision that declines to cleanly pick one side over the other in the unfolding theoretical fray.

3. Nevada: Mixed Messages in the Walker Lake Basin

The battle over the underlying legal theory of the public trust was gradually joined by another prior appropriations state, Nevada, in a decision that draws elements

---

Ackerman to explain the adoption of constitutional principles outside the formal amendment process (justifying, for example, the canonization of Fourteenth Amendment principles within the U.S. constitutional framework notwithstanding problems with the post-civil war amendment process). BRUCE ACKERMAN, WE THE PEOPLE: FOUNDATIONS 6–7, 110–11 (1991). Ackerman's theory, of course, has itself been the object of intense criticism. *See, e.g.*, Michael J. Klarman, *Review: Constitutional Fact/Constitutional Fiction: A Critique of Bruce Ackerman's Theory of Constitutional Moments*, 44 STANFORD L. REV. 759 (1992).

[202] *Id.*
[203] *See* Owen, *supra* note 9, at 1104–05.

from both the California and Idaho approaches. The litigation arose over appropriative withdrawals from the agriculturally important Walker River and their negative impact on Walker Lake at its terminus, another rare Great Basin lake not far from Mono Lake across the Nevada state line.[204] The farming community in western Nevada depends on these diversions, but they have caused Walker Lake to drop 160 vertical feet, increasing salinity and sedimentation, killing off its fish population, and destroying many of its public recreational and aesthetic values.[205] Ever since the California decision protecting Mono Lake, local environmentalists and indigenous people have attempted to apply the same legal logic to save Walker Lake by curbing upstream appropriative rights to the Walker River.[206] Their hopes had been raised when the Nevada Supreme Court previously recognized the doctrine as an inherent constraint on the state's sovereign authority over protected trust resources, following the first few footholds of the California approach.[207]

In *Mineral County v. Lyon County* (the *Walker Lake* case), decided late in 2020, the closely divided court dashed the hopes of these plaintiffs while also confusing analysts by issuing a decision with a clearly favorable outcome for appropriators but a somewhat mixed message for the future.[208] The Nevada Supreme Court doubled down on its Californian view of the public trust doctrine as a fundamental constraint on state authority, but it declined to follow the model to the point of unsettling appropriative rights that were clearly undermining a trust resource.[209] Instead, it followed Idaho's lead in holding that the public trust doctrine could not dislodge previously established water rights – but not because, as the Idaho legislature had reasoned, the public trust does not apply to appropriative water rights. For the Nevada high court, it was because all water rights established by state administrative processes had already conformed to the central public trust requirement that the state manage trust resources for the public benefit.[210]

It is a surprising decision – not quite a third way, but perhaps a middle ground – in that it draws from different elements of the two seemingly exclusive approaches taken by its neighbors. The court committed to an expansive reading of state obligations under the public trust doctrine, affirming application of the doctrine to all waters in the state, including those that are the subject of prior appropriation, and characterizing the trust as a constitutive limit on state authority to preserve trust

---

[204] Mineral Cnty. v. Lyon Cnty. (*Walker Lake*), 473 P.3d 418 (Nev. 2020).
[205] Kyle Roerink, *Can Walker River and Walker Lake Live in Harmony*, Sierra Nev. Ally, www.sierranevadaally.org/2020/09/29/can-walker-river-and-walker-lake-live-in-harmony/ (describing three decades of litigation over conflicting water uses in the Walker River Basin) (last visited Sept. 29, 2020).
[206] *Id.*; *Walker Lake*, 473 P.3d at 423–27.
[207] Lawrence v. Clark Cnty., 254 P.3d 606, 613 (Nev. 2011) ("The final underpinning of our formal adoption of the public trust doctrine arises from the inherent limitations on the state's sovereign power.").
[208] *Walker Lake*, 473 P.3d at 431; *see also* Roerink, *supra* note 205 (discussing local uncertainty following the decision).
[209] *Walker Lake*, 473 P.3d at 421–22.
[210] *Id.* at 427–29.

C. Ordinary Common Law or Quasi-Constitutional?   231

resources for the public benefit.[211] It explicitly recognized the doctrine as a sovereign constraint and a background principle of state law, writing that "the public trust doctrine applies to rights already adjudicated and settled under the doctrine of prior appropriation, such that the doctrine has always inhered in the water law of Nevada as a qualification or constraint in every appropriated right."[212] Its sweeping endorsement of public trust principles provides potential fodder for future environmental litigation, both to fortify challenges against new appropriative rights that threaten trust values and to defend environmental regulations against takings challenges by invoking the trust as a background principle of state law.

Nevertheless, the court declined to second-guess the challenged appropriative rights in the Walker Lake basin on grounds that they were allocated under water statutes that are already consistent with the public trust doctrine, and so everything that follows from them must also be so.[213] In a three-two split, the majority held that Nevada's comprehensive system of water law satisfies the state's public trust obligations because it was carefully designed to "constrain water allocations based on the public interest" and met all criteria for "the dispensation of public trust property" that the court had previously established.[214] Over a lively dissent, the justices in the majority acknowledged the grave threats to trust values at Walker Lake, but concluded that they could not grant the relief the plaintiffs sought:

> [W]hile we are sympathetic to the plight of Walker Lake and the resulting negative impacts on the wildlife, resources, and economy in Mineral County, we cannot use the public trust doctrine as a tool to uproot an entire water system, particularly where finality is firmly rooted in our statutes. We cannot read into the statutes any authority to permit reallocation when the Legislature has already declared that adjudicated water rights are final, nor can we substitute our own policy judgments for the Legislature's.[215]

While recognizing "the tragic decline of Walker Lake" and the associated environmental and economic harms to the surrounding community,[216] these justices reasoned that all established water rights satisfy the public trust doctrine by definition, because consideration of public trust values is built into the water allocation system itself.[217] If the rights were granted, goes the logic, the public trust must have been adequately considered, and values of finality must prevail.

Though finality is a legitimately important value in dispute resolution, the majority's reasoning here is confusing, given that the modern public trust doctrine was not

---

[211] *Id.* at 425–26, 430.
[212] *Id.* at 425.
[213] *Id.* at 429–30.
[214] *Walker Lake*, 473 P.3d at 426.
[215] *Id.* at 430.
[216] *Id.*
[217] *Id.*

given clear consideration in Nevada until this very Walker Lake dispute first arose thirty years ago – when the appropriative rights at issue had already been granted.[218] Although it recognized the public trust as an inherent limitation on state sovereign power predating its holding, the Nevada Supreme Court only formally adopted the doctrine in 2011,[219] nine years before holding here that all established water rights satisfy the state's trust obligations because the obliged considerations are built into the state's administrative process. The timing alone makes this proposition troubling. It is one thing to hold that trust values are accounted for on the front end through an administrative process designed to do so – as, for example, California's process arguably does today.[220] But the majority's argument here seems conveniently disinterested in genuine consideration of whether Nevada's administrative process matches the gravity that the rest of its decision places on the state's public trust obligations – especially the administrative process that took place before these obligations were formally recognized. The decline of Walker Lake may not be determinative of such a failing, but it is at the very least suggestive of it.

To that end, and writing for the remaining members of the court, the Chief Justice concurred in the parts of the decision expansively interpreting the Nevada public trust doctrine, but dissented vigorously from the conclusion that appropriative rights threatening trust resources could not be revisited.[221] He contended that the majority "fundamentally misapprehends the public trust doctrine and its constitutional and sovereign dimensions," invoking the California view of the constitutive nature of the doctrine while supporting his argument with references to the Nevada State Constitution and other expressions of state law.[222] He repeatedly referenced the *Audubon Society* decision in arguing that the public trust doctrine and private water allocation laws must be understood as independently functioning parts of the state's comprehensive water management system that must be balanced against one another.[223] In his view, and following the California approach, both the public trust and prior appropriations doctrines provide independent sources of regulatory value, both more important than finality, and neither doctrine can subsume or replace the contributions of the other.[224]

---

[218] Mineral Cnty. v. State, 20 P.3d 800, 807 (Nev. 2001) (en banc) (Rose, J., concurring) (in an earlier iteration of the Walker Lake dispute, urging the Nevada Supreme Court to clarify the scope of the doctrine in Nevada); *see also* Jason L. DeForest, *Lawrence v. Clark County and Nevada's Public Trust Doctrine: Reconsidering Water Rights in the Desert*, 13 NEV. L.J. 290, 297–99 (2012) (discussing the early history of the public trust doctrine in Nevada).
[219] Lawrence v. Clark Cnty., 254 P.3d 606, 613 (Nev. 2011) ("The final underpinning of our formal adoption of the public trust doctrine arises from the inherent limitations on the state's sovereign power.").
[220] *See generally* Owen, *supra* note 9 (considering the role of the public trust doctrine in the administration of California water rights).
[221] *Walker Lake*, 473 P.3d 418, 431–38 (Nev. 2020) (Pickering, C. J., concurring in part and dissenting in part).
[222] *Id.* at 433–34.
[223] *Id.* at 437–38.
[224] *Id.*

C. Ordinary Common Law or Quasi-Constitutional?

The battle over Walker Lake continues. While the court rejected the remedy the *Walker Lake* plaintiffs sought, its affirmation that public trust principles must undergird the state's water allocation laws may provide legal impetus for the State Engineer to act to protect threatened trust resources such as Walker Lake through administrative means – perhaps by encouraging state actors to free up additional water resources through conservation, where possible, or other means that do not disrupt established appropriations. Indeed, since the *Walker Lake* decision, the State Engineer has acted affirmatively to conserve trust resources, even approving water management plans that depart from the classic operation of the prior appropriation doctrine by requiring *all* rights holders in a designated critical management area to reduce groundwater withdrawals.[225] When such plans were drafted for the Diamond Valley basin of central Nevada, the Supreme Court of Nevada upheld them against subsequent challenge.[226] The State Engineer also acted to prohibit the drilling of new domestic wells in the Pahrump Artesian Basin near Death Valley, a decision also upheld by the Nevada Supreme Court.[227]

Nor are the *Walker Lake* plaintiffs fully precluded from taking further litigation to protect trust resources in the Walker Lake basin. The Ninth Circuit has indicated that it would not run afoul of the *Walker Lake* decision for plaintiffs to pursue legal remedies that would not disturb established prior appropriations of basin water rights.[228] Protecting threatened trust resources remains a tall order in a state as dry as Nevada, but the parts of the *Walker Lake* decision that reinforce the breadth of state obligations under the public trust doctrine may ultimately provide greater legal and political cover for such moves than had been available beforehand.

These fascinating doctrinal developments from Nevada highlight the ongoing debate in the western United States about the nature of the public trust doctrine and its relationship to the prior appropriations doctrine in the administration of water resources. The *Walker Lake* decision received criticism from neutral commentators for failing to clarify the law (and perhaps even muddying it with new sources of uncertainty),[229] but it reveals an effort by the highest jurists in the state

---

[225] See Diamond Nat. Res. Prot. & Conservation Ass'n v. Diamond Valley Ranch, LLC, 511 P.3d 1003 (Nev. 2022) (describing the State Engineer's challenged Diamond Valley plan).

[226] See id. (holding that the state legislature enacted NRS 534.037 and NRS 534.110(7) specifically to respond to water shortages, and that those statutes unambiguously allow the State Engineer to approve groundwater management plans that do not comport with the doctrine of prior appropriation).

[227] See Wilson v. Pahrump Fair Water, LLC, 481 P.3d 853 (Nev. 2021). The court held that notice and hearing were not required because water is a public resource and "a landowner's unilateral assumptions" that there is enough water "are not the sort of justified reliance that would demand a notice and hearing." Id. at 854.

[228] See Mono Cnty. v. Walker River Irrigation Dist., 2022 WL 314993 (D. Nev. 2022); Michael C. Blumm, *Walker Lake and the Public Trust in Nevada's Waters*, 40 Va. Env't L.J. 1 (2022) (briefly describing recent proceedings in the *Walker River Irrigation District* litigation and listing some of the twenty-four remedies sought by plaintiffs).

[229] Roerink, *supra* note 205 (noting that "the State Supreme Court's majority opinion has left considerable uncertainty for communities and more paperwork for water attorneys").

to bridge the deep cleavages between opposing views on how to allocate the scarce water resources of this dry desert state. The court's ruling confirmed the constitutive nature of the public trust doctrine and its foundational role in the state's water management system, but it also disempowered the doctrine by holding it subsumed into statutory allocation laws on a shaky presumption that all prior allocations were made faithfully to the state's trust obligations.

That presumption has resulted, at least in some instances, in a maintenance of the status quo. While the State Engineer has undertaken new plans for acute regional shortages, the Nevada State Water Plan has not been updated since March 1999.[230] And there appears to be no impetus to update it any time soon, because the *Walker Lake* decision implies that existing water regulations already represent an adequate consideration of the state's public trust obligations. In this regard, the Nevada approach seems to occupy a mushy midpoint between the warmer embrace of the doctrine in California and the colder renunciation of its force in Idaho.

The *Walker Lake* decision highlights the challenges of navigating the conflicting values in these cases – the environmental values that the California Supreme Court defended at Mono Lake; the economic interests that the legislature championed in Idaho; and the issues of finality, state obligations, and separation of powers with which the members of the Nevada Supreme Court so passionately wrestled. As the majority warned, securing finality in the assignment of rights is a critical value in implementing a regulatory system founded on scarcity, like the prior appropriations doctrine.[231] And yet, as the dissent intoned, "it cannot be that this state's affirmative fiduciary obligations over certain water sources – obligations supervised by the judiciary and founded on a century of common law, inherent sovereign authority, and the state constitution – are entirely subsumed by a handful of statutes governing the specific duties of an administrative agent."[232]

Each of the cases from these three states distills the conflict set in motion by the independent development of these two separate aspects of water law: the public trust doctrine's affirmation of public rights in waterways and the prior appropriations doctrine's affirmation of private rights to use of the water in those waterways.[233] Writ large, these stories also represent the conflict between environmental protection and

---

[230] *See* NEVADA STATE WATER PLAN, NEV. DIV. OF WATER PLAN. (1999), https://water.nv.gov/uploads/library-docs/SWP_Part_3.pdf.
[231] *Walker Lake*, 473 P.3d 418, 431 (Nev. 2020).
[232] *Id.* at 435.
[233] *See* Stevens, *supra* note 6, at 612–614 (discussing the relationship between the public trust and prior appropriations doctrines); Timothy J. Conway, National Audubon Society v. Superior Court: *The Expanding Public Trust Doctrine*, 14 ENV'T L. 617, 630–33 (1984) (analyzing the state court's reconciliation of the public trust and prior appropriations doctrines in *Mono Lake*); Craig A. Arnold & Leigh A. Jewel, *Litigation's Bounded Effectiveness and the Real Public Trust Doctrine: The Aftermath of the Mono Lake Case*, 14 HASTINGS W.-NW. J. ENV'T L. & POL'Y 1177, 1188–95 (2008) (same).

C. Ordinary Common Law or Quasi-Constitutional?

economic development.[234] And the clash between biocentric and anthropocentric environmental ethics, raised by the conflict between in-basin environmental values and the utilitarian needs of vast urban publics in distant places, and agricultural enterprises that feed the nation.[235] And doubtlessly others as well. These stories show how these two doctrines continue to create legal friction – but perhaps necessary friction, as we continue to struggle toward the uneasy, perhaps constantly shifting equipoise between legitimately conflicting values.

---

[234] See Gray, *supra* note 6, at 974 (discussing *Nat'l Audubon Soc'y*'s establishment of an environmental baseline in the management of public resources that exists in tension with continuing "economic and political pressures to expand existing water projects or to develop new sources").

[235] Cynthia L. Koehler, *Water Rights and the Public Trust Doctrine: Resolution of the Mono Lake Controversy*, 22 ECOLOGY L.Q. 541, 577–82 (1995) (discussing competing interests in the Water Board's reallocation decision-making process following the *Nat'l Audubon Soc'y* decision).

8

Beyond Mono Lake

The Development of the Public Trust across the United States

A.	The Planes of Public Trust Development across the United States	239
	1. Vindicating Public Trust Principles through Different Forms of Law	240
	a. Common Law Trusts	240
	b. Statutory Trusts	241
	c. Constitutional Trusts	245
	d. Executive Trusts	250
	e. Multiplatform Trusts	252
	2. Different Resources Protected by the Doctrine	253
	a. Waterways	254
	b. Beyond Water	255
	c. More Limited Application	257
	3. Different Values Protected by the Doctrine	259
	4. Different Legal Theories about the Nature of the Doctrine	261
	5. Different Public Trust Remedies	264
B.	The Public Trust in Federal Law	267
	1. The Doctrine as a Background Principle in Federal Takings Claims	268
	2. The Secret Supreme Court Public Trust Debate	272
	3. A Constitutive Constraint on Federal Authority?	274
	4. Stronger than Federal Law?	279

The *Mono Lake* case was followed by a surge of interest across the United States in use of the public trust doctrine as a tool of environmental advocacy – and in some jurisdictions, as a statement of environmental rights. Yet appeals to the doctrine have gone far beyond its role in litigation, and far beyond its American roots in water. While the *Mono Lake* case inspired many other environmental advocates to deploy the public trust principles as a sword in litigation against the state (and as discussed below in Part B, some states deploy them as a shield to defend their protection of public trust values against takings litigation), public trust principles have become just as important – and just as entrenched – in forward-looking environmental policy-making and implementation, preemptively ensuring that state action will be consistent with trust obligations.

Following Professor Sax's broad vision, advocates and policymakers sought to expand the application of public trust principles first to other water resources[1] and then to other critical public natural resource commons also subject to private expropriation.[2] In different jurisdictions, public trust principles have migrated from the common law to legislative and administrative realms.[3] States have constitutionalized various versions of the doctrine, some of which extend even broader protection to a wider array of trust resources than the original common law.[4] As noted, the doctrine has also become an increasingly important defense to Fifth Amendment takings claims targeting environmental and land use laws that protect public trust resources.[5] And as discussed further in Chapter 9, it has emerged at the center of

---

[1] See, e.g., Ralph W. Johnson, *Water Pollution and the Public Trust Doctrine*, 19 ENV'T L. 485, 486–88 (1989) (suggesting innovative application of the trust to nonpoint pollution sources left largely unregulated by the Clean Water Act); Danielle Spiegel, *Can the Public Trust Doctrine Save Western Groundwater?*, 18 N.Y.U. ENV'T L.J. 412, 414 (2010) (analyzing the public trust's extension to groundwater and concluding that western states where depletion is most problematic are least likely to do so); Carol N. Brown, *Drinking from a Deep Well: The Public Trust Doctrine and Western Water Law*, 34 FLA. ST. U. L. REV. 1, 2 (2006) (advocating for expansion of public trust doctrine to preempt prior appropriations in western states where water scarcity issues loom); Sam Brandao, *Louisiana's Mono Lake: The Public Trust Doctrine and Oil Company Liability for Louisiana's Vanishing Wetlands*, 86 TUL. L. REV. 759, 761–62 (2012) (comparing Louisiana's public trust doctrine to that of California following *Mono Lake* and arguing for its expansion to better protect Louisiana's coastal wetlands).

[2] See, e.g., Michael C. Blumm & Aurora Paulsen, *The Public Trust in Wildlife*, 2013 UTAH L. REV. 1437, 1440–41 (2013) (arguing that the public trust should be integrated into state wildlife protection law); Alexandra B. Klass, *Renewable Energy and the Public Trust Doctrine*, 45 U.C. DAVIS L. REV. 1021, 1026 (2012) (considering use of the doctrine within the field of renewable energy law); Robin K. Craig, *Adapting to Climate Change: The Potential Role of State Common-Law Public Trust Doctrines*, 34 VT. L. REV. 781, 781 (2010) (arguing that the doctrine could provide "legal support for adaptive management-based climate change adaptation regimes"); David D. Caron, *Time and the Public Trust Doctrine: Law's Knowledge of Climate Change*, 35 U. HAW. L. REV. 441, 442–43 (2013) (advocating that the doctrine be used to prevent sea level rise in the context of climate change).

[3] See, e.g., Ronald B. Robie, *Effective Implementation of the Public Trust Doctrine in California Water Resources Decision-Making: A View from the Bench*, 45 U.C. DAVIS L. REV. 1155, 1157 (2012) (reflecting on the impact of the case thirty years later and concluding that protection of the public trust should primarily rest with administrative actors); Dave Owen, *The Mono Lake Case, the Public Trust Doctrine, and the Administrative State*, 45 U.C. DAVIS L. REV. 1099, 1104–05 (2012) (considering the administrative ramifications of the case and its impacts on the California water board).

[4] See infra notes 58–68 and accompanying text (discussing state constitutional trusts); William D. Araiza, *Democracy, Distrust, and the Public Trust: Process-Based Constitutional Theory, the Public Trust Doctrine, and the Search for a Substantive Environmental Value*, 45 UCLA L. REV. 385, 394–95 (1997) (noting that many state constitutions have developed a conception of the public trust that is based on a more substantive commitment to preservation than most common law analogues); Jeffrey S. Silvyn, *Protecting Public Trust Values in California's Waters: The Constitutional Alternative*, 10 UCLA J. ENV'T L. & POL'Y 355, 356–57, 373 (1992) (comparing California's common law and constitutional public trust rights and concluding that the latter is more expansive).

[5] See infra Part (B)(1) ("The PTD as a Background Principle in Takings Litigation").

innovative climate advocacy seeking to extend public trust protection to the atmospheric commons.[6]

This chapter reviews the ongoing development of the public trust doctrine around the United States, focusing on the multiple paths of legal evolution it has followed in different state jurisdictions. In the years that have followed both the *Illinois Central* and *Mono Lake* cases, the doctrine has undergone remarkable differentiation along a number of common legal planes: the different forms of law through which public trust principles operate in different states, the different resources protected by the doctrine, the different values vindicated by the doctrine, and, as noted in Chapter 7, even different legal theories about the nature of the doctrine itself.

The array of doctrinal expressions across the country reveals there is no such thing as "the American public trust doctrine," only a tapestry of related but divergent implementations of the public trust principles at the core of the doctrine – that of state obligations for commons resources to be managed for the benefit of the public, and in most cases, public rights to hold the state to account for these obligations. In different states, the doctrine functions more as a vehicle for environmental protection and even a statement of environmental rights, especially in states that have constitutionalized public trust principles. In others, it functions more as a traditional constraint on sovereign ownership. With so much diversity, this chapter does not recapitulate scholarship cataloging doctrinal variation in every state.[7] Instead, the first half of the chapter traces the jurisdictional differentiation of the doctrine across the United States by focusing on the different legal planes along which it tends to vary – operation, resources, values, and theory – featuring snapshots from different regional states representing about a quarter of the nation. As Chapter 10 observes at the global level, the public trust is not a monolith; instead, it is a mosaic of these independent expressions of public trust principles.

The second half of the chapter considers the contested intersection between the public trust doctrine and federal law. While scholars and jurists continue to debate the existence of a federal public trust, the doctrine is increasingly recognized as a background principle of state property law for the purposes of federal takings

---

[6] See Chapter 9(B)(2) ("The Atmospheric Trust Project in U.S. Law").
[7] See, e.g., Robin K. Craig, *A Comparative Guide to the Eastern Public Trust Doctrines: Classifications of States, Property Rights, and State Summaries*, 16 PA. ST. ENV'T L. REV. 1 (2007) (comparing eastern states' public trust doctrines); Robin Kundis Craig, *A Comparative Guide to the Western States' Public Trust Doctrines: Public Values, Private Right, and the Evolution Toward an Ecological Public Trust*, 37 ECOLOGY L.Q. 53 (2010) (comparing western states' public trust doctrines) [hereinafter Comparative Western]; THE PUBLIC TRUST DOCTRINE IN FORTY-FIVE STATES (Michael C. Blumm et al., 2014), https://papers.ssrn.com/sol3/papers.cfm?abstract_id=2235329 (hereinafter "FORTY-FIVE STATES") (analyzing the public trust doctrines of 45 states); CTR. FOR PROGRESSIVE REFORM, RESTORING THE TRUST: AN INDEX OF STATE CONSTITUTIONAL AND STATUTORY PROVISIONS AND CASES ON WATER RESOURCES AND THE PUBLIC TRUST DOCTRINE (2009), https://progressivereform.org/publications/cpr-public-trust-doctrine-manual/.

litigation under the Fifth Amendment. The chapter recounts a little-known chapter of Supreme Court history, in which the justices negotiated *not* to address the public trust as a matter of federal law in one of its most influential takings decisions involving coastal wetlands, *Lucas v. South Carolina Coastal Council*.[8] While the Court has since referred to the trust as a doctrine of state law in dicta,[9] whether trust obligations should apply to federal decision-making remains an unsettled debate in the literature.

A. THE PLANES OF PUBLIC TRUST DEVELOPMENT ACROSS THE UNITED STATES

In the century-plus since *Illinois Central* was decided and the near-half-century since *Mono Lake*, the American public trust doctrine has developed and differentiated among the states, with different versions protecting different resources and values through different legal mechanisms, some even with different theories about the nature of the trust.[10] Some states apply the doctrine to only waterways, while others expand the resources protected by the trust to include groundwater, wildlife, beach access, other natural and cultural resources, and even atmospheric resources. Different trust values are protected in different states, some of which protect only the traditional fishing, swimming, and navigational values, while others add protection for the environmental, recreational, and cultural values of trust resources. In some states, the doctrine primarily operates through common law, while others have incorporated public trust principles into state statutory, regulatory, and constitutional law. In some states, especially those that have constitutionalized public trust principles, such as Pennsylvania and Hawaii, the doctrine serves as a veritable guarantor of environmental rights – while in others, such as the Idaho example reviewed in Chapter 7, the doctrine has been legislatively curtailed.

Given so much variety, the public trust doctrine is something of a genus from which countless differentiated species have evolved, though all from the same common law ancestor. This part reviews the different planes along which the trust has developed in different states, and, in so doing, provides brief snapshots of different jurisdictional versions of modern doctrine in roughly a third of the states: California, Colorado, Florida, Hawaii, Idaho, Louisiana, Massachusetts, Michigan, Minnesota,

---

[8] Lucas v. S.C. Coastal Council, 304 S.C. 376, 377 n.1 (1991), *rev'd*, 503 U.S. 1003 (1992); *see also infra* Part (B)(2) ("The Secret Supreme Court Public Trust Debate").
[9] PPL Mont., LLC v. Montana, 565 U.S. 576, 603 (2012). For fuller discussion, see *infra* text accompanying notes 274–76.
[10] *See, e.g.*, ALEXANDRA B. KLASS & LING-YEE HUANG, RESTORING THE TRUST: WATER RESOURCES AND THE PUBLIC TRUST DOCTRINE, A MANUAL FOR ADVOCATES 21–24 (2009), www.papers.ssrn.com/sol3/papers.cfm?abstract_id=1477556 (comparing the sources of various states' public trust doctrines and describing the differentiation of the public trust doctrine along constitutional and statutory lines).

New Hampshire, New Jersey, Nevada, Pennsylvania, Rhode Island, Oregon, South Carolina, Washington, and Wisconsin.

1. *Vindicating Public Trust Principles through Different Forms of Law*

The public trust doctrine operates through a variety of different legal mechanisms among the American states. The common law doctrine is the undeniable progenitor of public trust principles in the United States, as recognized by the U.S. Supreme Court in such cases as *Pollard v. Hagan, Illinois Central,* and *Shively v. Bowlby*.[11] Since then, however, public trust principles have been adopted in various state statutes and even ratified in state constitutions, sometimes working alongside the original common law doctrines and sometimes displacing them.[12] Perhaps for this reason more than any other, there is no single public trust doctrine in the United States. Many have evolved and continue to develop along entirely different lines of legal evolution, through these different mechanisms of law.

a. Common Law Trusts

Today, very few states operate from a purely common law trust unaccompanied by additional statutory, regulatory, or constitutional directives or counterparts, but the common law plays a relatively more important role in some than in others. Massachusetts, for example, maintains a fairly traditional common law doctrine, protecting traditional values of navigation, fishing, and swimming, mostly through judicial enforcement and elaboration.[13] Massachusetts courts have steadfastly enforced historic *jus publicum* encumbrances for public navigation and fishing.[14] The political branches are statutorily authorized to enforce public access to trust resources, but their performance remains subject to public oversight through the judicial system.[15] The state's highest court has held that the legislature must act as a "fiduciary for the public"[16] to ensure that public trust encumbrances on submerged lands remain acknowledged and open for use for designated trust

---

[11] *See* Shively v. Bowlby, 152 U.S. 1, 53–54 (1894); Ill. Cent. R.R. Co. v. Illinois, 146 U.S. 387 (1892); Pollard v. Hagan, 44 U.S. 212 (1845).

[12] *See* Alexandra B. Klass, *Modern Public Trust Principles: Recognizing Rights and Integrating Standards*, 82 NOTRE DAME L. REV. 699, 714 (2006).

[13] Butler v. Att'y Gen., 80 N.E. 688, 689 (Mass. 1907) ("In the seashore the entire property, under the colonial ordinance, is in the individual, subject to the public rights ... of navigation, with such incidental rights as pertain thereto. We think that there is a right to swim or float in or upon public waters as well as to sail upon them."); Commonwealth v. Alger, 61 Mass. 53, 91–93 (1851).

[14] Arno v. Commonwealth, 931 N.E.2d 1, 16–18 (Mass. 2010) (holding registration of certificate of title proceedings could not divest the public of its rights in tidelands).

[15] *Alger*, 61 Mass. at 91–93.

[16] *Arno*, 931 N.E.2d at 14 (holding registration of certificate of title proceedings could not divest the public of its rights in tidelands).

purposes.[17] The legislature has statutorily delegated much of its public trust authority to state administrative agencies, but these decisions remain subject to judicial review.[18] Even legislative determinations regarding public trust grants, uses, and purposes are reviewable by the Massachusetts courts.[19]

b. Statutory Trusts

In other states, public trust principles have been formally codified, shifting vindication of trust ideals from the common law to the constitution and the statutes it authorizes. The neighboring states of Michigan and Minnesota provide compellingly different examples of how statutory trusts independent of constitutionalized provisions can work. Notably, both sets of laws owe a direct debt to Professor Joseph Sax, the progenitor of the modern public trust movement, whose 1970 law review article, *The Public Trust Doctrine in Natural Resource Law: Effective Judicial Intervention*,[20] inspired the plaintiffs to bring the 1983 *Mono Lake* case itself. And just as Sax was inspiring the judicial application of public trust principles to protect the environment, he was also busily inspiring their legislative application.

In 1968, Joe Sax was a law professor at the University of Minnesota and Joan Wolfe was the leader of the West Michigan Environmental Action Council, a local environmental group trying to stop the U.S. Departure of Agriculture from spreading DDT, a toxic chemical used for pest control.[21] When Wolfe's group sued the Department, the federal district court dismissed the case because federal law did not

---

[17] Bos. Waterfront Dev. Corp. v. Commonwealth, 393 N.E.2d 356, 358–59, 367 (Mass. 1979) ("We therefore hold that the [Boston Waterfront Development Corporation] has title to its property in fee simple, but subject to the condition subsequent that it be used for the public purpose for which it was granted." This was a rejection of the longstanding precedent that the legislature possessed the power to convent submerged land free from the public trust because the *jus publicum*, the *jus privatum*, and all of Parliament's rights of regulation had devolved upon the state at the time of the Revolution.); *accord* United States v. 1.58 Acres of Land, 523 F. Supp. 120, 124–25 (D. Mass. 1981) (holding that the United States could take property below low-water mark in "full fee simple," however, the federal government was restricted in its ability to abdicate to private individuals its sovereign public trust in land). *But see* Op. of the Justs. to the Senate, 424 N.E.2d 1092, 1100, 1107 (Mass. 1981) (upholding, as a general proposition, the legislature's power to free land from the public trust and stated the two-thirds voting requirement applies to the disposition of all lands and easements taken or acquired for the stated purposes, regardless of when they were taken or acquired).

[18] Op. of the Justs. to the Senate, 424 N.E.2d at 1105.

[19] *Id.* at 1101 ("The question whether a particular legislative act, or an administrative decision pursuant to statutory authorization, serves a public purpose is for the Legislature to determine, and, although that legislative determination is entitled to great deference, it is not wholly beyond judicial scrutiny"); FORTY-FIVE STATES, *supra* note 7, at 364.

[20] *See generally* Joseph Sax, *The Public Trust Doctrine in Natural Resource Law: Effective Judicial Intervention*, 68 MICH. L. REV. 471 (1970).

[21] Jim Olson, *The MEPA Turns 50: Honoring the Michigan Environmental Protection Act of 1970, The World's First Environmental Citizen Suit Law*, FOR LOVE OF WATER BLOG (July 29, 2020), www.forloveofwater.org/the-mepa-turns-50/.

provide a means for them to contest the agency's use of pesticides.[22] Wolfe then read Sax's seminal article on the public trust doctrine and reached out to him to ask if the environmental rights Sax was writing about – especially the right to sue to prevent the degradation of the state's air, water, and natural resources – could be written into law.[23] In response, Sax drafted a model law stating that "any person could bring an action in court to protect the air, water, and natural resources or the public trust therein" from "likely pollution, impairment, or destruction."[24] The model law Sax drafted became the basis for the Michigan Environmental Protection Act of 1970, which itself was the model for similar laws in other states, including the Minnesota Environmental Rights Act of 1971.[25]

In 1970, the Michigan Environmental Protection Act (MEPA) was enacted, authorizing individuals and others to sue both government entities and private individuals "for the protection of the air, water, and other natural resources and the public trust therein, from pollution, impairment, or destruction."[26] The following year, Minnesota enacted its own Environmental Rights Act (MERA), which created a "civil remedy to protect air, water, land and other natural resources located within the state from pollution, impairment, or destruction" by establishing that "each person is entitled by right to the protection, preservation, and enhancement of air, water, land, and other natural resources located within the state and that each person has the responsibility to contribute to the protection, preservation, and enhancement thereof."[27] Two decades later, MEPA was replaced by the Natural Resources and Environmental Protection Act of 1994,[28] which incorporated much of the former statute and retained its public trust language.[29] However, the scope of statutorily conferred standing to bring public trust claims under the new law remains contested.[30]

---

[22] Id.
[23] Give Earth a Chance Team, *In Focus: Joe Sax*, MICHIGAN IN THE WORLD, www.michiganintheworld.history.lsa.umich.edu/environmentalism/exhibits/show/main_exhibit/1970s_activism/mepa/in-focus–joseph-sax.
[24] Id.
[25] Olson, *supra* note 21.
[26] MICH. COMP. LAWS ANN. § 691.1202(1) (repealed and replaced by MICH. STAT. ANN. § 324.1071(1).).
[27] MINN. STAT. § 116B.01.
[28] Natural Resources and Environmental Protection Act [NREPA], 1994 Mich. Pub. Acts 451.
[29] MICH. COMP. LAWS ANN. § 691.1202 (West) (indicating where the repealed features of MEPA can be found in the new statute).
[30] Michigan Citizens for Water Conservation v. Nestle Waters N. Am. Inc., 709 N.W.2d 174, 212 (Mich. Ct. App. 2005), aff'd in part, rev'd in part, 737 N.W.2d 447 (Mich. 2007) (in a public trust suit to enjoin water withdrawals by the Nestle corporation, holding that "to the extent that it confers standing broader than the limits imposed by Michigan's constitution [NREPA] is unconstitutional"). The court explained that standing doctrine in the Michigan courts is parallel to the federal doctrine in requiring "proper exercise of the judicial power and the separation of powers mandated by Michigan's constitution." Id. at 210 (citing Lee v. Macomb Co. Bd. of Comm'rs, 629 N.W.2d 900 [Mich. 2001]). That 2005 decision was restated in a later case and used to support a holding that invalidated statutorily conveyed standing in other Michigan statutes. Michigan Educ. Ass'n v. Superintendent of Pub. Instruction, 724 N.W.2d 478, 484 (Mich. Ct. App. 2006). However, a later case recognized *Michigan*

A. The Planes of Public Trust Development

MERA was modeled after MEPA but showcases important differences. For example, MERA exempts actions by state environmental or natural resource agencies from scrutiny,[31] while MEPA authorized plaintiffs to seek de novo judicial review of all agency actions alleged to have violated statutory obligations, even before exhausting all administrative remedies.[32] The Michigan law therefore created a far broader remedy for plaintiffs, involving much more sweeping judicial oversight of agency activity – even environmental agencies. In that regard, MEPA may have more accurately reflected Sax's vision of enabling judicial intervention on behalf of the environment when the state allegedly fails its public trust obligations – even, and perhaps especially, the parts of the state charged with overseeing natural resource management. Even so, ongoing controversy over the constitutionality of public trust standing under MEPA and its successor raises questions about the potential pitfalls of shifting too much power from political branches to the judiciary,[33] and whether MERA's enduring approach has achieved a more effective balance.

Yet MERA's statutory trust may have also weakened the potency of public trust principles in Minnesota for a wholly different, perhaps less obvious reason. After public trust principles that once existed only in the common law had been codified into state statutes, those statutes quickly become the far more salient avenue for the protection of public trust values in that state. Today, the Minnesota public trust doctrine relies largely on this statutory basis, with indirect constitutional support.[34] As these became the dominant source of protection for state natural resources, the development of the common law trust appears to have languished.[35] And the

---

Educ. Ass'n as overruled by implication of the Michigan Supreme Court when its overruled *Lee v. Macomb Co.* and its progeny, explaining that the narrow standing doctrine adopted in *Lee* "lacks a basis in the Michigan Constitution and is inconsistent with Michigan's historical approach to standing" and that state standing jurisprudence must be restored to be "consistent with Michigan's long-standing historical approach to standing." Council of Organizations & Others for Educ. About Parochiaid v. State, 931 N.W.2d 65, 72–73 (Mich. Ct. App. 2018) (quoting Lansing Sch. Educ. Ass'n v. Lansing Bd. of Educ., 792 N.W.2d 686 [2010]). Based on this ruling, it seems that statutorily conferred public trust standing is not unconstitutional *per se*, but limitations that may exist under state law remain unclear.

[31] MINN. STAT. § 116B.03(1). (exempting action undertaken "pursuant to any environmental quality standard, limitation, rule, order, license, stipulation agreement or permit" issued by listed state agencies, including the Pollution Control Agency and Department of Natural Resources).

[32] MICH. STAT. § 324.1704(2); *see also* § 16:53. Environmental Protection Acts, 2 State Environmental L.§ 16:53 (2023) (discussing this provision).

[33] For further discussion of the separation of powers critiques of the public trust doctrine, see Chapter 7(A)(2) ("The Legal Process Critique") and Chapter 11(B)(4) ("Separation of Powers and the Antidemocratic Critique").

[34] *See* MINN. CONST. art. II, § 2; MINN. STAT. ANN. § 116B.01-.13 (1986); MINN. STAT. ANN. § 116D.01-.11 (1986). Alexandra B. Klass, *The Public Trust Doctrine in the Shadow of State Environmental Rights Laws: A Case Study*, 45 ENV'T L. 431, 433–34 (2015).

[35] *See* Klass, *The Public Trust Doctrine in the Shadow of State Environmental Rights Laws*, *supra* note 34, at 457–59 (exploring how environmental rights statutes can effectively displace the common law public trust doctrine and limit its evolution as a tool for environmental protection); *see also* Klass,

common law trust, with its ability to gradually evolve over time to meet changing societal needs, may prove the more important vindicator of public trust principles.

Indeed, Professor Alexandra Klass has warned that overreliance on a statutory trust could displace more the flexible common law version of the doctrine, undermining the further development of public trust principles to respond to emerging problems through traditional common law processes.[36] An inadvertent result could be the calcification of the common law public trust, effectively freezing it in time by stifling the organic process of common law development that has thus far enabled the doctrine in other states to continue to evolve with the changing needs of the community.[37] In her research on the statutory codification of the public trust doctrine, Professor Klass specifically notes a dearth of Minnesota case law applying public trust principles, at least in comparison to states with stronger common law doctrines, signifying fewer opportunities for the common law trust to develop, and perhaps weakening the common law as a means of future protection if statutory protections are withdrawn or amended.[38]

Marking a different path from both Michigan and Minnesota, some states have more purposefully and forcefully limited the common law development of public trust principles through statutory law. As discussed in more fully in Chapter 7, Idaho's public trust doctrine exists in both common law and statutory law, without a clear presence in the constitution.[39] In direct response to rulings by the state supreme court suggesting that it might follow the California Supreme Court's interpretation of the doctrine in the Mono Lake decision, the Idaho legislature statutorily confined the doctrine to state ownership of submerged lands, limiting any further judicial elaboration.[40] Meanwhile, the Nevada public trust doctrine also appears in both common law and state statute.[41] Although it does not appear directly in the Nevada Constitution, the Nevada Supreme Court has interpreted the common law doctrine as an implied constitutional limit on sovereign authority, following the California model.[42] However, in response to litigation to protect Walker Lake (premised on the

---

Modern Public Trust Principles, supra note 12 at 721–26 (noting that Minnesota environmental statutes have channeled litigation into statutory claims instead of common law public trust doctrine claims).

[36] See Klass, *Modern Public Trust Principles*, supra note 12, at 726, 744–45 (discussing the limitations of both common law and statutory approaches to public trust governance and proposing an integrated approach).

[37] Klass, *The Public Trust Doctrine in the Shadow of State Environmental Rights Laws*, supra note 34, at 457–59.

[38] *Id.*

[39] See Chapter 7(C)(2) ("Idaho: Legislative Repudiation of the Constitutive Constraint"). *See also infra* footnotes 181–88 and accompanying text (discussing Idaho's statutory move in more detail).

[40] *Id.*

[41] Lawrence v. Clark Cnty., 254 P.3d 606, 612–14 (Nev. 2011) (citing State v. Bunkowski, 503 P.2d 1231, 1234 [Nev. 1972]); Nev. Rev. Stat. § 533.025 (1913) ("The water of all sources of water supply within the boundaries of the State whether above or beneath the surface of the ground, belongs to the public.").

[42] See Mineral Cnty. v. Lyon Cnty., 473 P.3d 418, 423–26 (Nev. 2020); *see also* Chapter 7(C)(3) ("Nevada: Mixed Messages in the Walker Lake Basin") (discussing recent developments in Nevada); *Lawrence*,

advocacy to save nearby Mono Lake), the court held that the state's administration of statutory water rights permits included sufficient consideration of the public interest to satisfy its obligations under the public trust doctrine – even though most had been granted before the state had recognized its public trust obligations – effectively preempting further common law development by indirect statutory means.[43]

c. Constitutional Trusts

In other states, the public trust doctrine has been elevated directly to the state constitution. Some constitutionalized versions look very similar to the common law statement of the public trust doctrine affirmed in *Illinois Central*. For example, Florida's Constitution includes a provision that recognizes public ownership of critical water commons and confers traditional protections for all submerged lands beneath navigable waters:

> The title to lands under navigable waters, within the boundaries of the state, which have not been alienated, including beaches below mean high water lines, is held by the state, by virtue of its sovereignty, in trust for all the people.[44]

Although Florida applies a generally conventional version of the common law trust, the state has modestly extended the doctrine by applying it not only to wet sand beaches below the mean high water line but also to "renourished" dry sand beaches hemmed in by the former high water line.[45] Beach renourishment is a strategy to combat coastal erosion by supplementing the dry sand portion of the beach seaward of the mean high water line with dredged sand, sustaining the beach against the forces of wave action and rising sea levels.[46] Under Florida law, beach renourishment does not change the boundary between public and private land, even though the renourished part will no longer be submerged (at least until it is eventually reclaimed). The Florida public trust has also been codified in the state's water allocation statute, now included as an element of the state's "public interest" criterion for water agency approval of permitted uses.[47]

Constitutionalization in other states has further broadened the scope and effect of the trust, sometimes far beyond the conventional *Illinois Central* version. For example, Article XI of the Hawaii Constitution declares that the state holds all of its

---

254 P.3d at 612 (interpreting the gift clause of the state constitution to constrain legislative alienation of trust lands).
[43] *Id. See also* text accompanying notes 189–190, *infra*, (discussing Nevada's interpretation of this conflict).
[44] FLA. CONST. art. X § 11; *See also* Trepanier v. Cnty. of Volusia, 965 So. 2d 276, 284 (2007) (affirming that the common law public trust doctrine is encoded in the Florida constitution).
[45] Walton Cnty. v. Stop the Beach Renourishment, Inc., 998 So. 2d 1102 (2008).
[46] *Stop the Beach Renourishment*, 998 So. 2d at 1106.
[47] FLA. STAT. § 373.223 (2023).

natural resources in trust for the public, including (but not necessarily limited to) land, water, air, minerals, and energy sources:

> For the benefit of present and future generations, the State and its political subdivisions shall conserve and protect Hawaii's natural beauty and all natural resources, including land, water, air, minerals and energy sources, and shall promote the development and utilization of these resources in a manner consistent with their conservation and in furtherance of the self-sufficiency of the State. All public natural resources are held in trust by the State for the benefit of the people.[48]

Codified in both the state constitution and state statutes, the Hawaiian public trust doctrine is widely considered to confer the strongest and broadest public trust protections for waterways of any U.S. state.[49] Like the California Supreme Court in the *Mono Lake* case,[50] the Hawaii Supreme Court has established that its public trust doctrine is not displaced by the statutory law of private water allocation.[51] However, it goes even further than California's public trust doctrine, and far further than the traditional *Illinois Central* version, in holding that all water resources – and not just navigable waterways – are protected by the doctrine.[52]

The Hawaii constitution burdens the state with an affirmative duty to protect the state's water resources for the benefit of the people,[53] and the state supreme court has specified that this duty requires the affirmative protection of the environmental values of state waters, including flow and purity, for the benefit of future generations.[54] In statute, Hawaii adds protection for "traditional and customary Hawaiian rights ... procreation of fish and wildlife, the maintenance of proper ecological balance and scenic beauty, and the preservation and enhancement of waters of the State for municipal uses, public recreation, public water supply, agriculture, and navigation."[55] Hawaii defines the "waters of the State" as "any and all water on or beneath the surface of the ground,"[56] and applicants for permits to use that water must demonstrate that the proposed use is consistent with the public interest.[57]

The Pennsylvania Constitution reveals a similarly expansive conception of the public trust, though in a much more contested political context. In 1971, Article 1 of

---

[48] Haw. Const. art. XI, § 1.
[49] Craig, *Comparative Western*, supra note 7, at 86, 88 (describing California and Hawaii as the states with the most robust public trust doctrines, but distinguishing Hawaii on the basis of its incorporation of two separate public trust doctrines – a navigable waters public trust and a water resources public trust – into its state constitution).
[50] Nat'l Audubon Soc'y v. Super. Ct., 658 P.2d 709, 712, 727–28 (Cal. 1983).
[51] *In re* Water Use Permit Applications (*Waiahole Ditch*), 9 P.3d 409, 445 (Haw. 2000) (holding that the state water code "does not supplant the protections of the public trust doctrine").
[52] *Id.* ("[T]he public trust doctrine applies to all water resources without exception or distinction").
[53] Haw. Const. art. XI, § 1.
[54] *See* Robinson v. Ariyoshi, 658 P.2d 287, 310 (Haw. 1982) (holding that the public trust doctrine imposes on the state "a concomitant duty to maintain the purity and flow of our waters for future generations").
[55] Haw. Rev. Stat. Ann. § 174C-2(c) (1999).
[56] *Id.* at § 174C-3.
[57] *Id.* at § 174C-49(a)(4).

A. The Planes of Public Trust Development

the Pennsylvania Constitution was amended to add Section 27, also known as "the Environmental Rights Amendment," constitutionally adding "natural, scenic, historic, and esthetic values" to the body of the state's public trust resources:

> The people have a right to clean air, pure water, and to the preservation of the natural, scenic, historic and esthetic values of the environment. Pennsylvania's public natural resources are the common property of all the people, including generations yet to come. As trustee of these resources, the Commonwealth shall conserve and maintain them for the benefit of all the people.[58]

In contrast to the simple affirmation of public ownership of natural resources in Florida, the Hawaii and Pennsylvania doctrines establish a substantive commitment to protecting the environmental values associated with public trust resources, and they partner that commitment with an unequivocal ethic of intergenerational equity.

Demonstrating the power of this substantive commitment, the Pennsylvania Supreme Court famously invoked the Environmental Rights Amendment to overturn a state law preventing local governments from regulating horizontal shale drilling and hydraulic fracturing ("fracking") through their authority to regulate land use planning.[59] Fracking is commonly used to extract natural gas reserves from the rich Marcellus shale resources of the state, but the operation uses a high volume of water and can threaten local water resources with contamination and overuse. Based on their zoning ordinances, many state municipalities had disapproved fracking operations that they feared would negatively impact local water supplies – prompting the state legislature to enact a statute preempting the local regulation of fracking.[60] In 2013, in *Robinson Township v. Commonwealth*, plaintiffs challenged the legality of the statute on a number of grounds – although without reference to the state's common law public trust doctrine.[61]

In response, the Pennsylvania Supreme Court invoked the Environmental Rights Amendment to protect local authority to regulate activities that pose a threat to local water and natural resources, including fracking.[62] In the *Robinson Township* decision, a plurality invalidated the state statute preempting the local zoning of fracking,[63] concluding that it conflicted with the state's obligation under the Environmental Rights Amendment to protect present and future generations' interests in public

---

[58] PA. CONST. ART. I, § 27. *See also* John C. Dernbach & Edmund J. Sonnenberg, *A Legislative History of Article 1, Section 27 of the Constitution of the Commonwealth of Pennsylvania*, 24 WIDENER L.J. 181 (2015).

[59] John C. Dernbach, *The Potential Meanings of a Constitutional Public Trust*, 45 ENV'T L. 463, 478, 481 (2015).

[60] *Id.* at 481–82 (describing how the challenged state statute interfered with "local regulation of oil and gas operations" under various state environmental and land use laws).

[61] *See Robinson Twp.*, 83 A.3d 901 (Pa. 2013).

[62] *Id.* at 981–82. The decision also noted potential problems associated with increased truck traffic, well-spacing congestion, and other public health and safety concerns.

[63] *See id.* at 901, 913, 980 (holding unconstitutional parts of Pennsylvania's Oil and Gas Act prohibiting local government water and air quality protections, on the basis of Article I, Section 27 of Pennsylvania's constitution, which provides for the public trust doctrine).

natural resources.⁶⁴ Notably, the high court invoked the public trust principles of the Environmental Rights Amendment *sua sponte* (on its own) to resolve the case, even though the parties had not raised it in their arguments.⁶⁵ The decision marked a turning point for Pennsylvania's constitutionalized trust, which had never before been used to invalidate state law (and was not previously understood as self-executing).⁶⁶

The move sharpened attention to other forms of state action that might also threaten public natural resources in violation of its constitutionalized public trust doctrine. Three years later, a majority of the high court confirmed that Pennsylvania is obligated to manage its state parks and forests, including the oil and minerals therein, as a trustee in accordance with the public trust principles of the Environmental Rights Amendment.⁶⁷ The court reasoned that the clear language of the Amendment expressly affirms both the right of the people to enjoy these public natural resources and the Commonwealth's obligation to maintain them.⁶⁸

Of note, municipalities in other states have attempted to assert local control over fracking with less success, especially in states without similarly robust public trust protections. For example, when two Colorado municipalities banned fracking within local limits, two separate state courts held their ordinances were preempted by contrary state law.⁶⁹ As discussed further below, Colorado's public trust doctrine is far more limited than Pennsylvania's expansive trust.⁷⁰ Because Pennsylvania's

---

⁶⁴ *Id.* at 981 ("In our view, the framers and ratifiers of the Environmental Rights Amendment intended the constitutional provision as a bulwark against enactments, like Act 13, which permit development with such an immediate, disruptive effect upon how Pennsylvanians live their lives. To comply with the constitutional command, the General Assembly must exercise its police powers to foster sustainable development in a manner that respects the reserved rights of the people to a clean, healthy, and esthetically-pleasing environment"); *see also id.* at 919–20 (noting, in its standing analysis, that "a political subdivision has a substantial, direct, and immediate interest in protecting the environment and the quality of life within its borders" and that "[t]he protection of environmental and esthetic interests is an essential aspect of Pennsylvanians' quality of life and a key part of local government's role").

⁶⁵ *See, e.g.*, Dernbach, *supra* note 59, at 478, 481.

⁶⁶ *Id.*; *ee also infra* notes 58–68 and accompanying text (discussing Pennsylvania's amendment); *See also* John C. Dernbach & Robert B. McKinstry, Jr., *Agency Statutory Authority and the Pennsylvania Environmental Rights Amendment*, 37 GEORGETOWN ENV'T L. REV. 1 (2024) (arguing that agencies can and should implement Article I, Section 27 as part of the exercise of their statutory authority).

⁶⁷ Pa. Env't Def. Found. v. Commonwealth, 161 A.3d 911, 916 (Pa. 2017).

⁶⁸ *Id.* The case arose from a challenge to the use of oil and gas lease funds. In 2009, the Governor allowed some of the lease funds to be directed to a General Fund rather than to environmental preservation programs. Through a reading of the plain language of Article I, Section 27, the Court determined that the section imposes fiduciary duties on the Commonwealth that align with state trust law, controlling how Pennsylvania may use "any proceeds generated from the sale of its public natural resources." *Id.* In its opinion, the Court overturned the three-part legal test that was previously used to interpret the Amendment and clearly solidified the Commonwealth's role as a trustee of the public natural resources. *Id.* at 930.

⁶⁹ *See* Order Granting Summary Judgment, Colo. Oil & Gas Ass'n v. City of Longmont, No. 2013CV63, at 17 (Colo. Dist. Ct. July 24, 2014); *see also* Order Granting Summary Judgment, Colo. Oil & Gas Ass'n v. City of Fort Collins, No. 2013CV031385, at 7, 9 (Colo. Dist. Ct. Aug. 7, 2014).

⁷⁰ *Compare* CTR. FOR PROGRESSIVE REFORM, *supra* note 7, at 2, 7 nn. 37–41 (noting that Colorado's public trust doctrine is limited to issues pertaining to "waters of every natural stream") *with* Robinson

constitutionalized doctrine is so encompassing, the same model may not be easily replicated elsewhere. Nevertheless, the Pennsylvania experience has galvanized interest among environmental advocates from states with strong public trust doctrines in applying the doctrine to regulate oil and gas extraction with impacts on water resources.[71] Perhaps more significantly, it has inspired advocates in other states to seek to amend their state constitutions with similar provisions.

As detailed further in Chapter 9, a handful of other state constitutions have been amended with environmental rights provisions that reflect many of the same underlying principles in different configurations.[72] These include the Montana Constitution's promise that "[t]he state and each person shall maintain and improve a clean and healthful environment in Montana for present and future generations,"[73] and most recently, the New York Constitution's Green Amendment of 2022, which guarantees New Yorkers "a right to clean air and water, and a healthful environment."[74] Some of these constitutions frame these provisions as statements of sovereign responsibility (such as Florida's), some as statements of public environmental rights (as New York's does), and some as both (like Pennsylvania). Yet as analyzed further in Chapter 9, they all partner the fundamental public trust principles, either overtly or implicitly, of sovereign obligations to protect natural resources for the benefit of a rights-bearing public.[75]

Constitutionalized versions of the doctrine thus provide additional means of protecting public trust resources and expanded recognition for new public trust values beyond those traditionally protected at common law. Nevertheless, there is always the risk that fixing a specific version of the doctrine in this super-statutory form could inadvertently calcify the continued evolution of the common law doctrine that otherwise might continue. As noted,[76] scholars such as Professor Alexandra Klass have warned that overreliance on the statutory adoption of public trust principles could inadvertently displace more flexible common law versions of the doctrine,[77] and the same may be true in the constitutional context.

For example, early in Florida's history, the Florida Supreme Court had observed that the public trust doctrine protected the "use and enjoyment" of Florida's trust

---

Twp. v. Commonwealth, 83 A.3d 901 (recognizing that Pennsylvania's public trust doctrine applies more broadly to natural resources affected by oil and gas).

[71] See Ellen M. Gilmer, *Enviros Push 'Public Trust' as Trump Card over Oil and Gas Influence*, E&E ENERGYWIRE (Aug. 15, 2014), www.eenews.net/stories/1060004530 (noting that in Michigan, environmental attorneys assert that "even if the doctrine is limited to navigable water issues … it places a duty on government to consider how fracking and horizontal drilling could affect the water").

[72] See Chapter 9(C) ("Climate Claims on State Constitutional Grounds").
[73] MONT. CONST. art. IX, §1.
[74] N.Y. CONST. ART. I, § 19.
[75] See Chapter 9(C) ("Climate Claims on State Constitutional Grounds").
[76] See supra Part (A)(1)(b) ("Statutory Trusts").
[77] Klass, *The Public Trust Doctrine in the Shadow of State Environmental Rights Laws*, supra note 34, at 457–59; *see also* Klass, *Modern Public Trust Principles*, supra note 12, at 726, 744–45 (discussing the limitations of both common law and statutory approaches to public trust governance, and proposing an integrated approach).

resources for "navigation and fishing and other implied purposes."[78] Over time, those uses were expanded through conventional common law processes beyond navigation, commerce, and fishing to include swimming, wading, and sunbathing.[79] Public-trust-like principles are also included in the state's statutory "public interest" criterion for approving use of water resources.[80] More recently, the doctrine has been invoked as a defense to takings claims.[81] Since constitutional codification in 1968,[82] however, the development of the doctrine seems to have slowed. And as discussed in Chapter 7, some states, such as Idaho, have committed the public trust doctrine to statute specifically to prevent the further development of the doctrine through the judicial common law process.[83]

d. Executive Trusts

In addition to statutory trust mandates for executive agencies discussed in Part A(1)(b) (and in Chapter 7 Part B(1)(b) regarding the role of trust administration in California), the public trust doctrine has also been invoked directly by state executive actors. For example, in 2020, the governor of Michigan relied on the public trust doctrine in revoking a nearly seventy-year-old easement permitting submerged oil pipelines underneath the Straits of Mackinac in Lake Michigan to prevent a potentially catastrophic oil spill from frequent anchor strikes by passing commercial shipping traffic.[84] The Office of the Governor announced that "[t]he state is revoking the 1953 easement for violation of the public trust doctrine. This body of law recognizes the State of Michigan as the 'trustee' of the public's rights in the Great Lakes and lays upon the state legal obligations to protect those rights from any impairment."[85] In a statement,

---

[78] State v. Black River Phosphate Co., 13 So. 640, 648 (Fla. 1893).
[79] White v. Hughes, 190 So. 446, 448–51 (Fla. 1939); Adams v. Elliot, 174 So. 731, 734 (Fla. 1937).
[80] FLA. STAT. § 373.223 (2016).
[81] For example, in *Krieter v. Chiles* a riparian property owner brought a taking claim after being denied a permit to build a dock on sovereign submerged lands. Krieter v. Chiles, 595 So. 2d 111, 112 (Fla. 3d Dist. Ct. App. 1992). The court held that the riparian owner's rights were subject to the public's interests and could not constitute a taking. *Id.* at 113.
[82] FLA. CONST. art.X, § 11 (1968).
[83] IDAHO CODE § 58-1201-1203 (1996). For a fuller discussion of the Idaho example, see Chapter 7(C)(2) ("Idaho: Legislative Repudiation of the Constitutive Constraint"); *see also* James M. Kearney, *Closing the Floodgates? Idaho's Statutory Limitation on the Public Trust Doctrine*, 34 IDAHO L. REV. 91, 94 (1997); Michael C. Blumm, Harrison C. Dunning, & Scott W. Reed, *Renouncing the Public Trust Doctrine: An Assessment of the Validity of Idaho House Bill 794*, 24 ECOLOGY L.Q. 461, 472 (1997) (noting that the new statute "was the legislature's response to judicial public trust declarations" in a series of Idaho Supreme Court cases).
[84] John Flesher, *Michigan Governor Seeks to Revoke Enbridge Easement*, STAR TRIB. (Nov. 13, 2020), www.startribune.com/michigan-governor-seeks-to-revoke-enbridge-easement/573072012.
[85] Press Release, State of Mich. Off. of the Governor, Governor Whitmer Takes Action to Shut Down the Line 5 Dual Pipelines Through the Straits of Mackinac After a Reasonable Transition Period to Protect the State's Energy Needs (Nov. 13, 2020), www.michigan.gov/whitmer/news/press-releases/2020/11/13/governor-whitmer-takes-action-to-shut-down-the-line-5-dual-pipelines-through-the-straits-of-mackina.

the governor explained that "the continued use of the dual pipelines cannot be reconciled with the public's rights in the Great Lakes and the State's duty to protect them," and that the pipeline operators had imposed "on the people of Michigan an unacceptable risk of a catastrophic oil spill in the Great Lakes that could devastate our economy and way of life."[86] Her actions were premised on Michigan's statutory expression of the trust discussed earlier,[87] but the executive invocation of the state's trust responsibilities represents a distinct usage of the trust, in contrast to reliance on the trust by citizens challenging government actions.

Another example of the executive use of the public trust is the increasing reliance of state attorneys general on the public trust doctrine in suits brought against defendants alleged to have harmed public trust resources. For example, in 2011, the New Hampshire state Attorney General (together with several other state attorneys general in their respective state courts) sued gasoline suppliers, refiners, and chemical manufacturers for contaminating state groundwater, asserting that it was acting as trustee for state citizens with regard to protecting the public water supply.[88] Notably, these suits sought damages for the costs of testing and remediating state water supplies and providing alternative sources of water due to the alleged contamination.[89] In a complex decision pairing the state's obligations under the public trust doctrine with its ability to vindicate quasi-sovereign interests at the margin of public trust jurisdiction (such as contamination of private wells that, in the aggregate, constitute public water supply), the court held that the state attorney general could pursue a damages remedy for this harm to state waters.[90] After settling with nineteen other corporate defendants, the state ultimately won a jury verdict of $200 million in damages from Exxon Mobil, in a decision affirmed by the New Hampshire Supreme Court.[91]

Similarly, in 2018, the Rhode Island Attorney General sued multiple oil companies for their contributions to climate change and its damaging effects on the

---

[86] *Id.* ("The state found that the 1953 easement violated the public trust doctrine from its inception because the easement does not make the necessary public trust findings. Moreover, the state also found that the continued use of the dual pipelines cannot be reconciled with the public's rights in the Great Lakes and the State's duty to protect them. Transporting millions of gallons of petroleum products each day through two 67-year old [sic] pipelines that lie exposed along the entire span of a busy shipping channel presents an extraordinary and unacceptable risk. The dual pipelines are vulnerable to anchor strikes, similar dangerous impacts, and the inherent risks of pipeline operations"). The statement goes on to list examples in which the pipelines were accidentally struck by commercial vessel anchors and repeated efforts by the state to win cooperation by the pipeline operators in meeting its obligations under the easement to avoid potential harm. *Id.*

[87] *See supra* text accompanying notes 24–30 (discussing the Michigan Natural Resources and Environmental Protection Act).

[88] State v. Hess Corp., 20 A.3d 212, 215–16 (N.H. 2011).

[89] *Id.* at 215.

[90] *Id.* at 216–21. *But see* Rhode Island v. Atlantic Richfield Co., 357 F. Supp. 3d 129, 144–45, 147 (D.R.I. 2018) (dismissing the state's claim because groundwater was not a public trust asset protected by the public trust).

[91] State v. Exxon Mobil Corp. 126 A.3d 266, 273, 312 (N.H. 2015) (affirming the jury's damages verdict and directing the defendant to pay the lump sum directly to the state's treasury).

state's infrastructure, communities, and coastal areas, the latter of which the state is responsible for protecting through state environmental laws and the Rhode Island public trust doctrine.[92] In addition to several other legal theories, the Attorney General had alleged that the companies "knew for decades that burning fossil fuels is damaging the earth's atmosphere but duped the public," which impaired Rhode Island's duties to protect public-trust resources.[93] The court declined the defendants' motion to dismiss on substantive grounds (that the state had failed to state a claim on which legal relief could be granted), but delayed disposition pending Supreme Court resolution of technical issues of jurisdiction that were also raised by the case.[94] Most recently, the New Jersey Attorney General attempted to bring suit against Exxon Mobil on a similar set of theories, including "impairment of the public trust."[95]

e. Multiplatform Trusts

Finally, some states have adopted public trust principles in so many different vehicles of law that they can best be described as multiplatform trusts. For example, as detailed in Chapter 7, California has simultaneously adopted public trust principles in its constitution, statutes, and regulatory law, in addition to its robust common law trust. Article X of the California Constitution codifies the doctrine in relation to water resources, including the sovereign ownership doctrine as it applies to tidelands[96] and rights of public access to all navigable waters.[97] The doctrine also appears in several sections of the California Water Code.[98] Section 102 states that "[a]ll water within the

---

[92] Rhode Island v. Shell Oil Prod. Co., 35 F.4th 44, 49 (1st Cir. 2022); *see also* State v. Chevron Corp., No. PC-2018–4716, 2023 WL 3274138, at *1–2 (R.I. Super. Ct. Apr. 28, 2023).

[93] *Shell Oil Prod. Co.*, 35 F.4th at 49.

[94] *Chevron Corp.*, 2023 WL 3274138, at *5. As this book goes to press, the case remains mired in complex litigation, moving back and forth between state and federal court and contesting issues of jurisdiction and discovery. *Id.*

[95] Platkin v. Exxon Mobil Corp., No. 22CV06733RKJBD, 2023 WL 4086353, at *1 (D.N.J. June 20, 2023) (states sue energy companies "alleging failure to warn, negligence, impairment of the public trust, trespass, public and private nuisance, and violations of New Jersey's Consumer Fraud Act."). On February 5, 2025, however, the New Jersey Superior Court granted a motion to dismiss the case. Platkin v. Exxon Mobile Corp., No. MER-L-001797-22, (N.J. Super. Ct. Feb. 5, 2025).

[96] CAL. CONST. art. X, § 3 (noting that "[a]ll tidelands within two miles of any incorporated city, city and county, or town in this State, and fronting on the water of any harbor, estuary, bay, or inlet used for the purposes of navigation, shall be withheld from grant or sale to private persons, partnerships, or corporations" with legislatively constrained exceptions as needed to protect the public interest).

[97] *Id.* § 4 ("No individual, partnership, or corporation, claiming or possessing the frontage or tidal lands of a harbor, bay, inlet, estuary, or other navigable water in this State, shall be permitted to exclude the right of way to such water whenever it is required for any public purpose, nor to destroy or obstruct the free navigation of such water; and the Legislature shall enact such laws as will give the most liberal construction to this provision, so that access to the navigable waters of this State shall be always attainable for the people thereof").

[98] CTR. FOR PROGRESSIVE REFORM, *supra* note 7, at 6; CAL. WATER CODE § 102, 104, 1201 (1943).

A. *The Planes of Public Trust Development* 253

State is the property of the people of the State,"[99] Section 104 deems the state responsible for determining how the state's water will be used,[100] and Section 1201 affirms that all unappropriated water is to be "public water of the State."[101] The California State Water Resources Control Board has also cited the public trust doctrine in its decisions,[102] albeit sometimes cursorily[103] and not always to prioritize environmental values.[104] Nevertheless, important California public trust developments continue to take place both judicially and administratively, by courts interpreting the common law doctrine and agencies observing regulatory public trust principles.[105]

These examples demonstrate how the public trust doctrine has shifted over time from serving solely as a judicially enforceable mandate for public access to its modern recognition as a background principle of state law – constitutionally, legislatively, and administratively obligating the state to protect public access and environmental values associated with trust resources – frequently with a thumb on the scale toward protecting environmental values, in light of the state's obligation to preserve them unimpaired for enjoyment by future generations.

2. *Different Resources Protected by the Doctrine*

Different states' public trust doctrines also protect different resources, although the common core of all of them remains navigable waterways. Still, states have increasingly

---

[99] CAL. WATER CODE § 102 (1943).
[100] *Id.* § 104.
[101] *Id.* § 1201.
[102] For a few examples of regulatory rulings, see Permit 20549, Ord. WR 2009-0015 (State Water Res. Control Bd. Mar. 17, 2009) (Order Approving Petitions for Change in Place of Use, Purpose of Use, Points of Re-Diversion, and Extension of time; and Issuance of Amended Permit), www.waterboards.ca.gov/waterrights/board_decisions/adopted_orders/orders/2009/wr2009_0015.pdf (requiring bypass flows "[f]or the protection of fish, wildlife, and public trust resources"); Application 31115, Decision 2010-0001 at 7–11 (State Water Res. Control Bd. Oct. 28, 2010) (decision denying application), www.waterboards.ca.gov/waterrights/water_issues/programs/applications/decisions/2010/dd2010_0001.pdf (citing the doctrine while rejecting a revised water rights permit and while inciting the early stages of a dam removal); Hidden Valley Lake Cmty. Serv. Dist., Ord. WR 2007-0032-DWR at 3–5 (State Water Res. Control Bd. Oct. 9, 2007) (order denying urgency change), www.waterboards.ca.gov/waterrights/board_decisions/adopted_orders/orders/2007/wr2007_0032_dwr.pdf (citing the doctrine as a reason for denying a temporary urgency change permit); License 9615, Ord. WR 2004-0040-DWR at 5–6 (State Water Res. Control Bd. Sept. 17, 2004) (order denying temporary urgency change in purpose and place of use) www.waterboards.ca.gov/waterrights/board_decisions/adopted_orders/orders/2004/wr2004_0040.pdf (citing an impact on public trust resources as a reason for denial).
[103] Owen, *supra* note 3, at 1130 n.186, 1132 n.192 (2012) (noting that the State Water Resources Control Board occasionally makes what appear to be "boilerplate" references to public trust principles).
[104] *Id.* at 1133–34.
[105] *See* Env't L. Found. v. State Water Res. Control Bd., 237 Cal. Rptr. 3d 393 (Cal. Ct. App. 2018), *rev. denied* (Nov. 28, 2018) (extending the *Mono Lake* doctrine to groundwater tributaries in the *Scott River* case); CAL. WATER CODE § 85023 (2009 amendment establishing the public trust doctrine as a foundational principle of state water policy that must inform state agency management decisions). *See also* Robie and Owen sources, *supra* note 3 (discussing administrative role of the doctrine in California).

applied the doctrine to protect different aspects of water resources and how the public might enjoy them, and some have extended it to protect resources far beyond water.

a. Waterways

The water resource, and especially navigable waterways, remains the lowest common denominator of public trust protection. For example, South Carolina statutorily defines navigable waters and the physical extent of the public rights in general waters and tidal waters.[106] In Louisiana, "running waters, the waters and bottoms of natural navigable water bodies, the territorial sea, and the seashore" are deemed "public things,"[107] and the state has also been deemed to own the "bayous, rivers, streams, lagoons, lakes and bays, and the beds thereof, not under the direct ownership of any person on August 12, 1910."[108] States calculate the boundaries of these submerged trust lands differently, with some states protecting slightly more or less land above and below the mean high water mark.[109] In a Washington case, the Ninth Circuit recognized that the natural processes that define the boundaries of submerged trust lands can lead them to shift over time, creating a sort of rolling easement with an "ambulatory boundary."[110]

Reminiscent of Hawaii, New Jersey applies the public trust doctrine to all waters of the state, erasing the traditional navigability requirement in protecting surface, ground, and even drinking water,[111] on grounds that clean potable water is necessary for societal function.[112] The New Jersey Supreme Court has taken a particularly flexible view of the potential for the doctrine to evolve to suit the changing needs of the public with regard to public trust resources, holding that "[T]he public trust doctrine, like all common law principles, should not be considered fixed or static, but should be molded and extended to meet changing conditions and needs of the public it was created to benefit."[113]

In contrast to most other states, New Jersey also extends public access rights implied by the trust from lands below the ordinary high water mark to even privately

---

[106] S.C. CODE ANN. § 49-1-10 (1976). Additionally, South Carolina case law protects access to navigable water whether or not there is a clearly defined public interest because of the amount of marshlands, intercoastal waterways, and shore that is protected under the specialized version of the trust. South Carolina *ex rel.* Medlock v. S.C. Coastal Council, 346 S.E.2d 716, 719 (S.C. 1986).

[107] LA. CIV. CODE ANN. art. 450 (1978).

[108] LA. STAT. ANN. § 9:1101 (1954).

[109] For example, in contrast to most states, which protect lands to the ordinary high-water mark under the doctrine, Ohio protects only those below the low water mark, the water's natural edge. See Blanchard's Lessee v. Porter, 11 Ohio 138, 139 (1841); Merrill v. Ohio Dept. Nat. Res., 955 N.E.2d 935, 949 (OH 2011).

[110] United States v. Milner, 583 F.3d 1174, 1188 (9th Cir. 2009).

[111] N.J. STAT. ANN. § 58:11A-3(g) (1977); Mayor of Clifton v. Passaic Valley Water Comm'n, 557 A.2d 299 (N.J. 1989).

[112] *Passaic Valley Water Comm'n*, 557 A.2d at 304–05.

[113] Borough of Neptune City v. Borough of Avon-By-The-Sea, 294 A.2d 47, 54 (N.J. 1972).

held dry sand beaches if needed to afford reasonable public access to submerged trust lands.[114] In a series of closely watched cases over the 1970s and 1980s, the state supreme court held that an oceanfront municipality may not exclude nonresidents from using its beach, including land seaward of the mean highwater line,[115] that the beach and open ocean waters must be open to all people equally,[116] and eventually, that public passage over even private beachfront property was required by the trust if necessary to enable state residents reasonable access to the ocean.[117] New Jersey legislatively codified this holding in 2019, giving the state some of the most expansive beach access protection in the nation.[118]

In Massachusetts, the doctrine has also been extended beyond traditional coastal assets to protect acquired public lands[119] (and even federally owned lands).[120] That said, the Massachusetts Supreme Court pointedly passed on the opportunity to recognize public trust rights to recreational activities in navigable waters[121] and cautioned against providing public access to private dry sand without compensation,[122] departing from the trajectory taken by other states with stronger protections, such as New Jersey and California.[123] Indeed, the court has used its interpretive discretion to limit the further development of trust values by both judicial and legislative actors, holding that the Massachusetts Constitution requires a two-thirds vote to approve the disposition of lands for any public trust purpose beyond those previously identified.[124]

b. Beyond Water

Other states have expanded the trust to other resources beyond waterways, especially states that include trust principles in statutory or constitutional law, such as Pennsylvania and Hawaii. As noted, Pennsylvania's constitutionalized doctrine protects all natural resources in the state, including waters, parklands, forests, and the oil and mineral resources within them.[125]

---

[114] *Neptune City*, 294 A.2d at 51.
[115] *Id.*
[116] *Id.* at 54.
[117] Matthews v. Bay Head Improvement Ass'n, 471 A.2d 355, 355–56 (N.J. 1984).
[118] *New law in NJ: Public has the right to access the beach*, ASSOCIATED PRESS, (May 4, 2019), www.nj1015.com/new-law-in-nj-public-has-the-right-to-access-the-beach/.
[119] *See* Gould v. Greylock Rsrv. Comm'n, 215 N.E.2d 114, 124–25 (Mass. 1966).
[120] *See* United States v. 1.58 Acres of Land, 523 F. Supp. 120, 124–25 (D. Mass. 1981).
[121] *See* Fafard v. Conservation Comm'n of Barnstable, 733 N.E.2d 66, 76 (Mass. 2000).
[122] Op. of the Justs. to the House of Representatives, 313 N.E.2d 561 (Mass. 1974) (rejecting beach access).
[123] *See* JOSEPH W. SINGER, BETHANY R. BERGER, NESTOR M. DAVIDSON & EDUARDO M. PEÑALVER, PROPERTY LAW: RULES, POLICIES, AND PRACTICES 75 (6th ed. 2014) (contrasting Massachusetts and New Jersey public trust law on beach access).
[124] Op. of the Justs. to the Senate, 424 N.E.2d 1092, 1100, 1107–08 (Mass. 1981) (affirming the legislature's power to free land from the public trust and stating that the two-thirds voting requirement applies to the disposition of all lands and easements taken or acquired for trust purposes).
[125] PA. CONST. art. I, § 27; Pa. Env't Def. Found. v. Commonwealth, 161 A.3d 911, 916 (Pa. 2017).

Hawaii arguably boasts the most expansive public trust doctrine in the United States, applying not only to all surface and ground water resources, but to all public natural resources in the state. The state constitution straightforwardly declares that "[a]ll public natural resources are held in trust by the State for the benefit of the people,"[126] and charges the state with the explicit duty to protect water resources for the benefit of the public.[127] State statutes further require the state to protect "traditional and customary Hawaiian rights" in the "procreation of fish and wildlife, the maintenance of proper ecological balance and scenic beauty, and the preservation and enhancement of waters of the State for municipal uses, public recreation, public water supply, agriculture, and navigation."[128]

The expansive doctrine has also been interpreted judicially, such as the Supreme Court of Hawaii's decision in *Robinson v. Ariyoshi*, which affirmed the state's "duty to maintain the purity and flow of our waters for future generations."[129] Protected at these three different levels of state law, the Hawaii doctrine imposes a duty on the state to protect an exhaustive array of resources and associated values, including cultural, ecological, recreational, scenic, and economic values for present and future generations. As discussed further in Chapter 9, Hawaii settled a 2024 constitutional claim by youth plaintiffs seeking greater protection of atmospheric resources with an agreement that "acknowledges the constitutional rights of Hawai'i's youth to a life-sustaining climate and confirms the commitment by [the Department of Transportation] to plan and implement transformative changes of Hawai'i's transportation system to achieve the state's goal of net-negative emissions by 2045."[130]

Other resources are occasionally looped in (and out). Oregon statutorily protects fish and wildlife under public trust principles.[131] California's public trust doctrine applies mostly to waterways but, in at least one case, was held to also apply to wildlife. In *Center for Biological Diversity v. FPL Group*, the California Court of Appeal held that public agencies must consider wildlife preservation under public trust principles when making decisions,[132] although it is the only California case allowing citizens to enforce public trust principles for wildlife protection.[133] In the

---

[126] HAW. CONST. art. XI, § 11.
[127] Id.
[128] HAW. REV. STAT. § 174C-2(c) (1999).
[129] Robinson v. Ariyoshi, 658 P.2d 287, 310 (Haw. 1982).
[130] Office of the Governor, *News Release: Historic Agreement Settles Navahine Climate Litigation*, Jun. 20, 2024, www.governor.hawaii.gov/newsroom/office-of-the-governor-news-release-historic-agreement-settles-navahine-climate-litigation/. See Chapter 9(C) ("Climate Claims on State Constitutional Grounds").
[131] See e.g., State v. Dickerson, 345 P.3d 447, 454–55 (Or. 2015) (*en banc*) (explaining that wildlife is a trust resource); Portland Fish Co. v. Benson, 108 P. 122, 124 (Or. 1910) (noting that the state holds fish in trust prior to capture).
[132] Ctr. for Biological Diversity, Inc. v. FPL Grp., 83 Cal. Rptr. 3d 588 (Cal. Ct. App. 2008).
[133] See id.

1970s codification of public trust principles in MEPA, later replaced by the Natural Resources and Environmental Protection Act of 1994, Michigan law held the trust to apply to atmospheric resources.[134] The Louisiana Constitution's public trust provision mandates that "[t]he natural resources of the state, including air and water, and the healthful, scenic, historic, and esthetic quality of the environment shall be protected, conserved, and replenished insofar as possible and consistent with the health, safety, and welfare of the people."[135]

c. More Limited Application

By contrast, many states of the interior West, such as Colorado and Idaho, have developed a much narrower doctrine, limiting its protections only to conventionally navigable waterways, and even then, sometimes begrudgingly.[136] Of all the United States, Colorado has taken the most restrictive view of the public trust doctrine, weakening it to the point of near impotence (although, as discussed below, it relies on other laws to effect related protections in some instances).

Like all states, Colorado gained title to all submerged lands at statehood,[137] presumably impressed with the same public trust doctrine that the Supreme Court recognized in *Illinois Central*.[138] However, the doctrine appears to have had little impact in judicial interpretations of the state constitution, statutes, or common law.[139] The Colorado Supreme Court has gone as far as to declare that all state waters were non-navigable[140] – notwithstanding the presence of

---

[134] Environmental Protection Act of 1970, MICH. COMP. LAWS § 691.1202(1) (extending the public trust to authorize legal actions "for the protection of the air" in addition to water and other natural resources), *repealed by* Natural Resources and Environmental Protection Act, 1994 Mich. Pub. Acts 451.

[135] LA. CONST. art. IX § 1. The Louisiana Supreme Court has interpreted this provision as articulating the state's public trust doctrine. La. Seafood Mgmt. Council v. La. Wildlife & Fisheries Comm'n, 719 So. 2d 119, 124 (La. Ct. App. 1998) ("Article IX, section 1 of the Louisiana Constitution sets forth this state's Public Trust Doctrine…").

[136] IDAHO CODE § 58-1203 (1996); In re German Ditch & Reservoir Co., 139 P. 2, 9 (Colo. 1914) (asserting that all Colorado streams are non-navigable); Stockman v. Leddy, 129 P. 220, 222 (Colo. 1912) (same), *overruled on other grounds by* United States v. City & Cnty. of Denver, 656 P.2d 1 (Colo. 1982) (disputing its treatment of non-navigable waters on federal lands); Craig, *Comparative Western*, supra note 7, at 71.

[137] *See* Pollard v. Hagan, 44 U.S. 212 (1845) (holding the shores of navigable waters, and the soils under them, were reserved to the states, and the new states have the same sovereignty and jurisdiction over these lands as the original thirteen states).

[138] *See* Chapter 1(B)(5) ("With Power Comes Responsibility: *Illinois Central Railroad Co. v. Illinois*").

[139] People v. Emmert, 597 P.2d 1025, 1027–29 (Colo. 1979) (limiting public recreational use of state waterways); Colo. Oil & Gas Conservation Comm'n v. Martinez, 433 P.3d 22 (Colo. 2019) (upholding the state's decision not to engage in proposed rulemaking to limit oil and gas drilling that could harm public trust resources).

[140] In re German Ditch, 139 P. at 9 ("The natural streams of the state are non-navigable within its limits…"); *Stockman*, 129 P. at 222. *But see* Bonelli Cattle Co. v. Arizona, 414 U.S. 313, 321 (1973) (implying that the Colorado River is a navigable river); Richard Gast, People v. Emmert: *A Step Backward for Recreational Water Use in Colorado*, 52 U. COLO. L. REV. 247, 267 (1981) (discussing the assertions

the mighty Colorado River[141] – in a decision that did not directly address the public trust doctrine, but still erects a formidable barrier to the potential incursion of public trust principles on the management of state waterways. Similarly, Colorado courts have never determined any state water to be "navigable."[142] In later litigation, the state supreme court clarified that to the extent there is a public trust doctrine in Colorado, it does not protect recreational values associated with waterways.[143]

Having generally disempowered the public trust doctrine as a formal matter, Colorado has nevertheless instituted several other programs to protect some environmental values protected by the public trust doctrine in other states, such as dedicating natural streams not previously appropriated for the use of citizens[144] and creating a trust fund to preserve state wildlife, parks, rivers, and open space.[145] The legislature also decriminalized recreationists floating on non-navigable waters on private property,[146] after recreational users were convicted for third-degree criminal trespass for floating and

---

in *Stockman* and *In re German Ditch* that Colorado waterways are non-navigable, but suggesting they are merely dicta).

[141] *Stockman*, 129 P. at 222 ("The federal government, by its lawmaking and executive bodies, knew that the natural streams of this state are, in fact, non-navigable within its territorial limits, and practically all of them have their sources within its own boundaries, and that no stream of any importance whose source is without those boundaries, flows into or through this state"). *But see*, Utah v. United States, 403 U.S. 9, 10 (1971) (concluding the Colorado River is navigable in fact); *Bonelli Cattle*, 414 U.S. at 319 (holding the Colorado River is a navigable river).

[142] *Stockman*, 129 P. at 222 ("the natural streams of this state are, in fact, non-navigable within its territorial limits"); *see also* United States v. Dist. Court, 458 P.2d 760, 762 (Colo. 1969) (holding that even though the Eagle River is a tributary of the Colorado River, it is non-navigable); People v. Emmert, 597 P.2d 1025, 1027–28 (Colo. 1979).

[143] *See, e.g., Emmert*, 597 P.2d at 1027 (declaring private landowner's ownership of the streambed of a non-navigable stream and thereby upholding a charge of criminal trespass against a recreationist who had floated down a non-navigable stream, occasionally touching the streambed). *But see* Hill v. Warsewa, No. 20CA1780 (Colo. Ct. App. Jan. 27, 2022), www.lede-admin.coloradosun.com/wp-content/uploads/sites/15/2022/02/20CA1780-Hill-v-Warsewa-01-27-2022.pdf (in which Judge Tow writes that it "may (or may not) be the case" that there is no public trust doctrine in Colorado).

[144] COLO. CONST. art. XVI, §5–7 (declaring natural streams not already appropriated as property of the public).

[145] *Id.* art. XXVII, § 1–3 (creating the Great Outdoors Colorado Program to preserve, protect, and manage wildlife, park, river, trail, and open space heritage funded by state-supervised lottery games). The state also imposes duties on its land management agency to manage school trust lands. *Id.* art. IX, § 10 (placing duties on the state board of land commissioners for the prudent management in protecting beauty, wildlife habitat, open space, and natural values of school lands that are held in public trust to benefit public schools).

[146] COLO. REV. STAT. ANN. § 18-4-504.5 (2020) (defining premises in the criminal trespass statute as "real property, buildings, and other improvements thereon, and the stream banks and beds of any non-navigable fresh water streams flowing through such real property." Notably, the statute excludes the water itself.); John R. Hill, *The "Right" to Float Through Private Property in Colorado: Dispelling The Myth*, 4 U. DENV. WATER L. REV. 331, 334 (2001) (referring to the Purpose and effect of C.R.S. 1973, 18-4-504.5 [1978 repl. Vol. 8]); Colo. Op. Att'y Gen. No. ONR8303042/KW 1 (Aug. 31, 1993) ("Woodward then concluded it was not a criminal trespass to float through private property so long as the floater does not touch the bed or banks").

fishing through private property traversed by the Colorado River.[147] The state supreme court had concluded that they had no right to float a non-navigable water through privately owned property without consent,[148] and that the task of decriminalizing floating through private lands was the job of the legislature.[149] The legislature responded, showing that there are avenues to protect natural resource values in the state other than the public trust doctrine, if there is a legislature committed to doing so.

Even so, floating on private riverbeds may still be subject to civil trespass,[150] as no appellate court yet has ruled on the issue.[151] Although the legislature contemplated right-to-float legislation, the bill was reportedly unsuccessful because of unconstitutional takings concerns.[152] As discussed further in Part (B)(1), the Colorado legislature's determination demonstrates the importance of the public trust doctrine as a potential background principle defense to such suits.

3. Different Values Protected by the Doctrine

As different states protect different resources, they also protect different trust values associated with protected resources. For example, California's Constitution contains public trust principles, preserving water for the public welfare and in the public interest,[153] and statutorily declares that "[a]ll water within the State is the property of the people of the State";[154] that the state is responsible for determining water use;[155] and that all unappropriated water is public water.[156] However, California case law explains that the water resource is protected for a set of express purposes or values, expanding traditional doctrinal protection for fishing, swimming, and navigational values to include environmental and scientific values.

---

[147] *Emmert*, 597 P.2d at 1026.
[148] *Id.* Emmert was a lawyer who trespassed "for the express purpose of testing whether the criminal trespass statute covered floating across private property." Memorandum from Felicity Hannay, Deputy Attorney General, to Ken Salazar, Attorney General, Re: Floating Access Issues at 2 (June 8, 1999) [hereinafter Hannay Memo]. Now, if only there was another brave attorney to see if civil trespass applies.
[149] *Emmert*, 597 P.2d at 1029 ("we note that in 1977, after the incident here in controversy had occurred, the legislature clarified the meaning of the word 'premises' by the enactment of section 18-4-504.5").
[150] *See* Gateview Ranch, Inc. v. Cannibal Outdoor Network, Inc., No. 01CV52, at 5–7 (Colo. Dist. Ct. Dec. 5, 2001); Arron Pettis, *Note: Takings and the Right to Fish and Float*, 89 IND. L. J. 473, 489 (2014).
[151] Pettis, *supra* note 150, at 489. One district court has expressly stated civil trespass still applies. *Gateview Ranch, Inc.*, No. 01CV52, at 5–7. Most of these suits, however, are settled out of court. Jessica Fender, *Rafting Compromise Diffuses Debate for Now*, DENVER POST (June 15, 2010), www.blogs.denverpost.com/thespot/2010/06/15/rafting-compromise-diffuses-debate-for-now/10578.
[152] HB 10-1188 (*Clarify River Outfitter Navigation Right*) *dies in Conference Committee*, COYOTE GULCH (May 15, 2020).
[153] CAL. CONST. art. X, § 2.
[154] CAL. WATER CODE § 102 (1943).
[155] *Id.* § 104.
[156] *Id.* § 1201.

First in *Marks v. Whitney*, and, most notably, affirmed in the *Mono Lake* case, the California Supreme Court held that the public trust protects ecological, scenic, and recreational uses associated with trust resources, and that the state must "protect public trust uses whenever feasible."[157] As noted, *Center for Biological Diversity* held that public agencies must also consider wildlife preservation when making decisions.[158]

Hawaii protects similar trust values, including recreational, ecological, and scenic values.[159] Nevada has also expanded on traditionally protected values to include recreational and ecological protections.[160] Other states' doctrines offer expanded protection for recreational values, but fewer explicit protections for environmental values. Montana's doctrine focuses on the traditional rights of navigation and fishing but includes some protection for recreational uses.[161] Oregon expressly protects public rights for recreation on all navigable-in-fact waters[162] and also specifies rights for commercial use.[163] New Jersey protects recreational values extensively, including beach access.[164] Florida expressly protects fishing, navigation, and commercial and recreational uses, such as swimming and sunbathing.[165] South Carolina's doctrine has been expanded past fishing rights to include "valuable floatage," defined broadly to include "all 'legitimate and beneficial public use,' including recreation."[166] In Michigan, as noted earlier, the Governor utilized the doctrine to avoid the risk of an oil spill. The state sought to protect public access and environmental values of trust resources, with an increasing thumb on the scale toward protecting environmental values because of the state's obligation

---

[157] Nat'l Audubon Soc'y v. Super. Ct., 658 P.2d 709, 719–28 (Cal. 1983); CTR. FOR PROGRESSIVE REFORM, *supra* note 7, at 4.

[158] Ctr. for Biological Diversity, Inc. v. FPL Grp., 83 Cal. Rptr. 3d 588 (Cal. Ct. App. 2008).

[159] *See supra* notes 126–129 (reviewing the Hawaiian public trust doctrine).

[160] Mineral Cnty. v. Dep't of Conservation & Nat. Res., 20 P.3d 800 (Nev. 2001) (reviewing petitions to prevent the state from granting more rights to withdraw water from the Walker River system and a writ of mandamus challenging the state's public trust obligations in managing the flows into Walker Lake). Justice Rose, in his concurrence, stated, "Although the original objectives of the public trust were to protect the public's rights in navigation, commerce, and fishing, the trust has evolved to encompass additional public values – including recreational and ecological uses." *Id.* at 807 (Rose, J., concurring).

[161] Erika A. Doot, *The Public Trust Doctrine in Montana*, *in* FORTY-FIVE STATES, *supra* note 7, at 467.

[162] Or. Op. Att'y Gen. No. 8281 (Apr. 21, 2005), www.doj.state.or.us/wp-content/uploads/2017/06/op8281.pdf.

[163] Guilliams v. Beaver Lake Club, 175 P. 437, 441–42 (Or. 1918) (considering whether Beaver Creek was navigable, the court was not convinced that the test for navigability should only include transportation of goods and that commerce could be construed to include the use of boats for pleasure).

[164] *See* Borough of Neptune City v. Borough of Avon-By-The-Sea, 294 A.2d 47 (N.J. 1972); *see generally* Part A(2)(a) ("Waterways").

[165] White v. Hughes, 190 So. 446, 448–51 (Fla. 1939) (detailing that "[t]here is probably no custom more universal, more natural or more ancient on the sea-coasts" than that of bathing in the ocean and enjoying the related recreation); Adams v. Elliott, 171 So. 731, 734 (Fla. 1937).

[166] Hughes v. Nelson, 399 S.E.2d 24, 25 (S.C. Ct. App. 1990); Casey Hill, *The Public Trust Doctrine in South Carolina*, *in* FORTY-FIVE STATES, *supra* note 7, at 760.

A. *The Planes of Public Trust Development* 261

to preserve them unimpaired for the enjoyment of future generations. Virginia's constitutionalized trust protects atmospheric resources as well as historic sites and buildings.[167]

Other states have expressly attempted to limit the expansion of the values protected by the doctrine. As noted earlier, in addition to minimizing the reach of the doctrine by eliminating recognition of its waterways as navigable, Colorado has disclaimed any protection by the doctrine for recreational values and has issued judicial decisions that effectively limit consideration under the doctrine of environmental values.[168] Idaho's common law and statutory law point in different directions, with judicial common law expanding trust resources beyond navigable waters and, seemingly, toward more protection of environmental values, but as discussed further below, the legislature has responded by statutorily limiting the trust to protect only the most traditional trust resources and values associated with navigation.[169]

4. Different Legal Theories about the Nature of the Doctrine

Over this period of doctrinal development and differentiation, states have even advanced different ideas about the nature of the doctrine itself, plumbing the public trust at the level of legal theory. As detailed in Chapter 7, a minority of states treat the doctrine as an ordinary feature of judicial common law – an extension of the police power to protect public health and safety that can be displaced or overridden by the legislature through enactment of contrary statutory law.[170] Others see the doctrine as a quasi-constitutional, "constitutive" doctrine

---

[167] VIRGINIA CONST., art. XI, Section 1 ("To the end that the people have clean air, pure water, and the use and enjoyment for recreation of adequate public lands, waters, and other natural resources, it shall be the policy of the Commonwealth to conserve, develop, and utilize its natural resources, its public lands, and its historical sites and buildings. Further, it shall be the Commonwealth's policy to protect its atmosphere, lands, and waters from pollution, impairment, or destruction, for the benefit, enjoyment, and general welfare of the people of the Commonwealth").

[168] *See, e.g.*, People v. Emmert, 597 P.2d 1025, 1027–29 (Colo. 1979) (defendants had no right under the Constitution of Colorado to float and fish on a non-navigable natural stream, stating, "Without permission, the public cannot use such waters for recreation"); Colo. Oil & Gas Conservation Comm'n v. Martinez, 433 P.3d 22 (Colo. 2019).

[169] *See, e.g.*, Walbridge v. Robinson, 125 P. 812, 814 (Idaho 1912) (indicating that the state may hold in its sovereign capacity all resources not suited to private appropriation, including light and air); Selkirk-Priest Basin Ass'n v. State ex rel. Andrus, 899 P.2d 949, 952–56 (Idaho 1995) (recognizing that, even if not public trust lands themselves, if the alienation of state land could adversely affect trust resources, private citizens have standing to challenge the sale under the public trust doctrine); *see* IDAHO CODE § 58-1201-1203 (1996) ("The public trust doctrine as it is applied in the state of Idaho is solely a limitation on the power of the state to alienate or encumber the title to the beds of navigable waters as defined in this chapter.... The public trust doctrine shall not be applied to any purpose other than as provided in this chapter").

[170] *See, e.g.*, Chapter 7(C)(2) ("Idaho: Legislative Repudiation of the Constitutive Constraint"); IDAHO CODE § 58-1201-1203 (1996) (quoted *supra* note 169).

that cannot be revoked through typical legislative or judicial means because it is an irrevocable limit on the authority with which the sovereign may govern.[171] This was an essential element of the Supreme Court's reasoning in the *Illinois Central* case, discussed in Chapter 1(B)(5), explaining why state legislation purporting to alienate the bed of Chicago Harbor was held to be ultra vires and thus void of legal effect.[172]

Support for the constitutive interpretation appears most famously in the California Supreme Court's decision in the *Mono Lake* case, which protected environmental values at Mono Lake from water withdrawals authorized under water allocation statutes.[173] As detailed in Chapters 3 and 5, Los Angeles had secured state permits to export the water decades earlier under statutory water allocation laws, and it had argued that the California legislature had abrogated the public trust doctrine when it enacted these water law statutes.[174] However, the California Supreme Court held that the statutory prior appropriations doctrine did not displace the public trust doctrine, and that the state had erred in granting these permits decades earlier because it lacked the authority to do so without considering its public trust obligations first.[175]

Many states have followed California's model, for example, Nevada,[176] Hawaii,[177] New Jersey,[178] and Washington,[179] all of which consider the public trust as a quasi-constitutional constraint on sovereign authority. Nevertheless, other states are less committed to the idea. Colorado law minimizes the role of the public trust in

---

[171] *See* Chapter 7(C) ("Ordinary Common Law or Quasi-Constitutional?"). *See generally* Ill. Cent. R.R. Co. v. Illinois, 146 U.S. 387 (1892) (discussing why state legislation purporting to alienate the bed of Chicago Harbor was held to be ultra vires and thus void of legal effect).

[172] *See generally* Ill. Cent. R.R. Co. v. Illinois, 146 U.S. 387 (1892); *see* Chapter 1(B)(5) ("With Power Comes Responsibility: *Illinois Central Railroad Co. v. Illinois*") (discussing *Illinois Central*); *see also* Ryan, *A Short History of the Public Trust Doctrine and its Intersection with Private Water Law*, 38 VA. ENV'T L.J. 135 (2020) [hereinafter *A Short History*], at 160–66 (interpreting *Illinois Central*).

[173] *See generally* Nat'l Audubon Soc'y v. Super. Ct., 658 P.2d 709 (Cal. 1983). Other states follow a similar approach. *See, e.g.*, San Carlos Apache Tribe v. Super. Ct. *ex rel*. Cnty. of Maricopa, 972 P.2d 179 (Ariz. 1999).

[174] *Nat'l Audubon Soc'y*, 658 P.2d 709.

[175] *Id.* at 728; *see also* Chapter 7(C)(1) ("California: A Constitutive Constraint") (discussing the significance of the case for the constitutive legal theory question).

[176] Lawrence v. Clark Cnty., 254 P.3d 606, 613 (Nev. 2011) ("The final underpinning of our formal adoption of the public trust doctrine arises from the inherent limitations on the state's sovereign power...").

[177] *In re* Water Use Permit Applications, 9 P.3d 409, 443 (Haw. 2000) ("[H]istory and precedent have established the public trust as an inherent attribute of sovereign authority....").

[178] E. Cape May Assocs. v. State Dep't of Env't Prot., 777 A.2d 1015, 1034 (N.J. Super. Ct. App. Div. 2001) ("[T]idally-flowed land has always been subject to the public trust doctrine[,] ... [which] provides that the sovereign never waives its right to regulate the use of public trust property[.]").

[179] Caminiti v. Boyle, 732 P.2d 989, 994 (Wash. 1987) ("The state can no more convey or give away this *jus publicum* interest than it can 'abdicate its police powers in the administration of government and the preservation of the peace'").

general,[180] and Idaho most famously rejected the California approach in protecting environmental values compromised by water rights granted under state allocation statutes.[181] Idaho case law had initially invited a broader interpretation of the public trust doctrine, considering application to light, air, public lands, and other natural resources,[182] but responsive legislative moves imposed a more traditional version of the doctrine, rejecting application to environmental values.[183] After the Idaho Supreme Court issued a series of public trust decisions converging on California's approach, the legislature expressly foreclosed the constitutive interpretation of the public trust doctrine by statute.[184] Idaho Code Title 58, Chapter 12 explicitly recognizes that the doctrine does limit the state's ability to alienate the title to the beds of navigable waterways,[185] but it expressly states that the trust will not impact the allocation of prior appropriative water rights or affect state decisions regarding the use of public trust waterways.[186] In so doing, Idaho also rejected California's

---

[180] See *supra* note 139 and accompanying text (discussing the Colorado Supreme Court's treatment of the public trust doctrine).

[181] See IDAHO CODE § 58-1201-1203 (1996); see also Chapter 7(C)(2) ("Idaho: Legislative Repudiation of the Constitutive Constraint") (discussing the significance of Idaho statutory law for the constitutive legal theory question).

[182] See, e.g., Walbridge v. Robinson, 125 P. 812, 814 (Idaho 1912) (indicating that the state may hold in its sovereign capacity all resources not suited to private appropriation, including light and air); Selkirk-Priest Basin Ass'n v. State *ex rel.* Andrus, 899 P.2d 949, 952–56 (Idaho 1995) (recognizing that, even if not public trust lands themselves, if the alienation of state land could adversely affect trust resources, private citizens have standing to challenge the sale under the public trust doctrine).

[183] See IDAHO CODE § 58-1201-1203 (1996) ("The public trust doctrine as it is applied in the state of Idaho is solely a limitation on the power of the state to alienate or encumber the title to the beds of navigable waters as defined in this chapter.... The public trust doctrine shall not be applied to any purpose other than as provided in this chapter."); see also Craig, *Comparative Western*, supra note 7, at 77 ("Idaho courts until 1996 were following the western 'modern trend,' indicated that water and 'proprietary rights to use water ... are held subject the public trust.' In 1996, however, Idaho's legislature invalidated this line of cases, instead defining (and confining) that state's public trust doctrine by statute.") (footnote omitted).

[184] IDAHO CODE § 58-1201-1203 (1996). *Compare* San Carlos Apache Tribe v. Super. Ct. *ex rel.* Cnty. of Maricopa, 972 P.2d 179, 199 (Ariz. 1999) Unlike Idaho, which permitted legislative abrogation of the trust, the Arizona Supreme Court struck down a legislative attempt to bar consideration of the public trust with respect to water rights and sovereign lands; see also Ariz. Ctr. for L. in the Pub. Interest v. Hassell, 837 P.2d 158, 168 (Ariz. Ct. App. 1991) (holding that "the state's responsibility to administer its watercourse lands for the public benefit is an inabrogable [sic] attribute of statehood itself"); Ariz. Dep't of Water Res. v. McClennan, 360 P.3d 1023, 1027 (Ariz. 2015) (holding that the state's obligation to hold water resources in trust for the public applies only to initial appropriations of water – not to the severance and/or transfer of existing water rights – but not commenting on the issue of whether the public trust doctrine is a constitutive constraint).

[185] IDAHO CODE § 58-1201(4), (6) (1996) (defining the public trust doctrine as guiding alienation of the title of the beds of navigable waters and clarifying that the purpose of the act is to define limits on the public trust doctrine); *id.* § 58-1203(1) (limiting the public trust doctrine to "solely a limitation on the power of the state to alienate or encumber the title to the beds of navigable waters").

[186] *Id.* § 58-1203(3) (stating that the trust does not limit the state to authorize public and private use or alienation of title to the beds of navigable waters if the state board of land commissioners determines that it is in accordance with Idaho statutes and constitution and for the purposes of navigation, commerce, recreation, agriculture, mining, forestry, or other uses).

interpretation in the *Mono Lake* case, finding instead that the prior appropriation doctrine does in fact override the public trust doctrine.[187] As now codified in statute, the Idaho doctrine applies only to navigable waters and not to any other trust lands or water rights.[188]

In an attempt, perhaps, to split the difference on the constitutive question, the Nevada Supreme Court in 2020 affirmed its understanding of the doctrine as a constitutive limit on sovereign authority regarding all waterways in the state – but also held that there can be no conflict between the state's obligations under the public trust doctrine and settled water allocation permits because state water law has always required that water permits only be granted when doing so serves the public interest.[189] In so holding, the Nevada Supreme Court affirmed the doctrine's sovereign ownership constraint as a quasi-constitutional limit on state sovereign authority, but foreclosed the constitutive interpretation of the doctrine as a guarantor of environmental values.[190]

5. *Different Public Trust Remedies*

Finally, it's worth considering the different legal remedies available under judicial administration of the public trust doctrine – or what it is, exactly, that public trust plaintiffs are asking courts to deliver when they initiate litigation that includes a public trust claim. In fact, the nationwide review of public trust activity above reveals that plaintiffs relying on the doctrine have sought every available form of judicial relief – declaratory, injunctive, and damages – especially in environmental litigation. The different "prayers for relief" that plaintiffs seek in litigation are more tied to their specific objectives than jurisdictional differences, with the exception of the use of the doctrine to seek or avoid financial remedies. But what exactly are these different legal remedies?

Sometimes, plaintiffs seek declaratory relief – asking the judiciary to clarify for everyone what the law actually says, and the different responsibilities it creates in the relevant legal actors or stakeholders. Declaratory relief is what plaintiffs desire when they want the court to say, once and for all, what the public trust means in a given circumstance. Other times, plaintiffs are more concerned with the conduct at issue. They seek injunctive relief when they want the court to "enjoin"

---

[187] See Chapter 7(C)(2) ("Idaho: Legislative Repudiation of the Constitutive Constraint"). The move prompted considerable scholarly controversy on this issue. *See* Kearney, *supra* note 83, at 94; Blumm, Dunning & Reed, *supra* note 83, at 472 (noting that the new statute "was the legislature's response to judicial public trust declarations" in a series of Idaho Supreme Court cases).

[188] IDAHO CODE § 58-1203 (1996).

[189] Mineral Cnty. v. Lyon Cnty., 473 P.3d 418, 425–27 (Nev. 2020); *see also* Chapter 7(C)(3) ("Nevada: Mixed Messages in the Walker Lake Basin") (discussing the significance of Nevada's treatment of the public trust doctrine for the constitutive legal theory question).

[190] *See* Chapter 7(C)(3) ("Nevada: Mixed Messages in the Walker Lake Basin").

the conduct of the defendant, or order them to either do something specific in light of the legal obligations created by the public trust, or else refrain from doing something that would violate public trust requirements. And sometimes, plaintiffs ask for money "damages" as compensation for harm to public trust resources that has already occurred. As the above executive branch trust examples demonstrate, attorney generals have sought damages when claiming that defendants have harmed public trust resources in a way that creates high costs for state remediation and response efforts.[191]

For some public trust plaintiffs, the most important goal is to set legal precedent going forward – the judicial declaration of the legal circumstances in which the public trust doctrine operates to protect trust resources. For a sidelong example, the state of Utah formally sought a declaration from the United States Supreme Court that the Great Salt Lake was a navigable water to establish state title to the submerged lands.[192] The Court held that because the Great Salt Lake was navigable when Utah became a state, therefore the Great Salt Lake had indeed been entrusted to the state.[193] While the state was more motivated to claim authority over the lake than responsibility for its protection, the decision nevertheless confers both – because the establishment of navigability for title, at least in this case, also established the Great Salt Lake as a public trust resource. More recently, Pennsylvania plaintiffs successfully sought a declaration by the state supreme court that the Commonwealth had violated its duty under the state's constitutionalized public trust doctrine by allowing oil and gas mining on public lands.[194]

However, public trust plaintiffs are often seeking to protect trust values from specific harmful conduct, so injunctive relief is a commonly requested remedy. For example, when a South Carolina resident blocked a canal traditionally used for fishing and recreation, the court agreed with the plaintiff's contention that the canal was a navigable waterway subject to the public trust doctrine and ordered that the canal be cleared to restore public access.[195] Similarly, plaintiffs in New Jersey have successfully sought injunctive relief in a series of public trust cases preventing beach clubs and communities from blocking public beach access over private uplands when other means of access are not reasonably available.[196]

---

[191] *See supra* Part (A)(1)(e) ("Executive Trusts"), discussing State v. Exxon Mobil Corp. 126 A.3d 266, 273, 312 (N.H. 2015) (discussing a jury's damage award of $200 million and directing the defendant to pay the lump sum directly to the state's treasury); Rhode Island v. Shell Oil Prod. Co., 35 F.4th 44, 49 (1st Cir. 2022); State v. Chevron Corp., No. PC-2018–4716, 2023 WL 3274138, at *1–2 (R.I. Super. Ct. Apr. 28, 2023); and other similar cases.

[192] Utah v. United States, 403 U.S. 9, 12–13 (1971).

[193] *Id.*

[194] Pa. Env't Def. Found. v. Commonwealth, 161 A.3d 911, 916, 925–26, 939 (Pa. 2017).

[195] Hughes v. Nelson, 399 S.E.2d 24, 24–26 (S.C. Ct. App. 1990).

[196] Matthews v. Bay Head Improvement Ass'n, 471 A.2d 355, 369–70 (N.J. 1984).

Often, public trust plaintiffs receive one or more of these remedies in combination. For example, in the *Mono Lake* case, the plaintiffs received something of a declaratory judgment that the public trust doctrine applies to the non-navigable tributaries of Mono Lake and also an injunction ordering the State Water Board to reconsider the original water licenses it had granted Los Angeles to divert from them, without considering the state's public trust obligations at Mono Lake.[197] While the plaintiffs had specifically asked only for the injunction,[198] the court was forced to first confront whether the streams were protected by the public trust doctrine as a question of first impression, yielding a judicial declaration of law as well.[199]

Finally, and especially when the plaintiffs are states or municipalities, public trust cases sometimes involve efforts to seek or avoid financial damages. As discussed earlier, state attorney generals in several states, including New Hampshire, have sued gasoline refineries and chemical manufacturers for contaminating state groundwater, seeking damages for the resulting costs of testing water for public safety, remediating the harm, and providing alternative public water supply.[200] Similarly, state attorneys general in Rhode Island, New Jersey, and other states have sued oil companies for their contributions to climate change and its damaging effects on state coastal areas and infrastructure, under a theory of impairment of public trust resources.[201]

Yet the doctrine has also been used by state and municipal defendants as a legal shield to avoid damages liability when confronted with private takings litigation, or claims that state conduct has deprived a private plaintiff of property rights protected by the Fifth Amendment to the constitution.[202] In contrast to the previous examples, the plaintiffs in these lawsuits may not even raise the public trust doctrine; more often, they argue that some specific state action or policy has violated other legal rights. As discussed further below in Part B(1), states are increasingly defending these lawsuits by asserting that the action the plaintiff is challenging is either privileged or obligated by the public trust doctrine.[203]

For example, state and municipal actors in Wisconsin have successfully used the public trust doctrine as a shield to defend against private takings claims. In 2001, the Wisconsin Supreme Court rejected a takings challenge to the state's denial of

---

[197] Nat'l Audubon Soc'y v. Super. Ct., 658 P.2d 709 (Cal. 1983).
[198] *Id.* at 712.
[199] *Id.* at 721.
[200] State v. Hess Corp., 20 A.3d 212, 215–16 (N.H. 2011).
[201] *See, e.g.,* State v. Chevron Corp., No. PC-2018-4716, 2023 WL 3274138, at *1 (R.I. Super. Ct. Apr. 28, 2023) (suing defendant oil company for impairment of public trust resources and also under theories of public nuisance, failure to warn, design defect, trespass, and violations of the State Environmental Rights Act).
[202] U.S. CONST. amend. V. (protecting "private property [from] be[ing] taken for public use, without just compensation").
[203] *See* Part (B)(1) ("The Doctrine as a Background Principle in Takings Law").

a marina's dredging permit because the developer lacked reasonable investment-backed expectations to fill wetlands, and because riparian rights are inferior to the public trust doctrine.[204] The Wisconsin Supreme Court emphasized that "[t]he public trust doctrine as an encumbrance on riparian rights is established 'by judicial authority so long acquiesced in as to become a rule of property.' It is part of the organic law of the state, and is to be broadly and beneficially construed."[205] More recently, in 2022, Wisconsin counties have defended claims for damages based on their public trust obligations when a dam was removed as a part of a water management plan.[206] There, the court determined that the government action did not constitute a taking, at least in part because the dam removal affected only areas that were already subject to the public trust.[207] Since the land was already public, it could not be a "taking" of private property.[208] Even some federal courts of appeal have allowed state actors use of the doctrine to defend takings claims seeking damages remedies.[209]

Lawsuits in which the state defends damages claims on the basis of its public trust obligations often arise when plaintiffs challenge state laws requiring public access to trust resources or regulating development on coastal areas or wetlands protected by the doctrine, or in some cases – like the *Mono Lake* case itself – when they challenge the allocation of water rights from a trust protected source. As noted in Chapter 5, Los Angeles brought a taking claim after its losses at Mono Lake, seeking compensation for lost water rights when the Water Board reconsidered them after the Mono Lake litigation, but its suit was dismissed in federal court.[210]

Which leads to the appropriate next question: what is the relationship, if any, between the public trust doctrine and federal law?

B. THE PUBLIC TRUST IN FEDERAL LAW

The public trust doctrine has long been recognized as a doctrine of state law, and the Supreme Court itself has stated, at least in dicta, that there is no federal public trust.[211] Nevertheless, a robust scholarly discourse disputes that claim, which

---

[204] R.W. Docks & Slips v. State Dep't of Nat. Res., 628 N.W.2d 781, 791 (Wis. 2001).
[205] *Id.* at 788 (internal citations omitted) (quoting Franzini v. Layland, 97 N.W. 499, 502 [Wis. 1903]).
[206] Kreuziger v. Milwaukee Cnty., 617 F. Supp. 3d. 970, 974–975 (E.D. Wis. 2022).
[207] *Id.* at 979.
[208] *Id.*
[209] *See* Esplanade Props., LLC v. City of Seattle, 307 F.3d 978, 980 (9th Cir. 2002) (affirming the city's refusal to allow construction of residences on an elevated platform above tidelands because the public trust doctrine vitiated any entitlement by the owner to build there).
[210] Petition for Writ of Certiorari, City of L.A. Dep't of Water & Power v. Nat'l Audubon Soc'y, 464 U.S. 977 (1983); *see also* Chapter 5(A)(3) & (4) ("The Legal Arguments"; "The California Supreme Court's Decision") (discussing the Court's denial of the petition).
[211] PPL Mont., LLC v. Montana, 565 U.S. 576, 603 (2012). For fuller discussion, see *infra* text accompanying notes 274–76.

has never been tested by the Supreme Court directly.[212] Federal law recognizes an analogous principle in Federal Navigational Servitude, a doctrine that authorizes the removal of any encroachment on navigable waterways, advancing many of the same values that underly the public trust doctrine.[213] Moreover, the doctrine plays an increasingly important role *adjacent* to federal law as advocates invoke it as a background-principles defense to takings claims against environmental and land use laws protecting trust resources. Recent revelations expose that the Supreme Court negotiated internally to keep the public trust doctrine out of its controversial suite of opinions in the *Lucas v. South Carolina Coastal Council*, a seminal takings case that expanded regulatory takings liability for regulations that leave owners without economically viable use of property – usually those preventing development on coastal or inland wetlands associated with the public trust, or requiring access to waterways impressed with the trust.[214]

This part reviews the role of the public trust doctrine in federal law, beginning with its role as a defense in takings litigation. Then it turns to the doctrine's "secret Supreme Court history," in which the justices negotiated to keep the relationship between the public trust doctrine and federal law unresolved. Finally, it explores the scholarly argument for finding a public trust in federal law, for the very same reasons the doctrine exists in state law.

1. *The Doctrine as a Background Principle in Federal Takings Claims*

From an environmental perspective, an important doctrinal development that cuts across jurisdictions is the increasing reliance by governments on the public trust doctrine as a defense against takings challenges to environmental regulations.[215] While it would take a century to become clear, the *Pollard v. Hagan*, *Shively v. Bowlby*, and *Illinois Central* decisions discussed earlier have arguably enshrined the public trust doctrine among what contemporary takings jurisprudence refers to as the "background principles" of state common law, or those built-in legal norms that constrain owners' legitimate expectations about the suitable uses of different kinds of property.[216] This intersection between the public trust doctrine and federal constitutional

---

[212] *See infra* Part (B)(3) ("A Constitutional Constraint on Federal Authority?").
[213] Kaiser Aetna v. United States 444 U.S. 164, 177–79 (1979).
[214] 505 U.S. 1003 (1992). *See infra* Part (B)(2) ("The Secret Supreme Court Public Trust Debate").
[215] *See* Ryan, *A Short History*, *supra* note 172 at 170–73.
[216] See Erin Ryan, *Palazzolo, The Public Trust, and the Property Owner's Reasonable Expectations: Takings and the South Carolina Marsh Island Bridge Debate*, 15 SE. ENV'T L.J. 121, 123 (2006) (analyzing how the public trust doctrine operates as a background principle of law that can constrain the reasonable expectations of a property owner alleging a taking); id. at 137–40 (discussing use of the public trust doctrine to defend takings claims by defusing the reasonableness of claimants' expectations); see also John D. Echeverria, *The Public Trust Doctrine as a Background Principles Defense in Takings Litigation*, 45 U.C. DAVIS L. REV. 931, 931–43 (2012) (analyzing use of the doctrine as a takings defense in light of two California cases in which the court did not allow it); J. Peter Byrne,

B. The Public Trust in Federal Law

law drew increasing recognition after the 1990s, when the Rehnquist Court issued a series of decisions that strengthened takings claims against regulations limiting property development.[217]

In a number of high-profile cases, the doctrine has been invoked in litigation brought under the U.S. Constitution's Takings Clause,[218] where governments defending environmental regulations argue that the trust sets forth something akin to environmental rights in the public that limit plaintiffs' reasonable expectations with regard to the use of trust resources. Not every court has allowed it, but some state and municipal governments have shielded themselves against regulatory takings claims on the grounds that the public trust doctrine obligates them to protect the environmental values of trust resources, especially wetland and coastal areas, as well as public access to those resources.[219]

In its 1992 decision in *Lucas v. South Carolina Coastal Council*, the Supreme Court clarified that takings liability applies whenever state regulation prevents all economically viable uses of private property,[220] sidestepping the usual regulatory takings balancing test that also requires consideration of the public interest in the regulatory prevention of harm,[221] and making it easier for owners to challenge environmental regulations limiting the development of fragile coastal or wetland property.[222] However, the Court also clarified that the *Lucas* rule does not apply if the regulation is a "background principle[]" of state property law – such as nuisance law – that already limits the owner's reasonable expectations about the permissible uses of property.[223] The Supreme Court's nineteenth century recognition in decisions like *Illinois Central* and others[224] that the public trust doctrine is a foundational element of American law thus took on new importance as its twentieth century takings jurisprudence expanded liability for environmental regulations that

---

The Public Trust Doctrine, Legislation, and Green Property: A Future Convergence?, 45 U.C. DAVIS L. REV. 915, 916 (2012) (suggesting that the doctrine be used as a defense to innovative regulatory takings claims and to "sustain environmental legislation against judicial hostility"). *But see* Barton H. Thompson, Jr., *Judicial Takings*, 76 VA. L. REV. 1449, 1532–33 (1990) (criticizing use of the doctrine to avoid just compensation for what otherwise looks like a taking).

[217] Richard H. Fallon, Jr., *The "Conservative" Paths of the Rehnquist Court's Federalism Decisions*, 69 U. CHI. L. REV. 429, 459–60 (2002) (noting that the Rehnquist Court "toughened judicial scrutiny of governmental action under the Takings Clause").

[218] U.S. CONST. amend.V. (protecting "private property [from] be[ing] taken for public use, without just compensation").

[219] *See* Ryan, A Short History, *supra* note 172, at 172–73.

[220] Lucas v. S.C. Coastal Council, 505 U.S. 1003, 1027–30 (1992); *see also* Palazzolo v. Rhode Island, 533 U.S. 606, 626–30 (2001).

[221] *Compare Lucas*, 505 U.S. 1003, *with* Penn Cent. Transp. Co. v. City of New York, 438 U.S. 104, 124 (1978) (describing the three-factor regulatory takings balancing test).

[222] *See* Ryan, A Short History, *supra* note 172, at 170–73.

[223] *Lucas*, 505 U.S. at 10297–30; *see also* Palazzolo, 533 U.S. at 626–30.

[224] *See* Ryan, A Short History, *supra* note 172, at 152–55 (discussing Martin v. Wadell, 41 U.S. 367 (1842), Pollard v. Hagan, 44 U.S. 212 (1845), and Shively v. Bowlby, 152 U.S. 1 [1894]).

interfere with economic use,²²⁵ confirming the doctrine as a "background principle[]" of state common law.²²⁶

Today, the doctrine is increasingly invoked by state and municipal parties defending takings claims against regulations involving construction on tidelands and wetlands, public access to waterways, and interference with water rights. Part A(5) offered examples of how Wisconsin has allowed state actors to defend takings claims on the basis of state public trust obligations, but a number of other states have made similar arguments in court. For example, the Hawaii Supreme Court rejected a takings challenge against the state's denial of water use permits because "the original limitation of the public trust" extinguished any claim the plaintiffs could make to an absolute right to water for purposes other than those protected by the trust. Quoting Professor Joseph Sax's influential public trust scholarship, the court explained that "[t]he state is not 'taking' something belonging to an owner, but is asserting a right it always held as a servitude burdening owners of water rights." Given the extensive history reported in this article and recited in these decisions, it seems difficult to argue that the public trust doctrine is *not* a background principle of state law that should impact reasonable expectations, even if it remains possible to argue over how, exactly, it should impact them.²²⁷

Hawaii's public trust doctrine may be idiosyncratically powerful, but even states with relatively weaker doctrines – and stronger protections for landowners against alleged takings – have allowed public trust-based defenses, such as Florida. All along the Florida peninsula, sea level rise and other changing climatic conditions have seriously exacerbated beach erosion, resulting in state policy to "renourish" disappearing public beaches by filling the eroding shoreline with dredged sand.²²⁸ When nearby private owners disadvantaged by these efforts challenged the state law authorizing beach renourishment as a taking, the Florida Supreme Court concluded that such activities could not constitute a taking of private rights, in part because the activity was affecting coastal areas subject to the public trust.²²⁹ In a complex decision that also addressed common law doctrines of accretion and reliction, the court held that the state statute providing for shoreline preservation "effectuates the State's constitutional duty to protect Florida's beaches," which are

---

²²⁵ Ryan, A Short History, supra note 172 at 172; see also Echeverria, supra note 216, at 931–34; Richard M. Frank, The Public Trust Doctrine: Assessing Its Recent Past and Charting Its Future, 45 U.C. DAVIS L. REV. 665, 682–84 (2012) (summarizing several courts' explorations of "the question of the extent to which the public trust doctrine represents just such a 'background principle' of state property law that immunizes from taking challenge government regulations that have a deleterious effect on private property use and/or value").

²²⁶ Ryan, A Short History, supra note 172, at 171 (defining "background principles" as "those built-in legal norms that constrain owners' legitimate expectations about the suitable uses of different kinds of property").

²²⁷ See Ryan, A Short History, supra note 172, at 172–73 (footnotes omitted).

²²⁸ Walton Cnty. v. Stop the Beach Renourishment, Inc., 998 So. 2d. 1102, 1105 (Fla. 2008).

²²⁹ Id. at 1120–21.

B. *The Public Trust in Federal Law* 271

held "in trust for all the people," based on clear state obligations under both the common law and constitutional public trust doctrine, as codified in Article X of the Florida Constitution.[230]

At present, courts in New Jersey,[231] Hawaii,[232] Wisconsin,[233] South Carolina,[234] Louisiana,[235] Rhode Island,[236] and the Ninth Circuit[237] have all accepted the public trust doctrine as a legitimate "background principles" defense to takings claims against environmental regulations – all implicitly recognizing an underlying right of the public in preventing environmental harm, even when it causes private economic harm. Some states, such as Florida, have invoked the public trust in takings claims independently of the background principles debate, while others have recognized the public trust as providing an analogous support even before the background principles issue had crystalized as a litigation strategy.[238] Nevertheless, the Court of Federal Claims has twice cast doubt on the background principles

---

[230] *Id.* at 1110–11 (citing Fla. Const. art. X, § 11); *see also id.* at 1120 (noting that the state statute, like the corresponding common law, "achieves a reasonable balance between public and private interests in the shore").

[231] *See* Nat'l Ass'n of Home Builders v. N.J. Dep't of Env't Prot., 64 F. Supp. 2d 354 (D.N.J. 1999) (rejecting a takings challenge to a state agency rule requiring developers of waterfront property to provide walkways along the water because the public trust doctrine prevents owners from claiming any entitlement to exclude).

[232] *See In re* Water Use Permit Applications, 9 P.3d 409 (Haw. 2000).

[233] *See* R.W. Docks & Slips v. State Dep't of Nat. Res., 628 N.W.2d 781 (Wis. 2001) (rejecting a takings challenge to the state's denial of a marina's dredging permit because the developer lacked reasonable investment-backed expectations to fill wetlands and because riparian rights are inferior to the public trust doctrine); *supra* notes 204–205 and accompanying text (discussing the case in more detail).

[234] *See* McQueen v. S.C. Coastal Council, 580 S.E.2d 116 (S.C. 2003) (holding that the public trust doctrine properly blocked tidelands development without compensation, even when the lands at issue became submerged after the owner took title).

[235] *See* Avenal v. State, 886 So. 2d 1085, 1088, 1102 (La. 2004) (rejecting a takings challenge against erosion-controlling freshwater diversion programs and holding that "the redistribution of existing productive oyster beds to other areas must be tolerated under the public trust doctrine").

[236] *See* Palazzolo v. State, No. WM 88-0297, 2005 WL 1645974, at *1 n. 2, *7, *15 (R.I. Super. Ct. July 5, 2005) (an unpublished decision on remand from the U.S. Supreme Court rejecting a takings challenge against the denial of permit to develop in coastal wetlands because, among other things *inter alia*, the public trust doctrine prevented the formation of reasonable investment-backed expectations to "fill or develop that portion of the site which is below mean high water").

[237] *See* Esplanade Props., LLC v. City of Seattle, 307 F.3d 978 (9th Cir. 2002) (affirming the city's refusal to allow construction of residences on an elevated platform above tidelands because Washington's public trust doctrine vitiated any entitlement by the owner to build there).

[238] *Compare* Walton Cnty. v. Stop the Beach Renourishment, Inc., 998 So. 2d 1102, 1110–11, 1120 (Fla. 2008) (discussed above) *with* Orion Corp. v. State, 747 P.2d 1062, 1072–73 (Wash. 1987) (determining that the public trust doctrine foreclosed a regulatory takings claim because the doctrine already applied to private property owner's tidelands prior to the adoption of a regulation prohibiting dredging and filling; remanded on factual question of whether private property owner uses land for any uses consistent with public trust doctrine, which could present a takings claim), *abrogated on other grounds*, Chong Yim v. City of Seattle, 451 P.3d 675, 682 (Wash. 2019). Even though it has been abrogated on other grounds, Orion still stands for the recognition that these principles could be applied to prevent a takings claim, even in 1987.

defense (though without clear support from the overseeing Federal Circuit),[239] the Massachusetts Supreme Court has implied hostility in clarifying that an extension of trust values would require compensation,[240] and the Texas Supreme Court also appears skeptical of the defense,[241] showing that for the time being, this use of the doctrine remains jurisdictionally unsettled.

2. The Secret Supreme Court Public Trust Debate

Although the Supreme Court has not weighed in directly on the public trust background principles debate, the issue was the subject of a notorious internal dispute in an important takings case from the Rehnquist Court Era involving coastal lands and municipal exactions. In *Nollan v. California Coastal Commission*, the majority concluded that the state was not entitled to require a private owner to allow public beach access by a trail easement along the edge of private waterfront land in exchange for permission to exceed existing land use regulations on building height.[242] Justice Brennan authored a lengthy dissent in which he briefly invoked the public trust doctrine in defense of the state's attempt to preserve public access to coastal waters: "The Court's insistence on a precise fit between the forms of burden and condition on each individual parcel along the California coast would penalize the Commission for its flexibility, hampering the ability to fulfill its public trust mandate."[243] For many years, however, the public was unaware of how substantially this published dissent departed from Justice Brennan's initial draft.

As was evident after other justices' papers became public, Justice Brennan had initially circulated a proposed dissent that began with a ten-page exposition of the public trust doctrine and its modern importance, citing it as the foundation for California's coastal regulatory policy and an independent basis for rejecting any

---

[239] *See, e.g.*, Tulare Lake Basin Water Dist. v. United States, 49 Fed. Cl. 313, 319 (2001) (upholding a takings claim by California irrigators after water delivery under a state contract was temporarily suspended while the state complied with restrictions under the Endangered Species Act); Casitas Mun. Water Dist. v. United States, 102 Fed. Cl. 443, 477–78 (2011) (in an opinion by the same judge as Tulare Lake Basin, on remand dismissing a water rights takings claim by a California irrigator that was itself required to create fish passage lanes to satisfy the Endangered Species Act on the ground that the issue was not ripe for adjudication, but noting that defendant did not preclude plaintiff's claim on theories of public trust or reasonable use); *aff'd by*, 708 F.3d 1340, 1360 (Fed. Cir. 2013) (affirmed on the ripeness grounds, and did not address the lower court's decision on the public trust issue).

[240] Op. of the Justs. to the House of Representatives, 313 N.E.2d 561 (Mass. 1974) (advising that legislation defining trust values to include beach access would require compensation as a taking).

[241] *See* Severance v. Patterson, 370 S.W.3d 705, 723 (Tex. 2012) ("[W]hile losing property to the public trust as it becomes part of the wet beach or submerged under the ocean is an ordinary hazard of ownership for coastal property owners, it is far less reasonable, and unsupported by ancient common law precepts, to hold that a public easement can suddenly encumber an entirely new portion of a landowner's property or a different landowner's property that was not previously subject to that right of use.").

[242] Nollan v. Cal. Coastal Comm'n, 483 U.S. 825, 828, 837, 841–42 (1987).

[243] *Id.* at 847 (1987) (Brennan, J., dissenting).

takings claim premised on the plaintiff's claimed right to exclude the public from the beach.[244] In reviewing the original draft (among the Papers of Justices Harry A. Blackmun and Thurgood Marshall that are on file at the Library of Congress), Professor Richard Lazarus reports that the dissent began by tracing the doctrine from the California constitution back to Roman law and ended with the conclusion that this historical understanding of public and private property rights in waterways forms the basis for intensive state regulation of coastal areas.[245] According to Lazarus, Brennan's initial dissent argued that the public trust doctrine "independently defeated any possible takings claim based on a private property right to exclude the public from the beach in front of the landowner's home."[246]

In Professor Lazarus's account of the judicial exchange behind closed doors, Justice Brennan's proposed dissent resulted in "a firestorm of controversy within and between chambers," prompting a series of negotiations between the Justices.[247] Justice Blackmun vehemently opposed Brennan's invocation of the public trust in support of a position being rejected by the majority, fearing that it would prompt a punishing response in Justice Antonin Scalia's majority opinion that could undermine the potential force of the doctrine in future jurisprudence.[248] He worried that even if the majority did not directly repudiate the doctrine, the central role that the doctrine would play in Justice Brennan's dissent would indirectly suggest that the Court had rejected it.[249] The two Justices and their clerks then engaged in a back-and-forth exchange of draft opinions in which Blackmun sought to persuade Brennan to eliminate his reliance on the public trust doctrine by threatening to specifically repudiate this analysis in a separate dissent that he would author himself.[250]

---

[244] Richard J. Lazarus, *Judicial Missteps, Legislative Dysfunction, and the Public Trust Doctrine: Can Two Wrongs Make It Right?*, 45 ENV'T L. 1139, 1146–47 (2015) [hereinafter *Judicial Missteps*] (citing Memorandum from Judicial Clerk, Supreme Court of the United States, to Harry A. Blackmun, Assoc. Justice, Supreme Court of the United States 1 [June 9, 1987] [on file with the Manuscript Division, Library of Congress, Papers of Harry A. Blackmun]).

[245] Posting of Richard J. Lazarus, to the Env't L. Professors Listserv, (Nov. 8, 2019) (on file with author) (telling the full story); E-mail from Richard J. Lazarus to author (July 7, 2019) (on file with author) (affirming permission for publication of this story).

[246] Lazarus, *Judicial Missteps supra* note 244, at 1146.

[247] *See id.* at 1146–47; Posting of Richard J. Lazarus, *supra* note 245; E-mail from Richard J. Lazarus, *supra* note 245.

[248] Lazarus, *Judicial Missteps, supra* note 244, at 1146 ("Justice Blackmun's chambers objected to Justice Brennan's inclusion of that discussion – not because of any substantive disagreement, but instead on purely tactical grounds").

[249] *Id.* at 1146–47 ("Justice Blackmun's clerk believed that any such discussion in Justice Brennan's dissent was ill-advised because it increased the odds that Justice Scalia might add language to the majority opinion expressly rejecting the doctrine or, even absent such a direct majority response, his opinion for the Court might more likely be read by the lower courts as implicitly doing so").

[250] *See id.*; Posting of Richard J. Lazarus, *supra* note 245; E-mail from Richard J. Lazarus, *supra* note 245. Richard Lazarus offered even more detail about the exchange in an account to the Environmental Law Professor's Listserv. This account includes so much more delightful intrigue than he reports in the published article that, with his permission, I thought it worth including here:

In the end, Justice Brennan's published dissent featured only the single reference to the doctrine, which signaled the importance of state obligations to protect public interests in coastal waters but in an understated way that did not prompt a response.[251] Justice Blackmun's bid to minimize the public trust discussion from Brennan's dissent succeeded in keeping the majority from repudiating the doctrine entirely, but Justice Scalia's majority decision troubled Blackmun enough that he nonetheless penned a separate dissent.[252] And within it, out of "an apparent abundance of caution,"[253] he took pains to stress that he did "not understand the Court's opinion in this case to implicate in any way the public-trust doctrine."[254]

3. A Constitutive Constraint on Federal Authority?

Even beyond the specific issue of constitutional takings, some scholars have argued that the doctrine is better understood not as an inherent limit on only state sovereign authority,[255] but as a quasi-constitutional "constitutive" limit on sovereign authority

> On June 9, Justice Blackmun's clerk for the case advised her Justice about what Brennan had done, with ominous words, and suggested he decline to join the dissent. Her concern was that "By featuring it so exhaustively in the dissent, Justice Brennan in effect incorporates the public trust doctrine into the position rejected by the majority. I regard this as unnecessary and unfortunate." The clerk accordingly recommended that Blackmun ask Brenna [sic] "to eliminate the first portion of this opinion and then to join the rest." The clerk further warned that she was not sure this would work – "I do not know if there is any hope of getting him to do this" but because "The Brennan clerk who worked on this case is known for launching grand strategies to order to get votes," and "they might be willing to modify the opinion in order to get your joinder."
>
> On June 12, Blackmun circulated his own first draft of a dissent just for himself saying not just [] what his final published dissent later said – "I do not understand the Court's opinion in this case to implicate in any way the public-trust doctrine" – but also a broadside complaint to Brennan for his then draft dissent: "I thus find Justice Brennan's reliance on this ground somewhat unusual, and I base my dissent on reasons independent of the public trust doctrine."
>
> Blackmun's ploy apparently worked. On June 15, Blackmun's clerk wrote her Justice that Brennan did now "remove the major section with the exposition of the public trust doctrine." She further explained in her memo that their "major goal is to prevent Justice Scalia from adding something to the majority that repudiates the public trust doctrine" and to that end, she recommended that Blackmun now withdraw his separate dissent and join Brennan's.
>
> On June 24, just before the final decision was published, the clerk wrote to Blackmun to say that the "case has gone from bad to worse" in light of more changes made by Scalia and there was no need to withdraw his (Blackmun's) separate dissent and still chiding Brennan's chambers, though happily the lengthy public trust discussion was now out of Brennan's dissent: "The damage has been done by Justice Brennan's dissent, not by your separate statement" though Blackmun should now take the last sentence of his draft out, to delete the reference to Brennan's extended public trust discussion, which was no longer there.
>
> Posting of Richard J. Lazarus, *supra* note 245 (published here with his permission).

[251] *Nollan*, 483 U.S. at 847 (1987) (Brennan, J. dissenting); *see also supra* text accompanying note 243.
[252] *See id.* at 865 (Blackmun, J., dissenting).
[253] Lazarus, *Judicial Missteps supra* note 244, at 1147.
[254] *Nollan*, 483 U.S. at 865.
[255] For a fuller discussion of this scholarship, see Chapter 7(C) ("Ordinary Common Law or Quasi-Constitutional?").

B. The Public Trust in Federal Law

in general, including federal authority.[256] As noted in Chapter 7, a constitutive limit is one that is "built into the fabric of sovereign authority, such that it cannot be extinguished through the normal judicial or legislative processes," as are ordinary exercises of sovereign power.[257] State supreme courts in California and Hawaii, among others, have already made this determination with regard to the role of the doctrine in state law.[258]

Pursuing the same intuition, scholars and advocates have often suggested that relevant federal sovereign authority should also be subject to public trust limits.[259] For example, Professor Gerald Torres and Nathan Bellinger argue that the public trust doctrine is an inherent right that predates the United States, and is therefore a preconstitutional constraint on the governance structure conferred by the U.S Constitution.[260] "After all," they contend, "the Constitution was not written on a blank slate but was written with certain principles and rights in mind. As the chalkboard on which the Constitution was written, the public trust doctrine provides the background and context for the Constitution."[261] Litigation following this argument has asserted that as an inherent limit on sovereign authority, the public trust doctrine may also be an implied feature of federal constitutional law.[262] If so,

---

[256] *See, e.g.,* Joseph Regalia, *A New Water Law Vista: Rooting the Public Trust Doctrine in the Courts*, 108 KY. L.J. 1, 6 (2020) ("Not only should litigants be able to argue for an expansion of trust duties in state courts under state constitutions, they should also be able to argue for this expansion in federal courts under the U.S. Constitution."); Michael C. Blumm & Mary C. Wood, *"No Ordinary Lawsuit": Climate Change, Due Process, and the Public Trust Doctrine*, 67 AM. U. L. REV. 1, 43–44 (2017) (arguing that the public trust doctrine is "an inherent constitutional limit on sovereignty"); Gerald Torres & Nathan Bellinger, *The Public Trust: The Law's DNA*, 4 WAKE FOREST J.L. & POL'Y 281, 288 (2014) (arguing that the public trust doctrine is an implied limit on federal authority because it "is the chalkboard on which the Constitution is written"); *see also* Chapter 7(C) ("Ordinary Common Law or Quasi-Constitutional?").

[257] *See* Chapter 7(C) ("Ordinary Common Law or Quasi-Constitutional?").

[258] *See supra* notes 126–129 and accompanying text.

[259] *See, e.g.,* MARY CHRISTINA WOOD, NATURE'S TRUST: ENVIRONMENTAL LAW FOR A NEW ECOLOGICAL AGE 133–36 (2014); Mary Christina Wood, *Advancing the Sovereign Trust of Government to Safeguard the Environment for Present and Future Generations (Part I): Ecological Realism and the Need for a Paradigm Shift*, 39 ENV'T L. 43, 74 (2009) [hereinafter Wood, Part I]; Mary Christina Wood, *Advancing the Sovereign Trust of Government to Safeguard the Environment for Present and Future Generations (Part II): Instilling a Fiduciary Obligation in Governance*, 39 ENV'T L. 91, 135–36 (2009) [hereinafter Wood, Part II] (suggesting avenues for Congress to meet its public trust responsibilities); Michael C. Blumm & Lynn S. Schaffer, *The Federal Public Trust Doctrine: Misinterpreting Justice Kennedy and Illinois Central Railroad*, 45 ENV'T L., 401, 401 (2015) (arguing that "there is considerable precedent applying the public trust doctrine to the federal government"); Blumm et al., *supra* note 83, at 494 ("[T]he public trust is grounded in the federal constitutional equal footing doctrine"); Richard A. Epstein, *The Public Trust Doctrine*, 7 CATO J. 411, 426 (1987) (asserting that the constitutional nature of the trust limits sovereign authority over public property in the same way the takings clause limits sovereign authority over private property).

[260] Torres & Bellinger, *supra* note 256, at 288.

[261] *Id.*; *see also* Chapter 7(C) ("Ordinary Common Law or Quasi-Constitutional?").

[262] *See, e.g.,* Blumm & Schaffer, *supra* note 259, at 403–06; *see also* Erin Ryan, *From Mono Lake to the Atmospheric Trust: Navigating the Public and Private Interests in Public Trust Resource Commons,*

goes this line of reasoning, then it may have application to waters under federal jurisdiction, and possibly to other natural resources that can be protected only by federal authority, such as the atmospheric commons under assault by greenhouse gas pollution.[263] As explored further in Chapter 9, this argument has met resistance in federal courts.

The argument proceeds along both logical and historical lines. The logical argument is that there is no principled reason to differentiate between the state and federal nature of the sovereign power rightfully constrained by the doctrine when the sovereign acts in a manner contrary to the public interest in trust resources.[264] Received as part of the English common law that forms the bedrock of all American legal institutions, the doctrine is neither a creature of state nor federal law, but a constraint on the sovereign authority delegated to each level of government within our federal system.[265] Whatever sovereign possesses legal authority over critical natural resource commons must match it with responsibility for protecting the public interests in them that have been recognized since ancient Rome.

The historical argument asserts that the public trust doctrine must constrain federal as well as state authority because there are neither logical nor historical grounds to differentiate their implicit origins. Except for the very first states, the trust obligations of most American states arose by delegation of federal authority over lands previously held in federal ownership. Today, the doctrine most often constrains state authority, because under the equal footing doctrine of the U.S. Constitution,[266] states own the submerged lands beneath navigable waterways,[267] and under the Submerged Lands Act,[268] they are the primary regulators of tidelands within three

---

10 GEO. WASH. J. ENERGY & ENV'T L. 39, 60–64 (2019) (discussing the argument as raised in atmospheric trust litigation, including *Juliana v. United States*); Juliana v. United States, 217 F. Supp. 3d 1224, 1254–55 (D. Or. 2016) (considering the argument), *rev'd*, Juliana v. United States, No. 24-684, D.C. No. 6:15-cv-1517, 2024 WL 5102489, 2024 WL 5102489, (May 1, 2024), *cert. denied*, 604 U.S. 645 (2025).

[263] *See* WOOD, NATURE'S TRUST, *supra* note 259, at 136 (arguing that federal trust obligations should apply to protect the atmosphere against private appropriation as a disposal site for greenhouse gas pollution).

[264] Blumm & Schaffer, *supra* note 259, at 401 ("The public trust doctrine, properly understood, is an inherent limit on all sovereigns – not merely state sovereigns"); WOOD, NATURE'S TRUST, *supra* note 259, at 133–36.

[265] *See* WOOD, NATURE'S TRUST, *supra* note 259, at 133–36.

[266] U.S. CONST. art. IV, § 3, cl. 1; Coyle v. Smith, 221 U.S. 559, 566 (1911) (interpreting the equal footing clause); *see also* Blumm et al., *supra* note 83, at 490–92 (1997) (discussing the relationship between the equal footing doctrine and the public trust doctrine); Harrison C. Dunning, *The Public Trust: A Fundamental Doctrine of American Property Law*, 19 ENV'T L. 515, 524 (1989) (also discussing the relationship between the equal footing doctrine and the public trust doctrine).

[267] *See* Pollard v. Hagan, 44 U.S. 212, 222, 230 (1845) (affirming under the equal footing doctrine that the state of Alabama owned the submerged land beneath its navigable waterways); *see also* Crystal S. Chase, *The Illinois Central Public Trust Decision and Federal Common Law: An Unconventional View*, 16 HASTINGS W.-NW. J. ENV'T L. & POL'Y 113, 121–22 (2010) (discussing the equal footing doctrine, as set forth in *Pollard*, as an analytical building block of the public trust doctrine).

[268] 43 U.S.C. § 1301–1315 (2012).

B. The Public Trust in Federal Law

miles of shore.[269] But other than the original thirteen colonies, all states inherited their trust obligations through the medium of federal sovereignty that applied before their lands were carved out of federal holdings.[270] The states must have inherited a preexisting trust obligation, goes this reasoning, because there is no clear legal moment when new trust obligations were expressly conferred. Therefore, the doctrine must have implicitly inhered at the federal level before it was transferred to the states, and by this theory, it remains there in application to all trust resources that were not delegated to the states.[271]

Advocates thus maintain that, by the logic underlying the doctrine and the history through which it came into effect, there is no persuasive reason to distinguish between state or federal sovereignty when they govern resources that are appropriately subject to the public trust.[272] The trust simply establishes a constraint on sovereign authority at whatever is the relevant level to protect public trust resources from private expropriation or monopolization. For submerged lands that remain under federal jurisdiction, or for other obligations the doctrine may be held to create, these scholars and litigants argue that the federal government should be equally bound as trustee.[273]

Nevertheless, the Supreme Court has not squarely considered the issue, leaving open to question the ultimate role of the doctrine as a limit on federal authority. To be sure, such a finding would have to overcome formidable hurdles in other Supreme Court dicta suggesting that there is no cognizable federal public trust.[274] In *PPL Montana, LLC v. Montana*, the Court considered a separate doctrine involving the role of navigable waterways in establishing state title, but the majority opinion noted that the public trust doctrine is a matter of state law.[275] That brief reference, suggesting that the doctrine is not an implied feature of federal constitutional law, weakens the argument that the public trust doctrine binds federal authority in the same way that it binds the states – but the reference appears as dicta, presenting a conclusion that was not properly presented or argued before the Court. It remains to be seen whether this *dicta* will hold firm over time or be dislodged by more directed Supreme Court litigation in the future.

---

[269] *Id.* § 1311–1312 (2012) (discussing state authority over submerged lands and seaward boundaries).

[270] One way of viewing this is that in the equal footing conveyances, the federal government itself imposed the trust on the states. See Blumm & Schaffer, *supra* note 259, at 403–07 (discussing Justice Kennedy's reference to the equal footing doctrine in Idaho v. Coeur d'Alene Tribe, 521 U.S. 261 (1997) and what it means for the public trust doctrine's origins).

[271] *See id.*

[272] *Id*; WOOD, NATURE'S TRUST, *supra* note 259, at 133–36.

[273] Blumm & Schaffer, *supra* note 259 at 430; WOOD, NATURE'S TRUST, *supra* note 259, at 133–36.

[274] PPL Mont., LLC v. Montana, 565 U.S. 576, 603–04 (2012). *Cf.* Alec L. *ex rel.* Loorz v. McCarthy, 574 U.S. 1047 (2014) (denying a petition for certiorari to the United States Court of Appeals for the District of Columbia).

[275] *PPL Mont., LLC*, 565 U.S. at 603 ("Unlike the equal-footing doctrine, however, which is the constitutional foundation for the navigability rule of riverbed title, the public trust doctrine remains a matter of state law.").

The issue was most recently raised, together with other novel claims, in *Juliana v. United States*,[276] the "Kid's Climate Case," in which youth plaintiffs in Oregon challenged state and federal regulatory failures to protect the air commons from private appropriation by greenhouse gas polluters.[277] The claim would have tested arguments about federal trust obligations, but as detailed in Chapter 9, it never reached a jury.[278] The federal district court judge twice agreed that the claim deserved its day in court, upholding the case against multiple motions to dismiss and writs of mandamus by the federal government, which was deeply resistant to the claim.[279] The Supreme Court declined the government's two invitations to weigh in, but it lightly interposed in its favor by suggesting that the Ninth Circuit intervene on interlocutory appeal,[280] The Ninth Circuit took the hint and ordered the case dismissed (over a vigorous dissent).[281] The plaintiffs unsuccessfully sought a rehearing before all the judges of the Ninth Circuit *en banc*,[282] and though the district court then allowed them to temporarily resurrect the claim by amending their complaint,[283] it was ultimately dismissed by the Ninth Circuit on another interlocutory appeal, and the Supreme Court declined the youth plaintiffs' petition for certiorari.[284]

The extraordinary ten-year journey of a claim that was never truly heard attests to the hurdles for American climate litigation in the absence of stronger federal foundations for environmental law, and as discussed further in Chapter 9, the potential importance of public trust principles as a surrogate. The labyrinthine procedural history in *Juliana* makes clear that the Supreme Court is not eager to entertain such a claim – but the extraordinary volley of litigation back and forth among the different federal courts testifies to the gravity of the issues, and the possibility that the Court may eventually have to consider some version of it in future litigation.

---

[276] Juliana v. United States, 217 F. Supp. 3d 1224 (D. Or. 2016). Here, federal district court Judge Ann Aiken initially ruled that the claim could go forward, engaging with the merits of a claim that would ultimately be dismissed on appeal. Juliana v. United States, No. 24-684, D.C. No. 6:15-cv-1517, 2024 WL 5102489, 2024 WL 5102489, (May 1, 2024), *cert. denied*, 604 U.S. 645 (2025).

[277] *Id.*; *see also* Erin Ryan, Mary Wood, Richard Frank, James Huffman, & Irma Russell, Juliana v. United States: *Debating the Fundamentals of the Fundamental Right to a Sustainable Environment*, 46 FLA. ST. U. L. REV. ONLINE 1 (2018), www.fsulawreview.com/article/juliana-v-united-states-debating-the-fundamentals-of-the-fundamental-right-to-a-sustainable-climate/ [hereinafter Ryan, et al., *Debating the Fundamentals of the Fundamental Right*] (analyzing both the atmospheric trust claim and the accompanying fundamental rights claim for climate stability).

[278] *See* Chapter 9(B)(4) ("*Juliana v. United States*") (recounting every stage of the decade-long litigation).

[279] Juliana v. United States, 947 F.3d 1159, 1164–66 (9th Cir. 2020).

[280] Order Denying Petition for Stay of Proceedings, *In re United States*, 586 U.S. 983 (2018) (No. 18A410), www.perma.cc/4GM6-W8BV (denying the petition while suggesting that relief might still be available from the Ninth Circuit).

[281] *Juliana*, 947 F.3d at 1175.

[282] Juliana v. United States, 986 F.3d 1295 (9th Cir. 2021) (mem.).

[283] Juliana v. Unites States, Civ. No. 15-CV-01517-AA, 2023 WL 3750334, at *8 (D. Or. June 1, 2023).

[284] Juliana v. United States, No. 24-684, D.C. No. 6:15-cv-1517, 2024 WL 5102489, 2024 WL 5102489, (May 1, 2024), *cert. denied*, 604 U.S. 645 (2025).

4. Stronger than Federal Law?

Even if the public trust doctrine has no force in federal law, at least one state has argued in federal court that it is an aspect of state law that is stronger than federal law, or at least more powerful than federal law can extinguish, even under the constitutional principle of federal supremacy. California took this argument all the way to the Ninth Circuit, after the United States took fee simple interest in 32.42 acres of state land on behalf of the Navy.[285] The Navy had continuously leased the parcel since 1949, and during that time, had filled the property "to expand the Navy's Training Station," such that only 4.88 of the original acreage remained submerged.[286] When the Navy sought to renew the lease in 1996 – after the *Mono Lake* story had galvanized the force of the California public trust – the State Lands Commission and San Diego Port District opposed the extension on public trust grounds.[287] The state argued, in essence, that the public trust doctrine was an aspect of state sovereignty that the federal government could not constitutionally extinguish.[288]

When the federal government sought to extinguish California's public trust rights in the property, California did not dispute the power of the U.S. government to take and use the land, but it protested its transfer to a private party free of trust restrictions.[289] California conceded that the United States was not subject to California's public trust restrictions while the federal government held title to the land, but it argued that during that time, the state trust restrictions simply fell "quiescent."[290] The state contended that when the United States seeks to transfer title of such land to a private party, then those trust restrictions would reemerge.[291] California argued that the federal government lacked authority to displace the public trust through eminent domain this way, because the public trust is an aspect of state sovereignty that federal power cannot extinguish.[292] The argument implies that that the rights protected by the public trust doctrine are just as foundational as the federal power of eminent domain.

The federal district court held that the 27.54 acres of former tidelands that had been filled by the United States to become dry land were now held without limitation and could "be conveyed to a private party free of any trust."[293] The 4.88 acres

---

[285] United States v. 32.42 Acres of Land, 683 F.3d 1030, 1032 (9th Cir. 2012).
[286] *32.42 Acres of Land*, 683 F.3d at 1033.
[287] *Id.*
[288] *Id.* ("The Lands Commission argues that [the *Illinois Central*] reasoning distinguishes California's title in 'sovereign public trust lands' from its interest in 'proprietary lands,' and that its public trust rights cannot be extinguished because they are an aspect of its sovereignty.").
[289] *Id.* at 1032.
[290] *Id.*
[291] *Id.*
[292] *Id.* at 1034. ("The Lands Commission contends that the public trust is an aspect of state sovereignty that the federal government is without power to extinguish, or at least has no power to extinguish in this case.").
[293] *Id.* at 1032.

that remained tidelands became subject to "a federal public trust" upon federal seizure and could not be conveyed to a private party.[294] The court did not expound on what it meant by "federal public trust" nor where it comes from, and it is notable that the federal court assumed there was such a doctrine.

The Ninth Circuit appeals court affirmed, reasoning that when the United States takes property by eminent domain within its legitimate constitutional powers, then it establishes a wholly new title, obliterating all previous interests.[295] California had cited *Illinois Central* to support its assertion that the public trust doctrine is an aspect of state sovereignty that cannot be overridden by federal power, and it further cited the *Mono Lake* case to illustrate the California Supreme Court's reliance on *Illinois Central* to establish the state's sovereign duties as trustee of public trust resources, but the Ninth Circuit was unconvinced.[296] Of note, it also mentioned the federal public trust doctrine, in the very same year that the Supreme Court cast doubt on its existence in the *PPL Montana* case, overtly noting the unresolved issue.[297]

These references to a "federal public trust doctrine" by a federal district court judge and a federal appellate panel of three judges reveal that that the courts are still in disarray on the precise relationship between the public trust doctrine and state sovereign authority. Perhaps they were ill-informed about the Supreme Court's contemporaneous contrary dicta, or perhaps they were simply persuaded by the reasoning championed by the public trust scholars described earlier. Either way, litigants continue to force the judiciary to consider the question, in ever more ambitious ways. Indeed, Chapter 9 explores the concerted efforts by environmental advocates to extend public trust principles to protect the atmospheric commons through both state and federal law, in hope of achieving affirmative obligations for effective climate governance. As this book goes to press, these efforts have met with only limited success in American courts when premised on the common law trust, but they have proved more successful when premised on state constitutional trusts and internationally, and they have accomplished notable successes in the policy arena. Perhaps just as important, they have mobilized millions of young people all around the world.[298]

---

[294] *Id.*
[295] *Id.* at 1038 ("Holding that California's public trust interest in the Property survives the federal government's attempt to condemn it would subjugate the federal government's eminent domain power to California's state law public trust doctrine … The Supremacy Clause Prevents this outcome.").
[296] *Id.* at 1037–38.
[297] *PPL Mont., LLC*, 565 U.S. 576 at 603 ("Unlike the equal-footing doctrine, however, which is the constitutional foundation for the navigability rule of riverbed title, the public trust doctrine remains a matter of state law."). The disjuncture between the Ninth Circuit and Supreme Court treatments of a federal public trust in the same year is noteworthy. The Ninth Circuit decided *32.42 Acres* on June 14, 2012, four months after the Supreme Court issued *PPL Montana* on February 22, 2012, and it duly cited the relevant *PPL Montana* dicta. However, in a footnote, the Ninth Circuit sidestepped the unresolved legal question, explaining that "[b]ecause the United States did not appeal from the district court's determination that a federal public trust arises in the 4.88 acres of the Property that currently remain tidelands, we do not address that determination." *Id.* at n.2.
[298] *See* Chapter 9(B) ("Trust-Rights Advocacy in Action: Atmospheric Trust and Climate Rights Litigation").

9

Public Trust Principles, Environmental Rights, and Trust-Rights Climate Advocacy

A.	Public Trust Principles and Environmental Rights in the Literature	287
	1. Searching for Environmental Rights in U.S. Law	288
	2. Public Trust Principles in Climate Advocacy	291
	3. The Scholarly Critics	293
	4. The Reciprocal Nature of Sovereign Obligations and Environmental Rights	297
B.	Trust-Rights Advocacy in Action: Atmospheric Trust and Climate Rights Litigation	300
	1. *Urgenda Foundation* and International Climate Claims	302
	2. The Atmospheric Trust Project in U.S. Law	310
	3. An Administrative Atmospheric Trust	315
	4. *Juliana v. United States*	318
	a. The *Juliana* Pleadings	319
	b. The Campaign to Dismiss	325
	c. The Amended Complaint	329
	d. *Juliana*'s Legacy	330
C.	Climate Claims on State Constitutional Grounds	333
	1. Trust-Rights Protections in State Constitutions	334
	2. Heeding the Lessons of *Juliana*	338
	3. Climate Stability as a State Fundamental Right	340
	4. Proposals for State Trust-Right Amendments	341
D.	Constitutional and Pragmatic Concerns with Emerging Climate Advocacy	344
	1. Separation of Powers Concerns	346
	2. The Atmospheric Trust and Negative Precedent	348
	3. Legal Strategy and Climate Advocacy	349
	4. In Defense of Trust-Rights Advocacy	351
	5. A Generational Divide?	357

While the ancient Roman common law statement of the public trust doctrine originally applied it to both air and water resources,[1] as described in Chapter 8, the American common law doctrine stands most firmly rooted in application to navigable waterways.[2] That doctrine continues to evolve in its application to different water contexts – including California's extension of the *Mono Lake* doctrine to groundwater tributaries,[3] the protection of public beach access in New Jersey,[4] public walking rights along Great Lakes shores,[5] and the protection of public drinking water from hydraulic fracturing under Pennsylvania's constitutionalized trust.[6] Yet scholars, litigants, and courts have continued to wrestle with questions about the scope of the doctrine. To which waterways does it apply – all of them, or only a subset?[7] Why would it bind only state and not federal authority?[8] And what about other public natural resources?

Indeed, the foundational public trust principle begs legitimate questions about why the same premise should not apply equally to other critical natural resource commons that are also susceptible to harmful private expropriation or monopoly. By the same rationale that requires sovereign oversight of the territorial seas, why not coral reefs, forests, or biodiversity – all intrinsically valuable features of the shared environment that also confer critical ecosystem services? American litigants applying the common law doctrine to these latter resources have encountered high hurdles, perhaps because they don't share the same fluid and fugitive common pool features as water, or draw less support from precedent.[9]

---

[1] See J. INST. PROEMIUM, 2.1.1 at 167 (T. Sandars trans., 4th ed. 1869) ("By the law of nature these things are common to mankind – the air, running water, the sea, and consequently the shores of the sea.").

[2] See, e.g., Ill. Cent. R.R. Co. v. Illinois, 146 U.S. 387, 452 (1892) (in a seminal Supreme Court public trust case, applying the doctrine to protect public interests in Chicago Harbor and affirming its long application as a constraint on state sovereignty to protect public interests in navigable waterways).

[3] See Env't Law Found. v. State Water Res. Control Bd., 26 Cal. App. 5th 844, 857–858 (2018), *rev. denied* (Nov. 28, 2018).

[4] See Matthews v. Bay Head Improvement Ass'n, 471 A.2d 355, 363 (N.J. 1984).

[5] See Glass v. Goeckel, 703 N.W.2d 58, 61 (Mich. 2005).

[6] See John C. Dernbach, *The Potential Meanings of a Constitutional Public Trust*, 45 ENV'T L. 463, 464 (2015); Robinson Twp. v. Commonwealth, 83 A.3d 901, 913 (Pa. 2013) (recognizing that Pennsylvania's public trust doctrine applies more broadly to natural resources affected by oil and gas).

[7] See, e.g., Kramer v. City of Lake Oswego, 395 P.3d 592, 612 (Or. Ct. App. 2017), aff'd in part, rev'd in part, 446 P.3d 1 (Or. 2019), *opinion adhered to as modified on reconsideration*, 455 P.3d 922 (Or. 2019) (declining plaintiff's request to clarify that the public trust doctrine applies to all submerged lands and overlying waters, not just those owned by the state). On appeal, the Oregon Supreme Court held that neither the city nor the state could restrict the public's right to enter public waters from abutting waterfront parks. Kramer v. City of Lake Oswego, 446 P.3d at 6.

[8] See Cathy J. Lewis, *The Timid Approach of the Federal Courts to the Public Trust Doctrine: Justified Reluctance or Dereliction of Duty?*, 19 PUB. LAND & RES. L. REV. 51, 76 (1998) (advocating that federal courts should make vigorous use of the public trust doctrine in natural resource cases).

[9] See, e.g., San Diego Cnty. Archaeological Soc'y, Inc. v. Compadres, 81 Cal. App. 3d 923, 925–26, (Ct. App. 1978), *disapproved of on other grounds by* City of Los Angeles v. Venice Peninsula Properties, 31 Cal. 3d 288, 644 P.2d 792 (1982) ("The [public trust] doctrine has been restricted to tidelands, navigable waters and situations where the government or public in general own the property.").

But if those are the relevant metrics, then what about the ocean of air that is the atmosphere, and the fragile climatic system it supports?

Given the premise of the fundamental public trust principle – that some natural resources are so critical to everyone that the sovereign must protect them for the public benefit – climate advocates have asserted that it should apply to the great air commons on which we all depend, certainly as dearly as we do the water commons.[10] They remind us that even the original Roman doctrine held that not only were the sea and the shores of the sea the common property of all the people, but also the air.[11] When Americans first received the doctrine from British common law centuries ago, the doctrine's protections expanded from focusing not only on the territorial seas but also the new nation's great navigable lakes and rivers, which would benefit for the same underlying reasons. Should the atmosphere become the next formal extension of the doctrine, also for the same underlying reasons? Should the core public trust principle be appropriately dispatched to address the natural resource crisis of our time, and one that threatens to eclipse all others – climate change?

This chapter reviews the adaptation of public trust principles in modern climate advocacy, exploring both the opportunities and the obstacles it poses for doctrinal development. It catalogs the explosion of atmospheric trust and other climate litigation that shares common roots with the public trust principles that are the subject of this book, addressing both the scholarly discourse that inspired the project and the pragmatic challenges litigators have faced attempting to use the doctrine in the climate context.

Moreover, it reveals a confluence of seemingly contrasting models of climate advocacy that are, in fact, one – claims for climate regulation based on (1) public trust sovereign obligations to protect the atmosphere, and (2) environmental rights held directly by members of the public. Climate litigants are increasingly asserting a mix of public trust principles – premised on the government's responsibility to protect atmospheric resources for the public – and public environmental rights to atmospheric stability – which, in turn, require sovereign vindication. Seldom acknowledged is the fact that each of these approaches to climate advocacy implies the same basic partnership between environmental rights and sovereign obligations.

As legal scholars have long understood, legal rights and duties are often different sides of the same coin: if a citizen has a right, then the state has an implicit duty to respect it.[12] By that same token, if the state has an obligation, the beneficiary of that obligation – the citizens – have rights.[13] For this reason, atmospheric trust litigation

---

[10] See *infra* Part B(2) ("The Atmospheric Trust Project in U.S. Law") (discussing these claims).

[11] See *supra* note 1 (quoting the Institutes of Justinian).

[12] Cf. WESLEY NEWCOMB HOHFELD, FUNDAMENTAL LEGAL CONCEPTIONS AS APPLIED IN JUDICIAL REASONING AND OTHER LEGAL ESSAYS 36–50 (1919) (making parallel arguments in the private law context).

[13] *Id.* Following the Hohfeldian model, "rights" are legal privileges to which the holder is entitled under the governing rules of law. In the private law context about which Hohfeld wrote, these rules of law

is premised on an implicit theory of environmental rights, and climate rights litigation is implicitly premised on a public trust theory of sovereign obligation. While individual lawsuits often brand themselves according to one or the other approach, they can be conceptually grouped together as "trust-rights" strategies.[14]

The fact that the plaintiffs in these suits are often children – speaking for themselves and members of future generations without more formal means of political participation – has made their claims all the more poignant. Beginning in the 2010s, American youth climate advocates began bringing atmospheric trust lawsuits and administrative petitions in every state and in federal court – each seeking to establish the atmosphere as a public trust resource on which we all depend, and which the government is therefore obligated to protect.[15] These lawsuits centered on the idea that the state should not permit, encourage, or enable greenhouse gas polluters to expropriate the public atmospheric commons for use as a private carbon sink.

International advocates brought both atmospheric trust litigation[16] and suits premised more directly on environmental rights, often drawn from national laws and treaties guaranteeing individual rights to life, dignity, and other values undermined by climate instability.[17] Beginning with the Dutch Supreme Court's groundbreaking conclusion in *Urgenda Foundation v. Netherlands*[18] that the nation had failed its duty under the European Convention on Human Rights (ECHR) to limit contributions to climate change,[19] these efforts inspired American advocates to experiment with partnering and even replacing trust claims with constitutional assertions of public rights to a stable climate. In the most famous example, *Juliana v. United States*,[20] the plaintiffs

---

are set forth as principles of tort, property, and contract law. In the public law context, they can be established by constitution, statute, or, as in the case of the public trust doctrine, common law.

[14] See generally Erin Ryan, *Public Trust Principles and Environmental Rights: The Hidden Duality of Climate Rights Advocacy and the Atmospheric Trust*, 49 HARV. ENVTL. L. REV. 225 (2025) [hereinafter *Public Trust Principles*] (coining the term "trust-rights" litigation and making this argument for the first time).

[15] See Anna Christiansen, *Up in the Air: A Fifty-State Survey of Atmospheric Trust Litigation Brought by Our Children's Trust*, 2020 UTAH L. REV. 867, 868 (2020); *Legal Proceedings in All 50 States*, OUR CHILD'S. TR., https://perma.cc/35XE-MXH8. See also James Conca, *Atmospheric Trust Litigation – Can We Sue Ourselves over Climate Change?*, FORBES (Nov. 23, 2014), https://perma.cc/V7UT-TK4C.

[16] See, e.g., Shrestha v. Off. of the Prime Minister, 074-WO-0283 (2018) (Nepal), https://perma.cc/X9SE-KZSH. See infra notes 109–120 (discussing the claim in more detail); Complaint at 14, La Rose v. Her Majesty the Queen, [2020] 2020 FC 1008 (Can.). See also infra notes 174–178.

[17] See infra Part B(1) ("*Urgenda Foundation* and International Climate Claims").

[18] Urgenda v. Netherlands, [2015] HAZA C/09/00456689 (Neth.) at 41, https://perma.cc/V7C5-VRAV (unofficial English translation).

[19] Urgenda v. Netherlands, [2015] HAZA C/09/00456689 (Neth.) at 41, https://perma.cc/V7C5-VRAV (unofficial English translation) (interpreting European Convention on Human Rights, arts. 2, 8, EU, Sept. 3, 1953, C.E.T.S. No. 213) ("Urgenda argues that under Articles 2 and 8 of the ECHR, the State has the positive obligation to take protective measures. Urgenda also claims that the State is acting unlawfully because, as a consequence of insufficient mitigation, it (more than proportionately) endangers the living climate (and thereby also the health) of man and the environment, thereby breaching its duty of care. Urgenda asserts that in doing so the State is acting unlawfully towards Urgenda.").

[20] Juliana v. United States, No. 24-684, D.C. No. 6:15-cv-1517, 2024 WL 5102489, (May 1, 2024), *cert. denied*, 604 U.S. 645 (2025) (Ninth Circuit's order granting the defendant's motion to dismiss and Supreme Court's denial of the plaintiffs' petition for certiorari).

partnered an atmospheric trust claim with environmental rights asserted under the substantive component of the U.S. Constitution's Due Process Clause.[21]

Other American claims for climate governance have proceeded directly from state laws and constitutional provisions guaranteeing rights to a healthy environment. Effective in 2022, the New York Constitution was amended to guarantee "a right to clean air and water, and a healthful environment."[22] In 2023, youth plaintiffs convinced a state court to recognize rights to climate stability under the Montana Constitution's promise of a healthy environment – the first recognition of climate rights in the United States – and the Montana Supreme Court resoundingly affirmed.[23] In 2024, Hawaiian youth plaintiffs succeeded in their claim that state practices favoring fossil fuel based transportation infringed their rights under the Hawai'i Constitution to a life-sustaining climate.[24] In the resulting consent decree, Hawai'i acknowledged these climate rights and enacted new climate governance infrastructure charged with achieving net zero emissions by 2045.[25] Inspired by these successes, climate advocates around the country are now advancing a series of state constitutional amendments to explicitly recognize both sovereign obligations and environmental rights.

This cascade of trust-rights climate litigation showcase common themes and opportunities, creating new levers for youth public participation, new tools for speech amplification, and new opportunities to reverse regulatory capture. Yet claims have also been vulnerable to similar hurdles associated with vagueness, redressability, and at least in the United States, the constitutional separation of powers. Especially domestically, claims have so far failed more often than they have succeeded in court.[26] While they proved successful at movement building, they have also generated substantial controversy among observers who assail them as rhetorical gestures that will, at best, be ineffective – and at worst, threaten the constitutional order.[27] Opponents critique these claims for their departure from established precedent, for practical problems created by the litigation

---

[21] Juliana v. United States, Civ. No. 15-CV-01517-AA, 2023 WL 3750334, at *9 (D. Or. June 1, 2023) (district court's order explaining that "plaintiffs seek declaratory relief that 'the United States' national energy system that creates the harmful conditions described herein has violated and continues to violate the Fifth Amendment of the U.S. Constitution and Plaintiffs' constitutional rights to substantive due process and equal protection of the law'").

[22] N.Y. CONST. art. I, § 19.

[23] Held v. Montana, 2024 MT 312, para. 30 (Dec. 18, 2024), *affirming* Held v. State of Montana, No. CDV-2020-307, slip op. at 17 (Mont. 1st Jud. Dist. May 23, 2023) ("Based on the plain language of the implicated constitutional provisions, the intent of the Framers, and Montana Supreme Court precedent, it would not be absurd to find that a stable climate system is included in the 'clean and healthful environment' and 'environmental life-support system' contemplated by the Framers.").

[24] Joint Stip. and Order Re: Settlement at 6, Navahine v. Hawai'i Dep't of Transportation et al., No. 1CCV-22-000063 (Haw. Cir. Ct. Jun. 20, 2024).

[25] *Id.* at 3. *See also* Office of the Governor of Hawaii-News Release-*Historic Agreement Settles Navahine Climate Litigation*, GOVERNOR JOSH GREEN, (June 20, 2024), https://perma.cc/4TAP-7SJA.

[26] *See infra* Part B(2) ("The Atmospheric Trust Project in U.S. Law") (discussing these claims).

[27] *See infra* Part A ("Public Trust Principles and Environmental Rights in the Literature") & Part D Constitutional and Pragmatic Concerns with Emerging Climate Advocacy") (discussing arguments by proponents and opponents).

strategy, and for the impracticability of some requested remedies given the nature of affirmative rights and the limits of the judicial role.[28] For others, the judicial role in trust administration raises a different set of constitutional concerns, on both sides of the political spectrum – from conservatives worried about judicial encroachment on legislative policymaking to liberals worried about the Supreme Court's rejection of administrative deference.[29] Still others worry more about the implications of *not* pushing these boundaries in the face of the looming harms associated with climate change.[30]

This chapter thus explores the intertwined evolution of "trust-rights" climate litigation strategies, the obstacles and opportunities for their future development, the critiques leveled against them, and the pragmatic hurdles for litigators attempting to deploy them. Part A begins with the origins of trust-rights litigation strategies in legal scholarship, reviewing the ongoing search for sources of environmental rights, consideration of public trust principles in application to climate advocacy, and scholarly critiques of the atmospheric trust project, even among environmental advocates. It also reveals the hidden duality of trust-rights climate claims, with reference to legal scholarship establishing the reciprocal nature of legal rights and duties. As explained in the Introduction, the core public trust principle is framed as a pairing of sovereign obligation with public environmental rights – making the public trust doctrine perhaps the *first* assertion of environmental rights in the western legal tradition. As a necessary corollary, pure statements of environmental rights are also variations of the core public trust principle, because they necessarily imply sovereign obligations to protect those rights.

Part B reviews the climate trust-rights advocacy that has followed, tracing the trajectory of atmospheric trust and environmental rights claims around the nation and the world. After reporting on successful examples of trust-rights litigation abroad, focusing on the Dutch *Urgenda Foundation* exemplar, it turns to the less successful track record of atmospheric trust advocacy in the United States, focusing on the American standard-bearer of *Juliana v. United States*. The *Juliana* plaintiffs were unable to get their claim before a federal jury despite a decade of preliminary litigation, demonstrating how the lacking constitutional foundations for U.S. environmental law makes it so comparatively difficult for U.S. environmental advocates to litigate claims in federal court. This section describes how the early atmospheric trust movement gave way to a newer generation of American litigation premising claims on both sovereign trust obligations and constitutional rights – and ultimately, environmental rights and obligations in state constitutions. Part C discusses significant trust-rights climate advocacy premised on state constitutional provisions, reporting

---

[28] *Id.*; *see also* Introduction, Part D: "Public Trust Principles and Environmental Rights" (discussing the limited role of affirmative rights in the American legal tradition and whether sovereign stewardship obligations are better understood as negative rights).

[29] *See infra* Parts A & D.

[30] *See, e.g.*, MARY CHRISTINA WOOD, NATURE'S TRUST: ENVIRONMENTAL LAW FOR A NEW ECOLOGICAL AGE 133–36 (2014) [hereinafter NATURE'S TRUST] (arguing that the atmospheric trust project is important because there is no more time to waste).

on developments in New York, Montana, Hawaii, Utah, Pennsylvania, and nine other states in which trust-rights amendments have been proposed.

Finally, Part D concludes with consideration of the jurisprudential and pragmatic arguments against – and in favor of – trust-rights advocacy, addressing both constitutional concerns about the separation of powers and practical concerns about bringing impact litigation in uncertain judicial venues. While these strategies offer heightened public participation opportunities for climate advocates who feel shut out of the political process, critics assail the vagueness and futility of the legal constraint these claims assert, as well as the extraordinary remedies they have sought. If the sovereign has an obligation to protect "the environment," what exactly does that require, and when do we know it has been violated? If citizens have a right to "a healthful environment," what specific action or inaction must the government undertake to vindicate that right? And even if these rights and obligations can be demonstrated, can the judiciary meaningfully redress alleged violations? Even if it can, is this the right time to further empower judicial oversight of environmental governance?

The chapter nevertheless concludes that trust-rights strategies play an important role in the overall democratic process, even when they lose. They help amplify the voices of ordinary advocates in a policymaking context dominated by more powerful stakeholders, and they offer opportunities to build public constituencies for more effective participation in the political arena. While climate advocacy of this sort should not replace conventional legal advocacy through the ordinary channels of policymaking, it provides a safety valve to address potential failures of the political process. The mixed reception of trust-rights litigation suggests a generational divide in environmental advocacy that also warrants our attention, in which an older generation appears to maintain more faith in conventional legal advocacy than those that have followed, as conventional tools and sources of law come increasingly under new forms of assault.[31]

A. PUBLIC TRUST PRINCIPLES AND ENVIRONMENTAL RIGHTS IN THE LITERATURE

Situating this analysis in the broader scholarly literature, this part discusses the array of legal scholarship has explored various legal bases for asserting public trust and rights-based claims to protect the natural environment, many arising long before public concerns over climate change began to eclipse most others. It reviews the academic exploration of potential legal foundations on which to premise claims for

---

[31] *See, e.g.*, West Virginia v. EPA, 597 U.S. 697, 732 (2022) (overturning Clean Power Plan regulations designed to reduce greenhouse gas emissions under the Clean Air Act without clearer authorization from a congress unlikely to provide it); Sackett v. EPA, 598 U.S. 651, 684 (2023) (overturning Clean Water Act regulations to protect wetlands without a continuous surface connection to conventionally navigable waterways for similar reasons); Loper Bright Enterprises v. Raimondo, 144 S.Ct. 2244, 2273 (2024) (overturning the *Chevron* doctrine of judicial deference to administrative interpretation by, among others, environmental agencies).

environmental rights and obligations that would protect climate stability, beginning with constitutional and statutory law, briefly addressing rights of nature scholarship, and then turning to scholarly advocacy for the application of public trust principles to the atmospheric commons. It also addresses scholarly criticism of public trust advocacy, its use in climate advocacy specifically, and climate litigation premised on environmental rights or obligations in general. Review of the literature addressing the atmospheric trust project and other environmental rights-based advocacy exposes longing among advocates for stronger legal foundations, but also dissensus among both proponents and opponents of stronger climate governance over the role trust-rights advocacy should play.

1. *Searching for Environmental Rights in U.S. Law*

In a 2003 book, Professors David Markell and Clifford Rechtschaffen confronted the problem of lacking constitutional foundations for U.S. environmental law in an exploration of what constitutional sources are available to ground environmental regulation.[32] Their account identified several constitutional provisions that offer at least indirect support for American environmental law, and on which federal environmental regulations are premised: (1) the Commerce Clause, (2) the dormant Commerce Clause, (3) Tenth Amendment limits on the power of the federal government to require state action, and (4) the Supremacy Clause and implied preemption.[33] While these constitutional provisions have grounded nearly half a century of critical environmental statutory law at the federal level, to date, none has produced an ironclad platform for holistic climate regulation that has survived judicial scrutiny,[34] nor have they grounded regulatory efforts to protect the nation's waterways beyond the point of navigability.[35]

In response to these limitations, the rights of nature discourse began gathering force in the United States after the Supreme Court rejected the idea that natural objects could assert legal rights in 1972.[36] In *Sierra Club v. Morton*, the Court held that harm to the natural environment itself was insufficient to confer standing in a suit to halt development plans for a Disney ski resort in the Sequoia National

---

[32] See CLIFFORD RECHTSCHAFFEN & DAVID L. MARKELL, REINVENTING ENVIRONMENTAL ENFORCEMENT & THE STATE/FEDERAL RELATIONSHIP 38–43 (2003).

[33] *Id.*

[34] *See, e.g.*, West Virginia v. EPA, 597 U.S. 697, 734–35 (2022) (concluding that the Clean Air Act did not clearly authorize EPA's plan to regulate certain large-scale greenhouse gas emissions, in a realm of environmental law that approaches the edge of constitutional comfort for the majority of the sitting Supreme Court).

[35] *See generally* Erin Ryan, *Sackett v. EPA and the Regulatory, Property, and Human Rights-Based Strategies for Protecting American Waterways*, 74 CASE W. RSRV. L. REV. 281 (2024); Erin Ryan, *How the Successes and Failures of the Clean Water Act Fueled the Rise of the Public Trust Doctrine and Rights of Nature Movement*, 73 CASE W. RSRV. L. REV. 425 (2022).

[36] Sierra Club v. Morton, 405 U.S. 727 (1972).

A. Public Trust Principles and Environmental Rights in the Literature

Forest.[37] While the plaintiff's effort to assert standing on behalf of the environment was unsuccessful, it launched a wave of scholarship contending that the Court had wrongly decided the underlying rights of nature issue.[38] This included Christopher Stone's seminal treatment in *Should Trees Have Standing?*, which argued for direct recognition of legal rights in natural objects and in nature as a whole.[39] Stone's work would eventually inspire a fully developed model of environmental rights that deprivileges human interests, embraced by the unfolding rights of nature movement.[40] Other environmentalists have objected to this line of reasoning, however, criticizing rights-of-nature approaches as unrealistic at best, and actively harmful at worst.[41]

Meanwhile, other scholars continued to explore legal principles on which to ground human rights in nature. In the early 1990s, Professor Joseph Sax, the intellectual progenitor of the public trust doctrine as a tool of environmental law, considered whether environmental rights should be grounded in the anthropocentric tradition of human rights or an ecocentric theory centered on the rights of nature itself.[42] He

---

[37] *Id.* at 729–30, 734–39.

[38] *See id.* at 735–36; *id.* at 739–42, 749–50 (Douglas, J., dissenting from the holding and inspiring the Western literature from which the contemporary Rights of Nature movement developed).

[39] Christopher D. Stone, *Should Trees Have Standing? – Toward Legal Rights for Natural Objects*, 45 S. Cal. L. Rev. 450, 455–56 (1972); *see also* Cormac Cullinan, *Do Humans Have Standing to Deny Trees Rights?*, 11 Barry L. Rev. 11, 11–12, 19–21 (2008) (referring to Stone's "seminal" article that "motivated the famous dissenting judgment by Justice Douglas in the case of *Sierra Club v. Morton*"). Stone urged that institutionalizing rights to nonhuman entities would jump start a long-term legal and cultural shift toward an understanding of humans as part of a greater whole, rather than at the center of the universe. *Id.* at 489–501.

[40] Erin Ryan et al., *Environmental Rights for the 21st Century: A Comprehensive Analysis of the Public Trust Doctrine and Rights of Nature Movement*, 42 Cardozo L. Rev. 2447, 2476 (2021) [hereinafter *Comprehensive Analysis*].

[41] For example, Professor Noah Sachs argues that its vague standards such as a right to "exist" or "flourish" are unenforceable and lack a limiting principle; that judges will lack the technical expertise required to adjudicate rights of nature claims; and that it is likely to create arbitrary and oppressive outcomes for humans while weakening protections for nature. Noah M. Sachs, *A Wrong Turn with the Rights of Nature Movement*, 36 Geo. Env't L. Rev. 39, 42, 51 (2023) (adding that as "[a]lmost every human activity … involves some harm to living organisms," a rights of nature based system has the potential to force a "remake" of the entire legal system). Cynthia Giagnocavo and Howard Goldstein worry that the rights of nature approach is overly optimistic; that it is a mistake to confuse "legal reform for the social change that we desire"; and that to define nature in terms of legal rights would give the legal community too much power in possessing the final word in defining the value of nature. *See* Cynthia Giagnocavo & Howard Goldstein, *Law Reform or World Reform: The Problem of Environmental Rights*, 35 McGill L.J. 315, at 361, 362–64 (1990). Mauricio Guim and Michael Livermore worry that rights of nature initiatives have the potential to undermine the success of environmental protection and may require impossible balancing when nonhuman interests are compared. *See* Mauricio Guim & Michael A. Livermore, *Where Nature's Rights Go Wrong*, 107 Va. L. Rev. 1347, 1366 (2021) (stating that if Rights of Nature efforts are ineffective it could "dissipate energy and create skepticism about future environmental advocacy efforts.").

[42] *See generally* Joseph L. Sax, *The Search for Environmental Rights*, 6 J. Land Use & Env't L. 93 (1990) [hereinafter, *Environmental Rights*]; *see also* Dinah Shelton, *Human Rights, Environmental Rights, and the Right to Environment*, 28 Stan J. Int'l 103 (1991). In Sax's seminal work advocating for use of the public trust to protect environmental interests, he suggested that the public

concluded that environmental rights could be pursued ecocentrically but that they are also deeply intertwined with human rights, given human interdependence with a healthy environment.[43] Pragmatically speaking, he recommended that advocating for them within the conventional framework of human rights would likely lead to greater legal recognition and more successful environmental enforcement.

At around the same time, Professor Dinah Shelton similarly concluded that the human rights-based approach of guaranteeing citizens' rights to environmental quality would be most successful at earning recognition from the courts.[44] In later work exploring the problem of developing substantive U.S. environmental rights in the absence of clearer constitutional guidance,[45] she observed that procedural environmental rights, which ensure participation and/or access to information, have been much easier to create and more successfully enforced than substantive environmental rights to a specified quality of environment.[46] Demonstrating the ongoing search for stronger foundations, her work suggests that in the absence of a substantive constitutional guarantee, a jurisdiction's statutory environmental laws may themselves establish substantive environmental rights.[47]

Professor James May reviewed domestic and international sources of law in search of potential sources of a substantive U.S. environmental right beyond the statutes considered by Shelton and the explicit constitutional provisions identified by Markell and Rechtschaffen.[48] He identified potential sources in express and implied constitutional recognition, recognition in domestic legislation, and recognition in international or regional law, expanding the potential range of legal foundation.[49] Yet he also identified major barriers to implementation of environmental rights on the basis of current law, including insufficient text, nonjusticiable remedies, and pragmatic hurdles for effective enforcement.[50] Thus far, these barriers have continued to preclude the recognition of environmental rights at the federal level, though as reported the final part of this chapter, they are increasingly being recognized the state level.[51]

---

trust doctrine should be used in place of environmental rights claims because environmental rights claims were overly ambitious and received inconsistent legal responses. Joseph Sax, *The Public Trust Doctrine in Natural Resource Law: Effective Judicial Intervention*, 68 MICH. L. REV. 471, 474 (1970). However, in the 1990 *Search for Environmental Rights* article, Sax reflected on subsequent developments in the discourse and sought to delineate potential legal bases for environmental rights.

[43] Sax, *Environmental Rights*, supra note 42.
[44] Dinah Shelton, *Human Rights, Environmental Rights, and the Right to Environment*, 28 STAN J. INT'L 103, 106 (1991).
[45] Dinah Shelton, *Developing Substantive Environmental Rights*, 1 J. HUM. RTS. & ENV'T 89 (2010).
[46] Id. at 90–92.
[47] Id. at 104.
[48] James R. May, *The Case for Environmental Human Rights: Recognition, Implementation, and Outcomes*, 42 CARDOZO L. REV. 983, 986–87 (2021).
[49] Id. at 990–1012 (2021).
[50] Id. at 1013–15.
[51] See infra Part D ("Constitutional and Pragmatic Concerns with Emerging Climate Advocacy").

Still other scholars declined to choose between a theory of environmental rights cleanly centered around humans or nature. In exploring the relationship between the public trust doctrine and environmental human rights in 2008, Professor David Takacs argued that the public trust doctrine asserts a normative principle in favor of preserving the environment, and that environmental human rights stand for the codification of this norm into positive law.[52] His recognition of the two sides of this coin sets the stage for this chapter's recognition of the partnership between the reciprocal principles at the heart of the public trust doctrine – the sovereign obligation it creates for environmental protection and the human rights it recognizes to demand performance of that obligation.

2. Public Trust Principles in Climate Advocacy

Pursuing the insight, first articulated by Joseph Sax, that the public trust doctrine obligates environmental protection of trust resources by the state,[53] many advocates have focused attention on the role that public trust principles should play in protecting the atmospheric commons from the greenhouse gas pollution most scientists believe is causing climate change. A number of scholars have argued that public trust principles could provide legal support for meaningful regulatory responses to climate change.[54] Professor Robin Craig has argued that it could support adaptive management-based regimes.[55] Professor David Caron has argued that it could support climate governance to forestall sea level rise.[56] Professor Jeff Thaler and Patrick Lyons suggest it could be used to promote offshore renewable energy as a means of

---

[52] David Takacs, *The Public Trust Doctrine, Environmental Human Rights, and the Future of Private Property*, 16 N.Y.U. ENV'T L.J. 711, 760 (2008). In later work favoring rights of nature principles, Takacs argued that both human and nonhuman needs must be balanced against one another to foster healthfully synergistic relationships within nature. David Takacs, *We Are the River*, 2021 U. ILL. L. REV. 545, 552 (2021).

[53] Sax, *supra* note at 556–57.

[54] *See generally* WOOD, NATURE'S TRUST *supra* note at 133–36; Rachel M. Pemberton & Michael C. Blumm, *Emerging Best Practices in International Atmospheric Trust Case Law*, 2022 UTAH L. REV. 941, 950–51 (2022) (addressing the shift to supporting atmospheric trust claims with state constitutional language); Patrick Parenteau, *The Atmosphere as a Global Public Good*, 16 U. ST. THOMAS J.L. & PUB. POL'Y 217, 220–21 (2023) (providing an overview of atmospheric trust litigation in the United States and abroad, arguing that an atmospheric trust could be a public good); Randall S. Abate, *Atmospheric Trust Litigation: Foundation for a Constitutional Right to A Stable Climate System?*, 10 GEO. WASH. J. ENERGY & ENV'T L. 33, 34–36 (2019) (explaining the development of atmospheric trust litigation); Bradford C. Mank, *Does the Evolving Concept of Due Process in Obergefell Justify Judicial Regulation of Greenhouse Gases and Climate Change?*: Juliana v. United States, 52 U.C. DAVIS L. REV. 855, 874–76 (2018) (providing an analysis of the Due Process claims in Juliana and Obergefell).

[55] *See* Robin Kundis Craig, *Adapting to Climate Change: The Potential Role of State Common-Law Public Trust Doctrines*, 34 VT. L. REV. 781, 781–82 (2010).

[56] *See* David D. Caron, *Time and the Public Trust Doctrine: Law's Knowledge of Climate Change*, 35 U. HAW. L. REV 441, 442–43 (2013).

combating climate change.⁵⁷ Professor Randall Abate frames the issue in terms of climate justice.⁵⁸ Most ambitiously, however, Professor Mary Wood has sought to apply the trust directly to atmospheric resources, reviving the Justinian concept of the public trust as encompassing not just the running waters and the sea, but also the air.⁵⁹

In her research and writings, Wood argues that we seek public trust protection for the atmospheric commons and the related climate system that enables life on earth as we have come to know it.⁶⁰ In urging use of the doctrine to protect this endangered commons, she argues that the state must curtail private appropriation of the atmosphere as a dumping ground for carbon pollution and other greenhouse gases.⁶¹ Together with Professor Michael Blumm, she argues that the government's failure to prevent this unprecedented private appropriation is enabling shortsighted destruction of the most important public commons of all, leading to the global threats associated with rapid climate change.⁶² Continuing our Chapter 1 metaphor from the Supreme

---

[57] See Jeffrey Thaler & Patrick Lyons, *The Seas Are Changing: It's Time to Use Ocean-Based Renewable Energy, the Public Trust Doctrine and a Green Thumb to Protect Seas from Our Changing Climate*, 19 OCEAN & COASTAL L. J. 241, 276 (2014).

[58] Randall S. Abate, *Atmospheric Trust Litigation in the United States: Pipe Dream or Pipeline to Justice for Future Generations?*, in CLIMATE JUSTICE: CASE STUDIES IN GLOBAL AND REGIONAL GOVERNANCE CHALLENGES 543, 543–569 (Randall S. Abate, ed., 2016).

[59] See generally WOOD, NATURE'S TRUST *supra* note 30; Mary Christina Wood, Atmospheric Trust Litigation, in CLIMATE CHANGE: A READER 1018, 1021 (W.H. Rodgers, Jr. et al., eds.) (2011); Mary Christina Wood, *Advancing the Sovereign Trust of Government to Safeguard the Environment for Present and Future Generations (Part I): Ecological Realism and the Need for a Paradigm Shift*, 39 ENV'T L. 43, 80–81 (2009) [hereinafter Wood, *Part I*] (criticizing the failure of modern environmental law to protect natural resources and proposing broader state responsibilities as trustee, especially to combat greenhouse gas pollution); Mary Christina Wood, *Advancing the Sovereign Trust of Government to Safeguard the Environment for Present and Future Generations (Part II): Instilling a Fiduciary Obligation in Governance*, 39 ENV'T L. 91, 93, 98, 139 (2009) [hereinafter Wood, *Part II*] (discussing the pragmatic duties of governmental trustees, the interaction between the public trust and statutory law, and the ramifications of the trust for property rights in an effort to "reframe what is currently government's *discretion* to destroy our atmosphere and other resources into an *obligation* to defend those resources") (emphases in original); Mary Christina Wood, *Tribal Trustees in Climate Crisis*, 2 AM. INDIAN L. J. 518, 518–19 (2014) (considering the federal trust obligation as the legal cornerstone of Indian law and suggesting how tribes can use their status as co-trustees with the federal government to combat climate change).

[60] See generally WOOD, NATURE'S TRUST, *supra* note 30; Mary Christina Wood, Atmospheric Trust Litigation, in CLIMATE CHANGE: A READER 1018, 1021 (W.H. Rodgers, Jr. et al., eds.) (2011), *supra* note 59; Wood, *Part I*, *supra* note 59; Wood, *Part II*, *supra* note 59; Wood, *Tribal Trustees in Climate Crisis*, *supra* note 59.

[61] Wood, *Part II*, *supra* note 59, at 93–98; *see also* Michael C. Blumm & Lynn S. Schaffer, *The Federal Public Trust Doctrine: Misinterpreting Justice Kennedy and Illinois Central Railroad*, 45 ENV'T L. 399 (2015) (arguing that the public trust doctrine is an inherent limit on both state and federal sovereign authority, and that *Illinois Central* represents an application of the Tenth Amendment's reserved powers doctrine).

[62] Michael C. Blumm & Mary Christina Wood, *"No Ordinary Lawsuit": Climate Change, Due Process, and the Public Trust Doctrine*, 67 AM. UNIV. L. REV. 1, 14–16, 43–44 (2017) [hereinafter Blumm & Wood]; Wood, *Part II*, *supra* note 59, at 97–98.

Court's 1892 decision in *Illinois Central*,⁶³ it's like giving away Chicago Harbor to self-interested private actors – only worse, because according to Wood and Blumm emphasize that countless lives, communities, cultures, places, and species will be lost if we don't act quickly to better protect the shared atmospheric commons.⁶⁴

This scholarship has helped ignite a worldwide movement to recognize the applicability of public trust principles, including both sovereign obligations and environmental rights, for preventing the destruction or expropriation of the air commons. In their earliest incarnation, these efforts in the United States became known as the atmospheric trust project.⁶⁵ Scholars have traced the deployment of atmospheric trust litigation across all fifty U.S. States.⁶⁶ The intuition behind the project – and the strong emotions it reflects – attracted significant public support, especially among young people.⁶⁷ Nevertheless, this public support has only rarely been matched by sought-after judicial outcomes.⁶⁸ This complex track record likely corresponds to the chaotic intersection between the strong public emotion that climate change inspires and the heavy doctrinal lifts that such litigation has required, extending common law precedents beyond the established zone of waterways and toward unconfirmed limits on federal authority. As discussed further in Chapter 10, scholars have observed that ambitious public trust advocacy often proves more successful in the political sphere than the judicial sphere,⁶⁹ but both the remedies sought and the losses sustained in court have raised concerns among both proponents and opponents of stronger environmental governance.

3. *The Scholarly Critics*

As popular as they have been among many young advocates, atmospheric trust claims have generated substantial controversy among legal scholars and observers. Opponents worry about the departure of these claims from established common law norms, given

---

⁶³ Ill. Cent. R.R. Co. v. Illinois, 146 U.S. 387, 452 (1892) (applying the common law public trust doctrine to protect public ownership of Chicago Harbor).
⁶⁴ Blumm & Wood, *supra* note 62, at 44–46; *see generally* WOOD, NATURE'S TRUST, *supra* note 30.
⁶⁵ *See* Erin Ryan, *The Public Trust Doctrine, Private Water Allocation, and Mono Lake: The Historic Saga of* National Audubon Society v. Superior Court, 45 ENV'T L. 561, 625–33 (2015) [hereinafter *Historic Saga*].
⁶⁶ Anna Christiansen, *Up in the Air: A Fifty-State Survey of Atmospheric Trust Litigation Brought by Our Children's Trust*, 2020 UTAH L. REV. 867 (2020).
⁶⁷ *See infra* text accompanying notes 338–339 and 327–331 (discussing public support for and the atmospheric trust cases like *Juliana*, especially among young people).
⁶⁸ *Id.*
⁶⁹ *See* Ryan et al., *Comprehensive Analysis*, *supra* note 40, at 2561–62. *See also* Paul Rink, *Conceptualizing U.S. Strategic Climate Rights Litigation*, 49 HARV. ENVTL. L. REV. 149 (2025) [hereinafter *Climate Rights Litigation*] (discussing how climate litigation that fails in court can still be a strategic tool of effective climate advocacy); Sam Bookman, *The Puzzling Persistence of Nature's Rights*, 2025 UTAH L. REV. 165 (2025) (discussing how even litigation doomed to loss in court can provide a win for the underlying political movement).

that the American public trust doctrine is mostly applied to state action impacting water resources, rather than state or federal action involving air resources.[70] Some have worried about the practical impacts of the advocacy strategy and the workability of the requested remedy – which would make it the responsibility of the court to order and then oversee ambitious legislative and executive activity.[71] The judicial remedy raises serious concerns for others about the horizontal separation of powers and the limits of sovereign authority.[72] Still others worry about the implications of newer constitutional strategies,[73] such as the fundamental rights claim made in *Juliana v. United States*,[74] which sought to reinvigorate judicial oversight of substantive due process claims,[75] and in its earliest incarnation, unenumerated fundamental rights.[76] At a time when judicial supremacy appears on the rise, some legitimately worry about further empowering courts at the expense of legislative and executive decision-making.[77]

---

[70] *See, e.g.*, Richard J. Lazarus, *Judicial Missteps, Legislative Dysfunction, and the Public Trust Doctrine: Can Two Wrongs Make it Right?*, 45. ENV'T L. 1139, 1152–54-56 (2015); *See also* Ryan, *Historic Saga*, *supra* note 65, at 617–22 (discussing related critiques of the public trust doctrine more generally).

[71] Lazarus, *supra* note 70, at 1155–61.

[72] *Id. See infra* Part D ("Constitutional and Pragmatic Concerns with Emerging Climate Advocacy") (discussing these concerns).

[73] *See, e.g.*, Dan Farber, *The Children's Crusade*, LEGAL PLANET, (Dec. 14, 2023) https://perma.cc/W8HH-MC3Y (arguing that the litigation has no chance of success because it "asks for major expansions of constitutional doctrines that the Court's majority has been downsizing: implied fundamental rights (slashed in the abortion case) and judicial protection for vulnerable groups (slashed in voting rights and affirmative action cases").

[74] Juliana v. United States, No. 15-CV-01517-AA, 2023 WL 3750334, at *9 (D. Or. June 1, 2023) ("plaintiffs seek declaratory relief that 'the United States' national energy system that creates the harmful conditions described herein has violated and continues to violate the Fifth Amendment of the U.S. Constitution and Plaintiffs' constitutional rights to substantive due process and equal protection of the law.").

[75] Substantive due process refers to the principle that the Due Process Clause of the Fourteenth Amendment "applies to matters of substantive law as well as to matters of procedure…. [A]ll fundamental rights comprised within the term liberty are protected by the Federal Constitution from invasion by the States." Planned Parenthood v. Casey, 505 U.S. 833, 846–47 (1992). Additionally, substantive due process "forbids the government to infringe certain 'fundamental' liberty interests at all, no matter what process is provided, unless the infringement is narrowly tailored to serve a compelling state interest." Reno v. Flores, 507 U.S. 292, 301-02 (1993). Relatedly, "[f]undamental liberty rights include both rights enumerated elsewhere in the Constitution and rights and liberties which are either (1) 'deeply rooted in this Nation's history and tradition' or (2) 'fundamental to our scheme of ordered liberty.'" Juliana v. United States, No. 6:15-CV-01517-AA, 2023 WL 9023339, at *16 (D. Or. Dec. 29, 2023) (quoting McDonald v. City of Chicago, 561 U.S. 742, 767 (2010)).

[76] A Ninth Amendment claim for an unenumerated fundamental right to climate stability was eventually dismissed from the *Juliana* litigation, although other elements of the claim were allowed to go forward. *Juliana*, No. 6:15-CV-01517-AA, at 20.

[77] *Cf.* Erin Ryan, *Sackett v. EPA and the Regulatory, Property, and Human Rights-Based Strategies for Protecting American Waterways*, 74 CASE W. L. REV. 281 (2023) (critiquing judicial immodesty in rejecting fifty years of executive expertise and legislative acceptance in the reach of Clean Water Act regulation); Allen C. Sumrall & Beau J. Baumann, *Clarifying Judicial Aggrandizement*, 172 U. PA. L. REV. ONLINE 24, 24, 42 (2023) (critiquing judicial aggrandizement by the Roberts Court); Josh Chafetz, *The New Judicial Power Grab*, 67 ST. LOUIS U.L.J. 635 (2023) (providing examples of judicial aggrandizement by the Supreme Court).

A. Public Trust Principles and Environmental Rights in the Literature

Several critics have subjected the public trust doctrine itself to scholarly scrutiny. Foremost among them, Professor James L. Huffman is skeptical of how the public trust doctrine has developed in the United States[78] and argues that its roots in Roman law should not be regarded as a basis for modern environmental uses of the doctrine. He contends that Roman law did not guarantee an inalienable public right to the sea and seashore and that Roman law considered these resources "common to all" only because supply was so abundant and demand so low that there was not enough competition to be comparable to the modern day.[79] Moreover, he contends that Roman law made no distinction between the public and the personal status of the ruler of the Empire, further confusing the analogy.[80]

The gap between the enthusiasm of advocates like Blumm and Wood and critics like Huffman prompted another pair of professors, legal scholar Fwiw, JB Ruhl and historian Thomas McGinn to carefully review the Roman origins of the doctrine in an attempt to provide a better clarity on the history. Acknowledging that Roman law is too complex to distill down to just the small portion that supports the modern public trust doctrine, they conclude that while Huffman and the other critics are correct that the modern doctrine has developed substantially since its roots in ancient Rome, the Roman trust was a well-established legal concept that likely even predated the Roman common law, and has gone on to influence both the civil codes in Europe and the common law of England and its former colonies.[81] Based on their careful historical analysis, they conclude that the Roman doctrine and the legal norms from which it emerged do provide some support for modern environmental invocations of the doctrine.[82]

Professor Richard Lazarus has long critiqued the use of the public trust doctrine in environmental law, beginning with a criticism not long after the environmental use of the doctrine emerged in the Mono Lake case.[83] Decades later, he reiterated similar concerns in his critique of atmospheric trust advocacy, warning that "it is a serious mistake to take the public trust doctrine far beyond its historic moorings … [p]urporting to glean from the doctrine legal obligations enforceable by the judiciary could shortcut the democratic processes for lawmaking that are central to our nation's values and system of government."[84] Considering its specific application in the context of climate advocacy, he critiques the hurdles of justiciability and

---

[78] J.B. Ruhl & Thomas A.J. McGinn, *The Roman Public Trust Doctrine: What Was It, and Does it Support an Atmospheric Trust?*, 47 ECOLOGY L.Q. 117, 123 (2020).

[79] James L. Huffman, *Speaking of Inconvenient Truths – A History of the Public Trust Doctrine*, 18 DUKE ENV'T L. & POL'Y F. 1, 14–18 (2007).

[80] *Id.*

[81] *See* J.B. Ruhl & Thomas A.J. McGinn, *The Roman Public Trust Doctrine: What Was It, and Does it Support an Atmospheric Trust?*, 47 ECOLOGY L.Q. 117, 165 (2020).

[82] *See id.* at 175–76 (2020).

[83] Richard J. Lazarus, *Changing Conceptions of Property and Sovereignty in Natural Resources: Questioning the Public Trust Doctrine*, 71 IOWA L. REV. 631, 641–44 (1986).

[84] Richard J. Lazarus, *supra* note 70, at 1152.

the problem of providing an appropriate judicial remedy, comparing atmospheric claims to the judicial relief sought in the pioneering civil rights decision in *Brown v. the Board of Education*:[85]

> The courts have struggled for more than sixty years to implement *Brown's* holding with "all deliberate speed." But imagine what would be required for climate change in light of its extraordinary temporal and spatial scope of cause and effect, and the corresponding complexity of the technological, economic, and social judgments that must be made in determining how to address the climate issue. The courts would be asked to embrace a judicial role that assigns them the primary responsibility of deciding the appropriate levels of greenhouse gas emissions in the United States. They would be asked to set legal rules governing how those emissions should then be allocated and when different levels would need to be achieved. The courts would have to develop the equivalent of the President's proposed Clean Power Plan ... consider the sweep of activities that would be affected over both time and space. Consider, too, the fundamental social and economic policy judgments that courts would have to make. The courts do not remotely possess the necessary competence or lawmaking legitimacy to answer those kinds of questions.[86]

Similarly, Professor Dan Farber argues that the claims have no chance of success, that they disparage federal regulators working hard to manage climate change from within environmental agencies, and that they might backfire by creating adverse precedent, "for instance, with a ruling that individuals never have standing based on harm from climate change."[87]

The thrust of these critiques is the concern that plaintiffs involving the public trust to respond to such pressing problems as disappearing natural resources and climate change are both unrealistic about their prospects of success and undermining the very environmental laws that stand a better chance at solving these problems. Frustrated attempts to cut through elaborate environmental laws and regulatory process crafted over many decades to get a court-ordered magical solution not only fails to anticipate why the courts will be unable to deliver on the vague directives they are being asked to consider, say the critics, they redirect scarce public resources and attention away from what environmental law can deliver, if we just let the process work.[88] Professor Dave Owen worries that these advocates placing their faith in these broad and aspirational legal doctrines are acting under an almost delusional "shared hope that heroic judges will cut through all the complexity of bureaucratic decision-making and just do what [] is right."[89] Assessing their attempt to wrest

---

[85] 347 U.S. 483 (1954).
[86] Lazarus, *supra* note 70, at 1156.
[87] Farber, *"The Children's Crusade," supra* note 73.
[88] Lazarus, *supra* note 70, at 1152–57; Email from Dave Owen, Professor of Law, University of California – San Francisco Law School (Mar. 6, 2024) (on file with author).
[89] Owen, *supra* note 88.

environmental decision-making away from the political process and into the courts, Professor Lazarus warns, "[t]he bottom line is that this is just not how we make laws of this nature under our constitutional framework."[90]

These critics herald instead the diligent work of devoted scientists and civil servants toiling away in state and federal agencies under the established authorities who make a meaningful differences every day – formulating total national ambient air quality standards and state renewable portfolio standards, while lawsuits brought under theories like the atmospheric trust "have yet to remove a single metric ton of carbon from the air."[91] Critics worry that atmospheric trust and environmental rights claims discredit the importance of these less mediagenic forms of environmental protection and may even misinform the public by suggesting that they are the only remaining hope for preventing a climate catastrophe.[92] Professor Lazarus specifically calls out some of the more passionate proponents of atmospheric trust advocacy for denigrating the invaluable contributions of countless state and federal employees who toil without recognition within the less glamorous infrastructure of modern environmental regulation that continues to protect the public and the environment from very real threats of harm.[93] These are serious critiques that cannot be taken lightly, and the book returns to them in Conclusion.

4. The Reciprocal Nature of Sovereign Obligations and Environmental Rights

Although scholars such as Joseph Sax and David Takacs considered the confluence of public trust principles and environmental rights, until now, the scholarly discourse has failed to consider the reciprocal relationship between them. For while the public trust doctrinal focuses on sovereign obligations and environmental rights focus on legal entitlements, as discussed in the Introduction, each is the mirror image of the other – necessarily implying a duality that connects all of these efforts. Each example of the climate advocacy that follows variously asserts some kind of

---

[90] Lazarus, *supra* note 70, at 1157.
[91] Oral communication from Professor Dave Owen to author (May 14, 2024). *Accord* Owen, *supra* note 88 (noting that "that there is no evidence that any case has led to any direct reduction in carbon emissions" in comparison to more conventional forms of environmental advocacy, which have accomplished a lot in the aggregate).
[92] Oral communication from Professor Dave Owen to author (May 14, 2024). *Accord* Owen, *supra* note 88.
[93] Lazarus, *supra* note 70, at 1157. ("[S]ome of the leading advocacy in favor of a judicially enforceable atmospheric trust doctrine has embraced a polarizing thesis that will make the necessary law reform even harder to accomplish. Such advocacy couples positive promotion of the atmospheric trust doctrine with a condemnation of existing environmental law, extending even to the good faith efforts of public servants in federal, state, and local governments who have sought to administer those laws. The gist of the argument is that courts must embrace and enforce an atmospheric public trust doctrine because of the failings of the legislative and executive branches. The rhetoric is surprisingly harsh. Environmental law becomes merely an "illusion" that purports to protect the environment but instead only perpetuates harm.").

sovereign obligation for protecting atmospheric resources, for the benefit of some kind of rights-bearing public, which recursively, can hold the sovereign accountable for its obligation.

While the scholarly discourse has thus far elided the reciprocal nature of trust-rights claims, the literature has long appreciated the reciprocal nature of rights and duties. As Professor Wesley Newcomb Hohfeld first recognized in the private law context, legal rights and duties are mirror images of one another.[94] When someone holds a legal right, the party against whom they hold that right has a legal duty to respect it, and the opposite is equally true. Hohfeld's central insight into the reciprocal nature of rights and applies in the public law context as well. When someone holds a public law right, the state is obligated to respect that right, whether it frames a positive entitlement (to a jury trial)[95] or a negative entitlement (to freedom of religion).[96] And by the same token, if the state has a legal obligation (to guarantee a republican form of government),[97] then the beneficiaries of that obligation, the citizens, have a legally cognizable right (to enjoy that republic).[98]

The claims for environmental rights reviewed here showcase the same reciprocal nature, generally partnering individual rights with state obligations.[99] If there is a sovereign duty (framed, for example, as a public trust obligation), then the public is impliedly empowered with the right to hold the state accountable for performance of that duty. If there is an environmental right held by members of the public, then the state is legally obligated to honor it. In the claims and constitutional provisions reviewed here, sometimes both the rights and obligations are acknowledged, while in other cases, only one side of the duality is specified – but they all represent different faces of the same single coin, stemming from the same fundamental principle of sovereign responsibility to protect public trust commons.

The Hohfeldian rights-duty model was conceived in the private law context of property, tort, and contract, but it is fitting to extend it to the public trust context,

---

[94] WESLEY NEWCOMB HOHFELD, FUNDAMENTAL LEGAL CONCEPTIONS AS APPLIED IN JUDICIAL REASONING AND OTHER LEGAL ESSAYS 36–50 (1919). This chapter focuses exclusively on the rights and duties aspect of Hohfeld's analysis that is most pertinent in the public law setting, setting aside Hohfeld's parallel consideration of privileges and immunities that has more purchase in the private law context he was originally writing for. Considering Hohfeld's theory in its entirety in this context would be an interesting thought experiment, but it would distract from the focus of this analysis, which is to discuss the reciprocal nature of environmental rights and sovereign obligations. I do not attempt to use Hohfeld's framework to construct a full portrait of the parties' legal relationships in every respect, including both the positive correlations (rights and duties) and negative correlations (privileges and immunities) that exist between private parties but apply less cleanly between private parties and the government.
[95] U.S. CONST. amend. VI.
[96] U.S. CONST. amend. I.
[97] U.S. CONST. art. IV, § 4 (the "Guarantee Clause").
[98] Id.
[99] See supra Part A(2) ("Public Trust Principles as Environmental Rights").

A. Public Trust Principles and Environmental Rights in the Literature 299

with doctrinal roots in the property fields of public property and trust obligations. While the Hohfeldian model applies cleanly to contexts in which there is a single party with a right and a single party with a duty, the public law context of environmental rights offers the additional parameter of common rights and reciprocal duties held by members of the public against (and reciprocally, toward) one another. There are thus environmental rights attached to the modern public trust doctrine (in states that have recognized an environmental dimension to the public trust doctrine),[100] and environmental rights that emerge from independent sources (for example, state constitutional environmental rights amendments, as discussed further below). Yet whatever its source, if the environmental right is coupled with an implied sovereign obligation of enforcement, it can be understood as an expression of the core public trust principles of public rights and responsibilities.[101]

The implication for assessing current climate advocacy is that what initially appears to be two independent models have much more in common than observers have thus far recognized. Sharing common principles and features, they each offer the same potential advantages of enabling citizens multiple ports of entry to the policymaking process, and amplifying citizen advocacy in contexts where the public choice dynamics of regulatory process may shut them out in comparison to repeat players with stronger influence on policymakers and regulatory agencies. They both provide a focal point for citizens to build constituencies and signal the importance of the issue to them in hope of influencing future policymaking where they may have fewer specifics to offer.

But they also have the same disadvantages, in many respects, for the same reasons. They are both vulnerable to critiques of vagueness and unenforceability. While the strategies may have rhetorical value as mechanisms for enhancing political speech, they can be put to no useful ends, because – even setting aside the possibility Professor Farber imagines of outright failure or negative precedent – the specific content of the rights and obligations at issue remain uncertain. After all, what exactly does it mean to have an individual right to a healthy environment, or a sovereign obligation to protect the atmosphere? What specific entitlements are conferred on the individual by a right to environmental health? What specific actions must the state take to defend it?

Of course, the litigants bringing these lawsuits may not know the specific action they want taken – they just want their leaders to understand how very badly they want different action from that taken to this point (and as Professor Lazarus notes, even

---

[100] See Ryan et al., *Comprehensive Analysis*, supra note 40, at 2461–76 (reviewing the different planes of the evolution of the doctrine in different states, including the consideration of environmental values).
[101] An interesting question left for another day is whether there can be sovereign obligations that are not paired with public rights of enforcement. Because the public trust doctrine does not fit that description, I leave the question idle for now, but there are certainly examples of constitutional texts considered non-self-executing.

if they did request specific relief, as the early atmospheric trust plaintiffs did, the courts will likely decline to deliver it).[102] New environmental scholarship has considered how losing litigation strategies under rights of nature theories and the atmospheric trust project exemplify a strategy of "winning through losing," or procuring sought after political, identity-based, or movement building results even when they are not successful in procuring the sought-after judicial remedy,[103] though critics worry about the demoralization costs of that strategy.[104] Others have specifically discussed the value of strategic climate litigation that fails in court, when it helps to galvanize social movements that then deliver results through the political process.[105] Which brings us to a review, in the section that follows, of how climate trust-rights claims have actually progressed.

B. TRUST-RIGHTS ADVOCACY IN ACTION: ATMOSPHERIC TRUST AND CLIMATE RIGHTS LITIGATION

Rising to the challenge framed by the scholarly discourse, grassroots advocates have attempted to leverage these theories beyond the ivory tower in a global campaign of independent and loosely coordinated environmental litigation. Having established that atmospheric trust and climate rights advocacy are both premised on public trust principles asserting sovereign obligations to protect public environmental rights, this part reports on the use of these strategies in domestic and international environmental litigation. Mixed results reveal that the strategies have thus far have proved more successful internationally than domestically, more successful administratively than judicially, and perhaps more successfully when framed as rights than as duties, notwithstanding their fundamental commonality. Most claims are expressly framed in terms of either public trust principles or fundamental rights, but having shown that they flow from the same core principles in either case, the analysis that follows reviews them holistically, in sequence geographically and over time.

Atmospheric trust claims and their environmental rights analogs have been brought in countries around the world,[106] including not only North and South

---

[102] Lazarus, *supra* note 70, at 1156.
[103] Douglas NeJaime, *Winning Through Losing*, 96 IOWA L. REV. 941, 941 (2011); Bookman, *supra* note 69 (applying NeJaime's thesis to the rights of nature movement); Ryan et al., *Comprehensive Analysis*, note 40, at 2560–63.
[104] Paul Rink, *Climate Rights Litigation*, *supra* note 69, at text accompanying note 304. ("Another risk is that courtroom losses for climate rights strategic litigation could have dampening indirect impacts on climate action more generally by disheartening climate activists. Judicial rulings that deride plaintiffs for contributing to their own harm or that sanction fossil fuel companies as providing a service to society could prove to be particularly demoralizing.").
[105] *Id.*; Ryan et al., *Comprehensive Analysis*, *supra* note 40, at 2561–62.
[106] *See Climate Change Litigation Databases*, SABIN CENTER FOR CLIMATE CHANGE LAW, https://perma.cc/J37S-6WDU.

America,¹⁰⁷ but also Africa,¹⁰⁸ Asia,¹⁰⁹ Europe,¹¹⁰ and Australia.¹¹¹ As discussed below, claims within the European Union have proceeded along clearer pathways of environmental rights, drawing on the more favorable platforms available to plaintiffs in European law. After the Dutch plaintiffs in *Urgenda v. Netherlands* convinced their highest court that European law compels sovereign climate governance obligations to protect citizens' fundamental rights,¹¹² plaintiffs around the world were inspired to frame climate-related claims as vindicating fundamental rights to environmental health and/or stability, or even basic human rights to life, privacy, and dignity.¹¹³ The first section of this section focuses on international climate claims, many of which, like *Urgenda*, have met with marked success in court.

The second section focuses on climate claims in the United States, where success has been more elusive. Inspired by Professor Mary Wood's vision of a trust for nature, and lacking comparable legal support for the environmental rights recognized in other countries, American advocates launched a loosely coordinated campaign of climate litigation premised on the idea of an atmospheric trust.¹¹⁴ In these lawsuits, plaintiffs have made different versions of the argument that the atmospheric commons is a congestible public resource that is being expropriated for the benefit of a select few, while the government has a duty to protect it for everyone.

Americans relying explicitly on the public trust principles contend that the government holds atmospheric resources in trust for the people – just as it holds navigable waterways in trust – and that governments at all levels are failing their sovereign obligations to protect the atmosphere from the greenhouse gas pollution that will destroy

---

¹⁰⁷ Future Generations v. Ministry of Env't, (2018) 11001-22-03-000-2018-00319-01, at 45 (Colom.).
¹⁰⁸ Mbabazi v. Att'y Gen. and Nat'l Env't Mgmt. Auth., (2015) Civil Suit No. 283, High Court of Uganda Holden at Kampala, Complaint, at 4 (Uganda) (decision pending) (the plaintiffs allege that "the government has failed in its duty to uphold the citizens [sic] right to a clean and healthy environment and neglected its duty as a public trustee"), https://perma.cc/H6W4-9UJE.
¹⁰⁹ Shrestha v. Off. of the Prime Minister et al., (2018) 074-WO-0283 at 3 (Nepal) (ordering the government to enact comprehensive climate regulation pursuant to constitutional obligations to protect the environment and citizens' rights to a clean and health environment and human dignity), https://perma.cc/X9SE-KZSH.
¹¹⁰ Urgenda v. Netherlands, [2015] HAZA C/09/00456689 (Neth.) at 32, https://perma.cc/V7C5-VRAV (unofficial English translation) ("This case is essentially about the question whether the State has a legal obligation towards Urgenda to place further limits on greenhouse gas emissions – particularly CO_2 emissions – in addition to those arising from the plans of the Dutch government, acting on behalf of the State.").
¹¹¹ *See generally* Pabai Pabai and Guy Kabai v Australia, VID622, 2021.
¹¹² Urgenda v. Netherlands, [2015] HAZA C/09/00456689 (Neth.) at 41, https://perma.cc/V7C5-VRAV (unofficial English translation) (interpreting European Convention on Human Rights, art. 2, 8, EU, Sept. 3, 1953, C.E.T.S. No. 213).
¹¹³ *See infra* Part B(1) ("*Urgenda Foundation* and International Climate Claims"), discussing Urgenda and its progeny in detail.
¹¹⁴ *See, e.g.*, Erin Ryan, Mary Wood, Jim Huffman, Irma Russel, & Rick Frank, Juliana v. United States: Debating the Fundamentals of the Fundamental Right to a Sustainable Environment, 46 FLA. ST. U. L. REV. ONLINE *1 (2018) [hereinafter Ryan et al., *Debating Juliana*] (analyzing the unfolding atmospheric trust litigation in the context of *Juliana v. United States*); Blumm & Wood, *supra* note 62 (discussing *Juliana v. United States* and all other atmospheric trust litigation and administrative actions); Abate, *supra* note 58.

climatic stability.[115] They claim that by failing to meaningfully regulate greenhouse gas production, governments are effectively allowing private polluters to appropriate the public air commons as a private dumping ground, and at the expense of present and future generations' interests in a livable world.[116] Implicit in this argument is the flip side of the core public trust principle: corresponding to the government's sovereign obligation to protect the atmospheric commons for the public is the public's fundamental right to this kind of environmental protection by the government.

Yet most of these efforts have not succeeded, at least not as initially conceived. Some have accomplished greater success in administrative spheres, and some have retooled their strategies to shift toward constitutional claims, at both the state and federal levels. The partnering of public trust and environmental rights assertions has evolved over the course of the American atmospheric trust project, from common law into statutory and constitutional premises, shifting explicit focus to both sides of the reciprocal rights-duties coin.

This section reports on the climate trust-rights litigation movement and considers both the promise and problems of these various legal campaigns. It begins with *Urgenda Foundation v. Netherlands*, the most famous example of successful trust-rights climate litigation, and other examples of international trust-rights claims. After briefly sketching the trajectory of the atmospheric trust movement in the United States, it then turns to the most famous domestic example, *Juliana v. United States*, recounting the decade-long efforts by its youth plaintiffs to have their claim heard, and imagining how a state plaintiff might succeed where the *Juliana* plaintiffs could not. Finally, it reviews the shift toward state constitutional advocacy and more narrowly tailored claims.

1. Urgenda Foundation *and International Climate Claims*

The first successful climate litigation resting on environmental rights and implied public trust principles was brought in the Netherlands in 2015 – a case eerily simultaneously to *Juliana v. United States*, though it was resolved much sooner.[117] In *Urgenda Foundation v. Netherlands*, the plaintiffs argued that the government's sovereign obligation to protect the environment required it to take immediate steps to reduce greenhouse gas emissions by 25 percent compared to 1990 levels.[118] The plaintiffs maintained that, based on the best available scientific models, the state had set insufficient targets to reduce greenhouse gas reductions.[119] They argued that the state,

---

[115] Juliana v. United States, 217 F. Supp. 3d 1224, 1253 (D. Or. 2016) (describing the plaintiffs' claims).
[116] See id. at 1233, 1245; see also Erin Ryan, From Mono Lake to the Atmospheric Trust: Navigating the Public and Private Interests in Public Trust Resource Commons, 10 GEO. WASH. J. ENERGY & ENV'T L. 39, 61 (2019).
[117] Urgenda v. Netherlands, [2015] HAZA C/09/00456689 (Neth.), https://perma.cc/V7C5-VRAV (unofficial English translation).
[118] Id. at 31–32 (interpreting European Convention on Human Rights, art. 2, 8, EU, Sept. 3, 1953, C.E.T.S. No. 213) ("This duty of care principally means that a reduction of 25% to 40%, compared to 1990, should be realised [sic] in the Netherlands by 2020.").
[119] Id. at 41.

B. Atmospheric Trust and Climate Rights Litigation

in failing to reduce emissions at a sufficient pace, was violating Articles 2 and 8 of the European Convention on Human Rights (ECHR), which protect the right to life and the right to respect for private and family life.[120] The defendant argued that the government had no legal obligation to achieve more aggressive reduction targets and that its current policy was not in violation of the ECHR or any other applicable law.[121]

In a resounding legal victory for the plaintiffs' argument, the court held that the state had an obligation to do its part to protect the atmospheric commons. It concluded that "given the high risk of hazardous climate change, the State has a serious duty of care to take measures to prevent it,"[122] and that the government had "acted negligently and therefore unlawfully" in implementing its low emissions reduction standards.[123] The court reasoned that "the possibility of damages ... [impacting] current and future generations of Dutch nationals[] is so great and concrete that given its duty of care, the State must make an adequate contribution, greater than its current contribution, to prevent hazardous climate change,"[124] and ordered a 25 percent reduction in current Dutch annual greenhouse gas emissions compared to 1990 levels.[125]

While *Urgenda* did not explicitly raise the public trust doctrine, the case was nevertheless premised on core public trust principles in its affirmation of fundamental rights to invoke sovereign responsibility for the protection of a shared natural resource commons for the benefit of the public. The court interpreted the fundamental rights to life and to respect for private and family life under European Law to include climate stability, leaving the state obligated to protect the atmospheric commons for the benefit of the public. Like every assertion of the core public trust principle in environmental advocacy, the case partnered an (implied) sovereign obligation with an (express) environmental right, enforceable by the citizens in court. At every level of litigation, as the case moved from the Hague District Court to the Court of Appeals and then finally on to the Dutch Supreme Court, all three bodies found for the plaintiffs – upholding both the environmental right and the sovereign obligation.[126] It was the first and highest profile example of successful trust-rights climate advocacy, and climate activists worldwide took note.

---

[120] *Id.* ("Urgenda argues that under Articles 2 and 8 of the ECHR, the State has the positive obligation to take protective measures. Urgenda also claims that the State is acting unlawfully because, as a consequence of insufficient mitigation, it (more than proportionately) endangers the living climate (and thereby also the health) of man and the environment, thereby breaching its duty of care. Urgenda asserts that in doing so the State is acting unlawfully towards Urgenda"). *See also* Spoelman, *infra* note 127, at 754.

[121] *Id.* at 32.

[122] *Id.* at 48.

[123] *Id.* at 54.

[124] *Id.* at 53.

[125] *Id.* at 57 (ordering the government "to limit the joint volume of Dutch annual greenhouse gas emissions, or have them limited, so that this volume will have reduced by at least 25% at the end of 2020 compared to the level of the year 1990").

[126] *See Urgenda Foundation v. The State of the Netherlands*, ENV'T L. ALL. WORLDWIDE, https://perma.cc/7UGP-2RQK.

For the first time anywhere in the world, *Urgenda* established as a legal matter that a government body bears a cognizable duty to prevent climate change, and that failing to take such action represents a violation of human environmental rights.[127] The decision prompted the Dutch government to adopt thirty of the plaintiffs' proposals from their "54 Climate Solutions Plan," drafted by Urgenda and a coalition of 800 Dutch organizations committed to reducing greenhouse gas emissions.[128] Adopted with substantial public support, the plan allocates billions of euros to fund renewable energy development, reduces the maximum speed on highways during daylight hours, reduces livestock numbers, and mandates more sustainable forest management practices.[129] In a press release, the UN High Commissioner for Human Rights noted that, because *Urgenda* relied upon the ECHR, the decision may implicate the activities of other European governments as well.[130]

While the decision does not have direct legal implications for the United States or other countries outside the European Union, *Urgenda* bolstered the international movement toward advancing public trust principles in climate governance more generally. After *Urgenda*, litigants across the globe brought related claims against their governments for failing to protect the environment – and climate stability in particular[131] – in other nations including Nepal,[132] Germany,[133] France,[134] India,[135] Switzerland,[136] Canada,[137] and Mexico.[138]

---

[127] Naomi Spoelman, *Urgenda: A How-To Guide for Enforcing Greenhouse Gas Emission Targets by Protecting Human Rights*, 47 ECOLOGY L.Q. 751, 751 (2020); *see also* Blumm & Wood, *supra* note 62, at 80–81 ("[T]he case was the first time a court intervened to pronounce the government's remedial efforts inadequate in light of the best available science.").

[128] Johnathan Watts, *Dutch Officials Reveal Measures to Cut Emissions After Court Ruling*, THE GUARDIAN (Apr. 24, 2020), https://perma.cc/C729-PZFH.

[129] *54 Actions for 17 Mtons of CO_2 Reduction*, URGENDA, https://perma.cc/S8TY-38Q9.

[130] *See Bachelet Welcomes Top Court's Landmark Decision to Protect Human Rights From Climate Change*, U.N. PRESS RELEASE (Dec. 20, 2019), https://perma.cc/A45D-YD6W; *see also* Spoelman, *supra* note 127, at 756–57 (noting that the *Urgenda* decision is only enforceable in the Netherlands but provides a roadmap for litigators in other European countries).

[131] *Cf.* Spoelman, *supra* note 127, at 757. *See also* the discussion that follows in this section.

[132] Shrestha v. Off. of the Prime Minister et al., (2018) 074-WO-0283 (Nepal), https://perma.cc/X9SE-KZSH. *See supra* notes 109–120 (discussing the claim in more detail).

[133] BVerfG, 1 BvR 2656/18 [Order of 24 March], https://perma.cc/B6F4-HMAC (official English Translation).

[134] Tribunaux Administratif [Administrative Court], Oct. 14, 2021, Nos. 1904967, 1904968, 1904972, 1904976/4-1, (Fr.) https://perma.cc/G9K3-SJYQ (unofficial English translation of *Notre Affaire à Tous v. France*).

[135] Pandey v. India, [2019] No. 187/2017, National Green Tribunal at Principal Bench, New Delhi, Order, at 2 (India).

[136] Verein KlimaSeniorinnen Schweiz v. Switzerland, [2024] 53600/20 Eur. Ct. H.R.; Isabella Kwai, *Heat Waves are Killing Older Women. Are They Also Violating Their Rights?*, N.Y. TIMES (Aug. 7, 2023), https://perma.cc/2VUT-4TYN.

[137] Complaint at 14, La Rose v. Her Majesty the Queen, [2019] 2020 FC 1008 (Can.). *See also infra* notes 174–178.

[138] *Jovenes v. Gobierno de Mexico*, OUR CHILD'S. TR., https://perma.cc/ZJF6-WPR8 reporting on the case). *See also infra* notes 179–181.

Nepal. In Nepal, for example, environmental plaintiffs successfully invoked public trust principles directly in the national constitution in a suit for climate action that ultimately produced comprehensive legal reform.[139] In 2017, the plaintiffs sought judicial relief to compel the government to enact climate mitigation and adaptation laws, claiming that persistent inaction violated constitutional protections for citizens' rights to a clean and healthy environment[140] and to live with dignity.[141] They argued that existing environmental laws were inadequate because they failed to address the specific challenges of climate change, resulting in grave harms to both the people and ecosystems of the nation.[142] In late December of 2018, the Court agreed that existing laws did not address the dire need for climate related regulations.[143] It concluded that action was required to satisfy the nation's constitutional obligations to protect its citizens' rights to a dignified life and a clean and healthy environment, its constitutional obligations to protect the environment more generally,[144] and as well, the nation's commitments to multilateral climate action under the U.N. Framework Convention on Climate Change and the Paris Agreement.[145]

Using a writ of mandamus, the Court ordered the government to enact and implement a new law to promote climate mitigation and adaptation; reduce fossil fuel consumption and increase low-carbon technology; and develop methods for compensating those harmed by environmental degradation, among other provisions.[146] The court further ordered the government to use available sources of authority to implement existing climate policy in the interim.[147] Within the year, the government complied with the court order by enacting the Environment Protection Act of 2019 and the Forest Act of 2019.[148]

Germany. In 2020, in Germany, a group of youth plaintiffs filed a legal challenge to their nation's federal climate law, arguing that its target of reducing GHGs from 1990 levels by 65 percent to 2030 was insufficient and therefore violated a series

---

[139] Shrestha v. Off. of the Prime Minister et al., [2018] 074-WO-0283 (Nepal), https://perma.cc/X9SE-KZSH.

[140] CONST. OF NEPAL, art. 30 ("Each person shall have the right to live in a healthy and clean environment.").

[141] Id. at art. 16 ("Each person shall have the right to live with dignity.").

[142] Shrestha v. Off. of the Prime Minister et al., [2018] 074-WO-0283 (Nepal), https://perma.cc/X9SE-KZSH.

[143] Id.

[144] CONST. OF NEPAL, art. 51(g).

[145] Shrestha v. Off. of the Prime Minister et al., [2018] 074-WO-0283 (Nepal), https://perma.cc/X9SE-KZSH.

[146] Id. at 13–14.

[147] Id. at 6 (The court directed the government "[t]o actively implement and renounce the sluggish attitude and plans and policies outlined in National Adaptation Program of Action 2010, Climate Change policy, 2011, National Framework for Local Adaptation Plan for Action 2011 in all local units, municipalities, wards and districts of all 7 provinces through forming local committees.").

[148] Summary, *Shrestha v. Off. of the Prime Minister et al.*, CLIMATE CASE CHART, https://perma.cc/X9SE-KZSH. Both statutes are https://perma.cc/X9SE-KZSH.

of human rights protected by German constitutional law.[149] The youth plaintiffs alleged conflicts with their constitutional right to "a future consistent with human dignity," as protected by Article 1, their fundamental rights to life and physical integrity protected by Article 2, and Article 20(a)'s requirement that the overall political process "protect the natural foundations of life in responsibility for future generations."[150] As in *Urgenda*, this case did not raise the public trust doctrine directly, but the constitutional claims mirror public trust principles in establishing sovereign responsibility for protecting human rights and related environmental "foundations for life" – in other words, a stable climate commons – for present and future generations. Like the Dutch case, the German case partners an implied sovereign obligation with an express environmental right, because the flip side of the citizen's environmental right is the state's duty to respect it.

On April 29, 2021, the Federal Constitutional Court agreed that parts of the Act violated the plaintiffs' fundamental rights by requiring emission cuts only through 2030, contrary to constitutional requirements that "environmental burdens [be] spread out between different generations."[151] Recognizing intergenerational equity concerns in this context for the first time, the Court invalidated those parts of the law, explaining that "[a]s intertemporal guarantees of freedom, fundamental rights afford the complainants protection against the greenhouse gas reduction burdens imposed by Art. 20a GG being unilaterally offloaded on to the future."[152] Holding that the legislature had failed to proportionally distribute the burden between current and future generations, the Court warned that "one generation must not be allowed to consume large portions of the CO_2 budget while bearing a relatively minor share of the reduction effort, if this would involve leaving subsequent generations with a drastic reduction burden and expose their lives to serious losses of freedom."[153] As significant as this decision appears, later German adjudicators have been reluctant to extend similar reasoning to statutes that lack similarly specific climate goals,[154] highlighting judicial reluctance to order specific acts of environmental governance without clearer constitutional authorization – a jurisprudential feature shared with atmospheric trust litigation in the United States.[155]

---

[149] BVerfG, 1 BvR 2656/18 at paras. 38, 193 [Order of 24 March], https://perma.cc/B6F4-HMAC (official English Translation). The federal climate law is the "Bundesklimaschutzgesetz" or "KSG," and the German Constitution is called the Basic Law, or "GG."

[150] *Id.*

[151] *Id.* at 193.

[152] *Id.* at 183.

[153] *Id.* at 192.

[154] *See Emma Johanna Kiehm et al. v. State of Brandenburg*, CLIMATE CASE CHART, https://perma.cc/5U7S-TKJP (noting that in later climate cases, plaintiffs lacked standing when the court did not find the clearly violated climate goals or proscribed generational burden shifting). *See also* BVerfG, 1 BvR 1565/21 Jan. 18, 2022, https://perma.cc/7XVM-BU94.

[155] *See infra* Part D ("Constitutional and Pragmatic Concerns with Emerging Climate Advocacy").

France. Meanwhile, in France in 2018, several nonprofits sued the French government for its failure to act appropriately in response to the threats of climate change in a claim that mixed domestic legal obligations and the same European obligations that the *Urgenda* plaintiffs invoked.[156] The French plaintiffs sought an injunction requiring the state to remedy its inadequate climate response on the basis of several specific duties to act.[157] These included climate governance obligations of the state under the French Environmental Charter,[158] characterized by the court as having constitutional significance,[159] and following in the footsteps of *Urgenda*, the European Convention "right to life" and "right to respect for private and family life."[160] They argued that France must implement a comprehensive policy framework and efficient practical measures to fight climate change.[161] Notably, they also requested compensation, both for ecological harm, and also for the intangible "moral harm" they themselves suffered as a result of state inaction, requesting "the symbolic sum of 1 euro."[162]

---

[156] Tribunal Administratif [Administrative Court], Feb. 3, 2021, Nos. 1904967, 1904968, 1904972, 1904976/4-1, (Fr.) https://perma.cc/Z2AW-9539 (unofficial English translation of *Notre Affaire à Tous v. France*).

[157] Tribunaux Administratif [Administrative Court], Oct. 14, 2021, Nos. 1904967, 1904968, 1904972, 1904976/4-1, at 27, (Fr.) https://perma.cc/G9K3-SJYQ ("[Plaintiffs seek] to order the Prime Minister and the competent ministers to take the necessary measures to repair the ecological damage[] linked to the surplus greenhouse gas emissions resulting from the State's failure to meet the first carbon budget and to stop the damage worsening and, in particular and as rapidly as possible, to take all useful steps to make it possible to meet the objectives that France set for itself in terms of the reduction of GHG emissions").

[158] *Id.* ("Finally, under the terms of Article 3 of the Environment Charter, which has constitutional value: 'Every person must, under the conditions defined by law, prevent damage to the environment or, failing that, limit the consequences thereof.'").

[159] *Id.*

[160] *Id.* at 2 ("[Plaintiffs argue that] the State has a legal obligation, in accordance with the principles of the right to life and the right to the protection of one's privacy and family life, as provided in article 2 and 8 of the European Convention on Human Rights, which presupposes the protection of the environment and the fight against climate change, the consequences of which jeopardize nearly 9.75 million people in France.").

[161] *Id.* at 3 ("[Plaintiffs argue that] the State is also bound by specific obligations related to its fight against climate change, as enshrined in international conventions, the laws of the European Union, and domestic law, each pertaining to the mitigation of greenhouse gas emissions and energy consumption, the development of renewable energies, the adoption of sector-specific measures, and the implementation of evaluation and monitoring measures").

[162] *Id.* at 17 ("[The plaintiff asked the court] 1) to order the State to pay him the symbolic sum of one Euro as compensation for the moral prejudice suffered, 2) to order the State to pay him the symbolic sum of one Euro for the ecological damage suffered, 3) to enjoin the Prime Minister and the competent ministers to put an end to all State failures to fulfill its general and specific obligations in the fight against climate change or to mitigate its effects, to put an end to the ecological damage, and in particular, within the shortest possible time to: [adopt the specific measures requested]."); *Id.* at 32 (holding that the French Environment Code allows plaintiffs to seek damages for "moral harm, caused by the harmful consequences of a wrongful failure by the administrative authority to demonstrate the existence and certain harm resulting, for that [plaintiff], from the fault committed by the State."); *see generally*, Vernon V. Palmer, *Moral Damages: The French Awakening in the Nineteenth Century*, 36 TULANE EUR. & CIV. L. FORUM 45, (2021) (discussing the development of "moral damages" as a

In early 2021, the Administrative Court of Paris concluded that state inaction on climate change had indeed caused ecological damage and awarded the plaintiffs the one euro requested in damages.[163] Interpreting Article 5 of the French Environmental Charter, the court reaffirmed that the government has an affirmative obligation to act "when the occurrence of any damage, albeit unpredictable in the current state of scientific knowledge, may seriously and irreversibly harm the environment."[164] Notably, the Environmental Charter places environmental obligations not only on the state, but also "every person" to "prevent damage to the environment, or failing that, limit the consequences thereof."[165] The French statement of environmental rights expands public trust principles from obligating the state as an entity to obligating the broader community of citizens who, in the aggregate, comprise the state. In so doing, the statement provides a potential stepping stone to the competing rights of nature frameworks currently emerging, which locate the beneficiary of environmental rights not in the citizens at all but in nature directly.[166]

Nevertheless, the court in Paris deferred its decision on whether an injunction was warranted – instead giving the government two months to disclose what steps it was taking to meet its climate targets.[167] The decision affirmed that the government could be held responsible for failing to meet its own climate and carbon budget goals under both EU and national law,[168] but it rejected the claim that the state could be forced to meet more specific targets or that these measures could be directly linked to clear ecological damage.[169] The court further declined the plaintiff's request for compensatory damages for ecological harm, concluding they had failed to show that the government would be unable to repair the alleged harm.[170]

French legal concept, which is similar to emotional damages in the United States and is used to demonstrate that the defendant has committed wrongful actions).

[163] Tribunal Administratif [Administrative Court], Feb. 3, 2021, Nos. 1904967, 1904968, 1904972, 1904976/4-1, (Fr.) https://perma.cc/Z2AW-9539 (unofficial English translation of *Notre Affaire à Tous v. France*).

[164] The Charter for the Environment (France), https://perma.cc/Q6T9-ZTWX.

[165] Tribunal Administratif [Administrative Court], Feb. 3, 2021, Nos. 1904967, 1904968, 1904972, 1904976/4-, at 27 (Fr.) https://perma.cc/Z2AW-9539 (unofficial English translation of *Notre Affaire à Tous v. France*).

[166] See Ryan et al., *Comprehensive Analysis*, supra note 40, at 2500-38.

[167] Tribunal Administratif [Administrative Court], Feb. 3, 2021, Nos. 1904967, 1904968, 1904972, 1904976/4-, at 27 (Fr.) https://perma.cc/Z2AW-9539 (unofficial English translation of *Notre Affaire à Tous v. France*). After the two-month period, the court upheld the steps the French government put in place following the first case. The court urged the government to "take all useful measures to repair the ecological damage and prevent it worsening for the share of greenhouse gas emissions not made good compared to the first carbon budget," by making changes in several sectors such as agriculture, transportation, and energy. Tribunal Administratif [Administrative Court], Oct. 14, 2021, Nos. 1904967, 1904968, 1904972, 1904976/4-1 at 44–45, (Fr.) https://perma.cc/G9K3-SJYQ (unofficial English translation of *Notre Affaire à Tous v. France*).

[168] *Id.* at 31–33.

[169] *Id.*

[170] *Id.* at 31.

B. Atmospheric Trust and Climate Rights Litigation

The French case highlights how litigants continue to experiment with all available legal tools to push for climate governance, including claims for injunctive and damages relief premised on public trust principles and environmental rights. But it also highlights the obstacles these claims face in courts that may affirm the interpretive principle but lack the tools or mandate to command the governance relief sought. As shown in Parts B(2) and B(4), atmospheric trust claims in the United States have failed to overcome related jurisprudential barriers of justiciability and redressability, albeit in suits premised on far less secure legal grounds than the French Environmental Charter.

India. Similarly, in India in 2019, a court summarily dismissed an atmospheric trust claim premised on international climate obligations on the grounds that "[t]here is no reason to presume that Paris Agreement and other international protocols are not reflected in the policies of the Government of India or are not taken into consideration in granting environment clearances."[171] And after a group of older Swiss women succeeded in a 2024 lawsuit claiming that their government's failure to curb emissions is violating the rights of older women, who are particularly physically vulnerable to the increased heat associated with climate change[172] – the Swiss Parliament later intervened to negate the court's decision.[173] As discussed further in Part D, separation-of-powers concerns over the judicial capacity to redress violations of public trust principles in the climate context pose an enduring challenge of the legal strategy.

Canada. In the Americas, climate trust-rights claims have faced even more barriers. Immediately following the Dutch and Nepali suits, a group of Canadian youth plaintiffs sued the federal government in 2019, alleging (among other claims) that it had failed to produce plans that would adequately fulfill Canada's "constitutional obligation to protect public trust resources" from the dangers of greenhouse gas emissions.[174] Matching their appeal to express sovereign obligations and implied environmental rights with an overt appeal to environmental rights with implied sovereign obligations, the plaintiffs also invoked rights to life and equal protection set forth in the Canadian Charter of Rights and Freedoms (similar to the American Bill of Rights).[175] They also

---

[171] *Pandey v. India*, [2019] No. 187/2017, National Green Tribunal at Principal Bench, New Delhi, Order, at 2 (India), https://perma.cc/XHD2-Z9LR (order dismissing the complaint on the grounds that "[t]here is no reason to presume that Paris Agreement and other international protocols are not reflected in the policies of the Government of India or are not taken into consideration in granting environment clearances").

[172] Verein KlimaSeniorinnen Schweiz v. Switzerland, [2024] 53600/20 Eur. Ct. H.R.; Isabella Kwai, *Heat Waves are Killing Older Women. Are They Also Violating their Rights?*, N.Y. TIMES (Aug. 7, 2023), https://perma.cc/2VUT-4TYN.

[173] Imogen Foulkes, *Swiss Parliament Defied ECHR on Climate Women's Case*, BBC NEWS (June 12, 2024), https://perma.cc/6P4H-2QYD.

[174] Complaint at 14, *La Rose v. Her Majesty the Queen*, [2019] 2020 FC 1008 (Can.).

[175] *Id.* at 15–16; CANADIAN CHARTER OF RIGHTS AND FREEDOMS § 7, 1982 (Can.) ("Everyone has the right to life, liberty and security of the person and the right not to be deprived thereof except in accordance with the principles of fundamental justice."); *id.* at § 15(1) ("Every individual is equal before and under the law and has the right to the equal protection and equal benefit of the law without

argued that the public trust doctrine is "both a common law obligation and an unwritten constitutional principle" governing federal action, seeking formal recognition of the constitutive understanding of public trust principles in Canada.[176] However, the lower court granted the government's motion to dismiss and an appeals court affirmed with prejudice.[177] A related Canadian claim is pending in one of Canada's provinces, mirroring the strategic turn to environmental federalism seen in the litigation taking place at multiple levels of regulatory scale in the United States.[178]

Mexico. In the same year, fifteen Mexican youth filed suit against their federal government, alleging that it too has failed to take concrete steps to uphold its constitutional and statutory obligations to ensure a healthy environment.[179] While the trial court initially dismissed the claim for lack of standing, the youth plaintiffs appealed and the Collegiate Court reversed, concluding that the plaintiffs did have standing.[180] As this piece goes to press, the case is still pending a final decision on the merits.[181]

2. The Atmospheric Trust Project in U.S. Law

Atmospheric trust cases in the United States have met with more limited success. Cases and administrative petitions were launched around the country at both the state and federal levels, with mixed judicial results and somewhat better results through the administrative process. As of yet, there has been no litigation yielding results approaching what the Supreme Court of the Netherlands delivered in *Urgenda*, although there have been notable administrative successes, especially in coastal states such as Washington, Massachusetts, and Hawai'i,[182] and as discussed further in Part C, trust-rights advocacy appears to be now shifting to the state constitutional realm.[183] In 2024, the *Juliana* case was dismissed before trial (for the umpteenth time), and the plaintiffs' appeal to the Supreme Court was denied,[184]

---

discrimination and, in particular, without discrimination based on race, national or ethnic origin, colour [sic], religion, sex, age or mental or physical disability.").

[176] Complaint at 62, *La Rose v. Her Majesty the Queen*, [2019] 2020 FC 1008 (Can.).

[177] *La Rose v. His Majesty the King*, [2023] 2023 FCA 241, at 6 (Can.) (reporting on the lower court's finding that the plaintiff's constitutional claims were not justiciable, and the public trust claims, while justiciable, "disclosed no reasonable cause of action."); *id.* at 11, 22–25 (dismissing all claims, including the public trust claims, on the grounds that they had "no reasonable prospect of success").

[178] *Mathur v. Ontario*, [2023] 2023 ONSC 2316 (Can.).

[179] *See Jovenes v. Gobierno de Mexico*, OUR CHILDREN'S TR., https://perma.cc/ZJF6-WPR8 (reporting on the case with case documents available in Spanish).

[180] *Id.*

[181] *Id.*

[182] Blumm & Wood, *supra* note 62, at 73–77 (discussing administrative relief in Massachusetts and Washington). *See also infra* Part C ("Climate Claims on State Constitutional Grounds") (discussing the *Navahine* settlement in Hawaii).

[183] *See infra* Part C ("Climate Claims on State Constitutional Grounds").

[184] *Juliana v. United States*, No. 24-684, D.C. No. 6:15-cv-1517, 2024 WL 5102489, (May 1, 2024), *cert. denied*, 604 U.S. 645 (2025).

ending the claim for good. Even so, the case deserves scrutiny as an exemplar of the atmospheric trust/environmental rights litigation strategy, and of what scholars have referred to as the "winning through losing"[185] virtues of "strategic climate litigation."[186]

Early atmospheric trust plaintiffs were inspired by a group of minors and their lawyers who, in 1993, convinced the Supreme Court of the Philippines to recognize their government's legal responsibility for intergenerational environmental equity.[187] Assisted in the United States by a nonprofit organization, Our Children's Trust,[188] youth plaintiffs organized nationwide to bring local lawsuits and administrative action seeking public trust protection for the atmosphere.[189] Beginning in the 2010s, atmospheric trust plaintiffs brought over fifty lawsuits and administrative petitions in every state and also in federal court, each seeking to establish that the atmosphere is subject to the public trust and that the relevant regulators must therefore act to protect it from further destructive appropriation by polluters, especially large-scale polluters.[190] When the agencies of government allow unfettered greenhouse gas emissions, these plaintiffs claimed, they are illegally enabling private actors to despoil the great air commons that belongs to all of us, in derogation of the public trust.[191] More recent claims have buttressed or replaced the original common law trust argument with claims arising under state constitutional trusts or independent provisions of the U.S. Constitution.[192]

---

[185] *See, e.g.*, Bookman, *supra* note 69 (discussing how even litigation doomed to loss in court can provide a win for the underlying political movement).

[186] *See, e.g.*, Paul Rink, *Climate Rights Litigation*, *supra* note 69, (discussing how climate litigation that fails in court can still be a strategic tool of effective climate advocacy).

[187] *See* OLIVER A. HOUCK, TAKING BACK EDEN: EIGHT ENVIRONMENTAL CASES THAT CHANGED THE WORLD 43–61 (2010) (discussing Minors Oposa v. Factoran, G.R. No. 101083, 224 S.C.R.A. 792 (1993), a decision by the Supreme Court of the Philippines recognizing a legal burden of intergenerational responsibility to protect the environment). *See also* Katy Scott, *Can 'Climate Kids' Take On Governments and Win?*, CNN (July 24, 2018), https://perma.cc/4LX6-KY2E (reporting that the *Juliana* youth plaintiffs were inspired by this case).

[188] *Our Mission*, OUR CHILD'S. TR., https://perma.cc/52SA-QXZ6 ("Our Children's Trust elevates the voice of youth to secure the legal right to a stable climate and healthy atmosphere for the benefit of all present and future generations.... We lead a game-changing legal campaign seeking systemic, science-based emissions reductions and climate recovery policy at all levels of government. We give young people, those with most at stake in the climate crisis, a voice to favorably impact their futures.").

[189] *See State Judicial Actions Now Pending*, OUR CHILD'S. TR., https://perma.cc/PF3G-DE6V (describing pending actions in Alaska, Hawaii, Montana, Utah, and Virginia).

[190] *See* Anna Christiansen, *Up in the Air: A Fifty-State Survey of Atmospheric Trust Litigation Brought by Our Children's Trust*, 2020 UTAH L. REV. 867 (2020); *Other Proceedings in all 50 States*, OUR CHILD'S. TR., https://perma.cc/35XE-MXH8; https://perma.cc/35XE-MXH8; *see also* James Conca, *Atmospheric Trust Litigation – Can We Sue Ourselves over Climate Change?*, FORBES (Nov. 23, 2014), https://perma.cc/S2N6-M8FK.

[191] *See generally* Christiansen, *supra* note 190.

[192] *See, e.g.*, Held v. Montana, 2024 MT 312, para. 30 (Dec. 18, 2024) (successfully challenging state laws preventing environmental assessment of greenhouse gas emissions under the state's constitutional protection for environmental rights to climate stability); Juliana v. United States, No. 15-CV-01517-AA,

A salient aspect of these lawsuits is that most of the plaintiffs have been children, at least at the time their initial claims were brought.[193] They argue that it is their future, and the well-being of the children that come after them, that is being squandered by sovereign failures to protect atmospheric resources today.[194] The named plaintiff in the case that got the farthest in federal court, *Juliana v. United States*, was a teenager when she and eighteen other youth plaintiffs first filed the case in 2015, and some plaintiffs have been even younger.[195] In addition to *Juliana*, as detailed below, this atmospheric trust advocacy included notably unsuccessful judicial appeals, such as *Alec L. v. Jackson*[196] in federal court and *Chernaik v. Brown*[197] in the Oregon Supreme Court, but also successful administrative actions, such as that leading to the Massachusetts Executive Order on Climate Change[198] and a Florida rule requiring electric utilities to use only renewable fuels by 2050.[199] (However, as this book was going to press, the Florida rule was repealed in July of 2024, revealing the inherent fragility of administrative successes.[200])

Most of the early judicial cases did not succeed in court, although there were some incremental successes. Many early claims were dismissed on displacement, preemption, or political question grounds.[201] In one of the very first atmospheric trust cases, *Blades v. California*, the plaintiffs sought a judicial declaration that the atmosphere is a public trust resource under California law and that the state has a public trust duty to limit greenhouse gas emissions – analogous to its duty to protect Mono Lake – but the claim was dismissed.[202] The plaintiffs in *Alec L. v. Jackson* brought the first atmospheric trust in federal court in Washington D.C., but the suit

---

2023 WL 3750334, at *19 (D. Or. June 1, 2023) ("[P]laintiffs seek declaratory relief that 'the United States' national energy system that creates the harmful conditions described herein has violated and continues to violate the Fifth Amendment of the U.S. Constitution and Plaintiffs' constitutional rights to substantive due process and equal protection of the law.").

[193] Sam Bliss, *These Teens Are Taking Their Climate Lawsuit All the Way to the Supreme Court*, GRIST (Oct. 22, 2014), https://perma.cc/43CH-YXMG.

[194] *Id.*

[195] Juliana v. United States, 217 F. Supp. 3d 1224 (D. Or. 2016).

[196] 863 F. Supp. 2d 11, 15 (D.D.C. 2012).

[197] 475 P.3d 68, 83–84 (Or. 2020).

[198] Mass. Exec. Order No. 569 (Sept. 16, 2016), https://perma.cc/RF7C-BYLN. On Sep. 16, 2016, the Governor of Massachusetts responded to a win in court by atmospheric trust youth plaintiffs by issuing Executive Order No. 569, establishing an Integrated Climate Change Strategy for the Commonwealth. *See Legal Updates*, OUR CHILD'S TR. (Sep. 16, 2016), https://perma.cc/77TT-GDUA; *see also* Blumm & Wood, *supra* note 62, at 72–74 (discussing Kain v. Mass. Dep't of Env't Protection, 49 N.E.3d 1124, 1128 (Mass. 2016), the litigation leading to this executive order).

[199] FLA. ADMIN. CODE ANN. r. 50-5.002 (2023) ("Each Electric Utility that produces or purchases energy should seek to achieve an increase in the amount of renewable energy produced or purchased to at least ... 100% renewable energy by 2050") (repealed Jul. 28, 2024).

[200] *Id.*

[201] *See, e.g.*, Alec L. v. Jackson, 863 F. Supp. 2d 11, 15 (D.D.C. 2012); Blades v. California, No. CGC11-510725 (Cal. Super. Ct. 2012); Reynolds v. Florida, No. 37 2018 CA 000819, at 1 (Fla. Cir. Ct. June 10, 2020), *aff'd*, 316 So.3d 813, 814 (Fla. Dist. Ct. App. 2021).

[202] No. CGC11-510725 (Cal. Super. Ct. 2012) (dismissing the claim without prejudice).

was dismissed on grounds that their common law claim was displaced by the Clean Air Act.[203] When the D.C. Circuit and then the Supreme Court affirmed the dismissal,[204] it was a great disappointment to atmospheric trust advocates – especially when subsequent Supreme Court precedent called into question the strength of federal authority even under the Clean Air Act to regulating greenhouse gas pollution.[205] Similar claims later failed in Pennsylvania,[206] Washington,[207] and Florida.[208]

Some later atmospheric trust cases seemed to erode some of the initially negative precedent that prevented claims from reaching court, but even so, few produced the results the plaintiffs were seeking. For example, in *Chernaik v. Kitzhaber*, an Oregon appellate court reversed a lower court's decision to dismiss an atmospheric trust claim based on the defendant's arguments that hearing the case would have violated the political question doctrine and separation of powers doctrine, which are jurisprudential rules that generally direct courts to refrain from deciding hot-button political issues that raise questions of legislative policy rather than judicially interpretable legal rights.[209] The appellate court also rejected the lower court's decision to dismiss on grounds that the court lacked the authority to grant the kind of relief the plaintiffs had requested.[210] It was a victory for the atmospheric trust plaintiffs to clear these initial hurdles, but the state supreme court would later vitiate all such claims by deciding against the atmospheric trust in Oregon – holding that the atmosphere is not a public commons resource within the state's public trust doctrine.[211]

Other decisions upholding atmospheric trust claims in the early stages of litigation also left plaintiffs empty-handed at the end. An Alaska court held that the political question doctrine did not foreclose the atmospheric trust claim, but nevertheless

---

[203] Alec L. v. Jackson, 863 F. Supp. 2d 11, 15 (D.D.C. 2012) (holding that the plaintiffs lacked standing in the first federal atmospheric trust case).
[204] Alec L. *ex rel.* Loorz v. McCarthy, 561 Fed. App'x 7, 8 (D.C. Cir. 2014) (affirming the dismissal on appeal), *cert. denied*, 574 U.S. 1047 (2014).
[205] West Virginia v. EPA, 142 U.S. 2587, 2616 (2022) (holding that EPA lacked authority under the Clean Air Act to regulate greenhouse gas pollution from power plants).
[206] *Pennsylvania*, OUR CHILD'S TR., https://perma.cc/E4WW-7JFE (Mar. 21, 2023).
[207] Aji P. *ex rel.* Piper v. State, 480 P.3d 438, 458 (Wash. Ct. App. 2021), *rev. denied*, 497 P.3d 350 (Wash. 2021). While the *Aji P.* case was on appeal, a separate group of youth activists attempted to sue the Washington State Department of Ecology for denying their petition for rulemaking, which would have required the agency to address greenhouse gas emission reduction. Foster v. Wash. Dep't. of Ecology, 2016 WL 11359472, at *1 (Wash. Super. Ct. 2016). While the trial court ordered the agency to initiate rulemaking to "adopt a rule to limit greenhouse gas emissions in Washington State," the appellate court reversed in an unpublished opinion. Foster v. Wash. Dep't. of Ecology, 2017 WL 3868481, at *7 (Wash. Ct. App. 2017).
[208] Reynolds v. Florida, supra note 201, at 1 (order granting defendant's motion to dismiss with prejudice).
[209] Chernaik v. Kitzhaber, 328 P.3d 799, 808 (Or. Ct. App. 2014).
[210] *Id.* at 805 ("In ruling otherwise, the trial court focused on the fact that plaintiffs had not alleged that defendants had violated 'a specific constitutional provision or statute.' To the extent that the court believed that a request for a declaration must be based on those kinds of written sources of law, as opposed to other doctrines, it misunderstood the scope of its statutory authority.").
[211] *Chernaik* 475 P.3d at 84 (holding that, while there may be room for the public trust holdings in Oregon to expand, the plaintiffs have not proposed a workable theory for expansion).

declined to provide the relief the plaintiffs asked for.[212] A Texas state court rejected the agency's determination that the public trust doctrine applies only to water and affirmed that the federal Clean Air Act provides "a floor, not a ceiling, for the protection of air quality," but that case was later vacated on unrelated grounds.[213] A Washington state court expressly held that the state public trust does includes air and atmosphere, but that case was also later reversed on other grounds.[214]

There have also been successes in court, though usually only partial successes. Several cases have provided potentially useful foundation for future success in atmospheric trust cases by recognizing the application of the public trust doctrine to the atmospheric commons. Some interpret constitutional provisions that are unique to each state, and some interpret the common law trust. For example, in 2015, an appellate court in New Mexico expressly affirmed that the state constitution recognizes public trust protection of the atmosphere: "We agree that Article XX, Section 21 of our state constitution recognizes that a public trust duty exists for the protection of New Mexico's natural resources, including the atmosphere, for the benefit of the people of this state."[215] However, it declined the requested injunctive relief on grounds that the state's air quality regulatory process provided a sufficient remedy.[216]

A few years before New Mexico judicially recognized the atmospheric trust under its state constitution, an appeals court in neighboring Arizona assumed (without deciding) that the atmosphere might be subject to protection under the state's common law public trust doctrine.[217] In *Butler v. Brewer*, the court affirmed (in an unpublished decision) that plaintiffs may seek a judicial determination of what resources are included in the public trust doctrine and whether the state has violated the doctrine, but ultimately dismissed the claim before it for lack of standing.[218] The court rejected legislative efforts like Idaho's to abrogate judicial authority to determine public trust protections,[219] but it was unpersuaded by the specific atmospheric trust claim before it, at least in this instance.[220]

---

[212] *See, e.g.,* Kanuk ex rel. Kanuk v. State, Dep't of Nat. Res., 335 P.3d 1088, 1091 (Ala. 2014).
[213] Bonser-Lain v. Texas Comm'n on Env't Quality, No. D-1-GN-11-002194, 2012 WL 2946041 (Tex. Dist. Ct. July 9, 2012), *vacated*, 438 S.W.3d 887, 895 (Tex. App. 2014).
[214] Foster v. Washington Dep't of Ecology, No. 14-2-25295-1 SEA, 2015 WL 7721362 at *4 (Wash. Super. Ct. Nov. 19, 2015), *rev'd* on other grounds, 200 Wash. App. 1035, 2017 WL 3868481 at *7 (2017).
[215] Sanders-Reed v. Martinez, 350 P.3d 1221, 1225 (N.M. Ct. App. 2015).
[216] *Id.* at 1227. The youth plaintiffs then submitted a rulemaking proposal to New Mexico's Environmental Improvement Board, but the Board opposed the proposal and denied the youth plaintiffs' request for a full hearing on the matter. *New Mexico,* OUR CHILD'S TR., https://perma.cc/BTX6-BY5Z (Mar. 21, 2023).
[217] *See* Butler v. Brewer, No. 1 CA-CV 12-0347, at 1, 3, 5-7 (Ariz. Ct. App. March 14, 2013) (notably, the court stated that "the [public trust doctrine] is '[a]n ancient doctrine of common law [that] restricts the sovereign's ability to dispose of resources held in public trust.'" Quoting Ariz. Ctr. For L. in the Pub. Interest v. Hassell, 172 P.2d 356, 364 (Ariz. Ct. App. 1991)).
[218] 2013 WL 1091209, at *1, *5-*7.
[219] *Id. See also* San Carlos Apache Tribe v. Super. Ct., 972 P.2d 179, 199 (Ariz. Sup. Ct. 1999). ("The public trust doctrine is a constitutional limitation on legislative power to give away resources held by the state in trust for its people.").
[220] *Butler,* No. 1 CA-CV 12-0347, at 7 ("we would be weaving 'a jurisprudence out of air' to hold that the atmosphere is protected by the [public trust] Doctrine and that state inaction is a breach of trust

B. Atmospheric Trust and Climate Rights Litigation

Since then, even though *Butler* did not establish an atmospheric trust and cannot be cited as precedential even within the state of Arizona, the case has been cited by other courts for both parts of its complex conclusion (rejecting legislative abrogation of the public trust doctrine but also rejecting the atmospheric trust claim that came before it). At least one Alaskan court cited the case in support of the proposition that atmospheric trust claims are indeed justiciable, which means that they are suitable for judicial review (overcoming the general counterarguments that such claims should be dismissed on political question, separation of powers, or other like grounds).[221] At the same time, other courts have taken *Butler's* cautious approach to mean that atmospheric trust claims are, in fact, nonjusticiable.[222]

3. *An Administrative Atmospheric Trust*

In contrast to lackluster results in court, atmospheric trust advocates have accomplished some noteworthy successes through administrative process.[223] Instead of asking a court to order regulatory agencies to take action to protect the atmospheric commons, which has raised potential issues of justiciability, these petitioners go directly to the regulators and ask for action directly. In some instances, they have met with great success.

For example, one group of atmospheric trust petitioners succeeded in persuading the Governor of Massachusetts to create an executive climate action plan by Executive Order.[224] Enacted in 2016, the resulting plan acknowledges that "climate

---

merely because it violates the [public trust] Doctrine without pointing to a specific constitutional provision or other law that has been violated"). *Id.* at 5 ("Not only is it within the power of the judiciary to determine the threshold question of whether a particular resource is a part of the public trust subject to the Doctrine, but the courts must also determine whether based on the facts there has been a breach of the trust").

[221] *See Kanuk*, 335 P.3d at n.62 (Alaska 2014) (holding that the claims are justiciable, based on the fact that other courts had recently reached the same conclusion).

[222] *See* Iowa Citizens for Cmty. Improvement v. State, 962 N.W.2d 780, 798 (Iowa 2021) ("other cases support the conclusion that environmental public trust litigation is a nonjusticiable political question") (*citing Butler*, No. 1 CA-CV 12-0347, 2013 WL 1091209); *Sanders-Reed*, 350 P.3d at 1225 ("A separate common law cause of action under the public trust doctrine would circumvent and render a nullity the process under the Air Quality Control Act that has established how competing interests are addressed and decisions are made regarding regulation of the atmosphere.").

[223] *See* Foster v. Washington Dep't of Ecology, No. 14-2-25295-1 SEA, 2015 WL 7721362 at *7-*9 (Wash. Super. Ct. Nov. 19, 2015) (holding that while the atmosphere may be protected by the public trust doctrine as enshrined in the state's constitution, administrative rulemaking is the proper venue for that action), *rev'd* on other grounds, Foster v. Washington Dep't of Ecology, 200 Wash. App. 1035 (2017), *abrogated* by Aji P. *ex rel*. Piper v. State, 480 P.3d 438, 458 (Wash. Ct. App. 2021), *rev. denied*, 497 P.3d 350 (Wash. 2021) ("we are not bound by [*Foster*] ... our analysis does not lead us to the conclusion that the public trust doctrine applies to the atmosphere"); *see also* Blumm & Wood, *supra* note 62, at 73–77 (discussing administrative relief in Massachusetts and Washington).

[224] On Sep. 16, 2016, the Governor of Massachusetts responded to a win in court by atmospheric trust youth plaintiffs by issuing Executive Order No. 569, establishing an Integrated Climate Change Strategy for the Commonwealth. The executive order was a response to the state supreme court's

change presents a serious threat to the environment and [state] residents, communities, and economy" and concludes that "only through an integrated strategy bringing together all parts of state and local government will we be able to address these threats effectively."[225] The order creates affirmative obligations for the Secretary of Energy and Environmental Affairs, the Department of Environmental Protection, and the Secretary of Public Safety, and orders the Secretary of each Executive Office to designate an existing employee to serve as the Climate Change Coordinator for that office.[226] Massachusetts further extended its commitment to fighting climate change in 2023 by creating a new Office of Climate Innovation and Resilience within the Office of the Governor, headed by a Climate Chief who will serve in the governor's cabinet.[227] Even though it was not a judicial determination of the state's public trust obligations, the Governor's acceptance of that burden likely buttresses future environmental advocacy premised on similar principles.

In Florida, a group of youth climate activists temporarily succeeded in convincing the Florida Department of Agriculture and Consumer Services (FDACS) to adopt a rule in 2022 that requires Florida's electric utilities to become 100 percent renewable by 2050, with the first accountability benchmark of 40 percent listed at 2030.[228] The state enacted the rule in settlement of an atmospheric trust lawsuit in which dozens of youth plaintiffs had claimed that the state's promotion of fossil fuels violated their constitutional rights.[229] The renewable energy plan was designed to be implemented in graded steps, with increasing shares of utilities becoming renewable.[230] FDACS Secretary Nikki Fried, then a candidate for Governor, acknowledged enforcement hurdles for the plan but nevertheless defended the settlement as "a monumental first step" in curbing greenhouse gas pollution from instate power generation.[231] "This is one of the most urgent issues of our time," she explained at

---

decision siding with OCT plaintiffs that the state environmental agency had failed its statutory obligation to limit sources of greenhouse gas emissions. Kain v. Dep't of Env't Prot., 49 N.E.3d 1124, 1127, 1142 (Mass. 2016). *See also* Anna Christiansen, *Up in the Air: A Fifty-State Survey of Atmospheric Trust Litigation Brought by Our Children's Trust*, 2020 UTAH L. REV. 867, 886–87 (2020) (discussing both the case and the executive order); Blumm & Wood, *supra* note 62, at 72–74 (discussing the litigation leading to this executive order).

[225] Mass. Exec. Order No. 569 (Sept. 16, 2016), https://perma.cc/4XWA-THFV.
[226] *Id.*
[227] Mass. Exec. Order No. 604 (Jan. 6, 2023), https://perma.cc/8LZU-CUCP.
[228] FLA. ADMIN. CODE ANN. R. 5O-5.002 (2023) ("Each Electric Utility that produces or purchases energy should seek to achieve an increase in the amount of renewable energy produced or purchased to at least ... 100% renewable energy by 2050."); *see* Press Release, *Strongest Climate Policy Enacted in Florida in Over a Decade*, OUR CHILD'S. TR. (August 9, 2022), https://perma.cc/XW48-HQAH. As this chapter went to press, the rule was repealed. FLA. ADMIN. CODE ANN. R. 5O-5.002 (2023) (repealed Jul. 28, 2024).
[229] *See* Curt Anderson, *Florida Seeks 100% Renewable Electricity by 2050*, AP (Apr. 21, 2022), https://perma.cc/2FJS-7U3G (describing the proposed settlement and noting that it was the result of a youth climate suit following the same model unfolding in other states).
[230] *Id.*
[231] *Id.*

a news conference; "[w]e can't afford to deny this reality and the urgency of what is happening to our state."²³² A few years later, after Fried lost her primary and retired from public office,²³³ the plan was ultimately repealed.²³⁴

In a celebrated Hawaii case discussed further in Part C,²³⁵ youth plaintiffs settled a trust-rights lawsuit when the state publicly recognized the constitutional climate rights the plaintiffs had asserted and the Department of Transportation agreed to establish a Climate Change Mitigation & Culture Manager, as well as a volunteer Youth Council, to help oversee state efforts to achieve "zero emissions in all ground transportation, and interisland sea and air transportation, by 2045."²³⁶

Other times, administrative petitioners have encountered hurdles distinct to the dynamic political process. For example, in Washington state, youth plaintiffs went to court to challenge the Department of Ecology's administrative decision to deny their petition for a rulemaking that would have required the agency to mandate limits on greenhouse gas emissions consistent with the best available science.²³⁷ The court ruled for the plaintiffs, requiring the agency to reconsider their petition, but the agency once again denied it.²³⁸ However, when the youth brought their now well-publicized petition directly to the Governor, he directed the Department to initiate a rulemaking to cap emissions.²³⁹

While the Washington example highlights the strength of public trust claims – and especially atmospheric trust claims – as a mobilizing force in the political process, politics are subject to shifting alliances and priorities. A few years later, the Governor's priorities changed again, and the Department dropped its rulemaking process, effectively lowering the standards the plaintiffs had sought to achieve.²⁴⁰ The trial court then ordered the agency to promulgate the rulemaking that it had started under the Governor's earlier order, but that decision was then overturned on appeal.²⁴¹ In the end, the Washington example epitomizes the confusingly

---

[232] *Id.*
[233] Tal Axelrod, *Charlie Crist Defeats Nikki Fried in Fla. Dem. Governor's Primary; Will Face DeSantis in November*, ABC NEWS (Aug. 23, 2022), https://perma.cc/78K3-4XXY.
[234] FLA. ADMIN. CODE ANN. R. 5O-5.002 (2023) (repealed Jul. 28, 2024), https://perma.cc/2G4Q-HPMW.
[235] See text accompanying notes 368–374 (discussing *Navahine* as an example of state constitutional trust-rights advocacy).
[236] Christopher Bonasia, *UK Activists Win Landmark Ruling on Oil Well's 'Inevitable' Emissions*, ENERGY MIX (June 26, 2024), https://perma.cc/8ZHG-86FZ. *See* Navahine v. Hawai'i Department of Transportation, No. 1CCV-22-0000631 (June 24, 2024); *see also Office of the Governor of Hawaii-News Release-Historic Agreement Settles Navahine Climate Litigation*, GOVERNOR JOSH GREEN (June 20, 2024), https://perma.cc/M8TV-YKFD.
[237] Foster v. Washington Dep't of Ecology, No. 14-2-25295-1, 2015 WL 7721362, at *1 (Wash. Super. Ct. Nov. 19, 2015).
[238] *Id.* at 2.
[239] *Id.* at 3.
[240] Blumm & Wood, *supra* note 62, at 76–77.
[241] Foster v. Wash. Dep't of Ecology, No. 14-2-25295-1, 2016 WL 11359472 at *1 (Wash. Super. Ct. 2016) (ordering DOE to "proceed with the rulemaking procedure to adopt a rule to limit greenhouse gas emissions in Washington state as directed by Governor Inslee in July 2015"), *rev'd* by Foster v. Wash.

vacillating trajectory that many atmospheric trust claims have faced while moving simultaneously through political and judicial processes.

Atmospheric trust advocates learned valuable lessons from this "first hatch" of cases. They experienced the advantages and disadvantages of proceeding through administrative channels, where they could bypass the separation of powers problems raised by asking courts to order specific legislative or executive acts, but the results they might achieve would be more vulnerable to shifting political winds. They also learned the distinct hurdles they could expect proceeding through judicial channels, especially when bringing a pure common law claim without the buttressing support of statutory or constitutional mandates, such as the text the New Mexico plaintiffs pointed to in their state constitution,[242] or the European treaty on which the *Urgenda* plaintiffs relied.[243] Later advocates attempted to apply these lessons in the next wave of atmospheric trust litigation, most famously in *Juliana v. United States*.[244]

4. Juliana v. United States

In 2015, just as *Urgenda* was getting underway, domestic atmospheric trust advocates launched a new claim in federal court with a novel approach, explicitly combining public trust sovereign obligation arguments with environmental rights claims premised on rights in the United States Constitution. The eighteen youth plaintiffs filed their suit in Oregon,[245] where University of Oregon Professor Mary Wood teaches and where the assisting NGO, Our Children's Trust, is based.[246] Alleging that the federal government had violated atmospheric trust obligations and the plaintiffs' constitutionally protected fundamental right to climate stability, the original complaint sought

---

Dep't of Ecology, 200 Wash. App. 1035, 2017 WL 3868481, at *8 ("[T]he trial court abused its discretion when it granted CR 60(b) relief ... we reverse.").

[242] N.M. CONST. art. XX, § 21 ("The protection of the state's beautiful and healthful environment is hereby declared to be of fundamental importance to the public interest, health, safety and the general welfare. The legislature shall provide for control of pollution and control of despoilment of the air, water and other natural resources of this state, consistent with the use and development of these resources for the maximum benefit of the people."); *see also Sanders-Reed v. Martinez*, 350 P.3d 1221, 1225 (N.M. Ct. App. 2015) (interpreting this provision as protecting the atmosphere as a public trust resource). Ten years later, however, a different appellate court concluded that the same provision does not provide a judicially enforceable right to a "beautiful and healthful environment." Atencio v. State of New Mexico, No. A-1-CA-42006, at 17 (N.M. Ct. App. 2025).

[243] European Convention on Human Rights, art. 2, 8, Sept. 3, 1953, C.E.T.S. No. 213 (Articles 2 and 8 of the European Convention on Human Rights contain the right to life and the right to privacy, respectively); *see also* Urgenda v. Netherlands, [2015] HAZA C/09/00456689 (Neth.) at 41, https://perma.cc/V7C5-VRAV (unofficial English translation).

[244] Juliana v. United States, No. 24-684, D.C. No. 6:15-cv-1517, 2024 WL 5102489, 2024 WL 5102489, (May 1, 2024), *cert. denied*, 604 U.S. 645 (2025).

[245] Juliana v. United States, 217 F. Supp. 3d 1224, 1233 (D. Or. 2016).

[246] *See* Sarah Adams-Schoen, *Juliana v. United States*, OR. HIST. SOC'Y – OREGON ENCYCLOPEDIA (Sep. 23, 2023), https://perma.cc/2VZW-82TM (discussing both Wood and Our Children's Trust as based in Oregon).

both declaratory relief – asking the court to affirm the environmental rights and sovereign obligations the plaintiffs alleged – and injunctive relief, ordering the government to take action in compliance with these rights and obligations.[247]

Kelsey Juliana, one of eighteen youth plaintiffs filing the lawsuit, explained her personal motivation behind bringing the case:

> Our nation's top climate scientists ... have found that the present [carbon dioxide] level is already in the danger zone and leading to devastating disruptions of planetary systems. The current practices and policies of our federal government include sustained exploitation and consumption of fossil fuels. We brought this case because the government needs to immediately and aggressively reduce carbon emissions and stop promoting fossil fuels, which force our nation's climate system toward irreversible impacts. If the government continues to delay urgent annual emissions reductions, my generation's well-being will be inexcusably put at risk.[248]

Bill McKibben, an internationally renowned environmentalist, famously called it "the most important lawsuit on the planet,"[249] as the plaintiffs fought off successive motions to dismiss the claim before the trial could even begin. In her order denying the government's first motion to dismiss, Federal District Court Judge Ann Aiken memorably began by observing: "This is no ordinary lawsuit."[250]

Even though the claim was ultimately unsuccessful, this section recounts the *Juliana* litigation in detail, both because it remains the standard-bearer trust-rights claim at the federal level in the United States, and because it highlights the consequences for environmental litigation of the poor constitutional foundations for U.S. environmental law identified in the introduction. The *Juliana* claim was repeatedly assailed by the defendants with unusual force during a decade of litigation, and the youth plaintiffs' dogged efforts to overcome each hurdle won international acclaim. Yet even after sequentially persuading trial judge that their claim at least deserved to be heard – and even as related international claims gained ground – the *Juliana* youth plaintiffs ultimately failed to ever get their proverbial day in court.

a. The *Juliana* Pleadings

The *Juliana* case was novel not only because it took on climate change, and not only because of the coordinated political advocacy that accompanied it, and not even because the primary advocates were all children at the time of its filing. It was

---

[247] Complaint at 94–95, Juliana v. United States, 217 F. Supp. 3d 1224 (D. Or. 2016) (No. 6:15-cv-01517-TC) (Plaintiffs asked the court to "[d]eclare that Defendants have violated and are violating Plaintiffs' fundamental constitutional rights," and asked the court to "[e]njoin Defendants from further violations of the Constitution").

[248] *Landmark U.S. Federal Climate Lawsuit: Details of Proceedings*, Our Child's. Tr., https://perma.cc/N354-9JBR.

[249] *Id.*

[250] *Juliana*, 217 F. Supp. 3d at 1234.

novel because it raised new legal claims involving issues of both common and constitutional law. The initial complaint relied on familiar public trust claims, alleging sovereign obligations to protect common pool natural resources, but like its sibling cases, it applied the doctrine in a wholly new way – alleging federal trust obligations to protect the atmospheric commons.[251] However, the *Juliana* plaintiffs attached a wholly new theory of constitutional rights and obligations to the public trust claim.[252] The plaintiffs argued that they held a fundamental right to a stable climate, and that the federal government's failure to protect it represented a violation of substantive due process (and at least in the original complaint, violations as well of equal protection and unenumerated rights claimed under the Ninth Amendment).[253] As the litigation unfolded and they confronted the same difficulties previous claimants had encountered on their common law atmospheric trust claim, their constitutional claims came to the forefront.[254]

Juliana inspired enormous international interest, especially among climate-conscious children,[255] but the merits of the claim would have to overcome serious problems of precedent. The first challenge was the plaintiffs' contention that public trust sovereign obligations attach to the federal government as well as the states, which, the plaintiffs argued, is the only level adequately positioned to regulate greenhouse gas pollution in the United States.[256] It was a difficult argument, given Supreme Court dicta characterizing the doctrine as a matter of state law just a decade earlier.[257] Nevertheless, the plaintiffs invoked scholars who distinguish

---

[251] Complaint at 83, *Juliana*, No. 6:15-cv-01517-TC (D. Or. Aug. 12, 2015) ("[O]ne principle of the public trust doctrine is: 'the public has fundamental rights and interests in natural resources such as the sea, shore, and the air.'").

[252] *Id.* at 92 ("Among the implicit liberties protected from government intrusion by the Ninth Amendment is the right to be sustained by our country's vital natural systems, including our climate system."); *id.* at 86 ("Defendants continue to knowingly enhance that danger by allowing fossil fuel production, consumption, and combustion at dangerous levels, thereby violating Plaintiff's substantive Fifth Amendment due process rights."); *see infra* note 272 (discussing that this element of the original complaint would eventually be dismissed).

[253] *Id.* at 92 ("Among the implicit liberties protected from government intrusion by the Ninth Amendment is the right to be sustained by our country's vital natural systems, including our climate system."); *id.* at 86 ("Defendants continue to knowingly enhance that danger by allowing fossil fuel production, consumption, and combustion at dangerous levels, thereby violating Plaintiff's substantive Fifth Amendment due process rights."); *see infra* note 272 (discussing that this element of the original complaint would eventually be dismissed).

[254] Juliana v. United States, No. 6:15-CV-01517 AA, 2023 WL 3750334, at *8 (D. Or. June 1, 2023) ("[P]laintiffs' proposed amendments are not futile: a declaration that federal defendants' energy policies violate plaintiffs' constitutional rights would itself be significant relief.").

[255] *See infra* text accompanying notes 338–340 and 327–331 (discussing public interest in *Juliana* and its sibling trust-rights cases, including the 36,000 children who signed an amicus brief in support of the *Juliana* claim while awaiting trial in 2018, and the 350,000 "intergenerational individuals" who signed petitions demanding that the Biden Administration stop opposing the case after the plaintiffs' 2024 appeal to the Supreme Court).

[256] *See* Juliana v. United States, 217 F.Supp.3d 1224, 1263–64 (D. Or. 2016).

[257] *See* PPL Montana, LLC v. Montana, 556 U.S. 576, 603 (2012).

that dicta based on its limiting context,[258] emphasizing that the public trust as an attribute of sovereign authority must apply to all sovereign authority, not just at the state level.[259] They also defended the existence of federal trust obligations on the historical grounds that every postcolonial American state that inherited the doctrine as an attribute of sovereignty upon statehood must have received it through sovereignty conferred by the federal government.[260] Federal sovereignty over prestate lands must have been bound by the same trust obligations that would ultimately pass to the new states. At a minimum, it established that federal sovereignty is not a complete stranger to trust obligations.

The more challenging doctrinal extension sought by the plaintiffs was their contention that public trust obligations apply to atmospheric resources.[261] The plaintiffs invoked Justinian references to the air commons, but they could point to no previous American common law precedent for this claim. Judge Aiken initially sustained this part of the claim against an early motion to dismiss, evading the novelty of the atmospheric trust claim by holding that the plaintiffs had also alleged cognizable claims of climate change related harm to coastal resources that are clearly the subject of public trust rights and obligations.[262] Over the course of the litigation, she repeatedly affirmed those aspects of the complaint alleging that ocean acidification caused by greenhouse gas pollution was harming the territorial seas, which are indisputably protected by the traditional public trust doctrine.[263]

---

[258] See *Juliana*, 217 F.Supp.3d at 1274. See also Ryan et al., *Debating Juliana*, supra note 114, at 17 (presenting Rick Frank's argument that the Court's passing statement in the *PPL Montana* dicta cannot resolve the larger issue in a fully different factual context).

[259] See *Juliana*, 217 F.Supp.3d at 1263–64; see also Erin Ryan, *A Short History of the Public Trust Doctrine and Its Intersection with Private Water Law*, 38 VA. ENV'T L. J. 135, 176–81 (2020) [hereinafter *A Short History*] (discussing ongoing scholarly debate over whether the trust extends to federal authority).

[260] See *Juliana*, 217 F.Supp.3d at 1274 ("Upon the acquisition of a territory by the United States ... the same title and dominion passed to the United States, for the benefit of the whole people, and in trust for the several states to be ultimately created out of the territory." quoting Shively v. Bowlby, 152 U.S. 1, 14 (1894)); see also Ryan, *A Short History*, supra note 259, at 178–79 (discussing the historic argument for a federal public trust doctrine); Michael C. Blumm & Lynn S. Schaffer, *The Federal Public Trust Doctrine: Misinterpreting Justice Kennedy and Illinois Central Railroad*, 45 ENV'T L. 399, 399–405 (2015) (discussing Justice Kennedy's reference to the equal footing doctrine in Idaho v. Coeur d'Alene Tribe and what it means for the public trust doctrine's origins).

[261] Complaint at 83, Juliana v. United States, No. 6:15-cv-01517-TC (D. Or. Aug. 12, 2015) ("[O]ne principle of the public trust doctrine is: 'the public has fundamental rights and interests in natural resources such as the sea, the shore, and the air.'"); see also Juliana v. United States, No. 6:15-CV-01517 AA, 2023 WL 3750334, at *6 (D. Or. June 1, 2023) ("Plaintiffs' Second Amended Complaint thus requests this Court to ... enter a judgment declaring that the United States' national energy system has violated and continues to violate the public trust doctrine.").

[262] Order Denying Petition for Mandamus, *In re* United States, 895 F.3d 1101, 1104 (9th Cir. 2018); *Juliana*, 217 F.Supp.3d at 1276.

[263] Opinion and Order at 46–48, Juliana v. United States, No. 15-CV-01517-AA (D. Or. Dec. 29, 2023) ("[P]laintiffs have alleged violations of the public trust doctrine in connection with the territorial sea. Because the Ninth Circuit did not reach the merits of plaintiffs' claims, the Court incorporates its analysis and legal conclusions, as stated *Juliana* (finding that plaintiffs' alleged injuries relate to the

However, in a dramatic departure from the "first hatch" pure atmospheric trust cases, the *Juliana* plaintiffs bolstered the public trust element of their lawsuit by adding a series of ambitious constitutional claims under the Equal Protection and Due Process Clauses of the Fourteenth Amendment and the unenumerated rights preserved by the Ninth Amendment.[264] In some respects, their most provocative claim rested on their invocation of the Constitution's promise of equal protection of the laws,[265] which they alleged was being violated because the burden of the government's failure to address climate change would fall disproportionately on the young and the future generations they represented.[266] Their contention was that the climate governance failures they alleged discriminated against their generation,[267] who would be most impacted by climate change but lacked the voting rights to influence climate policy through conventional political processes.[268] Even so lacking precedent for generational equal protection claims and facing problems of speculative evidence, they soon abandoned the equal protection claim to focus on the others.

The constitutional argument they took farthest was their claim that the federal government's failure to address climate change represented a violation of their fundamental right to a livable climate – an equally novel claim drawing on the rights to life, liberty, and property protected by the Fourteenth Amendment's Due Process Clause[269] and the Ninth Amendment's doctrine of unenumerated fundamental rights.[270] The Ninth Amendment adds to the Bill of Rights the clarification that "[t]he enumeration in the Constitution, of certain rights, shall not be construed to deny or disparage others retained by the people"[271] – at least theoretically leaving open the possibility that other fundamental rights, such as a right to climate stability, may also be worthy of legal protection. The *Juliana* claim had initially suggested that the right to a healthy climate may be one of these unenumerated rights that are also entitled to constitutional protection,[272] although in time, the plaintiffs would

---

effects of ocean acidification and rising ocean temperatures, thus pleadings adequately alleged harm to public trust assets…)") (internal citations omitted).

[264] Juliana v. United States, 217 F.Supp.3d 1224, 1263–64 (D. Or. 2016) (describing the plaintiffs' original claims).

[265] U.S. CONST. amend. XIV, §1, cl. 4 ("nor [shall any State] deny to any person within its jurisdiction the equal protection of the laws.").

[266] Complaint at 89-90, Juliana v. United States, 217 F. Supp. 3d 1224 (D. Or. Sep. 10, 2015) (No. 6:15-cv-01517-TC 217).

[267] Id.

[268] See Katy Scott, *Can 'Climate Kids' Take On Governments and Win?*, CNN (July 24, 2018), https://perma.cc/U5N9-3XF5.

[269] U.S. CONST. amend. XIV, §1, cl. 3 ("…nor shall any State deprive any person of life, liberty, or property, without due process of law.").

[270] U.S. CONST. amend. IX ("The enumeration in the Constitution, of certain rights, shall not be construed to deny or disparage others retained by the people.").

[271] Id.

[272] Complaint at 92, Juliana v. United States, 217 F. Supp. 3d 1224 (D. Or. Jun. 8, 2017) (No. 6:15-cv-01517-TC). This part of the claim would eventually be dismissed in late 2023, even as the public trust and substantive due process claim continued forward. Opinion and Order, Juliana v. United States,

B. Atmospheric Trust and Climate Rights Litigation

limit their focus to the Fourteenth Amendment argument that the government's failure to adequately regulate greenhouse gas pollution was implicitly violating their substantive Due Process rights to life, by denying them a livable climate.[273]

Although it relied on a different source for this claimed right to life, the *Juliana* plaintiffs' substantive due process claim was thus conceptually identical to the *Urgenda* plaintiff's claimed rights to life under the ECHR. Their requested outcome also mirrored that in *Urgenda*, but it differed from most previously successful public trust advocacy, which has generally sought negative relief – demanding that the government stop harming trust resources or allowing others to do so. The *Juliana* plaintiffs asked for more – not only demanding that the government stop allowing others to pollute the atmosphere, but also asking the government to take affirmative steps toward creating and implementing policy to protect climate stability.

In her memorable initial ruling in the case, rejecting the defendant's original motion to dismiss, Judge Aiken held that the plaintiffs could move forward with a suit claiming this kind of fundamental right – at a minimum, as a substantive component of due process – to a climate system capable of sustaining human life.[274] Analogizing to the fundamental right to marry that the Supreme Court had recognized earlier the same year,[275] Judge Aiken opined:

> [As to t]he idea that certain rights may be necessary to enable the exercise of other rights, whether enumerated or unenumerated.... Exercising my "reasoned judgment", I have no doubt that the right to a climate system capable of sustaining human life is fundamental to a free and ordered society. Just as marriage is the "foundation of the family," a stable climate system is quite literally the foundation "of society, without which there would be neither civilization nor progress."[276]

Judge Aiken did not conclude here that the alleged rights had actually been violated – only that the plaintiffs should have the opportunity to prove it in her court. For all the reasons noted earlier, that would have proven an exceptionally heavy lift legally, for both the novel atmospheric trust claim and the unprecedented constitutional claim. Yet recognition for a fundamental right to climate security would have been such a landmark ruling from a federal court at any level – whether under a substantive due process analysis or the conventional public trust argument that

---

Civ. No. 15-CV-01517-AA, at 45-46 (D. Or. Dec. 29, 2023) ("[T]he Ninth Amendment has never been recognized as independently securing any constitutional right ... this claim must be dismissed.").

[273] Second Amended Complaint at 133–40, Juliana v. United States, No. 6:15-CV-01517-AA, 2023 WL 3750334 (D. Or. June 1, 2023).

[274] Juliana v. United States, 217 F.Supp.3d 1224, 1249–50 (D. Or. 2016) ("Exercising my reasoned judgment, I have no doubt that the right to a climate system capable of sustaining human life is fundamental to a free and ordered society.") (internal citations omitted).

[275] Obergefell v. Hodges, 576 U.S. 644 (2015) (holding that the fundamental right to marry under the Due Process Clause of the Fourteenth Amendment applies equally, across all fifty states, to same-sex couples as it does to opposite-sex couples).

[276] *Juliana*, 217 F. Supp. 3d at 1249–1250.

Judge Aiken allowed in relation to the territorial seas. For that reason, even this initially sympathetic ruling, together with several others that would follow from Judge Aiken, were celebrated as an important incremental successes by the youth climate litigation movement.[277]

Even beyond these substantive legal hurdles, the *Juliana* claim raised sobering procedural hurdles relating to remedy the plaintiffs had requested, and how it should bear on their standing to even make these arguments in court. Even if the plaintiffs could prevail on the atmospheric trust or substantive due process claim, what exactly did they expect the court to do about it? What could they, both constitutionally and realistically, expect a court to do about it? The *Juliana* youth plaintiffs had high hopes. In their initial complaint, the plaintiffs specifically requested two things: "(1) a declaration [that] their constitutional and public trust rights have been violated and (2) an order enjoining defendants from violating those rights and directing defendants to develop a plan to reduce CO_2 emissions."[278] The first request for declaratory relief, interpreting alleged rights and obligations, falls within the traditional wheelhouse of a court. But the second request, for injunctive request on the basis of the requested interpretation of rights and duties, raised both eyebrows and concerns about redressability. Could the court order defendant agencies to regulate greenhouse gases this way?

Respecting the judicial lane within the constitutional separation of powers, courts are reluctant to engage in adjudication that veers toward untethered policymaking. Courts will order legislative or executive action when it is clearly required by the sources of law they are asked to interpret, but such jurisprudential constraints as the political questions doctrine and the standing doctrine of redressability counsel courts to err on the side of judicial restraint.[279] The defendants and critics of the lawsuit argued that these barriers exist to prevent exactly a claim like this one from moving forward, while the plaintiffs argued that they were simply asking the court to appropriately vindicate their alleged rights, as courts routinely do. They further contended that climate change, and the government's alleged complicity in creating it, constituted a unique exigency that weighed in favor of justiciability.[280] If the court would not order some kind of change, reasoned the plaintiffs, their rights would continue to be violated with no means of relief.

Their initial claim persuaded at least Judge Aiken that the defendant agencies possessed the power to redress their claim through existing regulatory resources, by

---

[277] See Ryan, *supra* note 116, at 62 (making this point).
[278] *Juliana*, 217 F. Supp. 3d at 1233 (quoted text); *see also id.* at 1246–48 (discussing redressability of plaintiff's claim).
[279] See Nat Stern, *The Political Question Doctrine in State Courts*, 35 S.C. L. Rev. 405, 414–15 (1984) (showing examples of courts exercising judicial restraint when confronted with jurisprudential constraints).
[280] See Ryan et al., *supra* note 114 (Jim Huffman and Mary Wood debating the requested remedy); Brief for Petitioner at 23–28, Juliana v. United States, No. 18-36082 (9th Cir. Feb. 26, 2019).

B. Atmospheric Trust and Climate Rights Litigation

developing a remedial plan to reduce greenhouse gas emissions.[281] However, the same argument did not persuade the higher courts, requiring sequential retooling of the case as it progressed through an epic legal obstacle course of motions to dismiss, interlocutory appeals, petitions for mandamus, and even Supreme Court intervention. Eventually, as described further below, the plaintiffs would have to address this problem by amending their complaint to seek only judicial recognition of the rights they claim violated.[282]

b. The Campaign to Dismiss

Before its final disposition in 2025, the *Juliana* claim endured an extraordinary volley of attempts to quash it, engaging every level of the multitiered federal judiciary. Judge Aiken had originally slated the case for trial in October of 2018, after denying several early motions to dismiss.[283] The Trump Administration then filed multiple petitions for the writ of mandamus, by which the Administration sought to convince the Ninth Circuit Court of Appeals to force Judge Aiken to dismiss the case after her decision otherwise.[284] Two of these petitions were appealed to the United States Supreme Court, which denied both of them. But in the latter denial, the Court offered the defendant (and the lower courts, who were paying close attention) a hint about how better to procure the dismissal it sought.[285]

Though the Supreme Court again declined the government's petition,[286] the second order suggested that this was because the defendants could seek the dismissal it wanted from a more appropriate judicial forum, understood by observers as the intermediate court of appeal.[287] The implication was that even though the justices did not wish to become involved at that point, the defendants could still seek to overturn Judge Aiken's refusal to dismiss by filing an interlocutory appeal with the

---

[281] Juliana, 217 F. Supp. 3d at 1247–48; *see also* Blumm & Wood, *supra* note 62, at 71–72.
[282] Juliana v. United States, No. 6:15-CV-01517 AA, 2023 WL 3750334, at *9 (D. Or. June 1, 2023).
[283] *See* Juliana v. United States – Major Court Orders and Filings, OUR CHILD'S. TR., https://perma.cc/EZ2A-7CZP (listing all motions).
[284] *Id.*; Adam Wernick, *Circuit Court Declines to Halt Climate Case Brought by Youth Plaintiffs*, WORLD (April 14, 2018), https://perma.cc/4654-45T3; *see also In re* United States, 884 F.3d 830, 838 (9th Cir. 2018).
[285] Order Denying Petition for Stay of Proceedings, *In re United States*, 586 U.S. 983 (2018) (No. 18A410), https://perma.cc/4GM6-W8BV.
[286] *Id.*
[287] The Court's order implied that the Ninth Circuit had previously dismissed the government's efforts to dismiss the case for reasons that may no longer be valid: "At this time ... the Government's petition for a writ of mandamus does not have a 'fair prospect' of success in this Court because adequate relief may be available in the United States Court of Appeals for the Ninth Circuit. ...Although the Ninth Circuit has twice denied the Government's request for mandamus relief, it did so without prejudice. And the court's basis for denying relief rested, in large part, on the early stage of the litigation, the likelihood that plaintiffs' claims would narrow as the case progressed, and the possibility of attaining relief through ordinary dispositive motions. Those reasons are, to a large extent, no longer pertinent. The 50-day trial was scheduled to begin on October 29, 2018, and is being held in abeyance only because of the current administrative stay." *Id.*

Ninth Circuit. An interlocutory appeal is a tool of civil procedure that enables a higher court to rule on a motion while the litigation still technically rests with a lower court (because there has not yet been a final result to appeal). Judge Aiken apparently understood the implications of the Court's second order as well, and she acknowledged it by certifying the question of whether the trial should proceed to the Ninth Circuit on interlocutory appeal.[288]

The case's unusually complicated procedural voyage continued from there. After an extended period of consideration and intense public interest,[289] and over a vigorous dissent by one of the three judges on the Ninth Circuit panel, the appeals court remanded the case back to the trial court with instructions to dismiss for lack of "redressability,"[290] a requirement of standing.[291] To qualify for judicial review, a case must be one for which the judiciary can provide meaningful "redress," and the majority concluded that some of what the plaintiffs had asked the courts to do in the initial case, such as ordering specific action by the political branches, was relief it should not provide.[292]

In response, in 2021, the youth plaintiffs filed a new motion to amend their complaint, removing their initial requests for the comprehensive court-ordered injunctive relief to which the Ninth Circuit had objected.[293] While retaining their substantive public trust and constitutional claims, they shifted legal strategy to seek primarily declaratory relief – an official interpretation of the law – which they hoped would fall more squarely within available judicial authority.[294] Highlighting national interest in the litigation, seventeen states attempted to intervene in opposition to the claims, indicating that they would object to any settlement between the plaintiffs and the sitting Biden Administration.[295] Their motion was denied in

---

[288] Certification of Interlocutory Appeal at 3–6, Juliana v. United States, No. 6:15-cv-01517-AA, 2018 WL 6303774 (2018).

[289] *See* Brandi Buchman, *Inaugural Hearing of House Climate Group Gathers Young Voices*, COURTHOUSE NEWS SERV. (April 4, 2019), https://perma.cc/DZE2-RTCZ (reporting on the public debate ahead of an anticipated trial).

[290] Juliana v. United States, 947 F.3d 1159, 1173–75 (9th Cir. 2020).

[291] *See* Lujan v. Def. of Wildlife, 504 U.S. 555, 560–61 (1992) (explaining that a plaintiff must satisfy each of three constitutional standing requirements to be heard in court: (1) injury in fact, (2) causation between the defendant's actions and the plaintiff's injury, and (3) redressability).

[292] *Juliana*, 947 F.3d at 1169–74.

[293] Motion to Amend Complaint at 10–19, Juliana v. United States, No. 6:15-cv-01517-AA (D. Or. Mar. 9, 2021), https://perma.cc/K9BN-9HJ8.

[294] *See* [Proposed] Second Amended Complaint for Declaratory and Injunctive Relief, Juliana v. United States, No. 6:15-cv-01517-AA (D. Or. Mar. 9, 2021). The youth plaintiffs sought a judgment declaring the violation of the public trust doctrine and plaintiffs' constitutional rights to substantive due process and equal protection of the law, an injunction "restraining Defendants from carrying out policies, practices, and affirmative actions that render the national energy system unconstitutional in a manner that harms Plaintiffs," award of attorneys' fees, and "such other and further relief as the Court deems just and proper." *Id.* at 144–45.

[295] *See Legal Actions*, OUR CHILD'S. TR., https://perma.cc/E648-S87W; Motion for Limited Intervention, Juliana v. United States, No. 6:15-cv-01517-AA (June 8, 2021). The Motion to Intervene was headed by Alabama and joined by Alaska, Arkansas, Georgia, Indiana, Louisiana, Mississippi, Missouri, Montana, Nebraska, North Dakota, Ohio, Oklahoma, South Carolina, Texas, Utah, and

March of 2023,²⁹⁶ although the court order indicated that they could refile later if the case moved forward.²⁹⁷

Eventually, Judge Aiken did allow the plaintiffs to amend their complaint in light of the redressability issue the Ninth Circuit had identified in its earlier grounds for dismissal, and she allowed some of those claims to move forward.²⁹⁸ Her order granting permission discussed three factors in her decision. First, she observed that the Ninth Circuit had not foreclosed the possibility of an amended complaint when it mandated the dismissal of their original complaint for lack of standing.²⁹⁹ Second, the plaintiffs cited a recent Supreme Court case offering an expansive interpretation of declaratory judgments that would support their standing to raise these claims.³⁰⁰ And finally, Judge Aiken noted that the modified complaint significantly narrowed the scope of injunctive relief that the plaintiffs were requesting.³⁰¹ Instead of asking for court-ordered substantive policy changes, the new complaint sought a more conventional injunction to restrain only further harm by the government³⁰² – preventing it "from carrying out policies, practices, and affirmative actions that render the national energy system unconstitutional in a manner that harms [the p]laintiffs" – and even then, only if the court deemed such injunctive relief "necessary, just, and proper."³⁰³ Even so, she allowed only the claims for declaratory relief to move forward.

In her ruling late in December of 2023, Judge Aiken dismissed all claims for injunctive relief, finding that even the narrowed prayer for injunctive relief would require the court to order a sweeping result that it could not grant.³⁰⁴ Although the requested order would satisfy the first prong of the redressability analysis by redressing the plaintiffs' alleged injuries,³⁰⁵ it would fail the second prong by requiring the

---

West Virginia. *Id.* Settlement negotiations between the youth plaintiffs, their attorneys, and the Department of Justice began in May 2021 but ended just five months later with no resolution. Press Release, *Settlement Talks End Without Resolution in Juliana v. U.S. Climate Case*, OUR CHILD'S TR (Nov. 1, 2021), https://perma.cc/QEF8-A6G4.

²⁹⁶ See *Legal Actions, supra* note 295.
²⁹⁷ *Id.*
²⁹⁸ Juliana v. Unites States, No. 15-CV-01517-AA, 2023 WL 3750334, at *8 (D. Or. June 1, 2023).
²⁹⁹ Opinion and Order at *12, Juliana v. United States, No. 15-CV-01517-AA, 2023 WL 9023339 (D. Or. Dec. 29, 2023).
³⁰⁰ *Id.* The plaintiffs pointed to *Uzuegbunam v. Preczewski*, in which the Supreme Court held that "a request for nominal damages satisfies the redressability element of standing where a plaintiff's claim is based on a completed violation of a legal right." Uzuegbunam v. Preczewski, 592 U.S. 279, 292 (2021).
³⁰¹ *Id.* (citing *Uzuegbunam v. Preczewski*). Judge Aiken noted that nominal damages are a form of declaratory relief, and that "*Uzuegbunam* illustrates that when a plaintiff shows a completed violation of a legal right, as plaintiffs have shown here, standing survives, even when relief is nominal, trivial, or partial." *Id.* at 30.
³⁰² *Id.* at 26–27.
³⁰³ *Id.* at 22.
³⁰⁴ *Id.* at 28.
³⁰⁵ Opinion and Order at 23–24, Juliana v. Unites States, Civ. No. 15-CV-01517-AA (D. Or. Dec. 29, 2023) ("Based on plaintiffs' alleged facts, an order to defendants to refrain from certain fossil fuel activities which are causing plaintiffs' injuries would redress those injuries.").

court to make complex policy decisions better left to the political branches.[306] She acknowledged that federal courts routinely issue injunctions against federal agencies,[307] including celebrated cases requiring the desegregation of schools, enforcing tribal treaty rights, and requiring prison reforms.[308] Yet she identified a critical difference between those "structural reform" cases and this one, which is that those cases required court-ordered conformity by a single agency, while the relief requested here would require the coordination of multiple decision-makers across multiple executive agencies,[309] positioning the court to "tread[] on ground over which [the] Ninth Circuit cautioned [her] not to step."[310]

Nevertheless, Judge Aiken allowed the plaintiffs to proceed on their key claims for declaratory relief, by which they seek judicial acknowledgement of the public trust violation and violations of their substantive due process rights to a stable climate. Judge Aiken reasoned that the Supreme Court "has long recognized that declaratory judgment actions can provide redressability, even where relief obtained is a declaratory judgement alone."[311] Moreover, she explained that courts have a "unique and singular duty to both declare constitutional rights and prevent political acts that would curb or violate those rights," and that "[d]eclaratory judgments are thus firmly sited within the core competences of the courts in ways that structural injunctions are not."[312] Finally, she laid out a vision for the process that could follow if the plaintiffs prevail in their claim, which could involve splitting the case into separate liability and remedy stages.[313]

---

[306] *Id.* at 24 (noting that the scaled-down injunction would still be "beyond a district court's power to award").

[307] *Id.* at 25 ("While crafting and implementing injunctions in cases involving longstanding agency shortcomings may require rigorous, adversarial fact-finding to penetrate questions of science, there is nothing exceptional about a federal court issuing injunctions against federal agencies.").

[308] *Id.* 26, Juliana v. Unites States, No. 15-CV-01517-AA, (D. Or. Dec. 29, 2023) 11 (noting that similar "structural injunctions" had been ordered in cases that "ordered busing to desegregate schools; the treaty rights cases that assured a fair share of fish for American Indian treaty fishers; cases instituting prison condition reform; and cases relating to land use and low-income housing"). Judge Aiken further noted that "the Ninth Circuit did not offer any explicit guidance on how to distinguish other structural injunction cases, where the district court has power to order specific, injunctive relief, from this case, where the relief necessary to redress plaintiffs' injuries is held to be too broad [by defendants]." *Id.*

[309] *Id.* at 27. This form of relief, Judge Aiken concluded, "would be more expansive than any case of which the Court is aware," and that while ordering plaintiffs to sue every agency individually may not "bring about the all-out course correction necessary to avoid the impending crisis," ordering "agencies to work together, outside their silos to oversee resolution of a complex, multiagency problem" is not "necessary – and is perhaps premature – at this point in the case." *Id.* at 27–28.

[310] Opinion and Order at 28, Juliana v. Unites States, Civ. No. 15-CV-01517-AA (D. Or. Dec. 29, 2023).

[311] *Id.* at 29–31 (concluding that a "declaration that defendants are violating plaintiffs' constitutional rights may be enough to bring about relief by changed conduct," satisfying the first prong of redressability).

[312] *Id.* 31–32 ("Declaratory judgments ask courts to declare actions lawful or unlawful, applying legal standards to a set of facts. Unlike structural injunctions, which envision an on-going dialogue between the court and the parties, the declaratory relief model facilitates a dialogue between the parties.").

[313] *Id.* at 33. In the liability stage, the court would lay out what obligations the government owes the plaintiffs, while the remedy stage would involve judicial oversight of the government as it adopts plans to comply with those obligations – potentially through a special master or a consent decree. *Id.*

c. The Amended Complaint

In the surviving complaint, then, the plaintiffs traded the possibility of a more immediately actionable remedy for the opportunity to make their novel constitutional and public trust claims in court. The complaint that then moved forward sought judicial affirmation of the plaintiffs' claim that the "United States national energy system that creates the harmful conditions described ... has violated and continues to violate the Fifth Amendment of the U.S. Constitution and plaintiffs' constitutional rights to substantive due process"[314] as well as judicial recognition of the ways that "the historical public trust doctrine" is implicated.[315] Judge Aiken dismissed the Ninth Amendment[316] and Equal Protection[317] claims, finding them insufficiently grounded in precedent, but she concluded that the complaint still framed a violation of constitutional and common law rights that were the proper subject of judicial review.[318] She allowed the public trust claim to continue because it addresses the serious harm of ocean acidification from excessive greenhouse gas pollution, connecting climate change to traditional public trust resources and bypassing at least one legal quandary.[319] As she concluded, the public trust claim could move forward independently of the controversy over extending trust protections to the atmosphere, because atmospheric climate change itself threatens the territorial seas that have been recognized as a public trust resource from the earliest days of the nation.[320]

In May of 2024, *Juliana* was once again dismissed by the Ninth Circuit, again for lack of standing, this time with prejudice (prohibiting the plaintiffs from revising their pleadings to revive their claim, as they had done after the Ninth Circuit dismissed their claim the last time).[321] The panel concluded that the plaintiffs had failed to raise a redressable claim, or one for which the judiciary could grant any

---

[314] *Id.* at 14.
[315] Opinion and Order at 2, Juliana v. Unites States, Civ. No. 15-CV-01517-AA (D. Or. Dec. 29, 2023).
[316] *Id.* at 45–46 ("[T]he Ninth Amendment has never been recognized as independently securing any constitutional right ... this claim must be dismissed.").
[317] *Id.* (noting that both the Supreme Court and the Ninth Circuit had rejected the contention that age could qualify as a "suspect class" that would subject a law challenged on equal protection grounds to strict scrutiny). This heightened form of judicial scrutiny of equal protection claims, normally required for the plaintiffs to prevail, is only available when the allegedly targeted group is one that the Supreme Court has identified as especially subject to unjustifiably different treatment.
[318] Juliana v. United States, No. 6:15-cv-01517-AA, 2023 WL 3750334, at *9 (D. Or. June 1, 2023).
[319] Opinion and Order at 47, *Juliana*, No. 6:15-cv-01517-AA (D. Or. Dec. 29, 2023) ("The Court has expended innumerable hours in research and analysis of plaintiffs' public trust claim and, in prior orders, determined that plaintiffs have alleged violations of the public trust doctrine in connection with the territorial sea."); *id.* ("Because the Ninth Circuit did not reach the merits of plaintiffs' claims, the Court incorporates its analysis and legal conclusions ... Accordingly, the Court finds that plaintiffs have stated a claim under a purported public trust doctrine.").
[320] *See* Ryan, *A Short History*, *supra* note 259, at 142–45 (reviewing the early Roman and English roots of the doctrine).
[321] Order at 4–5, Juliana v. United States, No. 24-684, D.C. No. 6:15-cv-1517, 2024 WL 5102489, (May 1, 2024) ("We held that the Juliana plaintiffs lack standing to bring their claims ... The district court

meaningful relief.[322] It also took issue with the district court's earlier ruling that the plaintiffs had leave to amend their complaint after the Ninth Circuit had granted the government's last petition for mandamus, dismissing the case the last time.[323] The new panel concluded that the plaintiffs should not have been able to reframe their claim, and that an intervening Supreme Court ruling that the plaintiffs had cited in support of their amended complaint did not provide a relevant change of law that would have enabled their amendment.[324] The plaintiffs unsuccessfully appealed the dismissal to the Ninth Circuit en banc,[325] and their petition for review by the U.S. Supreme Court was ultimately also denied.[326]

d. *Juliana*'s Legacy

Nevertheless, *Juliana* warrants academic consideration as the erstwhile standard-bearer of American trust-rights claims at the federal level, where advocates see climate governance as most necessary. Although the plaintiffs' decade-long, internationally watched campaign came to an end without ever reaching a formal trial, it measurably impacted the global conversation about climate governance at every stage. In 2015, when the case was in its infancy, respected journalist Bill Moyers produced a documentary about the atmospheric trust project, which he christened the Children's Crusade.[327] At various stages during the *Juliana* litigation, tens of thousands and even hundreds of thousands of supporters weighed in to show support for the claim, many (if not most) of them young people. In 2019, a "children's brief" signed by over 36,000 children was delivered to the Ninth Circuit Court of Appeals in support of the plaintiffs' claims,[328] beginning:

---

is instructed to dismiss the case forthwith for lack of Article III standing, without leave to amend."), https://perma.cc/2GHH-YYKZ.

[322] *Id.* at 3.
[323] *Id.* at 4.
[324] *Id.* ("We held that the Juliana plaintiffs lack standing to bring their claims and told the district court to dismiss. *Uzuegbunam* did not change that.").
[325] Order, Juliana v. United States, No. 24-684, D.C. No. 6:15-cv-1517, at 2 (9th Cir. July 12, 2024).
[326] Juliana v. United States, No. 24-684, D.C. No. 6:15-cv-1517, 2024 WL 5102489, 2024 WL 5102489, (May 1, 2024), *cert. denied*, 604 U.S. 645 (2025); Karen Zraick, *Youth Group Asks Supreme Court to Revive a Landmark Climate Lawsuit*, N.Y. TIMES (Sep. 12, 2024), https://perma.cc/3449-T6LW (discussing the Supreme Court appeal).
[327] Bill Moyers, *The Children's Climate Crusade*, MOYERS (Jan. 1, 2015), https://perma.cc/6VT7-3PSX.
[328] Brief of Zero Hour on Behalf of Approximately 32,340 Children and Young People as Amici Curiae Supporting Plaintiffs-Appellees, Juliana v. United States, 217 F. Supp. 3d 1224 (D. Or. 2016) at *12 [hereinafter Brief of Zero Hour]; *see also Join the Youth Legal Action for a Safe Climate*, JOIN JULIANA, https://perma.cc/CUW3-5XDC (noting that the brief was filed with over 36,000 names in support, and inviting continued signatories while the case works its anticipated way toward the U.S. Supreme Court) (the Zero Hour Movement has since moved their online operations to https://perma.cc/46UH-5YBD). The organization "This is Zero Hour" was instrumental in this petition campaign, and it now supports environmental issue awareness and letter writing campaigns to elected officials. *Current Actions*, THIS IS ZERO HOUR, https://perma.cc/83CQ-9X3D.

B. Atmospheric Trust and Climate Rights Litigation 331

> Children are people and citizens. The Constitution protects the fundamental rights of children as fully as it does the rights of adults. The Constitution states clearly it intends to "secure the Blessings of Liberty to ourselves and our Posterity." We *are* the Posterity the Constitution protects. Scientific studies show that government actions today, including its actions of authorizing greenhouse gas discharges and subsidizing fossil fuel extraction, development, consumption, and exportation, imperil plaintiffs' constitutional rights to life, liberty, and property. The government's fossil fuel policies and actions threaten to push our climate system over tipping points into catastrophe. We ask the Court to grant plaintiffs the opportunity to try their case and prove the harms caused and intensified by governmental action.[329]

The brief went on to address the importance of applying public trust principles to protect the atmosphere, on behalf of vulnerable youth today and voiceless generations yet to come:

> As the Constitution protects our fundamental rights, the public trust principle protects our inheritance of resources. It articulates the legal duty of the government, as the trustee of property held in common, to conserve our vital natural resources. The government holds and manages the public trust for us, the trust beneficiaries. The government is obligated to protect our inheritance of, and refrain from substantially impairing and alienating, the natural resources upon which all life and liberty depend. "The beneficiaries of the public trust are not just present generations but those to come."[330]

Five years later, after the *Juliana* plaintiffs appealed their 2024 dismissal by the Ninth Circuit to the Supreme Court, an even wider show of support from nearly 350,000 petitioners implored President Biden and Attorney General Merrick Garland to withdraw opposition by the Department of Justice to the lawsuit.[331]

The case also warrants consideration from the legal standpoint. Despite its substantial evolution after the initial filing in 2015, the central premise of the case remained its effort to vindicate a set of fundamentally paired rights and duties – environmental rights held by the public, in public natural resource commons that the state holds a sovereign obligation to protect. The *Juliana* plaintiffs retained the iconoclastic atmospheric trust claim, seeking to expand common law public trust protection to atmospheric resources, but they departed from the first wave of

---

[329] Brief of Zero Hour at 5–6, Juliana v. United States, 217 F. Supp. 3d 1224 (D. Or. 2016).

[330] *Id.* at 8–9 (quoting Ariz. Ctr. for L. in Pub. Int. v. Hassell, 837 P.2d 158, 169 (Ariz. Ct. App. 1991)).

[331] *Nearly 350,000 People Demand the Biden Administration and U.S. Department of Justice End the Opposition to Youth Climate Case*, FRIENDS OF THE EARTH (Sep. 12, 2024), https://perma.cc/CU44-XK57 ("Yesterday, two petitions signed by hundreds of thousands of intergenerational individuals were digitally delivered to President Biden and Attorney General Garland urging an end to the Department of Justice's (DOJ) relentless opposition to America's youth-led constitutional climate lawsuit, Juliana v. United States. Nearly 350,000 signatures were co-delivered by world renowned author and co-founder of 350.org and Third Act, Bill McKibben, and the youngest ever White House Environmental Justice advisor and Co-Founder of Waic Up, Jerome Foster II.") [hereinafter End Opposition to Youth Climate Case].

atmospheric trust suits to partner that claim with an independent assertion of fundamental rights to climate stability – an even broader trust-rights claim – through more established constitutional promises of fundamental fairness in governance under the Due Process Clause.

In this respect, the case highlights the potential for future trust-rights advocacy bridging both conventional and unconventional trust resources with more conventionally understood rights. The suit alleged that U.S. energy policy is unlawfully harming the atmosphere, a legal reach, but also the territorial seas, a long established public trust resources – and in violation of both the common law public trust doctrine and federally protected constitutional rights to due process. Even if the assertion of the atmosphere as a public trust resource never gains traction, the assertion of climatic impacts on the ocean revealed a lever for traditional public trust advocacy in pursuit of climate governance. And even if the substantive due process claim never advances federally, it has already inspired related constitutional advocacy at the state level, as described further below. The failure of *Juliana* to advance on redressability grounds has already inspired the next wave of climate trust-and-rights litigation to proceed in much narrower forms.[332] These suits, now shifting toward state constitutional claims, predicate more modest claims for relief on theories of the case that, if judicially affirmed, could create important trust-and-rights precedent for future climate advocacy.[333]

While the case may yet contribute to future climate advocacy, the loss stung for trust-rights plaintiffs today. Days after *Juliana* was dismissed, *G.B. v. EPA*, another version of the same suit brought by Our Children's Trust working with youth plaintiffs in California, was dismissed by a federal district court judge, citing the Ninth Circuit's grounds for dismissing *Juliana* (though allowing these plaintiffs leave to amend).[334] The history of these atmospheric trust and fundamental rights claims to date suggest they will continue to face hurdles as they moves through the legal system – and also that the Supreme Court is not eager to entertain the issue.[335]

Nevertheless, the extraordinary volley of litigation back and forth among the different levels of federal jurisdiction in *Juliana* testifies both to the gravity of the issue and the likelihood that the federal courts may eventually have to consider the substantive issues, one way or the other. For even if the standing analysis in the Ninth Circuit's 2024 dismissal precludes other private plaintiffs from bringing

---

[332] *See infra* Part C ("Climate Claims on State Constitutional Grounds").
[333] *Id.*
[334] Order Granting Defendant's Motion to Dismiss, G. B. v. EPA, No. CV 23-10345-MWF (AGRX), 2024 WL 1601807 (C.D. Cal., May 8, 2024).
[335] As noted above, the Supreme Court of Oregon has separately signaled that it does not consider the atmosphere to be a public trust resource as a matter of Oregon state law, which does not bear on the plaintiffs' federal claim (and even less so after the amended complaint), but it certainly lends no support to the public trust origins of the claim. *See* Chernaik v. Brown, 475 P.3d 68, 81-82 (Or. 2020).

similar suits, the fundamental arguments raised by the *Juliana* plaintiffs are not necessarily a dead letter. These same issues may yet reappear in a trust-rights climate suit brought by an American state as a plaintiff. A state plaintiff might succeed where private plaintiffs could not, based on the special standing that states hold to challenge erroneous federal actions that threaten unique state sovereign interests – arguably, including that of protecting public trust impressed state territory – from damage associated with global warming.[336] Moreover, as this book goes to press, youth plaintiffs in *Lighthiser v. Trump* are experimenting with similar arguments in attempting to challenge federal executive orders during the second Trump Administration not only for contravening the separation of powers but for violating their Fifth Amendment substantive due process rights to a livable climate and related fundamental rights under their state constitutions.[337] Although the suit faces hurdles at least as high as *Juliana*, it notably merges the ongoing attempt to pursue federal claims with a climate advocacy strategy currently proving more effective, based on state constitutional law

C. CLIMATE CLAIMS ON STATE CONSTITUTIONAL GROUNDS

The failure of so many of the early atmospheric trust cases satisfied many of the predictions of their critics. At the same time, they managed to engage the public in ways that appear to have exceeded previous strategies, especially across generations. As noted, over 36,000 youth signed an open amicus brief supporting the *Juliana* plaintiffs' claims that was shared with the Ninth Circuit Court of Appeals in 2019,[338] and another some 350,000 "intergenerational individuals" signed petitions delivered to the Biden Administration asking it to withdraw its opposition to

---

[336] See Ryan, *Public Trust Principles*, supra note 14, at 304–07 (introducing the idea). Because states are sovereign entities, federal courts grant states "special solicitude" when assessing state standing to bring suits challenging federal agency actions where Congress has created a procedural right in the authorizing statute. See Massachusetts v. EPA, 549 U.S. 497, 517–18 (2007) (quoting Lujan v. Def. of Wildlife, 504 U.S. 555, 572, n. 7 (1992)); *id.* at 520 (recognizing that states may meet the particularized injury, causation, and redressability requirements of standing in contexts where ordinary citizens cannot). The full exposition of this idea further considers and distinguishes these hypothetical facts from the limits on the "special solicitude" doctrine that the Court recently articulated in U.S. v. Texas, 599 U. S. 650, 676, 686 (2023). See Erin Ryan, Molly Adamo, and Nicola Strouse, *Environmental Rights, State Climate Claims, and Standing: Could a State Bring the* Juliana *Atmospheric Trust Lawsuit?* (2026) (providing a fuller treatment of this thought experiment).

[337] Complaint for Declaratory and Injunctive Relief, Lighthiser v. Trump, No. CV-25-54-BU-DLC (D. Mont. May 29, 2025) (claiming that three executive orders issued by the Trump Administration violate the youth plaintiffs' Fifth Amendment substantive due process rights, ultra vires assume powers reserved to and properly exercised by Congress, and harm their fundamental liberties protected by their state constitutions).

[338] Brief of Zero Hour at *12, Juliana v. United States, 217 F. Supp. 3d 1224 (D. Or. 2016); *supra* text accompanying notes 328–330, discussing and quoting the children's brief.

the suit in 2024.³³⁹ The youth plaintiffs in atmospheric trust cases helped jumpstart a public conversation about the importance of more effective climate governance and the responsibilities governments owe their citizens in response to serious environmental challenges.³⁴⁰ Given that many of these youth plaintiffs weren't even old enough to vote, speaking as litigants was their best means of participating in the political process – and the hundreds of thousands of petitioners supporting them suggest that their voices have indeed been heard. Even so, merely speaking is not as effective as actually winning, so American climate advocates have shifted strategy.

This part reviews how climate advocates have adapted to the challenges of the early atmospheric trust cases, partnering their public trust claims with constitutional claims that may find firmer legal footing, especially in states that have adopted trust-rights principles in their constitutions – or are now attempting to do so. Even critics of environmental advocacy based on the common law public trust doctrine acknowledge the comparative legal force of these claims when they are premised on, or partnered with, unambiguous commitments to environmental protection in state statutes and constitutions.³⁴¹ Assertion of public trust obligations and the environmental rights they imply – or conversely, assertions of environmental rights and the public trust obligations they imply – continue to motivate advocacy nationwide.

1. Trust-Rights Protections in State Constitutions

The notion that the government must protect the air commons for the benefit of the public has now spawned a series of new climate cases brought on specific state constitutional grounds.³⁴² This section reviews explicit protections for the environment and the climate in state constitutions from New York to Utah, as well as groundbreaking trust-rights advocacy on the basis of these provisions from Montana to Hawaii.

Juliana was among the first cases to make the argument that the environmental right to a stable climate is an unenumerated fundamental right of American citizenship (after *Urgenda* held that it was a basic human right under European law),³⁴³

---

³³⁹ *End Opposition to Youth Climate Case*, FRIENDS OF THE EARTH (Sep. 12, 2024), https://perma.cc/CU44-XK57; *supra* note 331. *See also* Bill Moyers, *The Children's Climate Crusade*, *supra* note 327.

³⁴⁰ Paul Rink, *Climate Rights Litigation*, *supra* note 69(discussing the impacts of strategic climate litigation, like Juliana, that loses in court but advances public discourse, among other potential benefits).

³⁴¹ *See, e.g.*, William D. Araiza, *Democracy, Distrust, and the Public Trust: Process-Based Constitutional Theory, the Public Trust Doctrine and the Search for a Substantive Environmental Value*, 45 UCLA L. REV. 385, 433 (1997) ("If there is to be justification for stringent judicial review under the public trust doctrine, it must therefore be found in some theory that accords a substantive preference for the preservation of public trust resources."); *id.* at 438–45 (proposing state constitutions as a source of these substantive environmental preferences).

³⁴² *Id.*

³⁴³ Juliana v. United States, No. 15-CV-01517-AA, 2023 WL 3750334, at *9 (D. Or. June 1, 2023); Urgenda v. Netherlands, [2015] HAZA C/09/00456689 (Neth.) at 41–42, https://perma.cc/V7C5-VRAV (unofficial English translation).

C. Climate Claims on State Constitutional Grounds

but similar arguments have now been made in the handful of states whose constitutions include positive environmental rights, such as Florida,[344] Hawaii,[345] Montana,[346] Utah,[347] Virginia,[348] and New York.[349] Expanding the pool to include state constitutions with substantive commitments to environmental protection that could arguably form the basis for related claims creates even broader opportunities for this kind of environmental advocacy. Nearly half the states include some such constitutional provision,[350] but the following discussion is limited to those with constitutional provisions expressly framed in terms of public trust obligations or public environmental rights.

New York is the most recent state to enact constitutional protections for the environment in its Green Amendment of 2022, which now guarantees New Yorkers "a right to clean air and water, and a healthful environment."[351] Similar language appears in the Massachusetts,[352] Illinois,[353] and Montana[354] constitutions. The Florida Constitution provides that the state shall "conserve and protect its natural resources and scenic beauty,"[355] and similar language appears in the Hawaii Constitution.[356] As described below, these state constitutional provisions have

---

[344] FLA. CONST. art II, § 7 ("[I]t shall be the policy of the state to conserve and protect its natural resources and scenic beauty. Adequate provision shall be made by law for the abatement of air and water pollution and of excessive and unnecessary noise and for the conservation and protection of natural resources.").

[345] HAW. CONST. art. IX, § 8 ("The State shall have the power to promote and maintain a healthful environment, including the prevention of any excessive demands upon the environment and the State's resources.").

[346] MONT. CONST. art. IX, § 1 ("The state and each person shall maintain and improve a clean and healthful environment in Montana for present and future generations.").

[347] *Natalie R. V. State of Utah*, OUR CHILD'S. TR., https://perma.cc/H5NY-GHQG.

[348] *Layla H. V. Commonwealth of Virginia*, OUR CHILD'S. TR., https://perma.cc/LW4Y-7XNV. In 2024, the Virginia Court of Appeals affirmed dismissal of the case for lack of standing, the plaintiffs' appeal was denied by the Virginia Supreme Court in 2025. Layla H. v. Virginia, No. 1639-22-2 (Va. Ct. App. June 25, 2024), *appeal denied*, No. 240684 (Va. Feb. 25, 2025).

[349] *See* Fresh Air for the East Side, Inc. v. New York, No. E2022-000699 (Sup. Ct. Monroe Cty. Dec. 20, 2022) (dismissed with prejudice, No. 23-00179 at 2 (N.Y. App. Div. 4th, July 26, 2024); *see also* Fresh Air for the Eastside, Inc. v. Town of Perinton, No. E2021-008617 (Sup. Ct. Monroe Cty. Dec. 8, 2022).

[350] *See* Araiza, *supra* note 341, at 451; John C. Dernbach, *The Environmental Rights Provisions of U.S. State Constitutions: A Comparative Analysis*, *in* ENVIRONMENTAL LAW BEFORE THE COURTS: A US-EU NARRATIVE 35 (Giovanni Antonelli et al. eds., 2023) (reviewing and analyzing judicial decisions on environmental rights provisions of U.S. state constitutions).

[351] N.Y. CONST. art. I, § 19.

[352] MASS. CONST. art. XCVII ("[T]he people shall have the right to clean air and water, freedom from excessive and unnecessary noise, and the natural, scenic, historic, and esthetic qualities of their environment; and the protection of the people in their right to the conservation, development and utilization of the agricultural, mineral, forest, water, air and other natural resources is hereby declared to be a public purpose.").

[353] ILL. CONST. art. XI, § 2 (Each person has the right to a healthful environment. Each person may enforce this right against any party, governmental or private, through appropriate legal proceedings subject to reasonable limitation and regulation as the General Assembly may provide by law.").

[354] MONT. CONST. art. IX, § 1.

[355] FLA. CONST. art. II, § 7.

[356] HAW. CONST. art. IX, § 8.

proven a source from which climate advocates are asserting both sovereign obligations and environmental rights, including the Montana youth who prevailed in their claim that the state constitution's promise of "a clean and healthful environment" were violated by state policies protecting the fossil fuel industry,[357] and the Hawaii youth who achieved a groundbreaking settlement for climate governance based on similar constitutional arguments.[358]

Montana. *Held v. Montana*, a case built on state constitution-based public trust principles was the first of its kind to go to trial in June 2023.[359] The case relied on a 1972 amendment to the Montana Constitution that provides that "[t]he state and each person shall maintain and improve a clean and healthful environment in Montana for present and future generations."[360] Montana's constitution is unusual for imposing obligations for environmental protection not only on the state as the collective representative of the public interest, but on all members of the public directly. Even so, and despite that constitutional provision, the state disputed that fossil fuels have contributed to climate change and that Montana has experienced unusual weather events that have been linked to temperature changes.[361]

The plaintiffs focused their lawsuit on a provision of the Montana Environmental Protection Act that requires state agencies to perform environmental review of proposed actions, but was amended to specifically forbid agencies from considering greenhouse gas emissions and climate-related environmental impacts.[362] In allowing the case to go to trial, Judge Seeley of the Montana First Judicial District Court denied the State's motion to dismiss[363] for lack of standing and failure to exhaust the administrative process.[364]

---

[357] David Gelles, *In Montana, It's Youth vs. the State in a Landmark Climate Case*, N.Y. TIMES (Mar. 24, 2023), https://perma.cc/3P8H-KXL7; *see also Montana Youth Win*, OUR CHILD'S. TR., https://perma.cc/GV9C-VSAJ.

[358] Clark Mindock, *Hawaii Transportation Department Must Face Kids' Climate Lawsuit, Judge Rules*, REUTERS (Apr. 7, 2023), https://perma.cc/M6GB-GX4A (reporting on the lawsuit); *Navahine F. v. Hawai'i Department of Transportation*, CLIMATE CASE CHART, https://perma.cc/5QS9-QPQF (reporting on the settlement and linking to the record of settlement).

[359] Held v. Montana, No. CDV-2020-307 at 102 (Mont. Dist. Ct. Aug. 14, 2023); Gelles, *supra* note 357; *see also Montana Youth Win*, OUR CHILD'S. TR., https://perma.cc/GV9C-VSAJ.

[360] MONT. CONST. art. IX, §1; *see also* Gelles, *supra* note 357.

[361] Gelles, *supra* note 357.

[362] Held v. Montana, 2024 MT 312, para. 30 (Dec. 18, 2024); *see also* Julia Jacobo, *Montana's New Law Banning Climate Impact Review Sparks Backlash from Environmental Experts*, ABC NEWS (May 26, 2023), https://perma.cc/V83Z-ZHAY (describing the new law, which "prevents weighing climate impacts in state environmental reviews").

[363] Rachel M. Pemberton & Micheal C. Blumm, *Emerging Best Practices in International Atmospheric Trust Case Law*, 2022 UTAH L. REV. 941, 956 (2022) ("While not explicitly using 'public trust' language, the court recognized that the inclusion of a state duty over natural resources in the Montana Constitution provides 'protections that are both anticipatory and preventative.'") (quoting Held v. State, No. CDV-2020-307, at *14 (Mont. Dist. Ct. Aug. 4, 2021).

[364] Order on Motion to Dismiss, Held v. State, No. CDV-2020-307 (Mont. Dist. Ct. Aug. 4, 2021), https://perma.cc/2KRH-3K3B; *see also* Order on Defendants' Motion to Dismiss for Mootness and for

C. Climate Claims on State Constitutional Grounds 337

On August 14, 2023, in a much celebrated win for climate advocacy, the trial court found in favor of the youth plaintiffs, holding that Montana citizens' rights to a clean and healthful environment under the state constitution includes the right to a stable climate, and that the challenged statutory provision harmed these rights.[365] With unequivocal support for the plaintiffs' claim on appeal, the Montana Supreme Court later concurred that "Montana's right to a clean and healthful environment and environmental life support system includes a stable climate system, which is clearly within the object and true principles of the Framers inclusion of the right to a clean and healthful environment," affirming the district court's conclusions that the plaintiffs had standing to challenge the statutes precluding assessment of climate impacts and that these statutes were unconstitutional.[366] Even before the high court's groundbreaking ruling, the case has already had an outsized impact on the discourse, inspiring advocates in nearly a fifth of all American states to file paperwork to advance similar environmental rights amendments to their state constitutions.[367]

Hawaii. In another iteration of this new wave of state constitutional climate litigation, youth climate activists in Hawaii sued the state Department of Transportation for failing to reduce harmful emissions in violation of the state's constitutionalized public trust doctrine and the environmental rights it implies.[368] In *Navahine v. Hawaii Department of Transportation*, the plaintiffs sought a declaration that the state had violated its duty under the public trust principles explicitly incorporated into the Hawaii Constitution,[369] contending that state practices favoring fossil fuel based transportation infringed their state constitutional rights to a healthy environment.[370] Given the historic strength of that state's public trust doctrine, the plaintiffs' claim survived a motion to dismiss[371] and resulted in an unprecedented

---

Summary Judgment slip op. 2-4, Held v. State of Montana, No. CDV-2020-307 slip op. at 2-4 (Mont. Dist. Ct. 23 May 2023) (declining to dismiss the case on prudential grounds, over protests from the state, even after the state amended the Environmental Policy Act).

[365] Held v. State, No. CDV-2020-307, slip op. at 101-02 (Mont. 1st Dist. Ct. Aug. 14, 2023), https://perma.cc/FWB3-5XA9.

[366] Held v. Montana, 2024 MT 312, para. 30, 73 (Dec. 18, 2024) (holding that the Montana Constitution's promise of a healthy environment included protections for climate stability, that the plaintiffs had standing on the basis of their injured state constitutional rights to challenge statutes precluding assessment of greenhouse gas emissions during environmental impact assessment, and that these statutes violated the state constitution).

[367] See infra notes 394–402 and accompanying text (describing proposed new state constitutional environmental rights amendments).

[368] Navahine v. Hawai'i Department of Transportation, No. 1CCV-22-0000631 (Haw. Cir. Ct. 2024); Clark Mindock, *Hawaii Transportation Department Must Face Kids' Climate Lawsuit, Judge Rules*, REUTERS (Apr. 7, 2023), https://perma.cc/M6GB-GX4A.

[369] *See* Complaint at 27–28, 67–70, Navahine v. Hawai'i Department of Transportation, No. 1CCV-22-0000631, (Haw. Cir. Ct. 2022) (detailing the constitutional public trust bases for the claim); Mindock, *Hawaii Transportation Department Must Face Kids' Climate Lawsuit*, supra note 368.

[370] *Navahine*, 1CCV-22-0000631 (Haw. Cir. Ct. 2024).

[371] *See* Mindock, *Hawaii Transportation Department Must Face Kids' Climate Lawsuit*, supra note 368.

consent decree with the state, approved by the overseeing court.[372] Under the terms of the settlement, the state will establish a Climate Change Mitigation & Culture Manager and a volunteer youth council, seating at least two of the youth plaintiffs,[373] all charged with overseeing an effort to achieve net-zero emissions in all ground and interisland sea and air transportation by 2045.[374]

2. Heeding the Lessons of Juliana

These state-based climate rights lawsuits have been more successful than their common law trust predecessors, both because the state constitutions at issue provide more robust support for the sovereign obligations and environmental rights claimed by the plaintiffs, and because the plaintiffs learned from the failures of the early cases. In particular, the newer claims have taken a more purposefully modest approach in their prayers for relief to avoid the redressability and justiciability issues raised in *Juliana* and earlier climate rights cases.[375] These claims seek less controversial judicial remedies that they hope will be more likely to support standing, while maintaining climate rights-based legal theories that they hope will preserve future opportunities for broader environmental advocacy in both the judicial and policy-making arenas.

For example, in contrast to *Juliana*'s initial pleadings, which sought judicial design and implementation of a national plan for reducing greenhouse gas pollution, the Montana plaintiffs in *Held* partnered their request for equally significant declaratory relief (interpreting the scope of their environmental rights under the state constitution to include climate stability) with more tailored injunctive relief, including the invalidation of a particular state law preventing state agencies from considering climate impacts when conducting legally required environmental review.[376] Like the *Juliana* plaintiffs, the Hawaiian plaintiffs in *Navahine* requested an emissions reduction plan, but they focused their complaint on the actions of one specific agency, the state Department of Transportation,[377] rather than the redesign of national climate policy initially sought in *Juliana*.

Other state law claimants have attempted to partner similar requests for declaratory relief with even more modest injunctive remedies tailored to specific projects

---

[372] *Office of the Governor of Hawaii-News Release-Historic Agreement Settles Navahine Climate Litigation*, GOVERNOR JOSH GREEN, (June 20, 2024), https://perma.cc/M8TV-YKFD.

[373] *Navahine*, 1CCV-22-0000631, 8–9 (Haw. Cir. Ct. 2024).

[374] *Office of the Governor of Hawaii-News Release-Historic Agreement Settles Navahine Climate Litigation*, GOVERNOR JOSH GREEN, (June 20, 2024), https://perma.cc/M8TV-YKFD (describing the terms of the settlement).

[375] Rink, *Climate Rights Litigation*, *supra* note 69, at Part II(d) ("Third Wave Climate Rights Strategic Litigation") (providing a comprehensive review of the climate-rights based claims noted here).

[376] Held v. Montana, No. CDV-2020-307, at 102 (Mont. Dist. Ct. Aug. 14, 2023).

[377] Complaint at 70, Navahine v. Hawai'i Department of Transportation, No. 1CCV-22-0000631 (Haw. Cir. Ct. 2022).

C. Climate Claims on State Constitutional Grounds 339

or decisions alleged to violate their alleged rights. For example, in *Fresh Air for the Eastside v. New York*, the plaintiffs premised their bid to close a specific local landfill emitting methane, a powerful greenhouse gas, on an alleged violation of environmental rights protected by the New York State Constitution.[378] A similar suit was filed in Alaska against a specific liquified natural gas terminal alleged to violate the plaintiffs' public trust and substantive due process rights under the state constitution.[379] In *Sagoonick v. Alaska*, plaintiffs sought an injunction against further action developing the terminal and a declaratory judgment that its operation violated their rights of equal access to public trust resources and to sustained yield of these resources, together with recognition of their fundamental right to a climate system that sustains human life, liberty, and dignity.[380] While neither of these claims has thus far proved successful,[381] similarly tailored lawsuits might still be better positioned to affirm the legal force of state-based environmental rights while surviving the standing hurdle that tripped *Juliana* and previous claims for broader injunctive relief.

Still other state-based environmental rights plaintiffs have requested only declaratory judgments recognizing harm to alleged constitutional rights, unpartnered with specific requests for injunctive relief. In *Clean Air Council v. Pennsylvania*, the plaintiffs have sought judicial intervention in greenhouse gas regulation, but only in the form of a declaratory judgment holding that abandoned oil and gas wells leaking greenhouse gases within the state violates state constitutional rights.[382] In a Virginia suit alleging public trust claims against state oil and gas infrastructure, the plaintiffs sought declaratory relief only and left the assignment of any appropriate equitable relief to the best judgment of the presiding court – but the claim was still dismissed for lack of standing.[383] In *Natalie R v. Utah*, plaintiffs following a similar strategy have argued that state fossil fuel development infringes their state-based

---

[378] Complaint, Fresh Air for the Eastside, Inc. v. State of New York, No. E2022000699 (Sup. Ct. Monroe Cty. Jan. 28, 2022).

[379] Complaint for Declaratory and Injunctive Relief, Sagoonick v. Alaska II, No. 3AN-24- (Alaska Sup. Ct. May 22, 2024).

[380] *Id.* at 40–44, 80–81.

[381] Sagoonick v. Alaska II, No. 3AN-24-06508 (Alaska Sup. Ct. Mar. 10, 2025) (dismissing the case as a nonjusticiable political question); Fresh Air for the Eastside, Inc. v. State of New York, No. 23-00179 at 2 (N.Y. App. Div. 4th, July 26, 2024) (dismissing the claim with prejudice). The New York plaintiffs brought a related action in federal court premised on statutory claims under the federal Resource Conservation and Recovery Act and state common law claims indirectly related to the earlier state court action, but that action was dismissed on procedural grounds. Fresh Air for the Eastside, Inc. v. Waste Mgmt. of N.Y., No. 18-CV-06588-FPG-MJP (W.D.N.Y. Apr. 18, 2024) (dismissing but with leave to amend).

[382] Petition for Review, Clean Air Council et al. v. Pennsylvania, No. 379 MD 2023 (Pa. Commw. Ct. 2023).

[383] Complaint for Declaratory and Injunctive Relief at 71–72, Layla H. v. Virginia, No. 1639-22-2 (Va. Ct. App. Feb. 9, 2022) (requesting a declaratory judgment of constitutional rights and any injunctive relief the court "deems necessary" to rectify alleged violations). Nevertheless, the claim was still dismissed for lack of standing. Layla H. v. Virginia, No. 1639-22-2, at 16-18 (Va. Ct. App. June 25, 2024), *appeal denied*, No. 240684 (Va. Feb. 25, 2025).

constitutional rights to life.[384] While the trial court initially dismissed their claim with prejudice – meaning that the problems with the claim were so foundational that the plaintiffs would be foreclosed from trying again – the Utah Supreme Court reversed that decision, allowing the plaintiffs to refile an amended claim that might yet achieve standing.[385] As this book goes to press, plaintiffs are working to reframe their suit.

3. Climate Stability as a State Fundamental Right

While climate plaintiffs in states with explicit constitutional environmental protections target those specific provisions, as the *Clean Air Council* Pennsylvania suit has done, plaintiffs in other states have attempted to imply environmental rights from more general constitutional provisions. The Utah and Virginia suits both claimed violations of fundamental rights under their respective state constitutions,[386] attempting variations of the novel federal claim in *Juliana* in state law contexts. The youth plaintiffs in Utah allege that the state has implemented environmental policies that violate life, liberty, and property under Utah's Due Process Clause.[387] The youth plaintiffs in Virginia had argued that the state's Gas and Oil Act constitutes an unconstitutional deprivation of life without due process, alleging that the defendants actions "violate Plaintiffs' substantive due process rights, secured by Virginia's Constitution," and as well that the defendant's claimed rights to "utilize[e] Virginia's coal, oil, and gas resources cannot and do not operate to secure, and are not narrowly tailored to achieve, a more compelling state interest than Plaintiffs' fundamental rights to life, liberty, and property."[388]

Like *Urgenda* and *Juliana*, these claims center on the idea that climate stability is a fundamental human right, whether or not it is specifically enumerated in constitutional text, for which there should be governmental accountability and judicial redress.[389] Similar claims have been recognized by judges, but thus far only

---

[384] Complaint for Declaratory Relief, Natalie R. v. Utah, No. 20230022-SC (Utah. Dist. Ct. Mar. 15, 2022).
[385] Natalie R. v. State, 2025 UT 5, 21-22 (Utah 2025).
[386] *See* Complaint for Declaratory Relief, Natalie R. v. Utah, No. 20230022-SC (Utah. Dist. Ct. Mar. 15, 2022); Plaintiff's Complaint for Declaratory Relief at 78-82, No. 220901658 (Utah Dist. Ct. Mar. 15, 2022); Plaintiff's Brief in Opposition to Defendant's Demurrer and Plea of Sovereign Immunity at 4, Layla H. v. Commonwealth, No. CL22000632-00, (Cir. Ct. Richmond, Aug. 26, 2022).
[387] Complaint at 78-82, Natalie R. v. State, No. 220901658 (Utah Dist. Ct. Mar. 15, 2022), https://perma.cc/6QS7-8KBS.
[388] Complaint at 65-67, Layla H. v. Commonwealth, No. CL22000632-00 (Va. Cir. Ct. Feb. 9, 2022), https://perma.cc/G3L6-YSA9.
[389] *Id.* at 66 (arguing that Virginia's contribution to harmful greenhouse gas emissions is depriving the youth plaintiffs of their "fundamental rights to life, liberty, and property"); *see* Urgenda v. Netherlands, [2015] HAZA C/09/00456689 (Neth.) at 41, https://perma.cc/V7C5-VRAV (unofficial English translation). ("This case is essentially about the question whether the State has a legal obligation towards Urgenda to place further limits on greenhouse gas emissions – particularly CO_2 emissions – in addition to those arising from the plans of the Dutch government, acting on behalf of the State."); *see*

C. Climate Claims on State Constitutional Grounds

in dissenting and concurring opinions. For example, even before *Navahine*, one Hawaii Supreme Court justice emphasized in a concurrence that "the right to a life-sustaining climate system is also included in the due process right to 'life, liberty, [and] property' enumerated in Article I, section 5 and the public trust doctrine embodied in Article XI, section 1's mandate that the State of Hawai'i 'conserve and protect Hawai'i's ... natural resources' '[f]or the benefit of present and future generations[.]'"[390] The same justice used his separate opinion to criticize the Ninth Circuit's opinion dismissing *Juliana* as an "abdicati[on of judicial] responsibility to leave future generations a habitable planet,"[391] and to critique the federal courts as a whole as "hostile" to climate claims.[392] Reasoning that the federal judiciary had abdicated its responsibility to respond to climate claims, he maintained the responsibility of state courts to take up the task.[393]

4. Proposals for State Trust-Right Amendments

As the next wave of climate litigation shifts to the states, many environmental advocates are acting quickly to facilitate constitutional reinforcement of environmental rights claims, following the success of the *Held* case in Montana and the *Navahine* case in Hawaii. At present, at least thirteen states have introduced bills to amend their state constitutions to include provisions that partner, either explicitly or implicitly, sovereign obligations and environmental rights.[394]

These proposed amendments follow from two different legal frameworks: one that explicitly emphasizes only the environmental rights held by individuals, such as Montana's constitution, and another that emphasizes both sides of the rights-and-duties legal coin – simultaneously recognizing the state's sovereign obligation to protect trust resources and guaranteeing the related environmental rights – as Pennsylvania's constitution does.[395] Most of the proposed amendments are framed

---

also Complaint at 94–95, Juliana v. United States, 217 F. Supp. 3d 1224 (D. Or. 2016) (No. 6:15-cv-01517-TC) (Plaintiffs asked the court to "[d]eclare that Defendants have violated and are violating Plaintiffs' fundamental constitutional rights," and asked the court to "[e]njoin Defendants from further violations of the Constitution").

[390] *In re* Haw. Elec. Light Co., Inc., 152 Haw. 352, 360 (Haw. 2023) (Wilson, J., concurring) (Justice Wilson's concurring opinion was not joined by the other justices of the Hawaii Supreme Court, and the majority opinion made no mention of the public trust doctrine, the atmospheric trust, or *Juliana*).

[391] *Id.* at 365.

[392] *Id.* at 367.

[393] *Id.* ("The stark failure of the federal judiciary to grant redress to present and future generations alleging knowing destruction of a life-sustaining climate system relegates implementation of the climate rule of law to state judiciaries.").

[394] Kate Burgess, *Issue Area: Green Amendment*, NATIONAL CAUCUS OF ENV'T LEGISLATORS, https://perma.cc/3VW2-RDQE (reporting on states considering or moving toward consideration of related constitutional amendments).

[395] PA. CONST. art. I, § 27 ("The people have a right to clean air, pure water, and to the preservation of the natural, scenic, historic, and esthetic values of the environment. Pennsylvania's public natural

in the latter model, explicitly recognizing both the public trust obligation of the state and the environmental rights of their citizens, including Arizona, Kentucky, New Jersey, New Mexico, Vermont, West Virginia, and Washington.[396] States considering exclusively environmental-rights framed constitutional amendments include California and Hawaii,[397] perhaps because these two states arguably already have strongly established public trusts doctrines reflected in different parts of their constitutions.

Although they share common roots, the proposals showcase fascinating variety. While California's proposed amendment is concise (noting that "[t]he people shall have a right to clean air and water and a healthy environment"),[398] proposals in sister states like Washington refer to the responsibilities of different state subdivisions, principles of environmental justice, and interpretive instructions to ensure that the provisions are procedurally self-executing (to ensure that individuals may invoke these guarantees without further legislative process):

> (a) The people of the state, including future generations, have the right to a clean and healthy environment, including pure water, clean air, healthy ecosystems, and a stable climate, and to the preservation of the natural, cultural, scenic, and healthful qualities of the environment. The state, including each political subdivision of the state, shall serve as trustee of the natural resources of the state, among them its waters, air, flora, fauna, soils, and climate. (b) The state, including each political subdivision of the state, shall conserve, protect, and maintain these resources for the benefit of all the people, including generations yet to come. (c) The rights stated in this section are inherent, inalienable, and indefeasible, are among those rights reserved to all the people, and are on par with other protected inalienable rights. The state, including each political subdivision of the state, shall equitably protect these rights for all people regardless of their race, ethnicity, tribal membership status, gender, geography, or wealth, and shall act with prudence, loyalty, and impartiality in fulfilling its trustee obligations. The provisions of this section are self-executing.[399]

---

resources are the common property of all the people, including generations yet to come. As trustee of these resources, the Commonwealth shall conserve and maintain them for the benefit of all the people."). *See also* John C. Dernbach, Kenneth T. Kristl & James R. May, *Recognition of Environmental Rights for Pennsylvania Citizens: Pennsylvania Environmental Defense Foundation v. Commonwealth of Pennsylvania*, 70 RUTGERS L. REV. 803, 845–52 (2018); *See* John C. Dernbach, *The Potential Meanings of a Constitutional Public Trust*, 45 ENV'T L. 436, 487–94 (2015) (noting that two explicit constitutional obligations in Pennsylvania are (1) the "duty to conserve and maintain public natural resources" and (2) the "duty to refrain from impinging upon public environmental rights.").

[396] S. Con. Res. 1031, 56th Leg., 2d Reg. Sess. (Ariz. 2024); B. Res. 1592, 24th Reg. Sess. (Ky. 2024); S. Con. Res. 43, 221st Leg., 2024 Sess. (N.J. 2024); H.R.J. Res. 4, 56th Leg., 2d Sess. (N.M. 2024); S. Proposal 5, 2024 Leg. (Vt. 2024); H.R.J. Res. 23, 2024 Reg. Sess. (W. Va. 2024); and H.R.J. Res. 4210, 68th Leg., 2024 Reg. Sess. (Wash. 2024). For the full text of all these proposed amendments, *see* Ryan, *Public Trust Principles*, *supra* note 14, at 316–17.

[397] Assemb. Const. Amend. 16, 2023-24 Reg. Sess. (Cal. 2024); S.B. 2933, 32d Leg. 2024 (Haw. 2024).

[398] Assemb. Const. Amend. 16, 2023–24 Reg. Sess. (Cal. 2024).

[399] H.J. Res. 4210, 68th Leg., 2024 Reg. Sess. (Wash. 2024).

C. Climate Claims on State Constitutional Grounds

Hawaii's proposed amendment would guarantee that the "inherent and inalienable rights of the people" to a healthy environment "shall not be infringed,"[400] invoking the force with which individual rights enshrined in the federal Bill of Rights are legally protected.[401]

The different formats these amendments take is itself a subject for further inquiry, and a fuller treatment would consider the strengths and weaknesses of the two main approaches. Some advocates for these amendments have emphasized the importance of pursuing the Pennsylvania model[402] – expressly affirming both sovereign obligations and environmental rights – presumably because it appears to maximize enforcement opportunities along two seemingly different legal theories. For example, some courts may be more amenable to enforce an individual right than a sovereign obligation, because courts are used to enforcing rights and reluctant to tell executive and legislative actors what to do. Nevertheless, the analysis in this chapter suggests that the choice between the two is truly irrelevant, because either exclusive formulation – framing the directive as only an environmental right or only a sovereign obligation – legally implies both.[403]

It is also worth considering the strategic advantages to adopting comparatively vague or specific directives in these amendments, perhaps in different political contexts. On the surface, it would seem that the stronger the political consensus about what these rights and obligations should entail, the greater the flexibility in that state to craft more specific directives of the sort proposed in Washington. Specific directives would theoretically be more easily enforced in courts reluctant to interpret vague directives in ways that could trigger the kinds of justiciability and redressability concerns that brought down the *Juliana* litigation.[404]

On the other hand, the Washington proposal is just that – a proposal – and to achieve the political consensus necessary to actually amend the state constitution, it may yet become necessary to capture only the vague premise on which there is political consensus, leaving the details of implementation in a given case or controversy to the professional judgment of the relevant state actors. It is noteworthy that some of the newest such amendments, such as that adopted in Montana and New York, are comparatively concise – and therefore more vague and open to interpretation than the Washington proposal. While that may initially seem like a hurdle, in this regard they resemble many of the amendments to the U.S. Constitution in the Bill of Rights, which have been successfully judicially interpreted for a quarter of a millennia. Framing public trust principles in constitutional terms may elide the vagueness and justiciability problems experienced by climate advocacy based on common law assertions of rights-and-trust principles.

---

[400] S.B. 2933, 32d Leg. 2024 (Haw. 2024).
[401] *See, e.g.*, U.S. CONST. amend. II.
[402] MAYA K. VAN ROSSUM, THE GREEN AMENDMENT: THE PEOPLE'S FIGHT FOR A CLEAN, SAFE & HEALTHY ENVIRONMENT (2d ed. 2022).
[403] *See supra* Part A(4) ("The Reciprocal Nature of Sovereign Obligations and Environmental Rights").
[404] *See infra* Part B(4) ("*Juliana v. United States*").

Even as creative climate litigation shifts to state constitutions, however, opponents of these claims remain equally creative, mounting nimble defenses that keep the legal status quo fluid. A common law-based action in *Honolulu et al. v. Sunoco*, for example, could undermine all other state claims if the plaintiff, the oil giant Sunoco, succeeds in persuading the U.S. Supreme Court to hold that the U.S. Constitution and the Clean Air Act preempt all state actions litigating over climate change. Sunoco had previously lost its bid to dismiss a common law climate change claim for lack of jurisdiction and failure to state a claim at the trial, appellate, and state supreme court levels. In February 2024, Sunoco then filed a writ of certiorari asking that the U.S. Supreme Court intervene to dismiss the case, arguing that the U.S. Constitution and the Clean Air Act preempt state actions for climate change. On June 10, 2024, the U.S. Supreme Court invited the Biden Administration to weigh in, and the outcome is still pending. If Sunoco succeeds, the conclusion could potentially invalidate related state-based claims, potentially even those made on state constitutional grounds.

D. CONSTITUTIONAL AND PRAGMATIC CONCERNS WITH EMERGING CLIMATE ADVOCACY

Climate advocates have thus deployed both trust- and rights-themed strategies in pursuit of effective climate governance, heralding the responsibilities of governments to protect public environmental values. On balance, these strategies have been more effective at rallying public support than winning in court – a fact that has drawn withering criticism from both supporters and opponents of the kinds of climate regulation these advocates seek. In this final section, the chapter considers these critiques, highlighting problems that have stymied the atmospheric trust cases and may also bedevil climate rights-based lawsuits, given their underlying commonalities. Trust-rights advocates have adapted to these challenges in different ways, partnering public trust claims with more explicitly framed assertions of environmental rights that may yet find firmer legal footing, especially in states that have expressly constitutionalized public trust principles.[405] The most recent wave grounded in these constitutional provisions may prove more robust than the first hatch of atmospheric trust claims, but even these require interpretation of relatively vague directives, raising common questions about justiciability, enforcement, and practical strategy.[406]

---

[405] See *infra* Part C ("Climate Claims on State Constitutional Grounds").

[406] *See, e.g.*, Lazarus, *supra* note 70, at 1159; Araiza, *supra* note 341, at 395, 445 ("These provisions have been plagued by courts' hesitation to construe them as imposing limits on governmental action, largely due to concern about both the vagueness of the provisions and judicial competence to evaluate difficult social policy decisions affecting the environment."); Lloyd R. Cohen, *The Public Trust Doctrine: An Economic Perspective*, 29 CAL. W. L. REV. 239, 275 (1992) (critiquing the inherent vagueness of the public trust directive to protect trust resources for the public benefit and the implied problems for judicial enforcement).

D. Constitutional and Pragmatic Concerns

The opportunities are clear. Trust-rights litigation offers climate advocates additional levers for heightened public participation and amplification of their political speech in a uniquely salient public forum – the courts. The strategy provides meaningful opportunities to push back against what public-choice theorists might call the "capture" of climate regulators by powerful fossil fuel industry players and their lobbyists.[407] Scholars have described lax regulation of fossil fuel emissions as a colossal example of market failure and manipulation of policymakers by the regulated industry, which has arguably facilitated enormous short-term profits for a concentrated minority of shareholders at the expense of the vast majority of stakeholders' long-term interests in a livable climate, including many future generations yet unborn.[408] The judicial forum provides a focused opportunity for citizens who view themselves as shut out by these political process failures to make their claim in a highly visible context, build coalitions in support of their cause, and try to effect legal change – if not through the judicial process itself, then potentially in settlement with the political branches, or through the wider electoral process that follows.[409] As one young supporter once exclaimed in class, "I have written letters to my representatives and decades later, I am still waiting to hear back from them – but if I get my day in court, at least I know I will be heard!"[410]

Yet the strategy remains vulnerable to criticisms that the implied rights and duties are too vague or ambitious to offer meaningful redress, especially in a judicial forum.[411] If the sovereign has an obligation to protect the environment, exactly what does that require? If citizens have an affirmative right to a healthful environment, what specifically does that right entail? In either case, what specific action or inaction must the government undertake? And is the judiciary the proper branch to entertain these questions? What can courts actually deliver in response? These claims face uphill battles once they reach the courtroom, many foreseen by the scholarly critics reported on in Part A(3) and by the affirmative-negative rights analysis in Part D of the Introduction, generating considerable dissensus about the wisdom of the approach. When atmospheric trust claims failed to gain traction for lack of established precedent, American climate advocates began shifting course to pursue environmental rights grounded in explicit constitutional text – but even there, the trust-rights strategy remains marked by constitutional and practical uncertainty.

---

[407] See, e.g., WOOD, NATURE'S TRUST, supra note 30 at 7, 32, 50, 52 (critiquing the "tight alliance" between environmental agencies and regulated industries).

[408] Id.; see also Dieter Helm, Government Failure, Rent-Seeking, and Capture: the Design of Climate Change Policy, 26 OXFORD REV. ECON. POL'Y 182, 182 (2010) (using public choice theory to trace market failure in climate policy).

[409] See generally WOOD, NATURE'S TRUST, supra note 30.

[410] Oral communication from Kevin Griffin to author (Feb. 26, 2024).

[411] See sources cited at supra note 406 (voicing these critiques); see also Introduction, Part D ("Public Trust Principles and Environmental Rights") (contrasting the treatment of affirmative and negative rights in American law and questioning the distinction in trust-rights contexts, where sovereign stewardship obligations may be better understood as a negative public right).

Debate has arisen within the environmental law community over whether the climate advocacy reviewed here, especially the atmospheric trust project, should be regarded as groundbreaking impact litigation – making use of all available legal tools to confront the climate crisis – or a foolhardy legal strategy that threatens to set back environmental jurisprudence for decades, or even longer.[412] Lawsuits by children on behalf of future generations yields haunting political imagery, but the legal arguments require a long reach. The original Justinian Code does provide support for the application of public trust principles to the air commons, but no common law precedent supports that claim in the United States,[413] and the extension sought by atmospheric trust plaintiffs faces stiff opposition from those who disfavored even the application of the traditional public trust doctrine to environmental values associated with waterways.[414] Even as courts begin to recognize environmental rights and sovereign obligations to protect the atmosphere, the task of responding with appropriate judicial remedies poses entirely different legal problems. Critics further allege that these mediagenic trust-rights lawsuits may be draining limited attention, funding, and energy that could be better focused on more promising forms of environmental advocacy.[415]

This part considers the theoretical implications of trust-rights litigation strategies, including potential constitutional ramifications for the separation of powers, the potential for creating harmful negative precedent, and potential ramifications of the strategy for the broader goals of environmental law.

1. Separation of Powers Concerns

While the Conclusion explores this issue in more detail, this section acknowledges the constitutional separation of powers concerns raised by trust-rights advocacy. Atmospheric trust litigation has especially prompted these concerns, as these cases have asked courts to make some of the heaviest interpretive lifts, but similar considerations could arise in climate advocacy seeking the judicial enforcement of broadly framed environmental rights.

In both contexts, advocates have asked courts to issue declaratory and injunctive relief in hope of changing the direction of state and national climate policies. Yet as Judge Aiken described in her 2023 decision limiting the *Juliana* claim only to declaratory relief,[416] climate policy is a complex tapestry of legislative and regulatory decision-making. Judges regularly interpret rights and obligations within legal relationships and enjoin the conduct of actors that violate them, both private and

---

[412] See *supra* Part A(3) ("The Scholarly Critics").
[413] See *supra* Part A(4) ("The Reciprocal Nature of Sovereign Obligations and Environmental Rights").
[414] See Ryan, *Historic Saga, supra* note 65, at 618–20 (discussing critiques from property rights advocates).
[415] See *infra* Part D(5) ("A Generational Divide").
[416] See *supra* Part B(4) ("*Juliana v. United States*").

public, but their comfort level declines as the requested relief approaches direct interference in substantive lawmaking.[417] Judges have always made new law through the conventional, incremental common law process, but outright judicial policymaking beyond the incremental interpretation of established sources of law threatens to exceed the constitutionally prescribed judicial role.[418]

When climate advocates ask courts to vindicate environmental rights and/or sovereign obligations by ordering changes to fossil fuel policy, these objectives can collide. Trust-rights suits legitimately ask the courts to interpret fundamental rights and obligations, but the extension to climate policy is an admittedly novel legal context. The ambitious injunctive relief requested by the early atmospheric trust claims attracted much criticism and contributed to their many losses in American courts. Standing challenges premised on issues of justiciability and redressability accounted for the legal gyrations these plaintiffs have made to preserve their claims, such as the transition from early trust-centered complaints seeking forceful injunctive relief to *Juliana*'s more constitutionally centered complaint seeking mostly declaratory relief.[419]

While the newest wave of state constitutional claims appears to have learned from *Juliana*'s difficulties by framing even narrower claims,[420] these suits may eventually request similar forms of relief, for the same essential reasons – climate advocates will want courts to transform judicial interpretations of their state constitutional rights into specific injunctive directions that impact climate policy. In each of these individual contexts, it will ultimately be the judiciary that interprets the demands of the alleged rights or obligations, and if they are violated, it will be the judiciary that decides on an appropriate remedy.

All of which raises two critical questions with which trust-rights advocacy must grapple, operating at two different levels of consideration. At the level of individual claims, it raises the question of what kinds of remedies successful trust-rights advocacy can realistically hope to accomplish. Providing formal interpretation of operative rights and duties is a conventional judicial task that may be within reach for these plaintiffs. Declaratory relief of this sort could significantly impact legislative, administrative, and even private law choices in the political process going forward,[421] so the value of a formal judicial declaration of rights or obligations should

---

[417] *See, e.g.,* Zivotovsky v. Clinton, 556 U.S. 189, 194–95 (2012) (explaining the political questions doctrine).
[418] *See generally* Antonin Scalia, *The Doctrine of Standing as an Essential Element of the Separation of Powers*, 17 SUFFOLK U. L. REV. 881 (1983).
[419] *See supra* Part B ("Trust-Rights Advocacy in Action: Atmospheric Trust & Climate Rights Litigation").
[420] *See supra* notes 359–380 and accompanying text (describing the newer wave of narrower claims).
[421] *Cf.* Evan Bianchi, Sean Di Luccio, Martin Lockman, & Vincent Nolette, *The Private Litigation Impact of New York's Green Amendment*, 49 COLUM. J. ENV'T L. 357, 408–22 (2024) (arguing that the Green Amendment could have a significant impact on even private law transactions going forward, even after a state court held that the amendment did not create a private right of action, by shaping the norms against which community standards and reasonableness expectations in contract and property law contexts will be measured).

not be underestimated. But is trust-rights litigation limited only to seeking declaratory relief, and is that enough to justify the potential downsides of this kind of litigation?

On a broader level, the separation-of-powers problems raised by trust-rights litigation begs the question whether the strategy is, as its proponents allege, a paragon of democratic governance, enabling citizens to access multiple forums for public participation and deliberation? Or, as critics contend, is the strategy fundamentally antidemocratic, distorting the judicial role at the expense of the wider political process? Is Professor Richard Lazarus correct in his ultimate assessment that "that this is just not how we make laws of this nature under our constitutional framework"?[422] At a time where the Supreme Court has been aggressively claiming new authority over environmental governance by rejecting its long tradition of deferring to the statutory interpretation by EPA and other federal agencies of the environmental laws they administer,[423] is further centering the judicial role in public trust administration a wise strategy for good environmental governance? As queried in the Introduction, Part D, will it meaningfully differ if the court is asked to administer the same claim framed as a disfavored affirmative right or a more familiar sovereign obligation?

While I return more fully to the constitutional separation of powers issue in Conclusion, for many environmentalists, trust-rights claims raise even more immediate questions of legal strategy.

2. The Atmospheric Trust and Negative Precedent

Counterbalancing criticisms from the opponents of environmental regulation, trust-rights advocacy also inspires criticism from the champions of environmental regulation, many of whom have bitterly opposed these lawsuits as bad legal strategy and as a misappropriation of scarce resources away from more promising avenues. These critics argue that trust-rights climate advocacy is dangerous to the very cause it seeks to advance, both because it threatens to create harmful future precedent, and because it is proverbially sucking up all the air in the room.

The first critique is that the losses these cases produce could undermine climate governance instead of advancing it, creating negative legal precedent that could stall the progress of environmental law for decades.[424] This contention was especially leveled against the atmospheric trust lawsuits, given the mass nationwide filings in the first wave of the strategy – which yielded a very small handful of incremental successes amidst a much larger tide of failure.

---

[422] Lazarus, *supra* note 70, at 1157. See also *supra* notes 83–93 and accompanying text (discussing these critiques).

[423] See Loper Bright Enterprises v. Raimondo, 144 S.Ct. 2244, 2273 (2024) (overturning the *Chevron* doctrine of judicial deference to administrative statutory interpretation).

[424] See *supra* Part A(3) ("The Scholarly Critics").

D. Constitutional and Pragmatic Concerns

While impact litigants often make careful decisions about when, where, and how to file novel claims in order to maximize their chances of success,[425] the first-hatch atmospheric trust project arguably carpet-bombed the nation with claims that made headlines but not a lot of helpful new law.[426] Bringing cases in every jurisdiction, all over the country, all at one time created a powerful rhetorical gesture – but it also ran the risk that at least some (and possibly many) of these claims would result in negative judgments that would make it difficult to bring more narrowly tailored public trust claims in the future. Some of these early cases may well have created precedent that future litigants with more promising claims may find difficult to overcome.

Critics thus assailed the strategy for recklessly threatening to set the cause of good climate governance back instead of forward.[427] Even Joseph Sax, in the very scholarship that midwifed the modern movement, counseled against overreaching legal arguments that might set back the development of public trust principles in environmental law.[428] Heeding this concern, the later wave of state constitutional claims have been more grounded in identifiable legal texts and appear more narrowly tailored to address individual aspects of wider climate policy.[429] For example, a recent lawsuit in Alaska sought redress for the limited grievance of how the operation of a single liquified natural gas terminal allegedly violated their constitutional rights,[430] rather than, say, seeking to alter national or even statewide oil and gas policy.

3. Legal Strategy and Climate Advocacy

Other environmental critics are concerned not only with the bad precedent these cases might set in court, but also with the bad strategy they portend more generally – by crowding out better strategies that might produce more meaningful climate governance more quickly, and by disillusioning youth advocates who repeatedly fail in the endeavor.

These critics worry that aspirationally vague trust-rights claims are distracting public attention and resources from the more conventional, incremental, and complex forms

---

[425] James E. Pfander, *Forum Shopping and the Infrastructure of Federalism*, 17 TEMP. POL. & CIV. RTS. L. REV. 355, 355 (2008) (discussing the use of forum shopping in deciding whether to bring impact litigation claims).

[426] *See supra* Part B(2) ("The Atmospheric Trust Project in U.S. Law").

[427] *See supra* Part A(3) ("The Scholarly Critics").

[428] *See* Sax, *supra* note 42, at 552–53 (cautioning against overly ambitious arguments that could create adverse precedent in his observation that a "litigation theory which begins with a sophisticated analysis of public trust principles ... is likely to obtain a far more sympathetic response from the bench than is one which takes a rigorous legal principle and squeezes it to death."). *See also* Lazarus, *supra* note 70, at 1160 (discussing Sax's warning).

[429] *See supra* Part C ("Climate Claims on State Constitutional Grounds").

[430] Complaint for Declaratory and Injunctive Relief at 40–44, 80–81, Sagoonick v. Alaska (Alaska Sup. Ct. May 22, 2024) II, No. 3AN-24.

of environmental governance that they believe are more likely to produce meaningful greenhouse gas reductions – even if not at the pace that young climate advocates contend is necessary.[431] They argue that a small group of climate advocates have hijacked the public conversation, diluting public confidence in the painstaking work of setting and enforcing emissions standards, best available technologies, renewable portfolios, and sustainable land use planning. As one critic has explained,

> I know the advocates will say they are raising awareness and enriching dialogue and serving an important expressive function, but I think it's also important to consider the possibility that they may be lowering awareness (for example, by working to discredit strategies that, while frustratingly political and technical and incomplete, might be our best hopes); reducing the quality of dialogue (again, by offering the siren song of a strategy that will just get the outcomes we want without dealing with the messiness of administrative governance); and sounding off without providing constructive expression.[432]

By contrast, he notes, the potentially displaced forms of environmental law include activities that have, collectively, made a lot of incremental progress toward the ultimate goal:

> Over the same time period, state and local governments have passed hundreds of climate-related laws. Federal agencies also have enacted lots of climate-related rulemakings. And climate attorneys have participated in many administrative proceedings, like utility ratemaking cases, leading to the adoption of rules promoting renewable energy. Activism focused on corporate energy policies also has produced major successes, helping dramatically advance the spread of renewable energy in otherwise skeptical red states. Climate attorneys and activists have also fought many defensive actions in these same realms. Not all of this work has been successful, and some of the results have been symbolic. But the aggregate result (along with the impact of new technologies and market trends) has been dramatic reductions in GHG emissions compared to a continuation-of-historic-trends scenarios. In other words, while the ATL attorneys have accomplished, at best, hardly anything, other strategies – which some ATL and environmental-rights attorneys openly disparage – have accomplished a lot.[433]

---

[431] *See supra* Part A(3) ("The Scholarly Critics"); Lazarus, *supra* note 70, at 1152 ("I think it is a strategic mistake to delude oneself – let alone the law students we teach – by suggesting [that this kind of advocacy can effect meaningful results through litigation]. Far better to accept the true difficulty of the lawmaking challenge we face, and to undertake the necessary hard work at the national – and no less important at the retail – level, than to pretend that the courts can provide quick fixes to rescue us from ourselves.").

[432] Email from Dave Owen, Professor of Law, University of California – San Francisco Law School (May 14, 2024) (on file with author). This quote and the next from the same exchange are published with Professor Owen's permission, although he notes that he expressed these ideas before the conclusion of the *Navahine* case in Hawai'i.

[433] Email from Dave Owen, Professor of Law, University of California – San Francisco Law School (May 6, 2024) (on file with author).

D. Constitutional and Pragmatic Concerns

Critics also worry that a strategy that continues to encounter defeats or extreme delays before reaching meaningful relief will lead young enthusiasts to become cynical about continuing to engage on the issue and in the political process more generally.

To be sure, these too are important concerns. It is critical that trust-rights advocacy not disillusion an entire generation or displace the elaborate mechanisms of environmental law that have accomplished enormous gains toward more breathable air, drinkable and swimmable water, and biodiversity preservation in just the few decades they have been operating at a national level.[434] Trust-rights advocacy could never deliver anything as complex or precise as the statutory programs accomplished through legislative and executive activity, such as the Inflation Reduction Act's advances toward renewable energy goals[435] or the President's Executive Order on environmental justice review.[436]

Yet there is no reason to think that environmental advocacy must be all or nothing, one way or the other, in support of either trust-rights or conventional advocacy. Most forms of environmental governance can only be accomplished through conventional political processes – like the Inflation Reduction Act and Environmental Justice review – but there are some forms better served by trust-rights advocacy, like movement-building of the sort to which the *Juliana* Children's Brief contributed;[437] the litigation-driven nudge toward climate planning that the *Navahine* plaintiffs accomplished in Hawaii,[438] and perhaps even true constitutional change, of the sort effected by the 1970s advocates for Pennsylvania's public trust amendment, and more recently, the 2020s advocates for New York's new environmental rights Green Amendment.[439]

4. In Defense of Trust-Rights Advocacy

The climate litigants' best response to the critique that they are crowding out conventional legal advocacy is that discrediting such forms of environmental governance is categorically the *opposite* of what they hope to accomplish. The contest for resources may or may not be significant; that is a claim hard to prove one way or the other. But there is no reason why trust-rights advocacy should cause onlookers to lose faith in conventional environmental governance, because in the end, that is what the litigants in every one of these suits have been seeking, in prayers for relief from the modest to the flamboyant.

---

[434] See Lazarus, *supra* note 70, at 1152–55 (describing the accomplishments of conventional environmental governance at the same time that most atmospheric trust cases were losing in court).

[435] Inflation Reduction Act of 2022, Pub. L. No. 117-169, 136 Stat. 1818.

[436] Exec. Order No. 12,898, 3 C.F.R. § 859 (1995), *reprinted as amended in* 42 U.S.C. § 4321.

[437] *See supra* text accompanying notes 327–331 (discussing widespread youth participation in the Children's Brief and the other 350,000 individuals who signaled their support of the *Juliana* claim to the Ninth Circuit).

[438] *See supra* text accompanying notes 368–374 (discussing *Navahine v. Hawai'i Dept. of Transportation*).

[439] *See* Part C(1) ("Trust-Rights Protections in State Constitutions") (discussing both the Pennsylvania and New York constitutional amendments).

For example, the judicial relief initially sought in *Juliana* was to compel more of exactly these kinds of traditional environmental regulation – just more than was happening to reduce greenhouse gas pollution. Even after retreating to a suit for declaratory relief alone (to overcome justiciability concerns), the plaintiffs' ultimate objectives were still to obtain this kind of conventional environmental lawmaking. Even if spurred by judicial recognition of a fundamental right to a livable climate, the endgame would have been lawmaking that would follow substantially the same processes of fact-finding, consensus-building, and fine-tuning that yielded the Clean Air and Water Acts.

The only difference is that this lawmaking would have taken place under a legal mandate alleged to be required by the public trust doctrine and Due Process Clause, a substantive requirement limiting the possibility that the political branches could simply opt out of the enterprise. While the substantive command would limit the range of possible outcomes (in a way most environmental advocates would approve), it would in no way obviate the need for the skill and expertise of the civil servants toiling away in the forgotten corners of environmental law. These lawsuits should always be seen as a supplement, and not a replacement, for conventional environmental law, to help overcome whatever political process failure is preventing governments from appropriately responding to a climate crisis that has already thrown countless lives, livelihoods, communities, economies, and vulnerable nations into chaos.

In seeking to refocus legislative and administrative attention on climate governance by asserting environmental rights and public trust responsibilities, litigants are attempting to overcome that barrier – whether a product of pure public choice theory, arbitrary and capricious administration, or outright political patronage – that has unreasonably diminished the speed and responsiveness of elected officials and confused or distracted fellow citizens. The strategy seeks merely to add incentives and reduce roadblocks preventing conventional environmental governance from addressing climate change. Yet without a specific set of legal mechanisms for following through on the relevant rights and obligations claimed by these plaintiffs, their suits would be of no inherent value.

In this regard, trust-rights litigation have used public trust principles in the way that has always been intended, relying on them as a legal device for starting a conversation among all branches of government about sovereign obligations to protect environmental rights. The public trust doctrine has always enabled ordinary citizens to put pressure on the political branches by invoking their rights to judicial review – a tool that is most important when the political branches don't seem to be listening. Used wisely, the doctrine can help "protect[] the public against legislative or executive abdication, strengthening the legitimacy of the democratic process with additional checks and balances."[440] As I have argued in prior work, the cross judicial-political dialogue

---

[440] Ryan, *The Historic Saga*, *supra* note 65, at 630; Gerald Torres, *Joe Sax and the Public Trust*, 45 ENV'T L. 379, 393–97 (2015).

D. Constitutional and Pragmatic Concerns 353

inspired by trust-rights litigation highlights why "the separation of powers" is not the same thing as those powers working in complete isolation.[441]

Citizens' appeals to the judicial process are rightly part of the wider political process. The ability to seek judicial review is especially important when citizens have felt silenced within the wider political process for unjust reasons, such as invidious discrimination or government corruption. The public trust doctrine thus facilitates a conversation between the three branches of government about the disposition of critical public natural resource commons in which all citizens have a stake, but which are often managed far beyond the reach of the average voter's influence. Viewed this way, it is not that the judiciary is antidemocratically second-guessing the political branches – any "second-guessing" at issue is by citizens legitimately invoking their rights to the judicial process. And especially for the *Juliana* plaintiffs and supporters, many of whom are too young to vote, it is one of their only means of democratic participation. In the ongoing and recursive dialectic between law and culture, a compelling case can sometimes change the conversation, even if it doesn't immediately change the law.[442]

For a recent example of the recursive dialectic between culture and law, consider the evolution of the Supreme Court's gay rights jurisprudence over the last thirty years – a stunning progression that tracked the evolution of cultural norms, themselves influenced by compelling examples of civil rights litigation.[443] For a more modern example in the climate context, consider the results of the Massachusetts, Florida, and Hawaii youth climate suits, leading to a Massachusetts executive climate strategy, a Florida pledge (later repealed) to generate 100 percent renewable electricity by 2050, and a Hawaii climate mitigation officer and youth council.[444] Even if the resulting climate governance strategies never fully deliver, they nevertheless represent remarkable shifts poised to alter the direction of public policy, in direct response to climate trust-rights advocacy. Even Professor Lazarus, who has strongly criticized the possibility that these strategies displace traditional

---

[441] *See* Ryan, *From Mono Lake to the Atmospheric Trust*, *supra* note 116, at 63–64.
[442] *Id.*
[443] *Compare* Bowers v. Hardwick, 478 U.S. 186, 190–96 (1986) (upholding state laws criminalizing gay sex), *with* Lawrence v. Texas, 539 U.S. 558, 578–79 (2003) (overturning *Bowers*), *and* Obergefell v. Hodges, 576 U.S. 644, 681 (2015) (establishing a constitutional right to gay marriage).
[444] *See supra* Part B(3) ("An Administrative Atmospheric Trust") (discussing Massachusetts and Florida examples) and Part C(1) ("Trust-Rights Protections in State Constitutions") (discussing the Hawaii example). The Florida pledge, repealed as this book was going to press, could nevertheless rise again if the political winds shift. FLA. ADMIN. CODE ANN. r. 50-5.002 (2023). Florida youth immediately filed new litigation to accomplish the same goal premised on state constitutional rights, following in the footsteps of *Held* and *Navahine*. Amy Green, *A Florida Commission Keeps Approving Utility Plans with Lots of Fossil Fuels. Now Young Adults Are Suing.* INSIDE CLIMATE NEWS (Dec. 18, 2024), perma.cc/V59X-424S (describing a suit by six young Floridians that "accuses the state commission overseeing Florida's electric providers of slowing the transition to cleaner energy by sanctioning utility plans that favor fossil fuels ... argu[ing that] the commission's actions violate state law and the constitutionally protected rights of the state's youth to a safe and livable future.").

environmental law, recognizes their value as a device for amplifying marginalized environmental concerns in the wider political process:

> I believe those lawsuits are best understood as part of an overall political strategy rather than as a viable, standalone litigation strategy. The filing of such lawsuits can serve a useful political purpose: they provide an opportunity for potentially effective political organizing and publicity with the ultimate goal of prompting legislatures to enact the laws we need... Fortunately, many of those who are championing the atmospheric trust litigation are very much focused on the positive political potential of their efforts in terms of influencing law- and policy-makers in both the legislative and administrative arenas, and wisely do not focus exclusively on litigation.[445]

Still, most trust-rights claims have not delivered the hoped-for environmental governance – yet. And in all fairness, most may never do so. That said, they have rallied countless youth to become more involved in a political process that so far, has not been responsive to their deep concerns about climate change.

Together with other focal points of youth activism, including the leadership of Swedish youth climate activist Greta Thunberg, trust-rights claims have helped inspire a worldwide youth movement.[446] In 2019, the same year in which 36,000 children signed on to an amicus brief in support of the *Juliana* claim, young people from every inhabited continent participated in an International Climate Strike, marching out of school to protest governmental failures to respond to the increasing urgency of the climate crisis.[447] As *Juliana* waited on appeal to the Supreme Court, 350,000 supporters asked the Biden Administration to get out of its way.[448]

The Climate Strike transitioned into a series of ongoing weekly protests, the Fridays for Future movement, joined by many thousands of additional young climate protestors around the world.[449] Around the same time, it was reported that at least 1,000 climate lawsuits had been filed in 24 nations, 888 of them from within the United States, many led by youth plaintiffs.[450] Not all of these cases were framed

---

[445] Lazarus, *supra* note 70, at 1157.
[446] *See, e.g., supra* notes 327–331 and 338–340 and accompanying text (documenting public support generated among youth and others for the atmospheric trust claims in *Juliana*).
[447] Harmeet Kaur & Madison Park, *Young Environmental Activists across the World Skip School in a Call to Action*, CNN (March 15, 2019), https://perma.cc/9CCF-N4ZP ("The movement, inspired by the actions of 16-year-old Swedish environmental activist Greta Thunberg, spanned more than 100 countries and 1,500 cities, where students gathered in the streets and at their state capitols to call for action."); *see also Pictures From Youth Climate Strikes Around the World*, N.Y. Times (March 15, 2019), https://perma.cc/7HAA-DFCQ ("From Sydney to Seoul, Cape Town to New York, children skipped school en masse Friday to demand action on climate change. It was a stark display of the alarm of a generation. It was also a glimpse of the anger directed at older people who have not, in the protesters' view, taken global warming seriously enough.").
[448] *End Opposition to Youth Climate Case*, *supra* note 331.
[449] *See* Seth Borenstein & Frank Jordans, *Afraid and Anxious, Young Protestors Demand Climate Action*, AP News (Sept. 23, 2022), https://perma.cc/4ZL6-2MQX.
[450] *See* Katy Scott, *Can 'Climate Kids' Take On Governments and Win?* CNN (July 24, 2018), https://perma.cc/ZRR5-TPNA (discussing climate cases filed against governments, corporations, and

D. Constitutional and Pragmatic Concerns

as trust-rights claims, but despite the outcomes in *Juliana* and many of its sibling litigation, these cases have helped coalesce a youth movement that cannot be undone.[451] (By contrast, most Americans seem not to understand what the Inflation Reduction Act was even about, let alone what it actually accomplished.[452])

For these reasons, trust-rights advocates should not focus exclusively on the litigation outcome, as Professor Lazarus recommends. Nor should they proceed blindly forward, without giving thought to the impacts of their claims on doctrinal development. Yet neither should they shy away from aspirational claims, if there is sufficient foundation for potential, if incremental, success. They might succeed, as the Massachusetts, Montana, and Hawaii youth plaintiffs did, and as the Florida plaintiffs administratively for a time (although they are now pressing forward with state constitutional claims premised on the Montana and Hawaii models).[453] Such advocacy may yield an administrative settlement that accomplishes the plaintiffs' goals, as the Hawaiian and Massachusetts lawsuits did. Or it might provide political leverage to help jumpstart the needed societal conversation about the importance of more effective climate governance, as the *Juliana* plaintiffs may yet do. It is a delicate line to walk – the line between pushing that conversation forward and triggering a judicial rejection that could entrench the status quo by validating the opposing view – but mindful of that line, careful trust-rights litigation can provide an additional means of entry into the political process for claimants otherwise sidelined. It may very well prove the lever that leads to the enactment or enforcement of the more conventional environmental statutes and regulations favored by trust-rights skeptics.

Even if a novel trust-rights lawsuit fails, then, it may provide advocates with political leverage to start a wider societal conversation about the management of trust resources – in this case, resources threatened by climate change. Such litigation provides an additional fulcrum into the political process, and into public dialogue. Even if no atmospheric trust case ever succeeds on the merits, children like the *Juliana* plaintiffs will have initiated an open conversation about climate change in terms that ordinary people can immediately understand, and to which many have responded with support.[454] The strategic critique elides the expressive power of the doctrine to spark meaningful grassroots change, translating losses in court to political momentum. After all, most successful legal movements are preceded by countless failures

---

individuals, and noting the role that youth activists have played at the forefront of many such high-profile cases).

[451] Alternatively, critics ask, "Did the Juliana plaintiffs make a positive contribution or just suck all the air out of the room – or some combination of both? I don't think we can assume the former just because they got a lot of media attention." Email from Dave Owen, Professor of Law, University of California – San Francisco Law School (May 6, 2024) (on file with author).

[452] *See, e.g.*, Mary Small, *Why Does No One Know What a Huge Success the Inflation Reduction Act Was?*, NEWSWEEK (Aug. 16, 2023), https://perma.cc/5Y5U-B93S.

[453] *See* Green, *supra* note 444 (describing the Florida lawsuit).

[454] *See, e.g., supra* notes 327–331 and 338–340 and accompanying text (discussing the Children's Brief and other substantial showings of public support for the Juliana plaintiffs).

before precedent eventually gives way to change, and their advocates seem more hardy than critics acknowledge. Civil rights pioneers did not give up when they did not immediately get their way, and neither should climate advocates. While pure atmospheric trust litigation across the U.S. may have reached a stalemate, the story of American trust-rights advocacy is only just beginning to be told.

Which is why, even if the legal argument may be too ambitious to succeed in the near term, the central premise of these suits warrants respect. Protecting a public commons from shortsighted private appropriation – as Professor Sax first urged in 1970 – is the same premise that motivated the *Mono Lake* decision, the *Illinois Central* decision before it, and the Supreme Court of India thereafter. It makes sense to understand the public trust doctrine as an attribute of sovereignty at all levels. The air commons was recognized as a public trust resource as early as ancient Rome – it is an equally essential public commons, and it is equally vulnerable to harmful private appropriation. Even if the American public trust only protects water resources, government would still be obligated to manage greenhouse gas emissions, not only to avoid further ocean acidification but also in light of the implications for navigable waters of the national mega-drought that has been forecast over the next century as a result of climate change.[455] Scientists project that extreme drought will threaten the public trust resources of virtually all the nation's navigable waterways[456] – just as diversions to Los Angeles have threatened Mono Lake.

For what it is worth, these are the same arguments that once motivated me, personally, to leave the idyllic life of a Mono Basin forest ranger to pursue the calling of law as a means of solving such critical societal problems. Recognizing this, I became a signatory on the law professor amicus briefs in the early atmospheric trust cases, notwithstanding concerns about the risky strategy. To be sure, these lawsuits are not without their own strategic craft; the very device of bringing suit with children as plaintiffs is arguably a strategic move. Yet the connection between these children and the future generations they represent is not opportunistic – it is literal. Concerns about precedent aside, there is something that goes beyond strategy, perhaps even beyond poetry, about children all around the country making this powerful public trust argument with a single voice, at this pivotal moment in time, because time appears to be running out. They may not win, but something about their argument is what the public trust doctrine was made for.

However the claims play out in court, these strategies play an important role in the overall democratic process, enabling citizens multiple ports of entry to the

---

[455] *See, e.g.*, NASA, *Megadroughts in U.S. West Projected to be Worst of the Millennium* (Feb. 2, 2015), https://svs.gsfc.nasa.gov/4270 (last visited Oct. 7, 2025) (discussing forecasted drought conditions that has already materialized across the western United States and other arid regions, and which is anticipated to worsen over the next century with shifting climate patterns); Raymond Zhong, *The West's Megadrought Might Not Let Up for Decades, Study Suggests*, N.Y. Times (July 16, 2025), www.nytimes.com/2025/07/16/climate/southwest-megadrought.html (last visited Oct. 7, 2025) (reporting on the study).

[456] *See supra* note 455 and accompanying text.

D. Constitutional and Pragmatic Concerns

political process, enabling them to build a constituency for more effective participation in the political arena, and amplifying their voices in policymaking contexts dominated by more powerful players with bigger and more expensive megaphones. Longshot legal strategies should by no means replace conventional legal advocacy – such as voting, lobbying for legislation, commenting on proposed rules, and suing to enforce conventional environmental statutes – all of which remain the gold standard of political participation by which citizens should pursue environmental objectives.

Even so, on a matter of such existential import as climate change, and as a means of amplifying the voices of the generations most voiceless in political channels – the young and the yet to be born – this kind of advocacy represents a legitimate, if desperate, part of the overall political economy. At best, it could prove a safety valve to address grave failures of the political process, and at worst, a safety valve to vent building public frustration. Either way, it makes a meaningful contribution to the overall conversation among the citizens and the branches of government that represent them. Additionally, if more states adopt these principles directly into their constitutions, then the rights and duties entailed may move beyond providing a mechanism for enhancing aggrieved political speech to providing a platform for genuinely improved climate governance. This, of course, is the great hope – and as sea levels rise around us, hope is much needed.

5. A Generational Divide?

This chapter has reviewed the emerging direction of climate advocacy along two seemingly distinct legal paths that are more unified than they may at first appear – the atmospheric trust movement, which casts the atmosphere as a resource protected by the public trust doctrine, and the pursuit of environmental rights to climate stability, under a set of potential sources that includes common law, statutory, constitutional, and treaty-based law. These paths may seem distinct, but in fact, both strategies appeal to the recursive legal premises of the core public trust principle, which asserts: (1) sovereign obligations to protect environmental resources for the benefit of the public, and (2) public rights to benefit from these resources and to hold the state to its protective obligations. Like reciprocal Hohfeldian rights and duties, the two strategies are the implied flip sides of the same theoretical coin, expressing the same underlying concepts regardless of which side faces up. Environmental rights presume sovereign vindication, and the sovereign obligation creates public environmental rights. And as two sides of a single coin, these different climate advocacy strategies herald similar advantages and disadvantages.

Reviewing the scholarly literature and key iterations of climate advocacy domestically and internationally provides an exploration of both the obstacles and opportunities for future development of trust-rights advocacy. Constitutional separation of powers concerns, issues of justiciability and redressability, and pragmatic concerns about impact litigation strategy have jointly shepherded American climate advocacy from the early atmospheric trust cases toward a newer generation premised on environmental rights and public trust obligations in state constitutions. While this modern trend may encounter familiar obstacles, the rapid evolution from one legal strategy to the next reveals the depth of frustration with the slow progress of conventional environmental regulation to cope with the looming threat of climate change.

Some critique the evolving trust-rights strategy as rhetorically satisfying but legally misguided, because these lawsuits must overcome serious constitutional and practical obstacles that have felled most of them thus far. But even when they do not succeed in court, these suits serve legitimate political purposes. Trust-rights advocacy helps facilitate a multifaceted conversation among the citizens and all three branches of government about the disposition of critical public natural resource commons in which all citizens have a stake, but which are managed far beyond the reach of the average citizen's influence. These plaintiffs, so many of them young people, are seeking their day in court because for them, court appears to be the only forum in which they will be heard on this matter of existential and time-sensitive importance. And indeed, for these youth plaintiffs and their supporters – many too young to vote – litigation may *truly* be their only means of democratic participation. Judicially asserting an environmental right, or affirming a sovereign obligation to protect it, enables youth plaintiffs to insist that the political branches take their concerns more seriously, even when they can't cast a ballot.

To that end, the youth trust-rights movement suggests a broader generational divide within environmental law, and one that warrants attention from commentators. Younger advocates have turned toward these newer strategies to move the levers of environmental law because the core public trust principles of sovereign environmental responsibility and public environmental rights make intuitive sense to them, at a moment when so much else in environmental governance does not. Still, as this generation turns toward trust-rights strategies, the architects and practitioners of the older, conventional mechanisms of environmental law worry that the focus on trust-rights advocacy will undermine the success of the comprehensive statutory schemes that have been critical tools of environmental law since the 1970s.

This generational divide is almost certainly facilitated by recent Supreme Court decisions weakening those comprehensive statutory programs, such as the weakening of the Clean Water Act in *Sackett v. United States*[457] and of the Clean Air Act in *West Virginia v. EPA*,[458] making statutes that seem like avatars to the older generation seem much more vulnerable and ineffective to the younger generation. The Court's 2024 decision in *Loper Bright Enterprises* to overturn the forty-year *Chevron* doctrine of judicial deference to agency expertise,[459] a cornerstone of robust environmental rulemaking under the big environmental statutes, further erodes the faith with which

---

[457] 598 U.S. 651, 684 (2023).
[458] 597 U.S. 697, 706, 735 (2020).
[459] Loper Bright Enterprises v. Raimondo, 603 U.S. 369, 410–13 (2024).

younger generations regard the traditional statutory pillars of environmental law and the regulations that implement them. *Corner Post*, a companion decision to *Loper Bright*, further weakened environmental (and other) regulations by loosening the statute of limitations in a way that facilitates more *Loper Bright* and major questions doctrine challenges to seemingly settled regulations.[460] These cases, unfolding one after another in the past three years, have deeply impacted young environmental advocates.[461] As a law professor, I have been surprised and dismayed by the erosion I see in many of my students' faith in conventional environmental law infrastructure and in the very rule of law as a guarantor of wise and fair environmental governance. I understand why many of them see the trust-rights litigation strategy as a necessary corrective.

Yet as younger advocates lose faith in the efficacy of the statutory avatars of federal environmental law to cope with climate change, many in the older generations, dismayed by the theoretical challenges and losing track records of trust-rights approaches, contend that the proven avatars are still the best bet. Having come of age during the emergence and development of these conventional strategies, they maintain an abiding faith in traditional environmental infrastructure that confers a greater buffer against the disappointment generated by cases like *West Virginia*, *Sackett*, and *Loper-Bright*. The elders may be right to place their bets where they do, but it's understandable that their younger counterparts are skeptical. These different generational perspectives make sense: the older generations reasonably place faith in legal infrastructure that they themselves helped build, participated in, and have seen work over many years, while the younger generation's thinner faith has been tested not only by the Supreme Court's recent decisions but also by political efforts to dismantle so much environmental law infrastructure during the Trump Administration.[462] On these facts, it would be surprising if there weren't a generational disconnect.

In the end, the elders are right to continue investing in conventional environmental law, but it's also important to understand the role that trust-rights advocacy plays

---

[460] Corner Post, Inc. v. Board of Governors of the Federal Reserve System, 603 U.S. 799, 804 (2024) (holding that the statute begins to toll at the date of the alleged injury, rather than the date of enactment, making it easier to bring new *Loper Bright* style claims against old regulations). See Erin Ryan, *The Four Horsemen of the New Separation of Powers: The Environmental Law Implications of* Loper Bright, West Virginia, Sackett, *and* Corner Post, 109 Minn. L. Rev. 2743 (2025) (exploring the horizontal and vertical separation of powers implications of the new concentration of judicial power in federal regulatory contexts, especially environmental law, and offering a proposal to protect judicial primacy in rights interpretation while sharing some authority over structural interpretation).

[461] My support for this proposition is anecdotal but widespread. It is a constant source of conversation in the environmental law classes that I and my colleagues teach and among students at the law schools I visit to lecture.

[462] *See supra* text accompanying notes 453–460. *See also* Nadja Popovich, Livia Albeck-Ripka & Kendra Pierre-Louis, *The Trump Administration Rolled Back More Than 100 Environmental Rules. Here's the Full List*, N.Y. Times (Jan. 20, 2021), https://perma.cc/2LGM-L859 ("[N]early 100 environmental rules [were] officially reversed, revoked or otherwise rolled back under Mr. Trump. More than a dozen other potential rollbacks remained in progress by the end but were not finalized by the end of the administration's term.").

within the overall political discourse, especially with these generational dynamics in mind. The movement represents, at best, the not-so-silent scream of the younger generation, calling out for their opportunity to be heard. For some youth advocates, given their age, it may feel like their *only* opportunity to be heard. And no matter what the elders may think about whether these strategies will win in court, it's important to stop and listen to what these young people are saying. The same holds true for the older participants in trust-rights litigation, who also play an important role. When there are that many voices raised in unison, and that much frustration spilling out into the public forum, just telling people to shut up is an equally problematic legal strategy.

For all these reasons, trust-rights strategies are simultaneously exciting and dangerous. For some, they offer a chance to speak truth to power and represent the last, best hope for mobilizing toward urgently needed change, while for others, they upset the constitutional order and threaten to displace our last, best hope for managing climatic crisis. But of course, both of these perspectives are missing the full view. Under the current circumstances of climate urgency, a diverse portfolio of approaches will be key, as is wisdom in their strategic deployment.

Trust-rights climate claims follow in the tradition of citizen suit provisions that justify a limited judicial forum in which private attorney generals help vindicate broader environmental concerns. For youth proponents, they represent a mechanism for enhancing their weakened political speech, with the expressive force of demanding adherence to baseline legal rights and responsibilities. When the judiciary weighs in on whether sovereign obligations have been failed or environmental rights violated, it is not antidemocratically second-guessing the political branches, but enabling young citizens to penetrate the political process by means that put them, at least for the moment, on equal footing with the institutional actors, lobbyists, and moneyed stakeholders that normally control it. Even unsuccessful claims provide a legitimate forum for movement building, political renegotiation, and agitating for the kinds of cultural change that ultimately lead to legal change. Still, it is critical that trust-rights strategies not eclipse or hamstring traditional mechanisms of environmental law, which remain bedrock tools for effecting meaningful environmental governance in concert with these rights and obligations.

In time, trust-rights claims premised on constitutionalized environmental rights and public trust principles may join the ranks of conventional environmental law. But even now, they form a legitimate part of the overall political economy of environmental advocacy, especially in addressing the climate crisis. Widespread generational support for these efforts among youth around the world provides an indication of the breadth of fear and the depth of frustration they feel with the slow pace of the political process in response thus far – frustration to which leaders at all levels of government should listen carefully. When that many children tell us that something is this wrong with the world we all share, we should all be listening carefully.

10

Environmental Rights around the World

Public Trust Principles and the Rights of Nature Movement

A.	Public Trust Principles around the World	364
	1. Oceania	364
	a. New Zealand and Australia	364
	2. Asia	365
	a. The Philippines	365
	b. India	367
	c. Nepal	368
	3. The Greater Middle East	369
	a. Pakistan	369
	b. Israel	370
	4. Africa	371
	a. Uganda	371
	b. Kenya	372
	c. Nigeria	372
	d. South Africa	373
	5. Europe	373
	a. England	374
	b. Scotland and Wales	375
	c. A Future British Trust?	375
	6. South America	376
	a. Brazil	376
	b. Ecuador	377
	7. North America	377
	a. Canada	377
	b. United States	378
B.	The Rights of Nature Movement	380
	1. A Whirlwind Tour of the Rights of Nature Movement	381
	a. International Initiatives	381
	b. U.S. and North American Tribal Initiatives	388

2. The Differentiating Development of the Rights
   of Nature Movement 400
   a. Parallel Planes of Jurisdictional Development 402
C. Comparing the Public Trust and Rights of Nature 405
   1. Philosophical Duality or False Dichotomy? 405
   2. Mosaics, Not Monoliths 409
   3. A Special Focus on Waterways 410
   4. Responding to the Failure of Conventional Environmental Law ... 411
   5. Leveraging the Political Arena 413
   6. Intuitive and Emotional Appeal 414
D. Which Is Better? 415
   1. Different Goals? 416
   2. Different Results? 418
   3. Mosaics in Progress 420

This chapter reviews the development of environmentally protective public trust principles across the globe – a quiet revolution in environmental rights – and then compares them to a competing vision of environmental rights that is on the rise globally, the rights of nature movement. The former affirms public rights to the environment, while the latter confers rights on the environment itself. Both reflect public dissatisfaction with the failure of more "conventional" environmental law – mostly, antipollution statutes that originated with the environmental movement of the 1970s and thereafter – to accomplish broader goals of environmental stewardship. The rise of public trust and rights of nature advocacy responds to challenges wrought by the weak foundations for environmental law identified earlier in this book – weak constitutional foundations, in the United States, and for other reasons elsewhere.

The development of public trust principles worldwide is notable but perhaps unsurprising. Despite its roots in ancient Roman law,[1] the doctrine is most closely associated with the United States, where constitutional constraints on sovereign authority have long been a distinguishing characteristic of American law.[2] Yet variations on the idea that people hold rights in natural resource commons have independently developed in numerous ancient legal systems. The Ottoman Civil Code, known as the Mejelle, details a related list of public commons resources that are free and open to all, including not only water and large waterways but also fire, grasses, certain trees and mushrooms, and all wild game.[3] Civil law nations

---

[1] *See* Chapter 1(A)(2) ("Early English Law: The Magna Carta, Forest Charter, and Common Law").
[2] *See, e.g.,* LAWRENCE M. FRIEDMAN, LAW IN AMERICA: A SHORT HISTORY 12–13 (2002) (discussing the uniquely American tradition of subjecting sovereign activity to constitutional review by the judiciary).
[3] *See* AL-MAJALLA AL AHKAM AL ADALIYYAH (THE OTTOMAN COURTS MANUAL (HANAFI)), book X (Joint Ownership), ch. IV (Jointly Owned Property Which is Free), art. 1234 *et seq.*, www.iium

often consider water resources under sovereign ownership,[4] likely reflecting shared roots in the Roman legal tradition that is the progenitor of both European common and civil law systems.[5] Perhaps for these reasons, public trust principles appear in legal systems throughout the world, including the examples detailed in Part A, from Oceania, Asia, the Greater Middle East, Africa, Europe, and the Americas.[6] In each case, these principles endow positive environmental rights in the public to enjoy either specified natural resources or a healthy environment more generally.

At the same time, a related environmental rights movement is developing from a contrasting ethical framework. The rights of nature movement locates actionable legal rights not in the people who benefit from natural systems, but directly in the natural systems that would benefit from legal protection.[7] In contrast to the public trust doctrine, the rights of nature approach deprivileges human needs in asserting the independent rights of ecosystems and their components to exist and thrive.[8] The rights of nature movement thus provides an unapologetically biocentric alternative to the inherent anthropocentrism of both the public trust doctrine and typical water allocation laws, which also locate rights to natural resource commons in human

---

.edu.my/deed/lawbase/al_majalle/al_majalleb10.html. In 1962, an Israeli court drew on the Mejelle to apply public trust-like principles in a case affirming public rights to access beaches, overturning the conviction of Moshe Puterman for trespassing on a public beach. CrimA (DC TA) 851/60 Puterman v. AG, PM 30, 7 (1962) (Isr.). For discussion of the case and the role of Ottoman law in the court's decision, see David Schorr, *The Israeli (and Ottoman and Islamic) Public Trust Doctrine*, ENV'T L. & HIST. (July 13, 2016), https://environmentlawhistory.blogspot.com/2016/07/the-israeli-and-ottoman-and-islamic.html (discussing the case and the role of Article 1234, *et seq.*, of the Ottoman Civil Code); Zafrir Rinat, *Thanks to This Man, You Don't Have to Pay to Go to the Beach in Israel*, HAARETZ (Oct. 4, 2018), www.haaretz.com/israel-news/.premium.MAGAZINE-this-man-is-the-reason-why-israeli-beach-entry-is-free-1.5387797 (describing the case and the Mejelle doctrine it applied).

[4] For example, Spanish law declares that rivers, riverbanks, shores, bays, springs, and streams are in the public domain. See *infra* note 76 and accompanying text (discussing Spanish law in more detail).

[5] Hessel E. Yntema, *Roman Law and Its Influence on Western Civilization*, 35 CORNELL L.Q. 77, 88 (1949) (describing Roman common law as the "fundamental body of legal doctrine" which is the "common element in the individual legal systems of much of Continental Europe, and its colonies").

[6] See Part A ("The Public Trust Doctrine Internationally"); *see also* Michael C. Blumm & Rachel D. Guthrie, *Internationalizing the Public Trust Doctrine: Natural Law and Constitutional and Statutory Approaches to Fulfilling the Saxion Vision*, 45 CAL. DAVIS L. REV. 742, 760 (2012) (reviewing the impact of the public trust doctrine internationally).

[7] See, e.g., Craig Kauffman, *Constructing Rights of Nature Norms in the US, Ecuador, and New Zealand*, 18 GLOB. ENV'T POL. 43 (2018); Meredith N. Healy, *Fluid Standing: Incorporating the Indigenous Rights of Nature Concept into Collaborative Management of the Colorado River Ecosystem*, 30 COLO. NAT. RES. & ENV'T L. REV. 327 (2019).

[8] See generally Erin Ryan & Holly Curry, *Environmental Rights, the Public Trust Doctrine and the Rights of Nature Movement*, 42 CARDOZO L. REV. 2447 (2021) (discussing constitutional, statutory, and local provisions conferring legal personhood on ecosystems, rivers, and even wild rice); *see also* Erin Ryan, Holly Curry & Hayes Rule, *Environmental Rights: A Comprehensive Analysis of the Public Trust Doctrine and Rights of Nature Movement*, 42 CARDOZO L. REV. 2447, 2541–48 (2021) [hereinafter Ryan et al., *Comprehensive Analysis*] (providing a more detailed look at the anthropocentric approach of the public trust doctrine).

beneficiaries.[9] Part B recounts notable international examples and domestic initiatives from within the United States, including North American indigenous tribes.

While the two approaches stem from distinct underlying principles, they are intriguingly evolving along similar legal pathways. The public trust doctrine has had more time to develop in comparison to the emerging rights of nature doctrine, but in recent decades, both have been diverging jurisdictionally along related legal planes regarding what is protected and how legal protections operate. These strikingly parallel developments appear to cut across even their underlying philosophical differences, as some advocates appear to rely on both approaches (in some places, even interchangeably) to resolve related environmental problems. Based on this global review of public trust principles and rights of nature initiatives, the Parts C and D offer a comparative analysis of the two approaches – contrasting the underlying ethics that divide them while recognizing the practical characteristics that unite them.

A. PUBLIC TRUST PRINCIPLES AROUND THE WORLD

To demonstrate the evolving reach of the public trust doctrine across the globe, this part introduces representative examples of public trust principles in operation on all inhabited continents, working roughly west from the International Date Line. Among nations that recognize the public trust, some base their legal doctrines on versions of the trust aligned with those found commonly in the United States, while others have developed versions wholly their own.

1. *Oceania*

The journey begins in Oceania, just east of the International Date Line. At present, rights of nature initiatives have eclipsed the development of the public trust doctrine in Australia and New Zealand. Yet even here, public trust principles have begun to appear in the wider environmental discourse.

a. New Zealand and Australia

The two largest nations in Oceania, Australia and New Zealand, are both British Commonwealth nations that root their formal legal systems in the same English common law as the United States. Unlike the wayward American colony, however, neither Australia nor New Zealand has extended the public trust doctrine beyond its early English origins toward environmental protection. Instead, both nations have addressed related concerns through the development of rights of nature principles, derived from the legal culture of their indigenous populations (discussed in the second half of this chapter).

---

[9] *See* sources cited *id.*

Nevertheless, it is worth noting that some Oceanian scholars have advocated for the expansion of the doctrine beyond its English origins to encompass vulnerable environmental values in their countries.[10] It has also been argued that environmentally protective elements of the doctrine are already in force in Oceania, even if they have not yet been formally recognized.[11] The Maori People of New Zealand, among the original progenitors of the modern rights of nature movement, have also attempted to utilize the public trust doctrine in their ongoing litigation against anthropogenic contributions to climate change.[12] The willingness of advocates to embrace both public trust and rights of nature principles in support of environmental goals is a notable phenomenon discussed further in Part B(4).

2. Asia

The public trust doctrine has received significant attention in Asia, especially the Philippines and India. Both nations have codified public trust principles in their constitutions, and both enable their citizens to seek judicial relief for violations of the trust.

a. The Philippines

The Philippines boasts one of the most comprehensive public trust doctrines in the world. The public trust has played an important role in the common law, statutory law, and constitution of the Philippines since the 1970s. The Water Code of 1976 declared that all waters belong to the State,[13] that the public held an easement along the banks of all rivers and streams for access, and that the public also held an easement for "recreation, navigation, floatage, fishing and salvage" on the shores of all seas and lakes.[14] One year later, the Philippines passed the 1977 Environmental

---

[10] Nicola Hulley, *The Public Trust Doctrine in New Zealand*, AUG. 2015 RES. MGMT. J. 31, 31; Nicola Hulley, New Zealand's Public Trust Doctrine (2018) (LLM Paper, University of Wellington), https://researcharchive.vuw.ac.nz/xmlui/bitstream/handle/10063/8072/thesis_access.pdf?sequence=1; Tim Bonyhady, *An Australian Public Trust*, in ENVIRONMENTAL HISTORY AND POLICY: STILL SETTLING AUSTRALIA 258–72 (Stephen Dovers ed., 2000); Bruce Thom, *Climate Change, Coastal Hazards, and the Public Trust Doctrine*, 8(2) MACQUARIE J. OF INT'L & COMPAR. ENV'T L. 21 (2012).

[11] See sources cited *id.*

[12] Patricia Quijano Vallejos & Lisa Anne Hamilton, *Maori Communities Bring Climate Claims Against New Zealand Under the Public Trust Doctrine*, CTR. FOR INT'L ENV'T L. (Nov. 1, 2017), www.ciel.org/maori-communities-bring-climate-claims-new-zealand-public-trust-doctrine.

[13] A Decree Instituting a Water Code, Thereby Revising and Consolidating the Laws Governing the Ownership, Appropriation, Utilization, Exploitation, Development, Conservation and Protection of Water Resources, Pres. Dec. No. 1067, art. 3 (Dec. 31, 1976) (Phil.), www.officialgazette.gov.ph/1976/12/31/presidential-decree-no-1067-s-1976. The code defines waters broadly to include surface water, groundwater, atmospheric water, and seawater. *Id.* art. 4.

[14] *Id.* art. 51.

Policy, which declared that the nation would "recognize, discharge and fulfill the responsibilities of each generation as trustee and guardian of the environment for succeeding generations ..."[15] Ten years later, the Filipino Constitution of 1987 constitutionalized these environmental rights, announcing that "[t]he State shall protect and advance the right of the people to a balanced and healthful ecology in accord with the rhythm and harmony of nature."[16]

The doctrine has also been developed judicially. In 1987, the Supreme Court ruled in *Oposa v. Factoran* that the new constitutional language did, in fact, codify public trust principles and was self-executing.[17] The Court held that a class of students challenging the state's grant of a timber license could sue the Department of Environment and Natural Resources for violating its public trust obligations under the Constitution.[18] In the end, the case had little effect on timber harvesting in the Philippines because the students failed to pursue the case.[19] However, in revisiting the issue fifteen years later, the Supreme Court clarified that the government did hold trust obligations under the Constitution.[20] Since then, the doctrine has been interpreted to include the conservation and management of natural resources to ensure their equitable distribution across present and future generations.[21]

The expansive Filipino public trust doctrine has been described as "encompassing terrestrial, aquatic, and marine resources, and providing public access for recreational and ecological purposes, as well as traditional public trust purposes."[22] While some public trust scholars point to the Filipino doctrine as an international model,[23] others have raised questions about the force of the aspirational doctrine in reality.[24]

---

[15] Philippine Environmental Policy, Pres. Dec. No. 1151, § 2 (June 6, 1977) (Phil.), www.officialgazette.gov.ph/1977/06/06/presidential-decree-no-1151-s-1977. One pair of scholars has observed that the policy is reminiscent of language in the U.S. National Environmental Policy Act (42 U.S.C. § 4331) (hereinafter NEPA). See Blumm & Guthrie, *supra* note 6, at 770 (referencing NEPA-like language at § 1 of the policy: "It is hereby declared a continuing policy of the State (a) to create, develop, maintain and improve conditions under which man and nature can thrive in productive and enjoyable harmony with each other, (b) to fulfill the social, economic and other requirements of present and future generations of Filipinos, and (c) to insure the attainments of an environmental quality that is conducive to a life of dignity and well-being.").

[16] CONSTITUTION 1987, art. II, § 16 (Phil.).

[17] Oposa v. Factoran, G.R. No. 101083 (July 30, 1993) (Phil.), *reprinted in* 30–31 UNITED NATIONS ENVIRONMENT PROJECT COMPENDIUM OF JUDICIAL DECISIONS IN MATTERS RELATED TO THE ENVIRONMENT, NATIONAL DECISIONS (1998) [hereinafter UN COMPENDIUM]; *see also id.* at 36 (Feliciano, J., concurring).

[18] *See* Dante B. Gatmaytan, *The Illusion of Intergenerational Equity: Oposa v. Factoran as a Pyrrhic Victory*, 15 GEO. INT'L ENV'T L. REV. 457, 467–68 (2003).

[19] Blumm & Guthrie, *supra* note 6, at 772; *see also* Gatmaytan, *supra* note 18, at 467–68.

[20] Blumm & Guthrie, *supra* note 6, at 772 (citing Metro. Manila Dev. Auth. v. Concerned Residents of Manila Bay, G.R. No. 171947-48, 574 S.C.R.A. 661 (Dec. 18, 2008) (Phil.)).

[21] *Id.* at 775.

[22] *Id.* at 774.

[23] *Id.*

[24] David L. Callies & Katie L. Smith, *The Public Trust Doctrine: A United States and Comparative Analysis*, 7 J. INT'L & COMP. L. 41 (2020) (while acknowledging that public trust principles are

b. India

Another nation that inherited its jurisprudence from English common law, India recognizes the public trust even more broadly than the United States,[25] guaranteeing the protection of public environmental rights in all natural resources nationwide. In India, the right to a healthy environment has been framed as a component of the constitutionally protected right to life,[26] as first recognized in the *Dehradun Quarrying* case.[27] After *Dehradun Quarrying*, the Supreme Court of India first articulated the Indian public trust doctrine in its 1997 decision in *M.C. Mehta v. Kamal Nath*, in which it cited the California Supreme Court's reasoning in the Mono Lake case to set forth an even more powerful version of the doctrine.[28]

In *M.C. Mehta*, a developer had sought to blast, dredge, reconstruct, and redirect the flow of a river threatening its resort,[29] and the plaintiffs sued to prevent it, arguing that the proposed action would encroach on a protected forest, cause harm to public lands, and threaten the community with landslides and flooding.[30] Affirming the public trust as "the law of the land" and that the public was the beneficiary of the "seashore, running waters, airs, forests and ecologically fragile lands," the *M.C. Mehta* court cited *Audubon Society* in siding with the plaintiffs.[31] Referring to the English common law roots of the public trust, the court held that the doctrine protected:

> The aesthetic use and the pristine glory of the natural resources, the environment and the ecosystems of our country ... [from being] eroded for private, commercial or any other use unless the courts find it necessary, in good faith, for the public good and in the public interest to encroach upon the said resources.[32]

Three years after *M.C. Mehta*, the Indian Supreme Court held that the doctrine was part of the Indian Constitution[33] and further extended its reach over all natural

---

evident throughout Filipino history, arguing that "the doctrine has never been unequivocally adopted," and that the words "public trust doctrine" are "not found anywhere in the common law, statutes or Constitution of the Philippines").

[25] *See, e.g.*, M.C. Mehta v. Kamal Nath, (1997) 1 SCC 388 (1996) (India), *reprinted in* UN COMPENDIUM, *supra* note 17, at 259, 269–70 (citing *Illinois Central*, the *Audubon Society* Mono Lake case, and Joseph Sax in establishing the public trust doctrine as "the law of the land"); *see also* Blumm & Guthrie, *supra* note 6, at 760.

[26] CONSTITUTION 1950, art. 21 (India).

[27] Rural Litigation and Entitlement Kendra, Dehradun v. State of Uttar Pradesh, 1985 AIR 652 (India).

[28] M.C. Mehta v. Kamal Nath, (1997) 1 SCC 388 (1996) (India), *reprinted in* UN COMPENDIUM, *supra* note 17, at 259.

[29] *Id.*

[30] *Id.* at 266–69.

[31] *Id.* at 269–70, 272.

[32] *Id.* at 273.

[33] Blumm & Guthrie, *supra* note 6, at 762 (quoting M.I. Builders Priv. Ltd. v. Radhey Shayam Sahu, (1999) 6 SCC 464, 518 (India)) ("The court agreed with a state high court that the public trust doctrine protected the park because of its 'historical importance and environmental necessity' and was

resources in the nation to include parklands.³⁴ Indian case law also gives citizens a right to enforce the doctrine, regardless of personal injury.³⁵ At least one scholar credits judicial use of the doctrine in the 1980s and 1990s with significant environmental justice gains in India, but suggests that reinforcement by formal environmental laws and regulations will be required to sustain them.³⁶

c. Nepal

In 2019, the Supreme Court of Nepal invoked public trust principles in its constitution and more generally in support of its decision to halt the construction of a 30-kilometer highway through Chitwan National Park.³⁷ The Park is a UNESCO World Heritage Site, one of few remaining tracts of wilderness in South Asia, and one of the last remaining refuges for the one-horned rhinoceros and Bengal tiger.³⁸ Home to endangered plants and animals and designated wetlands of international importance under the Ramsar Convention, the park is legally protected under the National Parks and Wildlife Conservation Act, enforced by units of the Nepalese army since 1975.³⁹ Article 30 of the Nepali Constitution also includes a provision guaranteeing citizens the right to a clean and healthy environment.⁴⁰

Environmental advocates filed suit to protect Chitwan National Park in 2012, after the government issued plans to construct a thirty kilometer highway through the park and the habitat of endangered species endemic to the park.⁴¹ UNESCO also issued a formal warning that the project would significantly harm regional biodiversity and cause the park to become listed on the World Heritage in Danger list, and in 2018, added a catalog of inadequacies to the state's environmental impact assessment for the project.⁴²

---

entrenched in Article 21 of the Constitution, which declares that '[n]o person shall be deprived of his life or personal liberty except according to procedure established by law.'").

34 *Id.* at 763.
35 *Id.* at 765 (citing Interview by Rachel Guthrie with Sairam Bhat, Professor, Nat'l L. Sch. of India at Bangalore, in Portland, Or. (Oct. 21, 2010)).
36 Naazima Kamardeen, *The Honeymoon Is Over: An Assessment of Judicial Activism in Environmental Cases in Sri Lanka*, 6 JINDAL GLOB. L. REV. 73 (2015).
37 Ramchandra Simkhanda et al. v. Nepal Government, Office of the Prime Minister and Council of Ministers, 068WO-0597, Decision Number 10204 (2019) (Nepal), https://climatecasechart.com/non-us-case/ramchandra-simkhanda-et-al-v-nepal-government-office-of-the-prime-minister-and-council-of-ministers/.
38 *Id.*
39 *Id.*
40 "Every citizen shall have the right to live in a clean and healthy environment." Constitution of Nepal, art. 30, https://lawcommission.gov.np/en/wp-content/uploads/2021/01/Constitution-of-Nepal.pdf.
41 Ramchandra Simkhanda et al. v. Nepal Government, Office of the Prime Minister and Council of Ministers, 068-WO-0597, Decision Number 10204 (2019) (Nepal), https://climatecasechart.com/non-us-case/ramchandra-simkhanda-et-al-v-nepal-government-office-of-the-prime-minister-and-council-of-ministers/.
42 *Id.*

A. Public Trust Principles around the World

In 2019, the Court sided with the plaintiffs and enjoined the project, holding that the proposed road would harm protected species, threaten to compound foreseeable harms from climate change, and contravene the constitutional right to a safe and healthy environment.[43] The Court invoked the public trust doctrine in reminding the government that it was responsible for the protection of public park resources and obligated to undertake due consideration of the environment when carrying out major projects, rather than cursorily approving "catastrophic environmental projects" for "short-term gain."[44]

The Nepali Supreme Court has sided with environmental plaintiffs in a number of other cases invoking constitutional protection of the right to a clean and healthy environment, including a suit against plans to excavate stone and gravel for export, which the Court held would be tantamount to "ecocide" on the Terai and Madhesh plains and would violate the norms of environmental justice and intergenerational equity,[45] and an even more ambitious suit demanding the state enact comprehensive climate change regulations (as discussed in Chapter 9).[46]

3. The Greater Middle East

In the Greater Middle East, at least two nations have framed environmental legal protections after the public trust doctrine. Relying on a mix of constitutional, statutory, and case law, both Pakistan and Israel have adopted public trust principles to protect access to clean drinking water and coastal waters.

a. Pakistan

There is no direct mention of the public trust doctrine in the constitution or statutes of Pakistan,[47] but the Supreme Court has concluded that public rights to environmental health are implied by critical language within Pakistan's constitution: "No person shall be deprived of life or liberty save in accordance with law."[48] This

---

[43] Id.
[44] Id. The Court also warned that the government must act in accordance with the UN Framework Convention on Climate Change and the Paris Agreement, explicitly noting that even a small nation like Nepal can make a meaningful contribution to the global goal of curbing the impacts of climate change. Id.
[45] Shailendra Prasad Ambedkar v. Office of Prime Minister et al., Writ no: 077-WC-0099 (2021) (Nepal), https://climatecasechart.com/non-us-case/shailendra-prasad-ambedkar-v-office-of-prime-minister-et-al/.
[46] Shrestha v. Office of the Prime Minister et al., 074-WO-0283 (2018) (Nepal), https://climatecasechart.com/non-us-case/shrestha-v-office-of-the-prime-minister-et-al/. See also Chapter 9(A)(1) ("Urgenda Foundation and International Climate Claims") (discussing the case in further detail).
[47] Blumm & Guthrie, supra note 6, at 766.
[48] CONSTITUTION 1973, art. 9 (Pak.); Blumm & Guthrie, supra note 6, at 766–68; see In re Hum. Rts. Case, (1994) 46 PLD (SC) 102 (1992) (Pak.), reprinted in UN COMPENDIUM, supra note 17, at 280; Zia v. WAPDA, (1994) 46 PLD (SC) 693 (Pak.), reprinted in UN COMPENDIUM, supra note 17, at 323.

language in Article Nine has been interpreted to contain public trust-like principles protecting public rights in the "clean atmosphere and unpolluted environment" against actions that would harm them.[49] Environmental advocates have used the doctrine to protect water resources from pollution, especially drinking water, but *West Pakistan Salt Miners Union v. Director of Industries & Mineral Development* suggested that it would apply as needed to protect "any environmental resources protected by the constitutional right to life."[50]

In one case, *In re Human Rights Case (Environmental Pollution in Balochistan)*, the Supreme Court held that industrial and nuclear waste dumping on coastal land violated Article Nine by creating "environmental hazard and pollution."[51] In *Shehla Zia v. WAPDA*, the Supreme Court further emphasized that the right to life included the right to environmental health, applying the doctrine to curtail potential environmental health hazards from electromagnetic energy and requiring that any future siting of electricity facilities be preceded by public notice and comment.[52]

b. Israel

Through a combination of different sources of law, Israeli law features public trust language seeking to protect environmental rights for present and future generations.[53] The Protection of Coastal and Environmental Law was enacted in 2004 to restore and preserve the coastal environment for the benefit and enjoyment of the public and future generations.[54] The law considers the sea and shore as integral pieces that extend three hundred meters inland from the country's territorial waters, essentially deeming the whole area a public resource to be protected from damage.[55] The Mejelle, referenced by Israeli case law, also states that "[w]ater, air, and light are free to all, and all people are joint owners in these three things."[56] The country has most famously applied the rule to guarantee public rights of access to beach and coastal areas in *Puterman v. AG*.[57]

---

[49] *Zia*, 46 PLD (SC), at 333–34.
[50] Blumm & Guthrie, *supra* note 6, at 769 nn.145–46 (citing Salt Miners Union v. Dir. of Indus. & Mineral Dev., (1994) SCMR (SC) 2061 (Pak.), *reprinted in* UN COMPENDIUM, *supra* note 17, at 286 and CONSTITUTION 1973, art. 9 (Pak.) (describing the constitutional right to life)).
[51] *In re Hum. Rts. Case*, 46 PLD (SC) 102.
[52] *Zia*, 46 PLD (SC) at 323; *see* Blumm & Guthrie, *supra* note 6, at 767–68 (citing the description of the word "life" in the *Zia* decision).
[53] *Guide to Law Online: Israel*, LIBR. CONG. (June 6, 2015), www.loc.gov/law/help/legal-research-guide/israel.php.
[54] *Protecting Israel's Coast*, MINISTRY OF ENV'T PROT. (Aug. 17, 2020), www.gov.il/en/departments/guides/coastal_environment_preservation; Tzvi Levinson, Julia Lietzmann & Gil Dror, *Protection of the Coastal Environment – A Step towards Sustainability*, 36 ENV'T POL'Y & L. 94 (2006).
[55] MINISTRY OF ENV'T PROT., *supra* note 54.
[56] Schorr, *supra* note 3.
[57] In 1962, an Israeli court drew on the Mejelle to apply public trust-like principles in a case affirming public rights to access beaches, overturning the conviction of Moshe Puterman for trespassing on

4. Africa

Several African countries have adopted public trust principles in their statutes and constitutions, signaling a commitment to protecting some of the most unique and important ecosystems on the planet. These include Uganda, Kenya, Nigeria, and South Africa. While some nations' trusts are more explicit than others (and some commitments have been operationalized more than others), the public trust in African law tends to be framed expansively, protecting resources that range from water to wildlife.

a. Uganda

Uganda's expansive public trust doctrine parallels the comprehensiveness of the Filipino and Indian doctrines, extending to natural resources far beyond navigable waterways.[58] The Ugandan Supreme Court first recognized the doctrine in its 2004 decision in *Advocates Coalition for Development and Environment v. Attorney General*,[59] where the plaintiff had challenged the government's approval of a fifty-year plantation permit for a forest reserve on public trust grounds.[60] The court ruled that the government had breached its public trust obligations by failing to perform an environmental impact assessment and had further failed its duty to obtain consent from the local community.[61] Since then, Ugandan constitutional and statutory laws[62] have codified and elaborated the Ugandan public trust doctrine to protect all surface water resources, wetlands, groundwater, public lands (including national parks, forests, and game reserves), wildlife, plant life, mineral resources, and "any other land reserved for ecological and touristic purposes for the common good ..."[63]

---

a public beach. CrimA (TA) 851/60 Puterman v. AG, PM 30, 7 (1962) (Isr.). For a discussion of the case and the role of Ottoman law in the court's decision, see Schorr, *supra* note 3; Rinat, *supra* note 3 (describing the case and the Mejelle doctrine it applied).

[58] Blumm & Guthrie, *supra* note 6, at 779 n.199 (comparing Ugandan law to parallel Indian and Philippine case law).

[59] Advocs. Coal. for Dev. & Env't v. Att'y Gen., Misc. Cause No. 0100 of 2004 (July 11, 2005) (Uganda), https://elaw.org/system/files/attachments/publicresource/ug.Acode_.v.AttorneyGeneral_o.pdf.

[60] *Id.* at *4–5.

[61] *Id.* at *23.

[62] CONSTITUTION 1995, objective XIII (Uganda); *id.* art. 39; *id.* art. 237(2)(b); *id.* objective XXVII (directing the state to "promote sustainable development and public awareness of the need to manage land, air, water resources in a balanced and sustainable manner for the present and future generations," and that "the natural resources of Uganda shall be managed in such a way as to meet the development and environmental needs of present and future generations of Ugandans; and ... take all possible measures to prevent or minimize [sic] damage and destruction to land, air and water resources resulting from pollution or other causes"); The Land Act, ch. 227, § 44 (2010) (Uganda); Blumm & Guthrie, *supra* note 6, at 777–78.

[63] CONSTITUTION 1995, art. 237(2)(b) (Uganda); The Land Act, ch. 227, § 44(1) (1998) (Uganda); Blumm & Guthrie, *supra* note at 779 (citing CONSTITUTION 1995, objective XIII (Uganda)).

More recently, Ugandan plaintiffs have attempted to expand public trust protections to include atmospheric resources, following the lead of the Dutch and American plaintiffs in the atmospheric trust litigation detailed in Chapter 9.[64]

b. Kenya

Kenya has interpreted the public trust doctrine as a legal means for vindicating the right to life that is expressly protected in the Kenyan Constitution.[65] In *Waweru v. Republic*, the High Court of Kenya allowed plaintiffs to rely on the doctrine in challenging the discharge of raw sewage into the Kiserian River, holding that the Kenyan Constitution entitles every citizen to the right to life and that the Environmental Management and Co-ordination Act grants citizens a right to a clean and healthy environment.[66] After *Waweru*, Kenya adopted a new constitution in 2010, which further expanded environmental protections by guaranteeing the right "to have the environment protected for the benefit of present and future generations through legislative and other measures."[67]

c. Nigeria

The public trust doctrine makes a brief but potentially significant appearance in Nigeria's Constitution of 1999, which declares that "[t]he State shall protect and improve the environment and safeguard the water, air and land, forest and wildlife of Nigeria."[68] As this book goes to press, it appears this provision has yet to be the subject of case law enforcing or interpreting it, but this constitutional language positions Nigeria to follow in the footsteps of other nations that have operationalized such aspirational statements of principle.

---

[64] Mbabzi v. Att'y Gen., Civil Suit No. 283 of 2012 (Uganda 2012) (sending the case to mediation); *see also* Callies & Smith, *supra* note 24, at 61 (discussing *Mbabzi*). As this piece goes to press, the plaintiffs are awaiting a scheduled hearing after failing to resolve the case in mediation and amending their complaint. *Uganda*, OUR CHILD'S TR., www.ourchildrenstrust.org/uganda.

[65] Waweru v. Republic, (2006) 1 K.L.R. 677, 688 (H.C.K.) (Kenya),www.kenyalaw.org/caselaw/cases/view/14988; *see also* Blumm & Guthrie, *supra* note 6, at 781–82 (discussing the case and its significance).

[66] *Waweru*, 1 K.L.R. at 687 (citing CONSTITUTION art. 26 (2010), art. 42 (Kenya), and Environmental Management and Coordination Act (1999) Cap. 8 § 3, 108).

[67] CONSTITUTION 2010, art. 42 (Kenya), www.klrc.go.ke/index.php/constitution-of-kenya/112-chapter-four-the-bill-of-rights/part-2-rights-and-fundamental-freedoms/208-42-environment ("Every person has the right to a clean and healthy environment, which includes the right – (a) to have the environment protected for the benefit of present and future generations through legislative and other measures, particularly those contemplated in Article 69; and (b) to have obligations relating to the environment fulfilled under Article 70."); *see also* Callies & Smith, *supra* note 24, at 62–63 (discussing the new provisions).

[68] CONSTITUTION 1999, ch. 2, § 20 (Nigeria).

d. South Africa

Like the constitutions of Kenya, Nigeria, India, and Pakistan, the South African Constitution protects the right to life.[69] South Africa goes even further in codifying public trust principles directly into its constitutional text, protecting the environment for the benefit of present and future generations (in Sections 11,[70] 24,[71] and 27[72]). In addition, the legislature codified public trust principles into the National Water Act of 1998, which states that water is a natural resource belonging to all people.[73] One scholar reports that the judiciary has also sought to confirm the force of the doctrine in litigation.[74] However, another South African researcher observes that while the nation's public trust was designed to free scarce water resources from the constraints of both private ownership and environmental regulation to meet basic human needs, it has yet to be "operationalized" with meaningful guidance for administrative decision-making.[75]

5. Europe

Conspicuously missing from the parade of nations developing public trust principles for environmental protection are many of the countries in Europe. As discussed further below, the British maintain the doctrine of sovereign ownership of submerged lands but have not developed it much beyond the common law principles reviewed in Chapter 1. Meanwhile, European civil law nations, such as Spain, have adopted

---

[69] CONSTITUTION (1996), §11 (S. Afr.).
[70] Id.
[71] Id. § 24 ("Everyone has the right – a. to an environment that is not harmful to their health or well-being; and b. to have the environment protected, for the benefit of present and future generations, through reasonable legislative and other measures that – i. prevent pollution and ecological degradation; ii. promote conservation; and iii. secure ecologically sustainable development and use of natural resources while promoting justifiable economic and social development.").
[72] Id. § 27 ("Everyone has the right to have access to … sufficient food and water …. The state must take reasonable legislative and other measures … to achieve the progressive realisation of … these rights.").
[73] National Water Act 36 of 1998 (S. Afr.).
[74] Andrew Blackmore, Note, *The Application of and the Prospects for the Public Trust Doctrine in South Africa: A Brief Overview*, 135 S. AFR. L.J. 631 (2018); *see, e.g.*, Minister of Water & Env't Affs. v. Really Useful Invs. 2017 (1) SA 505 (SCA) (S. Afr.); Clairison's CC v. MEC for Loc. Gov't Env't Affs. & Dev. Plan. & Bitou Mun. 2012 (3) SA 128 (CC) (S. Afr.); HTF Devs. v. Minister of Env't Affs. and Tourism 2006 (5) SA 512 (T) (S. Afr.); Thomas v. Gouveia 2008 (1) SA 392 (T) (S. Afr.).
[75] *See* Email Communications with Dr. Bill Harding, August 17, 2021 (on file with author) ("While our version of the trust has clear US 'roots,' it is quite a different beast and was deployed as a transformative and democratising instrument which, without challenge, dispensed with riparian rights to water and reallocated the whole of the resource in favour of meeting basic human needs and reallocating water to the most appropriate uses. The parallel intention was to remove obstacles to environmental protection, particularly with respect to water resource protection according to an ecosystem directed basis…. What our environmental body of law lacks is that the trust principles have yet to be built out to further their understanding, especially in guidance for administrative decision making."); *see also* Bill Harding, *Hydroecological Connectivity as a Normative Framework for Aquatic Ecosystem Regulation: Lessons from the U.S.A.* (2022) (Ph.D. thesis, University of Cape Town).

a related principle of sovereign ownership with shared roots in the Justinian *jus publicum*,[76] as Roman common law is also the progenitor of much of the continental European civil codes.[77] It may be that Europeans have felt less need to develop environmental rights under public trust principles because their legal systems, at least by comparison with many others across the globe, have protected environmental values more effectively by conventional statutory and regulatory means, especially under European Union law. This section briefly reviews related developments in Great Britain, given its special status as midwife to the American public trust.

a. England

While the principle of sovereign ownership of submerged tidelands continues to apply, public trust principles never developed in England the way they did in the United States.[78] The term "public trust doctrine" will not be recognized by the average English law scholar unless they have studied its development in the United States or corresponding principles of fiduciary obligations to public commons that bind the Crown in Canada.[79] Even resource commons protected under the Magna Carta's ancient Charter of the Forests have dwindled in importance.[80] Traditional forms of common property, such as common pasture lands for grazing, became less important as the British economy shifted from its feudal origins toward more entrenched and

---

[76] Las Siete Partidas, P. III, tit. 28, laws III, IV, VI; *see also* C.C. art. 407 (Spain) (declaring that rivers and their natural courses, springs, streams, and riverbeds are in the public domain); C.C. art. 339 (Spain) (declaring that rivers, riverbanks, shores, and bays are in the public domain). *See also* MERITXELL COSTEJÀ, NURIA FONT, ANNA RIGOL, & JOAN SUBIRATS, THE EVOLUTION OF THE NATIONAL WATER REGIME IN SPAIN (2002), https://citeseerx.ist.psu.edu/viewdoc/download?doi=10.1.1.472.731 9&rep=rep1&type=pdf (detailing the aspects of water that remain in the public domain after Spain's Civil Code was amended with multiple comprehensive pieces of water law legislation); Ker & Co. v. Couden, 223 U.S. 268 (1912) (in interpreting a case about ownership of submerged lands, noting that under Spanish civil law, the seashore flowed by the tides was public property, belonging, in Spain, to the sovereign). Of note, several Florida cases also discuss the Spanish roots of the Florida sovereign ownership aspect of the public trust doctrine. *See, e.g.*, Apalachicola Land & Dev. Co. v. McRae, 98 So. 505, 517–18 (Fla. 1923); Geiger v. Filor, 8 Fla. 325, 336–37 (1859); Bd. of Trs. v. Webb, 618 So. 2d 1381, 1382 (Fla. Dist. Ct. App. 1993). Other Florida cases also cite the English common law roots of the Florida public trust doctrine. *See, e.g.*, Broward v. Mabry, 50 So. 826, 829 (Fla. 1909).

[77] *See* Yntema, *supra* note 5, at 88 (describing Roman common law as the "fundamental body of legal doctrine" which is the "common element in the individual legal systems of much of Continental Europe, and its colonies").

[78] *See* Anne Bottomley, *Beneath the City: The Forest! Civic Commons as Practice and Critique*, 5 BIRKBECK L. REV. 1, 18–19 (2018) (distinguishing the American and English approaches to common property).

[79] *See id.*

[80] *See* SARAH NIELD, FOREST LAW AND THE VERDERERS OF THE NEW FOREST 5–8, 13 (The New Forest Research and Public Trust 2005) (discussing the waning lands and resources protected under English Forest Law from the Middle Ages to the New Forest Act of 1964); Sarah Nield, *The New Forest: Ancient Forest and Modern Playground*, *in* MODERN STUDIES IN PROPERTY LAW 294 (Elizabeth Cooke ed., 2d ed. 2003).

widespread privatization.[81] In assessing the devolution of English commons to private property, Professor Anne Bottomley has observed that "patterns of enclosure and privatisation" were substantially altering the landscape by the seventeenth century and had overwhelmingly changed it by the late eighteenth century.[82]

b. Scotland and Wales

Nevertheless, the historic trend toward privatization of natural resource commons is increasingly meeting with reversals in Great Britain, especially in Scotland and Wales. In both Wales and England, recent statutory law enables both public authorities and private individuals to proactively designate land they already own as a "registered commons" to purposefully preserve common rights of access overlying more conventional forms of ownership.[83] This approach enables the creation of broader forms of public commons than are currently recognized under most applications of the American public trust doctrine, but these statutory commons do not hold the foundational, quasi-constitutional character of the pre-statutory public trust doctrine as a constraint on sovereign authority.[84] Meanwhile, Scotland has embarked on an even more ambitious program of reasserting public natural resource commons in its adoption of the 2003 Land Reform Act, which establishes access rights over much of the country's open land and inland water resources, even those privately owned.[85]

c. A Future British Trust?

Notably, some predict that environmental law in Great Britain will likely get weaker after Brexit, the British exit from the European Union, because environmental

---

[81] See NIELD, FOREST LAW AND THE VERDERERS OF THE NEW FOREST, supra note 80, at 12–23 (discussing the gradual privatization of the sovereign forest commons); Daniel R. Coquillette, *Mosses from an Old Manse: Another Look at Some Historic Property Cases About the Environment*, 64 CORNELL L. REV. 761, 807–09 (1979) (discussing the development of the "enclosure movement" and the historical trend away from public commons and toward exclusivity in the use and ownership of natural resources).

[82] See Bottomley, supra note 78, at 5; see also id. at 16 ("It is no surprise that commons, as the state of nature, was understood in so much European political philosophy as simply being in a state-of-waiting to be made into, reduced into, property by the inventive intrusion of the human.").

[83] Id. at 19–20.

[84] Id. at 18–19 (differentiating between the English and Welsh approaches to public commons and the public trust approach taken in the United States).

[85] Land Reform (Scotland) Act 2003, (ASP 2) pt. 1; see also John A. Lovett, *Progressive Property in Action: The Land Reform (Scotland) Act 2003*, 89 NEB. L. REV. 739, 741 (2011) ("In Part I of the Land Reform (Scotland) Act 2003 (the LRSA), just the latest in a series of sweeping property law reform initiatives in Scotland, the Scots have created a new kind of property interest and a detailed property regime to contextualize this interest. At the heart of this regime is the right of *responsible* access. It is a right to go almost anywhere in Scotland, on most land and inland water, whether privately owned or public, without a motorized vehicle, for purposes of recreation, education, and passage, as long as one acts responsibly.").

harm will no longer be the subject of stricter E.U. laws overseen by the Court of the European Union.[86] If environmental protection becomes weakened in this way, it could present an opportunity for the British to readdress the role of the public trust doctrine as a common law constraint with implications for environmental protection.[87] Some scholars suggest that English courts adopt the American version of the doctrine that has developed since its departure from English origins, referencing American public trust cases where analogous claims have arisen in the U.K.[88] In this way, public trust principles emphasizing environmental values may yet cross the pond in the opposite direction, bringing the development of the common law doctrine full circle.

6. South America

Given their proximity to Amazon rainforest, it is perhaps no surprise that several countries in South America have adopted sweeping public trust principles into their constitutions. The doctrine in Brazil's constitution is expansive, though untested, while Ecuador had constitutionalized significant environmental protections even before its heralded codification of rights of nature principles in recent amendments.

a. Brazil

Public trust principles are both an explicit and implicit feature of Brazil's 1993 constitution, which affirms the sovereign ownership of submerged lands and tidelands, mineral resources, archaeological sites, caves, and energy sites,[89] but also adopts the core environmental rights of ecological protection, intergenerational equity, public environmental rights, and the sovereign responsibility of the government as trustee of these rights and resources.[90] Brazil's constitution also protects ecological processes, genetic wealth, fauna, and flora – recognizing the "national wealth"

---

[86] Marc Willers & Emily Shirley, *The Public Trust Doctrine's Role in Post-Brexit Britain*, GARDEN CT. CHAMBER (Mar. 31, 2017), www.gardencourtchambers.co.uk/news/the-public-trust-doctrines-role-in-post-brexit-britain.

[87] *Id.*

[88] *See, e.g.*, Bottomley, *supra* note 78, at 17–19. Nevertheless, other scholars considering the matter have noted that English statutory law may already obviate some of the more ambitious environmental applications of the trust, such as the atmospheric trust project, which some may argue has been preempted by the Climate Change Act of 2008 that sets legally binding carbon reduction targets for the country. Bradley Freeman & Emily Shirley, *England and the Public Trust Doctrine*, J. PLAN. & ENV'T L. 839, 845 (2014).

[89] CONSTITUIÇÃO FEDERAL [CONSTITUTION] 1988, art. 20 (Braz.).

[90] *Id.* art. 5; *id.* art. 225 ("All have the right to an ecologically balanced environment, which is an asset of common use and essential to a healthy quality of life, and both the Government and the community shall have the duty to defend and preserve it for present and future generations.").

and key resources of the Amazon Forest, Atlantic Woodlands, and the coastline.[91] However, the public trust doctrine has not thus far been the subject of litigation in Brazilian courts.[92]

b. Ecuador

In 2008, Ecuador arguably ratified the most ambitious set of constitutional protections for environmental rights in the world.[93] The 2008 Ecuadorian Constitution incorporated public trust principles extending well beyond waterways to include nearly all natural resources.[94] Still, as discussed further below, Ecuador went further than codifying the public trust doctrine, becoming the first nation to explicitly recognize the legal rights of nature constitutionally. In addition to assigning sovereign responsibility for protecting conventional public trust principles, the constitution declares the fundamental rights inherent in nature, including rights to exist, persist, and flourish, and grants all persons the right to "call upon public authorities to enforce the rights of nature."[95]

7. North America

In contrast to nations that have codified public trust principles constitutionally or in national level statutes, North American nations have acted less affirmatively in support of them, at least at the national legislative level. Yet as reported in Chapter 8, the doctrine has been enthusiastically embraced at the subnational level in the United States by all three branches of government, and the Canadian judiciary has formally protected public trust values relating to fishing rights, forest values, and environmental assessment.

a. Canada

Canada has endorsed public trust principles without formally affixing them into law. Reflecting the common roots of American and Canadian law in the public trust principles of the Roman *jus publicum* and English Magna Carta, Canadian courts have allowed suit against the government for failure to maintain common rights to

---

[91] *Id.* art. 20; *id.* art. 225 (also listing the Serra do Mar and the Pantanal Mato-Grossense and prohibiting the alienation of "unoccupied" lands if "necessary to protect the natural ecosystems").
[92] Blumm & Guthrie, *supra* note 6, at 794.
[93] CONSTITUCIÓN DE LA REPUBLICA DEL ECUADOR [CONSTITUTION] 2008, art. 71 (Ecuador).
[94] *Id.* art. 12; *id.* art. 375, cl. 8. The constitution refers to "[t]he unique and priceless natural assets of Ecuador includ[ing], among others, the physical, biological and geological formations whose value from the environmental, scientific, cultural, or landscape standpoint requires protection, conservation, recovery and promotion." *Id.* art. 404.
[95] *Id.* art. 71.

fish in Atlantic waters.[96] Beyond that, Canadian law has not more formally developed the public trust in the ways that American states have.

Even so, references to public trust principles have surfaced in disputes over public access and private obstructions to navigable waterways and other environmental values. For example, in considering whether a mining project was exempt from environmental assessment requirements, the Newfoundland Court of Appeal held for the environmental plaintiffs on grounds that public trust principles protecting future generations were an important element of the governing environmental legislation.[97] Similarly, in addressing a forest fire public nuisance claim in *British Columbia v. Canadian Forest Products*, the court discussed the evolution of the American public trust doctrine and opined that the public trust principles at stake in this case granted the federal government damages for the forest fire, which was caused by a Crown licensee's negligence.[98]

b. United States

Finally, we return full circle to the United States. Although Chapter 8 extensively reviewed the development of the doctrine across individual states and its intersections with federal law, this discussion briefly revisits the potential for future public trust developments at the national level. As noted previously, while the U.S. Supreme Court has not considered the issue directly, it has indicated in dicta that the doctrine operates only as a matter of state law, and not federal law.[99] That said, both environmental and scholarly advocates continue to maintain that there is no legitimate reason to distinguish between the implications of the doctrine for state and federal authority. That is to say, if the doctrine limits sovereign authority to alienate or compromise essential public commons, it should not matter at what level that authority is operating, and federal sovereign authority should also

---

[96] P.E.I. v. Canada (2005), 256 Nfld. & P.E.I.R. 343 para. 6, 37 (Can. P.E.I. Sup. Ct.) (relying in part on B.C. v. Canadian Forest Prods. Ltd., (2004) 2 S.C.R. 74 (Can.), the court explained that if a government can sue "as guardian of the public interest, to claim against a party causing damage to that public interest, then it would seem that in another case, a beneficiary of the public interest ought to be able to claim against the government for a failure to properly protect the public interest," as "[a] right gives rise to a corresponding duty").

[97] Labrador Inuit Ass'n v. Newfoundland (1997), 155 Nfld. & P.E.I.R. 93 para. 11, 80 (Can. Nfld. C.A.) ("If the rights of future generations to the protection of the present integrity of the natural world are to be taken seriously, and not to be regarded as mere empty rhetoric, care must be taken in the interpretation and application of the legislation. Environmental laws must be construed against their commitment to future generations and against a recognition that, in addressing environmental issues, we often have imperfect knowledge as to the potential impact of activities on the environment.").

[98] *Canadian Forest Prods. Ltd.*, 2 S.C.R. at para. 1, 46, 78–80 (the Crown sued for damages both in its capacity as landowner and as representative of the public interest).

[99] PPL Mont., LLC v. Mont., 565 U.S. 576, 603 (2012); *see also* Chapter 8(B)(3) ("A Constitutive Constraint on Federal Authority?") discussing arguments that the public trust is also a constraint on federal authority).

A. Public Trust Principles around the World 379

be subject to the responsibilities imposed by the doctrine.[100] The argument rests on the idea that the doctrine is an implied feature of federal constitutional law,[101] both because there is no reason to differentiate between state and federal actors in this area, and because all post-thirteen-colony states inherited their trust obligations through federal sovereignty.[102]

The effort to expand recognition of the public trust constraint on federal sovereign authority is a foundation of the atmospheric trust project discussed in Chapter 9 – a coordinated effort to sue state and federal actors for violating sovereign public trust obligations to protect the atmosphere, referencing Justinian's recognition of trust resources in not only the sea and the shores of the sea, but also the air.[103] Among the most famous of these efforts was *Juliana v. United States*, the "Kid's Climate Case," in which youth plaintiffs invoked the doctrine to protect the atmosphere from greenhouse gas pollution and vindicate their fundamental right to climate stability.[104] Over an exceptionally complex nine-year period of litigation, detailed in Chapter 9, the plaintiffs unsuccessfully sought a judicial declaration that the United States' failure to address the dangers of climate change violated both their rights under the public trust doctrine and the Constitution.[105]

Yet in both the United States and elsewhere, even as some avenues to protect critical environmental values and ecosystems under the public trust doctrine appear

---

[100] For full discussion of these arguments, see Chapter 8(B)(3); *see also* Mary Christina Wood, Nature's Trust: Environmental Law For a New Ecological Age 133–36 (Cambridge University Press, 2014); Michael Blumm & Lynn S. Schaffer, *The Federal Public Trust Doctrine: Misinterpreting Justice Kennedy and Illinois Central Railroad*, 45 Env't L. 399, 401 (2015); Gerald Torres & Nathan Bellinger, *The Public Trust: The Law's DNA*, 4 Wake Forest J.L. & Pol'y 281, 288 (2014); Mary Christina Wood, *Advancing the Sovereign Trust of Government to Safeguard the Environment for Present and Future Generations (Part II): Instilling a Fiduciary Obligation in Governance*, 39 Env't L. 91, 135–36 (2009); Michael C. Blumm, Harrison C. Dunning, & Scott W. Reed, *Renouncing the Public Trust Doctrine: An Assessment of the Validity of Idaho House Bill 794*, 24 Ecology L.Q. 461, 494 (1997); Richard A. Epstein, *The Public Trust Doctrine*, 7 Cato J. 411, 426 (1987).

[101] See Chapter 8(B)(3) ("A Constitutive Constraint on Federal Authority?"). *See also* Blumm & Schaffer, *supra* note 100, at 403–07.

[102] One way of viewing this is that in the equal footing conveyances, the federal government itself imposed the trust on the states. See Blumm & Schaffer, *supra* note 100, at 403–407 (discussing Justice Kennedy's reference to the equal footing doctrine in Idaho v. Coeur d'Alene Tribe, 521 U.S. 261 (1997) and what it means for the public trust doctrine's origins).

[103] J. Inst. 2.1.1 (Thomas Collett Sandars trans., Longmans, Green & Co. eds., 4th ed. 1869).

[104] Juliana v. United States, 217 F. Supp. 3d 1224 (D. Or. 2016), *rev'd*, Juliana v. United States, No. 24-684, D.C. No. 6:15-cv-1517, 2024 WL 5102489, (May 1, 2024), *cert. denied*, 604 U.S. 645 (2025). *See also* Chapter 9(B)(4) ("*Juliana v. United States*").

[105] Juliana v. United States, Civ. No. 15-CV-01517-AA, 2023 WL 3750334, at *9 (D. Or. June 1, 2023) ("'[P]laintiffs seek declaratory relief that 'the United States' national energy system that creates the harmful conditions described herein has violated and continues to violate the Fifth Amendment of the U.S. Constitution and Plaintiffs' constitutional rights to substantive due process and equal protection of the law.'"); *Id.* at *6 ("Plaintiffs' Second Amended Complaint thus requests this Court to … enter a judgment declaring that the United States' national energy system has violated and continues to violate the public trust doctrine").

foreclosed, environmental advocates have also embraced a new argument for environmental protection: the obligation to protect the rights of nature itself.

B. THE RIGHTS OF NATURE MOVEMENT

Just as the public trust doctrine has been gathering steam as a means of protecting public environmental values associated with trust resources, a wholly different conception of environmental rights – the rights of nature movement – has been gathering force as an alternative approach to stewardship. The rights of nature have long been recognized in indigenous legal systems, but since the turn of the twenty-first century, the movement has gathered considerable force in nonindigenous legal systems, first in international contexts,[106] and more recently in the United States[107] – especially at the local level, and especially as a means of protecting vulnerable waterways.

While the public trust doctrine assigns legally protected rights in waterways and other trust resources to the public, the rights of nature doctrine assigns rights directly to features of the natural environment itself. There are important differences between the two models of environmental rights, most notably the contrasting philosophical ethics that undergird them.[108] Like most U.S. environmental laws (and most laws in the Western tradition), the public trust doctrine takes a utilitarian approach, focusing on the benefits that waterways and other trust resources confer on the people designated as holding legally protected rights.[109] By this anthropocentric ethic, a natural resource management decision is right if it produces the maximum benefit for the maximum number of people. In contrast, the rights of nature movement is premised on very different environmental ethics – the principles of biocentrism (valuing all living things) and ecocentrism (valuing ecosystems and all components within them), considering features of the natural world worthy of protection in and of themselves, without reference to human needs.[110] Under this approach, a decision is right if it protects nature, or at least that part of nature designated with legal personhood or other rights.

Despite these starkly different philosophical starting points, the two models showcase a surprising amount in common pragmatically. Especially in comparison with public trust paradigms that consider future generations, both approaches manifest as something approximating environmental stewardship. Over their respective periods of evolution, they have also taken interestingly similar paths of development and differentiation among the different jurisdictions that have adopted them,

---

[106] Id. at 2514–21.
[107] Ryan et al., *Comprehensive Analysis*, supra note 8, at 2501, 2521–38.
[108] See generally id. at 2541–55.
[109] Id. at 2541–48.
[110] Id. at 2548–55.

both domestically and internationally. These analogous pathways of differentiation include the different legal mechanisms by which they operate, the different resources they have been held to protect, the different values that they serve, and the different underlying legal theories that give them meaning.[111]

This part briefly introduces the rights of nature movement, compares it with its public trust counterpart, and considers how the rise of both approaches responds to the failure of conventional environmental laws to protect waterways. After providing a whirlwind tour of rights of nature initiatives globally and domestically, the chapter concludes with a comparison of the two approaches on both a philosophical and practical level.

1. A Whirlwind Tour of the Rights of Nature Movement

To provide context for the comparative analysis that follows, this section provides a brief review of significant rights of nature initiatives unfolding around the world, highlighting examples both internationally and domestically.[112] These examples showcase an array of legal approaches with as many differences as commonalities, but what most unites them is their underlying biocentric or ecocentric environmental ethics. In contrast to anthropocentric environmental laws that strive to preserve the natural environment for human enjoyment, the rights of nature movement confers positive environmental rights directly on nature itself.

Like the variations of the public trust doctrine reviewed in Chapter 8, the rights of nature movement has been organically developing across jurisdictions independently, spawning variations best illustrated by example. As this book goes to press, the movement is moving too quickly to catalog with accuracy, so the following discussion covers early movers and noteworthy examples both internationally and domestically, rather than attempting a comprehensive global catalog that will almost instantaneously become out of date.

a. International Initiatives

I. GLOBAL FIRST MOVER: ECUADOR'S CONSTITUTIONAL COMMITMENT

Perhaps the most famous rights of nature example is the world's most ambitious initiative: Ecuador's blanket constitutional protection for all of nature. In 2008, drawing deeply on the core values of its Indigenous cultures, the Ecuadorian Constitution was amended by public referendum to protect a pantheon of environmental rights associated with nature in general.[113] The new provisions set forth that Pacha Mama, or

---

[111] See id. at 2461–76 (discussing the public trust doctrine), 2506–14 (discussing the rights of nature movement).
[112] For a more thorough review of rights of nature initiatives in both contexts, see id. at 2500–39.
[113] CONSTITUCIÓN DE LA REPUBLICA DEL ECUADOR [CONSTITUTION] 2008, art. 71 (Ecuador).

Mother Earth, "has the right to integral respect for its existence and for the maintenance and regeneration of its life cycles, structure, functions and evolutionary processes," and further recognizes the right of nature to exist, persist, maintain, and regenerate its vital cycles.[114] It then goes on to describe who is empowered or obligated to act on these rights: "All persons, communities, peoples and nations can call upon public authorities to enforce the rights of nature."[115] Further, "[t]he State shall apply preventive and restrictive measures on activities that might lead to the extinction of species, the destruction of ecosystems and the permanent alteration of natural cycles."[116]

Ecuador is the first country to explicitly recognize the rights of nature at the constitutional level, and the rights it created have proved meaningful, thus far enforced primarily through litigation.[117] Between 2008 and 2016, one study identified thirteen cases in which the rights of nature were invoked in litigation.[118] Of those thirteen cases, ten were successful – a yield of 76.9 percent.[119] For example, three years after ratification of the new constitutional provisions, two Americans living near the Vilcabamba River successfully sued on behalf of the river to stop a proposed road-widening project[120] on grounds that the construction altered the river's natural flow.[121] The Constitutional Court of Ecuador later heard arguments on proposed mining projects in the Los Cedros Protected Forest,[122] holding in December of 2021 that the mining projects violated the rights of nature and banning all extractive activities in the Protected Forest.[123] The case was the first rights of nature case to reach Ecuador's highest court, and it could have significant implications for extraction projects in Ecuador's other 186 Protected Forests.[124]

II. SOUTH AMERICAN EXAMPLES: BOLIVIA AND COLOMBIA

Ecuador's constitutional amendment rapidly inspired the adoption of similar principles around South America and, soon afterward, the world. Following Ecuador's

---

[114] *Id.* art. 71.
[115] *Id.* art. 71.
[116] *Id.* art. 73.
[117] Craig M. Kauffman & Pamela L. Martin, *Can Rights of Nature Make Development More Sustainable? Why Some Ecuadorian Lawsuits Succeed and Others Fail*, 92 WORLD DEV. 130, 133 (2017).
[118] *Id.* at 133–34.
[119] *Id.* at 134.
[120] Mihnea Tanasescu, *When a River Is a Person: From Ecuador to New Zealand, Nature Gets Its Day in Court*, THE CONVERSATION (June 19, 2017), https://theconversation.com/when-a-river-is-a-person-from-ecuador-to-new-zealand-nature-gets-its-day-in-court-79278.
[121] María Valeria Berros, *Defending Rivers: Vilcabamba in the South of Ecuador*, 6 RACHEL CARSON CTR. PERSPS. 37, 38 (2017).
[122] Rebekah Hayden, *Rights of Nature in Ecuador*, THE ECOLOGIST (Nov. 6, 2020), https://theecologist.org/2020/nov/06/rights-nature-ecuador.
[123] Press Release, Ctr. for Biological Diversity, Ecuador's Highest Court Enforces Constitutional 'Rights of Nature' to Safeguard Los Cedros Protected Forest (Dec. 2, 2021), https://biologicaldiversity.org/w/news/press-releases/ecuadors-highest-court-enforces-constitutional-rights-of-nature-to-safeguard-los-cedros-protected-forest-2021-12-02/.
[124] *Id.*

B. The Rights of Nature Movement

example, Bolivia adopted rights of nature provisions legislatively in the 2010 Law of the Rights of Mother Earth.[125] The law states that Madre Tierra, Mother Earth, is entitled to life, biodiversity, water, clean air, balance, restoration, and to be free from pollution.[126] Bolivia's move was the first statutory recognition of the rights of nature worldwide, but it was critiqued for failure to include sufficient guidance or mechanics for enforcement.[127] Accordingly, the legislature expanded its effort in 2012 with enactment of the Framework Law of the Mother Earth and Integral Development for Living Well, specifically designed to operationalize the specific rights in Mother Earth that had been set out in the 2010 law.[128] In 2010, Bolivia hosted the World People's Conference on Climate Change and the Rights of Mother Earth, resulting in the *Universal Declaration on the Rights of Mother Earth*, which was issued by the Conference and submitted to the United Nations for its consideration.[129]

In Colombia, the rights of nature were first articulated by the judiciary after a series of legal challenges resulted in the judicial recognition of rights for certain national parks, rivers, and lakes.[130] The Colombia Constitutional Court, which is specifically tasked with resolving constitutional issues, first recognized the rights of the Atrato River in 2016 as "an entity subject to rights of protection, conservation, maintenance and restoration."[131] In 2018, responding to a suit by youth plaintiffs against the government for the right to a healthy environment, the Colombian Supreme Court built on the Atrato River decision to recognize the Amazon River as "an entity subject of rights."[132] In addition to creating an Intergenerational Pact

---

[125] *See generally* Paola Villavicencio Calzadilla & Louis J. Kotzé, *Living in Harmony with Nature? A Critical Appraisal of the Rights of Mother Earth in Bolivia*, 7 TRANSNAT'L ENV'T L. 397 (2018) (extensively detailing the legislative history of Bolivia's rights of nature laws).

[126] Ley de Derechos de la Madre Tierra [Law of the Rights of Mother Earth], 2010 (Law No. 71) ch. III, art. 7 (Bol.).

[127] For example, when Indigenous resistance to roadbuilding through the Isiboro Ségure Indigenous Territory and National Park led to violence, lawmakers were forced to recognize that the new law lacked any means by which authorities were required to account for or protect the Rights of Mother Earth when threatened. *See* Pablo Sólon, *The Rights of Mother Earth*, *in* THE CLIMATE CRISIS: SOUTH AFRICAN AND GLOBAL DEMOCRATIC ECO-SOCIALIST ALTERNATIVES 107, 121–24 (Vishwas Satgar ed., 2018); *See also* Calzadilla & Kotzé, *supra* note 125, at 404–05 (noting that while the Bolivian Constitution recognizes the importance of protecting nature, it does not constitutionally entrench the rights of nature as firmly as the Ecuadorian counterpart).

[128] *See* Ley Marco de la Madre Tierra y Desarrollo Integral para Vivir Bien [Framework Law of the Mother Earth and Integral Development for Living Well], 2012 (Law No. 301) (Bol.); Anna Hernandez, *Defending Mother Earth in Bolivia*, CULTURAL SURVIVAL (June 19, 2016), www.cultural survival.org/news/defending-mother-earth-bolivia.

[129] Sólon, *supra* note 127, at 122–23.

[130] *Rights of Nature Law and Policy*, HARMONY WITH NATURE, U.N., http://harmonywithnatureun.org/rightsOfNature (listing recent legal decisions regarding the rights of nature in Colombia).

[131] Corte Constitucional [C.C.] [Constitutional Court], November 10, 2016, Sentencia T-622/16 (Colom.) (Dignity Rts. Project trans., 2019), https://delawarelaw.widener.edu/files/resources/riveratratodecision englishdrpdellaw.pdf.

[132] Corte Suprema de Justicia [C.S.J.] [Supreme Court], Sala. Civ. Apr. 5, 2018, M.P. Luis Armando Tolosa Villabona, STC4360-2018, Radicación n. 11001-22-03-000-2018-00319-01 (Colom.),

for the Life of the Colombian Amazon, the Supreme Court required Amazonian municipalities to create and implement territorial land use plans respecting the rights of the Amazon and required action plans to combat deforestation and mitigate the impacts of climate change.[133] The similarity between this youth suit seeking a healthy environment and the trust-rights litigation described in Chapter 9 is striking – as is the strikingly different reception.[134]

III. EXAMPLES FROM OCEANIA: NEW ZEALAND AND AUSTRALIA

As in South America, the rights of nature movements in Oceania have been driven by the core values and cultural identities of local Indigenous cultures. Departing from the broad grants of rights enacted for nature in Ecuador and Bolivia, however, the nations of Oceania have set forth specific rights in identified natural features.

Over the past decade, New Zealand has recognized the legal personhood of three specific natural features. In 2014, the New Zealand Parliament first granted legal personhood to Te Urewera National Park,[135] "the homeland and the heartland of the Tūhoe people"[136] and a historic source of conflict between the Crown and the tribe.[137] The statute recognizes that Te Urewera "has all the rights, powers, duties, and liabilities of a legal person"[138] and transfers ownership of the land from the Crown to Te Urewera itself.[139] The statute also establishes a legal guardian for the protected park, the Te Urewera Board.[140] The Board is composed of nine members – six appointed by the trustees of Tūhoe Te Uru Taumatua and three appointed by the Minister of Conservation – and is empowered to exercise and protect the rights set forth in the law.[141] The Te Urewara Act is conceived as a return to the

---

www.dejusticia.org/wp-content/uploads/2018/01/Fallo-Corte-Suprema-de-Justicia-Litigio-Cambio-Clim%C3%A1tico.pdf?x54537; *Colombian Supreme Court Rules to Protect Future Generations and Amazon Rainforest in Climate Change Case*, ESCR-Net (Jan.11, 2019), www.escr-net.org/caselaw/2019/stc-4360-2018; *see also* Ryan et al., *Comprehensive Analysis, supra* note 8, at 2516–17.

[133] *See* Nicholas Bryner, *Colombian Supreme Court Recognizes Rights of the Amazon River Ecosystem*, INT'L UNION FOR THE CONSERVATION OF NATURE (Apr. 20, 2018), www.iucn.org/news/world-commission-environmental-law/201804/colombian-supreme-court-recognizes-rights-amazon-river-ecosystem (quoting the Supreme Court opinion, which is written in Spanish and translated in this article).

[134] *See* Chapter 9(B) ("Trust-Rights Advocacy in Action: Atmospheric Trust and Climate Rights Litigation"); Juliana v. United States, 217 F. Supp. 3d 1224 (D. Or. 2016), *rev'd*, Juliana v. United States, No. 24-684, D.C. No. 6:15-cv-1517, 2024 WL 5102489, (May 1, 2024), *cert. denied*, 604 U.S. 645 (2025).

[135] Te Awa Tupua (Whanganui River Claims Settlement) Act 2017, subpt. 12 (N.Z.); *see also* Ryan et al., *Comprehensive Analysis, supra* note 8, at 2517–18. Separately, New Zealand also recognized legal personhood in a specific mountain, Mt. Taranaki, and the Te Urewera National Park. *Id.*

[136] TE KAWA O TE UREWERA [TE UREWERA MANAGEMENT PLAN], 43 TE UREWERA BD. (2017).

[137] *See generally* Vincent O'Malley, *Tūhoe-Crown Settlement – Historical Background*, MĀORI L. REV. (Oct. 2014) (discussing the turbulent history behind the Tūhoe-Crown Settlement).

[138] Te Urewera Act 2014, subpt. 11(1) (2014) (N.Z.).

[139] *Id.* subpt. 12(3).

[140] *Id.* subpts. 16–20.

[141] *Id.* subpts. 19, 21(2).

B. The Rights of Nature Movement 385

philosophy of environmental rights that have always been part of Tūhoe culture.[142] As the Te Urewera Board's management plan observes, "The Act does not establish the Te Urewera identity rather it liberates it from human speculation in order that nature and the natural world return to its primal role, revered and served by those of her children she has given life to."[143]

In 2017, three years after the recognition of Te Urewera, the New Zealand Parliament granted legal personhood to the Whanganui River (Te Awa Tupua) watershed, resolving a legal fight by the local Māori people that dates back to 1873.[144] The legislation grants legal personhood to the river as "an indivisible and living whole, comprising the Whanganui River from the mountains to the sea, incorporating all its physical and metaphysical elements,"[145] and creates the office of Te Pou Tupua, a body of two representatives, one appointed by the Crown and one appointed by the Māori communities, to act as legal guardians on behalf of the river.[146] Finally, New Zealand has also granted personhood to a specific mountain, Mt. Taranaki,[147] a dormant volcano on the west coast of the North Island.[148] This legislation appoints a joint entity composed of both Māori tribes and representatives of the British Commonwealth Crown as "the human face of" of Mt. Taranki, to "act in the name of" the mountain as legal guardians.[149]

Neighboring Australia began recognizing limited rights to specific natural areas shortly after New Zealand pioneered the concept at Te Urewera National Park in 2014. In 2017, the Australian state of Victoria recognized the Yarra River as "one living and integrated natural entity."[150] Victoria mandated the development and implementation of a Yarra Strategic Plan, as well as the creation of the Birrarung Council, a statutory advisory board designated to speak and advocate for the Yarra River.[151] Like the rights of nature efforts in New Zealand, the Victorian law incorporates traditional Australian Aboriginal values.[152] But unlike the New

---

[142] TE UREWERA BD., *supra* note 136, at 24.
[143] *Id.*
[144] Yarra River Protection Act 2017 (Vict.) subpt. 5(b) (Austl.); *see also* Ryan et al., *Comprehensive Analysis*, *supra* note 8, at 2518–19; Erin L. O'Donnell & Julia Talbot-Jones, *Creating Legal Rights for Rivers: Lessons from Australia, New Zealand, and India*, 23 ECOLOGY & SOC'Y 1, 4 (2018).
[145] Te Awa Tupua (Whanganui River Claims Settlement) Act 2017, subpt. 12 (N.Z.).
[146] *Id.* at subpt. 20.
[147] Record of Understanding for Mount Taranaki, Pouākai, and the Kaitake Ranges (Dec. 20, 2017) (N.Z.) [hereinafter Record of Understanding], www.govt.nz/assets/Documents/OTS/Taranaki-Maunga/Taranaki-Maunga-Te-Anga-Putakerongo-Record-of-Understanding-20-December-2017.pdf.
[148] Global Volcanism Program, Taranaki (241030), SMITHSONIAN INST., https://volcano.si.edu/volcano.cfm?vn=241030.
[149] Record of Understanding, *supra* note 147, at subpts. 5.14–5.15.
[150] Yarra River Protection Act 2017 (Vict.) subpt. 5(b) (Austl.).
[151] *Id.* at pts. 4, 5.
[152] Katie O'Bryan, *Indigenous Rights and River Rights: Australia and New Zealand*, GLOB. WATER F. (June 7, 2018), https://globalwaterforum.org/2018/06/07/indigenous-rights-and-river-rights-australia-and-new-zealand.

Zealand model, the Australian corollary was passed at the state level, rather than the national level. More importantly, it does not grant full legal personhood to the river, but protects environmental rights associated with the river basin by requiring the development of a strategic plan to inform the future management of the region.[153] Some proponents of the rights of nature have advocated that Australia broaden its rights of nature initiatives to create legal rights in the Great Barrier Reef,[154] the world's largest coral reef system off the Australian east coast,[155] and the Great Artesian Basin, the largest and deepest artesian groundwater basin in the world,[156] from which most of inland Australia draws its drinking water.[157] However, these efforts have yet to materialize into legislative action.[158]

IV. IN ASIA: INDIA AND BANGLADESH

In 2017, in the northern Indian state of Uttarakhand, traversed by the Himalayas, the High Court of Uttarakhand granted legal personhood to the Ganges and Yamuna Rivers.[159] Ten days later, the same court granted legal rights to the Gangotri and Yamunotri Glaciers above these rivers.[160] The court observed that the rights granted "shall be equivalent to the rights of human beings and the injury/harm caused to these bodies shall be treated as harm/injury caused to the human beings."[161] The Supreme Court of India ultimately stayed the lower court rulings on the Ganges and Yamuna Rivers,[162] as well as the Gangotri and Yamunotri Glaciers.[163] Despite the Supreme Court's ruling, rights of nature initiatives have continued to develop in India, especially in the North. In 2018, the Uttarakhand High Court acted once

---

[153] Id.
[154] U.N. Secretary-General, *Harmony with Nature*, ¶ 46, U.N Doc. A/74/236 (July 29, 2019) (noting that in 2018, one Australian Senator "called for the adoption of rights of Nature laws, in particular for iconic ecosystems such as the Great Barrier Reef, the Murray-Darling Basin and the Great Artesian Basin").
[155] *Great Barrier Reef*, ENCYCLOPEDIA BRITANNICA (June 18, 2021), www.britannica.com/place/Great-Barrier-Reef.
[156] *Great Artesian Basin Strategic Management Plan*, DEP'T OF AGRIC., WATER & THE ENV'T (Austl.) (June 18, 2021), www.agriculture.gov.au/sites/default/files/documents/strategic-management-plan.pdf.
[157] Id.
[158] *Rights of Nature*, AUSTL. EARTH L. CTR., www.earthlaws.org.au/aelc/rights-of-nature (last visited Nov. 20, 2023).
[159] Mohd. Salim v. State of Uttarakhand (2017) Writ Petition (PIL) No. 126 of 2014 (UTT H.C.) (India), www.nonhumanrights.org/content/uploads/WPPIL-126-14.pdf.
[160] Lalit Miglani v. State of Uttarakhand (2017) Writ Petition (PIL) No. 140 of 2015 (UTT H.C.) (India), www.indiaenvironmentportal.org.in/files/living%20entity%20Gangotri%20Himalaya%20Uttarakhand%20High%20Court%20Order.pdf.
[161] Id. at *65.
[162] *India's Ganges and Yamuna Rivers Are "Not Living Entities,"* BBC (July 7, 2017), www.bbc.com/news/world-asia-india-40537701.
[163] Stellina Jolly & K.S. Roshan Menon, *Of Ebbs and Flows: Understanding the Legal Consequences of Granting Personhood to Natural Entities in India*, TRANSNAT'L ENV'T L. 1, 2 n.5 (2021) (explaining that the appeals of both the river and glacier decisions have been grouped together and stayed).

again to declare that animals are "legal entities."[164] In 2019, the Punjab and Haryana High Court also declared animals to be legal persons,[165] and the following year, it declared Chandigarh's Sukhna Lake to be a living entity.[166]

In Bangladesh, all rivers in the country have been granted legal personhood.[167] In 2019, following several years of environmental litigation over serious water pollution and illegal riverbank development,[168] the Bangladeshi Supreme Court granted all of its rivers the same legal status as human beings and called for the removal of all illegal establishments on their banks.[169] In 2016, a nongovernmental organization had filed suit over pollution and illegal construction on the Turag River, the upper tributary of the major Buriganga River in the Dhaka region in the center of the country.[170] By 2019, the case made its way to the High Court of Bangladesh, which resolved the case with reference to both the public trust doctrine and emerging rights of nature principles. It held that the government had an obligation under the public trust doctrine to protect the river, but it also declared that the river, together with all other rivers within the country, are "living entit[ies]" entitled to rights as "legal persons."[171]

V. IN AFRICA: UGANDA

In 2019, Uganda became the first nation in Africa to enact national rights of nature legislation in adopting the National Environment Act,[172] fifteen years after the Ugandan Supreme Court first recognized the public trust doctrine.[173] The National

---

[164] *See* Vineet Upadhyay, *Animals Have Equal Rights as Humans, Says Uttarakhand High Court*, TIMES OF INDIA (July 5, 2018) https://timesofindia.indiatimes.com/city/dehradun/members-of-animal-kingdom-to-be-treated-as-legal-entities-ukhand-hc/articleshow/64860996.cms.

[165] Karnail Singh v. State of Haryana, 2019 SCC OnLine P&H 704 (India), www.livelaw.in/pdf_upload/pdf_upload-361239.pdf. Appeals to some (but not all) Indian rights of nature decisions remain pending as this essay goes to press.

[166] Court on Its Own Motion v. Chandigarh Administration, CWP No. 18253 of 2009 (P&H H.C.) (2020) (Unreported), www.livelaw.in/pdf_upload/pdf_upload-370827.pdf.

[167] *See* Rina Chandran, *Fears of Evictions as Bangladesh Gives Rivers Legal Rights*, THOMSON REUTERS FOUND. NEWS (July 4, 2019), https://news.trust.org/item/20190704113918-rzada; *see also* Ryan et al., *Comprehensive Analysis, supra* note 8, at 2516–21.

[168] *See Protecting Rights of Rivers: Turning Intention into Action*, DAILY STAR (Nov. 20, 2020), www.thedailystar.net/law-our-rights/news/protecting-rights-rivers-turning-intention-action-1998201.

[169] *See* Chandran, *supra* note 167.

[170] *Legal Rights of Rivers – An International Trend?*, CLIENTEARTH (Mar. 13, 2019), www.clientearth.org/projects/access-to-justice-for-a-greener-europe/updates/legal-rights-of-rivers-an-international-trend.

[171] Mari Margil, *Bangladesh Supreme Court Upholds Rights of Rivers*, MEDIUM (Aug. 24, 2020), https://medium.com/@mari_margil/bangladesh-supreme-court-upholds-rights-of-rivers-ede78568d8aa; Chandran, *supra* note 167.

[172] *See Uganda Recognises Rights of Nature, Customary Laws, Sacred Natural Sites*, THE GAIA FOUND. (Mar. 29, 2021), https://gaiafoundation.org/uganda-recognises-rights-of-nature-customary-laws-sacred-natural-sites/.

[173] Advocs. Coal. for Dev. & Env't v. Att'y Gen., Misc. Cause No. 0100 of 2004 (July 11, 2005) (Uganda), https://elaw.org/system/files/attachments/publicresource/ug.Acode_.v.AttorneyGeneral_o.pdf.; *see supra* text accompanying notes 58–64 (discussing the public trust doctrine in Uganda).

Environment Act follows Ecuador's model in declaring that "Nature has the right to exist, persist, maintain and regenerate its vital cycles, structure, functions and its processes in evolution."[174] Critics contend that the nation's adherence to environmentally harmful oil and gas policies contradict this commitment,[175] but indigenous Bagungu communities in western Uganda have responded with localized efforts to enact legislation that protects sacred natural sites and advances rights of nature principles in accordance with customary Bagungu laws.[176]

VI. IN EUROPE: SPAIN AND SUSSEX, ENGLAND

Last among inhabited continents, the movement has now found a foothold in Europe. Spain became the first European nation to enact a rights of nature law in 2022, when it established legal personhood for the Mar Menor Lagoon near its southeastern Mediterranean coast, perhaps Europe's largest saltwater lagoon, which has suffered severe environmental harm from coastal development and agriculture.[177] The law, spurred by a ballot initiative signed by 600,000 citizens and later approved by the national Senate, establishes the lagoon's right "to exist as an ecosystem and to evolve naturally," recognizing associated rights to environmental protection, conservation and restoration.[178] While Spain provides a national example to match its Asian and South American counterparts, the U.K. appears to be following the more American model of municipal experimentation, starting with the English town of Lewes's 2023 decision to grant legal rights to the River Ouse in Sussex.[179]

b. U.S. and North American Tribal Initiatives

This flurry of international activity since Ecuador's dramatic 2008 constitutional embrace also spurred growing interest in rights of nature initiatives in the United States.[180] A raft of municipal rights of nature ordinances have been proposed, mostly to protect waterways, some more successfully than others. In contrast to the international examples listed earlier, some of the most celebrated initiatives undertaken

---

[174] National Environmental Act, 2019 (Act No. 5/2019) part I, section 4 (Uganda), https://static1.squarespace.com/static/5e3f36df772e5208fa96513c/t/5fbd12907dd1bd0a7624e251/1606226577880/UGANDA+National-Environment-Act-2019.pdf.

[175] Jack Losh, *Uganda Joins the Rights-of-Nature Movement but Won't Stop Oil Drilling*, NAT'L GEOGRAPHIC (Jun. 2, 2021), www.nationalgeographic.com/environment/article/uganda-joins-the-rights-of-nature-movement-but-wont-stop-oil-drilling.

[176] See THE GAIA FOUND., *supra* note 172.

[177] Joseph Wilson, *Spain Gives Personhood Status to Mar Menor Salt-Water Lagoon*, AP NEWS (Sep. 21, 2022), https://apnews.com/article/science-spain-climate-and-environment-government-politics-a7952765649ad9d171b0ada314e34bcd.

[178] *Id.*

[179] Frankie Elliot, *Sussex River to be the First in England to Have Its Own Rights*, SUSSEX WORLD (Feb. 22, 2023), www.sussexexpress.co.uk/news/people/sussex-river-to-be-the-first-in-england-to-have-its-own-rights-4037652.

[180] For a fuller account, see Ryan et al., *Comprehensive Analysis*, *supra* note at 2514–39.

B. The Rights of Nature Movement

by American municipalities were judicially overturned or legislatively preempted afterward, indicating the significant hurdles that rights of nature approaches face within the U.S. legal system.

This section briefly reviews the emerging rights of nature initiatives around the United States, noting examples from Pennsylvania, Ohio, California, and Florida before reviewing examples from Tribal Nations within the United States and Canada. In North America, the most successful examples of rights of nature legal initiatives have taken place among native communities within Indian Tribes and First Nations, which have enacted a set of rights of nature laws less likely to meet resistance within indigenous legal systems.[181] Yet as the examples below reveal, even rights of nature initiatives that fail in litigation can continue to impact public decision-making through the political process.

1. Pennsylvania – Tamaqua Borough, City of Pittsburgh, and Grant Township

Tamaqua Borough's Sewage Ordinance

Ecuador's constitutional recognition in 2008 may be the most famous rights of nature initiative in the world, but the first community in the world to formally recognize legal personhood for nature is a small town of 7,000 people in central Pennsylvania: Tamaqua Borough.[182] The effort was inspired in the mid 2000s by opposition to a proposed sewage sludge dumpsite in the town, which is northwest of Allentown, Pennsylvania.[183] In 2006, after lobbying by community advocates, the Borough Council adopted the Tamaqua Borough Sewage Sludge Ordinance, prohibiting the land application of sewage sludge and recognizing that "natural communities, and ecosystems shall be considered 'persons' for purposes of the enforcement of the civil rights of those residents, natural communities, and ecosystems."[184]

City of Pittsburg's Anti-Fracking Ordinance

Tamaqua's action motivated the larger Pennsylvania City of Pittsburgh to adopt rights of nature principles in 2010 in a bid to stop hydraulic fracking within its boundaries. Hoping to circumvent state preemption of municipal oil and gas regulations, the city adopted an ordinance that not only prohibited fracking, but also granted the "inalienable and fundamental rights to exist and flourish" to "[n]atural communities and ecosystems, including, but not limited to, wetlands, streams,

---

[181] Id. at 2536–38.

[182] *Timeline*, Glob. All. for Rts. of Nature, https://therightsofnature.org/timeline (noting that Tamaqua Borough was the first place in the world to officially recognize the rights of nature).

[183] Madeleine Sheehan Perkins, *How Pittsburgh Embraced a Radical Environmental Movement Popping Up in Conservative Towns across America*, Bus. Insider (July 9, 2017) www.businessinsider.com/rights-for-nature-preventing-fracking-pittsburgh-pennsylvania-2017-7.

[184] Tamaqua Borough, Pa., Tamaqua Borough Sewage Sludge Ordinance, Ordinance No. 612 (Sept. 19, 2006).

rivers, [and] aquifers ...."[185] Doug Shields, former President of the Pittsburgh City Council, observed, "We not only banned fracking, but we asserted our right to self-government. We asserted nature's rights, and our obligation to protect the ecosystems that sustain us."[186]

Four years after the adoption of Pittsburgh's anti-fracking ordinance, as discussed in Chapter 8, the Pennsylvania Supreme Court invalidated the fracking preemption statute under the state constitution, which codifies an expansive version of the public trust doctrine.[187] While not a party to the suit, the City of Pittsburgh had filed an amicus curiae brief and argued that the preemption prohibited local governments from meeting their civic obligations to protect public health and welfare through local zoning regulations.[188] While the city did not raise the public trust doctrine or the rights of nature directly in its brief, the court situated the city's understanding of civic duty as within the constitutional recognition of these public trust obligations.

The Pennsylvania fray over fracking thus presents a rare example where the rights of nature and public trust doctrine have been deployed simultaneously to resolve the same underlying issue. The fact that the court raised the public trust doctrine sua sponte suggests that the parties did not think the doctrine offered a viable legal argument on which to fight the preemption in the legal arguments they raised in their briefs – perhaps explaining why Pittsburgh turned to the untested rights of nature as an alternative. It will be interesting to see whether the court's action has changed the environmental legal calculus there going forward.

Anti-Fracking Home Rule Charter of Grant Township. Rights of nature principles continue to play a notable role in the ongoing regulatory battles over fracking the Marcellus Shale in Pennsylvania. In 2020, the small community of Grant Township won one of the most high-profile and hard-fought victories for rights of nature principles in the state. In 2014, Pennsylvania General Energy (PGE) had received an initial permit to convert an existing gas well into a fracking wastewater injection well in Grant Township, a tiny town of fewer than one thousand people.[189] The proposal to inject 42,000 gallons of fracking wastewater a day was met with opposition from these residents.[190] The Township responded by adopting a Community Bill of Rights Ordinance in 2014, prohibiting the disposal of fracking waste within the township, restricting corporate personhood, and recognizing the rights of "[n]atural communities and ecosystems within Grant Township, including but not limited to, rivers, streams, and aquifers ... to exist, flourish, and naturally

---

[185] PITTSBURGH, PA., CODE § 618.03 (2010).
[186] *Doug Shields from We the People 2.0 – The Second American Revolution*, CMTY. ENV'T LEGAL DEF. FUND (Oct. 19, 2016), https://celdf.org/2016/10/doug-shields-people-2-0-second-american-revolution.
[187] Robinson Twp. v. Commonwealth, 83 A.3d 901, 976–78 (Pa. 2013).
[188] Amicus Curiae Brief of Council of the City of Pittsburgh at 3, *id.* (No. 284 M.D. 2012).
[189] Pa. Gen. Energy Co. v. Grant Twp., No. 14-209ERIE, 2017 WL 1215444, at *3 (W.D. Pa. Mar. 31, 2017).
[190] Justin Nobel, *How a Small Town Is Standing Up to Fracking*, ROLLING STONE (May 22, 2017), www.rollingstone.com/politics/politics-news/how-a-small-town-is-standing-up-to-fracking-117307.

evolve."[191] When the ordinance was challenged by PGE, a group of local environmental advocates, the East Run Hellbenders Society, unsuccessfully attempted to intervene as legal guardians on behalf of the Little Mahoning Watershed.[192]

The community rights ordinance was eventually struck down in federal court as "run[ning] afoul of constitutional protections afforded corporations such as PGE and attempt[ing] to immunize Grant Township from clashes with current federal and state law."[193] The Township responded by enacting a Home Rule Charter that incorporated the same prohibition on fracking waste, limits on corporate personhood, and a rights of nature provision included in the original ordinance.[194] In 2017, PGE was granted a permit to inject fracking waste into an existing natural gas well,[195] but after a prolonged legal battle, the permitting agency reversed course, citing the Home Rule Charter's ban on injection wells for fracking.[196] The impact of the charter in this instance highlights the efficacy of rights of nature initiatives in the political sphere, often in comparison to litigation. Indeed, PGE again filed suit against Grant Township in 2020,[197] seeking to establish that the Home Rule Charter is unconstitutional and unenforceable.[198] The trial court concluded that the charter was legally void, and the township has appealed to the Pennsylvania Supreme Court.[199] At the time this book goes to press, it is not yet clear whether Grant Township's rights of nature charter will remain in force.

II. SANTA MONICA'S BILL OF RIGHTS FOR SUSTAINABILITY

In 2013, the City Council of Santa Monica, California, unanimously approved the "Bill of Rights for Sustainability," granting "[n]atural communities and ecosystems ... fundamental and inalienable rights to exist and flourish" within the city limits.[200] The ordinance also allows city residents to bring legal actions on behalf of "groundwater aquifers, atmospheric systems, marine waters, and native species" within the city.[201] Santa Monica is a rare example of a proactive rights of nature ordinance that was not adopted in response to an immediate environmental threat. To

---

[191] Grant Twp., Pa., Community Bill of Rights Ordinance §§ 2(d), 3(a), 5(a) (June 1, 2014).
[192] Pa. Gen. Energy Co. v. Grant Twp., 658 F. App'x. 37, 42–43 (3d Cir. 2016).
[193] *Pa. Gen. Energy*, 2017 WL 1215444, at *16.
[194] Grant Twp., Pa., Home Rule Charter §§ 105, 107, 301, 401 (Nov. 21, 2015).
[195] Laura Legere, *Pa. DEP Revokes Permit for Grant Twp. Oil and Gas Waste Well*, PITT. POST-GAZETTE (Mar. 27, 2020), www.post-gazette.com/business/powersource/2020/03/27/Pennsylvania-DEP-revokes-permit-oil-gas-waste-well-Grant-home-rule-charter/stories/202003260151.
[196] *Id.*
[197] Complaint, Pa. Gen. Energy Co. v. Grant Twp., No. 20-cv-00351 (W.D. Pa. Dec. 9, 2020).
[198] *Id.* at 3.
[199] However, some speculate that the injection well will be "plugged" by PGE to avoid further litigation. John Hurdle, *A Pennsylvania Community Wins a Reprieve on Toxic Fracking Wastewater*, INSIDE CLIMATE NEWS (June 13, 2023) https://insideclimatenews.org/news/13062023/pennsylvania-fracking-wastewater-injection-wells/.
[200] SANTA MONICA, CAL., MUN. CODE § 12.02.030(b) (2019).
[201] *Id.*

date, neither the city nor its citizens have utilized the ordinance to bring an action on behalf of nature, but neither has the ordinance been challenged.

III. OHIO: THE (ERSTWHILE) LAKE ERIE BILL OF RIGHTS

In 2014, the same year that the Flint, Michigan, water crisis began,[202] the City of Toledo, Ohio, was forced to warn local residents not to use their tap water for drinking, bathing, or cooking.[203] A harmful algae bloom in Lake Erie, the source of the city's drinking water, had rendered the water toxic. The algae produce microcystin, a toxin that causes gastrointestinal, respiratory, neurological, and dermatological health effects.[204] For three days, the 400,000 city residents had to rely on bottled water instead.[205]

After this three-day tap water ban, Toledo residents successfully launched a multiyear effort to amend their city charter with the Lake Erie Bill of Rights (LEBOR), one of the most ambitious rights of nature initiatives in the United States. In its own words, LEBOR was created by residents to "reclaim, reaffirm, and assert our inherent and inalienable rights, and to extend legal rights to our natural environment in order to ensure that the natural world ... [is] no longer subordinated to the accumulation of surplus wealth and unaccountable political power."[206] LEBOR asserted three different sets of rights: (1) the rights of the Lake Erie ecosystem, (2) the rights of the residents to a clean and healthy environment, and (3) the right of local community self-governance.[207] Under LEBOR, Lake Erie and its watershed "possess the right to exist, flourish, and naturally evolve," and any local resident (or the city itself) has the right to sue to enforce these rights.[208]

LEBOR also engaged one of the more powerful rhetorical foils of the rights of nature movement – the idea that corporations are granted legal personhood while natural systems are not. While LEBOR explicitly granted legal personhood to the Lake Erie ecosystem, it also expressly restricted legal personhood for corporations that violate the law, stating that "[c]orporations that violate this law, or that seek to violate this law, shall not be deemed to be 'persons' to the extent that such treatment would interfere with the rights or prohibitions enumerated by this law."[209]

---

[202] Merrit Kennedy, *Lead-Laced Water in Flint: A Step-by-Step Look at the Makings of a Crisis*, NAT'L PUB. RADIO (NPR) (Apr. 20, 2016), www.npr.org/sections/thetwo-way/2016/04/20/465545378/lead-laced-water-in-flint-a-step-by-step-look-at-the-makings-of-a-crisis.

[203] Toledoans for Safe Water's Amicus Brief re Motions for Judgment on the Pleadings at 7, Drewes Farms P'ship v. City of Toledo, 441 F. Supp. 3d 551 (N.D. Ohio 2020) (No. 19-cv-00434).

[204] Elizabeth D. Hilborn et al., *Algal Bloom-Associated Disease Outbreaks among Users of Freshwater Lakes – United States, 2009–2010*, 63 MORBIDITY & MORTALITY WKLY. REP. 11 (2014).

[205] Michael Wines, *Behind Toledo's Water Crisis, a Long-Troubled Lake Erie*, N.Y. TIMES (Aug. 4, 2014), www.nytimes.com/2014/08/04/us/toledo-faces-second-day-of-water-ban.html.

[206] TOLEDO, OHIO, MUN. CODE ch. XVII, § 253 (2019).

[207] *Id.* § 254(a)-(c).

[208] *Id.* § 254(a), (d).

[209] *Id.* § 257(a).

B. *The Rights of Nature Movement*   393

The day after Toledo voters approved the measure, the city was sued by agricultural interests.[210] The plaintiff, Drewes Farms, alleged primarily that LEBOR exceeded Toledo's authority as a municipal arm of the state, was unconstitutionally vague, and violated due process.[211] Drewes Farms argued that by applying fertilizer on their land, they might run afoul of LEBOR's protections and expose their operations to liability, despite legally operating under a certificate by the Ohio Department of Agriculture.[212] While the case was winding its way through federal court, the Ohio State Legislature acted directly to preempt the initiative and specifically prohibited any person from bringing a legal action on behalf of an ecosystem.[213] In 2020, the federal district court agreed with the plaintiff's arguments and invalidated LEBOR, noting that it was "well-intentioned" but unconstitutionally vague and beyond the power of local government.[214] The City of Toledo initially fought the decision, but in May 2020, it voluntarily dismissed its appeal, citing budgetary constraints.[215]

IV. FLORIDA

Like Pennsylvania, Florida provides an interesting example of a state in which the rights of nature movement and public trust doctrine could intersect in the context of unfolding environmental law. As detailed in Chapter 8, Florida has codified the public trust doctrine in both the state constitution and statutory law, emphasizing the sovereign ownership of submerged lands.[216] However, the Florida public trust has thus far not played a significant role in environmental advocacy. Unlike New Jersey, Florida has not applied the doctrine to protect its upland beaches or drinking

---

[210] Complaint at 2–3, Drewes Farms P'ship v. City of Toledo, 441 F. Supp. 3d 551 (N.D. Ohio 2020) (No. 19-cv-00434) (alleging violations of the First Amendment, the Equal Protection Clause, the Fifth Amendment (for vagueness), and deprivation of rights without due process).

[211] Order Invalidating Lake Erie Bill of Rights, *Drewes Farms*, 441 F. Supp. 3d at 556.

[212] *Id.*

[213] H.R. 166, 133d Gen. Assemb., Reg. Sess. § 2305.011 (Ohio 2019).

[214] *Drewes Farms*, 441 F. Supp. 3d at 557–58.

[215] Tom Henry, *City Quietly Drops Appeal of Lake Erie Bill of Rights Ruling*, BLADE (May 11, 2020), www.toledoblade.com/local/environment/2020/05/11/toledo-quietly-drops-appeal-of-lebor-ruling-lake-erie/stories/20200511082.

[216] Article X, Section 11 of the Florida Constitution reads:

> The title to lands under navigable waters, within the boundaries of the state, which have not been alienated, including beaches below mean high water lines, is held by the state, by virtue of its sovereignty, in trust for all the people. Sale of such lands may be authorized by law, but only when in the public interest. Private use of portions of such lands may be authorized by law, but only when not contrary to the public interest.

> FLA. CONST. art. X, § 11; *see also* Broward v. Mabry, 50 So. 826, 829–30 (Fla. 1909) (affirming the sovereign ownership aspect of the public trust doctrine); Coastal Petrol. Co. v. Am. Cyanamid Co., 492 So. 2d 339, 342–43 (Fla. 1986) (holding that the trust imposes a legal duty on the state to preserve and control navigable rivers, lakes, and tidelands for public navigation, fishing, swimming, and other lawful uses).

water resources.[217] Unlike California, it has not explicitly required the balancing of environmental values against other values associated with state waterways in the state's ambitious water management system.[218] Yet as advocates have noted, the lack of an environmentally dynamic public trust doctrine in Florida is not for lack of need; the state is beset by environmental woes as relevant laws struggle to keep pace with explosive development and population growth.[219] Florida's complex matrix of waterways and aquifers is also uniquely vulnerable, given the local importance of these groundwater resources, which are not explicitly protected by the state's public trust doctrine.[220]

Given the ineffectiveness of public trust protections and permissive environmental laws that have allowed the degradation of so many state waterways, advocates have increasingly sought environmental protection through rights of nature initiatives. In a first for the nation, explicit reference to the rights of nature was even included in the platform of one of the state's two main political parties. In October 2019, the Florida Democratic Party became the first state-level political party to incorporate the rights of nature into their platform, declaring "to adequately protect our waters, we support communities' rights in reclaiming home rule authority and recognizing and protecting the inherent rights of nature, as we have done for corporations ..."[221]

The rights of nature movement emerged in Florida after several ecological disasters involving emergency declarations responding to toxic algal blooms that closed beaches, killed marine life, threatened homes, and shuttered businesses dependent

---

[217] Mayor of Clifton v. Passaic Valley Water Comm'n, 557 A.2d 299 (N.J. 1989) (applying the public trust doctrine to all water resources in the state, including surface, ground, and drinking water).

[218] Nat'l Audubon Soc'y v. Super. Ct., 658 P.2d 709 (Cal. 1983); *see also* Dave Owen, *The Mono Lake Case, the Public Trust Doctrine, and the Administrative State*, 45 U.C. DAVIS L. REV. 1099, 1116–17 (2012), (detailing the many provisions of the California Water Code that protect public trust doctrine values, including water quality, fisheries, and wildlife).

[219] Approximately one thousand new residents move to Florida every day. DEMOGRAPHIC ESTIMATING CONFERENCE EXECUTIVE SUMMARY, FLA. OFF. OF ECON. & DEMOGRAPHIC RSCH. (2021), http://edr.state.fl.us/Content/conferences/population/demographicsummary.pdf. In 1960, Florida was home to 8 percent of the nation's coastal population; by 2008, that number had already doubled to more than 16 percent. STEVEN G. WILSON & THOMAS R. FISCHETTI, COASTLINE POPULATION TRENDS IN THE UNITED STATES: 1960 TO 2008, U.S. CENSUS BUREAU 5–6 (2010), www.census.gov/prod/2010pubs/p25-1139.pdf.

[220] Groundwater remains unprotected by the public trust doctrine in many states, although, this is an aspect of trust-related environmental protection that is evolving. For example, Hawaii's trust has long protected groundwater, and California courts have recently recognized the application of the trust to groundwater resources that are tributaries of trust-protected navigable waterways. *See* CTR. FOR PROGRESSIVE REFORM, RESTORING THE TRUST: AN INDEX OF STATE CONSTITUTIONAL AND STATUTORY PROVISIONS AND CASES ON WATER RESOURCES AND THE PUBLIC TRUST DOCTRINE 8–9, 9 n. 62 (2009); Env't L. Found. v. State Water Res. Control Bd., 237 Cal. Rptr. 3d 393, 399–403 (Cal. Ct. App. 2018) *cert denied*, 2018 Cal. LEXIS 9313 (Cal. 2018) (concluding that the public trust doctrine protected groundwater tributaries of navigable waters).

[221] Scott Powers, *Florida Democratic Party Adopts 'Rights of Nature' into Platform*, FLA. POL. (Oct. 16, 2019), https://floridapolitics.com/archives/308603-florida-democratic-party-adopt-rights-of-nature-into-platform.

B. *The Rights of Nature Movement* 395

on water-related tourism, a central driver of Florida's economy.[222] Harm from algal blooms, agricultural pollution, and water withdrawals for commercial uses impact inland waterways and both the Atlantic and Gulf coasts, impairing 82 percent of all lakes in the state, more than 50 percent of the assessed rivers, and 32 percent of Florida's bays.[223] Concern over the issue cuts across conventional interest groups, engaging environmentalists, recreationalists, impacted homeowners, and small business owners. In 2019 and 2020, stakeholders thus launched a flurry of rights of nature initiatives to protect threatened waterways,[224] including the Santa Fe River and Indian River Lagoon in Brevard County,[225] the Caloosahatchee River near Fort Myers,[226] the Kissimmee River in Osceola County,[227] and even Pensacola Bay in the corner of the panhandle.[228]

Of all these efforts, however, the most noteworthy took place in Orange County, north of Orlando, to protect the Wekiva and Econlockhatchee Rivers, which had

---

[222] Pam Wright, *Florida Algae Blooms Send People to Hospital, Kill Marine Wildlife*, WEATHER CHANNEL (July 31, 2018), https://weather.com/science/environment/news/2018-07-31-florida-algae-blooms-red-tide-health-wildlife.

[223] *Waters Assessed as Impaired Due to Nutrient-Related Causes*, U.S. ENV'T PROT. AGENCY, www.epa.gov/nutrient-policy-data/waters-assessed-impaired-due-nutrient-related-causes (noting that, in Florida's most recent Water Quality Assessment Report, only 20 percent of rivers were assessed).

[224] For the full details of these Florida stories, see Ryan et al., *Comprehensive Analysis*, supra note 8, at 2529–36.

[225] The Santa Fe River Bill of Rights was inspired by a proposal to increase groundwater withdrawals for Nestlé water bottling from the Indian River Lagoon, one of the Santa Fe River's springs, a 156-mile-long estuary already struggling with agricultural nutrient pollution and persistent harmful algal blooms. Greg Allen, *The Water Is Already Low at a Florida Freshwater Spring, but Nestlé Wants More*, NAT'L PUB. RADIO (NPR) (Nov. 8, 2019, 6:00), www.npr.org/2019/11/08/776776312/the-water-is-already-low-at-a-florida-freshwater-spring-but-nestl-wants-more. In periods of wet weather, highly polluted water from Lake Okeechobee is diverted into the lagoon through the St. Lucie Canal to prevent flooding, altering estuarine salinity and carrying toxic blue-green algae blooms out to the coast. Max Chesnes, *What Are Lake Okeechobee Discharges? A Multimedia Primer and Historical Data*, TREASURE COAST NEWSPAPERS (Mar. 11, 2021), www.tcpalm.com/story/news/local/indian-river-lagoon/2021/01/07/lake-okeechobee-discharges-into-st-lucie-indian-river-lagoon-graphic/6567907002.

[226] Similar facts to the Indian River Lagoon story inspired the local effort to declare rights for the Caloosahatchee River on Florida's Gulf Coast, a waterway also stressed by polluted freshwater releases from Lake Okeechobee, a regional catch basin for large-scale agricultural runoff, and which receives restricted freshwater flows during periods of drought. *Ripple Effect*, CONSERVANCY SW. FLA., https://conservancy.org/ripple-effect/ (last visited Apr.11, 2024) (providing overview of ecological impacts from Lake Okeechobee discharges and altered hydrology).

[227] After extensive ecological damage to the Kissimmee River from Army Corps of Engineers flood control measures in the 1960s, local environmental advocates responded to insufficient remediation efforts with a rights of nature initiative, the Kissimmee River Bill of Rights. Tamia Streeter, *Legislation Proposed to Grant Kissimmee River Rights*, NEWS STAR (Sept. 15, 2019), www.thenewsstar.com/story/news/2019/09/15/legislation-proposed-grant-kissimmee-river-rights/2333791001. As local organizer Barbara Cady explained to the public, "Our river was destroyed in the name of flood control, killing the wildlife it supported. A Kissimmee River Bill of Rights will ensure that this living breathing ecosystem will never be assaulted again." Press Release, Cmty. Env't Legal Def. Fund, Florida: Flurry of Rights of River Ballot Initiatives Proposed to Save Drinking Water, Ecosystems (Sept. 11, 2019).

[228] Cmty. Env't Legal Def. Fund, *supra* note 227.

long suffered declining water levels and increasing nutrient pollution from septic tanks, agricultural waste, and lawn fertilizer.[229] In 2020, Orange County made national news when it enacted a county charter amendment to grant legal protections directly to the two rivers.[230] The resulting Wekiva River and Econlockhatchee River Bill of Rights, or WEBOR, recognized the right of the two rivers to "exist, [f]low, to be protected against [p]ollution and to maintain a healthy ecosystem" while creating standing for citizens of Orange County to bring actions on behalf of the rivers.[231] After eleven public hearings, the 2020 Charter Review Commission approved WEBOR to appear on the ballot in November 2020.[232]

Roughly eight months before the election, and before the proposed amendment had even qualified for the ballot, the Florida Legislature moved decisively to preempt it and all other rights of nature efforts in Florida, enacting statutory language clarifying that

> [a] local government regulation, ordinance, code, rule, comprehensive plan, charter, or any other provision of law may not recognize or grant any legal rights to a plant, an animal, a body of water, or any other part of the natural environment that is not a person or political subdivision ... or grant such person or political subdivision any specific rights relating to the natural environment not otherwise authorized in general law or specifically granted in the State Constitution.[233]

At the time, approximately half a dozen rights of nature initiatives had been proposed at the municipal level, including those reported earlier. Within two months, identical language prohibiting local governments from taking any action to "recognize or grant any legal rights to a plant, an animal, a body of water, or any other part of the natural environment" was incorporated into four separate bills, a clear indicator that the preemption was a top legislative priority.[234]

---

[229] Rebecca Renner, *In Florida, A River Gets Rights*, SIERRA CLUB (Feb. 9, 2021), www.sierraclub.org/sierra/2021-2-march-april/protect/florida-river-gets-rights (discussing the sharply declining water level and increasing pollution load).

[230] *Id.*; ORANGE COUNTY, FLA., CHARTER art. VII, § 704.1(A)-(B).

[231] *Id.*

[232] 2020 ORANGE CNTY. CHARTER REV. COMM'N, RIGHTS OF THE WEKIVA RIVER AND ECONLOCKHATCHEE RIVER COMMITTEE (2020), www.occompt.com/wordpress/wp-content/uploads/2020/01/2020-01-22-Rights-of-the-Wekiva-River-and-Econlockhatcee-River-Final-Report.pdf.

[233] FLA. STAT. § 403.412(9)(a) (2020) (proposed as Senate Bill 712). It was an impressive legislative feat, requiring swift coordination. The Florida Legislature had preempted many local environmental protection efforts in recent years, including statewide preemption of local plastic-bag bans, local polystyrene foam foodware bans, local plastic straw bans, and local reef protection ordinances banning the sale and use of certain chemical sunscreens found to damage coral reefs. However, the statewide legislative effort to preempt rights of nature ordinances stood out for the speed with which the legislature acted. *See* Ryan et al., *Comprehensive Analysis*, *supra* note 8, at 2533, and accompanying notes.

[234] S. 712, 2020 Leg., Reg. Sess., at 48 (Fla. 2020), http://laws.flrules.org/2020/150 (amending Section 403.412 to include Subsection 9). Representative Blaise Ingoglia, the Republican House sponsor of the original measure, urged passage on grounds that the proposed rights of nature initiatives would undermine the economy, framing them as enabling suits on behalf of a fern or anthill. HB 1199,

B. The Rights of Nature Movement

Despite the preemption, Orange County kept WEBOR on the ballot. In November, electors approved the charter amendment by nearly 90 percent.[235] The margin of victory is noteworthy in a county that cleaves, like the rest of the state, fairly evenly along partisan lines, indicating bipartisan support for this novel legal idea – even after legislative preemption.[236] Supporters argued that the preemption was unconstitutional and unenforceable, and immediately brought suit under the ordinance to stop the destruction of wetlands for 1,900-acre housing development on grounds that it violated the rights of the protected water bodies to exist, flow, and "maintain a healthy ecosystem."[237] Their claim was dismissed at trial and is on appeal as this book goes to press,[238] but the lawsuit immediately gained national and even international attention.[239] Emboldened by WEBOR's success at the ballot box, advocates proposed similar ordinances in at least twenty-eight counties and municipalities throughout Florida, even after the preemptive legislation.[240]

House-Judiciary Committee (Fla. Feb. 12, 2020), www.myfloridahouse.gov/Sections/HouseSchedule/houseschedule.aspx?calendarListType=Interim&date=02-12-2020 (click "Watch Archived Stream" under the "Judiciary Committee" subheader) (video of state house committee hearing that includes statement of Rep. Blaise Ingoglia, R-Spring Hill). The preemption language was ultimately grafted onto SB 712, a massive water quality bill dubbed the "Clean Waterways Act." Fla. S. Appropriations Comm., Committee Meeting Expanded Agenda 2–3 (2020), www.flsenate.gov/Committees/Show/AP/ExpandedAgenda/4919 (proposed committee substitute for CS/SB 712). The bill passed and was signed into law on June 30, 2020, just weeks after WEBOR qualified for the ballot.Orange Cnty., Fla. Elections, 2020 Official Results 7 (2020), www.ocfelections.com/sites/default/files/media/forms/Election%20Records%20and%20Turnout/election%20records/10866-2020%20GENERAL%20ELECTION/10866-official-election-results-summary.pdf (showing that 89.2 percent voted yes and 10.8 percent voted no).

[235] Orange Cnty., Fla. Elections, 2020 Official Results 7 (2020), www.ocfelections.com/sites/default/files/media/forms/Election%20Records%20and%20Turnout/election%20records/10866-2020%20GENERAL%20ELECTION/10866-official-election-results-summary.pdf (showing that 89.2 percent voted yes and 10.8 percent voted no).

[236] Joseph Bonasia, *Voters Approve Charter Amendment and Make Florida the Epicenter of Rights of Nature*, Fla. Today (Nov. 6, 2020), www.floridatoday.com/story/opinion/2020/11/06/florida-epicenter-rights-nature-opinion/6189196002 ("In a county in which the breakdown of Democrats, Republicans, and Independents is 36.6%, 34.2% and 24.3%, respectively, the amendment results may reflect the sentiments of residents throughout the state.").

[237] Plaintiffs sued on behalf of a series of Florida waterbodies associated with the protected rivers, Lake Hart, Lake Mary Jane, Wilde Cypress Branch, Boggy Branch, and Crosby Island Marsh, attempting to block the dredge and fill of approximately 115 acres of Orange County waters and wetlands for road construction, development, and stormwater pond construction. Complaint, Wilde Cypress Branch v. Beachline S. Residential, L.L.C. (Fla. 9th Cir. Ct. Apr. 26, 2021).

[238] Brief for Appellant at 15, Wilde Cypress Branch v. Beachline S. Residential, L.L.C., No. 6D23-1412, 2023 WL 2580263 (Fla. 6th DCA 2023).

[239] *See generally* Isabella Kaminski, *Streams and Lakes Have Rights: A U.S. County Decided. Now They're Suing Florida*, The Guardian (May 1, 2021), www.theguardian.com/environment/2021/may/01/florida-rights-of-nature-lawsuit-waterways-housing-development; Anagha Srikanth, *Streams and Lakes Have Rights – And They're Suing Florida*, The Hill (May 3, 2021), https://thehill.com/changing-america/sustainability/environment/551513-streams-and-lakes-have-rights-and-theyre-suing.

[240] Efforts are currently underway in Leon County, Alachua County, Seminole County, Lee County, Palm Beach County, Santa Rosa County, Miami-Dade County, Pinellas County, St. Lucie County,

Indeed, as this book goes to press, statewide efforts are underway to overturn that preemptive legislation by incorporating rights of nature principles into a state constitutional amendment.[241] Advocates have also begun gathering signatures to qualify a statewide rights of nature citizen ballot initiative, the "Florida Right to Clean Water" measure,[242] recognizing a right to clean water for Floridians and an additional right to the waters themselves to be clean. Like WEBOR, the ballot measure proposes rights for waters to "exist, flow, be free from pollution, and maintain a healthy ecosystem."[243] The proposed amendment also grants any Florida resident, governmental entity, and nongovernmental entity the right to sue for enforcement of the rights.[244]

V. NORTH AMERICAN TRIBAL NATIONS

Even as American municipalities and state legislatures skirmish over the legality of rights of nature initiatives, North American tribes and First Nations have acted swiftly and purposefully to codify a number of diverse and far-reaching rights of nature laws. While these newly recognized rights represent a significant shift in the western legal landscape, they intersect with broader cultural and natural law traditions that have developed over millennia among many indigenous peoples. For many tribes, rights of nature initiatives simply codify what they have always held to be true – that nature is sacred and that people and the environment are inextricable.[245]

Ho-Chunk Nation and Menominee Tribe of Wisconsin

In 2015, the Ho-Chunk Nation of Wisconsin proposed an amendment to its Tribal constitution to affirm that "[e]cosystems, natural communities, and species within the Ho-Chunk Nation territory possess inherent, fundamental, and inalienable rights to naturally exist, flourish, regenerate, and evolve."[246] In 2018, 86.9 percent of

---

Martin County, Volusia County, Maitland, Davenport, Haines City, Winter Springs, Pensacola, Apalachicola, Peace River, Satellite Beach, New Smyrna Beach, Altamonte Springs, Venice, Sarasota, Cocoa, Naples, Punta Gorda, and Northport. Telephone Interview with Chuck O'Neal, Chairman, Fla. Rts. of Nature Network (Jan. 5, 2021).

[241] Deidra Funcheon, *Group Wants to Amend the Florida Constitution to Protect Waters*, AXIOS MIAMI (Jun. 12, 2023), www.axios.com/local/miami/2023/06/12/florida-constitutional-amendment-protect-waters; Valerie Vande Panne, *"Rights of Nature" Proposed for Florida Constitution*, WGCU PUB. MEDIA (Jun. 3, 2021), https://news.wgcu.org/news/2021-06-03/rights-of-nature-proposed-for-florida-constitution.

[242] *Florida Needs the Right to Clean and Healthy Waters*, FLORIDARIGHTTOCLEANWATER.ORG, www.floridarighttocleanwater.org/ (last visited January 8, 2024).

[243] *Id.*

[244] *Id.*

[245] *See generally* James D. K. Morris & Jacinta Ruru, *Giving Voice to Rivers: Legal Personality as a Vehicle for Recognizing Indigenous Peoples' Relationships to Water?*, 14 AUSTL. INDIGENOUS L. REV. 49, 58 (2010) (discussing the strong connections between Indigenous people and freshwater rivers).

[246] Resolution to Amend the Ho-Chunk Nation Constitution and Provide for Rights of Nature, Gen. Council Res. 09-19-15 (Ho-Chunk Nation 2015), https://d3n8a8pro7vhmx.cloudfront.net/honorearth/pages/2098/attachments/original/1446129806/HoChunk_RightsOfNature_Resolution_Sep2015.pdf?1446129806; Press Release, Cmty. Env't Legal Def. Fund, Ho-Chunk Nation General Council

the General Council of the Ho-Chunk Nation voted to proceed with the rights of nature amendment.[247] The proposed amendment still needs final approval from the full membership.[248] In 2020, the Menominee Indian Tribe of Wisconsin asserted the rights of the Menominee River in an effort to stop proposed mining.[249]

Ponca Nation of Oklahoma
In 2017, the Ponca Nation of Oklahoma passed a statute recognizing the rights of nature to protect tribal lands from fracking.[250] Casey Camp-Horinek, a Ponca Nation councilwoman, observed, "The Ponca Nation has chosen to follow the rights of nature, the immutable rights of nature by ... recognizing that we as human beings are not separate from but part of this sacred system of life."[251]

White Earth Band of Ojibwe in Minnesota
In 2018, the White Earth Band of Ojibwe, part of the Minnesota Chippewa Tribe, adopted legal rights for *manoomin* (wild rice) and the freshwater resources where it is found.[252] This was the first law to recognize the rights of a plant species.[253] The resolution asserts that *manoomin* has "inherent rights to exist, flourish, regenerate, and evolve, as well as inherent rights to restoration, recovery, and preservation."[254] In August of 2021, the White Earth Band filed suit to stop the Minnesota Department of Natural Resources from issuing a water use permit for a new oil pipeline that it alleged would violate the protected rights of *manoomin*, in a suit currently pending in the White Earth Band of Ojibwe's Tribal Court.[255] Uniquely, the protections also

---

Approves Rights of Nature Constitutional Amendment (Sept. 17, 2018), https://celdf.org/2018/09/press-release-ho-chunk-nation-general-council-approves-rights-of-nature-constitutional-amendment.

[247] Press Release, Cmty. Env't Legal Def. Fund, *supra* note 246.

[248] *Id.*

[249] Amelia Cole, *Wisconsin Tribe Recognizes Menominee River Rights*, GREAT LAKES ECHO (Mar.13, 2020), https://greatlakesecho.org/2020/03/13/wisconsin-tribe-recognizes-menominee-river-rights.

[250] Alex Brown, *Cities, Tribes Try a New Environmental Approach: Give Nature Rights*, PEW STATELINE (Oct. 30, 2019), www.pewtrusts.org/en/research-and-analysis/blogs/stateline/2019/10/30/cities-tribes-try-a-new-environmental-approach-give-nature-rights.

[251] Casey Camp-Horinek, Councilwoman, Ponca Tribe of Okla., Keynote Address at the 2019 Bioneers Conference: Aligning Human Law with Natural Law (Oct. 20, 2019), https://bioneers.org/casey-camp-horinek-aligning-human-law-natural-law-zstfi911.

[252] 1855 Treaty Auth., Resolution Establishing Rights of Manoomin, Res. 2018-05 (Dec. 5, 2018), https://whiteearth.com/assets/files/public_documents/Letter%20to%20Tim%20Walz%20re%20Rights%20of%20Manoomin.pdf (see same URL for subsequent citations); White Earth Rsrv. Bus. Comm., Res. 001-19-009 (Dec. 31, 2018); White Earth Rsrv. Bus. Comm. Res. 001-19-010 (Dec. 31, 2018).

[253] *Advancing Legal Rights of Nature: Timeline*, CMTY. ENV'T LEGAL DEF. FUND, https://celdf.org/rights-of-nature/timeline (noting that the Rights of the Manoomin is the "first law to secure legal rights of a particular plant species").

[254] White Earth Band of Ojibwe Res. 0001-19-0009 and 0001-19-101 (2018), https://whiteearth.com/assets/files/public_documents/Letter%20to%20Tim%20Walz%20re%20Rights%20of%20Manoomin.pdf.

[255] *See* Dan Gunderson, *Advocates Hope White Earth Wild Rice Case Will Boost 'Rights of Nature,'* MINN. PUB. RADIO (Sept. 1, 2021), www.mprnews.org/story/2021/09/01/advocates-hope-white-earth-wild-rice-case-will-boost-rights-of-nature.

include a right to a healthy climate system and a right to be free from genetic engineering from "seeds that have been developed using methods other than traditional plant breeding."[256]

Yurok Tribe of California
In 2019, the Tribal Council of the Yurok Tribe of Northern California adopted a resolution establishing the rights of the Klamath River to "exist, flourish, and naturally evolve; to have a clean and healthy environment free from pollutants ...."[257] After adoption of the resolution, one member of the Yurok Tribal Council stated, "We are sending a strong message that we now have an additional legal mechanism to shield the Klamath against those who might harm our most sacred resource. It is and always will be our responsibility to defend this river by any means necessary."[258]

Innu Council of Ekuanitship and Minganie County, Quebec
As this book goes to press, the Innu Council of Ekuanitship and the Minganie Regional County Municipality have granted legal rights to the Magpie River in northern Quebec.[259] Through tandem resolutions, the Indigenous council and municipality confer nine rights to the river, including the right to flow, the right to maintain its natural biodiversity, and the right to sue.[260] This is the first instance in which rights have been recognized in natural objects in Canada.[261]

2. The Differentiating Development of the Rights of Nature Movement

While the public trust doctrine was founded upon Justinian principles, the historical origins of the rights of nature movement are rooted in indigenous cultures worldwide, where these principles have circulated culturally and legally for generations.[262]

---

[256] 1855 Treaty Auth., Resolution Establishing Rights of Manoomin, Res. 2018-05 § 1(a) (Dec. 5, 2018), https://whiteearth.com/assets/files/public_documents/Letter%20to%20Tim%20Walz%20re%20Rights%20of%20Manoomin.pdf.

[257] *Testimony Regarding Natural Solutions to Cutting Pollution and Building Resilience: Hearing before the H. Select Comm. on the Climate Crisis*, 116th Cong. 8 (2019), https://docs.house.gov/meetings/CN/CN00/20191022/110110/HMTG-116-CN00-Wstate-MyersF-20191022.pdf (statement of Frankie Myers, V. Chairman, Yurok Tribe).

[258] *Tribe Passes Powerful Resolution*, YUROK TODAY (Yurok Tribe, Klamath, Cal.), May 2019, at 3; see also John Anhi Schertow, *The Yurok Nation Just Established the Rights of the Klamath River*, CULTURAL SURVIVAL (May 21, 2019), www.culturalsurvival.org/news/yurok-nation-just-established-rights-klamath-river#:~:text=%E2%80%9CWe%20are%20sending%20a%20strong,on%20the%20Yurok%20Tribal%20Council (reporting on the same story).

[259] *See* Jack Graham, *Canadian River Wins Legal Rights in Global Push to Protect Nature*, REUTERS (Feb. 24, 2021), https://news.trust.org/item/20210224174810-i75ms [https://perma.cc/H5WY-6RXQ]; *see also* Morgan Lowrie, *Quebec River Granted Legal Rights as Part of Global "Personhood" Movement*, CBC (Feb. 28, 2021), www.cbc.ca/news/canada/montreal/magpie-river-quebec-canada-personhood-1.5931067.

[260] *See* Graham, *supra* note 259; *see also* Lowrie, *supra* note 259.

[261] *See* sources cited *id*.

[262] *See also* Ryan et al., *Comprehensive Analysis*, *supra* note 8, at 2502–03, 2502 n.289.

B. The Rights of Nature Movement

In the Western tradition, the legal history of the rights of nature likely begins with the Supreme Court's dismissal of the idea in 1972 in Sierra Club v. Morton,[263] a case rejecting the notion that harm to the natural environment itself was sufficient to confer standing in a suit to halt development plans for a Disney ski resort in the Sequoia National Forest.[264] While the claim was unsuccessful, it launched a wave of scholarship contending that the Court had wrongly decided the rights of nature issue, including Christopher Stone's famous treatment in Should Trees Have Standing?, which argued for direct recognition of legal rights in natural objects and in nature as a whole.[265]

The resulting rights of nature discourse has produced results in the legal systems of countries in every inhabited continent of the world, including the aforementioned examples.[266] As noted, the embrace of rights of nature reasoning reflects growing dissatisfaction with the utilitarian environmental ethics underpinnings conventional Western legal systems and the results of environmental management within them.[267] Where the public trust doctrine protects environmental values to maximize social welfare, or to ensure "the greatest good for the greatest number of people," the rights of nature movement rejects the anthropocentric advancement of human interests only to advance ecocentric protections for nature and natural systems directly.[268] Instead of assigning legal rights to enjoy natural systems to human members of the public, rights of nature proponents ask the law to protect the rights of ecosystems and their components to exist – assigning them something akin to "legal personhood."

Nevertheless, the shift to a rights of nature approach raises its own philosophical and practical challenges. Perhaps the core challenge for the use of rights of nature principles in environmental advocacy remains a pragmatic one – who speaks for nature, when rights-holders cannot themselves speak? And what if the people speaking on their behalf do not all agree?[269]

Different jurisdictions have taken a variety of approaches to resolve these and other dilemmas. As a result of simultaneous but diverging developments in the

---

[263] Sierra Club v. Morton, 405 U.S. 727 (1972).
[264] See id. at 735–36, 739–42, 749–50 (Douglas, J., dissenting).
[265] Christopher D. Stone, Should Trees Have Standing? – toward Legal Rights for Natural Objects, 45 S. CAL. L. REV. 450, 455–56 (1972); see also Cormac Cullinan, Do Humans Have Standing to Deny Trees Rights?, 11 BARRY L. REV. 11, 11–12, 19–21 (2008) (referring to Stone's "seminal" article that "motivated the famous dissenting judgment by Justice Douglas in the case of Sierra Club v. Morton"). Stone urged that institutionalizing rights to nonhuman entities would jump start a long-term legal and cultural shift toward an understanding of humans as part of a greater whole, rather than at the center of the universe. Id. at 489–501.
[266] For a fuller account of rights of nature initiatives worldwide, see Ryan et al., Comprehensive Analysis, supra note 8, at 2500–39.
[267] See id. at 2548–55.
[268] Ryan et al., Comprehensive Analysis, supra note 8, at 2500–01.
[269] See id. at 2509–10.

emerging international discourse, the rights of nature movement has begun to differentiate jurisdictionally along legal planes that bear resemblance to some of the variations on public trust principles described in Chapter 8.[270] Previous scholarship provides a fuller snapshot of what the rights of nature movement looks like internationally and domestically, but this section provides a summary of the different approaches taken to such open questions as what in nature has received legal rights, who speaks for rights holders, by what legal mechanisms are those rights vindicated, and which rights are receiving protection.[271]

a. Parallel Planes of Jurisdictional Development

I. WHAT ELEMENTS IN NATURE SHOULD RECEIVE LEGAL PROTECTION?
Reviewing the development of rights of nature principles in different jurisdictions, the first axis on which initiatives differ is their answer to the question of what elements in nature should receive legal protection.[272] In some contexts, like the Constitution of Ecuador, all of nature receives legal protection.[273] In others, specific ecosystems receive protection – for example, river systems have received legal protection in Oceania and Bangladesh, and Indian states have even proposed giving legal rights to glaciers.[274] In others, specific species have received protection, such as the *manoomin* species of wild rice protected by the White Earth Band of Ojibwe in Minnesota.[275]

Even so, in cataloging these initiatives worldwide, one important theme that bears highlighting is how often the features in nature designated for legal personhood or protection are *waterways*.[276] As indicated by the list of examples reported earlier, these include the Atrato and Amazon River systems in Colombia; the Whanganui and Yarra Rivers in New Zealand and Australia, respectively; Sukhna Lake in Chandigarh, India; the Mar Menor Lagoon in Spain; the River Ouse in England; and every single river in the nation of Bangladesh.[277] In the United States, nearly every reported rights of nature initiative launched at the municipal level and reported earlier was undertaken to protect a river or waterway.

II. WHO SPEAKS FOR RIGHTS HOLDERS?
One question that all rights of nature jurisdictions must grapple with is the matter of who speaks legally for rights holders that cannot, themselves, speak – and here, too,

---

[270] *See* Chapter 8(A) ("The Planes of Public Trust Development across the United States").
[271] Ryan et al., *Comprehensive Analysis*, *supra* note 8, at 2448.
[272] *Id.* at 2506–07.
[273] *Id.* at 2514; Constitución De La Republica Del Ecuador [Constitution] 2008 (Ecuador).
[274] Ryan et al., *Comprehensive Analysis*, *supra* note 8, at 2518–21.
[275] Resolution Establishing Rights of Manoomin § 1(a), 2018 (Res. No. 2018-05) (Chippewa).
[276] *Id.* at 2559–60.
[277] *See supra* notes 113–128 and accompanying text; *see also* Ryan et al., *Comprehensive Analysis*, *supra* note 8, at 6–21.

B. *The Rights of Nature Movement* 403

there is jurisdictional differentiation. The Constitution of Ecuador clarifies that virtually everyone has the right to speak on behalf of nature, and perhaps the obligation to do so.[278] Elsewhere, rights of nature laws designate a specific local community with a special relationship to the protected resource to act legally in support of its rights, an approach widely taken in the U.S. municipalities that have enacted rights of nature ordinances.[279] In other nations, special guardians have been appointed to protect the rights of the resource, as New Zealand has done in appointing a Pou Tupua Council to protect the Whanganui River.[280]

III. WHAT LEGAL MECHANISMS VINDICATE THE RIGHTS OF NATURE?

Jurisdictions also differ in specifying the legal mechanisms that will operate to vindicate the rights of nature recognized by their legal systems. Ecuador elevates the rights of nature to a constitutional principle, and there has been speculation that Sweden might follow.[281] In other nations, such as Bolivia, and North American tribes and First Nations, rights of nature principles have been codified through legislative action.[282] Within U.S. states, the predominant vehicles for enacting rights of nature principles have been municipal ordinances.[283] In Bangladesh, rights of nature protections have been conferred by courts as a judicial remedy.[284]

IV. WHICH RIGHTS OF NATURE ARE PROTECTED?

Finally, and perhaps most interestingly, there is jurisdictional variation on the question of which rights are actually being protected under different rights of nature initiatives. Internationally, rights of nature initiatives are often framed as conferring legal personhood on the rights holder.[285] For example, New Zealand has conferred legal personhood on rivers, mountains, and national parks,[286] and in the Punjab and Haryana regions of India, animals have been granted the same legal rights that a person would hold.[287]

However, other jurisdictions recognize special, nature-specific rights that people do not actually have. For example, the Constitution of Ecuador and the Ugandan National Environmental Act grant rights to nature to both exist and evolve (as did

---

[278] CONSTITUCIÓN DE LA REPUBLICA DEL ECUADOR [CONSTITUTION] 2008 (Ecuador).
[279] Ryan et al., *Comprehensive Analysis*, *supra* note 8, at 2509–10.
[280] *Id.* at 2510; Te Awa Tupua (Whanganui River Claims Settlement) Act 2017, subpt. 20 (N.Z.).
[281] Ryan et al., *Comprehensive Analysis*, *supra* note 8, at 2510–11 (noting that Swedish MP, Rebecka Le Moine, proposed a constitutional amendment to recognize rights of nature in 2019, but it was unsuccessful); Press Release, Cmty. Env't Legal Def. Fund, Rights of Nature Constitutional Amendment Introduced in Sweden's Parliament (Oct. 8, 2019), https://celdf.org/2019/10/media-release-rights-of-nature-constitutional-amendment-introduced-in-swedens-parliament/.
[282] Ryan et al., *Comprehensive Analysis*, *supra* note 8, at 2515, 2536–38.
[283] *Id.* at 2522; *see also id.* at 2522–35.
[284] *Id.* at 2520–21; *see also supra* note 128 and accompanying text.
[285] Ryan et al., *Comprehensive Analysis*, *supra* note 8, at 2512.
[286] *Id.* at 2517–18; *see also supra* Part (A)(1)(a) ("New Zealand and Australia") (describing rights of nature initiatives in New Zealand).
[287] Ryan et al., *Comprehensive Analysis*, *supra* note 8, at 2517, 2520.

the Lake Erie Bill of Rights, before it was preempted), even though there is no comparable legally recognized right of a person to evolve.[288] In other jurisdictions, rights of nature initiatives are framed more modestly, in terms that resemble a form of strong but conventional environmental protection, such as the Australian requirement of a strategic plan to protect the Yarra River.[289]

These different assertions of rights in nature raise pressing questions about what the rights of nature really mean, whether they are consistent with human rights or a wholly different model, or whether they are really just a strong form of conventional environmental protection. Either way, it is fascinating to observe the ways in which these jurisdictionally differentiating planes of development reflect similar planes of jurisdictional differentiation in the development of public trust principles across the United States and the world, inviting further comparison of these seemingly distinct approaches to pursuing related goals of environmental protection.

V. WHAT REMEDIES ARE REQUESTED AND GRANTED?

As in the public trust context, rights of nature advocates have used their legal accomplishments to request different forms of relief, ranging from declaratory relief, establishing the legal obligation to protect a designated rights holder; to injunctive relief, to block a development project that might threaten a protected rights holder; and perhaps even allowing for damages in cases where rights-holders have been harmed by illegal conduct. For example, courts in India have awarded declaratory relief when they have used judicial authority to acknowledge legal rights in animals and specific geographic landmarks.[290] Courts award injunctive relief when they prevent action that would harm rights-holders within nature, as the Constitutional Court of Ecuador did when it banned all extractive activities in the Los Cedros Protected Forest.[291] Sometimes a court will grant both declaratory and injunctive relief, as the Supreme Court of Bangladesh did when it established legal status for its rivers and ordered the removal of illegal establishments from the banks.[292]

At present, damages remedies are less identifiable in association with rights of nature litigation, although they could potentially be used to redress illegal conduct

---

[288] *Id.* at 2513.

[289] *Yarra River Protection Act 2017* (Vic.) divs 4–9 (Austl.).

[290] *See* Vineet Upadhyay, *Animals Have Equal Rights as Humans, Says Uttarakhand High Court*, TIMES OF INDIA (July 5, 2018) https://timesofindia.indiatimes.com/city/dehradun/members-of-animal-kingdom-to-be-treated-as-legal-entities-ukhand-hc/articleshow/64860996.cms; *see also* Karnail Singh v. State of Haryana, 2019 SCC OnLine P&H 704 (India), www.livelaw.in/pdf_upload/pdf_upload-361239.pdf. Appeals to some (but not all) Indian rights of nature decisions remain pending as this essay goes to press.

[291] Press Release, Ctr. for Biological Diversity, Ecuador's Highest Court Enforces Constitutional 'Rights of Nature' to Safeguard Los Cedros Protected Forest (Dec. 2, 2021), https://biologicaldiversity.org/w/news/press-releases/ecuadors-highest-court-enforces-constitutional-rights-of-nature-to-safeguard-los-cedros-protected-forest-2021-12-02/.

[292] *See* Chandran, *supra* note 167; *see also* Ryan et al., *Comprehensive Analysis*, *supra* note 8, at 2516–21.

that requires costly restoration, or to exact punitive damages in order to deter future such violations. Still, it seems likely that remedies in international rights of nature litigation will be less connected to damages than domestic public trust litigation because the public trust is increasingly used as a defense against damages remedies sought in takings litigation under the U.S. Constitution's Fifth Amendment. As in the public trust context, the evolving patterns of remedies remains a developing doctrinal area.

C. COMPARING THE PUBLIC TRUST AND RIGHTS OF NATURE

As the public trust doctrine and rights of nature approaches to environmental protection continue to develop across the globe, a comparison between them yields sharp contrasts but also surprising commonalities. Perhaps the most important lesson in reviewing the foregoing plethora of rights of nature movements erupting across the globe is that they are not one thing – there is so much variety among these efforts, let alone the unfinished definition that characterizes many of them, that it is more accurate to see them not as "the rights of nature movement," but, though less poetically, as "a series of loosely related movements for reconceptualizing legal protections for different components of nature."[293] Indeed, the same thing can be said of the rapidly evolving public trust principles across the globe detailed in Part A of this chapter, foreshadowing the most important observation in this comparative analysis – which is that both of these unfolding legal movements are not monoliths, but mosaics.

While the differences in underlying environmental ethics remain powerful, the two approaches also reveal unexpected points of overlap in what they focus on, when advocates appeal to them, and the kind of work each doctrine does within the larger political context, explored in the following section.

1. *Philosophical Duality or False Dichotomy?*

In analyzing these contrasting models of environmental rights, the most striking contrast seemingly lies in the mutual exclusivity of their underlying ethical frameworks, flowing from the different legal roots from which the two approaches begin. The public trust doctrine derives normative direction primarily in reference to human needs, reflecting the anthropocentrism that underlies most of the common law tradition from which it stems, and which is manifest today across modern regulatory law.[294] By contrast, and consistent with many indigenous traditions, the rights

---

[293] Ryan et al., *Comprehensive Analysis*, *supra* note 8, at 2539–48.
[294] *Id.* at 2541–48 (discussing examples from across the regulatory spectrum). For example, in the *Audubon Society* case, the California Supreme Court clarifies that in meeting the state's obligations under the doctrine, the water agency must balance the public trust values of ecology, scenery, and

of nature movement considers human interests only as one component of the overall natural system, in which people are merely one constituent part.²⁹⁵

For rights of nature adherents, the anthropocentrism of the public trust doctrine leads to dangerous indeterminacy in how it will prioritize among the competing human interests in trust resources. They worry whether it will protect environmental values when they are pitted against contrary human concerns, such as the exploitation of natural resources for economic development.²⁹⁶ Conventional environmental advocates are more daunted by the unfinished development of rights of nature principles, especially regarding who speaks for nature when nature cannot speak for itself. Rights of nature critics worry about the uncertainty regarding who should be legally privileged to act on behalf of the nonhuman components of a protected ecosystem – especially when human spokespeople disagree on what nature's rights require, be it more solar arrays or more desert tortoise habitat, more wind farms or migratory birds, or which of two competing endangered species should take priority.²⁹⁷ It is perhaps noteworthy that the core theoretical challenge for each approach boils down to different forms of indeterminacy.

Yet observing public trust and rights of nature advocacy in action raises provocative questions about the significance of the ethical distinction when the two models are applied on the ground, in real legal controversies. For one thing, when public trust principles are understood as protecting future generations, then public trust governance follows a stewardship ethic that loosely approximates the goals of the more moderate rights of nature models. When rights of nature models are applied, human beings still generally assume the role of steward (and the meaningful question becomes which human beings will call the shots).

For another, it is not always clear that the advocates organizing under each of these banners truly see the world in strictly anthropocentric or biocentric terms. While anthropocentrism and ecocentrism are incompatible frameworks of analysis on the theoretical plane, not all of us are strict theorists, and even theorists can struggle for consistency outside the ivory tower. While there are clearly examples of

---

recreation in the Mono Basin against countervailing public interests in transferring its water hundreds of miles to the south for uses associated with economic and residential development in Los Angeles. *Id.* at 2547–48. *See also* Ryan et al., *Comprehensive Analysis, supra* note 8, at 2539–48 (discussing anthropocentrism in U.S. law).

²⁹⁵ *See* Ryan et al., *Comprehensive Analysis, supra* note 8, 120 at 2548–55 (discussing examples from U.S. indigenous and federal environmental law). For example, when the California Yurok Tribe ascribed legal personhood to the Klamath River in 2019, it represented a more ecocentric move, recognizing not just the rights of the living things that depend on the river, but of the entire river system itself. *Id.* at 2548–49.

²⁹⁶ *See* Richard J. Lazarus, *Changing Conceptions of Property and Sovereignty in Natural Resources: Questioning the Public Trust Doctrine*, 71 IOWA L. REV. 631, 715–16 (1986); *see also* Ryan et al., *Comprehensive Analysis, supra* note 8, at 2454 n. 12 and accompanying text.

²⁹⁷ *See, e.g.,* Mauricio Guim & Michael A. Livermore, *Where Nature's Rights Go Wrong*, 107 VA. L. REV. 1347 (2021) (critiquing rights of nature approaches as theoretically problematic and difficult to implement).

C. Comparing the Public Trust and Rights of Nature

faithful adherents in the literature,[298] the ordinary citizens bringing actual lawsuits and ballot initiatives are not always so doctrinaire. Even the great naturalist Aldo Leopold, one of the forefathers of ecocentric ethics in American environmental law, wavers on the question at times,[299] and so, it would seem, do many of us.

When pressed, many ordinary people will give voice to both ethics simultaneously, even though they are, strictly speaking, mutually exclusive ethical directives.[300] It is highly plausible that many of the atmospheric trust champions passionately advocating for the expansion of the public trust doctrine to protect the atmospheric commons against greenhouse gas pollution[301] would subscribe to a rights of nature perspective if it were legally available to them – just as many rights of nature advocates for the Sewage Sludge Ordinance in Tamaqua, Pennsylvania[302] probably also subscribe to the public trust principles enshrined in the Pennsylvania Constitution's Environmental Rights Amendment.[303] Behavioral economics has demonstrated that human beings are not nearly as rational as we like to think we are, and that we often hold inconsistent beliefs at the same time.[304] Human tolerance of cognitive dissonance, in which people hold inconsistent ideas simultaneously, has been well documented in the social science literature.[305] My own experience teaching hundreds

---

[298] *Compare* the unapologetically anthropocentric writings of WILLIAM F. BAXTER, PEOPLE OR PENGUINS: THE CASE FOR OPTIMAL POLLUTION 4–9 (1974) (Baxter's writings are unapologetically anthropocentric) *with* the pioneering ecocentric Deep Ecologists BILL DEVALL & GEORGE SESSIONS, DEEP ECOLOGY: LIVING AS IF NATURE MATTERED 67 (1985) (the Deep Ecologists were pioneers in modern ecocentrism).

[299] Earlier writings showed greater tolerance for the displacement of nature so long as not all of it was lost to human development. ALDO LEOPOLD, A PLEA FOR WILDERNESS HUNTING GROUNDS (1925), *reprinted in* ALDO LEOPOLD'S SOUTHWEST 155, 159 (David E. Brown & Neil B. Carmony eds., 2003) (noting that it might be legitimate to develop five out of six vacant lots for housing, "but when we build houses on the last one, we forget what houses are for. The sixth house would not be development at all, but rather it would be mere short-sighted stupidity"). *Cf.* ALDO LEOPOLD, A SAND COUNTY ALMANAC AND SKETCHES HERE AND THERE at 224–25 (1949) (arguing that "A thing is right when it tends to preserve the integrity, stability, and beauty of the biotic community. It is wrong when it tends otherwise.").

[300] After decades of teaching environmental ethics to hundreds of law students, I can personally attest to this phenomenon.

[301] *See, e.g.*, Juliana v. United States, 217 F. Supp. 3d 1224 (D. Or. 2016), *rev'd*, Juliana v. United States, No. 24-684, D.C. No. 6:15-cv-1517, 2024 WL 5102489, (May 1, 2024), *cert. denied*, 604 U.S. 645 (2025); *see also* Chapter 9(B)(2) ("The Atmospheric Trust Project in U.S. Law").

[302] Tamaqua Borough, Pa., Tamaqua Borough Sewage Sludge Ordinance, Ordinance No. 612 (Sept. 19, 2006).

[303] PA. CONST. art. I, § 27 ("The people have a right to clean air, pure water, and to the preservation of the natural, scenic, historic and esthetic values of the environment. Pennsylvania's public natural resources are the common property of all the people, including generations yet to come. As trustee of these resources, the Commonwealth shall conserve and maintain them for the benefit of all the people.").

[304] *Cf.* RICHARD H. THALER, MISBEHAVING: THE MAKING OF BEHAVIORAL ECONOMICS (2015) (reviewing how behavioral economics revealed the many fallacies and irrationalities of human thinking).

[305] *See generally* LEON FESTINGER, A THEORY OF COGNITIVE DISSONANCE (1957).

of law students environmental ethics over nearly two decades has demonstrated this for me personally time and time again (and if I am honest, I can hardly claim not to demonstrate the same behavior myself).[306]

Moreover, in many parts of the world, it may oversimplify the rights of nature movement to frame it as a purely ecocentric or biocentric enterprise, in contrast to anthropocentrism, because some movements have emerged within cultural traditions that lovingly anthropomorphize components of the ecosystem that rights of nature initiatives protect. Some people, and some cultures, hold a Gaia conception of nature as a person.[307] For example, when the Māori people of New Zealand assign legal personhood to a river system, it is because they consider the river part of their family.[308] They see the river system as not just a legal person, but a person – their grandmother, so to speak.[309] If the river is part of the people, and the people are part of the river, then the bifurcation between people and nature that the anthropocentric vs. ecocentric dichotomy presumes begins to break down.

Even among academics, the dichotomy can break down. Some scholars inspired by Christopher Stone's seminal work have nevertheless declined to choose between a theory of environmental rights cleanly centered around humans or nature. In the early 1990s, Professor Joseph Sax, the intellectual progenitor of the modern public trust doctrine, considered whether they should be grounded in anthropocentric human rights or an ecocentric theory centered on nature itself.[310] He concluded that environmental rights are inextricably intertwined with human rights, but pragmatically advised that centering them within the human rights tradition

---

[306] *See supra* note 300.
[307] *See, e.g.,* JAMES LOVELOCK, GAIA: A NEW LOOK AT LIFE ON EARTH 9–10 (1979) ("[T]he entire range of living matter on Earth, from whales to viruses, and from oaks to algae, could be regarded as constituting a single living entity, capable of manipulating the Earth's atmosphere to suit its overall needs and endowed with faculties and powers far beyond those of its constituent parts.... [Gaia can be defined] as a complex entity involving the Earth's biosphere, atmosphere, oceans, and soil; the totality constituting a feedback or cybernetic system which seeks an optimal physical and chemical environment for life on this planet.").
[308] Catherine J. Iorns Magallanes, *Nature as an Ancestor: Two Examples of Legal Personality for Nature in New Zealand*, 10 VICTORIA U. WELLINGTON LEGAL RSCH. PAPERS 1, 1–3 (2020) (observing that plants, animals, and natural features are treated as "kin" by the Māori).
[309] *Id.*
[310] Joseph L. Sax, *The Search for Environmental Rights*, 6 J. LAND USE & ENV'T L. 93 (1990); *see also* Dinah Shelton, *Human Rights, Environmental Rights, and the Right to Environment*, 28 STAN. J. INT'L 103 (1991). In Sax's seminal work advocating for use of the public trust to protect environmental interests, he suggested that the public trust doctrine should be used in place of environmental rights claims because environmental rights claims were overly ambitious and received inconsistent judicial response. Joseph Sax, *The Public Trust Doctrine in Natural Resource Law: Effective Judicial Intervention*, 68 MICH. L. REV. 471, 474 (1970). However, in his later 1990 article, *The Search for Environmental Rights*, Sax reflects on the evolution of the discourse since his original publication in 1970. *Supra* at 93. He notes that during this time, significant efforts were made "to formulate an environmental right." *Id.* By 1990, Sax recognized the necessity for identifying the basis for an environmental right, prompting him to write this article delineating the basis for such a right. *See id.*

would lead to greater recognition and enforcement.[311] Dinah Shelton similarly concluded that as sources of law increasingly guarantee citizens' rights to environmental quality, the human rights-based approach would be most successful,[312] further observing that procedural environmental rights (guaranteeing rights to participation and information) have been more successful than substantive environmental rights (guaranteeing specific environmental criteria).[313] Professor David Takacs argues that both human and nonhuman needs must be balanced against one another to foster healthfully synergistic relationships within nature,[314] characterizing his normative vision as "an eco-anthropocentric hybrid."[315]

2. Mosaics, Not Monoliths

Notwithstanding philosophical differences, the public trust and rights of nature models share a lot in common on the practical level. As noted, in many (though not all) cases, both approaches strive toward a governance model of environmental stewardship. Another key parallel is the enormous doctrinal variety each has spawned in different jurisdictional contexts. Neither approach means just one thing – there is enormous variation in the public trust doctrine as it has independently developed in the states, and even more variation in what the rights of nature mean to different movements in different parts of the world. Neither can be understood as a monolith – instead, both are mosaics of related but diverging legal doctrines.

For example, in Colorado, the public trust doctrine barely protects navigational and commercial values in waterways,[316] while in Hawaii, the doctrine protects all water in the state for purposes that range from navigational access to

---

[311] Sax, *supra* note 42, at 103, 170.
[312] Shelton, *supra* note 42, at 106.
[313] Dinah Shelton, *Developing Substantive Environmental Rights*, 1 J. Hum. Rts. & Env't 90–92 (2010). She further notes that in the absence of a constitutional substantive guarantee, a jurisdiction's environmental laws may establish substantive environmental rights. *Id.* at 104. Professor James May identifies various sources of substantive environmental rights, including (1) express constitutional recognition, (2) implied constitutional recognition, (3) recognition in domestic legislation, (4) recognition in international law, and (5) recognition in regional law. James R. May, *The Case for Environmental Human Rights: Recognition, Implementation, and Outcomes*, 42 Cardozo L. Rev. 983, 990–1012 (2021). May also identifies three major barriers to effective implementation of these rights: language, remedies, and enforceability. *Id.* at 1013–15. *See also* Clifford Rechtschaffen & David L. Markell, Reinventing Environmental Enforcement & The State/Federal Relationship 38–43 (2003).
[314] David Tackacs, *We Are the River*, 2021 U. Ill. L. Rev. 545, 552 (2021).
[315] *Id.* at 604. Tackacs highlights that the voices of local and indigenous communities would be centered in the RoN approach, as these people would serve as the stewards of the nonhuman entities. *Id.* at 603. Of note, Takacs has also argued that environmental rights under the public trust doctrine and other sources of environmental human rights trump contrary state and local laws. David Takacs, *The Public Trust Doctrine, Environmental Human Rights, and the Future of Private Property*, 16 N.Y.U. Env't L.J. 761 (2008).
[316] *See* Ryan et al., *Comprehensive Analysis*, *supra* note 8, at 2469–70 (discussing Colorado law).

environmental protection,[317] and in Pennsylvania, it protects all natural resources in the state, even beyond waterways.[318] Meanwhile, although Ecuador has assigned constitutional protection for nature,[319] New Zealand and India have focused on protecting specific waterways,[320] Santa Monica protects sustainability interests,[321] and the Minnesota White Earth Band of Ojibwe protects individual plant species of wild rice.[322]

This rich variety is a result of the ongoing doctrinal development described earlier, which points to another important shared feature of the two approaches: their propensity to evolve pragmatically, sometimes rapidly, in response to changing legal circumstances. Moreover, because neither approach means just one thing, both are less absolutist than they may at first appear, leaving open the possibility of multiple meanings and the contradictory impulses that motivate some advocates who appeal to them.[323] Doctrinal variety not only diffuses the absolutism that can accord more dogmatic approaches, but it also adds to the core theoretical challenges of indeterminacy, discussed earlier, that both approaches feature for different reasons.[324]

3. A Special Focus on Waterways

Another key similarity is that while both public trust and rights of nature principles have been applied to protect various natural resources and ecosystems, the predominant focus in both legal contexts has been waterways.

The public trust doctrine is overwhelmingly focused on the protection of water and waterways.[325] This repeated emphasis has been evident since the ancient Roman recognition of the sea and its shores as public commons, to the Magna Carta's specific protection of public navigation, to the early English and American doctrines of sovereign ownership of submerged lands and resources, to the more recently articulated protections for groundwater, recreational access to waterways, and the ecological values associated with them.[326] Similarly, while different communities have

---

[317] See id. at 2468 (discussing the Hawaiian doctrine).
[318] See id. at 2463, 2469 (discussing Pennsylvania's trust).
[319] See Part (A)(6)(b) ("Ecuador") (discussing Ecuador's constitution).
[320] See Part (A)(1)(a) ("New Zealand and Australia") (New Zealand); Part (A)(2)(b) ("India").
[321] See supra notes 200–201, and accompanying text (discussing Santa Monica's ordinance); see also Ryan et al., *Comprehensive Analysis*, supra note at 2527.
[322] See supra notes 152, 160 and accompanying text (discussing the protection of manoomin); see also Ryan et al., *Comprehensive Analysis*, supra note at 2537–38.
[323] See Part (B)(2)(a) ("Duality or False Dichotomy") (discussing the possibility of a false dichotomy).
[324] See id. (discussing indeterminacy).
[325] See Ryan et al., *Comprehensive Analysis*, supra note at 2509–10; see also Erin Ryan, *A Short History of the Public Trust Doctrine and its Intersection with Private Water Law*, 38 VA. ENV'T L.J. 135, 149–50 (2020) [hereinafter *A Short History*].
[326] See Chapter 1 ("The Historical Origins of the Modern Public Trust Doctrine"); see generally Ryan, *A Short History*, supra note 325.

established rights of nature protection for resources ranging from full ecosystems to wild rice, the majority thus far have been applied to river systems.[327] Testifying to this, Professor David Takacs entitles his recent review of international rights of nature initiatives simply *We Are the River*.[328]

The shared emphasis of the public trust and rights of nature on protecting waterways likely reflects the intrinsic centrality of water and waterways to the ecosystems and natural resources that advocates see as needing protection. Just as likely, it suggests something important about the shortcomings of conventional environmental law to protect them. In this regard, both approaches reflect efforts by communities of interest to better protect the most critical and legally vulnerable aspects of natural systems – the water.

4. Responding to the Failure of Conventional Environmental Law

It is noteworthy that the rise of both approaches appears to respond directly to the failure of conventional environmental laws to protect waterways, illustrating a central failure of American water governance more generally. That failure is the artificial disconnect that has developed between our legal treatment of water *quality* and water *quantity* – how clean is the water in a waterway vs. how much water is in the waterway – when every expert understands that they are, in fact, inextricably intertwined. Not only does greater quantity ensure greater quality by diluting pollution to an acceptable level, water pollution control becomes meaningless if there is no longer a waterway to protect from pollution.[329]

Until recently, most water allocation laws were not concerned with the environmental values associated with instream flow, and most water pollution laws left problems of water quantity largely unaddressed. For example, the Clean Water Act,[330] the primary environmental law protecting U.S. waterways, seeks to "restore and maintain the chemical, physical, and biological integrity of the Nation's waters," ensuring they remain safe for drinking, fishing, and swimming by shielding water quality from threats of pollution.[331] It protects waterways by limiting pollutant discharges from discrete, end-of-pipe "point sources,"[332] but it lacks any legal

---

[327] *See* Ryan et al., *Comprehensive Analysis*, supra note 8, at 2514–21.
[328] *See generally* Takacs, supra note 314.
[329] Erin Ryan, *How the Successes and Failures of the Clean Water Act Fueled the Rise of the Public Trust Doctrine and the Rights of Nature Movement*, 73 CASE WEST. RSRV. L. REV. 475, 478 (2022) ("As the advocates for stressed waterways increasingly remind us, water pollution control becomes meaningless if there is no longer a waterway to protect from pollution.") [hereinafter Ryan, *Successes and Failures*].
[330] *See generally* Clean Water Act, 33 U.S.C. §§ 1251–1389 (formerly amended by Federal Water Pollution Control Act Amendments of 1972, Pub. L. No. 92-240, 86 Stat. 47, then amended by Clean Water Act of 1977, Pub. L. 95-217, 91 Stat. 1566).
[331] 33 U.S.C. § 1251(a).
[332] *Id.* § 1342(a).

mechanism to ensure that sufficient quantities of water actually remain instream to preserve the waterway itself.[333] As population growth, industrial demands, migration patterns, and climate change further stress our waterways, environmental laws must do more to consider the amount of water left within them – and water allocation laws must ensure that the allocation of rights to remove water leaves a sufficient amount behind. Recent decisions limiting the jurisdictional reach of the Clean Water Act have cast further doubt on the ability of the statute to meet the environmental needs of the moment.[334]

For these reasons and others, advocates are increasingly embracing the public trust and rights of nature as alternative models for environmental protection that may offer stronger tools for protecting threatened natural resources, or at least different tools. The growing popularity of these approaches domestically and internationally reflects the desperation of advocates seeking to protect waterways that will cease to function ecologically if sufficient water is not left instream, despite the application of conventional environmental laws that focus on pollution. While neither alternative would supplant the Clean Water Act and similar laws in other countries, they highlight the inadequacies of such laws to protect waterways against existential threats unrelated to pollution.

To that point, both public trust and rights of nature principles are routinely invoked as arguments of last resort, by constituents who are openly unsatisfied with the level of protection conventional environmental law has provided for the critical natural resources they see under siege. As one Floridian told the press after passage of the WEBOR Rivers Bill of Rights ordinance, the "mandate ... demonstrates that an overwhelming majority of Orange County citizens have lost faith in a state government and a regulatory system that have failed to protect the basic rights of people as well as the natural world."[335]

In this respect, both approaches function, as much as anything else, as signaling tools for legal desperation. Indeed, the Mono Lake advocates in California did not appeal to the public trust doctrine until all other legal avenues had been explored,[336] just as the Kissimmee River Bill of Rights initiative in Florida was launched only

---

[333] Ryan, *Successes and Failures, supra* note at 483 ("If there is not enough water in the waterways, then we are not protecting the physical, biological, or chemical integrity of the water, as Congress charged us under the CWA. But in the entire statute, perhaps only one section specifically protects waterways *as* waterways, rather than just protecting the water within them.").

[334] *See, e.g.*, Sackett v. Env't Prot. Agency, 598 U.S. 651, 657 (2023); Rapanos v. United States, 547 U.S. 715 (2006); Solid Waste Agency of N. Cook Cnty. v. U.S. Army Corp. of Eng'rs, 531 U.S. 159 (2001).

[335] Joseph Bonasia, *Voters Approve Charter Amendment and Make Florida the Epicenter of Rights of Nature in the U.S.*, SUN SENTINEL (Nov. 6, 2020), www.sun-sentinel.com/opinion/commentary/fl-op-com-invading-sea-orange-county-charter-natural-rights-20201109-yehr2rulu5bi3cdf7jampdbtdm-story.html ("In a county in which the breakdown of Democrats, Republicans, and Independents is 36.6%, 34.2% and 24.3%, respectively, the amendment results may reflect the sentiments of residents throughout the state.").

[336] *See* Chapter 5 ("*National Audubon Society*: The 'Mono Lake Case'").

after all other legal options had failed.[337] In the end, the Mono Lake advocates had more luck than those seeking to protect the Kissimmee River, but all were desperate before trying these novel strategies.

5. Leveraging the Political Arena

A related feature that both concepts hold in common is that while they have not always resulted in legal successes, they very often facilitate political successes. That is to say, even where public trust and rights of nature advocacy has failed to produce the results sought in court, the movements have succeeded in building public awareness and concern to accomplish their goals in the political arena. For example, the atmospheric trust movement has not been terribly successful in court so far, but it has resulted in notable political successes, for example, the gubernatorial creation of climate action plans in the states of Massachusetts and Hawaii, and galvanized public advocacy for climate governance, especially among the young.[338]

Similarly, even though the rights of nature-oriented Community Bill of Rights ordinance enacted by Pennsylvania's Grant Township was struck down in federal court, the community nevertheless accomplished its substantive goal of preventing harm to local waterway by proposed fracking operations.[339] Although the ordinance proved unenforceable, the movement to establish and protect the rights of nature ordinance galvanized public opinion against the injection well that PGE was seeking to dispose of fracking wastewater. Even after the ordinance was invalidated in court, the community doubled down on a Home Rule Charter that incorporated many of the original provisions from the ordinance, which ultimately helped the community defeat the proposed injection well.[340]

These examples reveal an important, dynamic relationship between judicially enforceable constraints on political branch decision-making, such as those set forth in public trust and rights of nature lawmaking, and the larger political process. As noted in Chapter 9's discussion of the atmospheric trust project, one of the most powerful features of the public trust doctrine is the way that it implicates the separation of powers controversy, but with a twist: enabling citizens to use the levers made available by the horizontal separation of powers to increase their efficacy in democratic participation, by enabling them to invoke judicial review of legislative or executive action that violates legal rules. That's why, even though the *Juliana* plaintiffs did not succeed in their lawsuit, the very act of these children bringing it – generating

---

[337] See Ryan et al., *Comprehensive Analysis, supra* note 8, at 2532.
[338] See Chapter 9(B) ("Trust-Rights Advocacy in Action"); Chapter 9(C) (Climate Claims on State Constitutional Grounds).
[339] See Ryan et al., *Comprehensive Analysis, supra* note 8, at 2524–25.
[340] See *supra* notes 193–199 and accompanying text.

international interest and support for their cause – amplifies their voices as individual voters and constituents in the broader political process.[341]

When public trust and rights of nature advocates fail in the judicial sphere but succeed politically, it may be construed not as a design flaw in the system, but instead as a design feature. Scholars are beginning to study the overlooked importance of litigation loss as a galvanizing force in political movements that are later successful, such as the campaigns for LGBTQ and religious rights.[342] Failed campaigns for environmental rights, under the banners of both the public trust and the rights of nature, may well prove another example.

6. *Intuitive and Emotional Appeal*

Finally, it is important to acknowledge that both the public trust and rights of nature approaches do more than just appeal to advocates based on principle – they also appeal to advocates on an intuitive, emotional level. These relatively open-ended doctrines, by virtue of being so ill-defined, have allowed people to pour into them their hopes and dreams for the kind of environmental protection unavailable to them under conventional regulation. As these doctrines have emerged as flexible reservoirs for advocates' uniquely unsatisfied hopes and dreams for environmental law, so have they been pushed to evolve further in different directions, completing the spiral of their rapid differentiation and development.

Indeed, both approaches resonate with something in proponents that goes beyond whether the idea is actionable in court, giving voice to concerns otherwise underserved by the legal system under existing environmental management regimes. In both public trust and rights of nature contexts, environmental advocates appeal to these strategies not only because they are desperate, but because they are drawn to the seemingly straightforward principles at their core. The public trust doctrine's admonition that "the river belongs to all of us," or the rights of nature's recognition that "the river is valuable in and of itself," appears to speak more powerfully to the average decision-maker, and on a more meaningful level, than the Clean Water Act's regulation of "total maximum daily loads." The *Juliana* atmospheric trust litigation and the various rivers' bill of rights movements in Florida have engaged proponents looking for new legal tools and vocabulary in an emotional, almost spiritual, way – speaking to people on levels that conventional legal doctrines do not. Advocates often approach their efforts with the zeal of a mission that exceeds ordinary legal advocacy.[343]

---

[341] *See* Chapter 9(D)(4) ("In Defense of Trust-Rights Advocacy").
[342] Douglas NeJaime, *Winning through Losing*, 96 Iowa L. Rev. 941 (2011) (analyzing the productive function of litigation loss toward successful social movements).
[343] For example, in his statement of principles that would inspire the Earth Jurisprudence movement, Thomas Berry referred not only to "the physical need of humans[,] but also the wonder needed by human intelligence, the beauty needed by human imagination, and the intimacy needed by

These novel legal strategies offer hope for saving beloved natural resources that advocates feel have been under-protected by environmental law and undervalued by cost-benefit analyses that fail to account for the full array of values at stake. But even beyond that, people turn to these approaches because their central premises make sense to them. Public trust and rights of nature principles seem able to speak to lay people on an intuitive plane that conventional environmental law cannot always reach. At their core, both principles reduce to the premise that vulnerable natural systems should be protected against annihilation in service of shortsighted economic interests. The intuitive draw of the public trust doctrine was evident in the nationwide coalition of 36,000 young people inspired to join the atmospheric trust project (even as the litigation struggled to make headway in court),[344] just as the intuitive appeal of the rights of nature movement was demonstrated by the 90 percent of voters in a politically divided Florida county that supported the Orange County WEBOR Rivers Bill of Rights initiative (even as the state legislature voted to preempt it).[345]

Whatever one's critique may be of either the public trust doctrine or the rights of nature movement – or both – one would be wise to heed the critique this level of engagement suggests for the rest of environmental law. While conventional environmental laws like the Clean Air and Water Acts have made important strides in containing pollution, they are not designed to protect public natural resource commons of the sort that the public trust and rights of nature initiatives are now targeting. Conventional environmental law is not working in many such cases, especially with regard to waterways, and the rise of these novel legal strategies suggests that the people most impacted by these failures are getting restive.

D. WHICH IS BETTER?

Those seeking to protect natural resource systems, especially the waterways that are so often the subject of both approaches, may ask the bottom line question – which approach is better? But the answer, at best, is unclear. The first problem we face in grappling with this question, of course, is that we have to be more specific. Which rights of nature initiative? Which public trust doctrine? As demonstrated amply earlier, there is enormous jurisdictional variation in both arenas, as both approaches continue to differentiate and diversify along multiple planes simultaneously. One cannot speak of the public trust doctrine or the rights of nature movement as if either one is a monolith, when as noted earlier, they are emphatically mosaics. Even beyond that, both mosaics suffer from drawbacks that make it hard to choose a clear winner.

---

human emotions for personal fulfillment." THOMAS BERRY, THE ORIGIN, DIFFERENTIATION, AND ROLE OF RIGHTS, Principle 10 (2001), www.ties-edu.org/wp-content/uploads/2018/09/Thomas-Berry-rights.pdf.

[344] *See* Chapter 9(B)(4)(d) ("*Juliana*'s Legacy") (discussing the 36,000 youth who signed an open amicus brief in support of *Juliana v. United States*).

[345] *See supra* note 232 and accompanying text.

1. Different Goals?

In part, it depends on the goals of the observer. Even from the standpoint of providing more environmental protection, the answer seems unclear. To be sure, the public trust doctrine may be a precarious vehicle if the jurisdiction discounts the interests of future generations and public sympathies shift away from long-term environmental values in service of shorter-term economic needs. People clearing forests for agriculture in the Amazon are making an anthropocentric choice that may better their interests today, though it will surely harm them, and especially future generations, over time. If the arbiters of public trust decision-making are human beings in the moment, the doctrine is vulnerable to short-term choices to pave paradise and put up a parking lot[346] whenever parking becomes especially short. As shown earlier, environmental advocates have often turned to the rights of nature movement when the public trust doctrine has proved insufficient to confer needed environmental protection, often because it has been interpreted narrowly or to prioritize other human interests.

Yet ecocentrism may be equally problematic to confer environmental protection when we do not fully understand who should interpret for nature in legal contexts. The early *Sierra Club v. Morton* case first framed this dilemma in terms of legal standing in court, denying natural objects independent standing to sue to prevent harm.[347] Accordingly, an early move by rights of nature proponents was to secure legal personhood for natural objects, unquestionably providing them standing in court, independent of the people acting to protect them. But if we confer standing or legal personhood on natural objects that cannot speak for themselves, how do we reconcile the problem of voice? *Who speaks for nature?* As Professor Stone asked at the beginning of the American movement, *who speaks for the trees?*[348]

It is an especially puzzling problem when different people might come to very different conclusions about how to prioritize the interests of other members of the biotic community. Many believe that to protect nature, we must act quickly to foster wind energy generation to stabilize the climatic foundations of the overall biotic community,[349] while others believe wind turbines cause unacceptable harm

---

[346] See Joni Mitchell, *Big Yellow Taxi*, on LADIES OF THE CANYON (Reprise Recs. 1970).
[347] Sierra Club v. Morton, 405 U.S. 727 (1972).
[348] Cf. DR. SEUSS, THE LORAX (1971) (suggesting that the Lorax speaks for the trees). In his seminal work, *Should Trees Have Standing?*, Stone originally proposed a guardianship system whereby individuals or committees would be put in charge of holding the nonhuman object in trust, with the nonhuman object itself as beneficiary. Stone, *supra* note 39, at 464–67, 471–73.
[349] See, e.g., *Renewable Energy: A Key Climate Solution*, INT'L RENEWABLE ENERGY AGENCY, www.irena.org/-/media/Files/IRENA/Agency/Publication/2017/Nov/IRENA_A_key_climate_solution_2017.pdf?la=en&hash=A9561C1518629886361D12EFA11A051E004C5C98#:~:text=Analysis%20by%20the%20International%20Renewable,the%20Paris%20Agreement%20climate%20goals (last visited Apr. 21, 2023) ("Renewable technologies could generate more than 80% of all electricity by 2050.").

D. Which Is Better?

to vulnerable populations of birds and other wildlife whose habitat they disrupt.[350] In this scenario, who speaks for nature? The proponents of renewable energy or the proponents of birds? In a system such as that in the United States, the representational problem is compounded by procedural problems, as the first movers in litigation may determine how legal efforts to protect nature will unfold, even if they are not the best representatives.

This conundrum for the unfolding rights of nature movement is similar to the classic debate between animal rights activists and conventional environmental advocates for wildlife. Conventional wildlife advocates protect populations, willing to sacrifice individual animals who may be harmed by a larger regulatory program in service of species preservation, as the Endangered Species Act anticipates through the safety valve of incidental take permits. By contrast, animal rights advocates protect individuals, treating each animal as an individual worthy of protection and not just a representative of a larger species of biodiversity – just as human rights advocates fight for the sacred rights of individual human beings, rejecting utilitarianism that would sacrifice innocents in service of goals like swift justice or forced organ donation. When people speak for nature in a rights of nature regime, should they represent nature at the level of individual animals or plants or wetlands? Or are they representing the natural system as a whole, even if there are adverse consequences for individuals within those ecosystems?

And of course, in natural systems, there are always adverse consequences for individuals, as they compete for scarce resources within the food chain and other constraints of the habitat. To that end, what will rights of nature proponents say about those elements of the food chain that feed humans, and other non-endangered species? If wild rice should have rights, what about cows and pigs, or the deer and beavers who want to eat rights-bearing wild rice? What about other survival conflicts between the human and nonhuman members of the biotic community – if a bear attacks a hiker on a trail, whose interests should prevail? How should we balance the competing rights of different individuals and other components of nature, and what exactly are we balancing, then – humans against all of nature, or a specific species, or a specific organism?[351]

Some environmental scholars have criticized the rights of nature movement as unrealistic at best, and materially harmful at worst.[352] A common critique from

---

[350] *See, e.g., Conventional Wind Energy – A Design Deadly for Birds*, AM. EAGLE FOUND, www.eagles.org/take-action/wind-turbine-fatalities ("Wind turbines present an ever-present danger to not only eagles and other birds of prey, but also to any migratory bird that passes through areas where wind turbine farms have been constructed.").

[351] *See* Guim & Livermore, *supra* note 297, at 1378, 1387–95, 1380 (discussing the problems of balancing rights when the interests of nonhuman entities are involved).

[352] *See* Noah M. Sachs, *A Wrong Turn with the Rights of Nature Movement*, 36 GEORGETOWN ENV'T L. REV. (2023); Cynthia Giagnocavo & Howard Goldstein, *Law Reform or World Reform: The Problem of Environmental Rights*, 35 MCGILL L.J. 315 (1990); *see* Guim & Livermore, *supra* note 297, at 1347.

environmental lawyers is that the movement is just too inchoate – that it all seems so vague and unactionable, and if it is actionable, to what ultimate end?[353] It has been anecdotally reported that now that rivers in India have rights, some people in India are suing a river for flooding their lands. If rivers are legal persons, do they have responsibilities as well as rights? How far does the legal personhood construct really go? Some assert that the movement has the potential to undermine the success of environmental protections that have worked.[354] Others worry that the movement threatens to debase the spiritual mysticism of nature by giving the legal community the final word on defining its value through the arbitration of rights.[355] Thus far, the rights of nature movement has not answered these questions, although they surely will have to be answered at some point.[356] But even then, the answer will likely be different in different jurisdictions, representing different points in the constellation of differing planes of development.

2. Different Results?

In wrestling with this kind of comparative assessment, we might also ask where we could expect to see the two approaches yielding concretely different results within the same jurisdiction. And as suggested earlier, we can easily imagine circumstances in which public trust principles would be less protective than the rights of nature. The trust might be sufficient to protect some public interests in a protected resource but insufficient to protect ecological values where they conflict with other compelling public interests. For example, the public trust might protect river flows that are sufficient to protect kayakers and anglers, but it might balk at the anthropocentric flows needed to maintain the integrity of an ecosystem supporting endangered mussels. The rights of nature approach may be tangentially worried about kayakers but more wholesomely concerned about the mussels.

---

[353] *See generally* Sachs, *supra* note 352 (arguing that it is difficult to implement vague standards such as a right to "exist" or "flourish" and worrying that there is no limiting principle to the granting of such rights, threatening the existing legal order). Sachs worries that as judges lack the technical expertise required to adjudicate rights of nature claims, the system may create arbitrary and oppressive outcomes for human beings while weakening more effective legal protections for nature. *Id.*

[354] *See id.*; *see also* Guim & Livermore, *supra* note 297, at 1366 (worrying that unsuccessful rights of nature initiatives could sap the energy supporting more successful environmental advocacy and erode confidence in future environmental advocacy).

[355] *See* Giagnocavo & Goldstein, *supra* note 352, at 361 (cautioning that the rights of nature approach is overly optimistic and warning against confusing "legal reform for the social change that we desire."). They argue that defining nature in the language of legal rights would limit its mysticism and give lawyers too much power in assessing what is valuable in nature. *Id.* at 362–64.

[356] Christopher Stone, in his seminal *Should Trees Have Standing?* rights of nature article, analogized to conventional anthropocentric law in clarifying that nonhuman rightsholders would not have absolute rights, because even important rights held by humans are not absolute and may be worked around with the proper procedure. Stone, *supra* note 39, 482–83.

D. Which Is Better?

Even under an ecologically protective version of the public trust doctrine, as adopted in California, rights of nature principles would be implicated far earlier, at a more nature-protective threshold. Before litigants could invoke the public trust doctrine, they would need to affirmatively demonstrate potential impacts to cognizable trust values – for example, a loss of recreational access, impacts to a vulnerable species, or negative impacts on navigation. Under a rights of nature approach, however, any alternation of flow or impact to the natural ecosystem, no matter the magnitude, could theoretically be sufficient to warrant a claim. Taken to its extreme, *any* alteration of natural flow could be held to violate the rights of nature – creating a potential conflict reminiscent of the anthropocentric pressure that caused the original English common law rule of "natural flow" riparian rights to give way to the more modern American "reasonable use" doctrine, as described in Chapter 1.[357]

That said, the differences become more muted in states with the strongest public trust doctrines, like Hawaii. Hawaii provides an especially interesting example, because the state's strong public trust doctrine is at least partly informed by Native Hawaiian legal principles, which share some of the rights of nature values that are common to wider Polynesian cultures, including the New Zealand Māori people, who have led on rights of nature initiatives. Hawaii may be a good place to look for how these doctrines coexist and work together, and for the interplay between subsistence and environmental justice values in both traditions. By contrast, Florida provides an example of a state with an environmentally weak public trust doctrine in which the rights of nature movement has been invoked to fill the gaps left open by the inability of the public trust doctrine to protect environmental values of surface and groundwater taken together. Yet Pennsylvania provides an example of a state with an environmentally strong public trust doctrine where rights of nature initiatives have also emerged to fill gaps.

For that reason, evaluating which is the "better" approach is an almost impossible project. The answer probably hinges not only on deep philosophical questions about our underlying goals, but also pragmatic factors, like path dependence within an existing legal system. Perhaps the better choice is whichever one fits more seamlessly into the legal tradition at hand, or the political circumstances of the day. The public trust doctrine continues to command force because it has been the law of the land for hundreds (if not thousands) of years in common law countries, especially the United States. The rights of nature commands force in Indigenous communities where that has been the prevailing norm for hundreds, and possibly thousands, of years. And in communities where conventional environmental tools have failed, rights of nature approaches may provide an opportunity to organize around the protection of a resource that has been failed by more conventional means. Even if the rights of nature approach fails in court, it may serve to galvanize political support for

---

[357] *See* Chapter 1 ("The Historical Origins of the Modern Public Trust Doctrine"); *see also* Ryan, *A Short History, supra* note 325, at 185–86. It would be interesting to see, centuries later, if such a transformation could truly be unmade; it would certainly be a very uphill battle ... or a very upstream journey.

the sought result – an effective organizing tool to persuade decision-makers in office to heed public concerns.

A more interesting question is whether there is value to be had in mixing and matching these approaches within one legal system. Can the two doctrines ever be used to support one another from these contrasting ethical approaches, or are they destined only to undermine one another? Perhaps more interesting still is the question of whether they may support one another asymmetrically. The public trust doctrine might provide oblique support to a rights of nature initiative, if only by constraining sovereign decisions to alienate a trust resource, but will rights of nature initiatives openly conflict with public trust principles by reorienting the discussion toward an ecocentric ethical perspective that is ultimately incompatible with the public trust and surrounding legal system in which these laws are embedded?

Where both doctrines are operating, environmental advocates may appreciate that the two offer different but complementary layers of protection. The public trust doctrine may remain the primary tool for protecting traditional values associated with navigability and public enjoyment, but where the trust fails to address ecological concerns, rights of nature principles can be invoked to protect an aquifer, or a habitat, or biodiversity. It is also possible that, in the end, the doctrines may offer complementary protections that are simply aimed at different goals, with the public trust doctrine protecting water resources for human needs and the rights of nature protecting water resources for their inherent ecological value.

Indeed, a frequently observed feature of multilevel environmental governance within a federal system of governance is the advantage of redundancy of multiple sources of authority. History has shown that it is very useful to have two or more available avenues for environmental protection when the path is blocked for political reasons at one level on the jurisdictional scale. The scholarship on environmental federalism is especially cognizant of this benefit, previously described as the "regulatory backstop" feature of American federalism.[358] It may be that simultaneous efforts toward environmental protection rooted in both of these environmental ethics can provide a paradoxical source of checks and balances in natural resource protection. Even if the redundancy cannot be legally or philosophically justified, because the two underlying ethical frameworks are fundamentally irreconcilable, there may still be political advantages to redundancy.

3. Mosaics in Progress

The worldwide rise of these two parallel approaches to environmental rights continues to unfold, as nations across the globe struggle to address the problem of weak legal foundations for environmental protection or missing environmental rights

---

[358] Erin Ryan, *Environmental Federalism's Tug of War Within*, in THE LAW AND POLICY OF ENVIRONMENTAL FEDERALISM: A COMPARATIVE ANALYSIS 355, 364 (Kalyani Robbins ed., 2015).

D. Which Is Better?

in constitutional systems. The rich jurisdictional differentiation described earlier suggests that neither approach is "finished."[359] It reminds us that there is really no such thing as the "public trust doctrine" or the "rights of nature movement," but rather, multiple doctrines and multiple movements.[360] The principles outlined in these emerging environmental theories are more mosaics than they are monoliths, and we can expect them to evolve further as they continue to develop across the lands.[361]

The public trust doctrine is oriented toward anthropocentric injuries, but it has been in legal operation for hundreds if not thousands of years, and it has been steadily evolving to address ecological concerns in many jurisdictions. In theory, rights of nature initiatives may provide even more robust ecological protections, but at least domestically, they remain largely inchoate. In many cases, advocates have turned to either or both approaches to resolve the same problems, in many cases seeking the same substantive results, even though the two approaches operate from fundamentally different ethical frameworks. It will be fascinating to observe how these different approaches will provide different answers to the same legal questions over time, and even more so, how the public trust and rights of nature regimes will interact.

However we should understand those beliefs, it is notable that the two approaches each seem to resonate with people on an ethical and even emotional level that goes beyond the reach of most other environmental laws. The ideas at their heart are simple. At the core, the public trust doctrine holds that the river – or the lake, or the harbor, or whatever the trust resource may be – is so precious that it must be preserved for everyone's benefit. The rights of nature movement holds that the river, as a part of nature, is so precious that it must be preserved for its own intrinsic value. These principles seem to galvanize communities to accomplish environmental stewardship goals outside of court, which can be every bit as important as what happens in court – and, as the political mobilization that preceded the Mono Lake litigation and the political advocacy that followed it both demonstrate, sometimes even more so.

---

[359] Ryan et al., *Comprehensive Analysis*, supra note 8, at 2575–76; Ryan, *A Short History*, supra note 325, at 205–06.
[360] Ryan et al., *Comprehensive Analysis*, supra note 8, at 2558–59.
[361] *Id.*

Conclusion

A Quiet Revolution in Environmental Law

A.	Foundations for Environmental Governance	423
B.	Open Questions	426
	1. The Force and Flexibility of the Doctrine	426
	2. The Legal Nature of the Doctrine	429
	3. The Public Trust's "Public"	430
	4. Separation of Powers and the Antidemocratic Critique	432
	a. Judicial Trust Administration in a Time of Judicial Ascendance	432
	b. Environmental Claims as Generalized Harms	437
	c. Citizen Suit Provisions and the Public Trust	440
	d. Separation of Powers and the Constitutive Constraint	443
C.	The Mono Lake Story, beyond California	445
	1. Great Salt Lake	445
	2. The Sea of Galilee and the Dead Sea	450
	a. The Sea of Galilee (Lake Kinneret)	450
	b. The Dead Sea	453
	3. The Aral Sea	456
D.	Coda: Save Mono Lake?	459

This chapter concludes the book, but the book concludes only midway through the ongoing legal revolution that modern public trust advocacy has engendered. This final discussion considers the quiet revolution that the Mono Lake litigation inspired by advancing public trust principles as a source of environmental law – and even environmental rights. Recognizing the underlying duality of the public trust as a mandate for sovereign protection of natural resources – and a guarantor of public rights within them – offers a new way of understanding modern environmental advocacy, as well as a new paradigm for conceiving responsible environmental governance. Part A begins with a brief summary of the public trust history recounted in this book, and reflection on the role of the doctrine in providing needed support for environmental protection amid weak foundations for environmental law, especially in the United States.

Part B turns to the open questions that remain for future consideration, including the appropriate flexibility of the doctrine, which resources should be protected, and most importantly, the principled objection that the judicial role it invites may threaten the constitutional separation of powers. With prolonged attention to the suggestion that the doctrine may prove antidemocratic, it considers the critique that environmental claims raise the kind of generalized harms that jurisprudential standing limitations are intended to prevent – but also the counterargument that the public trust doctrine may be the original "citizen suit" provision of the common law, appropriately deputizing private attorneys general to litigate diffuse environmental harms in suits that might otherwise be precluded by public choice factors favoring private expropriators and special interests.

Finally, Part C ponders the stakes at hand by sketching out what the world might look like *without* meaningful public trust governance – visiting parallel Mono Lake stories unfolding in other parts of the world without straightforward public trust recourse. It considers the struggles of imperiled waterways at the Great Salt Lake in Utah, the Sea of Galilee (Lake Kinneret) and the Dead Sea straddling Israel and Jordan, and the Aral Sea between Kazakhstan and Uzbekistan, before returning at last in Part D to the ongoing story unfolding at Mono Lake itself. The conversations in each of these parts press us to reflect carefully on the panoply of issues raised throughout the book, and to reach hard for the lessons we can draw to build an environmentally sustainable future.

A. FOUNDATIONS FOR ENVIRONMENTAL GOVERNANCE

Since time immemorial, public trust principles have thus played a pivotal role in balancing protections for the public and private interests that collide within critical shared natural resources.[1] All natural resource commons – such as the waterways and air that sustain us – are complicated by the demands individuals place on their share of the common pool. Sometimes the common pool is more easily disaggregated, as when one individual takes an acre-foot of water from a waterway, or a single member from a species of plants or animals, or even a breath of fresh air. Other times it may be harder to share out the commons, as when one user's river weir prevents all else from passage, or one polluter's carbon emissions equally compromises the atmosphere for everyone. But in all cases, over-exploitation of the commons by a small number of individuals can compromise the resource for all – or in the worst case, destroy it.

As detailed in Chapter 1, the public trust doctrine represents one of the earliest known mechanisms for regulating these natural resource commons problems.[2] The doctrine first did so by legally recognizing such resources *as* public commons, belonging to everyone equally, as set forth in ancient Roman law. Later, it added

---

[1] *See* Chapter 1 ("The Historical Origins of the Modern Public Trust Doctrine").
[2] *See* Chapter 1(A) ("Roots in Early Roman and English Law").

recognition of the sovereign authority to maintain these resources for the public, as affirmed by early British and American law. More recently, it has been understood to confer responsibility on the government to affirmatively protect these resources for the public, as recognized by the Mono Lake case (explored in Chapters 2–5) and its progeny (explored in Chapters 6–8).[3] And now, as the principle is increasingly read or infused into statutory and constitutional texts, that sovereign responsibility can be even more easily been recognized as creating explicit or implicit environmental rights in the public – or alternatively, as the implicit enforcement mechanism for expressly constitutionalized state environmental rights (explained in Chapter 9).[4]

Today, as described in Chapters 8–10, public trust principles can and do support environmental governance initiatives where they are most needed. Public trust models that take seriously the needs of future generations provide grounding for stewardship-oriented environmental governance where legal foundation is lacking.[5] In many jurisdictions, the public trust frames not only a judicially vindicated sovereign obligation and corresponding public environmental right, but also a best practice for statutory and administrative environmental governance. While the Mono Lake plaintiffs deployed the doctrine in court to defend trust resources against government abdication, Chapters 7–8 explored how California, Michigan, and other states build public trust principles into legislative and administrative process, to help ensure that future state action is consistent with state trust obligations. Although administrative adoption may be the least visible manifestation of public trust governance, it has the potential to be the most important. As discussed in Chapter 9, the doctrine provides further pragmatic support for good environmental governance as a strategic lever for achieving the enactment of more specific statutory and regulatory environmental protections.

The embrace of the modern public trust doctrine is not the only manifestation of public frustration with environmental governance that too often fails to protect the environment. The rise of the rights of nature movement described in Chapter 10 follows similar dissatisfaction with the status quo, revealing another modern attempt to leverage an old idea from a different legal tradition to solve the same underlying problem. While the rights of nature movement borrows from indigenous legal systems and ecocentric environmental ethics, the public trust doctrine is squarely rooted in the western legal tradition, reaching back to some of its earliest progenitors in the Roman Empire. Each approach fits more easily within the legal tradition

---

[3] *See* Chapter 2 ("Building the Los Angeles Aqueduct"); Chapter 3 ("The Mono Basin Extension"); Chapter 4 ("Saving Mono Lake: The Political Mobilization"); Chapter 5 ("*National Audubon Society*: The 'Mono Lake Case'"); Chapter 6 ("In the Wake of *Audubon*: The Legal and Political Aftermath"); Chapter 7 ("The *Mono Lake* Doctrine"); Chapter 8 ("Beyond Mono Lake: The Development of the Public Trust across the U.S.").

[4] *See* Chapter 9(A)(4) ("The Reciprocal Nature of Sovereign Obligations and Environmental Rights"); Chapter 9(C) ("Climate Claims on State Constitutional Grounds").

[5] *See* Introduction Part B ("The Public Trust as an Emerging Foundation for Environmental Governance"); Chapter 10(C)(4) ("Responding to the Failure of Conventional Environmental Law").

from which it flows (though with further legal evolution, these traditions may yet find points of convergence). In the meanwhile, public trust principles likely provide the firmer foundation for stewardship-based environmental governance in mostly western legal systems, like the United States.

The quiet revolution, already in progress, thus continues. But it has been a relatively gradual revolution, and the final outcome remains uncertain. To be clear, that revolution is the incremental recognition of public trust ideals as a guarantor of environmental rights and responsibilities – within legal systems chronically short on both – and accordingly, as an additional foundation for wise environmental governance. The Mono Lake litigation became the inflection point in this new trajectory of the old public trust idea, advancing the doctrine as a source of environmental law that could help fill gaps left open by poor constitutional foundations in the United States, and for different reasons abroad.[6] These developments have followed a long and measured process – perhaps more "evolution" than "revolution" – but their potential significance should not be underestimated.

At this point, our inquiry returns full circle to where it began, grappling with important questions about the role public trust ideals can play in establishing better foundations for environmental governance of public natural resource commons. In the contexts explored in this book, public trust principles provide a self-reinforcing partnership of sovereign environmental obligations and corresponding environmental rights, jointly requiring the protection of environmental values associated with public natural resources. The resources protected will differ depending on whether the public trust principle arises from common law, legislative, regulatory, or constitutional sources, prompting the acknowledgement that in reality, there is no such thing as "the public trust doctrine" – only a mosaic of environmental rights and duties, all following the underlying principle of sovereign obligation to protect natural resources for the public.[7]

The public trust principle is itself so ancient and foundational – undergirding legal systems from ancient Rome through the Ottoman Empire to modern common and civil law countries across the globe – that it may be rightly considered an implicit legal premise of human civilization.[8] Even so, we continue to grapple with unresolved problems raised by the doctrine, including who and what it protects, how it does and should operate, and even whether it is inherently antidemocratic. Concluding our inquiry, we turn to these problems, although more to provoke further reflection than to resolve them definitively, in recognition that the public trust doctrine continues to evolve independently throughout the United States and the world.

---

[6] See Introduction Part A ("The Missing Constitutional Foundations of Environmental Law"); Chapter 10(A) ("The Public Trust Doctrine Internationally").

[7] See Chapter 8(A) ("The Planes of Public Trust Development across the United States"); Chapter 10(C)(1) ("Mosaics, Not Monoliths").

[8] See Chapter 1(A) ("Roots in Early Roman and English Law"); Chapter 10(A) ("The Public Trust Doctrine Internationally").

B. OPEN QUESTIONS

As explored in the preceding chapters, the public trust doctrine raises as many questions as it answers. How firm, fixed, or flexible are the rights and obligations it creates? Which resources are subject to its protection? Public trust conflicts like the Mono Lake story also force us to consider the contested nature of the doctrine itself. Is the public trust doctrine an expression of the common law of property? An element of the state's police power? A quasi-constitutional doctrine? Which sources of sovereign authority are encumbered with the trust, and who is the relevant "public"? To that end, what are the responsibilities of the operative legal institutions – the legislature, courts, administrative agencies, and citizens – for carrying out public trust obligations? Does the doctrine facilitate democratic governance by providing multiple ports of entry to the deliberation of environmental policy, or is a doctrine that empowers courts to second-guess political branches – and litigants to challenge broader public policy – inherently antidemocratic?

This part considers these open questions, though as Chapters 8–10 have amply demonstrated, there is no single answer to them, because again – there is no one public trust doctrine.[9] Instead, there is a tapestry-in-progress of jurisdictional approaches, each differentiating along distinct legal planes, all embracing the core public trust principle of sovereign responsibility for protecting public natural resources. In recognition of the public trust continuum that makes these questions unintelligible except in the context of a specific jurisdiction, we take them on with preferential reference to the doctrine as it was articulated by the touchstone case of the book, the *Audubon Society* decision at Mono Lake.

1. *The Force and Flexibility of the Doctrine*

First, how firm is the public trust doctrine? How fixed, flexible, and/or forceful is its protection of trust resources, and which resources should be protected? In California, where the doctrine was successfully deployed to protect the public trust values at Mono Lake (and later, the Scott River), doctrinal protection was firm, but the jurisprudence nevertheless acknowledges the balancing act at the heart of so much environmental governance. As the California Supreme Court recognized in *Audubon Society*, the doctrine does not foreclose private use of public trust commons.[10] The Mono Lake case affirmed a variety of legitimate private uses of the water commons at issue there – recreational use, scientific inquiry, commercial exploitation, and sheer aesthetic beauty, among others – so long as these private uses did not compromise the sustainability of the underlying *res*, the thing held in trust.

---

[9] *See* Chapter 8(A) ("The Planes of Public Trust Development across the United States"); Chapter 10(C)(1) ("Mosaics, Not Monoliths").
[10] Nat'l Audubon Soc'y v. Super. Ct., 658 P.2d 709, 727 (Cal. 1983).

For example, the public trust doctrine did not prevent the state's decision to allocate Mono Basin water for municipal use in Los Angeles – so long as doing so did not destroy the environmental values at Mono Lake.

Yet the Mono Lake case and its progeny still leave much to resolve in interpreting the force of the doctrine going forward – for example, its flexibility. Acknowledging that legislative applications of public trust principles can be directed to whatever resources the body politic sees fit, what about common law versions of the doctrine? How fast or far should the common law trust evolve?

Audubon Society applied the doctrine squarely within the traditional public trust purview of navigable waterways – but the case extended the protections of the California doctrine to new environmental values, farther up the watershed, and farther out in time. Later, the Scott River case extended the *Mono Lake* doctrine itself, protecting non-navigable tributaries to groundwater tributaries of a dependent navigable waterway.[11] Developments like these highlight the flexibility of a doctrine about which the New Jersey Supreme Court famously exclaimed: "like all common law principles, [it] should not be considered fixed or static, but should be molded and extended to meet changing conditions and needs of the public it was created to benefit."[12] The New Jersey courts went on to interpret the trust into new doctrinal territory, extending its protection of public beach access to extend over both public and private lands if trust resources could not otherwise be reached.[13]

Later advocates have attempted to apply public trust principles in wholly new natural resource contexts, such as the atmospheric commons, and wholly new forms of law, such as administrative regulations and state constitutions. Indeed, Chapters 8–10 reveal how different legal systems have embedded the core public trust principle into different vehicles of law and in application to vastly different resources around the country and the world.[14] State actors, once only defendants in public trust lawsuits, are now using the doctrine to defend constitutional takings claims against regulations protecting trust resources.[15] The common feature among all these interpretations? A sovereign obligation to protect public natural resources for the public, and the corresponding rights implied in the public to insist on performance of that obligation.

But what about other management contexts, beyond natural resources, in which public and private interests collide? Could public trust principles bear on, say, the legal

---

[11] Env't L. Found. v. State Water Res. Control Bd., 26 Cal. App. 5th 844, 858 (Cal. Ct. App. 2018).
[12] Borough of Neptune City v. Borough of Avon-by-the-Sea, 294 A.2d 47, 54 (N.J. 1972) (and accordingly having "no difficulty in finding that, in this latter half of the twentieth century, the public rights in tidal lands are not limited to the ancient prerogatives of navigation and fishing, but extend as well to recreational uses, including bathing, swimming and other shore activities").
[13] Matthews v. Bayhead, 471 A.2d 355, 369–70 (N.J. 1984) (extending the doctrine of access to quasi-private beaches); Raleigh Ave. Beach Ass'n v. Atlantis Beach Club, Inc., 879 A.2d 112, 121–25 (N.J. 2005).
[14] *See* Chapter 8(A) ("The Planes of Public Trust Development across the United States"); Chapter 10(C)(1) ("Mosaics, Not Monoliths").
[15] Chapter 8(B)(1) ("The Doctrine as a Background Principle in Takings Claims").

treatment of intellectual property? Enthusiasts occasionally toy with the idea, because there are compelling elements to the analogy.[16] This is another legal realm characterized by chronic public-private tensions, for example, between inventors' interests in maintaining the artificial monopoly that patents provide and the public interest in accessing invention benefits that patent law is designed to promote. Still, the analogy is limited, in part because of the distinguishing feature of creativity in the creation of intellectual property. Natural resources are distinct because they are innately valuable without human manufacture, and thus less amenable to private claims based on creativity or labor. Moreover, unlike created objects, trust resources are often non-fungible – we cannot replace our reliance on water, and especially waterways, with a different resource. And for many natural resources contemplated by trust principles, we cannot easily make more. Applying the doctrine in non-environmental contexts raises many more vexing questions about limiting principles and competing public interests.

By contrast, public trust management of waterways has been universal for over a thousand years – and with good reason. To understand its durability, one need only imagine what the world might have looked like *without* the doctrine – a world in which powerful individuals could monopolize the non-fungible, non-manufacturable lifeblood of advanced civilization, excluding others from waterways necessary for sustenance, migration, transportation, commerce, and even survival. Part C provides a sobering picture of the fate of several ailing waterways that have *not* benefited from strong public trust management, and are now disappearing from the world. For related reasons, as reviewed in Chapter 8, some jurisdictions apply public trust principles to protect other critical natural resources that are also vulnerable to private expropriation or degradation, including wildlife, the atmosphere, and public forests, lands, and energy resources.

Even so, the development of the common law public trust doctrine remains relatively constrained in most U.S. jurisdictions. While state constitutionalized versions of the doctrine have embraced every variety of natural resources (and some have even protected cultural resources),[17] substantive extensions of the common law doctrine to natural resources beyond waterways have been few and far between, and those few that have succeeded have continued to face high legal hurdles after early successes.[18] At present, attempts to deploy the public trust for environmental purposes remain firmest in application to water resources, and weakest in applications beyond that (such as the atmosphere), at least without express statutory or constitutional expansion beyond the common law. The doctrine is thus flexible enough to evolve through the conventional common law process of reasoning by analogy, but not so flexible as to lose its foundations within a precedential system of law.

---

[16] *See, e.g.*, Deirdré A. Keller, *Limiting Lessons from Property: Reimagining the Public Domain in the Image of the Public Trust Doctrine*, 107 KY. L.J. 629 (2019).

[17] Chapter 8(A)(2) ("Differing Resources Protected by the Doctrine").

[18] Chapter 9(C)(4) ("Proposals for State Trust-Right Amendments").

2. The Legal Nature of the Doctrine

The public trust doctrine also prompts consideration of its core, infrastructural features. What is the underlying legal nature of the public trust constraint? To what sources of authority does it apply? Does it make a difference whether we conceive of it as an affirmative public right or a negative sovereign constraint? These are some of the most interesting and difficult questions raised by the Mono Lake case and its progeny. *Audubon Society* established the nature of the trust as something beyond the ken of ordinary common law, without fully resolving the question of its constitutive status.[19] As discussed in Chapter 7, the extent to which the doctrine exceeds conventional common law limitations remains debated, although most states follow the California approach of placing it beyond the reach of ordinary statutory abrogation.[20] This approach seems most consistent with a negative-rights doctrine that meaningfully constrains sovereign authority over public trust resources – limiting what the sovereign can and cannot do – because a constraint that the sovereign can easily extinguish has no real force.

As for whose sovereign authority it constrains – state or federal or both – at present, the doctrine has been confirmed only in application to state sovereign authority.[21] However, the most theoretically and historically consistent answer is that it should be understood to constrain *all* sovereign authority, no matter its source. Based on centuries of settled U.S. and state case law, the doctrine clearly constrains state authority. But if it is appropriately understood as a limit on sovereign authority over public commons, then as an intellectual matter, why should it matter whose sovereign authority is at issue? Logically, as reviewed in Chapter 8, it constrains whatever authority governs the relevant commons.[22]

As further elaborated in Chapter 8, this answer also best accounts for the history of state and federal turn-taking on managing public trust resources, given that most states inherited their trust-impressed resources through the intervening medium of federal sovereign authority, by which the U.S. government held these resources until they could be disbursed to new states.[23] The Supreme Court's dicta in *PPL Montana* characterizing the doctrine as a feature of state law remains problematic for claims that depend on federal trust obligations – but that passing, out-of-context reference should not be authoritative when the Court properly considers this issue for the first time.[24] After the Supreme Court declined to hear the *Juliana* plaintiffs'

---

[19] Chapter 7(C)(1) ("California: A Constitutive Constraint").
[20] Chapter 5(B) ("Unpacking the *Mono Lake* Decision: Legal Elements and Innovations").
[21] Chapter 8(B) ("The Public Trust in Federal Law").
[22] *Id.*
[23] *Id.*
[24] *See supra* Chapter 8(B)(3) ("A Constitutive Constraint on Federal Authority?"). The Court may well choose to confront this question, if the *Juliana* petition for certiorari is accepted. Indeed, the judicial effort required to keep the substantive *Juliana* claim away from federal adjudication may attest to the anxiety that resolving that question one way or the other has raised for many jurists.

appeal of their dismissal,[25] it is less certain when that claim will be raised, but it seems inevitable at some point.

Meanwhile, the reciprocal version of the public trust principle increasingly evident in statutes, treaties, and constitutions – which implies a sovereign constraint through an overt public right – is framed expressly as an affirmative right, in contrast to the more familiar negative rights of the western legal tradition. As discussed in Chapter 9, the environmental rights provisions in several American state constitutions and international analogues fit this model. Yet as considered in the Introduction, Part D, and Chapter 9(A)(4), both sides of the public trust coin are the necessary implication of the other – lacking legal meaning without the implied partnership between them.[26] Different expressions of public trust principles may emphasize one side of the coin over the other, but as revealed throughout the book, both sides must be in operation for either version to have any force. Understanding public trust principles expressed as both negative sovereign constraints and positive environmental rights as conceptual mirror images raises questions about how much weight the distinction between positive and negative rights can really bear, at least in the public trust context.

3. The Public Trust's "Public"

Whether framed as a sovereign constraint or a public environmental right, it is the public that benefits. Yet we might also consider who, exactly, is the public trust doctrine's "public?" Who gets to vindicate implied environmental rights in trust resources as beneficiaries of the trust? Whose interests count when assessing the "public" interests protected by the doctrine, and on what scale? For example, in the Mono Lake story told in Chapters 3–6, was the relevant "public" the town of Lee Vining? The state of California? The United States Forest Service? The *Audubon Society* and scientific community? Should we understand the public interest as a mere aggregation of individual private interests? Does "the public" include nature itself, independently from human members of the biotic community, as the rights of nature movement reviewed in Chapter 10 would contend?[27]

In the context of the Mono Lake case, many different publics were operating, and they appeared to have different interests. But at least in the United States, most public trust cases suggest that the relevant public is the population of the relevant sovereign, usually the state. The New Jersey Supreme Court reached this conclusion explicitly in the beach access cases, in which it determined that the interests

---

[25] Juliana v. United States, No. 24-684, D.C. No. 6:15-cv-1517, (May 1, 2024), cert. denied, 604 U.S. 645 (2025).
[26] *See* Chapter 9(A)(4) ("The Reciprocal Nature of Sovereign Obligations and Environmental Rights"); Introduction, Part D ("Public Trust Principles and Environmental Rights").
[27] Chapter 10(B)(1) ("A Whirlwind Tour of the Rights of Nature Movement").

of state citizens who lived far away from the beach must be protected, even at the expense of the contrary interests among the more local beachfront communities.[28] In *Audubon Society*, the court invoked the interests of the entire state of California in preserving Mono Lake[29] – even though millions of Los Angelenos lost some of their former access to water that will now remain in a basin where only a few hundred live.

That uncertain utilitarian calculus suggests that the public trust's "public interest" must be more than just the aggregation of the individual private human interests most impacted, at least when measured by conventional economic means.[30] Even though the original common law trust sounds in the concept of ownership, the modern doctrine has incorporated an ethic of environmental stewardship, starting at Mono Lake (and perhaps that recognition mitigates against the fear that a fickle public will one day choose to pave paradise to put up another parking lot).[31] One important difference between the state's public trust obligations and its more general police powers to protect public welfare is that the public trust frames a specific, unwaivable obligation, while the police power is a broader and more flexible reservoir of discretionary authority applied in many different contexts. The public trust doctrine may also require greater focus on the welfare of future generations (and in many jurisdictions, constrains use of the police power for conflicting reasons). In that way, the "public" of the public trust doctrine may uniquely force consideration of intergenerational equity, balancing the property law roots of the common law doctrine with undertones of sustainability.

Nevertheless, the Mono Lake decision also invoked utilitarian reasoning in affirming the need to move water great distances to the south, even when doing so causes harm to the basin of origin.[32] The balancing act remains complex. By assigning the balancing act to the Water Board, the California Supreme Court invited conventional means of public consultation and consensus building, inviting DWP, the *Audubon Society*, the Forest Service, the scientific community, and all

---

[28] Matthews v. Bayhead, 471 A.2d 355, 363–64 (N.J. 1984).

[29] Nat'l Audubon Soc'y v. Super. Ct., 658 P.2d 709, 722 (Cal. 1983) ("The ownership of the navigable waters of the harbor and of the lands under them is a subject of public concern to the whole people of the State").

[30] Environmental economists seeking to measure the non-market existence, option, and bequest values of preserved nature that humans may never experience directly may yield a different utilitarian calculus, though these tools are still rough. See Ryan, Curry, Rule, *Environmental Rights for the 21st Century*, 42 CARDOZO L. REV. 2447, 2545–46 (2021) (discussing environmental economists efforts to value non-priced ecological values in cost-benefit analysis).

[31] Joni Mitchell, BLUE (A&M Studios 1971); *see also* Chapter 7(A)(3) ("The Environmental Critique") n. 70 and text accompanying note (discussing this critic of the public trust doctrine).

[32] *Nat'l Audubon Soc'y*, 658 P.2d at 727–28 ("[T]he Water Board ... has the power to ... permit an appropriator to take water from flowing streams and use that water in a distant part of the state, even though this taking does not promote, and may unavoidably harm, the trust uses at the source stream." "[A]ppropriation may be necessary for efficient use of water despite unavoidable harm to public trust values ....").

other stakeholders to voice their interests as public participants.[33] With that in mind, perhaps the public trust "public" isn't even a discrete collection of people; perhaps it is best understood as a process of public deliberation and expression. Cynically, one could conclude that the role of the public in public trust controversies is therefore to be played by whoever turns out to be most successful at mobilizing the political process, by whatever means is effective. Less cynically, how else is democracy intended to work?

4. Separation of Powers and the Antidemocratic Critique

Which brings us to the final question: is the public trust doctrine a paragon of democratic governance, enabling citizens to access multiple forums for public participation and deliberation? Or is it antidemocratic at its core, distorting the judicial role at the expense of the wider political process? The public trust doctrine asks us to consider the rightful roles of all the different legal actors in accomplishing the complex decision-making it requires: the courts, the legislature, executive agencies, even individual citizens. Citizens usually bring trust lawsuits, generally against the legislature or executive agencies they allege are violating trust obligations – although as detailed in Chapter 8, some legislatures and agencies have codified trust principles themselves, and states are increasingly invoking the doctrine as a defense against citizens' takings claims challenging environmental regulation of trust resources.[34] In both contexts, however, it is ultimately the judiciary who interprets the demands of the trust in a given context. And for that reason, as discussed in Chapter 7 and again in Chapter 9,[35] the judicial role in administering the public trust doctrine has always prompted separation-of-powers concerns.

a. Judicial Trust Administration in a Time of Judicial Ascendance

The public trust doctrine has always prompted separation-of-powers concerns about the role of the courts in policing the acts of the other branches on matters that, for some, stray uncomfortably close to matters of pure policy.[36] When a court invalidates

---

[33] Chapter 6(A) ("Protecting the Mono Bain Land").
[34] Chapter 8(B)(1) ("The Doctrine as a Background Principle in Takings Claims").
[35] Chapter 9(D)(1) ("Separation of Powers Concerns").
[36] *See, e.g.*, Richard J. Lazarus, *Judicial Missteps, Legislative Dysfunction, and the Public Trust Doctrine: Can Two Wrongs Make it Right?*, 45. ENV'T L. 1139, 1155–56 (2015) (noting that environmental protection requirements "are exclusively the product of the common law and statutory law," and without the constitutional support analogous to equal protection claims, there is "therefore far less force to the premise that courts can legitimately supplant the lawmaking prerogatives of the legislative and executive branches."); see also William D. Araiza, *Democracy, Distrust, and the Public Trust: Process-Based Constitutional Theory, the Public Trust Doctrine and the Search for a Substantive Environmental Value*, 45 UCLA L. REV. 385, 395, 445 (1997) (critiquing the judicial role in public trust administration);

state action for violating trust obligations, the court is overriding presumptively deliberated decision-making by the political branches. Is the judicial vindication of public trust principles an appropriate check on legislative or executive action, or does it usurp policymaking authority better exercised by the political branches? In the context of protecting natural resource commons, does empowering judicial review guarantee vulnerable public interests, or does it threaten the constitutional order by coopting the conventional political process?

At bottom, the question is how much power courts should have over the actions taken by other branches of government to vindicate core public trust rights and obligations, and it is a question about which reasonable minds have long disagreed. In his seminal critique of atmospheric trust advocacy, Professor Lazarus argues that the courts should always be seen as, at best, "secondary players" in the broader effort to actualize effective climate governance:

> Courts can, as in *Massachusetts v. U.S. Environmental Protection Agency*, properly cajole and push executive branch agency recalcitrance in the face of statutory commands. But the courts possess neither the competency nor the legitimacy necessary to play a far greater role and should avoid substituting their policy judgment regarding the proper level of environmental protection for that of the legislature or executive branch agencies acting pursuant to legislative charges of such lawmaking responsibility. For this reason, I think it is a strategic mistake to delude oneself – let alone the law students we teach – by suggesting otherwise. Far better to accept the true difficulty of the lawmaking challenge we face, and to undertake the necessary hard work at the national – and no less important at the retail – level, than to pretend that the courts can provide quick fixes to rescue us from ourselves.[37]

Lazarus is right that the importance of fighting for responsible environmental governance through the political process at all levels of jurisdictional scale must never be taken for granted. He is right that the judiciary will never be able to provide a quick fix that obviates that important work, nor should we ask this of judicial actors. Courts cannot, as he memorably warns, "rescue us from ourselves." But can they at least help us move the ball forward, when the matter involves the enforcement of environmental rights and obligations? Is it possible, or even desirable, to call on what the judiciary *can* do in an effort to save ourselves and the future generations put at risk by the threat of unremediated global warming?

Lloyd R. Cohen, *The Public Trust Doctrine: An Economic Perspective*, 29 CAL. W. L. REV. 239, 275 (1992) (critiquing the problems of the vague public trust directive for judicial enforcement); Chapter 9(A)(3) ("The Scholarly Critics"); Erin Ryan, *The Public Trust Doctrine, Private Water Allocation, and Mono Lake: The Historic Saga of* National Audubon Society v. Superior Court, 45 ENV'T L. 561, 621–22 (2015) [hereinafter Historic Saga] (discussing these concerns with regard to traditional trust advocacy); Erin Ryan, *From Mono Lake to the Atmospheric Trust: Navigating the Public and Private Interests in Public Trust Resource Commons*, 10 GEO. WASH. J. ENERGY & ENV'T L. 39, 62–64 (2019) (discussing them with regard to the atmospheric trust project).

[37] Lazarus, *supra* note 36, at 1152.

It is a genuinely troubling question – especially now. Climate litigation is raising these questions at a time of environmental exigency, but also a controversial moment of ascendancy for judicial power. In recent years, the Supreme Court in general (and the Roberts Court in particular) has been criticized for aggrandizing power to itself at the expense of all other federal actors[38] – the executive agencies, by weakening judicial deference to agency discretion;[39] the legislature, by promulgating new clear statement rules at a time of legislative paralysis;[40] and even previous Supreme Courts, by breezily disregarding past precedents.[41] Within that context, is it really wise to entrust judges with yet more power to second-guess political actors, especially as the doctrine continues to expand? Is advocacy attempting to engage the courts in climate governance on public trust grounds, especially in the absence of constitutional grounding, dangerously antidemocratic?

These are legitimate, even wrenching, concerns.

And yet, public trust principles remain an integral part of the legal system, at an arguably foundational level. Most states that have considered the issue treat the public trust doctrine as a quasi-constitutional constraint on sovereign authority, operating beyond the reach of normal legislative processes to undo.[42] Constitutional or constitutive constraints, which structure the space within which normal legislation takes place, typically *are* the proper subject of judicial interpretation and intervention.[43] Even the famously libertarian Professor Richard Epstein has noted that the public trust doctrine has a constitutional dimension,[44] undermining casual disregard

---

[38] *See, e.g.,* Allen C. Sumrall & Beau J. Baumann, *Clarifying Judicial Aggrandizement*, 172 U. PA. L. REV. ONLINE 24, 24, 42 (2023) (concluding that "the Roberts Court's exceptional feature is judicial self-aggrandizement, its demeaning rhetoric about other constitutional actors and vague judicial standards that together reify judicial importance and justify centralized power in the judiciary"); Josh Chafetz, *The New Judicial Power Grab*, 67 ST. LOUIS U.L.J. 635 (2023) (providing examples of judicial aggrandizement by the Roberts Court, and other Supreme Courts, in multiple arenas of law); Erin Ryan, *Sackett v. EPA and the Regulatory, Property, and Human Rights-Based Strategies for Protecting American Waterways*, 74 CASE W. RSRV. L. REV. 281, 284 (2023) (critiquing the Court for self-aggrandizement in the environmental law context by "invoking a new 'clear statement' doctrine during an unusually intense period of legislative paralysis (in which Congress appears unlikely to achieve clarity on any major question)," enabling the Court to "unselfconsciously substitute[] its own judgment for that of the political branches on a scientific matter in which judicial capacity approaches its nadir.").

[39] Loper Bright Enters. v. Raimondo, 144 S.Ct. 2244 (2024).

[40] West Virginia v. EPA, 142 S. Ct. 2587 (2022); Sackett v. EPA, 598 U.S. 651 (2023).

[41] Dobbs v. Jackson Women's Health Org., 597 U.S. 215 (2022) (overturning the precedent set decades earlier in *Roe v. Wade*, recognizing a constitutional right to abortion).

[42] *See* Erin Ryan et al., *Environmental Rights for the 21st Century: A Comprehensive Analysis of the Public Trust Doctrine and Rights of Nature Movement*, 42 CARDOZO L. REV. 2447, 2472–76 (2021) [hereinafter *Comprehensive Analysis*] (discussing the majority approach adopting the public trust as a constraint on sovereign authority, but also Idaho's minority approach rejecting this rationale).

[43] *See* Erin Ryan, *A Short History of the Public Trust Doctrine and its Intersection with Private Water Law*, 38 VA. ENV'T L. J. 135, 176–81 (2020) [hereinafter *A Short History*] (discussing academic discourse on the public trust as a constitutive constraint.

[44] Richard A. Epstein, *The Public Trust Doctrine*, 7 CATO J. 411, 426–28 (1987).

for the judicial role in its implementation and enforcement. The doctrine creates serious sovereign obligations, and as this book has argued, reciprocally meaningful environmental rights. If the judiciary were not available to interpret and defend these rights and obligations, they would become devoid of all power and all legal meaning.

The judiciary has long been understood as the proper vindicator of rights and enforcer of obligations. The law of trusts has always been interpreted and enforced by courts, for exactly the reason of this unique judicial capacity.[45] Who better than judges to oversee the public beneficiary's interest in trust resources against the potentially self-serving or neglectful management by a legislative or executive trustee? While the government is always under a police power duty to protect the public, and decisions made under the police power generally receive judicial deference, sovereign obligations under the public trust are less open to interpretation and thus the proper subject of judicial scrutiny.[46] Given the trust obligation to protect specific trust values even when they are in conflict with other public interests, courts may be the best and only venue for evaluating government decisions that fall short.[47]

The antidemocratic critique may also discount the ways that judicial review of public trust governance legitimately empowers democratic participation in the wider political process, because of the intricately braided dance between citizens and the three branches of government within that process.[48] Most policymaking is appropriately legislative, because the elected legislature is the operative democratic device for achieving consensus among competing considerations and diverse interest groups. Administrative agencies are often involved, usually by legislative invitation in broadly framed requests for implementation given agencies' superior subject matter expertise.[49] Courts adjudicate related disputes by interpreting the operative legal constraints and the past judicial precedents that help make sense of them. And most important of all, the citizens oversee the political process, variously

---

[45] *See generally* Edward A. Zelinsky, *Situating the Modern Public Trust Doctrine in Trust Law: The Duty of Loyalty and the Case for Bifurcated, De Novo Judicial Review*, 42 VA. ENV'T L. J. 1 (2024).

[46] In the Mono Lake case, first affirming public trust responsibilities for environmental protection, the California Supreme Court specifically rejected the state's argument that the trust obligation was satisfied so long as the state was acting in the public interest, an interpretation that would have rendered the public trust doctrine coterminous with the police power. Nat'l Audubon Soc'y v. Super. Ct. of Alpine Cnty. (Mono Lake), 658 P.2d 709, 712 (Cal. 1983).

[47] *See* Samuel H. Ruddy, *Finding a Constitutional Home for the Public Trust Doctrine*, 43 ENVIRONS ENV'T L. & POL'Y J. 139, 160–61 (2020) (arguing that separation of powers concerns about the public trust doctrine can be defeated for various reasons, including that its use for environmental protection "comports with accepted understandings of the proper judicial role in our constitutional system" because the doctrine corrects for "structural imbalance in political access by raising judicial scrutiny when government dispositions of trust resources appear to favor particular interests at the expense of the general public").

[48] Part of this analysis expands on an argument in Ryan, *Historic Saga, supra* note 36, at 637–39.

[49] *Cf.* Chevron, U.S.A., Inc. v. Nat. Res. Def. Council, Inc., 467 U.S. 837, 864–66 (1984) (discussing the importance of the administrative role), overruled by Loper Bright Enters. v. Raimondo, 144 S. Ct. 2244 (2024).

participating as voters, jurors, public commenters, editorial writers, legislative office visitors – and occasionally, as plaintiffs.

As I have previously argued, the best way to understand trust-based advocacy is that it engages all players in the democratic process within their usual role.[50] The legislative and executive branches coordinate in policy making and implementation until a citizen objects, filing a claim against the state for allegedly violating some core public trust constraint. The court assesses whether the government has abdicated a sovereign obligation or contravened an environmental right. If it agrees with the complaint, most courts will, at a minimum, declare that the challenged government activity was *ultra vires* – beyond its authorized powers – and the sovereign actor will be required to revisit its decision. Importantly, the reviewing court doesn't invalidate these policy choices of its own volition; it simply interprets whether the challenged action was authorized – whether the applicable public trust principles either allowed or prevented the challenged action from having legal force.[51] In this regard, a court issuing a declaratory judgment should easily pass separation-of-powers matters. Presumably, and in keeping with the judicial role of enforcing rights and obligations, so would appropriately tailored requests for injunctive relief necessitated by the rights and obligations recognized by the court (although more ambitious requests for injunctive relief raise additional questions and may warrant additional scrutiny).

Concerns about the judicial role are even more muted when public trust principles are based on constitutional or legislative sources of law, because then courts are interpreting a statutory command and performing a constitutionally mandated function. But even when a court interprets the common law public trust doctrine, as articulated by previous courts, the judicial role should survive scrutiny. Just as *Marbury v. Madison* had to invent judicial review of congressional acts to protect the constitutional order,[52] so the public trust doctrine was necessary to protect sovereign regulation of critical public commons from capture by private interests. As described in Chapter 7, the common law doctrine itself may even be quasi-constitutional in nature – or at least an inherent limit on sovereignty warranting constitutional recognition, even if it is not expressly set forth in the text.[53] (After all, the Constitution nowhere mentions the words "equal footing," and yet we uncontroversially consider that a constitutional doctrine.)[54] The Supreme Court does not presently favor this view,[55] but as does the common law, constitutional interpretation may gradually evolve over time.

Moreover, it is worth noting that – especially after the failure of the *Juliana* litigation in federal court – the overwhelming majority of trust-rights claims are likely

---

[50] Ryan, *Historic Saga*, *supra* note 36, at 637.
[51] Id.
[52] Marbury v. Madison, 5 U.S. 137, 177 (1803).
[53] Chapter 7(C) ("Ordinary Common Law or Quasi-Constitutional?").
[54] Id.
[55] PPL Montana, LLC v. Montana, 132 S. Ct. 1215 (2012).

to be raised in state courts, rather than federal courts. Most of the contemporary critiques of judicial aggrandizement have been focused on the federal courts, and the Supreme Court in particular[56] – not the state courts that, as courts of general jurisdiction, will hear most of these claims, likely premised on state constitutions, the common law public trust doctrine, statutory trust applications, or a mix of all three. While it is too early to say anything definitive in this regard, one could imagine that state court decisions may even prove a helpful counterbalance to federal judicial aggrandizement, as the very kind of constitutional check-and-balance that the vertical separation of powers has always intended.[57]

b. Environmental Claims as Generalized Harms

Even so, the separation-of-powers critique remains especially potent when the public trust doctrine is invoked to protect environmental values, because the public nature of these claims triggers a separate critique about the antidemocratic abuse of judicial process. Courts serve a constitutionally assigned role in balancing legislative and executive power, and they are arguably the only meaningful enforcer of counter-majoritarian rights against a potentially indifferent majority.[58] But when trust-rights claims are made to protect environmental rights, they seem less like counter-majoritarian rights in the classical sense.[59] Do climate lawsuits represent claims to vindicate individual rights that must be honored even if the majority would prefer otherwise, like an individual right to free speech or free exercise? Or are they better understood as claims to protect the generalized but diffuse interests of the public?[60]

---

[56] See supra notes 38–41 and accompanying text.
[57] See ERIN RYAN, FEDERALISM AND THE TUG OF WAR WITHIN 39–44 (2012) [hereinafter RYAN, TUG OF WAR].
[58] Raines v. Byrd, 521 U.S. 811, 828–29 (1997) ("The irreplaceable value of the power articulated by Mr. Chief Justice Marshall [in Marbury v. Madison, 1 Cranch 137, 2 L.ED. 60 (1803),] lies in the protection it has afforded the constitutional rights and liberties of individual citizens and minority groups against oppressive or discriminatory government action. It is this role, not some amorphous general supervision of the operations of government, that has maintained public esteem for the federal courts and has permitted the peaceful coexistence of the counter-majoritarian implications of judicial review and the democratic principles upon which our Federal Government in the final analysis rests.") (quoting United States v. Richardson, 418 U.S. 166, 192 (1974) (Powell, J. concurring)). See also Erin Ryan, *The Four Horsemen of the New Separation of Powers: The Environmental Law Implications of Loper Bright, West Virginia, Sackett, and Corner Post*, 109 MINN. L. REV. ___ (2025) (in an article exploring the horizontal separation of powers implications of the concentration of judicial power in environmental regulatory contexts, offering a proposal to protect the judicial primacy in counter-majoritarian rights interpretation while sharing some authority over constitutional structural interpretation with the political branches).
[59] Cf. Araiza, supra note 36, at 415, 427 (distinguishing public trust concerns from the concerns of discrete and insular minorities that warrant heightened equal protection scrutiny).
[60] Cf. Joseph Sax, *The Public Trust Doctrine in Natural Resource Law: Effective Judicial Intervention*, 68 MICH. L. REV. 471, 560 (1970).

Setting aside concerns about requests for ambitious injunctive relief, even if courts are constrained to merely undoing wrongful political action, critics of trust-rights climate claims might argue that such litigation violates the separation of powers for essentially the same reason that the jurisprudential standing doctrine limits the judicial role.[61] As explained in Chapter 9,[62] plaintiffs must meet a strict set of standing requirements to access the court system, including the requirements of a particularized and redressable injury. To meet them, plaintiffs must show that the harm at issue is unique to them in a way that deserves individual judicial inquiry (rather than a generalized grievance shared by all members of the public), and also that it is a harm the court can actually redress (rather than a public policy matter that is the proper subject of the political process).[63] These standing requirements are more than mere legal technicalities. The late Justice Antonin Scalia famously maintained that strict application of the standing doctrine – which, he argued, vindicates the constitutional separation of powers by properly distinguishing courts from legislators – is a bedrock protection for liberal democracy.[64]

While the debate over the judicial role with regard to generalized injuries is broader than the debate over judicial administration of trust-rights claims, they raise similar separation-of-powers issues because both involve the potential for judicial intervention in decision-making realms otherwise reserved for policymakers. As Justice Scalia explained in legal scholarship published in 1983, the same year that the *Audubon Society* public trust decision saving Mono Lake launched the modern environmental public trust movement[65]

> [T]he law of standing roughly restricts courts to their traditional undemocratic role of protecting individuals and minorities against impositions of the majority, and excludes them from the even more undemocratic role of prescribing how the other two branches should function in order to serve the interest *of the majority itself*.[66]

Scalia's article differentiates between particularized injuries, for which plaintiffs should always have access to judicial review, and the kinds of majoritarian injuries – often raised by administrative and environmental law plaintiffs – which he

---

[61] This line of reasoning raises similar concerns to arguments for preempting public trust claims on standing grounds, as the Ninth Circuit did in dismissing multiple iterations of the *Juliana* atmospheric trust claim. Order Granting Motion for Writ of Mandamus, Juliana v. United States, No 24-684 (9th Cir. May 1, 2024).
[62] See Chapter 9(B)(4) ("*Juliana v. United States*") (describing the standing challenges confronted by atmospheric trust litigants).
[63] See Lujan v. Defs. of Wildlife, 504 U.S. 555, 560–61 (1992) (explaining that a plaintiff must satisfy each of three constitutional standing requirements to be heard in court: (1) injury in fact, (2) causation between the defendant's actions and the plaintiff's injury, and (3) redressability).
[64] See generally Antonin Scalia, *The Doctrine of Standing as an Essential Element of the Separation of Powers*, 17 SUFFOLK U. L. REV. 881 (1983).
[65] Id.
[66] Id. at 894.

B. Open Questions

disdains as antidemocratic.[67] For him, harms that concern everyone equally should be resolved strictly through conventional political processes, such as voting and lobbying.[68] Pursuing this reasoning, he points favorably to 1920s era Supreme Court jurisprudence denying taxpayer standing to pursue a generalized policy grievance in court,[69] and he critiques later 1960s era jurisprudence allowing it for qualifying constitutional claims.[70]

To be clear, trust-rights plaintiffs must meet the same standing requirements as any other plaintiffs to access the courts, just like plaintiffs suing under conventional environmental laws.[71] Indeed, the application of these standing requirements to preclude plaintiffs from vindicating the broader public interest in environmental cases has prevented environmentalists from pursuing claims on behalf of wildlife and ecosystems in a number of seminal cases for the development of standing doctrine and environmental law[72] (and in so doing, indirectly fomenting the Rights of Nature movement as an alternative conception of environmental rights[73]).

Yet the public trust doctrine really *does* invite members of the public to use the judiciary to second-guess legislative policies relating to resources that are, by definition, important to everybody. The U.S. Supreme Court confirmed this when it revoked a nineteenth century legislative conveyance of Chicago Harbor to a private railroad in a seminal statement of the public trust doctrine,[74] and a century later, the California Supreme Court did the same in rejecting the executive licensing of water exports destroying Mono Lake.[75] Concerns about judicial empowerment are thus legitimate issues with which trust-rights advocacy must contend. To the extent that

---

[67] *Id.* at 894, 897.
[68] *Id.* at 894–897.
[69] Frothingham v. Mellon, 262 U.S. 447, 487–89 (1923) (denying taxpayer standing to prevent certain federal government expenditures alleged to violate the Tenth Amendment, because the plaintiff did not suffer particularized harm.) *Accord* United States v. Richardson, 418 U.S. 166, 175 (1974) (denying taxpayer standing to challenge the exemption of CIA spending from public auditing because the interest was too generalized).
[70] Flast v. Cohen, 392 U.S. 83, 105–06 (1968) (holding that federal taxpayers can have standing for claims that federal tax money is being used in contravention of constitutional limits in certain circumstances, here in violation of the Establishment Clause).
[71] Lujan v. Defs. of Wildlife, 504 U.S. 555, 560–61 (1992) (setting forth the modern standing requirements of concrete and particularized injury specifically to preempt a public interest environmental claim).
[72] See *id.*; Sierra Club v. Morton, 405 U.S. 727 (1972) (denying environmental advocates standing in their suit to prevent a ski resort from developing a pristine ecosystem in the Sierra National Forest because they represented only the generalizable public interest and lacked a particularized injury.
[73] Justice Douglas's dissent in *Sierra Club v. Morton*, 405 U.S. at 741–42 (Douglas, J., dissenting), prompted Christopher Stone's famous article, *Should Trees Have Standing? – Toward Legal Rights for Natural Objects*, 45 S. CAL. L. REV. 450 (1972), considered one of the most important progenitors of the modern Rights of Nature movement. *See also* Ryan, *Comprehensive Analysis*, *supra* note 42, at 2503–06.
[74] Ill. Cent. R.R. Co. v. Illinois, 146 U.S. 387, 452 (1892).
[75] Nat'l Audubon Soc'y v. Super. Ct. of Alpine Cnty. (*Mono Lake*), 658 P.2d 709, 727 (Cal. 1983).

these lawsuits protect widespread public interests and empower judicial intrusion in policymaking spheres, they confirm the very anxiety about the runaway judicial role that Justice Scalia famously critiqued in the standing context.

c. Citizen Suit Provisions and the Public Trust

Nevertheless, there is a reason why Justice Scalia's argument especially targeted environmental cases as blurring the lines that the separation of powers should maintain. For the same reason public trust principles threaten to blur these lines, Congress itself has blurred them by the inclusion in environmental statutes of "citizen suit" provisions that specifically authorize individual plaintiffs to enforce public environmental claims in the courts – even in suits against the government. These citizen suits provide insight into why environmental plaintiffs invoking public trust principles are also operating on the right side of the constitutional line, even if it is a blurry one.

Citizen suit provisions are not exclusive to environmental law, but they are endemic there. To take a prominent example, the Endangered Species Act authorizes any person to bring a civil suit to enjoin anyone else – including the state and federal government – alleged to be in violation of the Act or its implementing regulations, or to compel enforcement of the Act by the government.[76] Similar citizen suit provisions exist in the Clean Air Act,[77] the Clean Water Act,[78] and at least sixteen other major federal environmental statutes.[79] Plaintiffs must still show a particularized injury to satisfy standing requirements in these cases,[80] but these claims often vindicate generalizable concerns, aiming for judicial intervention within realms of executive and legislative discretion. The Administrative Procedures Act similarly invites plaintiffs to challenge failures in agency decision-making if they can show they have been affected, even if the alleged harm represents a more generalized kind of concern.[81]

It is no accident that so many environmental statutes are specifically crafted with citizen suit provisions that invite this kind of partnership between individual plaintiffs and judicial enforcement. These provisions are designed to recruit private plaintiffs to serve as "private attorneys general," to ensure vigorous enforcement of

---

[76] Endangered Species Act, 16 U.S.C. § 1540(g).
[77] Clean Air Act, 42 U.S.C. § 7604.
[78] Clean Water Act, 42 U.S.C. § 7604.
[79] *See* James R. May, *The Availability of State Environmental Citizen Suits*, 18-SPG NAT. RES. & ENV'T. 53, 53 (2004); (*The Role of Citizen Enforcement*, NAT'L ENV'T L. CENTER, www.nelc.org/get-involved/citizen-enforcement/#:~:text=The%20citizen%20suit%20provisions%20of,violations%2C%20payable%20to%20the%20government.
[80] *See, e.g., Lujan*, 504 U.S. at 560–62 (establishing the modern standing requirements of showing a concrete injury in fact, effectively limiting public interest environmental claims without a showing of unique personal harm).
[81] 5 U.S.C. § 702.

environmental laws protecting widespread public interests against the anticipated pushback from economic actors that benefit from continued environmental harm and regulatory failures to contain them.[82] These strong countervailing forces combine due to the political process failure known as "regulatory capture," well documented by both public choice theorists[83] and environmental scholars,[84] in which the political branches fail to vindicate widespread public interests because, through a variety of means, they become "captured" by powerful industries seeking weaker regulation, which gain influence over regulators and policymakers by lobbying, funding, and even staffing them.

In passing these environmental statutes with citizen suit provisions, Congress recognized the importance of protecting such public natural resource commons as waterways, the atmosphere, and biodiversity. But after centuries of environmental degradation and the political process failures that enabled it, Congress also understood how easy it is for the intense interests of a few focused appropriators to overcome the diffuse interests of the general public in environmental protection.[85] So legislators made it easier for members of the public to assist environmental enforcement by seeking judicial review. These statutes invite citizens (who must still be able to meet the applicable standing requirements) to seek enforcement of even generalizable public concerns in a purposeful, carefully constructed partnership with the judiciary.

Public trust principles work in the same way, for many of the very same reasons. In fact, the public trust doctrine is probably the historical progenitor of the "citizen suit" as a legal device – the original common law citizen suit provision – enabling judicial intervention by private attorneys general to enforce the protection of wider public interests in natural resource commons. Centuries ago, the common law

---

[82] Regan v. Cherry Corp., 706 F. Supp. 145, 149 (D.R.I. 1989) ("Congress intended to establish a citizens suit provision through which the public could prod the executive branch into zealously enforcing hazardous waste laws. In addition, Congress intended that § 310 establish private attorneys general to supplement administrative action and aid in attacking CERCLA violators."). *See also* James R. May, *The Availability of State Environmental Citizen Suits*, 18 SPG NAT. RES. & ENV'T 53, 53 (2004); (discussing how citizen suit provisions "invite citizens to sue as 'private attorneys general' to force compliance, or to force agencies to perform mandatory statutory duties").

[83] *See, e.g.*, James M. Buchanan, *What is Public Choice Theory?*, 32 IMPRIMIS No. 3, at 3–5 (March 2003) (describing the mechanics of public choice theory and agency capture); Robert C. Ellickson, *Taming Leviathan: Will the Centralizing Tide of the Twentieth Century Continue into the Twenty-First?*, 74 S. CAL. L. REV. 101, 114 (2000) (same); MANCUR OLSON, THE LOGIC OF COLLECTIVE ACTION (1965).

[84] *See, e.g.*, Sax, *supra* note 60, at 560 (1970) (describing the circumstances in which "self-interested and powerful minorities often have an undue influence on the public resource decisions of legislative and administrative bodies and cause those bodies to ignore broadly based public interests"); Lazarus, *supra* note 36, at 1160–61 (discussing Sax's understanding of regulatory capture, and affirming how public choice dynamics, in which the diffuse public interest cannot compete with politically power special interests, "regularly arises with environmental lawmaking").

[85] *Cf.* May, *supra* note 82, at 53 (quoting Nat. Res. Def. Council v. Train, 510 F.2d 692, 700 (D.C. Cir. 1974).

recognized the importance of facilitating judicial review for exactly these kinds of claims,[86] which often stack intense private economic interests against diffuse public harms, where the public choice incentives to facilitate private appropriation of a commons resource are much stronger than the incentives to resist it.[87] To protect widespread public interests in these critical natural resources, including those of future generations, the public trust doctrine appropriately draws on the branch of government that can partner with private attorney general enforcers of public environmental values (who, in modern times, can also show enough private harm to meet the jurisprudential requirements of standing).

For these reasons, a defining feature of the common law public trust doctrine is the way it empowers ordinary citizens to seek redress for public trust violations in court.[88] Even statutory and constitutionalized public trust principles invite this kind of partnership between private attorney general plaintiffs and judicial enforcement. Separation-of-powers critics are right to worry about judicial capacity, the antidemocratic critique, and especially about further empowering the judiciary at a moment when growing judicial power is already worrisome at the federal level – but in this unique legal context, the judicial role seems appropriate to the task (if for no other reason, because there is no ready alternative).

In the absence of firmer foundations for environmental law, as described in the Introduction, advocates have similarly turned to trust-rights advocacy for lack of better alternatives. If it is not the ultimate answer, perhaps it is at least an element of the corrective, bringing issues to the public fore through this unique perch within the larger political process, ideally helping to inspire appropriate legislative and executive responses with the appropriate application of litigation-based pressure. Perhaps this justifies taking the long view on empowering judges at a time when judicial power is already rising – a view that looks past the political winds of this single moment in time and instead toward time immemorial. The core public trust principle, after all, is thousands of years old. There must be some reason for that, and we would do well to consider it.

For the same reason, the judicial role in administering the trust should not be seen as antidemocratic – instead it is a democratic corrective. As Chapter 9 recognized, the separation of powers does not require that citizens engage with those powers in isolation.[89] Judicial review is the citizen's last stand in a democracy – the last opportunity to be heard within the complex political process that includes checks, balances, and multiple ports of entry to the broader public conversation in which policies are conceived, deliberated, enacted, and refined. The platforms

---

[86] See, e.g., Ill. Cent. R.R. Co. v. Illinois, 146 U.S. 387, 452 (1892).
[87] Sax, supra note 60, at 560.
[88] See, e.g., Araiza, supra note 36, at 437–38 (acknowledging the centrality of judicial review to effectuating the public trust doctrine while struggling to understand what that review should be based upon).
[89] Chapter 9(D) ("Constitutional and Pragmatic Concerns").

for public discourse and organizing enabled by public trust litigation are important components of the overall political process, even when that litigation is premised on theories that may lose in court (such as the many losing atmospheric trust cases).[90] When citizens invoke the judicial process this way, the lawsuits themselves become part of the wider political process, enabling them to speak their truth to sources of power, communicate with other citizens about their grievances, and build support for ongoing policymaking through conventional political channels. In this way, as noted in Chapter 9, the doctrine "facilitates a conversation between the three branches of government about the disposition of critical public natural resource commons in which all citizens have a stake, but which are often managed far beyond the reach of the average voter's influence."[91]

If the premise of the doctrine is that public trust resources must be protected, then the public must be able to check political activity that falls prey to patronage, capture, oversight, or other shortsighted impulses to allow the destruction of trust values.[92] The ballot box, alone, has proved inadequate to this critical task. Throwing elected representatives out of office is an insufficient corrective if they have already forfeited an irreplaceable trust resource – as the Illinois legislature forfeited Chicago Harbor in the late nineteenth century,[93] the California Water Board forfeited Mono Lake in the twentieth,[94] and government actors at many levels are arguably forfeiting atmospheric integrity today.[95] But within the constitutional order, the only other avenue for aggrieved citizens to vindicate public trust rights and responsibilities is to invoke judicial review of these political decisions and get their day in court.

d. Separation of Powers and the Constitutive Constraint

Separation of powers questions about trust administration intersect with the ultimate question raised by the Mono Lake case regarding which doctrine should

---

[90] See supra Chapter 7(B)(2) ("Impacts of the Mono Lake Case in Other States"), Chapter 9(D)(1) ("Separation of Powers Concerns"); see Paul Rink, *Conceptualizing U.S. Strategic Climate Rights Litigation*, 49 HARV. ENV'T L. REV. 149 (2024); Ryan, *From Mono Lake to the Atmospheric Trust*, supra note 36, at 60–64; Erin Ryan, *The Hidden Duality of Emerging Climate Advocacy: Environmental Rights and the Atmospheric Trust*, 49 HARV. ENV'T L. REV. 225 (2025).

[91] See Rink, *Climate Rights Strategic Litigation*, supra note 90; Ryan, *Historic Saga*, supra note 36, at 629–31; see also Chapter 9 ("Public Trust Principles, Environmental Rights, and Trust-Rights Climate Advocacy").

[92] Cf. Chapter 9(D)(3) ("Legal Strategy and Climate Advocacy").

[93] Ill. Cent. R. Co. v. Illinois, 146 U.S. 387, 459 (1892); see also Chapter 1(B)(5) ("With Power Comes Responsibility: *Illinois Central Railroad Co. v. Illinois*") (discussing the case in detail).

[94] Nat'l Audubon Soc'y v. Super. Ct., 658 P.2d 709, 722 (Cal. 1983); see also Chapter 5 ("*National Audubon Society*: The 'Mono Lake Case'") (discussing the Mono Lake case in detail).

[95] Juliana v. United States, 217 F. Supp. 3d 1224, 1233 (D. Or. 2016), rev'd, Juliana v. United States, No. 24-684, D.C. No. 6:15-cv-1517, 2024 WL 5102489(May 1, 2024), cert. denied, 604 U.S. 645 (2025). See also Chapter 9(B)(4) ("*Juliana v. United States*") (discussing the case in detail).

trump – the common law public trust doctrine, interpreted by judges, or the statutory doctrine of prior appropriations, ratified by the legislature. As noted earlier and detailed in Chapter 5, this was a tricky question, because when statutes conflict with the common law, we normally conclude that the common law has been abrogated by the statute.[96] The judge-made precedents of the common law are what the legal system uses to answer questions on which the legislature hasn't spoken – and they are usually preempted uncontroversially when the legislature gets around to saying otherwise. So when the court determined that the public trust doctrine had *not* been displaced by statutory water law, it was a significant legal moment – revealing what sets the public trust doctrine apart.

The decision affirmed that the common law public trust doctrine is special, because it doesn't just state a principle – it acts as a formidable constraint on government action, limiting what it may or may not do with its authority. It establishes a line beyond which the state cannot go. As repeatedly discussed in Chapters 1, 5, 7, and 8, it acts as a limit on sovereign power.[97] With that in mind, should the sovereign be able to free itself from that limit by destroying it with a statute? A few states may have come to that conclusion, by abolishing or limiting the common law public trust doctrine, as Idaho famously did by legislative enactment.[98] Still, most have not done so, and like California, have honored the principle that the public trust can't be so easily abrogated.

In states with strong common law doctrines, then, judges bear a heightened responsibility to act carefully, because what they decide cannot easily be undone by casual legislative response. In this respect, as even the famously libertarian Professor Richard Epstein has noted, the public trust doctrine has a constitutional dimension.[99] When a court renders a statutory interpretation the legislature doesn't like, it can always amend the statute. But when the high court determines that a legislative act violates the applicable constitution, the legislature has no recourse but to accept the court's judgment. Judicial public trust determinations have similar force, and must be taken equally seriously. And yet, so they are – and the sky has not fallen.

Constitutional interpretation, while important, is not exotic; it is what we regularly ask of our courts, and by and large, they are good at it. All of us can point to a judicial decision we don't like, but that hardly invalidates the system. That the doctrine evolves through the normal common law process of judicial elaboration is necessary

---

[96] *See* Chapter 5(B)(4) ("The Nature of the Public Trust Doctrine").
[97] *See supra* Chapter 1(B)(4) ("With Power Comes Responsibility: *Illinois Central Railroad Co. v. Illinois*"); *see also* Chapter 5(B)(4) ("The Nature of the Public Trust Doctrine"); *see also* Chapter 7(C) ("Ordinary Common Law or Quasi-Constitutional"); *see also* Chapter 8(B)(3) ("A Constitutive Constraint on Federal Authority?").
[98] IDAHO CODE ANN. § 58-1203 (West 2012). *See also* Chapter 7(C)(2) ("Idaho: Legislative Repudiation of the Constitutive Constraint").
[99] Richard A. Epstein, *The Public Trust Doctrine*, 7 CATO J. 411, 426–28 (1987).

for the same reason the common law has always evolved.[100] Times change, and with them, the circumstances. The public interest evolves with new circumstances, and so courts evaluating public trust claims must have flexibility to adjust. The same insight underlies hallowed legal doctrines hostile to dead-hand control, such as presumptions against perpetuities and unreasonable restraints on alienation, which are disfavored for empowering the dead over the living.[101] We have long held out our constitutional system of judicial review as a model for the world, so perhaps we should have more faith in the judicial administration of the public trust doctrine. The common law doctrine has continued to develop incrementally, like most others.

C. THE MONO LAKE STORY, BEYOND CALIFORNIA

The importance of the public trust sentry is highlighted now, more than ever, by the many environmental catastrophes that have not benefited from trust safeguards, demonstrated by copycat Mono Lake stories unfolding all over the world.

After the Mono Basin victories in the Mono Lake litigation and administrative implementation described in Chapters 5 and 6, the lake is still not yet "saved," but things are looking better than they have in more than eighty years.[102] Yet even as Mono Lake reaches a point of legal (if not ecological) equipoise, different versions of the Mono Lake story are taking place across the nation and even the world – many just as heartrending as the original, and often with fewer reasons for hope. The saga at Mono Lake is just one iteration of the same conflict playing out in countless places around the globe where cultural, environmental, and economic values clash over the management of precious waterways.

This part reviews several selected Mono Lake stories unfolding beyond Mono Lake, at the Great Salt Lake in Utah, the Sea of Galilee (Lake Kinneret) in Israel and the Dead Sea that straddles the nations of Israel and Jordan, and the forsaken Aral Sea between Kazakhstan and Uzbekistan. Each offers important counterpoints to the Mono Lake story in California, revealing common natural resource challenges, different management strategies, and the different results that follow. These stories demonstrate the importance of public trust principles in guiding environmental governance, and the severe environmental and social costs that accrue when public trust principles are forsaken.

1. Great Salt Lake

A particularly tragic rendition of the Mono Lake story is rapidly unfolding in Utah, where Mono Lake's more famous cousin, the Great Salt Lake, is in the process of

---

[100] *Cf.* Matthews v. Bayhead, 471 A.2d 355, 361–63 (N.J. 1984) (discussing the evolution of the public trust doctrine).
[101] *See* JOSEPH WILLIAM SINGER, et al., PROPERTY LAW RULES, POLICIES, AND PRACTICES 639–48, 783–806 (2017) (discussing the rule against perpetuities and the canon against unreasonable restraints).
[102] *See supra* Chapter 5(A) ("The Historic Mono Lake Case: *Audubon Society v. Superior Court*"); *see also supra* Chapter 6(E) ("A Reprieve for Mono Lake?").

evaporating away. As source waters that once fed the great water body are increasingly diverted to other purposes, the Great Salt Lake is disappearing at an astonishing rate. In the Great Salt Lake Basin, population growth, irrigated agriculture, and other demands have increasingly stressed water supplies since the region began attracting greater settlement in the late 1800's.[103] Since then, the lake has lost 67 percent of its volume to water-intensive development, aggravated by a crippling drought that portends a future of restricted water supply due to climate change.[104] Comparing aerial maps of the lake today and just a few decades earlier reveals the astonishing change: two-thirds of the lake has simply disappeared.

Wide-ranging ecological and human health impacts are following the decline of the Great Salt Lake just as they did at Mono Lake, and by the exact same mechanisms. The depletion of the lake has destroyed wildlife habitat and produced toxic air quality for surrounding communities.[105] In a direct parallel to the Mono Lake story, as the shrinking Great Salt Lake condenses into an ever saltier brine, the brine shrimp at the base of the food chain face dramatic population decline.[106] As at Mono Lake, these tiny crustaceans are a staple for the millions of birds that rely on the Great Salt Lake during heroic migrations and that are also an important contributor to the regional economy.[107] And just like Mono Lake, the exposed Great Salt lakebed left behind as its waters recede is laced with arsenic and other heavy metals, which then threaten local public health as they are routinely whipped into the air as toxic dust storms.[108]

But in contrast to the California crisis, where advocacy to save Mono Lake was mostly driven by public love for the Mono Basin resources and ecosystem, advocacy to restore water to the Great Salt Lake is mostly driven by fears regarding the public health impacts of toxic air pollution in the major population centers adjacent to the lake.[109] Over one million people live in the surrounding Salt Lake Valley, about

---

[103] See Wayne A. Wurtsbaugh & Somayeh Sima, *Contrasting Management and Fates of Two Sister Lakes: Great Salt Lake (USA) and Lake Urmia (Iran)*, 14 WATER 3005 (2022).

[104] See Wayne A. Wurtsbaugh & Somayeh Sima, *Contrasting Management and Fates of Two Sister Lakes: Great Salt Lake (USA) and Lake Urmia (Iran)*, 14 WATER 3005 (2022). See Sarah E. Null & Wayne A. Wurtsbaugh, *Water Development, Consumptive Water Uses, and Great Salt Lake*, in GREAT SALT LAKE BIOLOGY, 1 (Bonnie Baxter & Jaimi Butler, eds. 2020) (noting that "consumptive water uses in the watershed have depleted inflows by approximately 39%, with 63% used by agriculture, 11% by cities, 13% by solar ponds, and 13% by other uses [which have] lowered the lake by 3.4 m, decreased its area by 51%, and reduced its volume by 64% as of 2019. Projected water development of the lake's primary tributary could lower the lake approximately 1.5 m more.").

[105] See Wayne A. Wurtsbaugh et al., *Decline of the World's Saline Lakes*, 10 NATURE GEOSCIENCE 816 (2017).

[106] Aimee Van Tatenhove, Increasing Great Salt Lake Salinity Predicted to Impact Utah Brine Shrimp, KSLTV (Oct. 3, 2022), https://ksltv.com/507570/increasing-great-salt-lake-salinity-predicted-to-impact-utah-brine-shrimp/#:~:text=SALT%20LAKE%20CITY%20%E2%80%94%20New%20research,waters%20of%20Great%20Salt%20Lake.

[107] Id.

[108] See Wurtsbaugh & Sima, *supra* note 103.

[109] See Christopher Flavelle, *As the Great Salt Lake Dries Up, Utah Faces an 'Environmental Nuclear Bomb,'* N.Y. TIMES, www.nytimes.com/2022/06/07/climate/salt-lake-city-climate-disaster

one-third of the population of the state of Utah.[110] There are serious concerns that if the lake continues to recede, the resulting air pollution will render the state capital and surrounding communities uninhabitable.[111] While there are certainly many Utahans who cherish the Great Salt Lake in the same way the *Audubon Society* plaintiffs cherished Mono Lake, for the average citizen, the problem is not so much preserving the lake itself as preserving the livability of the most densely populated region of the state.[112] As more of the lake bottom becomes exposed, the regional air will "occasionally turn poisonous," as windstorms carry these toxic particulates into the lungs of regional residents.[113] One Utah rancher and Republican state lawmaker explained, "We have this potential environmental nuclear bomb that's going to go off if we don't take some pretty dramatic action."[114]

Another important difference between the Great Salt Lake and Mono Lake crises is that there is no one dominant party taking the water that would otherwise be destined for the Great Salt Lake. There is no analogous "Los Angeles" character in the Great Salt Lake story, which, if only their diversions were stopped or reduced, could produce the sudden resolution to the crisis. In the Great Salt Lake story, the same threat of water depletion by diversion is occurring, but here it is a slow death by a thousand cuts – or many tens of thousands of smaller diversions. The problem is the same – even the extensive human health harms created by releasing toxic sediments to the air from the receding alkaline shores – but there is no single diverter to sue, and no single hero to make a dramatic change to save the lake. It is a problem of cumulative impacts – many agriculturalists, many industrialists, and many households all drawing the regional water supply steadily down, leaving the lake at the bottom of the watershed, below the myriad diversion points, to slowly die of thirst.

For this reason, a Mono Lake-like attempt to protect Great Salt Lake through litigation has been slow to emerge. The public trust doctrine exists in Utah through

---

.html#:~:text=Most%20alarming%2C%20the%20air%20surrounding,leaders%20seem%20reluctant%20to%20do. (last updated June 22, 2023); Jessie Torrisi, *Why We're in Court to Protect the Great Salt Lake*, EARTHJUSTICE (Sept. 17, 2024), https://earthjustice.org/article/saving-utahs-great-salt-lake-toward-off-an-ecological-collapse-and-public-health-disaster (explaining that millions of people could wind up breathing in toxic dust and the effects on human health).

[110] *Quick Facts: Salt Lake County, Utah*, UNITED STATES CENSUS BUREAU, www.census.gov/quickfacts/fact/table/saltlakecountyutah/PST045224 (last visited Apr. 9, 2025) (reporting a population of about 1.2 million); *Quick Facts: Utah, United States*, UNITED STATES CENSUS BUREAU, www.census.gov/quickfacts/fact/table/UT,US (last visited Apr. 9, 2025) (reporting a state population of around 3.5 million).

[111] Flavelle, *supra* note 109; Kirk Siegler, *Climate Change and a Population Boom Could Dry Up the Great Salt Lake in 5 Years*, NPR (Feb. 3, 2023), www.npr.org/2023/02/03/1153550793/climate-change-and-a-population-boom-could-dry-up-the-great-salt-lake-in-5-years.

[112] *See* Torrisi, *supra* note 111.

[113] *See* Flavelle, *supra* note 109 (comparing the impending Salt Lake air pollution crisis to the Owens Valley catastrophe).

[114] *Id.* (quoting Joel Ferry).

state common law[115] and receives some recognition in state statute.[116] Although the full doctrine was never expressly constitutionalized in Utah, Article XX, section 1 of the state constitution analogously states that "all lands of the State that have been ... granted to the State ... are declared to be the public lands of the State; and shall be held in trust for the people ... for the respective purposes for which they [were] ... acquired"[117] – and though these sovereign lands include submerged lands, there is no overt constitutional protection for state water resources.

The Friends of Great Salt Lake, a local environmental advocacy group inspired by the Mono Lake Committee, has considered taking legal action under the banner of the public trust doctrine, but they recognize how much more difficult a case that would be.[118] As one local observed, it's not clear "how, exactly, the public trust doctrine would solve the Great Salt Lake's problems," with no villain to oppose:[119] "At Mono Lake, the culprit depleting the lake was clear: a single utility in L.A. that could be obliged to reduce its consumption. In Utah, a patchwork of cities, towns, agricultural fields and industries across the watershed have dropped the Great Salt Lake by as much as 11 feet, according to a Utah State University analysis."[120]

Applying the Mono Lake logic to the Great Salt Lake's dilemma would require that its limit be imposed uniformly to every tributary in the wider watershed, extending from the Bear, Weber, Jordan, and Provo rivers, and "everything in between."[121] Moreover, Utah's distinctive history, politics, and culture set it apart from California, leaving the result of a Mono Lake style lawsuit uncertain, even if a litigation strategy could be forged.[122] Even so, as this book goes to press, a coalition of conservation groups is attempting a full-scale Mono Lake lawsuit on the issue, holding the state to account for its sovereign responsibility to manage Great Salt Lake as a trust resource and its constitutional obligation to mitigate the adverse health

---

[115] See Robin Kundis Craig, *A Comparative Guide to the Western States' Public Trust Doctrines: Public Values, Private Rights, and the Evolution Toward an Ecological Public Trust*, 37 ECOLOGY L.Q. 53, 93–194 (2010) (providing a comprehensive summary of various State's public trust doctrine at the time the article was written); see also Brandon S. Fuller, *Pure as Running Water: A Constitutional Argument for Utah's Public Trust Doctrine*, 2019 UTAH L. R. 481, 482 (2019). This note also examines the key cases in Utah's public trust history. See id. at 490–97.

[116] UTAH CODE ANN. § 23-21-4(1) (2022) ("There is reserved to the public the right of access to all lands owned by the state, including those lands lying below the official government meander line ... of navigable waters, for the purpose of hunting, trapping, or fishing."). Elsewhere, the code qualifies public trust assets as those "lands lying below the ordinary high-water mark of navigable bodies of water at the date of statehood and owned by the state by virtue of its sovereignty." ULRA § 65A-1-1(6) (2022).

[117] UTAH CONST. art. XX, §1.

[118] Leia Larsen, *Why the Courts Could Have the Final Say on the Great Salt Lake's Future*, THE SALT LAKE TRIB. (Oct. 11, 2022), www.sltrib.com/news/environment/2022/10/11/why-courts-could-become-great/.

[119] Id.

[120] Id.

[121] Leia Larsen, *The Public Trust Doctrine Prevented Mono Lake from Drying Up. Could it Be Used to Save the Great Salt Lake?*, KSL NEWS RADIO (Oct. 11, 2022), https://kslnewsradio.com/1976907/the-public-trust-doctrine-prevented-mono-lake-from-drying-up-could-it-be-used-to-save-the-great-salt-lake/.

[122] Id.

impacts of toxic alkali dust emerging from relicted state sovereign lands.¹²³ For these advocates, it makes no difference whether the task at hand is hard, or controversial among those who believe their best bet is to work with the agricultural community outside of court.¹²⁴ As beneficiaries of the state's trust obligation to the public, they are entitled to enforce it. They are, in effect, vindicating environmental rights.

In addition, a coalition of environmental groups is pursuing a novel strategy to protect the Great Salt Lake – securing water rights for the lake itself.¹²⁵ A mining, smelting, and refining company, Rio Tinto Kennecott, has an excess of water for its mining demands and has promised to donate 21,000 acre-feet of water every year for the next ten years to the Great Salt Lake.¹²⁶ The state Division of Wildlife Resources, which will help administer the donation of rights, has indicated that this "is believed to be the first time this has happened,"¹²⁷ reflecting the legal tradition of prior appropriations jurisdictions, in which water rights could not be secured for instream use, and which donations to NGOs or even public agencies are still exceptional.¹²⁸ Advocates are also attempting to use provisions under a new state Water Banking Act, adopted in 2020, to reallocate water from existing appropriative rights toward the protection of environmental values at the lake.¹²⁹ In 2022, the state legislature also enacted a statute creating a $40 million trust fund to increase water supply for the lake and improve upstream habitat, and another requiring the state water agency to study the five watersheds that feed the lake.¹³⁰

Let us all hope these strategies will suffice to rescue the Great, if ailing, Salt Lake. Let us also note that even if a Mono-Lake style lawsuit does not prove the means to end the conflict, public trust principles have informed the conduct and expectations of both the lake advocates and key state actors. The Division of Wildlife Resources coordination of water rights donations for the lake, the legislative Water Banking Act, and the $40 million trust fund all reflect an understanding of the state's sovereign obligation to protect the ailing Great Salt Lake, for the benefit of the citizens, some of whom prepared to go to court to vindicate their rights, while others are donating precious water rights to do their part as fellow citizens. Even if the trust is

---

¹²³ Interview with Earthjustice attorneys planning the lawsuit (August 23, 2023) (notes on file with author).
¹²⁴ Krik Siegler, *Farmers Accused of Drying up the Imperiled Great Salt Lake Say They Can Help Save It*, NPR (Mar. 11, 2024), www.npr.org/2024/03/11/1235980748/farmers-accused-of-drying-up-the-imperiled-great-salt-lake-say-they-can-help-sav.
¹²⁵ Ben Winslow, *Environmentalists Secure Water Rights for Great Salt Lake*, Assoc. Press (Oct. 18, 2021), https://apnews.com/article/lakes-environment-utah-water-rights-great-salt-lake-aa16b99235e0eb37684499c47c4073db.
¹²⁶ Id.
¹²⁷ Id.
¹²⁸ *See* Chapter 1(C)(2) ("Prior Appropriations").
¹²⁹ Sarah E. Null, *Water Banking Can Help Great Salt Lake*, PERC (Sept. 27, 2022), www.perc.org/2022/09/27/water-banking-can-help-great-salt-lake/.
¹³⁰ Utah Governor Spencer J. Cox, *3 Ways We're Working to Preserve Great Salt Lake*, Utah.gov (June 10, 2022), https://governor.utah.gov/2022/06/10/3-ways-were-working-to-preserve-great-salt-lake/.

never judicially enforced by litigation, the values that underlie the trust are operating in full force, and they may yet serve to facilitate the balancing acts required to forestall the total loss all fear.

2. The Sea of Galilee and the Dead Sea

While Mono and the Great Salt Lake represent the two most famous examples of the Mono Lake phenomenon in the United States, the same issues haunt watersheds in arid climates around the world. Two especially famous examples are unfolding in the notoriously arid Middle East: the Sea of Galilee, of Biblical renown, and the Dead Sea, a wonder of the world. Like Mono Lake, both are mortally threatened by the out-of-basin removal of water from the watersheds of origin – but these stories bear very different lessons. The Sea of Galilee offers a hopeful counternarrative to the Mono Lake story, in which the state honored its responsibility to protect the treasured waterway before it was too late. The Dead Sea offers the opposite – a counternarrative to the Mono Lake story in showing what happens when a treasured waterway is forsaken.

a. The Sea of Galilee (Lake Kinneret)

The Sea of Galilee, known by Israelis as Lake Kinneret, is a large freshwater body in northern Israel, the largest in the nation, located beside the Golan Heights and the border with Syria. At nearly 700 feet below sea level, the 64-square mile waterbody has long been considered the lowest freshwater surface lake in the world, and is second only to the saline Dead Sea at the bottom of the Jordan River watershed in terms of all lakes globally.[131] The lake is supported by underground springs and the Jordan River, which runs along the borders of several nations, including Lebanon, Syria, and Jordan.

Kinneret is a rare freshwater source in the desert region of the Levant, and it serves as a cherished tourist destination for both its ecological and religious significance.[132] In the New Testament, Jesus reportedly performed many miracles near the Sea, which today supports a commercial fishery and unique aquatic ecosystem.[133] Over the past two decades, a series of factors, including the expansion of irrigated

---

[131] *Sea of Galilee*, NEW WORLD ENCYCLOPEDIA, www.newworldencyclopedia.org/entry/Sea_of_Galilee (last visited Feb. 16, 2024) (noting that the recently discovered sub-glacial Lake Vostok in Antarctica challenges both records for non-surface bodies).

[132] Anna Skinner, *Climate Change Threatens Sea of Galilee as Israelis Attempt to Save Waters*, NEWSWEEK (Aug. 8, 2022), www.newsweek.com/sea-galilee-lake-kinneret-israeli-attempts-save-waters-1735267#:~:text=Climate%20change%20has%20tightened%20its,feedback%20loop%20with%20global%20warming.

[133] Michael L. Wine et al., *Agriculture, Diversions, and Drought Shrinking Galilee Sea*, 651 SCI. TOTAL ENV'T 70, 71 (2019).

agriculture, the doubling of groundwater pumping within the watershed, decreasing flows from the Upper Jordan River, and increasing impoundments of water within the basin, has caused serious declines at the lake.[134] The waterway is prone to fluctuations between alarmingly low and normal levels, but these factors, combined with a severe drought in 2017, brought it to the lowest levels seen in a century.[135]

Until recently, the lake was Israel's main source of fresh drinking water, supplying about one-third of the nation's annual water requirement.[136] However, due to the impacts of these diversions on the lake level, it was abandoned as a source of drinking water and instead became the subject of a national conservation effort. The government acted in apparent appreciation of a sovereign obligation to protect the lake, perhaps drawing on public trust elements in British and Ottoman legal traditions that have become part of the stew of Israeli law.[137]

To preserve the lake and stabilize its water supply, Israel constructed five major desalination plants along the Mediterranean Sea over the span of a decade, and the government worked hard to redirect agricultural waste away from Lake Kinneret.[138] Residential, commercial, and agricultural water conservation, always a priority in these desert lands, became an even higher national priority. To channel water dependence away from Lake Kinneret, the government began recycling nearly 90 percent of all municipal wastewater, meticulously piping it out to rural agricultural operations.[139] Then, on December 22, 2022, Israel became the first country in the world to channel desalinated water into a natural lake via a $264 million pipe to bridge the lake to a system of water infrastructure that links it and the five desalination plants into a unified system of water production and transport.[140] The

---

[134] *Id.*

[135] Skinner, *supra* note 132; *see also* Hadassah Brenner, *Is the Sea of Galilee's Recent Water Rise Dangerous?*, THE JERUSALEM POST (March 29, 2021), www.timesofisrael.com/sea-of-galilee-thriving-remains-close-to-maximum-capacity/#:~:text=The%20Sea%20of%20Galilee%20%E2%80%94%20Israel%27s,11%20feet)%20lower%20than%20today (reporting on the much needed rainfall reprieve that nearly caused the Jewish state to open a dam to lower the lake level).

[136] Tomer Ovadia, *12 Facts About the Sea of Galilee*, POLITICO (Aug. 20, 2012), www.politico.com/story/2012/08/12-facts-about-the-sea-of-galilee-079885.

[137] The Israeli Judicial Authority, *The History of Law and Judgement* (Oct. 25, 2022), www.gov.il/en/pages/the_judiciary_authority_history ("This law included a mosaic of laws, which included, among others: Ottoman laws that were absorbed into the laws of the British mandate and remained in force at the time of the establishment of the state, religious laws, laws of the British mandate and British laws – including, 'the principles of common law and the foundations of the laws of equity practiced in England.'").

[138] Brenner, *supra* note 135.

[139] *AWWA Members Among Delegates Exploring Israeli Water Recycling Programs*, AM. WATER WORKS ASSOC. (Jan. 25, 2023), www.awwa.org/AWWA-Articles/awwa-members-among-delegates-exploring-israeli-water-recycling-programs#:~:text=Israel%20is%20a%20global%20leader,industrial%20sector%2C%20among%20other%20uses.

[140] Toi Staff & Sue Surkes, *Pioneering Plan Inaugurated to Top Up Sea of Galilee with Desalinated Water*, TIMES OF ISRAEL (Dec. 28, 2022), www.timesofisrael.com/pioneering-plan-inaugurated-to-top-up-sea-of-galilee-with-desalinated-water/.

infrastructure is reported to have the potential to raise the lake's level by half a meter each year – all with desalinated Mediterranean seawater.[141]

The import of desalinated water to Lake Kinneret will also enable Israel to export more water to Jordan, facilitating a fractious political relationship that has been eased, in part, by water diplomacy.[142] Jordan has water resources estimated to sustain around two million people, but a population that has surpassed ten million, especially with the addition of more than a million humanitarian refugees fleeing a civil war in Syria (which was itself fueled by drought and resulting food shortages).[143] One of the most water-stressed nations in the world, it is extracting groundwater at twice the rate at which it is cyclically renewed,[144] so there is an acute need for new sources of supply. The neighboring nations signed a peace treaty in 1994 that relied heavily on an agreement by Israel to supply some 50 million cubic meters of potable water to Jordan each year[145] – a pledge that was doubled in 2021, in exchange for 600 megawatts of solar generating capacity that Jordan has promised Israel.[146] Reportedly, construction is underway to double the promised water exports again, until Israel provides Jordan with 200 cubic meters of water annually, comparable to the amount used by the five biggest Israeli cities combined.[147]

Israel's population is also approaching ten million people,[148] who are also primarily relying on desalinated water. Israelis are keenly interested in the Mono Lake story because of its parallels with Kinneret, and I was fortunate to be invited there in 2018 to teach water law and lecture about the Mono Lake story. It was hard not to be impressed by the many examples there of brilliant water conservation, sustainable water policy, and committed water discipline practiced by ordinary people – while also sobering to see the ramifications of water inequity in the region. When I visited Lake Kinneret, I was moved by the success of the mission, and even more by the promise of Middle East water diplomacy and high hopes for increased international cooperation over scarce water and energy resources.

The political situation in Israel and Palestine has deteriorated since my visit, and the suffering associated with the full-scale war that erupted in October of 2023 has proved heartbreaking in every respect, including increasing scarcity of potable water

---

[141] Ari Rabinovitch, *Israel Refills the Sea of Galilee, Supplying Jordan on the Way*, REUTERS (Jan. 3, 2023), www.reuters.com/business/environment/israel-refills-sea-galilee-supplying-jordan-way-2023-01-30/#:~:text=The%20Sea%20of%20Galilee%2C%20whose,south%20to%20the%20Dead%20Sea.

[142] *Id*.

[143] *After Years of Delays, Jordan Said to Nix Red Sea-Dead Sea Canal with Israel, PA*, TIMES OF ISRAEL (June 17, 2021), www.timesofisrael.com/after-years-of-delays-jordan-said-to-nix-red-sea-dead-sea-canal-with-israel-pa/.

[144] *Id*.

[145] *Id*.

[146] *Id*.

[147] *Id*.

[148] *Israel Population 2023*, WORLD POPULATION REV., https://worldpopulationreview.com/countries/israel-population (last visited March 31, 2023) (citing a population of 9,134,682 in 2023).

in Gaza. That war continues as this book goes to press, making it a poignantly sad time to reflect on water diplomacy as a tool for achieving peace in the Middle East. Certainly, from any vantage point in this conflict, peace cannot come fast enough.

Even so, the Israeli efforts at Kinneret represent a monumental commitment to preserve an ecosystem with cultural relevance that matches its ecological relevance. It's hard to miss the distorted parallel – how the pipeline returning salvaged water to struggling Lake Kinneret stands in opposition to the Los Angeles Aqueduct that draws water away from struggling Mono Lake, both of them in desert environments where water resources remain scarce for domestic, economic, and ecological purposes. It will be fascinating to see how this infrastructure changes the trajectory of what once seemed a doomed waterway – and perhaps even the complex political landscape of the Levant conflict. Unfortunately, it will be much harder to save the other most famous waterway along the River Jordan, the Dead Sea.

b. The Dead Sea

Mono Lake has often been referred to as the Dead Sea of California, a nod to the notorious characteristics of the true Dead Sea, the otherworldly hypersaline lake at the bottom of the Jordan River watershed between Israel and Jordan. The defining geographical feature of the Holy Land, the Dead Sea is also referenced in biblical accounts of the apocryphal destruction of Sodom and Gomorrah, two cities along the lake destroyed for their wickedness.[149] Encrusted in salt and mined for potash, magnesium, and other chemicals, the Lake is ten times saltier than the earth's oceans, and three times saltier than Mono Lake.[150] But like Mono Lake, the Dead Sea is falling as irrigation projects, the mineral industry, and other diversions carry water geologically destined for the lake elsewhere. The River Jordan remains its primary source, but far fewer waters now reach the Dead Sea.[151]

The lowest body of water on the earth's surface, lying between the hills of Judaea and the Transjordanian plateaus, the surface level of the lake hovered around 1,300 feet below sea level in the mid twentieth century.[152] At the time, the lake was 394 square miles in surface area.[153] Yet as Israel and Jordan began diverting the Jordan

---

[149] *Genesis* 18:16-19:29 (*The Bible: King James Version*).

[150] *The Saltiest Pond on Earth*, NASA, https://earthobservatory.nasa.gov/images/84955/saltiest-pond-on-earth#:~:text=The%20Dead%20Sea%20has%20a,average%20salinity%20of%203.5%20percent (last visited Apr. 20, 2023) (noting that the Dead Sea has a salinity of 34 percent and the Earth's oceans have a salinity of 3.5 percent); *Water Chemistry*, MONO LAKE COMM., www.monolake.org/learn/aboutmonolake/naturalhistory/chemistry/ (last visited Apr. 20, 2023) (describing Mono Lake as 2–3 times saltier than the world's oceans, depending on fluctuations in the lake's water levels).

[151] *See Rates of Decline*, U.S. GEO. SURV., https://eros.usgs.gov/media-gallery/earthshot/rates-of-decline (last visited Nov. 1, 2022).

[152] Kenneth Pletcher, *The Dead Sea*, ENCYCLOPEDIA BRITTANICA, www.britannica.com/place/Dead-Sea (last visited March 31, 2023).

[153] *Id.*

River's flow over the second half of that century, like Mono and Kinneret, the Dead Sea began to decline precipitously. Within fifty years, the Dead Sea had lost at least 100 vertical feet, now measuring closer 1,410 feet below sea level, and it is reported to continue to drop an average of three feet per year.[154] The U.S. Geological Survey reports a drop in surface level of closer to 45 meters, and the rate of decline is increasing.[155]

The Dead Sea has now become so saline that it is "virtually devoid of microbial communities,"[156] providing habitat for almost nothing, let alone human populations. There remains thriving interest from tourists and active commercial exploitation of the chemical precipitates from Dead Sea water, but as the surface level drops, sinkholes appearing around the waterway are causing increasingly dangerous conditions for adjacent development.[157] I visited the Dead Sea while teaching water law nearby, and I can attest that it remains a wonder of the world. But in contrast to generations past, it takes far more work just to find the edge of the water, which requires traversing endless empty and hazardous salt flats where the Sea itself once stood. And while I was used to the mild alkaline sting of Mono's unique chemistry, I could only forebear immersion in the increasingly hostile waters of the Dead Sea for a short time.

Over the last decade, Israelis and Jordanians have discussed a plan to solve the problem of the dying Dead Sea by means similar to the rescue of Lake Kinneret. Debate has centered over plans to construct a desalination plant and canal to connect the Red Sea to the Dead Sea, and potentially the Mediterranean.[158] Ideally, the plan would generate additional potable water resources and electricity through the force of dropping that water through a hydroelectric power plant into the Dead Sea.[159] The same infrastructure could also be used to desalinate seawater for drinking or irrigation purposes, filling the Dead Sea with its leftover brine.[160] But reports are mixed on the likely success of the effort, both politically and environmentally.[161]

---

[154] *Id.*

[155] *See* U.S. GEO. SURV., *supra* note 151 ("From 1930 to 1973, the sea declined 17 centimeters per year. From 1974 to 1979, it dropped 62 centimeters per year, and from 1981 to 1990, 79 centimeters per year. From 1994 to 2001, the sea declined 100 centimeters per year. A 2018 report by Israel's Ministry of Environmental Protection notes a rate of decline of 1.2 meters per year.")

[156] Ittai Gavrieli & Aharon Oren, *The Dead Sea as a Dying Lake*, *in* 36 DYING AND DEAD SEAS. CLIMATIC VERSUS ANTHROPIC CAUSES. NATO SCI. SERIES: IV: EARTH AND ENV'T SCI. 287, 288 (Jacques C.J. Nihoul, Peter O. Zavialov, Philip P. Micklin, eds. 2004).

[157] *See* U.S. GEO. SURV., *supra* note 151; Yoseph Yechieli, *Sinkhole "Swarms" along the Dead Sea Coast: Reflection of Disturbance of Lake and Adjacent Groundwater Systems*, 118 GSA BULLETIN 1075 (2006).

[158] Nir Hassan, *Israel Promotes Giant, Controversial Dead Sea Infrastructure Project*, HAARETZ ISRAEL NEWS (June 22, 2022), www.haaretz.com/israel-news/2022-06-22/ty-article/.premium/israels-environment-ministry-backs-controversial-project-to-restore-dead-sea-water-levels/00000181-87be-da94-a9ff-efbf1c700000/.

[159] RED SEA – DEAD SEA CANAL AND THE FEASIBILITY STUDY OF THE WORLD BANK, GLOB. NAT. FUND (Dec. 2013), www.globalnature.org/bausteine.net/f/8005/RedSea-DeadSeaCanalandFeasibilityStudyoftheWorldBank.pdf?fd=2.

[160] *Id.*

[161] TIMES OF ISRAEL, *supra* note 143.

C. The Mono Lake Story, beyond California

In 2015, Israel and Jordan sought international bids for the Red Sea–Dead Sea Water Project, a pipeline to carry water 120 miles between the two bodies of water.[162] The plan would include a desalination plant in the Jordanian port city of Aqaba, intended to produce 65–85 million cubic meters of freshwater annually that the two nations would divide, combined with imported freshwater from the Sea of Galilee.[163] It received 94 bids from around the world, including China, South Korea, France, Canada, Israel, Egypt, and Lebanon.[164] The Israeli Ministry of Regional Cooperation pitched the idea to potential investors, gaining support from the World Bank and the U.S. government, among others.[165]

However, scientists worried that desalination brine could harm the unique geochemistry of the Dead Sea and its surrounding biological communities, because the biochemical content of Red Sea water is very different.[166] Some warned that the addition of Red Sea water to the Dead Sea could trigger an algal bloom that would turn the surface of the Dead Sea red or cause a chemical reaction precipitating gypsum that would turn it white.[167] Others worried that the project would only exacerbate the expanding sinkholes in the region, already exceeding 4,000, threatening to further corrupting local aquifers and streams.[168] In 2016, a geology consultant tracking the project warned: "If this Red–Dead nonsense happens, the operation will be successful but the patient will absolutely die…. You cannot preserve the [lake's] level by using seawater. You will lose the qualities of the Dead Sea."[169]

In 2021, after several additional years of delay, Jordan reportedly decided to pull out of the project in favor of a more straightforward desalination project in Aqaba that would not extend to the Dead Sea.[170] The TIMES OF ISRAEL reported that Jordan blamed a lack of sincere interest on the part of Israel, which would have spent $1 billion on a project with the chiefly noneconomic return of improving regional political stability.[171] Given the need for more immediate water resources in Jordan, and the scientific concerns about harm to the Dead Sea, the collapse of this plan may have been for the best – but it remains unclear how, and whether, the Dead Sea can be preserved. Unlike the previous examples, the Dead Sea faces the additional challenge of a bisecting international boundary, further complicating the already fraught legal context.

---

[162] Todd Pitock, *Could Water from the Red Sea Help Revive the Dead Sea?*, NAT. RES. DEF. COUNCIL (Jan. 23, 2017), www.nrdc.org/stories/could-water-red-sea-help-revive-dead-sea#:~:text=The%20Red%20Sea–Dead%20Sea,sell%20the%20rest%20to%20Israel.
[163] *Id.*
[164] *Id.*
[165] *Id.*
[166] *Id.*
[167] Pitock, *supra* note 162.
[168] *Id.*
[169] *Id.* (quoting Eli Raz).
[170] TIMES OF ISRAEL, *supra* note 143.
[171] *Id.*

Given evermore ambitious regional water infrastructure around the world, the Red-Dead strategy will likely not be the last we hear of such a plan. China is also working on previously unimaginable water infrastructure through its fifty-year South-North Water Project to unite the country in a national water grid, including the world's largest hydropower project, the Three Gorges Dam.[172] Here in the United States, formerly fantastical talk about shipping Alaskan glaciers to southern California on barges is beginning to sound feasible. The extent to which technology can alleviate the conflict between economic and environmental demands on scarce water resources remains to be seen.

3. The Aral Sea

Yet surely the most alarming Mono Lake Story is the tragedy that has so recently befallen the Aral Sea, a waterway the size of Bavaria that straddles the boundary between Kazakhstan to the north and Uzbekistan to the south, at the bottom of a watershed that also drains parts of Afghanistan, Iran, Kyrgyzstan, Tajikistan, and Turkmenistan.[173] Once the world's third largest lake, the Aral Sea covered over 26,000 square miles until the 1960s, when Soviet engineers began diverting the entirety of its supplying rivers for irrigation projects elsewhere[174] – just as Los Angeles had diverted the Owens River away from the Owens Valley beginning in the 1910s,[175] and the Mono Basin creeks away from Mono Lake beginning in the 1940s.[176] The result was the same, except startlingly more quickly, on an exponentially larger scale, and to the existential detriment of many more human and ecological communities.

The Aral Sea has been a focal point in human history for more than a thousand years. It was considered the western frontier of the Chinese Empire during the Tang dynasty that ruled for nearly three hundred years beginning in the seventh century.[177] It was the subject of Muslim scientific study in the fifteenth century and Russian exploration in the nineteenth, earning a Russian naval presence by the end of that century.[178] At its peak, its fishing industry yielded nearly 50,000 tons of

---

[172] *South-to-North Water Diversion Project*, WATER TECH., www.water-technology.net/projects/south_north/; Zhang Wenjing et al., *The Next Phase of China's Water Infrastructure: A National Water Grid*, CHINA DIALOGUE (March 16, 2022), https://chinadialogue.net/en/cities/the-next-phase-of-chinas-water-infrastructure-a-national-water-grid/.
[173] Rick Livingston, *Aral Sea*, ENCYCLOPEDIA BRITTANICA, www.britannica.com/place/Aral-Sea (last visited Nov. 17, 2024).
[174] *Id.*
[175] *See* Chapter 2(B) ("The Early 1900s: Tapping the Owens River Valley").
[176] *See* Chapter 3(B) ("Acquiring the Mono Basin Water Rights").
[177] CHUNSONG GAN, A CONCISE READER OF CHINESE CULTURE 24 (2019).
[178] RENATO SALA, QUANTITATIVE EVALUATION OF THE IMPACT ON ARAL SEA LEVELS BY ANTHROPOGENIC WATER WITHDRAWAL AND SYR DARYA COURSE DIVERSION DURING THE MEDIEVAL PERIOD, 95–121 (2019).

fish a year, and accounted for one-seventh of the overall catch of the entire Soviet Union.[179] But canals built in the early twentieth century began to channel away tributaries that would have replenished the freshwater sea against evaporation.[180] Water was largely exported to raise cash crop cotton in Uzbekistan.[181] Starting in the 1960s, when diversions doubled, tripled, and then quadrupled, the lake began to recede, leaving behind a poisonous dust barrens, economic dislocation and despair, and mortality rates unheard of in the western world.[182] As it concentrated, it grew ten times saltier than the ocean, becoming inhabitable to all native species of fish.[183]

In the fifty years that followed, the sea declined by 90 percent, descending into four much smaller lakes – the North Aral Sea, separate eastern and western remnants of the former South Aral Sea, and a much smaller Barsakelmes Lake in Kazakhstan.[184] In 2005, Kazakhstan attempted to protect local portions by erecting the Dike Kokaral dam to replenish part of the North Aral Sea, enabling the restoration of sufficient water to resuscitate the local fishing industry in some seaside towns.[185] However, the southern portions of the sea continued to shrivel unimpeded.[186] By 2009, the southeastern portion had disappeared entirely, and the southwestern portion was no more than a crescent at the western boundary of the drainage.[187] In 2014, NASA satellite images documented that the eastern basin of the Aral Sea was completely dry.[188] That basin is so irretrievably desiccated that it is now known as the Aralkum Desert.[189]

Where the Aral Sea had once been a thriving ecological and economic wellspring for the region, since 2010 – only a half century since diversions began – the sea has been largely gone.[190] In its place was left a polluted desert expanse surrounded by ghost towns and littered with abandoned fishing boats of the once

---

[179] Dene-Hern Chen, *Once Written Off for Dead, the Aral Sea Is Now Full of Life*, NAT. GEO. (Mar. 16, 2018), www.nationalgeographic.com/science/article/north-aral-sea-restoration-fish-kazakhstan.

[180] Ryszard Kapuscinski, IMPERIUM 255–60 (1995).

[181] Tansy Hoskins, *Cotton Production Linked to Images of the Dried up Aral Sea Basin*, THE GUARDIAN (Oct. 1, 2014), www.theguardian.com/sustainable-business/sustainable-fashion-blog/2014/oct/01/cotton-production-linked-to-images-of-the-dried-up-aral-sea-basin.

[182] Rick Livingston, *Aral Sea*, ENCYCLOPEDIA BRITTANICA, www.britannica.com/place/Aral-Sea (last visited Nov. 17, 2024).

[183] Phillip Micklin and Nikolay V. Aladin, *Reclaiming the Aral Sea*, SCIENTIFIC AMERICAN (2008).

[184] *Id.*

[185] *Aral Sea Reborn*, AL-JAZEERA (Jul. 8, 2013), www.aljazeera.com/program/earthrise/2013/7/8/aral-sea-reborn

[186] *Id.*

[187] *Id.*

[188] Tansy Hoskins, *Cotton Production Linked to Images of the Dried up Aral Sea Basin*, THE GUARDIAN (Oct. 1, 2014), www.theguardian.com/sustainable-business/sustainable-fashion-blog/2014/oct/01/cotton-production-linked-to-images-of-the-dried-up-aral-sea-basin.

[189] Caitlin Dempsey, *Aralkum Desert: The World's Newest Desert*, GEOGRAPHYREALM (May 28, 2014), www.geographyrealm.com/aralkum-desert-worlds-newest-desert/.

[190] Rick Livingston, *Aral Sea*, ENCYCLOPEDIA BRITTANICA, www.britannica.com/place/Aral-Sea (last visited Nov. 17, 2024).

thriving regional industry.[191] Just as the retreating Owens and Mono exposed toxic alkali dust from the lakebeds, the exposed Aral seabed has highly polluted the surrounding communities.[192] But the detritus beneath the Aral Sea is far worse. The exposed barrens contain not only toxic salts and fine particulate matter, but also toxic chemicals from weapons testing, industrial projects, PCB and heavy metal contamination, pesticides, and fertilizer runoff.[193] Pollutant concentrations spiked in the soil, remaining water resources, and windborne dust, spreading widely throughout the region.[194] Human intake of these toxins through direct inhalation and absorption by plants and livestock food sources have led to staggering public health impacts.[195] The region is plagued by high rates of cancer, drug resistant tuberculosis and other respiratory illnesses, digestive disorders, infectious diseases, and anemia, as well as liver, kidney, and eye problems.[196] Child and maternal mortality rates have soared to rates unheard of in the western world, as high as 75 child and 12 maternal deaths per 1,000 live births, respectively.[197] The combined ecological and economic catastrophe prompted a regional migration crisis as entire communities have fled.[198]

In 2011, United Nations Secretary General Ban Ki-moon lamented the Aral Sea catastrophe as one of the worst environmental disasters on the planet.[199] UNESCO, the United Nations Educational, Scientific, and Cultural Organization, has documented the Aral Sea story in its official Memory of the World Register, to highlight its significance as human heritage and facilitate ongoing research into what has happened.[200] Yet what happened here is not a mystery. The extinction of the Aral Sea was foreseen and approved by its Soviet administrators long before the catastrophe became unstoppable.[201] In 1964, Soviet hydro engineers publicly acknowledged that the lake was doomed and this had been considered and greenlighted in the official five-year plans approved by the relevant ministerial councils

---

[191] *Id.*
[192] *Id.*
[193] S. Jensen, Z. Mozhi, & R. Zetterstrom, *Environmental Pollution and Child Health in the Aral Sea Region in Kazakhstan*, 206 SCIENCE TOTAL ENV'T 187–193 (1997).
[194] *Id.*
[195] *Id.*
[196] *The Aral Sea Crisis*, COLUMBIA UNIV. (2008), www.columbia.edu/~tmt2120/impacts%20to%20 life%20in%20the%20region.htm#:~:text=This%20region%20has%20the%20highest,120%20 women%20per%2010%2C000%20births.
[197] *Id.*
[198] *Id.*
[199] *Aral Sea "One of the Planet's Worst Environmental Disasters,"* THE TELEGRAPH (Apr. 5, 2010), www.telegraph.co.uk/news/earth/earthnews/7554679/Aral-Sea-one-of-the-planets-worst-environmental-disasters.html
[200] *Aral Sea Archival Fonds,* UNESCO (2011), www.unesco.org/en/memory-world/aral-sea-archival-fonds?hub=1081.
[201] Michael Wines, *Grand Soviet Scheme for Sharing Water in Central Asia is Foundering*, NEW YORK TIMES (Dec. 9, 2002), www.nytimes.com/2002/12/09/world/grand-soviet-scheme-for-sharing-water-in-central-asia-is-foundering.html.

and overseeing Politburo. Public trust principles did not play a role in the adjudication of the Aral Sea's fate.[202]

The horrific management of the erstwhile Aral Sea betrays the worst abdication of public trust principles in environmental governance, leading to the very environmental and humanitarian catastrophes the doctrine is pledged to prevent. UNESCO has now added the Aral Sea tragedy to its Memory of the World Register, in hope that we learn how not to repeat it.[203] But we seem to be struggling with the lesson.

What happened to the Aral Sea is the same thing that happened to Owens Lake, except grotesquely magnified along every axis of scale. It is what will happen to the Dead Sea between Israel and Jordan if nothing in its present trajectory changes. It is what is threatening the Great Salt Lake in Utah, despite admirable late-breaking efforts to forestall it. It is the opposite of what happened to the Sea of Galilee, however, at least for now. And it is the fate that the Mono Lake litigation forestalled in California, at least for now, thanks to the famous public trust advocacy that intervened – and that helped inspire the different present approaches to protect the Great Salt Lake and Sea of Galilee. What happens from here to these places, and to so many countless others around the world, is now up to us.

D. CODA: SAVE MONO LAKE?

The preceding chapters recount the story of how the public trust doctrine developed as a focal point for broader environmental advocacy, how Mono Lake became the turning point of this trajectory, and how underlying public trust principles continue to infuse environmental law domestically and around the world. The Introduction situated this analysis in the context of the weak foundations for broader environmental law, and how the core public trust principles of sovereign responsibility for public environmental rights have been deployed to fill that gap.

After plumbing the development of the public trust doctrine through old Roman and British common law to its reception in the United States, the early chapters explored the Mono Lake story in detail, tracing the history of the L.A. Aqueduct in the Owens Valley and then the Mono Basin, and narrating the organic political mobilization to protect Mono Lake that would lead to the *Audubon Society* case. The middle chapters plumbed the Mono Lake litigation and its aftermath, from the state Water Board's resolution to protect the Lake to the legal implications of *Audubon Society* in the scholarly literature and other jurisdictions. The later chapters shifted focus from Mono Lake to the differentiating development of public trust principles around the United States and globally, with special focus on their use in emerging models of climate

---

[202] *Id.*
[203] *Aral Sea Archival Fonds*, UNESCO (2011), www.unesco.org/en/memory-world/aral-sea-archival-fonds?hub=1081.

advocacy and contrasting them with the ecocentric rights of nature movement. The Conclusion has considered the questions of legal theory, meaning, and strategy that the trust continues to prompt, while also considering what the world might look like without public trust-based environmental governance, through sketches of contemporary Mono Lake stories playing out elsewhere.

Here, at last, we return to the original Mono Lake story out in the Mono Basin itself – the historic saga still unfolding. Now more than a century after the opening of the Los Angeles Aqueduct, nearly a half century after the California Supreme Court's *Audubon Society* decision, and some thirty years since the Water Board's famous Decision 1631 implementing it, it is a good time to revisit that story. For like all public trust tales, the Mono Lake story continues to raise as many questions as it answers, not only about what did or should have happened in the past, but also about what will and should happen in the future.

The lake is in better shape now than it was before the litigation that launched a thousand public trust claims, but the epic tale continues. Mono Basin water continues to flow back into the lake, but at least for now, it also continues to flow south to Los Angeles. Decision 1631 directed management efforts in anticipation that the lake would reach its target level in 2014, but even these many years later, that has never come close to happening.[204] In a late-breaking 2025 reprieve, the city recognized that new reclaimed water generated in Los Angeles could meaningfully change the trajectory of the lake's recovery – providing genuine cause for hope and celebration among all who have worked so hard to change the fate of this cherished natural treasure.[205] But until it actually happens, the twists and turns in Mono Lake's story over so many years cautions ongoing vigilance.

In the intervening thirty years, the lake level has risen and fallen. Today, it remains only halfway to the healthy level mandated by Decision 1631. Ongoing diversions and intense dry periods have resurrected ecological threats and temporarily curtailed exports all the way back to the severest restrictions that immediately followed the original litigation, which few had expected to see again.[206] Yet California precipitation has become less predictable in recent decades. Reservoirs alternate between all-time lows and unseasonably swollen, and when the rains do come, they come down in torrential atmospheric rivers that drown the parched earth instead of the blanketing snowpack more evenly released over the rest of the year.[207] Climatic projections show that the state will swing unpredictably from very wet to

---

[204] *See* Chapter 6(E)(1) ("Mono Lake after Decision 1631").

[205] *See id.; see also* Ian James, *Los Angeles Will Nearly Double Recycled Water for 500,000 Residents*, L.A. TIMES (Oct. 31, 2025), www.latimes.com/environment/story/2025-10-31/los-angeles-wastewater-recycling (last visited Nov. 2, 2025) (reporting on plans to double water reclamation at the Donald C. Tillman Water Reclamation Plant in Van Nuys, "enable[ing] the city to stop taking water from Sierra streams that feed Mono Lake").

[206] For example, on April 1, 2015, the lake had receded to 6,380 feet. *See* Chapter 6(E)(1) ("Mono Lake after Decision 1631").

[207] *See* Chapter 6(E)(1) ("Mono Lake after Decision 1631").

extremely dry, facing drought that will put previous shortages to shame.[208] Mono Lake's survival in this changing climate depends on recovery from nearly a century of drought by diversion. Even in this hopeful moment, as Los Angeles announces best-faith effort to stop drawing water from the Mono Basin except in emergencies, we cannot discount the pressures of urgent future circumstances.

Perhaps the state's duty of ongoing supervision has finally led to the protection of Mono Lake that advocates have sought for over half a century – or perhaps it will eventually require that even the current plans be revisited because of prolonged drought conditions.[209] Such a drought would cause hardship for both Mono Lake and Angelenos, and both would factor into reconsiderations. Indeed, this is the state's delicate balancing act – its ongoing task to negotiate between Los Angeles's legitimate needs for municipal water supplies and the competing environmental, cultural, and economic reasons to keep it in the Mono Basin. The requirement of environmental values in the balance is itself a substantial achievement, in contrast to the negligent environmental management that preceded.

In the meanwhile, conflicts between public and private claims on water resources and other natural resource commons will doubtlessly continue to drive the evolution of environmental law, just as new principles of environmental rights – framed as anthropocentric human rights[210] or ecocentric rights of nature[211] – emerge to challenge the dominant theoretical models of the legal systems we have come to rely on. Public trust sovereign obligations and the reciprocal environmental rights that flow from them will be developed through advocacy, litigation, scholarship, and policymaking. The dynamic co-development of public trust principles and rules of private allocation, of resource conservation and resource exploitation, of environmental protection and natural resource management, will inexorably press forward.

Hopefully, the public trust doctrine will continue to help frame the overarching structure of environmental governance in a way that facilitates democratic and accountable public processes. Environmental lawmaking should begin from public trust principles, promoting reasonable policies of conservation, stewardship, and intergenerational fairness. Public trust litigation provides a corrective for failures of the political process that betray these underlying principles. Public trust norms encouraged by good environmental governance will reinforce cultural traditions that facilitate environmental responsibility in the private and commercial realms. When all is in order, public trust principles are internalized as a legal, cultural, and ethical imperative.

---

[208] *See, e.g.*, Nathan Rot, *Study Finds Western Megadrought is the Worst in 1,200 Years*, NPR (Feb. 14, 2022), www.npr.org/2022/02/14/1080302434/study-finds-western-megadrought-is-the-worst-in-1-200-years.

[209] *Cf.* Chapter 5(B)(3) ("Duty of Ongoing Supervision").

[210] *See* Chapter 9(A)(1) ("Searching for Environmental Rights in U.S. Law"); Chapter 9(A)(4) ("The Reciprocal Nature of Public Trust Principles and Environmental Rights").

[211] *See* Chapter 10(B) ("The Public Trust Doctrine and Rights of Nature Movement").

And so, the quiet revolution, already in progress, will continue. Our cherished natural world – together with the natural resources within it on which we all rely – have never been under more pressure from human decision-making than they are right now. The challenges are daunting, and the stakes are high. But we are not without the tools, strength, or will to respond. We are the agents of our own future. May we continue to find resolve and inspiration to move forward in the importance of the task.

Index

54 Climate Solutions Plan, 304

Aarhus Convention, 8
Abate, Randall, 292
Ackerman, Bruce, 229
administrative atmospheric trust, 315–18
Administrative Procedures Act, 440
Africa
  public trust doctrine in, 371
    Kenya, 372
    Nigeria, 372
    South Africa, 373
    Uganda, 371–72
  rights of nature initiatives in, 387–88
Air Quality Control Act, 315
Alaska
  atmospheric trust claims in, 313
  constitutional environmental protection in, 339
Alfonso X, 33
American environmental law, 4–7, 9, 288
  California Environmental Quality Act, 9
  Clean Air Act, 7, 10–11
  Clean Power Plan, 7
  Clean Water Act, 7, 9–10
  Endangered Species Act, 6, 7
  Minnesota Environmental Rights Act, 9
American public trust doctrine, 223–25, 238–39, 282–83, 375, 378–80
  adoption of public trust doctrine, 14, 35–36
    definitive Supreme Court statement (*Shively v. Bowlby*), 40–42
    equal footing doctrine (*Pollard v. Hagan*), 38–40
    state common law (*Arnold v. Mundy*), 36–37
    Supreme Court, affirmation by (*Martin v. Waddell*), 37–38
    trustee power and responsibility for resource protection (*Illinois Central Railroad Co. v. Illinois*), 42–48

California, 225–27, 256, 259–60, 262
Colorado, 257–59, 261
as common law doctrine. *See* common law doctrine
constitutional trusts, 245–50
damages, compensation for, 265, 266–67
declaratory relief, 264, 265, 266
for environmental governance, 3–4, 13–16
environmental law, U.S. Constitution and, 288
and environmental rights, 17–21
  as background principle, 268–72
  environmental stewardship obligations and, 20–21
  U.S. Constitution and, 18–20
executive trusts, 250–52
in federal law. *See* federal law, public trust doctrine in
Florida, 245–46, 249–50, 260, 270–71, 393–94
Hawaii, 219, 245–46, 255–56, 260, 270, 419
Huffman's critics on Roman origin of, 295
Idaho, 227–29, 244, 261, 263–64
injunctive relief, 264–66
judicial relief, 264–67, 294
as legal shield for defending against private takings claims, 266–67
legal theories about nature of, 261–64
Massachusetts, 240–41
Michigan, 241–44, 260–61
Minnesota, 241–44
Montana, 260
multiplatform trusts, 252–53
Nevada, 229–34, 244–45, 260, 264
New Jersey, 254–55, 260
Oregon, 260
Pennsylvania, 246–49
as quasi-constitutional doctrine. *See* quasi-constitutional doctrine
remedies, 264–67
resources protection by, 253–54

463

American public trust doctrine (cont.)
   natural resources, 255–56
   waterways, 254–55
   wildlife protection, 256
   restricted protections, 257–59
   South Carolina, 260
   by state attorneys general, use of, 251–52
   statutory trusts, 241–45
   trust-associated values protection by, 259–61
American River, 213
animal rights advocates, 417
anthropocentric public trust doctrine, xiv, 24, 363, 405, 406
antidemocratic critique, 24, 204, 207, 435, 442
Anti-Fracking Home Rule Charter of Grant Township, 390–91, 413
Araiza, William, 206, 209
the Aral Sea, 456–59
Arizona, atmospheric trust claims in, 314–15
Articles of Confederation, 5
Asia
   public trust doctrine in, 365
      India, 367–68
      Nepal, 368–69
      Philippines, 365–66
   rights of nature initiatives in
      Bangladesh, 387
      India, 386–87
atmospheric commons, public trust protection for, 292
atmospheric river event, 187
atmospheric trust, 207
atmospheric trust claims, 300–1
   in Alaska, 339
   in Canada, 309–10
   in Florida, 316–17, 335
   in France, 307–9
   in Germany, 305–6
   in Hawaii, 335, 337–38
   in India, 309
   in Massachusetts, 315–16
   in Mexico, 310
   in Montana, 336–37, 338
   in Nepal, 305
   in Netherlands, 302–4
   in New York, 335, 339
   in Pennsylvania, 339
   scholar's criticism of, 293–97
   in U.S., 301–2, 310–15, 318–33
   in Utah, 339–40
   in Virginia, 339, 340
   in Washington, 317–18
atmospheric trust litigation, 283, 284–85, 291
atmospheric trust project, 293, 310–15, 330, 346, 349, 379, 413

Australia
   public trust doctrine, 364–65
   rights of nature initiatives in, 385–86

background principle, public trust doctrine as, 268–72
Bangladesh, rights of nature initiatives in, 387
Bellinger, Nathan, 224, 275
Berry, Thomas, 414
Bill of Rights, 5, 322, 343
Blumm, Michael, 209, 210, 292
Bolivia, rights of nature initiatives in, 383
Bottomley, Anne, 375
Brazil Constitution, 4, 376
   Article 225, 4
Brazil public trust doctrine, 376–77
Bundesklimaschutzgesetz (KSG), 306
Byzantine Empire, public trust principles in, 30–31

California
   environmental-rights, proposed amendments for, 342–43
   Gold Rush, 83, 89, 90, 91, 113, 148
   public trust doctrine, 225–27, 252–53, 262
      atmospheric trust claims and, 312
      values protection by, 259–60
      wildlife protection by, 256
California, *Mono Lake* doctrine impacts in, 211–12
   American River litigation, 213
   appropriative water rights and riparian water rights litigation, 214–15
   judicial, 213–17
   legislative and executive, 212–13
   non-navigable waterways, public trust doctrine protection to, 216
   to groundwater resources, 217
   Putah Creek litigation, 214
   Scott River case, 217–20
   wildlife, public trust protection in, 215–16
California Constitution, 139, 252
   Article I, 126
   Article X, 58, 95, 127, 137, 168, 212, 252
California Environmental Quality Act (CEQA), 9, 103, 156, 195
California Fish and Game Code, 166, 167, 168, 171, 214
California State Water Resources Control Board (SWRCB), 253
California Water Code, 127, 138, 142, 181, 211, 212, 213, 218, 252–53, 394
California Wilderness Act, 162
CalTrout litigation, 166–70
Canada
   climate claims in, 309–10
   public trust doctrine, 377–78

Canadian Charter of Rights and Freedoms, 309
Caron, David, 291
CEQA. *See* California Environmental Quality Act (CEQA)
Children's Brief, 330–31, 351
citizen suit provisions, 440–43
Clean Air Act, 7, 10–11, 77, 98, 111, 145, 288, 313, 314, 344
Clean Power Plan, 7, 296
Clean Water Act, 7, 9–10, 111, 120, 145, 171, 198, 237, 294, 411, 412, 414
climate advocacy, public trust principles in, 291–93
climate rights litigation, 284, 285–86
climate stability, 340–41
climate trust-rights advocacy/litigation. *See* trust-rights climate advocacy/litigation
Cohen, Lloyd, 203
Colombia, rights of nature initiatives in, 383–84
Colorado public trust doctrine, 261
　restricted protection in, 257–59
Colorado River Aqueduct, 63
Commerce Clause, 6, 7, 12
common law doctrine, 223–25, 240–41, 243, 244, 245, 253, 261
　California, 225–27
　Idaho, 227–29, 244, 263–64
　Massachusetts, 240–41
　Minnesota, 241–44
　Pennsylvania, 246–49
common law nuisance, 120, 126, 145, 171, 209
constitutive limit, 224, 275
constitutional trusts, 245–50
conventional wildlife advocates, 417
Cook, Paul, 89
Craig, Robin, 291
Crowley Lake, 96

Dahlgren litigation, 165–66
damages, compensation for, 265, 266–67, 309, 404
Dana, Gayle, 104
Davis, Martha, 178, 180
Dead Sea of California, 453–56
Decision 1631, 183, 185, 197, 216
　6,392 as new Mono Lake level target, 174–77
　Los Angeles decision forgoing appeal against Water Board's, 178
　Los Angeles' water conservation and reclamation projects after, 178–80
　Mono Lake after, 182–89
Decision 1641, 217
declaratory relief, 264, 265, 266, 294, 319, 352, 404
Delta Reform Act, 213
Dernbach, John C., 199, 247, 248, 282, 342
Dodge, Bruce, 129, 133, 170

Doyle, Arthur Conan, Sir, 42
Due Process Clause, 285, 294, 322, 323, 332, 340, 352
Dunning, Harrison, 122

East Valley Reclamation Project, 173
Eaton, Fred, 64, 67, 68
ECHR. *See* European Convention on Human Rights (ECHR)
Ecuador public trust doctrine, 377
Ecuadorian Constitution, 377, 402, 403
　Article 71, 4, 6, 8
　and environmental law, 7
　rights of nature initiatives in, 381–82
Endangered Species Act, 6, 7, 417, 440
England public trust doctrine, 374–75
English common law, public trust doctrine in, 32–33, 34, 367, 419
English law, public trust doctrine in, 31–33
Environment Protection Act of 2019 (Nepal), 305
environmental governance, 349–51, 423–25
environmental human rights, 288–91
environmental law, constitutional foundations of
　Brazil Constitution, 4
　Ecuador Constitution, 4, 6, 7, 8
　Nepal Constitution, 7
　Swiss Constitution, 6, 7
　U.S. Constitution, 4–7
　U.S. state constitutions, 8
Environmental Management and Co-ordination Act (Kenya), 372
environmental rights, 17–21
　climate trust-rights advocacy/litigation. *See* trust-rights climate advocacy/litigation
　David Takacs on, 291
　Dinah Shelton on substantive, for quality of environment, 290
　Hohfeldian rights-duty model, 298–99
　James May on recognition of, 290–91
　Joseph Sax on human rights and, 289–90
　nature, rights of, 288–89
　reciprocal nature of sovereign obligations and, 297–300
　in U.S. law, 288–91
the Environmental Rights Amendment, 247, 248
Epstein, Richard, 434
equal footing doctrine, 38–40, 41, 52, 153, 225, 276
Europe
　public trust doctrine in, 373–74
　　England, 374–75
　　Scotland and Wales, 375
　rights of nature initiatives in, 388
European Convention on Human Rights (ECHR), 303, 307, 318, 323
Executive Order No. 569, 315
executive trusts, 250–52

Farber, Dan, 296, 299
federal law, public trust doctrine in, 267–68
  as background principle in federal takings claims, 268–72
  federal authority, constitutional constraint of, 274–80
  secret Supreme Court public trust debate, 272–74
Federal Navigational Servitude, 268
federal reserved water rights doctrine, 58
Fifth Amendment, 239
Filipino public trust doctrine, 365–66
Florida
  atmospheric trust claims in, 316–17, 335
  public trust doctrine, 245–46, 249–50, 260, 270–71, 393–94, 419
  tribal rights of nature initiatives in, 393–98
Florida Constitution, 271
  Article II, 20, 335
  Article X, 393
  trust-rights protections in, 335
Florida Right to Clean Water, 398
Forest Act of 2019 (Nepal), 305
Forest Charter, 32, 35
Framework Law of the Mother Earth and Integral Development for Living Well, 383
France, climate claims in, 307–9
Frank, Richard, 113, 115
French Environmental Charter, 307, 308, 309

Gaines, David, 133
  campaigns on saving Mono Lake, 107
  and Mono Basin Research Group, 103–4
  Mono Lake Committee, 105–8
Gaines, Sally, 105, 107, 129, 133. *See also* Mono Lake Committee
Gaining Responsibility on Water Act, 220
German Constitution, 306
Germany, climate claims in, 305–6
Giagnocavo, Cynthia, 289
Goldstein, Howard, 289
Great Britain, public trust doctrine in, 374–76
the Great Middle East, public trust doctrine in, 369
  Israel, 370
  Pakistan, 369–70
Great Outdoors Colorado Program, 258
Great Salt Lake Basin, 445–50
Grinnell, Joseph, 66
Guim, Mauricio, 289

Hale, Matthew, Sir, 32
Hart, John, 164
Hawaii
  atmospheric trust claims in, 335, 337–38
  environmental-rights, proposed amendments for, 343
  public trust doctrine, 219, 245–46, 260, 270, 419
  natural resources protection by, 256
Hawaii Constitution, 245
  Article IX, 335
  based climate litigation, 337–38
  trust-rights protection in, 335
Henry III, King, 32
Herbst, David, 104
Ho-Chunk Nation (Wisconsin), 398
Hohfeld, Wesley Newcomb, 298
  rights-duty model, 298–99
Hot Creek fish hatchery agreement, 95
Huffman, James L., 206
  on Roman public trust doctrine, 295
Huffman, Jim, 34
human rights, 5

Idaho
  approach to *Mono Lake* doctrine, 153–54, 222–23
  public trust doctrine, 227–29, 244, 261, 263–64
Illinois Constitution, Article XI, 335
India
  climate claims in, 309
  public trust doctrine, 367–68
  rights of nature initiatives in, 386–87
Inflation Reduction Act, 351, 355
injunctive relief, 264–66, 309, 319, 404, 438
Innu Council of Ekuanitship (Quebec), 400
Institutes of Justinian, 30–31, 34
Integrated Climate Change Strategy for the Commonwealth, 315
Inyo National Forest, xii, 22, 84, 92, 161, 162
Inyo-Los Angeles Long Term Water Agreement, 191, 194, 195
Israel public trust doctrine, 370

judicial relief, 264–67, 294, 296, 305
judicial review critique, public trust doctrine, 204–7
Juliana case (*Juliana v. United States*), 318–19, 338
  amended complaint, 329–30
  Children's Brief, 330–31, 351
  declaratory relief claims, 328
  government petitions, dismissal of, 325
  injunctive relief claims, dismiss of, 326–28
  interlocutory appeal, 325–26
  legacy, 330–33
  Ninth Circuit in 2024, dismissal by, 329–30
  pleadings, 319–25
  redressability issue, 326, 327, 328

jus privatum, 43, 112
jus publicum, 30, 31, 34, 112, 240, 374, 377
Justinian Code, 346
Justinian I, 30

Kenya public trust doctrine, 372
Kenyan Constitution, 372
　Article 42, 372
Kissimmee River Bill of Rights, 395, 412
Klass, Alexandra, 211, 244, 249
Klein, Christine, 51
Kootzaduka'a/Kutzadika'a (Mono Lake indigenous people), 88–89

Lajoie, Kenneth, 103, 106
Lake Erie Bill of Rights (LEBOR), 392–93, 404
Lake Front Act of 1869, 44, 45
Lake Kinneret, 450–53
Land Reform Act 2003 (Scotland), 375
Lange, Charlotte, 89
Las Siete Partidas, 33
Layzer, Judith, 207
Lazarus, Richard, 207, 273, 353, 355, 433
　atmospheric trust advocacy, critique of, 295–96, 297
　environmental critics of public trust doctrine, 208–9
LEBOR. *See* Lake Erie Bill of Rights (LEBOR)
Lee Vining, California, xii, xiii, 90, 91, 107
Lee Vining Indian and Community Center, 89
legal process critique, Mono Lake doctrine, 204–7
Leopold, Aldo, 407
Libecap, Gary, 73, 94, 203
　Los Angeles Aqueduct, assessment on, 73–75
Lippincott, Joseph, 64, 67, 68, 72
Livermore, Michael, 289
Los Angeles, 61
　Inyo County lands for landfill, ownership of, 195–96
　water scarcity in, 61–64
Los Angeles Aqueduct, 16, 22, 60, 63
　Aberdeen diversion dam, 69, 72
　consequences of, 72, 75–78
　　decline in Owens Valley agriculture, 75–76
　　Environmental Impact Report (EIR) on, 76
　　fine alkali salts and dust storm in Owens Valley, 77–78
　　Great Basin Unified Air Pollution Control District, agreement with, 78
　　Oroville Dam failure, 81–82
　　Owens Dry Lake, 76–77
　　St. Francis Dam disaster, xiii, 22, 60, 61, 78–81
　construction of, 69–70
　Crowley Lake, 96
　Decision 1631, 174
　　6,392 as new Mono Lake level target, 174–77
　　Los Angeles decision forgoing appeal against Water Board's, 178
　　Los Angeles' water conservation and reclamation projects after, 178–80
　　Mono Lake after, 182–89
　Gary Libecap assessment on, 73–75
　groundwater export through Mono Craters Tunnel, 186–87
　Inyo-Los Angles Long Term Water Agreement, 191, 194, 195
　litigation against, 76, 118–22
　　CalTrout, 166–70
　　Dahlgren, 165–66
　　for exposed Owens Dry Lake bed, 192–93
　　National Audubon Society. *See* Mono Lake case (*National Audubon Society v. Superior Court*)
　Lower Owens River, restoring dewatered portions of, 69
　on Mono Basin, water exports impacts, 97–100, 117
　　air quality problem and dust storm, 98
　　Benchmark Tufa towers appearance, 97–98
　　on ecosystem, 98–99
　　surface area shrinkage, 99
　in Mono Basin and acquiring water rights, 93
　　constraints on water rights after Decision 1631, 185
　　Mono Basin Extension (1940), 93–96
　　Second Barrel (1970), 96–97, 99, 110, 117, 167
　Mono Basin Restoration Plan, 181–82
　Mono Lake level and water exports percentage during drought seasons, 182–85, 188–89
　Owens Lake Scientific Advisory Panel, 193
　Owens Lake Trails recreational project, 194
　Owens Valley, 60, 63, 64–67
　　devastation due to Aqueduct, 75–78
　　gravity-powered design, 67
　　Lower Owens River Project, 191–92
　　self-powering design of, 67–68
　　water rights, acquiring, 70–73
　Owens Valley Committee effort in restoring water, 191–92, 193–94
　San Fernando Valley, 68–69
Los Angeles River, 61–62
Lower Owens River Project, 191–92
Lyons, Patrick, 291

Magna Carta, 14, 31–32, 34, 224, 374, 377, 410
　Forest Charter, 32, 35
　Jim Huffman critique on, 35
Māori people, 408

Markell, David, 288
Massachusetts
  atmospheric trust claims in, 315–16
  public trust doctrine, 240–41
  waterways protection, 255
Massachusetts Constitution, 255
  Article XCVII, 335
May, James, 290, 409
McGinn, Thomas, 34, 295
McKibben, Bill, 319
mean high-water mark (MHWM), 35
Mejelle, 362, 370
Menominee Indian Tribe (Wisconsin), 399
MEPA. *See* Michigan Environmental Protection Act (MEPA) of 1970
MERA. *See* Minnesota Environmental Rights Act (MERA) of 1971
Mexico, climate claims in, 310
Michigan Environmental Protection Act (MEPA) of 1970, 242, 243–44
Michigan public trust doctrine, 241–44, 257
  executive use of, 250–51
  values protection by, 260–61
Minganie Regional County Municipality (Quebec), 400
Minnesota Environmental Rights Act (MERA) of 1971, 9, 242, 243–44
Minnesota public trust doctrine, 241–44
modern public trust doctrine. *See* public trust doctrine
Mono Basin Extension (1940), 93–96
Mono Basin National Forest Scenic Area, 93, 98, 123, 158, 161–65
Mono Basin National Forest Scenic Area Comprehensive Management Plan, 164
Mono Basin Research Group, 103
Mono Basin Restoration Plan, 181–82
Mono Craters, 86–87, 91, 93, 96, 186
Mono Lake Basin, xi–xiv, 84–85
  age, 84
  Decision 1631. *See* Decision 1631
  during drought seasons, 182–85, 187
    emergency regulations by Water Board, 188
  economy, 91–93
  ecosystem, 85–87
    alkali fly and brine shrimp in, 85–86
    Barroeca monosierra in, 87
    California gulls breeding in, 86, 104
    choanoflagellates in, 87
    Los Angeles Aqueduct impacts on, 98–99
    Mono Craters, 86–87, 91, 93, 96
    NASA research of GFAJ-1 arsenic bacteria in, 87
    as National Monument, 92
    Pacific Flyway, 86
  European settlement in, 89–90
  Kootzaduka'a (indigenous people), 88–89
  Lee Vining, xii, xiii, 90, 91
    resident employment, 91
  legislation for protecting, 122–23
  litigations, 425
    CalTrout, 166–70
    Dahlgren, 165–66
    In re Mono Lake Water Rights cases, 169–72
    National Audubon Society v. Superior Court. *See Mono Lake* case (*National Audubon Society v. Superior Court*)
  Los Angeles Aqueduct impacts on, 97–100
    air quality problem and dust storm, 98
    Benchmark Tufa towers appearance, 97–98
    on ecosystem, 98–99
    surface area shrinkage, 99
  Los Angeles Aqueduct in, 93
    Mono Basin Extension (1940), 93–96
    Second Barrel (1970), 96–97, 99, 110, 117, 167
  Los Angeles decision forgoing appeal against Water Board's Decision 1631, 178
  Los Angeles' water conservation and reclamation projects after, 178–80
  as Outstanding National Resource Water, 175
  political advocacy. *See* political advocacy, Mono Lake Basin
  population decline in, 92–93
  protecting land of, 159
    Mono Basin National Forest Scenic Area, 93, 98, 123, 158, 161–65
    Mono Lake Tufa State Natural Reserve, 123, 159–61
  saltwater terminal lake, 84
  source of industry, 91–92
  state/federal funding for water conservation, 172–73
  surface area and depth of, 84
  yearly measurements of surface level, 188
Mono Lake Basin Restoration Settlement Agreement, 185
Mono Lake case (*National Audubon Society v. Superior Court*), 2–3, 16–17, 28, 48, 50, 60, 85, 91, 93, 94, 96, 99–100, 105, 117, 118–22, 125–26, 169–72, 197, 201, 202, 206, 209, 221, 226, 246, 253, 260, 262, 266, 394, 426–27, 431, 435, 439, 443
  attorneys, 128–32
    defense (Los Angeles), 130
    plaintiff (Mono Lake), 129
    State of California, 130–31
    U.S., 131–32
  California Supreme Court's decision, 141–45
  legal arguments, 133–34, 140–41
    Los Angeles defendants, 136–38

Mono Lake plaintiffs, 134–36
  State of California, 138–40
litigations against Los Angeles Department of Water and Power (DWP), 118–22
Los Angeles defense statement, 127–28
Morrison & Foerster contribution to, 117
plaintiff's allegation on violation of water rights, 126–27, 133–34
pleadings, 126–28
private water allocation, 59
public interest in, 430–31
and public trust doctrine, 15, 16–17, 26–27, 126, 134–36, 140, 144, 145
settlement negotiations, 132–33
water allocation law, 27
Mono Lake Committee, 100, 102, 105–8, 128, 165
  campaigns for gaining public attention on, 107–9
  David Winkler's effort on saving California Gull population, 107
  legislation policy advocacy, 109–10
  Martha Davis effort on lake water level restoration, 178
  Outdoor Experiences educational program, 109
  rural–urban partnership, 108–10
  settlement negotiation, rejecting, 133
Mono Lake doctrine, 146, 197–98, 211
  Buzz Thompson critics, 206
  California, impacts in, 211–12
    American River litigation, 213
    appropriative water rights and riparian water rights litigation, 214–15
    judicial, 213–17
    legislative and executive, 212–13
    non-navigable waterways, public trust doctrine protection to, 216, 217
    Putah Creek litigation, 214
    Scott River case, 217–20
    wildlife, public trust protection in, 215–16
  environmental critique, 207–11
  environmental public trust values, protection of, 146–47
  Gary Libecap critique on, 203
  Hawaii, ongoing oversight in, 151
  James Huffman critics, 206
  legal process critique, 204–7
  Mary Wood critique on legal process, 205
  nature of public trust doctrine, 152–54
  Nevada, ongoing oversight in, 151
  to non-navigable tributaries, 147–49
  ongoing supervision of public trust resources, duty of, 149–52, 206, 223
  other states, impacts in, 220–23

Alaska, 221
Arizona, 221
Idaho, *Mono Lake* doctrine in, 222–23
Minnesota, 221
Montana, 221
Nevada, 222
North Dakota, rejection of *Mono Lake* doctrine in, 222
South Dakota, 221–22
Vermont, 221
property rights critique, 201–4, 220
as quasi-constitutional rule, 223
revisiting water management and allocation decisions, 149–51
as substantive and procedural doctrine, 155–57
William Araiza critics, 206
Mono Lake Task Force (Lajoie), 103
Mono Lake Tufa State Natural Reserve, 123, 159–61, 163, 183
Montana
  atmospheric trust claims in, 336–37, 338
  public trust doctrine, 257, 260
Montana Constitution, 249, 341
  Article IX, 8, 335
  based climate litigation, 336–37, 338
  and environmental law, 8, 19
Montana Environmental Protection Act, 336
Moore, Tredwell, 89
Moskovitz, Adolph, 130, 143
Mulholland, Bill, 64, 67, 68, 70
Mulholland, William, 63, 72, 80
multiplatform trusts, 252–53

National Environmental Policy Act (NEPA), 7, 155
National Water Act of 1998 (South Africa), 373
Natural Resources and Environmental Protection Act of 1994, 242, 257
nature, rights of, 288–89
Negit Island, 86, 99, 104, 107
Nepal
  climate claims in, 305
  public trust doctrine, 368–69
Nepal Constitution, 368
  Article 30, 305
  and environmental law, 7
Netherlands, climate claims in, 302–4
Nevada
  ongoing oversight in, 151
  public trust doctrine, 229–34, 244–45, 260, 264
New Jersey public trust doctrine, 254–55, 260
New Mexico, atmospheric trust claims in, 314, 335, 339
New Mexico Constitution, Article XX, 318

New York Constitution
 based climate litigation, 339
 and environmental law, 8, 19
 trust-rights protections in, 335
New York's Green Amendment, 351
New Zealand
 public trust doctrine, 364–65
 rights of nature initiatives in, 384–85
Newsom, Gavin, 187
Nigeria Constitution, 372
Nigeria public trust doctrine, 372
Ninth Amendment, 294
North America
 public trust doctrine in, 377
  Canada, 377–78
  United States. *See* American public trust doctrine
 tribal rights of nature initiatives in, 398
  Ho-Chunk Nation and Menominee Tribe (Wisconsin), 398–99
  Innu Council of Ekuanitship and Minganie County (Quebec), 400
  Ponca Nation (Oklahoma), 399
  White Earth Band (Ojibwe), 399–400
  Yurok Tribe (California), 400

Oceania
 public trust doctrine in, 364–65
 rights of nature initiatives in, 384
  Australia, 385–86
  New Zealand, 384–85
Ohio, tribal rights of nature initiatives in, 392–93
ongoing oversight doctrine, 149–52
ordinary low water mark (OLWM), 35
Oregon
 atmospheric trust claims in, 313
 public trust doctrine, 260
Oroville Dam failure, 81–82
Ottoman Civil Code, 362
Our Children's Trust, 311
Owen, Dave, 210, 296
Owens Dry Lake, 76–77
 litigations against Los Angeles Aqueduct for exposed, 192–93
 Owens Lake Scientific Advisory Panel, 193
Owens Lake, 65–67, 76, 135
Owens Lake Scientific Advisory Panel, 193
Owens Lake Trails recreational project, 194
Owens Valley, 60, 63, 64–67
 for agricultural use, 71
 climate in, 65
 depth of, 67
 gravity-powered design, 67
 Los Angeles Aqueduct

 Inyo-Los Angles Long Term Water Agreement, 191, 194, 195
 Owens Lake Trails recreational project, 194
 Los Angeles Aqueduct consequences on
  decline in agriculture, 75–76
  fine alkali salts and dust storm in, 77–78
  litigation against, 76
  Owens Dry Lake, 76–77
 Lower Owens River Project, 191–92
 Owens Lake, 65–67
 Owens Valley Committee effort in restoring water, 191–92, 193–94
 Pacific Flyway in, 66
 self-powering design of, 67–68
 surface area of, 64
Owens Valley Committee, 190, 191–92, 193–94

Pakistan public trust doctrine, 369–70
Pennsylvania
 public trust doctrine, 246–49, 419
 tribal rights of nature initiatives in
  Pittsburgh's anti-fracking ordinance, 389–91
  Santa Monica's Bill of Rights for Sustainability, 391–92
  Tamaqua Borough's Sewage Ordinance, 389
Pennsylvania Constitution, 19, 246, 247, 341, 407
 Article I, 341, 407
 based climate litigation, 339
 and environmental law, 8
 and environmental rights, 19
Pennsylvania Oil and Gas Act, 247
Philippine Environmental Policy, 366
Philippines public trust doctrine, 365–66
Pittsburgh's anti-fracking ordinance, 389–91
political advocacy, Mono Lake Basin, 101–2
 David Gaines and Mono Basin Research Group, 103–4
 David Winkler on salinity of lake water, 104–5
 Kenneth Lajoie's Mono Lake Task Force, 103
 Mono Lake Committee, 100, 102, 105–8
  campaigns for gaining public attention on, 107–9
  David Winkler's effort on saving California Gull population, 107
  legislation policy advocacy, 109–10
  rural–urban partnership, 108–10
 Morrison & Foerster, 117
 "Save Mono Lake" campaign, 102, 108, 110
 Tim Such, 116–17
Ponca Nation (Oklahoma), 399
prior appropriations doctrine, 27, 54–58, 126, 136, 137, 140, 141, 143, 146, 151, 152, 168, 204, 226, 228, 229, 231, 233, 234, 262, 264
 advantages of, 55
 first-in-time rights, 54, 55

privatization approach to resource allocation, 56
public trust doctrine vs., 49–50
return flows, 55
temporal priority of users, 55, 57
use-it-or-lose-it features, 132, 136, 177
private property rights, Mono Lake doctrine and, 201–4, 220
Privileges and Immunities Clause, 12–13
Protection of Coastal and Environmental Law (Israel), 370
public trust advocacy, 3, 15, 18, 21
public trust doctrine, xii, xiii, xiv–xv, 1–2, 14, 26–27, 28–30, 153, 181, 198–201, 236–40, 263, 423, 426
  anthropocentrism of, xiv, 24, 363, 405, 406
  in climate advocacy, 291–93
  climate trust-rights advocacy/litigation. See trust-rights climate advocacy/litigation
  as common law doctrine. See common law doctrine
  constitutional trusts, 245–50
  conventional historical account, critique of, 34–35
  core principles, 17–18, 286
  in early English common law, 32–33
  in early English law, 31–33
  in early Spanish law, 33
  environmental critique, 207–11
  for environmental governance, 3–4, 13–16, 423–25
  and environmental rights, 17–21
  executive trusts, 250–52
  in federal law. See federal law, public trust doctrine in
  forcibility and flexibility of, 426–28
  Forest Charter, 32, 35
  government as trustee for resource protection, 43–44
  judicial relief, 264–67, 294
  Las Siete Partidas, 33
  legal nature of, 429–30
  legal process critique, 204–7
  Magna Carta, 31–32, 34, 35
  multiplatform trusts, 252–53
  property rights critique, 201–4, 220
  public interest of, 430–32
  as quasi-constitutional doctrine. See quasi-constitutional doctrine
  in Roman and Byzantine Empires, 14, 30–31
  Roman origin of, 295
  separation-of-powers critique. See separation-of-powers critique, public trust doctrine
  statutory trusts, 241–45

  United States. See American public trust doctrine
  vs. prior appropriations doctrine, 49–50
  water allocation law conflicts. See water allocation law
The Public Trust Doctrine in Natural Resource Law: Effective Judicial Intervention (Sax), 110, 241
public trust doctrine vs. rights of nature movement, 380–81, 405
  anthropocentrism vs. ecocentrism, 405–9
  environmental law failure, response to, 411–13
  intuitive and emotional appeal, 414–15
  nature of, 409–10
  philosophical difference, 405–9
  political arena, leveraging, 413–14
  waterways, protection of, 410–11
Putah Creek, 214

quasi-constitutional doctrine, 223–25, 261–62, 434, 436
  California, 225–27, 262
  Hawaii, 245–46
  Nevada, 229–34, 244–45, 264

Rechtschaffen, Clifford, 288
Red Sea–Dead Sea Water Project, 454–56
regulatory capture, 441
res communis, 33
rights of nature movement, 363–64, 365, 380, 381, 415–21, 423
  international initiatives
    in Africa, 387–88
    in Asia, 386–87
    in Australia, 385–86
    in Bangladesh, 387
    in Bolivia, 383
    in Colombia, 383–84
    in Ecuador, 381–82
    in Europe, 388
    in India, 386–87
    in New Zealand, 384–85
    in Oceania, 384–86
    in South America, 382–84
    in Spain, 388
    in Uganda, 387–88
  jurisdictional development, differentiation in, 400–2
  legal protections, 400–2
  protections of rights of nature, 403–4
  remedies, 404–5
  rights to speak for rights holders, 402–3
  vindication of, legal mechanisms for, 403
  North American tribes and First Nations initiatives, 398

rights of nature movement (cont.)
  Ho-Chunk Nation and Menominee Tribe (Wisconsin), 398–99
  Innu Council of Ekuanitship and Minganie County (Quebec), 400
  Ponca Nation (Oklahoma), 399
  White Earth Band (Ojibwe), 399–400
  Yurok Tribe (California), 400
  public trust doctrine vs. See public trust doctrine vs. rights of nature movement
  U.S. tribal initiatives
    in Florida, 393–98
    in Ohio, 392–93
    in Pennsylvania, 389–92
Riordan, Richard, 178
riparian rights doctrine, 28, 50–54, 58
  advantages of, 52
  core principles for reasonable water allocation, 51
  de-privileging riparian ownership, 50, 52
  disadvantages of, 52
  natural flow doctrine, 52–53
  reasonable use of, 50–51, 53
  regulated riparianism, 52, 53, 57
Rogers, J. David, 80
Roman common law, 374
Roman Empire, public trust principles in, 14, 30–31, 295
Rose, Carol, 209
Ruhl, J. B., 34, 295

Sachs, Noah, 289
Sacramento-San Joaquin Delta Reform Act, 212
San Fernando Valley, 68–69
Santa Fe River Bill of Rights, 395
Santa Monica's Bill of Rights for Sustainability, 391–92
"Save Mono Lake" campaign, 102, 108, 110
Sax, Joseph, 100, 110, 241, 270, 289, 291, 297, 349, 356, 408
  on public trust doctrine, 110–12
scholarly analysis, public trust doctrine, 207–11
  Alexandra Klass, 211
  atmospheric trust claims, scholarly critics of, 293–97
  Carol Rose, 209
  Dan Farber, 296, 299
  Dave Owen, 210
  Harrison Dunning, 122
  J. B. Ruhl, 34, 295
  James Huffman, 34, 35, 206, 295
  Judith Layzer, 207
  Mary Wood, 210
  Michael Blumm, 209–10
  Richard Lazarus, 208–9, 295–96, 297
  Thomas McGinn, 34, 295
  William Araiza, 209
Scotland public trust doctrine, 375
Scott River case, 148, 187, 217–20
Sea of Galilee, 450–53
separation-of-powers, 318, 346–48
separation-of-powers critique, public trust doctrine, 204–7, 432
  citizen suit provisions, 440–43
  and constitutive constraint, 443–45
  environmental claims, 437–40
  judicial trust administration, 432–37
Shelton, Dinah, 290, 409
South Africa public trust doctrine, 373
South America
  public trust doctrine in, 376
    Brazil, 376–77
    Ecuador, 377
  rights of nature initiatives in, 382–84
    Bolivia, 383
    Colombia, 383–84
South Carolina public trust doctrine, 260
Spain, rights of nature initiatives in, 388
Spanish law, public trust doctrine in, 33
St. Francis Dam disaster, xiii, 22, 60, 61, 78–81
statutory trusts, 241–45
Stevens, Jan, 224
Stone, Christopher, 289, 401, 408, 416, 418
substantive due process, 294, 320
substantive environmental rights, 409
Such, Tim, 116–17, 134
Supremacy Clause, 225
Swiss Constitution
  Article 74, 6, 7
  and environmental law, 7

Takacs, David, 291, 297, 409, 411
Takings Clause, 269
Tamaqua Borough Sewage Sludge Ordinance, 389
Te Urewara Act, 384
Texas, atmospheric trust claim in, 314
Thaler, Jeff, 291
Thompson, Buzz, 206
Three Gorges Dam, 456
Thunberg, Greta, 354
Torres, Gerald, 224, 275
traditional common law doctrine, 52, 244
Treatise on English Maritime Law, 32
trust-right amendments, proposals for, 341–44
trust-rights climate advocacy/litigation, 284, 285–86, 287, 288, 300–2, 357–58, 436
  in Alaska, 313

in Arizona, 314–15
in California, 312
in Canada, 309–10
constitutional and pragmatic concerns of, 344–46
generational perspective, difference in, 358–60
legal and political environmental advocacy, 351–57
legal strategy and climate advocacy, 349–51
negative legal precedent, 348–49
separation-of-powers, 346–48
in Florida, 316–17
in France, 307–9
in Germany, 305–6
in India, 309
in Massachusetts, 315–16
in Mexico, 310
in Nepal, 305
in Netherlands (*Urgenda Foundation v. Netherlands*), 302–4
in New Mexico, 314
in Oregon, 313
state constitutions based, 334–35
   Alaska, 339
   Florida, 335
   Hawaii, 335, 337–38
   Montana, 336–37, 338
   New York, 335, 339
   Pennsylvania, 339
   Utah, 339–40
   Virginia, 339, 340
in Texas, 314
in U.S., 310–15
   Juliana v. United States, 318–33
in Washington, 314, 317–18
youth trust-rights movement, 354–55
Twain, Mark, 85

Uganda
   public trust doctrine, 371–72
   rights of nature initiatives in, 387–88
Uganda Constitution, 371
Ugandan National Environmental Act, 387, 403
U.N. Universal Declaration of Human Rights, 18
United States, tribal rights of nature initiatives in
   in Florida, 393–98
   in Ohio, 392–93
   in Pennsylvania, 389–92
Universal Declaration on the Rights of Mother Earth, 383
Urgenda case (*Urgenda Foundation v. Netherlands*), 302–4

U.S. Constitution, 5, 11, 18, 269, 275, 311, 322, 343
   amending national constitution, 11
   Articles of Confederation, 5
   Bill of Rights, 5
   Commerce Clause, 6, 7, 12
   Due Process Clause, 285
   and environmental rights, 18–20
   federal laws, 6–7
   Privileges and Immunities Clause, 12–13
   Takings Clause, 269
U.S. state constitutions, 8
   trust-right amendments, proposals for, 341–44
   trust-rights protections in, 334–35
      Alaska, 339
      Florida, 335
      Hawaii, 335, 337–38
      Montana, 336–37, 338
      New York, 335, 339
      Pennsylvania, 339
      Utah, 339–40
      Virginia, 339, 340
Utah Constitution, 448
   based climate litigation, 339–40

Vining, Leroy, 90
Vining, Thomas, 90
Virginia Constitution
   Article XI, 261
   based climate litigation, 339, 340

Wales public trust doctrine, 375
Walker Lake case, 229–34
Walston, Roderick "Rod," 121, 128, 131, 139, 140, 145, 178
Washington
   atmospheric trust claims in, 314, 317–18
   environmental-rights, proposed amendments for, 343
water allocation law, 28, 49–50
   prior appropriations, 27, 54–58
   riparian rights, 28, 50–54
Water Commission Act, 94
Water Conservation Emergency Regulations, 188
water law, 48–49
Water Quality Control Plan for the Bay-Delta, 217
Water Resources Act, 221
waterways protection, 254–55
WEBOR. *See* Wekiva River and Econlockhatchee River Bill of Rights (WEBOR)

Wekiva River and Econlockhatchee
  River Bill of Rights (WEBOR), 396–97,
    415
White Earth Band (Ojibwe), 399–400
wildlife, public trust protection in, 215–16
Wilkinson, Charles, 224
Winkler, David, 104, 105
  efforts on saving California Gull population,
    107
  on salinity of lake water, 104–5
Wolfe, Joan, 241

Wood, Mary, 301, 318
  atmospheric commons, public trust protection
    for, 292
  environmental critique, 210
  legal process, critique on, 205

Yosemite National Park, xii, 3, 16, 22, 63, 84, 89,
    91, 107, 162
Yurok Tribe (California), 400, 406

Zero Hour Movement, 330

For EU product safety concerns, contact us at Calle de José Abascal, 56–1°, 28003 Madrid, Spain or eugpsr@cambridge.org.

www.ingramcontent.com/pod-product-compliance
Lightning Source LLC
LaVergne TN
LVHW011753060526
838200LV00053B/3586